LANDMARK CASES IN EU LAW, VOLUME 1

From *Van Gend en Loos* and *Costa v ENEL* to *Cassis de Dijon* and *Consten and Grundig*, *Landmark Cases in EU Law* explores the most important and well-known EU law cases in two volumes. These volumes show how the European Court of Justice has played a fundamental role in the construction of the European Union in the past 70 years. Many EU 'landmark' cases have been controversial, yet no-one can deny that they have been essential in defining the Union legal order as we find it today.

Volume 1 explores the 'constitutional' cases that have come to define the legal nature and competences of the Union, its judicial architecture as well as its fundamental rights system. Each of the twenty cases within this volume is placed in its historical and doctrinal context, and each chapter also presents the history of its reception by the Court and academia.

Landmark Cases in EU Law

Volume 1: Constitutional Cases

Edited by
Paul Craig
and
Robert Schütze

•HART•
OXFORD • LONDON • NEW YORK • NEW DELHI • SYDNEY

HART PUBLISHING

Bloomsbury Publishing Plc

Kemp House, Chawley Park, Cumnor Hill, Oxford, OX2 9PH, UK

1385 Broadway, New York, NY 10018, USA

Bloomsbury Publishing Ireland Limited, 29 Earlsfort Terrace, Dublin 2, D02 AY28, Ireland

HART PUBLISHING, the Hart/Stag logo, BLOOMSBURY and the Diana logo are trademarks of Bloomsbury Publishing Plc

First published in Great Britain 2025

A catalogue record for this book is available from the British Library.

A catalogue record for this book is available from the Library of Congress.

Library of Congress Control Number: 2025933470

ISBN: HB: 978-1-50995-412-4
ePDF: 978-1-50995-414-8
ePub: 978-1-50995-413-1

Typeset by Compuscript Ltd, Shannon

For product safety related questions contact productsafety@bloomsbury.com

To find out more about our authors and books visit www.hartpublishing.co.uk. Here you will find extracts, author information, details of forthcoming events and the option to sign up for our newsletters.

CONTENTS

CONTRIBUTORS

Albertina Albors-Llorens is Professor of European Union Law, Faculty of Law, University of Cambridge and Fellow of St John's College

Roberto Caranta is Professor of Law, University of Turin Law School

Paul Craig is Emeritus Professor of English Law, St John's College, Oxford

Marise Cremona is Professor Emerita, European University Institute, Florence

Gareth Davies is Professor of EU law, Vrije Universiteit Amsterdam

Bruno de Witte is Professor Emeritus of European Law, Maastricht University, formerly Professor of Law at the European University Institute

Sionaidh Douglas-Scott is the Anniversary Chair in Law, Queen Mary University of London

Sara Drake is Reader in Law, Cardiff University's School of Law and Politics

Christina Eckes is Professor of European Law, University of Amsterdam and Director of the Amsterdam Centre for European Law and Governance (ACELG)

Eleni Frantziou is Associate Professor in Public Law and Human Rights, Durham Law School, University of Durham

José Gutiérrez-Fons is Legal Secretary, Court of Justice of the European Union

Alexander Kornezov is Judge at the General Court of the European Union

Panos Koutrakos is Jean Monnet Professor of EU Law, The City Law School, City St George's, University of London

Jasper Krommendijk is Professor of Human Rights Law and Director of the Research Centre for State and Law (SteR), Radboud University

Koen Lenaerts is President of the Court of Justice of the European Union

Tobias Lock is Professor of Law, Maynooth University (National University of Ireland, Maynooth)

Joana Mendes is Professor of Comparative and Administrative Law, University of Luxembourg

Michal Ovádek is Lecturer in European Institutions, Politics and Policy, University College London

Laurent Pech is Professor of Law at Sutherland School of Law, University College Dublin

Sacha Prechal is Honorary Professor in Law, Utrecht University, and was a Judge at the Court of Justice of the European Union from 2010 to 2024

Kai Purnhagen is Professor of Law, University of Bayreuth, and Director of the Research Centre for German and European Food Law

Daniel Sarmiento is Professor of EU Law, Universidad Complutense de Madrid and Editor-in-Chief of EU Law Live

Robert Schütze is Professor of European and Global Law, Durham University and LUISS (Rome)

Takis Tridimas is Professor and Director of the Luxembourg Centre for European Law, University of Luxembourg

TABLE OF CASES

Belgium

Canada

Czech Republic

Denmark

France

Germany

Italy

European Court of Human Rights (ECHR)

EFTA Court

Malta

Netherlands

Permanent Court of International Justice

Poland

Spain

Switzerland

UK

UN Human Rights Committee

United States

Introduction

PAUL CRAIG AND ROBERT SCHÜTZE

I. Landmark Judgments in the EU Legal Order

While it was perfectly possible to read all European Union (EU) law cases in the Union's 'foundational' period, this task has become considerably harder today.[1] The Court of Justice has become 'a prolific juggernaut'.[2] Very few academic or judicial court-watchers will be able to follow all of the Court's jurisprudence, with most of us aiming to read and study the most important – landmark – cases decided by the Court.

What, then, are the EU's major landmark cases, and how many are they? Pedagogically, one could simply define landmark cases as those cases that every serious student of the law has read or ought to have read. How do we find them? Courts will of course generally quote them, academic textbooks will sanctify them;[3] and, sometimes, broader theoretical superstructures will arise from them.[4] And yet, when selecting them, it is often not logic but experience that dictates choice. For a classic can often simply not be defined in purely qualitative or quantitative terms. To Pierre Pescatore, there were only four 'classic' constitutional cases,[5] to others there may be 10,[6] or 100. We have settled on 40 cases and have here followed our personal experiences.[7] There will of course be 'gaps' and 'omissions', yet we think that our selection offers an excellent starting point for anyone interested in the Union legal order and its problems in the past and present.

[1] There were only four cases in 1958 and 36 cases in 1962; yet by the end of the transitional period, there were about 100 cases per year. In 2023 alone, the CJEU registered 811 ECJ cases and 1196 General Court cases.

[2] M Jacob, *Precedents and Case-based Reasoning in the European Court of Justice* (Cambridge University Press, 2014) 2.

[3] For a quantitative view using network analysis to identify the top 10 EU landmark cases in, respectively, EU law textbooks and ECJ judgments, see M Derlén and J Lindholm, 'Goodbye van Gend en Loos, Hello Bosman? Using Network Analysis to Measure the Importance of Individual CJEU Judgment' (2014) 20 *European Law Journal* 667.

[4] See, for example, M Maduro's *We the Court: The European Court of Justice and the European Economic Constitution* (Hart, 1998), which can be viewed as a complex elaboration of the Court's *Keck* judgment.

[5] These cases were: *Commission v Luxembourg & Belgium (Gingerbread)*; *Van Gend en Loos*; *Costa v ENEL*; *and Consten & Grundig*. See A Vauchez, 'EU Law Classics in the Making: Methodological Notes on Grands arrêts at the European Court of Justice' in F Nicola and B Davies, *EU Law Stories: Contextual and Critical Histories of European Jurisprudence* (Cambridge University Press, 2017) 21, 26 for this reference to Pescatore's 'Aspects judiciaries de l'acquis judiciare' (1981) 17 *Revue trimestrielle de droit européen* 617.

[6] Derlén and Lindholm (n 3).

[7] We, the editors, in fact originally decided to each blindly draw up a list with 40 cases as a first point of reference, and to our mutual surprise, they were almost identical.

We must nonetheless identify the nature of these important cases in the broader landscape of EU law. Landmark cases are meant to 'mark' and 'signpost' an important part within the jurisprudence of the Court. While there is some truth in the assertion that '[a] court's jurisprudence cannot be immediately ascertained by looking at individual cases',[8] certain cases may in fact be identified with a broader jurisprudential principle *or even with the nature of the legal order as a whole*. The study of such landmark cases has a long tradition in EU law, even in those Member States that follow a 'civilian' legal tradition. It is, then, important – at the very outset – to reflect on the core meaning of a landmark judgment, more especially so given the centrality of the concept to this volume and other volumes in the series.

A. Landmark Cases: Foundations of a New Legal Order

Leaving aside architectural connotations, the principal non-architectural dictionary meaning of the term 'landmark' is an event or development that marks a turning point or a stage in a particular area or sphere. This is readily comprehensible within the legal arena; and most legal scholars will proceed on the assumption that it is meaningful to consider judgments that are landmark, as conceived in terms of their importance as a turning point or stage in the development of a particular area or sphere. This, of course, still leaves a plethora of more specific inquiries as to what judgments should qualify in this respect – a point to which we shall return below.

The idea of landmark cases has however also been contested. There might, for example, be historical legal scholarship in which the alleged landmark status of a leading judgment is debunked or questioned, the argument commonly being that its importance within the particular legal area has been overplayed.[9] Alternatively, there might be scholarship that assumes that all cases are equally significant in the development of the legal order, or any particular area therein. To us, this second and more general criticism of the landmark idea is clearly wrong, for it assumes a false equivalence of legal rulings that is not borne out in legal theory and practice.

What, then, about judicial landmarks in the EU legal order? To us, the landmark status of cases within EU law is especially distinctive when compared to other legal spheres or areas of law. It is unique and compelling in equal measure. The European Economic Community (EEC) was created by the Rome Treaty. It was a new political venture with an extraordinarily extensive legal base. There were, however, important issues not explicitly covered by the Treaty, such as the relative primacy of EEC law and national law in the event of a clash, and there were many Treaty articles framed in broad terms, the interpretation of which was not preordained in advance.

The initial rationale for recognition of an European Court of Justice (ECJ) decision as a landmark case is therefore that it played a seminal role in fashioning the very nature of the Community legal order in the years immediately following 1957. It is for this very

[8] M Maduro and L Azoulai (eds), *The Past and Future of EU Law: The Classics of EU Law Revisited on the 50th Anniversary of the Rome Treaty* (Hart, 2010) xiii.

[9] See, eg, R Schütze, '"Re-Reading" *Dassonville*: Meaning and Understanding in the History of European Law' (2018) 24 *European Law Journal* 376.

reason that cases such as *Van Gend*,[10] *Costa*[11] and *Cassis de Dijon*[12] are clearly deserving of the status of landmark cases. They each, albeit in different ways, made seminal contributions to the Community legal order, which had profound second order consequences for the nature of the emergent Community political order.

Their importance in this regard is an admixture of reasoning and result. The very fact that the result of *Van Gend* was that individuals could generally derive rights from the constituent EEC Treaty was highly significant; so too the fact that the result in *Costa* was to establish that Community law had primacy over national law in the event of a clash. The result in *Cassis de Dijon* for the reach of the internal market was equally compelling. To focus purely on the result is nonetheless to miss the significance of the reasoning. It is the combination of reasoning and result that warrants their place as landmark cases within the Community legal order. It is therefore worth dwelling a little longer on this dimension of the issue.

There is very little in legal reasoning that is a priori preordained. This is a fortiori true in the context of an emergent legal order, where the judges come from six legal systems, the traditions of which varied, notwithstanding the fact that they were all part of the civil law family. We may be accustomed to the Court's purposive and teleological reasoning, but it would be mistaken to believe that it was inevitable at the outset. There was in reality nothing inexorable in this regard. The Court made a choice as to the result that should be reached, and as to the reasoning that should inform this conclusion. The significance of these judgments resided in the combination of reasoning and result.

Take *Van Gend*,[13] by way of example, whose result was far-reaching. The Court rejected the analogy with ordinary international treaties pressed by the Member States, whereby individuals commonly have no enforceable legal rights, even if they are directly impacted by the treaty. The Court transformed the Community legal and political order by the general inclusion of individuals as litigants with cognisable legal rights. The Court's reasoning was however equally significant, for it was willing to justify the conclusion through argumentation flowing from the nature of the political Community, and the mention of individuals at various points in the founding Treaties. It brushed aside a central Member State argument that there was no need for direct effect because the Treaty already contained provision for public enforcement by the Commission, the Court tersely responding that the fact that the Treaty provided this enforcement mechanism did not thereby preclude enforcement at the behest of individuals.

Consider, by way of further example, the result and reasoning in *Costa*.[14] The result was crucial for the development of the Community as a viable international project. If Community law did not have primacy in the event of a clash with national law, then the very objectives central to the EEC project would be stultified at the Community's inception. Once again, the ECJ's reasoning was equally important. This is not the place to rehearse the argumentation used by the Court; suffice it to say in this regard that the Court deployed a range of functional, analytical and normative arguments to justify

[10] Case 26/62 *van Gend & Loos* EU:C:1963:1.
[11] Case 6/64 *Costa v ENEL* EU:C:1964:66.
[12] Case 120/78 *Rewe-Zentral AG v Bundesmonopolverwaltung für Branntwein* EU:C:1979:42.
[13] Case 26/62 (n 10).
[14] Case 6/64 (n 11).

the conclusion that Community law should take precedence in the event of a clash with national law. It is, moreover, noteworthy in this regard that while the traditional academic focus has been on instances of intentional recalcitrance by Member States, the empirical reality is that the danger of divergence between national law and Community law was more likely to be from unintentional mismatch flowing from the complexity of the respective provisions.

B. Landmark Cases: Foundations of a Particular Institutional Area

There is a second group of cases that warrants the label 'landmark' for reasons that are related to, albeit distinct from, the cases considered thus far. An emergent constitutional regime, such as the EEC, is shaped not only by foundational case law that has wide-ranging implications across the entire legal and political order, as evidenced by the case law on direct effect and primacy. There are also foundational decisions that warrant this appellation because of their centrality in laying the intellectual fundamentals of a particular constitutional or substantive area of the law. This is exemplified by cases such as *Internationale Handelsgesellschaft*,[15] *Plaumann*,[16] *Francovich*[17] and *Tobacco Advertising*[18] in the institutional domain, and by decisions such as *Bosman*,[19] *Keck*,[20] *Consten and Grundig*[21] and *Continental Can*[22] in the substantive domain.

The more particular contribution of the four constitutional cases mentioned is perforce varied, but the reasoning and result was again significant. *Internationale Handelsgesellschaft*[23] was important in three different respects. The Court built on *Costa* and pushed back against the suggestion emanating from the German courts that the primacy of EEC law would be bounded by the scope of national constitutional provisions. At the same time – indeed, in the very next paragraph of its judgment – it sought to prevent a damaging constitutional clash by making clear that fundamental rights were a part of the Community legal order, and that it, the ECJ, would review Community regulations, directives and decisions to ensure compliance with such rights-based precepts. It thereby played a seminal role in making fundamental rights part of EEC law, a foundation built on in subsequent jurisprudence. However, the decision was also important in a third institutional respect, less well-known than the preceding two. The Court's reasoning established that general principles of law were indeed general, insofar as that connoted application across all spheres of Community law, and were not dependent on the wording of a particular Treaty article. We are accustomed to this being the norm, but it was not so during previous years, when then there was considerable contestation as to the very meaning and incidence of general principles of law.

[15] Case C-11/70 *Internationale Handelsgesellschaft* EU:C:1970:114.
[16] Case 25/62 *Plaumann* EU:C:1963:17.
[17] Cases C-6 and 9/90 *Francovich* EU:C:1991:428.
[18] Case C-376/98 *Germany v European Parliament and Council* EU:C:2000:544.
[19] Case C-415/93 *Bosman* EU:C:1995:463.
[20] Cases C-267 and 268/91 *Keck and Mithouard* EU:C:1993:905.
[21] Cases 56 and 58/64 *Consten and Grundig* EU:C:1966:41.
[22] Case 6/72 *Continental Can* EU:C:1973:22.
[23] Case 11/70 (n 15).

Plaumann[24] was also significant in a particular institutional sphere, this being the capacity of an individual to contest the legality of Community law directly via what is now Article 263 of the Treaty on the Functioning of the European Union (TFEU). It is indicative of the truism that a case may properly be regarded as foundational while also being controversial. The ECJ's construction of Article 263 TFEU was not pre-ordained, nor was it determined by the precise Treaty text, which could perfectly well have accommodated a more liberal construction of standing. The Court's determination of when individual litigants should have *locus standi* to contest the legality of Community action was driven by an underlying policy view as to when non-privileged actors should be able to have direct recourse to the ECJ, or more latterly the Court of First Instance. It was controversial from the outset, and remains so today. It had important second order implications for other Treaty provisions, since Article 267 TFEU became ever more important in contesting the legality of Community action by individuals.

Francovich[25] deserves recognition as a landmark case in the constitutional domain because of its practical and normative contribution to the idea of responsibility that underpins the Community legal order. The conjunction of reasoning and result are, once again, worthy of note. The result cast in terms of state liability in damages was sharp and designed to catch the attention of recalcitrant Member States. The factual backdrop was non-implementation of a directive, and it was not fortuitous. The inclusion of directives in the constituent EEC Treaty furnished a valuable method by which Community goals could be advanced, through the stipulation of ends, while giving Member States choice as to form and method of implementation. It nonetheless carried the attendant danger that Member States would not fulfil their obligations, or do so imperfectly, as attested to by the Commission league table listing good and bad Member States in this regard.

The Treaties contained a mode of public enforcement, via a Commission action under what is now Article 258 TFEU. But the Commission's enforcement resources were limited, and the remedy relatively weak, more especially in the first 30 years of the Community's existence. This was the judicial rationale for the supplementation of public enforcement, with private enforcement at the behest of the individual, with the added bite that the sanction was framed in hard-edged monetary terms, which was more likely to get Member State attention as compared to a declaratory judgment of illegality. The Court's reasoning to justify its desired conclusion was set at a relatively high level, but it was nonetheless persuasive. It connected analogically with ideas of considerable historical provenance that could be found in national law, whereby national courts developed doctrine based on the conjunction between *ubi jus, ibi remedium*.

Tobacco Advertising[26] was central to the institutional discourse concerning the limits of harmonisation pursuant to what is now Article 114 TFEU. The issue was controversial and remains so, more especially in academic discourse, to the present day. The Community project was predicated on an admixture of negative and positive integration. The principal legal vehicles for negative integration were the Treaty articles on the four freedoms. However, the Community project could only be attained if this was complemented by positive integration, which legitimated enactment of harmonisation measures to complete the internal market. *Tobacco Advertising* was famous for setting boundaries

[24] Case 25/62 (n 16).
[25] Cases C-6 and 9/90 (n 17).
[26] Case C-376/98 (n 18).

to such harmonisation initiatives, the standard story being that the Court beforehand had softened the conditions, and interpreted them liberally, thereby allegedly fostering competence creep and unwarranted incursion into Member State autonomy. There is moreover no doubt that the Court has since weakened the conditions laid down in *Tobacco Advertising*. There is, however, room for considerably greater contestation as to whether the result should be cast in terms of competence creep and incursion into Member State autonomy, given, inter alia, the fact that the Member States voted for the contested measure, and given also the definition of the scope of competence in Article 114 TFEU.

C. Landmark Cases: Foundations of a Particular Substantive Area

A decision may, as noted above, also be regarded as foundational because of its centrality to a particular *substantive* area of the law, as exemplified by decisions such as *Bosman*, *Keck*, *Consten and Grundig* and *Continental Can*. They can be properly regarded as a significant turning point or stage in the particular area.

We should pause at this juncture and take note of a fact that is both trite and important in equal measure. At the outset, the remit of the EEC as determined by the Rome Treaty was already broad. It has expanded markedly since then. Not all Treaty revisions are equally important, whether judged in terms of scale of ambition or result. There is, nonetheless, a feature that is common across all such developments, including the Single European Act, and the Treaties of Maastricht, Amsterdam, Nice and Lisbon. The scope of EU competence has expanded either through the inclusion of new heads of competence, or the expansion of an existing head. The Treaty covers a very broad range of substantive areas ranging from trade to crime, social welfare to family law, consumer protection to the environment and intellectual property to competition, with much else besides. While there have been some limits placed on the exercise of such competence, through subsidiarity, this does not alter the point being made here. There has also been greater calibration as to the type of EU competence, most notably in the Lisbon Treaty, but this does not affect the relevance of the ensuing analysis.

The salient point for present purposes is simple and compelling. There will inevitably be cases that are foundational for each substantive area, where the Court's ruling can properly be regarded as a significant turning point or stage in its legal development. The judgments may have implications for other substantive areas, and may have important political consequences. The four cases considered briefly in this introduction are merely examples of this phenomenon.

Bosman[27] was foundational in the development of the free movement of workers. The ECJ had to decide in relation to each of the four freedoms whether it applied to measures that were not directly or indirectly discriminatory. The issue was addressed in the context of free movement of workers in the famous *Bosman* ruling, in which the transfer system developed by national and transnational football associations was found to be in breach of Article 45 TFEU. The contested transfer system applied equally to players

[27] Case C-415/93 (n 19).

moving from one club to another within a Member State, as well as to players moving between states. The player's nationality was irrelevant. The ECJ nonetheless held that the transfer regime affected players' access to the employment market in other Member States and was thus capable of impeding freedom of movement for workers. The decision represented the beginning of a new strand of jurisprudence concerning such free movement, whereby the Court had to adjudicate on possible impediments to market access, and the scope of any public interest defence where such impediments were found to exist.

The ruling in *Keck*[28] was noteworthy in several respects. It represents a rare instance where the ECJ consciously and explicitly shifted judicial direction when seeking to define the contours of the free movement of goods. The ruling in *Cassis de Dijon*[29] had expanded the reach of Article 34 TFEU by making clear that it was not confined to direct or indirect discrimination. The conceptual shift to mutual recognition was predicated on home state control. Goods produced in accord with the lawful requirements of the home state could be exported to any other Member State, subject only to mandatory requirements imposed by the host state, provided that the ECJ regarded the national rule as falling legitimately within that category. This naturally led to questions concerning the outer boundaries of Article 34 TFEU, and to related inquiries as to the best way for such boundaries to be delineated. These questions persisted in the years following the *Cassis de Dijon* ruling, with the ECJ taking different approaches to the problem. This led in turn to the ruling in *Keck and Mithouard*, in which the ECJ introduced the dichotomy between rules that related to selling arrangements and those that related to the goods themselves. Rules of the former kind did not fall within the scope of the Treaty, provided that they applied to all affected traders and provided also that they affected in the same manner, in law and fact, the marketing of domestic products and those from other Member States. The soundness of this distinction continues to divide commentators, as evident in the substantial academic commentary. The decision generated a steady flow of case law in which the ECJ articulated the contours of selling arrangements, and the circumstances in which the rules had a disparate impact such as to come within the Treaty remit.

Competition law constitutes an important area over which the EU has had competence from the very inception of the Rome Treaty. The principal Treaty provisions have retained their central characteristics through subsequent Treaty amendments, although they have been complemented by regulations specifying in greater detail various procedural and substantive dimensions of the subject. The reach of competition law is shaped by interpretive choices that are commonly not predetermined by the strict letter of the Treaty provisions. The consequence is that such choices are for the courts to decide, which in the context of the Union meant the ECJ and more latterly the Court of First Instance (CFI) and General Court (GC). The early ruling in *Consten and Grundig*[30] tackled central issues relating to the distinction between vertical and horizontal competitive restraints. It also had implications for whether EU law could be said to have a rule of

[28] Cases C-267 and 268/91 (n 20).
[29] Case 120/78 (n 12).
[30] Cases 56 and 58/64 (n 21).

reason. The debate in this regard, both as to what the law is and what it ought to be, has continued over the subsequent decades.

The early ruling in *Continental Can*[31] was equally foundational for competition law, albeit for different reasons. The Treaty provisions did not deal expressly with mergers. The Member States recognised the significance of mergers for the overall efficacy of competition policy, but negotiation of a first EEC Merger Regulation was protracted, and it proved difficult to secure consensus in the Council as to the precise content of such a measure. It was inevitable that the ECJ would be faced with the issue as to whether the existing Treaty provisions could cover a merger, more especially where it created or strengthened the dominant position of an undertaking in the internal market. This was the issue presented to the Court in *Continental Can*. The decision can readily be regarded as a landmark, in the sense of a development that marked a turning point or a stage in this particular area. It is, as with many other cases considered in these two volumes, the conjunction of reasoning and result that was especially significant. The ECJ's willingness to interpret the constituent Treaty so as to cover action that was detrimental to the competitive market structure, as well as that which was more directly harmful to consumers, was important in the subsequent interpretation of Article 102 TFEU. The decision also reveals the interplay between institutional and substantive law that is often a feature of landmark cases. In this instance, the backdrop to the ruling was the fact that the political organs had not yet directly addressed mergers. The ruling in *Continental Can* showed that the Court was willing to deal with this issue through legal interpretation of the primary Treaty text, pending an outcome from the political forum.

II. Structure and Style of EU Judgments

In many modern societies, courts are not allowed to make law, but must only interpret and apply the law. This civilian tradition contrasts strikingly with the common law tradition in which courts have the power to make law. Textually, the Court of Justice of the European Union seems to stand in the civilian tradition. For, according to Article 19 TEU, the Court shall 'ensure that in the interpretation and application of the Treaties the law is observed'.[32] The European Court is here portrayed as an interpreter and an applier of European law, but not as a 'maker' of its own.

However, this invites the inquiry as to the way in which legal 'interpretation' is different from legal 'creation'. The process of interpretation is generally seen as a process of expressing implicit meaning that lies between art and science: it is creative in its construction of meaning; yet, by insisting on judicial 'rules' of construction, it is claimed to have a scientific soul. Moreover, according to civilian logic, the scientific creation of legal meaning is not the same as law-making, even where the Court uses the most powerful teleological interpretation method. For the law, the EU Treaties and all secondary law adopted pursuant thereto, is seen to be created by the Member States, or

[31] Case 6/72 (n 22).
[32] Art 19(1) TEU.

the Union legislature and executive. When viewed in this way, all the European Court is supposed to do is 'deduction and nothing but deduction'.[33]

This civilian portrayal of the European judiciary as the mere 'mouth of the law' has historic roots. When the Court was first created in 1951, French administrative law was considered the dominant inspiration, and the French *Conseil d'État* became the European Court's first role model.[34] This also explains the extreme brevity of earlier EU judgments. For once upon a time, judgments issued by the European Court were very brief, as exemplified by the judgment in *Van Gend en Loos* that contains approximately 2,000 words, which is not more than an undergraduate essay. This world of short 'French' judgments is today gone. While ECJ judgments are still, generally, much shorter than US Supreme Court judgments or decisions of the German Constitutional Court, they have undoubtedly become longer.[35]

This textual development might be linked with two major developments of the Union legal order. First, with every enlargement of the Union, a new national legal tradition has entered the Union and its Court. With the 1973 arrival of two common law jurisdictions, a 'mixed' style of judicial reasoning came to dominate within the Court,[36] although it was not only the common law's clear penchant for argument and detail that were decisive.[37] Secondly, in contrast to the early days of the ECJ, EU Treaties have become much more complex, and there has been a very significant increase in EU legislation, which has dramatically changed the legal situation. This move to the interpretation of technical legislation is a very important factor in explaining the length and comprehensiveness of modern EU judgments.[38]

This has not necessarily made ECJ judgments easier to read and understand, because every ECJ judgment is a 'collective' or 'collegiate' judgment. Unlike the US Supreme Court, no dissenting Opinions by a minority of judges are allowed. All judicial differences must thus be settled in the (majority) decision of the Court, which often turns a judgment into a complex 'edited collection'. Disagreements within the Court must be settled by weaving diverse threads of reasoning into a single judicial texture, and the simplest way to remove disagreements is to remove those legal 'reasons' in a chain of argumentation over which no collective agreement could be

[33] JL Goutal, 'Characteristics of Judicial Style in France, Britain and the U.S.A' (1976) 24 *American Journal of Comparative Law* 43, 45.

[34] C Schönberger, '"Mi-attendu, mi dissertation": Le style des decisions de la Cour de justice de l'Union européenne' (2015) 91 *Droit er Société* 505, 511.

[35] A typical judgment issued today will, on average, be four to five times as long as *Van Gend*. In the worst-case scenario, a judgment, especially in the area of EU competition law, may be as long as 100,000 words – a book of about 300 pages.

[36] Schönberger (n 34) 514.

[37] On the relationship between the 'common law' and the length of judgments, see Goutal (n 33) 56, 'A Common Law case is sometimes forty or eighty pages long; a fifteen-line French case is nothing unusual.'

[38] There is a third reason why EU judgments have become much longer, which has to do with a change in the presentation of the judgment. The shortness of early judgments was partly due to a structural division the judgment made between the 'Issues of Fact and of Law' (or later: 'Report for the Hearing'), which set out the facts, procedure and the arguments of the parties, on the one hand, and the 'Grounds of Judgment' on the other. Only the latter constituted the judgment *sensu stricto* and this was often very short indeed. Modern judgments, by contrast, have come to integrate much of the facts and the parties' arguments into the main body of a 'single' judgment, and this has especially made many direct actions much longer and much more repetitive.

found. This sometimes creates significant argumentative gaps that require Herculean hermeneutic powers.[39]

This leads to the issue of how the judgment is generally structured. After a brief summary of how the case came to the Court in the first paragraphs, the judgment will turn to the 'Legal Context' in which the relevant provisions of European and national law that will be important to the case are presented. This has the undoubted advantage that readers will not need to track and produce them themselves, although this 'civilian' beginning might test the impatient reader.

This is followed by the most important part: the presentation of the 'action', whether this is a direct action or a preliminary ruling. This is where a reader should best start because the Court here presents the 'problem' of the case and the scenario that led to the litigation. The following sections will subsequently deal with specific questions relating to the legal problem(s) identified. In direct actions, the Court will deal successively with the 'arguments of the parties', before offering its own 'findings'. Each of these 'findings' will conclude an argumentative step, which the Court draws together in its 'grounds' at the end of the judgment.

An additional key to deciphering a judgment may be the 'Opinion' of the Advocate General.[40] The institution of Advocate General is a French trademark of the European judicial system. The Treaties define their function as follows: 'It shall be the duty of the Advocate General, acting with complete impartiality and independence, to make, in open court, reasoned submissions.'[41] According to this role, an Advocate General produces an 'Opinion' that is designed to inform the Court of ways to decide a case in advance. The Court sometimes expressly agrees or disagrees with the case's Advocate General in its final judgment. For the retrospective reader, it may thus offer clues and reasons – potentially omitted in the judicial decision – to explain the meaning of the judgment.

The foregoing prompts a further inquiry as to the legal nature of an EU judgment. According to the common law view, ECJ judgments are legal precedents that are generally binding (though not necessarily on the European Court).[42] This view seems to gain strong support from the Court's own judicial practice. For the Court often tries to 'signpost' a particular doctrinal position through the citation of a previous judgment (or special 'formulas') that indicate a 'settled jurisprudence'. A good example here is *Fransson*, where the Court held:[43]

> [I]t is settled case-law that a national court which is called upon, within the exercise of its jurisdiction, to apply provisions of European Union law is under a duty to give full effect to

[39] A case in point is here the *Zambrano* judgment discussed in Volume II, ch 9. See also, N Nic Shuibhne, 'Seven questions for seven paragraphs' (2011) 36 *European Law Review* 161.

[40] Art 19(2) TEU. Today, not every case before the Court of Justice will be accompanied by the Opinion of an Advocate General. For all landmark cases, this will however almost inevitably be the rule even today.

[41] Art 252(2) TFEU.

[42] A Trabucchi, 'L'Effet "erga omnes" des décisions préjudicielles rendues par la cour de justice des communautés européennes' (1974) 10 *Revue Trimestrielle de Droit Européen* 56.

[43] Case C-617/10 *Åklagaren v Hans Åkerberg Fransson* EU:C:2013:105, para 45. The case is extensively discussed in Volume I, ch 17. On the Court's special formulas, see P Pescatore, *Vade-mecum: Recueil de Formules et de conseil pratique à l'usage des rédacteurs d'arrêt* (Bruylant, 2007). The perhaps most famous 'formula' is the *Dassonville* formula.

> those provisions, if necessary refusing of its own motion to apply any conflicting provision of national legislation, even if adopted subsequently, and it is not necessary for the court to request or await the prior setting aside of such a provision by legislative or other constitutional means.

This confidence in its case law is underlined by the absence of academic and doctrinal argumentation.[44] The Court only refers to itself. A particular judgment therefore assumes the role of an 'authority' or 'precedent' for a particular legal principle. In that sense, there is no doubt that the ECJ has adopted a precedent-driven jurisprudence.[45] This is also where the very idea of a 'landmark' case comes from. It is a case that 'formulated' a legal position, or 'changed' an anterior legal position and 'made' new law.

Interestingly, however, the Court seems to still prefer the 'civilian' position according to which even these landmark cases do not formally create new legal principles. Every judgment thus only offers an interpretation of EU law; and, in the words of the Court:

> The interpretation which … the Court of Justice gives to a rule of [European] law clarifies and defines where necessary the meaning and scope of that rule as it must be or ought to have been understood and applied from the time of its coming into force.[46]

Following this version of the declaratory theory, judgments are seen to only clarify pre-existing law. The legal effects of Court judgment are therefore seen as being always mediated through the positive law interpreted, and not, as the common law view asserts, through a doctrine of binding precedent.[47]

This does not, in reality, diminish the importance of the Court's own jurisprudence. Thus, even if one thinks of judgments as 'not sources but authoritative evidence of [European] law', they will necessarily affect the legal position and the meaning of EU law.[48] A Court's new interpretation of an old norm will thus signal a major change of direction, and for that reason, the Court sometimes expressly renounces its former jurisprudence.[49] A 'landmark case' here signals and signposts a turning point. We thus think of *Van Gend* as the case that 'introduced' direct effect into the EU legal order, and of *Plaumann* as the case that 'established' the standing requirements for private party applicants, whereas *Cassis de Dijon* is seen as having 'invented' the principle of

[44] M de S.-O.-L'E Lasser, *Judicial Deliberations: A Comparative Analysis of Judicial Transparency and Legitimacy* (Oxford University Press, 2004), 110. The absence of 'la doctrine' is striking when compared to other constitutional courts.

[45] M Derlén and J Lindholm, 'Peek-A-Boo, It's a Case Law System! Comparing the European Court of Justice and the United States Supreme Court from a Network Perspective' (2017) 18 *German Law Journal* 647.

[46] Case 61/79 *Amministrazione delle finanze dello Stato v Denkavit* [1980] ECR 1205, para 16; and somewhat more recently, Case C-453/00 *Kühne & Heitz v Productschap voor Pluimvee en Eieren* [2004] ECR I-837, para 21.

[47] It has, consequently, been claimed by various Advocates General, that 'in European Union law, the Court's judgments do not constitute binding precedents'. See eg Opinion of Advocate General Kockott in Case C-163/09 *Repertoire Culinaire Ltd v The Commissioners of Her Majesty's Revenue & Customs* EU:C:2010:434, para 61.

[48] A Toth, 'The Authority of Judgments of the European Court of Justice: Binding Force and Legal Effects' (1984) 4 *Yearbook of European Law* 1, 70–74.

[49] Most famously in Cases C-267 and 268/91 *Criminal proceedings against Bernard Keck and Daniel Mithouard* EU:C:1993:905. The case will be discussed in Volume II, ch 3.

mutual recognition.[50] Each case has indeed effected an informal constitutional change through which the Court readjusts the Union legal order.

III. Structure of the Two Volumes

It might be helpful to say a brief word at the end of this Introduction concerning the divide between the two volumes of Landmark Cases. It is largely self-explanatory. The cases considered in Volume 1 are concerned with constitutional dimensions of EU law broadly conceived, while those analysed in Volume 2 deal with substantive dimensions of the subject. This divide is meaningful, but it should also be qualified in certain respects.

Thus, it is trite but important nonetheless to acknowledge that every constitutional case necessarily arises from a dispute grounded in a certain substantive area over which the EU has competence. The reverse side of this coin is equally significant. Landmark cases that warrant this status primarily because of their substantive impact can also have important constitutional implications, as exemplified by *Cassis de Dijon*,[51] which shaped the way in which the Union pursued positive integration after the Single European Act (SEA), and embodied normative precepts as to the respective powers of home and host state within the emerging legal order. To take another example, *Bosman* dealt with internal market matters and also the principle of horizontal direct effect. By parity of reasoning, *Van Gend* and *Costa* are constitutional cases that emerged from fact situations concerning the internal market.

There are other ways in which the constitutional dimensions interrelate with the substantive. Developments in a particular substantive area are frequently the testing ground for the application of particular constitutional precepts, such as direct effect, horizontal and vertical, and the primacy of EU law. There are also significant instances where the catalyst for constitutional doctrine has been malaise in the political process that prevents or impedes attainment of certain substantive goals through standard legislative procedures.

Nonetheless, and with this caveat in mind, Volume I explores the constitutional cases that have defined the nature of EU law (Part A), the vertical and horizontal division of Union competences (Part B), the judicial architecture of the Union (Part C), and the question of fundamental rights (Part D). By contrast, Volume II covers the substantive cases, and begins with the internal market (Parts A and B), moves to competition law (Part C) and finally explores the landmark cases on the Union's main internal and external policies (Part D).

Each of the 40 cases will be analysed along four dimensions, namely: (1) its historical and doctrinal context; (2) the 'case' itself and its judgment; (3) its judicial and academic reception history; and (4) famous potential follow-up cases to the landmark judgment.

[50] Some cases may even represent more than just 'one' important constitutional idea. Consider for example 'ERTA', which stands for at least two important constitutional principles, namely the doctrine of parallel powers (today: Art 216 TFEU) and the doctrine of subsequently exclusive powers (Art 3(2) TFEU).

[51] Case 120/78 (n 12).

The reasons behind these four dimensions are easy to grasp. Many landmark cases will have a historical and doctrinal past whose 'logic' they will often escape. And each landmark case will, as a case, represent a much thicker 'story',[52] whose specific facts may exert a strong normative force, especially where a Court wishes to balance abstract against concrete considerations of justice. Finally, a landmark case may be born as such, as was the case with *Keck*, but it may only be with the effluxion of time that the case becomes a bright star within the European judicial firmament. In both scenarios, the reception history, be it judicial or academic, will here be paramount, also as regards the path towards future landmark cases.

[52] For a wonderful collection of such 'thick' stories behind some EU landmark cases, see: Nicola and Davies (n 5). For the US constitutional order, see the 'Landmark Law Cases and American Society' Series (Kansas University Press), which offers book-length thick description of particular cases.

PART A

The Nature of European Law

1

van Gend en Loos: A Star is Born

KOEN LENAERTS AND JOSÉ GUTIÉRREZ-FONS*

I. Introduction

Fifteen years after the end of his mandate as President of the Court of Justice, Robert Lecourt wrote a thought-provoking article asking the following rhetorical question:[1] What would the European Union (EU, then the European Economic Community (EEC)) have become without the judgments of the Court of Justice in *van Gend en Loos* and *Costa v ENEL*?[2] Describing a counterfactual scenario, his article gives us valuable insight into the minds of one of the judges who sat in both cases. *Without those two judgments*, he wrote, the value of the EEC Treaty would have been reduced to that of a simple agreement amongst the Member States that was limited to laying down rules for their mutual cooperation and for their relationship with the EU institutions. Individuals would have played no role in building the internal market, and an exclusive reliance on infringement proceedings would not have sufficed to keep defaulting Member States in line. *Without those two judgments*, the preliminary reference mechanism would have become an 'empty shell', since the Member States could have made the application of that mechanism subject to conditions incompatible with the principle of primacy. *Without those two judgments*, the uniform interpretation and application of EU law would have been no more than a 'utopian' dream. He thus concluded that *van Gend en Loos* and *Costa v ENEL* enabled the EEC to become a 'Community of Peoples and States' with its own institutions and competences, governed by the rule of law.

We could not agree more with those wise words. Compared by some scholars to the legendary *Marbury v Madison* ruling,[3] the significance of *van Gend en Loos* and its legacy cannot be overstated. This judgment is so important to the case law of the Court of Justice that for its fiftieth anniversary, the latter organised a conference and published

* All opinions expressed herein are strictly personal to the authors.

[1] Robert Lecourt was judge at the Court of Justice from 18 May 1962 to 9 October 1967, and President from 10 October 1967 to 25 October 1976. See R Lecourt, 'Quel eût été le droit des Communautés sans les arrêts de 1963 et 1964?'in *L'Europe et le droit. Mélanges en hommage à Jean BOULOUIS* (Dalloz, 1991) 349.

[2] Case 26/62 *van Gend en Loos* EU:C:1963:1; and Case 6/64 *Costa v ENEL* EU:C:1964:66.

[3] *Marbury v Madison*, 5 US (1 Cranch) 137 (1803). See, in this regard, D Halberstam, 'Constitutionalism and Pluralism in *Marbury and Van Gend*' in M Poiares Maduro and L Azoulai (eds), *The Past and Future of EU Law: The Classics of EU Law Revisited on the 50th Anniversary of the Rome Treaty* (Hart Publishing, 2010) 26.

a book inviting scholars to comment on it.[4] Since it is probably the most examined judgment in the history of the Court of Justice, we face the challenge of exploring it without repeating what has already been written. To that end, this chapter will focus on two elements that are worth taking into account when revisiting that judgment.

In the first place, in the past decade, legal historians have become increasingly interested in studying the early case law of the Court by having recourse to archive material, both public and private.[5] As Davies and Rasmussen point out, 'the new historical research can be used by legal scholars and practitioners to improve their understanding of the broader societal context within which European law has historically operated'.[6] That is why we have decided to refer to some of their main findings in this chapter. In the second place, we shall also look at the impact of that judgment from three different, albeit intertwined, perspectives. First, it is submitted that 'structural considerations' weighed heavily in the Court's reasoning. As a theory of constitutional adjudication, structuralism has underpinned the case law of the Court of Justice from the early years to the present day. Second, the notion of autonomy, understood in both its positive and negative conceptions, played an important role in that judgment insofar as the Court sought to draw a distinction between the EEC Treaty and ordinary international agreements.[7] Third and last, *van Gend en Loos* is, in our view, the foundation stone that enabled the principle of effective judicial protection of EU rights to become a living truth. In that regard, we support the contention that by introducing the second subparagraph of Article 19(1) of the Treaty on European Union (TEU), the authors of the Treaty of Lisbon gave new impetus to the principle of direct effect so that it is no longer accurate to say that this principle is entirely judge-made.

II. Historical and Doctrinal Context

The judgment of the Court of Justice in *van Gend en Loos* was delivered on 5 February 1963, that is, only five years after the entry into force of the EEC Treaty, and only three weeks after President de Gaulle had vetoed the UK's accession to the EU. The initial 'feverish legislative and administrative activity' at EU level had come to a halt,[8] announcing grimmer times of inactivity brought about by the policy of the empty chair and the Luxembourg compromise.[9] The customs union was a work in progress and the Common (now Internal) Market was no more than a distant dream.

[4] A Tizzano, J Kokott and S Prechal (eds), *50th Anniversary of the Judgment in* van Gend en Loos *1963–2013*, Conference Proceedings, Luxembourg, 13 May 2013 (Luxembourg, Office des publications de l'UE, 2013).

[5] See, eg, B Davies and M Rasmussen, 'Towards a New History of European Law' (2010) 21 *Contemporary European History* 305.

[6] M Rasmussen, 'Revolutionizing European law: A History of the *Van Gend* en Loos judgment' (2014) 12 *International Journal of Constitutional Law* 136, 138.

[7] See K Lenaerts, J-A Gutiérrez-Fons and S Adam, 'Exploring the Autonomy of the European Union Legal Order' (2021) 81 *Zeitschrift für ausländisches öffentliches Recht und Völkerrecht* 47, and K Lenaerts and J-A Gutiérrez-Fons, 'Epilogue. High Hopes: Autonomy and the Identity of the EU' (2023) 8 *European Papers* 1495.

[8] Sk, 'Case annotation' (1963) 1 *Common Market Law Review* 88.

[9] See J Ziller, 'Les réactions des milieux institutionnels, nationaux et scientifiques de l'époque' in Tizzano, Kokott and Prechal (eds) (n 4) 37.

At the beginning of 1963, the EEC had yet to clarify whether it was to speak the language of international law just like any ordinary international agreement, or whether it would speak a new language imbued with supranational elements. The very nature of the common legal order and its law needed clarification. This was, in part, because the EEC Treaty was silent on the key question of whether its provisions may produce direct effect and thus prevail over conflicting national law.

At international level, the Permanent Court of International Justice (PCIJ, the predecessor of the International Court of Justice) had, in its Advisory Opinion *Jurisdiction of the Courts of Danzig*, settled the question of direct effect.[10] In that case, the PCIJ held that 'according to a well-established principle of international law, … an international agreement, cannot, as such, create direct rights and obligations for private individuals'. It is, however, otherwise where 'according to the intentions of the Contracting Parties' the very object of the international agreement at issue is to produce direct effect.[11] Thus, that Advisory Opinion endorsed a general – yet rebuttable – presumption against direct effect.

At national level, there was no consensus amongst the six founding members of the EEC as to the way in which international law was to be incorporated into national law.[12] On the one hand, the Netherlands and Luxembourg favoured a 'monist approach', meaning that there was no need for an international agreement to be translated into domestic law. Moreover, international agreements prevailed over national laws. On the other hand, Germany and Italy followed a 'dualist approach', meaning that legislation was required in order for an international agreement to be considered 'the law of the land'. In Italy and Belgium, since their constitutions were silent on the legal value of international agreements, they enjoyed the same legal status as laws. This opened the door to the application of the principle of '*lex posterior derogat legi priori*'. For its part, France, which had recently adopted a new constitution embracing a monist approach, faced resistance from national courts that were reluctant to uphold an international agreement where it was in conflict with the '*volonté générale*' represented by the French Parliament. Yet, despite that lack of consensus, the Member States seemed to agree that the question of direct effect was a matter pertaining exclusively to the purview of national constitutional law.[13]

That said, legal historians have, in the light of archive material, observed that the traditional understanding of direct effect was being challenged in academic circles as well as within the Commission Legal Service when the order for reference in *van Gend en Loos* arrived at the Court of Justice. From 1958 to 1962, the idea that the authors of the EEC Treaty had incorporated supranational elements that made it different from ordinary international agreements began to gain momentum.[14] For example, in preparing the second edition of the FIDE Congress that was to take place in October 1963 at The Hague, both the Commission Legal Service and the Dutch section of FIDE

[10] Permanent Court of Justice, Advisory Opinion in *Jurisdiction of the Courts of Danzig* of 3 March 1928, PCIJ 1928, Series B, No 15.

[11] ibid 17 and 18.

[12] B de Witte, 'Direct Effect, Primacy, and the Nature of the Legal Order' in P Craig and G de Búrca (eds), *The Evolution of EU Law*, 3rd edn (Oxford University Press, 2021) 187.

[13] ibid 188.

[14] Rasmussen (n 6) 146–56.

requested that the FIDE board chose as a topic the question of direct effect.[15] Similarly, perhaps due to the 1956 constitutional reform (that facilitated the application of directly effective provisions of international law) and to a 1962 ruling of the *Hoge Raad* (holding that the question whether a treaty provision produced direct effect was a matter of treaty interpretation),[16] Dutch lawyers were particularly active in urging Dutch courts to make use of the new opportunities offered by the preliminary reference mechanism.[17] In particular, those references would operate as a means of clarifying the question of direct effect.[18] The winds of change had begun to blow.

Similarly, within the Court of Justice, the question of direct effect had already been examined by Advocate General Lagrange in the very first preliminary reference ever made under Article 177 EEC (now Article 267 of the Treaty on the Functioning of the European Union (TFEU)). In his Opinion in *Bosch*,[19] he pointed out that Article 85 EEC (now Article 101 TFEU) produced direct effect. Most importantly for present purposes, he wrote that 'Since the Treaty, by virtue of its ratification, is incorporated into the national law, it is the function of national courts to apply its provisions, except when powers are expressly conferred on [EU] organs.'[20] The Court concurred with Advocate General Lagrange in that 'Article 85 EEC [had] been applicable from the time of entry into force of the Treaty'.[21] However, unlike the Advocate General, it 'did not connect its finding about [that Treaty provision] to a broader vision of the status of the Treaty' regarding the question of direct effect.[22] That constitutional question was left for another day.

III. Facts and Judgment in the Case

That day came on 5 February 1963 when the Court of Justice delivered its judgment in *van Gend en Loos*. The facts of the case may be summarised as follows. On 9 September 1960, van Gend en Loos, a Dutch company, imported from Germany a chemical substance that is used for making glue (urea-formaldehyde). The Dutch customs authorities decided to apply an *ad valorem* import duty of eight per cent to the product in question. That decision was based on a new customs tariff classification that had been introduced by virtue of an international agreement ratified by the Benelux countries (the 1958 Brussels Protocol) and had entered into force on 1 March 1960. van Gend en Loos challenged that decision on the ground that the Brussels Protocol modified the tariff headings, resulting in the application of a higher import duty to the

[15] A Vauchez, 'The transnational politics of judicialization. *Van Gend en Loos* and the making of EU polity' (2010) 16 *European Law Journal* 1, 10.

[16] Hoge Raad (Dutch Supreme Court), 18 May 1962, *De Geus en Uitenbogerd v Bosch GmbH*.

[17] Vauchez (n 15) 10 (who observes that 'out of the first 18 preliminary rulings notified to the Court during the first six years of the Rome treaties, 15 were from Dutch tribunals').

[18] Rasmussen (n 6) 147 (referring to Case 26/62 *van Gend en Loos* (n 2) and Joined Cases 28/62 to 30/62 *Da Costa and Others* EU:C:1963:6).

[19] Opinion of AG Lagrange in Case 13/61 *de Geus en Uitdenbogerd v Bosch e.a.*, not published, EU:C:1962:3.

[20] ibid 65.

[21] Case 13/61 *de Geus en Uitdenbogerd v Bosch e.a.* EU:C:1962:11, 51.

[22] W Phelan, *Great Judgments of the European Court of Justice: Rethinking the Landmark Decisions of the Foundational Period* (Cambridge University Press, 2019) 37.

product in question: whilst before 1 March 1960 the product in question was subject to an import duty of three per cent, after that date a rate of eight per cent was applied by customs authorities.[23] The applicant posited that such an increase was contrary to Article 12 EEC (a standstill clause), which prevented the Member States from increasing the customs duties applicable at the time when the EEC Treaty entered into force.[24]

The Tariefcommissie, a Dutch administrative court of last resort in revenue cases, made a reference to the Court of Justice asking two questions. First, it asked whether Article 12 EEC produced direct effect. Second, in the event of an affirmative reply to the first question, it asked whether the application of an import duty of eight per cent represented an 'unlawful increase', since such an increase was not due to the application of a higher rate but resulted from a modification of the tariff classification. The parties to the proceedings – the Dutch, Belgian and German Governments as well as the Commission – submitted written observations.

A. First Question

Before examining the merits of the case, the Court of Justice had to deal with the objections put forward by the Dutch and Belgian Governments regarding the admissibility of the first question referred. The former argued that the Court enjoyed jurisdiction to examine an alleged infringement of EU law by national authorities only under infringement proceedings. It lacked jurisdiction to do so under the preliminary reference procedure, as such an infringement related not to the interpretation of EU law but to its application.[25] For its part, the Belgian Government contended that the case boiled down to resolving a conflict between two international agreements, that is, the 1958 Brussels Protocol and the EEC Treaty. Such a conflict had nothing to do with the interpretation of EU law but was a matter for Dutch constitutional law alone and fell within the exclusive jurisdiction of the Dutch courts.[26] In addition, the Belgian Government argued that the first question referred was not relevant for the main proceedings, since regardless of the answer provided by the Court of Justice, the referring court would still have to decide, under the Dutch constitution, which of the two Treaties prevailed.[27]

In his Opinion, Advocate General Roemer took a different view.[28] He conceded that 'it [was] impossible to clarify exhaustively the real legal effects of an international agreement on the nationals of a Member State without having regard to the constitutional law of that Member State'.[29] However, this did not mean that the latter constitutional

[23] Those authorities argued that there was no increase of import duties given that prior to the entry into force of the EEC Treaty, the goods at issue were already subject to a 10% rate. The Tariefcommissie had not taken a formal decision in that regard when it referred the case to the Court of Justice. That may explain why the Court replied 'in law' to the second question.

[24] That provision read as follows: 'Member States shall refrain from introducing between themselves any new customs duties or imports or exports or any charges having equivalent effect and from increasing those which they already apply in their trade with each other.'

[25] Case 26/62 *van Gend en Loos* (n 2) 6.

[26] ibid.

[27] ibid.

[28] Opinion of AG Roemer in Case 26/62 *van Gend & Loos*, not published, EU:C:1962:42.

[29] ibid 18–19.

law applied exclusively in this matter, since – according to Advocate General Roemer – the interpretation of Article 12 EEC provided by the Court of Justice would clarify the intentions of the authors of the EEC Treaty (the contracting parties) as to whether Article 12 EEC produced direct effect. That said, in his view, the Court should limit itself to interpreting that Treaty provision, but 'without reaching a conclusion on the question how national constitutional law incorporates the intended effects of the [T]reaty into the national legal system'.[30] In addition, he argued that the Court of Justice had no jurisdiction to examine the relevance of the preliminary question in the proceedings before the national court, save in exceptional cases where the evaluation by the national court is 'manifestly wrong'. This was not so in this case, since it was not possible to determine how the referring court would resolve the conflict between the two international agreements at issue.[31]

For its part, the Court of Justice drew a distinction between interpretation and application,[32] which still holds true today.[33] Whilst it is for the national courts to apply the EU law provision in question to the case at hand, it is for the Court to interpret that provision. Since the Court was asked to interpret Article 12 EEC and, in particular, to determine its effects on individuals, it enjoyed jurisdiction to examine the first question. As to the additional argument put forward by the Belgian Government, the Court agreed with Advocate General Roemer that it fell within the jurisdiction of national courts to determine the choice of questions and their relevance for the main proceedings.[34]

As to the merits of the first question, the views of the Commission and those of the Member States that submitted written observations 'were not unanimous'.[35] On the one hand, the Commission opined that Article 12 EEC produced direct effect, putting forward three sets of arguments. First, in the light of 'the legal structure of the Treaty and of the legal system which it establishes', it argued that the Member States did not only intend to undertake mutual commitments but to establish a system of EU law that could be applied by national courts.[36] That Treaty was a 'far-reaching legal innovation' the nature of which could not be measured by traditional standards of 'the law of nations'.[37] Second, since EU law must be applied effectively and uniformly throughout the EU, national courts must apply that law directly and ensure that it prevails over conflicting provisions of national law. Third and last, the Commission argued that Article 12 EEC was 'perfectly clear' in that it contained 'a specific unambiguous obligation' that did not require any implementing measures.[38]

On the other hand, the Member States argued that Article 12 EEC did not produce direct effect. First, the Dutch Government drew a distinction between 'internal effect' (*interne werking*) and 'direct applicability' (*rechtstreekse toepasselijkheid*). Internal

[30] ibid 19.

[31] ibid.

[32] Case 26/62 *van Gend en Loos* (n 2) 11.

[33] See, eg, Case C-396/09 *Interedil* EU:C:2011:671, para 29 (holding that 'the Court is empowered to rule on the interpretation or validity of a rule of [EU] law on the basis of the facts which the national court or tribunal puts before it, and it is for the national court or tribunal to apply that rule to the specific case before it').

[34] Case 26/62 *van Gend en Loos* (n 2) 11.

[35] Opinion of AG Roemer in Case 26/62 *van Gend & Loos* (n 28) 20.

[36] Case 26/62 *van Gend en Loos* (n 2) 7.

[37] Opinion of AG Roemer in Case 26/62 *van Gend & Loos* (n 28) 20.

[38] Case 26/62 *van Gend en Loos* (n 2) 7.

(direct) effect relates to the question whether, in the light of the intention of the contracting parties and its content, a provision laid down in an international agreement contains rights that individuals may invoke and enforce. Direct applicability relates to the question whether an international agreement may, under national law, be relied upon before the national courts. Without internal direct effect (a right), there cannot be direct applicability (a remedy).[39] Since the wording of Article 12 EEC only imposed an obligation on the Member States, it did not produce internal direct effect. Second, since the EEC Treaty was no different from a standard international agreement, it was for national courts – and not for the Court of Justice – to decide, in the light of their own constitutions, whether that Treaty was directly applicable in their respective territories.[40] Third, if Article 12 EEC were to have direct effect, it would change the nature of the preliminary reference mechanism, which was not designed to examine whether a Member State acted in breach of the Treaties.[41] For their part, the Belgian and German Governments argued that Article 12 EEC did not produce direct effect, since it only imposed an obligation on the Member States and required national implementing measures.[42]

In his Opinion, Advocate General Roemer sided with the Member States. He appeared to follow, albeit implicitly, the conceptual distinction between 'internal effect' and 'direct applicability' put forward by the Dutch Government. First, he examined whether Article 12 EEC could produce 'direct internal effect'. To that end, he began by noting that:

> Anyone familiar with [EU] law knows that in fact it does not just consist of contractual relations between a number of States considered as subjects of the law of nations. The [EU] has its own institutions, independent of the Member States, endowed with the power to take administrative measures and to make rules of law which directly create rights in favour of and impose duties on Member States as well as their authorities and citizens.

He thus observed that some Treaty provisions could produce direct effect. To that end, he embarked on a horizontal analysis of the wording and content of the provisions contained in the EEC Treaty.[43] He found that, although some Treaty provisions 'are clearly intended to be incorporated in national law and to modify or supplement it', 'large parts of the Treaty clearly contain only obligations of Member States, and do not contain rules having a direct internal effect'.[44] This finding was consistent with the fact that the authors of the Treaty had introduced the infringement action as the way of dealing with defaulting Member States. If the principles of direct effect and primacy were seen as 'fundamental principle[s]' of EU law, infringement actions would become 'superfluous'.[45] Next, he examined the wording of Article 12 EEC and concluded that it only imposed a legal obligation on the Member States. This was, in part, because it did not contain terms such as 'prohibition', 'prohibited', 'inadmissible' or 'without effect' that were to be found in other Treaty provisions.[46]

[39] ibid 7–8.
[40] ibid 8.
[41] ibid.
[42] ibid.
[43] Opinion of AG Roemer in Case 26/62 *van Gend & Loos* (n 28) 20–21.
[44] ibid 21.
[45] ibid.
[46] ibid 22.

Second, as to the incorporation of EU law into the national legal orders, he observed that the constitutional laws of the Member States were far from uniform. There was no consensus as to the determination of the relationship between EU law and subsequent national legislation. Whilst in some Member States directly effective provisions may prevail over later national law,[47] in others this was not so clear.[48] That lack of consensus would give rise to 'an uneven development of the law involved in the principle of direct application' in relation to Article 12 EEC, which is a provision of great importance to customs law. This would be at odds with the intention of the authors of the Treaties.[49] Even among the Member States where international law prevails over national law, uniformity would not be guaranteed given that the same normative conflict might not be solved in the same fashion. The preliminary ruling mechanism would not be of much assistance either, since it is limited to questions of interpretation and does not grant jurisdiction to the Court of Justice to examine the compatibility of national law with EU law.

The Court of Justice did not follow the Opinion of the Advocate General, holding instead that Article 12 EEC produced direct effect. Its reply to the first question referred by the Tariefcommissie is contained in a passage of 12 paragraphs. That passage constitutes a true 'constitutional moment' in the history of European integration. Contrary to the arguments put forward by the Dutch Government and by the Advocate General, the Court rejected the contention that it was for the constitutional laws of the Member States to determine the way in which Treaty provisions are incorporated into their national legal orders. To use the terms in which the Dutch Government sought to frame the debate, both 'the internal effect' and 'the direct applicability' of Treaty provisions are questions of EU law falling within the jurisdiction of the Court of Justice. That may explain why the Court first looked at the 'the spirit, the general scheme and the wording of [the] provisions' of the EEC Treaty and only then, examined Article 12 EEC. In our view, the reply of the Court may be divided into three parts.[50]

To begin with, the Court of Justice examined the objective of the EEC Treaty, which was to establish a Common Market. That objective implies that that Treaty 'is more than an agreement which merely creates mutual obligations between the Contracting States'. That implication was confirmed by three findings. First, 'the preamble to the Treaty … refers not only to governments but to peoples'. Second, the fact that the Treaty had established institutions with 'sovereign rights' the exercise of which 'affect[ed] not only the Member States but also their citizens'. Third and last, nationals of the Member States were to participate together in the functioning of the EU 'through the intermediary of the European Parliament and the Economic and Social Committee'.[51] Moreover, the fact that the authors of the Treaties had entrusted to the Court the task of securing, by means of the preliminary reference mechanism, the uniform interpretation of EU

[47] This was the case for the Netherlands and Luxembourg. France would also fall within this category but AG Roemer found that the French Constitution was not so clear regarding 'later laws' and subjected the supremacy of international law to reciprocity.

[48] In Belgium, international agreements had 'the same status as national laws'. In Italy and Germany, the question of the supremacy of international law was subject to question.

[49] Opinion of AG Roemer in Case 26/62 *van Gend & Loos* (n 28) 24.

[50] See P Pescatore, '*Van Gend en Loos*, 3 February 1963 – A view from Within' in Poiares Maduro and Azoulai (eds) (n 3) 3, 5.

[51] Case 26/62 *van Gend en Loos* (n 2) 12. See also R Lecourt, *L'Europe des juges* (Bruylant, 1976) 249 (who argued that it is individuals more than the Member States who make the Common Market into an everyday reality).

law showed that '[EU] law has an authority which can be invoked by [Member State] nationals before [national] courts and tribunals'. In the light of the objective of the EEC Treaty, the Court came to the following conclusion which has become the 'mantra' of EU law and merits quotation in full:

> [T]he [EU] constitutes a new legal order of international law for the benefit of which the States have limited their sovereign rights, albeit within limited fields, and the subjects of which comprise not only Member States but also their nationals.

In that part of the judgment, the Court of Justice further rejected two arguments put forward by the Member States. It held that EU law not only imposes obligations on individuals but also confers rights on them. That is so 'Independently of the legislation of Member States'. Thus, contrary to the views of the Member States and those of Advocate General Roemer, national constitutional laws were not decisive in deciding the question of direct effect. The Court also rejected the 'uncoupling' of obligations and rights favoured by the Member States, holding that EU law rights are not only those 'expressly granted by the Treaty, but also by reason of obligations which the Treaty imposes in a clearly defined way upon individuals as well as upon the Member States and upon the institutions of the [EU]'.

Next, the Court of Justice looked at the 'general scheme of the Treaty', by examining the Treaty provisions relating to customs duties and charges having equivalent effect. It held, in view of Article 9 EEC (now Article 28 TFEU), that the EU is based upon a customs union, the establishment and proper functioning of which bans customs duties and charges having equivalent effects between the Member States. Article 12 EEC is to be understood in the light of that ban. The Court of Justice found that 'the wording of Article 12 contains a clear and unconditional prohibition which is not a positive but a negative obligation', which 'makes it ideally adapted to produce direct [effect]'. The Court also rejected the arguments put forward by the Member States concerning the need for implementing measures at national level, holding that Article 12 EEC did not require legislative intervention on the part of national authorities.

Last but not least, the Court of Justice went on to explain the relationship between infringement actions and the principle of direct effect. The former are not incompatible with the latter. Rather, both contribute to securing compliance with EU law. Otherwise, if the views of the Member States and those of the Advocate General were to be upheld, 'all direct legal protection of the individual rights' would be removed. Moreover, the Court found that infringement actions were 'ineffective' to secure protection of those rights when they are brought after the implementation of a conflicting national measure. That is why the EEC Treaty established a 'dual vigilance' system for safeguarding individual rights, under which individuals may act to protect their rights before national courts, whereas the Commission – and the Member States – do the same directly before the Court of Justice by bringing infringement actions.

B. Second Question

The Belgian and Dutch Governments argued that this question was inadmissible, since the applicant in the main proceedings and the Dutch customs authorities had different views as to whether there had actually been an increase in customs duties and the referring court had not yet given a formal decision on that question. Whilst acknowledging that the existence or absence of such an increase was a factual matter to be decided by the referring court in the light of Dutch law alone, the Court of Justice noted that the second question sought to clarify, in law, whether an increase arising from a modification of the tariff was compatible with Article 12 EEC.

As to the merits of the second question, the Court of Justice ruled that 'it [was] of little importance how the increase in customs duties occurred when, after the [EEC] Treaty entered into force, the same product in the same Member State was subjected to a higher rate of duty'. Such an increase could arise both from a modification of the tariff or an increase in the rate of customs duty applied.

IV. Reception History: Judicial and Academic

A month after it delivered its judgment in *van Gend en Loos*, the Court of Justice took the opportunity to confirm its previous findings. In *Da Costa and Others*, the Court was confronted with identical questions.[52] Awarding to *van Gend en Loos* the value of a binding precedent, it ruled that 'there [was] no ground for giving a new interpretation of Article 12 [EEC]'. This bears witness to the fact that the Court had settled the question of direct effect for good, even though we now know that the judges sitting in that case did not share the same views at first. Legal historians tell us that Léon Hammes (the reporting judge), André M Donner (the then President) and Otto Riese were, at first, inclined to follow the Opinion of Advocate General Roemer. However, in a memorandum ('*note en délibéré*'), Alberto Trabucchi, who had recently arrived to the Court, put forward the idea that the EU was a new legal innovation that placed individuals centre stage. Together with the active support of Robert Lecourt, also a newcomer, he managed to convince the two remaining judges – Louis Delvaux and Rino Rossi – to rule in favour of direct effect.[53]

Interestingly, the judges of the Court of Justice – even those who had originally taken a different view – acted with great institutional loyalty following the ruling, actively participating in 'spreading the word' about the birth of a new legal order, both in conferences and academic journals.[54] For example, in the first issue of the *Common Market Law Review*, President Donner wrote that that judgment was 'of cardinal importance for the entire operation of the EEC Treaty'.[55] Outside the Court, Michel Gaudet, the Director of the Commission Legal Service, who was the mastermind behind that institution's observations in *van Gend en Loos*, and the President of the Commission, Walter Hallstein, also stressed the significance of that judgment.[56]

[52] Joined Cases 28/62 to 30/62 *Da Costa and Others* (n 18).

[53] M Rasmussen, 'The Origins of a Legal Revolution – The Early History of the European Court of Justice' (2008) 14 *Journal of European Integration History* 77, 94. See, in this regard, P Gori, 'Souvenirs d'un survivant' in Tizzano, Kokott and Prechal (eds) (n 4) 29, 30 (who was the legal secretary of Judge Trabucchi and observes that the judgment was the result of a four-judge majority).

[54] For a full account, see Ziller (n 9) 37. See also Vauchez (n 15).

[55] Ziller (n 9) 40 (referring to AM Donner, 'National law and the case law of the Court of Justice of the European Communities' (1963) 1 *Common Market Law Review* 1, 13).

[56] Ziller (n 9) 39–41.

Academics broadly welcomed the judgment of the Court in *van Gend en Loos*, focusing their attention on the relationship between EU law and international law, and on that between the Court of Justice and national courts. Many scholars found the reasoning of the judgment solid and noted that it had broken away from conventional wisdom regarding treaty interpretation. Indeed, the judgment had 'reversed' the presumption against direct applicability of international agreements.[57] However, they rightly observed that the Court had not addressed the elephant in the room, that is, the question whether EU law prevails over conflicting provisions of national law. They attributed that silence to the sensitivity of that question or to the fact that the referring court had not explicitly asked the Court of Justice to address it.[58] Be that as it may, a year later, in its seminal ruling *Costa v ENEL*, the Court seized the opportunity to hold that EU law prevails over conflicting provisions of national law, 'however framed'.[59] Drawing on its main findings in *van Gend en Loos*, it dispelled any doubts regarding the primacy of EU law.

Unlike the principle of primacy, the principle of direct effect did not provoke a strong reaction from national courts and, some exceptions notwithstanding, faced little resistance.[60] Perhaps this was due to the fact that the direct effect doctrine was seen by national courts as a matter pertaining to treaty interpretation with which national courts were already familiar and did not require a 'clean break with their past habits'.[61]

More recently, academic debates have revolved around the judicial reasoning that the Court of Justice followed when it decided *van Gend en Loos*. Some scholars argue that the Court embarked on judicial activism in establishing the principle of direct effect, whilst others support the contention that the reasons in the judgment are sufficiently convincing to justify the Court's approach. The Neill–Edward debate may illustrate this point. In a long article, Patrick Neill, then Warden of All Souls College, Oxford, accused the Court of Justice of judicial activism, arguing that its case law was more the result of a self-empowering agenda than logic or reason. The judgment in *van Gend en Loos* was the first example where the Court 'carried [EU] law far beyond the written text of the various provisions' since it 'thought that an innovatory decision was called for'.[62] Favouring the textualist approach of Advocate General Roemer, he criticised the Court for disregarding 'the customarily accepted discipline of endeavouring by textual analysis to ascertain the meaning of the language of the relevant provision'.[63] In his reply to Neill's article, David Edward, at the time of his response a Judge of the Court of Justice, argued that the ruling of the Court did not come out of the blue but was progressively

[57] See, eg, F Rigaux, 'Note à l'arrêt van Gend en Loos' (1963) *Journal des Tribunaux* 190, 191.

[58] See J Bréban, 'Note à l'arrêt Van Gend en Loos' (1963) *Recueil Dalloz* 623, 626.

[59] Case 6/64 *Costa v ENEL* (n 2). See de Witte, ch 2 in this volume (who posits that 'primacy was unproblematic from the point of view of a Dutch court … The occasion for the [Court of Justice] to affirm the principle of primacy was offered, shortly after, by a preliminary reference from a modest but recalcitrant judge from a dualist country, in Case 6/64 *Costa v ENEL*.').

[60] Ziller (n 9) 42; and de Witte (n 12) 212.

[61] See de Witte (n 12) 212.

[62] P Neill QC, 'The European Court of Justice: A Case Study in Judicial Activism' (1995) *European Policy Forum/Frankfurter Institut – Stiftung Marktwirtschaft und Politik* 1, 3–4.

[63] ibid 47.

built on previous case law.[64] Notably, he observed that ECSC case law had already made clear that the EEC Treaty was 'both an international contract and the Charter of the [EU]'. That case law also showed that the Court had previously had recourse to contextual and teleological interpretations where the wording of a provision of EU law did not suffice to build a convincing reasoning.[65] In his reading, that ECSC case law was known to the authors of the EEC Treaty who 'did not feel it necessary to instruct the Court to modify its approach to interpretation'. Consequently, and legitimately, that approach continued when the EEC Treaty entered into force and led to the findings of the Court in *van Gend en Loos*.[66] Between the positions of those two scholars, others argued that *van Gend en Loos* was a difficult case where there was no clear answer to the question of direct effect,[67] and that the outcome therefore largely depended on the method of interpretation favoured by the Court (literal v teleological).[68]

As to the doctrine of direct effect, it is worth noting that the criteria enabling a provision of EU law to produce that effect – its content must be clear, precise and unconditional – have remained almost perfectly constant over time.[69] By contrast, the scope of that doctrine has progressively been expanded by the Court of Justice in three different ways.[70] First, the Court abandoned the distinction between negative and positive obligations, the latter also being capable of producing direct effect.[71] Second, an individual may rely on a directly effective provision of EU law not only against public authorities (vertical direct effect), but also – as far as Treaty provisions and regulations are concerned – against another individual (horizontal direct effect).[72] Third and last, the doctrine of direct effect covers not only Treaty provisions but also secondary EU legislation, including regulations, decisions and directives.[73]

However, directives may not produce horizontal direct effect, even if the provision in question is clear, precise and unconditional.[74] That said, the Court has ruled that

[64] D Edward, 'Judicial Activism – Myth or Reality? *Van Gend en Loos, Costa v. ENEL* and the *Van Duyn* Family Revisited' in A Campbell and M Voyatzi (eds), *Legal Reasoning and Judicial Interpretation of European Law: Essays in the Honour of Lord Mackenzie-Stuart* (Trenton Publishing, 1996) 29, 40ff.

[65] ibid 40 (referring to the following judgments: Case 1/54 *France v High Authority* EU:C:1954:7; Joined Cases 7/54 and 9/54 *Groupement des industries sidérurgiques luxembourgeoises v High Authority* EU:C:1956:2; and Case 8/55 *Fédération charbonnière de Belgique v High Authority* EU:C:1956:11).

[66] ibid 40–43 (referring to the following judgments: Joined Cases 27/58 to 29/58 *Compagnie des hauts fourneaux and fonderies de Givors and Others v High Authority* EU:C:1960:20; Case 6/60-IMM *Humblet v Belgian State* EU:C:1960:48; Case 13/61 *de Geus en Uitdenbogerd v Bosch e.a.* (n 21); and Joined Cases 2/62 and 3/62 *Commission v Luxembourg and Belgium* EU:C:1962:45).

[67] See, eg, R Schütze, *European Union Law*, 3rd edn (Cambridge University Press 2021) 153 (who points out that 'all judicial arguments [in the judgment] marshalled to justify a monistic reading of European law are debatable').

[68] H Rasmussen, *On Law and Policy in the European Court of Justice: A Comparative Study in Judicial Policymaking* (Brill, 1986) 12.

[69] It is worth noting that in Case 26/62 *van Gend & Loos* (n 2) 13, the Court of Justice used the expressions 'clear and unconditional'.

[70] E Stein, 'Lawyers, Judges, and the Making of a Transnational Constitution' (1981) 75 *American Journal of International Law* 1, 16–22 (who observes that the doctrine of direct effect underwent a 'triple expansion' since the judgment of the Court in *van Gend en Loos*). See, generally on the principle of direct effect, D Gallo, *Direct Effect in EU Law* (Oxford University Press, 2025).

[71] Case 57/65 *Lütticke* EU:C:1966:34.

[72] Case 43/75 *Defrenne* EU:C:1976:56.

[73] As to decisions, see Case 9/70 *Grad* EU:C:1970:78. Regarding directives, see Case 41/74 *Van Duyn* EU:C:1974:133.

[74] Case C-91/92 *Faccini Dori* EU:C:1994:292.

both general principles of EU law and provisions of the Charter may produce horizontal direct effect, even if directives giving concrete expression to those general principles or to those Charter provisions do not.[75] The Court of Justice has also applied the principle of direct effect to international agreements and to customary international law.[76] However, in relation to international agreements, the Court follows a two-step analysis, drawing a distinction between direct applicability and direct effect.[77] First, it examines whether the contracting parties intended the agreement at issue as a whole to be directly applicable before domestic courts (direct applicability).[78] If that question has not been expressly dealt with by the contracting parties, the Court of Justice will examine the nature and the broad logic of that agreement. If the requisite intention is present, the Court will, in a second step, examine whether the provision of the agreement in question is clear, precise and unconditional (direct effect).[79]

Moreover, it took more than 50 years for the Court of Justice to clarify the relationship between the twin principles of direct effect and primacy, putting to rest a long-standing academic debate.[80] In *Popławski II*,[81] it held that

> a national court's obligation to disapply a provision of its national law which is contrary to a provision of EU law, if it stems from the primacy afforded to the latter provision, is nevertheless dependent on the direct effect of that provision in the dispute pending before that court. Therefore, a national court is not required, solely on the basis of EU law, to disapply a provision of its national law which is contrary to a provision of EU law if the latter provision does not have direct effect.[82]

In order for such a provision to produce direct effect, it must be sufficiently clear, precise and unconditional. Moreover, primary EU law may rule out the possibility that

[75] Regarding general principles of EU law, see Case C-144/04 *Mangold* EU:C:2005:709 and Case C-555/07 *Kücükdeveci* EU:C:2010:21. As to the Charter, see Case C-414/16 *Egenberger* EU:C:2018:257; Case C-68/17 *IR* EU:C:2018:696; Joined Cases C-569/16 and C-570/16 *Bauer and Willmeroth* EU:C:2018:871; Case C-684/16 *Max-Planck-Gesellschaft zur Förderung der Wissenschaften* EU:C:2018:874; and Case C-193/17 *Cresco Investigation* EU:C:2019:43.

[76] As to the use of customary law for the purposes of challenging an EU act, see Case C-366/10 *Air Transport Association of America (ATAA) and Others* EU:C:2011:864, para 107 and the case law cited.

[77] JA Winter, 'Direct Applicability and Direct Effect: Two Distinct and Different Concepts in Community Law' (1972) 9 *Common Market Law Review* 425. It is worth noting that the two-step analysis mirrors, to some extent, the arguments put forward by the the Dutch Government in *van Gend en Loos*.

[78] As to the use of an international agreement for the purposes of challenging an EU act, see Case C-149/96 *Portugal v Council* EU:C:1999:574, paras 42–48; and Joined Cases C-401/12 P to C-403/12 P *Council and Others v Vereniging Milieudefensie and Stichting Stop Luchtverontreiniging Utrecht* EU:C:2015:4, para 54.

[79] Case C-366/10 *ATAA and Others* (n 76) paras 73–78.

[80] Prior to that judgment, academics had drawn a distinction between situations where the provision of EU law is sufficiently clear, precise and unconditional in order to set aside and replace the conflicting national measure at issue (in French, '*invocabilité de substitution*') and situations where the provision of EU law is sufficiently clear in order to set aside the conflicting national measure at issue without replacing it (in French, '*invocabilité d'exclusion*'). In their view, in relation to the latter situations, a conflicting provision of national law could be set aside, even if the provision of EU law did not produce direct effect. See, in this regard, Opinion of AG Saggio in Joined Cases C-240/98 to C-244/98 *Océano Grupo Editorial and Salvat Editores* EU:C:1999:620. See generally on this debate, CWA Timmermans, 'Directives: their Effects within the National Legal Systems' (1979) 16 *Common Market Law Review* 533; D Simon, *La directive européenne* (Dalloz, 1997); and S Prechal, 'Member State Liability and Direct Effect: What's the Difference After All?' (2006) 17 *European Business Law Review* 299.

[81] Case C-573/17 *Popławski II* EU:C:2019:530.

[82] ibid para 68.

a provision of EU law produces direct effect, as it is the case of a Framework Decision such as that at issue in *Popławski II*.

V. The Legacy of *van Gend en Loos*

A. Structuralism

In our view, a structural reasoning underpins the judgment of the Court of Justice in *van Gend en Loos*.[83] This seems logical since, when it delivered that judgment, the Court was beginning to expound its understanding of the 'new legal order' established by the EEC Treaty.[84] The Court, one may say, was looking at 'the big picture', and identified three elements of the constitutional framework that the authors of the Treaties intended to establish.

First, the Court of Justice observed that the EEC Treaty established institutions that are endowed with 'sovereign rights, the exercise of which affects Member States and also their citizens'. Unlike ordinary international agreements, the EU legal order has an institutional framework with autonomous regulatory powers, 'albeit within limited fields'. Second, the Court refers to the preliminary reference procedure as a mechanism that secures the uniform interpretation of EU law by national courts. It is 'the linchpin connecting the legal systems of the supranational and national legal orders'.[85] As the Court of Justice would later emphasise that mechanism is the 'keystone of the judicial system established by the Treaties'.[86] Third and last, the Court read the EEC Treaty as establishing a system of dual vigilance.

Whilst the centralised enforcement of EU law lies in the hands of the Commission – and, exceptionally, the Member States – by virtue of the principle of direct effect, any individual across Europe may also seek judicial protection of his or her EU rights before national courts. The Court was right to say that infringement actions were not sufficient to secure effective judicial protection of directly effective rights. That is because the Commission brings such actions after the infringement takes place and, in deciding whether or not to do so, may often take account of political factors. Moreover, private complainants cannot oblige it to bring such an action no matter how obvious and egregious the breach of EU law is. Conversely, political considerations play

[83] In US constitutional law, structuralism is a method of interpretation that 'refers to the constitutional relationships between the national government and the states, the branches of the national government, the government and the people and, in sum, the general arrangement of offices, powers, and relationships allegedly manifest in the Constitution's text and the settled facts of constitutional history. A strong concern for elaborating and maintaining proper governmental structures has been a prominent feature of constitutional debate in America. And few will deny that American judges should exercise their power in ways that maintain constitutional structures'. See, in this regard, SA Barber and JE Fleming *Constitutional Interpretation: The Basic Questions* (Oxford University Press, 2007).

[84] US scholars note that during the foundational years, structural considerations played a prominent role in the reasoning of the US Supreme Court. They refer to cases such as *Marbury v Madison* (n 3); *Martin v Hunter's Lessee*, 14 US (1 Wheat) 304 (1816); and *McCulloch v Maryland*, 17 US (4 Wheat) 316 (1819). See, in this regard, LH Bloom, *Methods of Interpretation* (Oxford University Press, 2009) 170ff.

[85] Halberstam (n 3) 113.

[86] *Opinion 2/13 (Accession of the European Union to the ECHR)* EU:C:2014:2454, para 198.

no role in the decentralised enforcement of EU law, as national courts become the '*juges de droit commun du droit de l'Union*' (courts of general jurisdiction for EU law). EU law confers directly effective rights on individuals 'which national courts must protect'.[87] As Halberstam observes, 'those five words changed the Union', as they have the effect of mobilising national courts to take an active part in the process of European integration.[88]

Over the years, the case law of the Court of the Justice has striven to complete that big picture by adding new elements, arising either from new cases or from Treaty amendments. Soon afterwards, for example, the Court first referred to the principle of primacy,[89] the principle of effective judicial protection,[90] the system of protection of fundamental rights[91] and, albeit considerably later, to the principle of mutual trust.[92] Simultaneously, it has also focused on describing those elements in greater detail. The evolution of the principle of effective judicial protection illustrates this point. The Court has consistently held that, in the absence of EU harmonisation, it is for national procedural law rules to provide for the relevant remedy, provided that those rules comply with the twin principles of equivalence and effectiveness.[93] However, it is by developing its case law that the Court fine-tuned that proviso. In so doing, the Court sought to strike the right balance between the need to provide for remedies that do not exist in national law,[94] and respect for national procedural autonomy.[95] Even today, the principle of effective judicial protection continues to evolve, since the effectiveness of national remedies is more often than not examined in the light of Article 47 of the Charter.[96]

Once the main features of the constitutional framework established by the Treaties have been sufficiently developed in respect of a particular issue, the Court of Justice then uses a structural reasoning in order to protect that framework. Since the EU constitutional structure places individual rights centre stage, such a reasoning also seeks to enhance the legitimacy of the EU over time.[97] Two recent examples taken from the case law illustrate this point, both relating to national courts.

First, the body of case law on the judicial independence of national courts is grounded in structural considerations.[98] That case law has made clear that the EU's constitutional structure would collapse without independent courts, given that those courts are an essential building block of that structure. Without independent courts, there cannot be effective remedies, nor judicial dialogue, nor mutual trust. Without them,

[87] Case 26/62 *van Gend en Loos* (n 2) 16.
[88] Halberstam (n 3) 114.
[89] Case 6/64 *Costa v ENEL* (n 2).
[90] Case 106/77 *Simmenthal* EU:C:1978:49.
[91] Case C-11/70 *Internationale Handelsgesellschaft* EU:C:1970:114.
[92] Those elements are summarised in *Opinion 2/13* (n 86) paras 157–77.
[93] Case 33/76 *Rewe-Zentralfinanz and Rewe-Zentral* EU:C:1976:188, and Case 45/76 *Comet* EU:C:1976:191.
[94] Case C-213/89 *Factortame and Others* EU:C:1990:257; and Joined Cases C-46/93 and C-48/93 *Brasserie du pêcheur and Factortame* EU:C:1996:79.
[95] Case C-432/05 *Unibet* EU:C:2007:163.
[96] See, in this regard, F Episcopo, 'The Vicissitudes of Life at the Coalface: Remedies and Procedures for Enforcing Union Law Before National Courts' in Craig and de Búrca (eds) (n 12) 275.
[97] Halberstam (n 3) 116.
[98] For a more detailed account of this argument, see K Lenaerts and JA Gutiérrez-Fons, *Les Méthodes d'interprétation de la Cour de justice de l'Union européenne* (Larcier, 2020) 67ff.

it would thus be impossible to guarantee that EU rights are properly exercised; to secure the uniform application of EU law; and to ensure the free movement of judicial decisions in the Area of Freedom, Security and Justice.[99]

Second, in *IS*,[100] the Court of Justice recalled that the judicial dialogue between itself and a lower court must be free from external interference, including interference exerted by the supreme court of the Member State concerned.[101] It is true that Article 267 TFEU does not preclude an order for reference from being challenged under national law. However, that Treaty provision precludes 'a decision of a supreme court, by which a request for a preliminary ruling is declared unlawful on the ground that the questions referred are not relevant and necessary for the resolution of the dispute in the main proceedings'.[102] That was so despite the fact that the referring court was not required to withdraw the order for reference. The Court reasoned that such a decision encroached upon its exclusive jurisdiction to rule on the admissibility of the questions referred for a preliminary ruling. By qualifying the order for reference as 'unlawful', the decision of the supreme court at issue also undermined the authority of the answers that the Court would provide to the referring court and the ruling that the latter would adopt implementing those answers. More broadly, that decision had the systemic effect of deterring national courts of the Member State concerned from referring questions to the Court, since national courts will naturally not wish for their orders for reference to be challenged by the parties or to be subject to an appeal in the interest of the law.[103] Most importantly, the Court observed that the decision of the supreme court at issue would undermine the system of dual vigilance set out in the Treaties. Referring expressly to its judgment in *van Gend en Loos*, it held that 'Limitations on the exercise by national courts of the jurisdiction conferred on them by Article 267 TFEU would have the effect of restricting the effective judicial protection of the rights which individuals derive from EU law'.[104]

B. Autonomy

As noted by Pernice, *van Gend en Loos* heralded the principle of autonomy of the EU legal order vis-à-vis international law.[105] In the following years, the Court of Justice continued to distance itself from international law. For example, whilst in *van Gend en Loos*, the Court wrote that 'the [EU] constitutes a new legal order *of international law*',[106] in subsequent judgments, the expression 'of international law' was abandoned

[99] See, in this regard, K Lenaerts 'On Checks and Balances: the Rule of Law within the EU' (2023) 29 *Columbia Journal of European Law* 25.

[100] Case C-564/19 *IS* (*Illegality of the order for reference*) EU:C:2021:949.

[101] See, eg, Case C-689/13 *PFE* EU:C:2016:199.

[102] Case C-564/19 *IS* (n 100) para 82.

[103] ibid paras 72–75.

[104] ibid para 76.

[105] I Pernice, 'The Autonomy of the EU Legal Order – Fifty Years After *Van Gend*' in Poiares Maduro and Azoulai (eds) (n 3) 55, 56.

[106] Case 26/62 *van Gend en Loos* (n 2) 12 (emphasis added).

by the Court. Similarly, in *Commission v Luxembourg and Belgium*,[107] decided a year and a half later, the Court of Justice rejected the contention that the principle of international law according to which 'a party, injured by the failure of another party to perform its obligations, [may] withhold performance of its own' (the so-called '*exceptio non adimpleti contractus*') was applicable under EU law. The Court wrote:

> [T]he Treaty is not limited to creating reciprocal obligations between the different natural and legal persons to whom it is applicable, but establishes *a new legal order* which governs the powers, rights and obligations of the said persons, as well as the necessary procedures for taking cognisance of and penalising any breach of it.[108]

In the same way, in *Costa v ENEL*, the Court ruled that

> [by] contrast with ordinary international treaties, the EEC Treaty has created its *own legal system* which, on the entry into force of the Treaty, became an integral part of the legal systems of the Member States and which their courts are bound to apply.[109]

However, that change in the Court of Justice's legal discourse should not be seen as an attempt to insulate the EU from its international law origins. That is because autonomy must not be confused with complete detachment. In the light of *van Gend en Loos* and the cases that followed, the Court strives to define the EU constitutional space, but without denying the fact that EU law influences and is influenced by the legal orders that surround it.[110] Fifty years ago, Pescatore observed that there are still remnants of EU law's international law origins in the Treaties,[111] namely the fact that Member States retain the 'treaty-making power'; that a Member State may bring an infringement action against another Member State; and that EU law 'allows certain supplementary agreements about matters peripheral to the main [EU] activities'.[112] More recently, de Witte has argued that 'the autonomy of EU law is not absolute but relative [since EU law has not] ceased to belong to international law'.[113] This can be illustrated by the fact that the Court has interpreted Treaty provisions bearing in mind the 1969 Vienna Convention. This is the case of the withdrawal clause contained in Article 50 TEU, which has its origins in the Treaty establishing a Constitution for Europe, and was drafted taking into account the 1969 Vienna Convention – in particular its Article 68 – which 'allows for the revocability of withdrawal notifications at any time before the withdrawal takes effect'.[114]

[107] See, eg, Joined Case 90-91/63 *Commission v Luxembourg and Belgium* EU:C:1964:80, 631.
[108] ibid (emphasis added).
[109] Case 6/64 *Costa v ENEL* (n 2) (emphasis added).
[110] See, in this regard, Lenaerts, Gutiérrez-Fons and Adam (n 7).
[111] P Pescatore, 'International Law and Community Law – a Comparative Analysis' (1970) 7 *Common Market Law Review* 167.
[112] ibid 180. See, eg, Case C-370/12 *Pringle* EU:C:2012:756 (in relation to the ESM Treaty).
[113] B de Witte, 'European Union Law: How Autonomous is its Legal Order?' (2010) 65 *Zeitschrift für öffentliches Recht* 155.
[114] Opinion of AG Campos Sánchez-Bordona in Case C-621/18 *Wightman and Others* EU:C:2018:978, point 108. See also Case C-812/79 *Burgoa* EU:C:1980:231, para 8; and Case C-264/09 *Commission v Slovakia* EU:C:2011:580, para 41.

C. Individual Rights and National Courts

The judgment of the Court of Justice in *van Gend en Loos* put individuals at the heart of the European integration project. By virtue of the principle of direct effect, the enforcement of EU law is not the exclusive purview of the EU institutions and the Member States which may, as political actors, be guided by the need to compromise. That enforcement may also take place before national courts where political considerations are not relevant in order to provide effective judicial protection. The idea that the EU is, first and foremost, a 'Union of rights' has been confirmed by the fact that the 'legal heritage' – to which the judgment in *van Gend en Loos* refers – has been enriched with every successive Treaty reform. The incorporation into the Treaty of provisions on EU citizenship by the Treaty of Maastricht and the fact that the Treaty of Lisbon elevated the Charter to the status of primary EU law, illustrate this point.

To conclude, had *van Gend en Loos* been decided today, we believe that the Court of Justice would also have relied on the second subparagraph of Article 19(1) TEU. That Treaty provision provides a solid, written authority, on the constitutional level, for the principle that the Treaties are capable of producing direct effect, and that the enforcement of EU law is based on a system of dual vigilance. Introduced by the Treaty of Lisbon, that Treaty provision reads as follows: 'Member States shall provide remedies sufficient to ensure effective legal protection in the fields covered by Union law.' That provision, which imposes a positive obligation on the Member States to provide for effective remedies, would lose much of its meaning without the principle of direct effect. Indeed, why would national courts be required to provide remedies protecting rights that are not enforceable before them in the first place? It would be like putting the cart before the horse. In our view, since the second subparagraph of Article 19(1) TEU obliges the Member States to provide effective remedies, that Treaty provision is necessarily based on the premise that EU law confers directly effective rights on individuals.

Accordingly, we support the contention that the principle of direct effect – and thus the judgment of the Court in *van Gend en Loos* – has found expression in the Treaties so that it is no longer accurate to say that that principle is entirely judge-made. What is more, coming full circle in a sense, the Court of Justice has ruled that the second subparagraph of Article 19(1) TEU itself produces direct effect.[115]

[115] Case C-824/18 *AB and Others (Appointment of judges to the Supreme Court – Actions)* EU:C:2021:153, para 146.

2

Costa and the Primacy of Union Law

BRUNO DE WITTE

I. Introduction

In cases brought before a national court in a European Union (EU) Member State, EU law must prevail over national law in the case of conflict. This simple idea goes under the name of the primacy of EU law, and is now generally recognised as an essential element of the EU legal order. The primacy rule, also often called the primacy *principle*, was not contained in the original Community Treaties and is still not contained in the current text of the EU Treaties.[1] It was, rather, established by the European Court of Justice (ECJ), as a 'product of judicial creativeness'.[2] This was done in an early judgment of 1964, *Costa v ENEL*, which is the subject of this chapter.[3] Following the general format of this volume, this chapter will successively discuss the historical and doctrinal context in which the *Costa* judgment arose (section II), the content of the judgment itself (section III), the reception of the primacy rule established in *Costa* by the national courts of the Member States (primarily those of Italy where the case originated) and by the national governments (section IV), and finally the further evolution of the primacy rule, which has been a frequent object of refinements and extensions in the 60 years since *Costa* (section V).

II. Historical and Doctrinal Context

Prior to the European Court judgment of 15 July 1964 in *Costa v ENEL*, the primacy of European Community law over national law was not firmly established. According to the dominant view in judicial practice and academic writing, this was not a matter to be determined by Community law itself but by the domestic legal orders of each of its six Member States, based on the broader idea that the status of international legal rules

[1] Except for a non-binding Declaration annexed to the Final Act of the Lisbon Treaty; see below section IV.
[2] F Mancini, 'The Making of a Constitution for Europe' (1989) 26 *Common Market Law Review* 595, 599.
[3] Case 6/64 *Costa v ENEL* EU:C:1964:66.

within the domestic legal order was to be determined by the constitutional rules of each country.[4] The fact that treaty obligations are binding on the states that have ratified a given treaty (a legal principle rendered by the expression '*pacta sunt servanda*', which stems from Roman contract law) implied that states could not invoke their national law as an excuse for failing to perform their treaty obligations towards the other contracting parties. As the Permanent Court of International Justice had put it in an inter-war case, it was 'a generally accepted principle of international law that in the relations between powers who are Contracting Parties to a treaty, the provisions of municipal law cannot prevail over those of the treaty'.[5] However, that principle applied to 'relations between powers', that is, it merely implied that an international treaty prevailed over national law on the *international* plane, whereas states remained free to organise their domestic legal order in the way they wished, possibly subject to incurring state responsibility under international law if they did not manage to ensure compliance with the treaty. Whether treaties could have *internal primacy* within a national legal order was a matter for that national legal order.[6]

On this question, the six Member States of the early European Community were divided into two groups, adhering to different conceptions of the relation between international law and national law: Germany and Italy were dualist, whereas France and the three Benelux countries were monist. In the dualist countries, courts and legal writing took the view that international treaties cannot, as such, display legal effects in the municipal sphere, so that their norms must be transformed into national law before they can become operational there. As the EEC Treaty had been duly transformed into national law in the dualist member states Germany and Italy, nothing prevented their courts from applying some of the norms contained in that Treaty to individual cases brought before them, 'as national law'. Indeed, already in 1962 (that is, prior to the *Van Gend en Loos* judgment of the Court of Justice), the Italian *Consiglio di Stato* had applied a 'transformed' provision of the EEC Treaty in an administrative law dispute.[7] However, the dualist perspective hinders the recognition of the primacy of international (or European) law. The relation between a norm of international origin and a purely national norm becomes, through the transformation of the former, a matter pertaining to the internal cohesion of the domestic legal order, and conflicts are to be solved according to the ordinary conflict rules applying within that order. As treaties are usually transformed by an act of the legislator, they will take precedence over conflicting administrative regulations and earlier legislative acts, but will be superseded in turn

[4] For a broad survey of the practice of domestic courts prior to the creation of the European Communities, see F Morgenstern, 'Judicial Practice and the Supremacy of International Law' (1950) 27 *British Yearbook of International Law* 42. For a comparative constitutional law study reflecting also the early (pre-*Costa*) national reception of EEC law, see M Waelbroeck, *Traités internationaux et juridictions internes dans les pays du Marché commun* (Pédone, 1969). For a retrospective view of the pre-*Costa* situation, see also M Claes, *The National Courts' Mandate in the European Constitution* (Hart Publishing, 2006) ch 2.

[5] Permanent Court of International Justice, *Greek and Bulgarian Communities*, Series B, No 17, 32.

[6] Today, the position in international law has not changed: the effect of a treaty within the legal system of the participating states is determined by the constitutional law of each particular country. See, inter alia: A Nollkaemper, *National Courts and the International Rule of Law* (Oxford University Press, 2012) ch 4; and Y Iwasawa, 'Domestic Application of International Law' (2016) 378 *Collected Courses of the Hague Academy of International Law* 21.

[7] Judgment of 7 November 1962, *Foro Italiano* (1963-III) 143.

by later legislative acts according to the rule *lex posterior derogat priori*. This was, at any rate, the received wisdom in both Germany and Italy in the early 1960s.

In the four monist countries of the early European Community, courts and legal writing took the view that international legal norms are, upon their ratification and publication, received within the national legal order while *preserving* their nature of international law. However, only in the Netherlands and Luxembourg did the courts occasionally recognise the primacy of international law in the case of conflict with purely national law. Although France, ever since the adoption of the Constitution of the Fourth Republic in 1946, had a very advanced constitutional provision recognising the primacy of international treaty law over subsequent legislation, the courts continued to adhere to the traditional separation-of-powers view that 'no French court is entitled to question the popular will as expressed by the representative assembly'.[8] The prevailing opinion was that the constitutional provision was addressed solely to the legislator and not to the courts, who were not allowed to set aside French laws conflicting with an earlier treaty. The same approach prevailed in Belgium.

III. Facts and Judgment in the Case

In the judgment of 1963 in *Van Gend en Loos*, the Court of Justice had affirmed and explained the doctrine of the direct effect of Community law, but it had not discussed the related question of the primacy of Community law, because that question had not been put to it by the referring Dutch court. Indeed, under Dutch constitutional law at the time, if a treaty provision was self-executing, it could prevail over conflicting national law. In other words, primacy was unproblematic from the point of view of a Dutch court, whereas direct effect of EEC Treaty norms was a matter on which it wanted to seek enlightenment from the European Court.

The occasion for the ECJ to affirm the principle of primacy was offered, shortly after, by a preliminary reference from a modest but recalcitrant judge from a dualist country, in *Costa v ENEL*.[9] Flaminio Costa had refused to pay a bill of the newly created national electricity corporation, ENEL, and argued before the *Giudice Conciliatore* of Milan (a local magistrate dealing with small disputes) that the Act of Parliament of 1962, by which the electricity industry had been nationalised, conflicted with the EEC Treaty. In an earlier dispute about the payment of electricity bills between the same two parties, another local judge had decided to refer questions about the constitutionality of the Electricity Nationalisation Act to the Italian Constitutional Court. That court, in its own *Costa v ENEL* judgment, which was handed down on 7 March 1964, some months before the European Court's, took the view that the Italian Constitution, in its

[8] G Bermann, 'French Treaties and French Courts: Two Problems in Supremacy' (1979) 28 *International and Comparative Law Quarterly* 458, 461.

[9] For a detailed study of the legal context in which the case emerged, and the role of some key actors, such as Costa's lawyer Stendardi, see A Arena, 'From an Unpaid Electricity Bill to the Primacy of EU Law: Gian Galeazzo Stendardi and the Making of *Costa v ENEL*' (2019) 30 *European Journal of International Law* 1017. An almost contemporary discussion of the case against its Italian legal background was written by E Stein, 'Toward Supremacy of Treaty-Constitution by Judicial Fiat: On the Margin of the *Costa* Case' (1965) 63 *Michigan Law Review* 491.

Article 11, allowed for limitations of sovereignty in favour of international organisations such as the European Community, but that this provision did not affect the domestic status of the European treaties or the rules produced by the Community institutions. It held that the existing rules about the domestic effect of international obligations should be applied in all dualist orthodoxy so that the EEC Treaty, which had been transformed into national law in 1957, could not prevail over the later Electricity Nationalisation Act of 1962.[10]

With the fresh support offered by its Constitutional Court, the Italian Government intervened before the ECJ in *Costa*, and submitted that the preliminary reference was 'absolutely inadmissible': as the Milan court had no power, under Italian law, to set aside the Electricity Act for breach of EEC law, its questions about the interpretation of EEC law could not serve a valid purpose. This open challenge to its jurisdiction encouraged the Court of Justice to formulate its doctrine of the primacy of Community law.

The judgment in *Costa* thus consists of two parts: the first part deals with the plea of inadmissibility raised by the Italian Government and contains the formulation of the primacy doctrine, whereas the second part deals with the substantive question of how to interpret the provisions of the EEC Treaty, which Costa had invoked in support of his claim. That second part did not come to a clear conclusion of incompatibility and is of anecdotal interest, whereas the first part acquired historical importance. The final ruling of the Court on the plea of inadmissibility was simple and clear: '[A]s a subsequent unilateral measure cannot take precedence over Community law, the questions put by the Giudice Conciliatore, Milan, are admissible in so far as they relate in this case to the interpretation of provisions of the EEC Treaty.'

The ECJ's task in *Costa* to establish the primacy rule was not an easy one. As was mentioned above, a duty for national courts to give precedence to norms of international law could arise under national constitutional law, but was not imposed by international law itself. If national courts failed to enforce international treaty norms, this could contribute to a situation whereby their state failed to comply with its treaty obligations and could incur state responsibility under international law, even though that possibility was, in practice, a very remote one. However, one of the original features of the EEC Treaty, when it was concluded in 1957, was to grant to the ECJ a jurisdictional competence that was then unique in the panorama of international law, namely that of guiding the activity of national courts while they are applying EU law by means of the preliminary rulings procedure. This procedure gave the ECJ a window of opportunity to intervene in pending national court cases and to direct those national courts to respect the precedence of EU law over national law. In order to seize that opportunity and arrive at that conclusion, the European Court used a vast array of arguments,[11] but insisted in particular on the special nature of the EEC Treaty, implying that by adopting a treaty like the EEC Treaty, with its focus on market integration, the Member States had accepted that its provisions should effectively apply within their national legal orders

[10] Italian Constitutional Court, judgment of 7 March 1964, No 14/64. See Arena (n 9) 1023–26.

[11] One can identify in the Court's reasoning a combination of contractarian, functional, egalitarian and analytic arguments for primacy, according to P Craig and G de Búrca, *EU Law – Text, Cases and Materials*, 7th edn (Oxford University Press, 2020) 305.

without being blocked by conflicting national laws. Here is the key part of the Court's reasoning:

> By contrast with ordinary international treaties, the EEC Treaty has created its own legal system which, on the entry into force of the Treaty, became an integral part of the legal systems of the Member States and which their courts are bound to apply. … The integration into the laws of each Member State of provisions which derive from the Community, and more generally the terms and the spirit of the Treaty, make it impossible for the States, as a corollary, to accord precedence to a unilateral and subsequent measure over a legal system accepted by them on a basis of reciprocity. Such a measure cannot therefore be inconsistent with that legal system. The executive force of Community law cannot vary from one State to another in deference to subsequent domestic laws, without jeopardizing the attainment of the objectives of the Treaty set out in Article 5 (2) and giving rise to the discrimination prohibited by Article 7. The obligations undertaken under the Treaty establishing the Community would not be unconditional, but merely contingent, if they could be called in question by subsequent legislative acts of the signatories. … It follows from all these observations that the law stemming from the Treaty, an independent source of law, could not, because of its special and original nature, be overridden by domestic legal provisions, however framed, without being deprived of its character as Community law and without the legal basis of the Community itself being called into question.[12]

The Court of Justice uses strong language in this passage, for example when stating that it is 'impossible' for the States to give precedence to a subsequent national law over EC law. It is clearly possible for them to do so, as in fact the preceding judgment of the Italian Constitutional Court showed. The ECJ meant to say that it is *impermissible* for States do so. The internal primacy of Community law is clearly something that only the national courts themselves could ensure and the ECJ could not have the ambition to change this. But what it could do, and did in *Costa*, is to impose an obligation under EC law on all national courts to give precedence to Community law in the case of conflict.

IV. Reception History

The crucial element for the effective application of primacy is the attitude of national courts and authorities. It is not enough for the Court of Justice to proclaim that EU law rules should have direct effect and should prevail over national law: 'to put it bluntly, the ECJ can say whatever it wants, the real question is why anyone should heed it'.[13] There is therefore a second dimension to the matter, which is decisive for determining whether the Court's doctrines have an impact on legal reality: the attitude of national courts and other institutions. The ruling in *Costa* was directly addressed to the *Giudice Conciliatore* of Milan, but beyond that local magistrate, to all Italian courts as well as the courts of all other Member States. Indeed, general legal statements made in a preliminary ruling have general authoritative value.

[12] Case 6/64 *Costa* (n 3) 593-594.
[13] KJ Alter, 'The European Court's Political Power' (1996) 19 *West European Politics* 458, 459.

A. Reception by the Italian Courts

On the merits of the *Costa* dispute, the interpretations by the ECJ of the various EEC Treaty provisions seemed to imply that the Italian nationalisation law was compatible with EU law. Nevertheless, the referring judge in Milan decided the dispute in favour of Mr Costa, who was dispensed from paying his electricity bill.[14] But nothing much else happened in the short run. The nationalisation law remained on the statute books, and continued to be enforced in Italy and, more generally, the Italian courts did not suddenly start reviewing the compatibility of national legislation with Community law. No further preliminary references came from Italy in the next few years. Indeed, the duty imposed on national courts by the *Costa* judgment went well beyond what the mainstream constitutional doctrine, at that time, was prepared to accept in terms of the domestic force of international treaty law. However, the Court of Justice had suggested, by distinguishing EEC law from ordinary international law in its *Costa* judgment, that the Italian courts might, with some creativity, find the constitutional resources needed for recognising the primacy of *Community law* whilst conserving their well-established dualist perspective on *international law* generally. This is indeed what eventually happened, nine years after *Costa*. In its *Frontini* judgment of December 1973, the Italian Constitutional Court came to recognise the primacy of Community law over national legislation, on the basis of its special nature which distinguishes it from other international treaties.[15] Article 11 of the Italian Constitution became the constitutional peg on which to hang the primacy of Community law, or, to quote another frequently used metaphor, the instrument piercing the barrier of dualism and allowing Community law to have effect within the Italian legal order.

The reasoning adopted by the Constitutional Court in *Frontini* ran as follows: Article 11 of the Constitution allows for limitations of sovereignty in favour of international organisations; the particular limitation accomplished by the ratification of the EEC Treaty is a restriction of the Italian Parliament's power to legislate in the domains transferred to Community competence or to legislate in contrast with Community law norms. Therefore, if, in the course of a dispute before an Italian court, a conflict emerged between Community law and a piece of legislation adopted later in time, the latter would be a breach of Article 11 of the Constitution. As ordinary courts could not themselves declare legislation void or inapplicable for violation of the Constitution, they needed to refer the case to the Italian Constitutional Court which would then declare the legislative act void and thereby ensure the application of Community law in the underlying dispute.

This complicated arrangement met the ECJ's demands only half way. The ECJ had required in *Costa* that *any* national court should be able to give precedence to Community law over national legislation. The *Simmenthal* case, another reference from

[14] See Arena (n 9) 1030–31.

[15] Italian Constitutional Court, decision no 183/73, *Frontini*. For a discussion of the gradual evolution in the Constitutional Court's position on the primacy of European law, see M Cartabia, 'The Italian Constitutional Court and the Relationship between the Italian Legal System and the European Union' in AM Slaughter, A Stone Sweet and J Weiler (eds), *The European Court and National Courts. Doctrine and Jurisprudence* (Hart Publishing, 1997) 133; and M Claes, *The National Courts' Mandate in the European Constitution* (Hart Publishing, 2006) 188–95.

a low-ranking judge (the *Pretore* in Susa) gave the ECJ an opportunity to push the Italian Constitutional Court further. The ECJ stated, in that well-known judgment from 1978, that the procedural detour imposed by the Constitutional Court in *Frontini* was not permissible and that *all* courts should have the immediate power to disapply national legislation when it conflicts with EU law norms:

> [A] national court which is called upon, within the limits of its jurisdiction, to apply provisions of Community law is under a duty to give full effect to those provisions, if necessary by refusing of its own motion to apply any conflicting provision of national legislation, and it is not necessary for the court to request or await the prior setting aside of such provision by legislative or other constitutional means.[16]

It then took another six years before the Italian Constitutional Court accepted the *Simmenthal* ruling; in its *Granital* judgment,[17] it held that, in the case of a conflict arising before any Italian court, the conflicting national norm should be deemed 'inapplicable', leaving room for the application of the EC law norm, without the need to eliminate the national norm from the statute books through an intervention of the Constitutional Court. The obligation formulated in *Costa*, and specified in *Simmenthal*, could now (20 years after *Costa*) be fully implemented in the Italian legal order. Beyond the particular case of Italy, the *Simmenthal* ruling had the broader effect of imposing to all Member States the decentralised enforcement of EU law – that it, the obligation for *any* national court seized with a dispute involving a directly effective norm of EU law to give it precedence over conflicting national law.[18]

B. Reception by National Courts in Other Countries

The *Costa* judgment was also, indirectly, addressed to the five fellow Member States of Italy. The way in which the German Constitutional Court hesitantly paved the way for the reception of *Costa* bears quite some similarity with what its Italian counterpart had done. It required a painful recalibration of the traditional dualist view of international law, as well as a recognition that all national courts could acquire a new power to review national legislation, as regards its compatibility with Community law.[19] No special efforts for the reception of the '*Costa* duty' were required from the courts in the Netherlands and Luxembourg, where the primacy of international treaty provisions over national legislation was accepted prior to 1957. The courts in Belgium reacted promptly and loyally to the European Court's injunction. Although the Belgian Constitution was silent on the domestic effect of international or European law (or precisely because of this absence of written rules) the Belgian supreme court (the *Cour de Cassation*)

[16] Case 106/77 *Amministrazione delle Finanze dello Stato v Simmenthal* EU:C:1978:49, para 24.

[17] Italian Constitutional Court, decision no 170/84, *Granital*. See the English translation of the core passages of the judgment, with an annotation by G Gaja, in (1984) 21 *Common Market Law Review* 756.

[18] On this broader significance of *Simmenthal*, see for instance D Piqani, 'The *Simmenthal* revolution revisited: what role for constitutional courts?' in B De Witte et al (eds), *National Courts and EU Law – New Issues, Theories and Methods* (Edward Elgar, 2016) 26.

[19] For a detailed study of the judicial and doctrinal acceptance of the *Costa* ruling in Germany, see K Alter, *Establishing the Supremacy of European Law: The Making of an International Rule of Law in Europe* (Oxford University Press, 2003) ch 3.

adopted the principle of primacy as it had been formulated in *Costa*, and based it on the nature of international law and (a fortiori) of EC law.[20] The other Belgian courts soon followed the same line.

In France, although the text of Article 55 of the Constitution recognised the priority of international treaties even over later French laws, the courts were surprisingly slow to accept that this constitutional provision could actually be used as a conflict rule in real cases and controversies. The *Cour de Cassation*, taking the lead of all ordinary courts, came forward in the 1975 *Cafés Jacques Vabre* judgment.[21] The *Conseil d'Etat* (and the administrative courts subject to its authority) followed suit only much later, with the *Nicolo* decision (1989) – that is, a full 25 years after the *Costa* judgment.[22]

For the 22 countries that joined the European Community (or the EU) after *Costa*, the situation was rather different. For them, unlike for the original six, recognising primacy did not require ex-post constitutional creativity, but was a matter of voluntary acceptance as part of the *acquis communautaire* upon their accession. As Lord Bridge put it in his speech in *Factortame (No 2)*

> if the supremacy within the European Community of Community law over the national law of member states was not always inherent in the EEC Treaty it was certainly well established in the jurisprudence of the Court of Justice long before the United Kingdom joined the Community.[23]

Following the lead of *Costa* thus became an implicit part of the *acquis communautaire* that all new members were expected to accept.

By and large, 'ordinary' primacy of Union law, that is, primacy over national *legislation* and sources of national law lower in rank than legislation, seems now firmly anchored in the national legal orders of all Member States, although with some important exceptions. In Denmark and Sweden, in particular, there is no other basis for the application of EU law than the statute which confers domestic effect on EU law, and EU law therefore remains in the best dualist tradition, at the mercy of a later, conflicting, statute, so that primacy remains a logical problem in those countries even if actual conflicts rarely arise.[24] Primacy over national *constitutional* law is quite another matter, on which there is no similar quasi-consensus across all EU states. Already in the *Costa* case, the Court held that Community law 'cannot be overridden by domestic legal provisions, *however framed*',[25] but the dispute before the Italian court concerned an act of the Italian Parliament and not the Constitution. The classic assertion of the precedence of Community law over even the highest ranking sources of national law came in the *Internationale Handelsgesellschaft* case in 1970. Faced with a challenge to the

[20] Cour de Cassation (Belgium), 27 May 1971, *SA Fromagerie franco-suisse 'Le Ski'*, 27 May 1971 (1971) *Revue trimestrielle de droit européen* 495.

[21] Cour de Cassation (France), *Jacques Vabre*, 23 May 1975 (1975) *Revue trimestrielle de droit européen* 336.

[22] Conseil d'Etat, *Nicolo*, 20 October 1989 (1989) *Revue trimestrielle de droit européen* 771. On the slow judicial acceptance of primacy in France, see Alter (n 19) ch 4.

[23] House of Lords, *Factortame (No 2)* [1991] 1 AC 603 (HL), 658.

[24] See the analysis by C Lebeck, 'Supranational Law in a Cold Climate: European Law in Scandinavia' (2010) *STALS Research Papers* No 4.

[25] Emphasis added. The original French text of the judgment is clearer: Community law '*ne peut se voir opposer de norme interne quelle qu'elle soit*'.

validity of a Community regulation for violation of the German Basic Law, the Court of Justice held that

> the validity of a Community measure or its effect within a member State cannot be affected by allegations that it runs counter to either fundamental rights as formulated by the constitution of that state or the principles of a national constitutional structure.[26]

The main reason offered by the Court was, very much in the spirit of *Costa*, that the unity and efficacy of Community law would be gravely affected if one allowed a review of its validity on the basis of particular national legal standards. However, extending the primacy of EU law even over national constitutions takes the logic of the *Costa* judgment into a more difficult terrain. Indeed, today, more than 50 years after the *Internationale Handelsgesellschaft* judgment, the view articulated by the ECJ, that Union law has primacy even over national constitutional provisions, is not generally accepted by national constitutional and supreme courts. As those courts have recognised the 'ordinary' primacy of EU law by grace of their own constitutional rules, they are unlikely to recognise that EU law might prevail over the very foundation from which its legal force derives.

Almost everywhere in Europe, the national constitution remains at the apex of the hierarchy of legal norms, and EU law is allowed to trump national law only under the conditions, and within the limits, set by the national constitution.[27] Most of the time, national courts apply the 'constitutional reservations' doctrine cautiously, if necessary by putting mild pressure on the Court of Justice through a 'judicial dialogue' conducted by means of the preliminary reference mechanism, but without challenging the validity itself of EU law. In some cases, though (notably in Germany, Denmark, Poland, the Czech Republic and Romania), national supreme or constitutional courts have refused to follow rulings by the Court of Justice, and have denied the primacy of EU law when that law was held to be in conflict with national constitutional law. Such contestations show the ultimate fragility of the principle of primacy: its effective recognition and application continues to depend on the willingness to cooperate from the side of the national courts of the Member States. Despite the formal authority of its judgments, the Court of Justice is not able to invalidate or set aside the judgments of national courts.

C. Reception by the Member State Governments

Whereas the message formulated in *Costa* was addressed to the national courts, one could also have expected the national governments and parliaments to react. In some

[26] Case C-11/70 *Internationale Handelsgesellschaft* EU:C:1970:114, para 3.

[27] For comparative studies of those national constitutional limits to the application of EU law, see P Craig and G de Búrca, *EU Law – Text, Cases and Materials*, 7th edn (Oxford University Press, 2020) 317–45; S Griller, L Papadopoulou and R Puff (eds), *National Constitutions and European Integration* (Hart Publishing, 2022); M Claes and B De Witte, 'The Roles of Constitutional Courts in the European Legal Space' in *Constitutional Adjudication: Common Themes and Challenges*, Max Planck Handbooks in European Public Law, Vol IV (Oxford University Press, 2023) 495, 517–25.

countries, especially among those acceding later to the EU, constitutional provisions were indeed enacted to expressly recognise the primacy of EU law, but in most countries the task of organising the smooth reception of the *Costa* rule was left to the national courts themselves. However, the governments of the Member States took one important common initiative in the framework of the Convention on the Future of the Union, in 2002–03. During that Convention, a consensus was reached fairly quickly and without much controversy on incorporating the principle of primacy into the Treaty text, as part of the Convention's general aim of 'simplifying' EU law by enhancing the visibility of its basic norms for the citizens. The relevant provision was incorporated in the opening part of the Treaty establishing a Constitution for Europe of 2004, as its Article I-6: 'The Constitution and law adopted by the institutions of the Union in exercising competences conferred on it shall have primacy over the law of the Member States.'[28] The article fell by the wayside when the ratification process of the Constitutional Treaty was interrupted in 2005. When the governments meeting in the European Council decided, in June 2007, to turn the Constitutional Treaty into a deconstitutionalised 'Reform Treaty', they considered that a deletion of the primacy article would fit in their strategy to weaken (or hide) the constitutional features of the treaty text. The principle of primacy was removed again from the text of the founding Treaties, and instead a new and much longer Declaration was adopted and attached to the Treaty of Lisbon, which is as follows:

> The Conference recalls that, in accordance with well settled case law of the Court of Justice of the European Union, the Treaties and the law adopted by the Union on the basis of the Treaties have primacy over the law of Member States, under the conditions laid down by the said case law.
>
> The Conference has also decided to attach as an Annex to this Final Act the Opinion of the Council Legal Service on the primacy of EC law as set out in 11197/07 (JUR 260):
>
> Opinion of the Council Legal Service of 22 June 2007
>
> It results from the case-law of the Court of Justice that primacy of EC law is a cornerstone principle of Community law. According to the Court, this principle is inherent to the specific nature of the European Community. At the time of the first judgment of this established case law (Costa/ENEL, 15 July 1964, Case 6/64) there was no mention of primacy in the treaty. It is still the case today. The fact that the principle of primacy will not be included in the future treaty shall not in any way change the existence of the principle and the existing case-law of the Court of Justice.[29]

So, the only written trace of the primacy principle in primary EU law is to be found in a non-binding annexed declaration, but that declaration does refer to the *Costa* judgment, which is thereby singled out as the one Court judgment mentioned in the European Treaty instruments.

[28] On the wording and significance of this provision, see P Craig, 'The Constitutional Treaty and Sovereignty' in C Kaddous and A Auer (eds), *Les principes fondamentaux de la Constitution européenne* (Bruylant, 2006) 117.

[29] Declaration (No 17) concerning primacy, attached to the Final Act of the Treaty of Lisbon [2008] OJ C115/344.

V. Conceptual Developments and Follow-Up Cases

The primacy case law of the Court of Justice has broadened and deepened over time. Two of the main extensions of *Costa* happened in the *Simmenthal* and *Internationale Handelsgesellschaft* judgments, as mentioned above (section IV). A further important extension happened in 1989 with the *Costanzo* judgment, where the ECJ held that the duty to disapply national legislation that is contrary to EU law is owed not only by national courts, but also by all other organs of the state, including administrative authorities when they decide claims based on EU law.[30]

Further ramifications of the primacy doctrine continue to happen, and the Court of Justice still uses *Costa* when developing its case law on the primacy of EU law. In the *Euro Box* judgment of 2021, the elaborate restatement of primacy starts with a nutshell summary of the *Costa* judgment. In that summary, the Court uses a curious mixture of the past and present tenses, which make it sound as if the EEC Treaty still existed in the year 2021:

> In the judgment of 15 July 1964, Costa … the Court laid down the principle of the primacy of Community law, which it understood to enshrine the precedence of Community law over the law of the Member States. In that regard, it found that the establishment by the EEC Treaty of the Community's own legal system, accepted by the Member States on the basis of reciprocity, means, as a corollary, that they cannot accord precedence to a unilateral and subsequent measure over that legal system or rely on rules of national law of any kind against the law stemming from the EEC Treaty, without depriving the latter law of its character as Community law and without the legal basis of the Community itself being called into question. In addition, the executive force of Community law cannot vary from one Member State to another in deference to subsequent domestic laws, without jeopardizing the attainment of the objectives of the EEC Treaty or giving rise to discrimination on grounds of nationality prohibited by that treaty.[31]

The reason for this detailed (and exceptional) rehearsal of the *Costa* judgment lies probably in the last sentence, in which the Court recalls the passage from *Costa* in which non-discrimination on grounds of nationality was mentioned as one of the justifications for imposing the duty of primacy. Indeed, in the following paragraph of the *Euro Box* judgment, the Court of Justice insists on the equality between the Member States as an important foundation of primacy:

> It must be added that Article 4(2) TEU provides that the Union is to respect the equality of Member States before the Treaties. However, the Union can respect such equality only if the Member States are unable, under the principle of the primacy of EU law, to rely on, as against the EU legal order, a unilateral measure, whatever its nature.[32]

This argument from equality had been launched the year before, in an unusual press release published by the ECJ in response to the *PSPP* judgment of the German

[30] Case 103/88 *Fratelli Costanzo v Comune di Milano* EU:C:1989:256, para 31. This has been confirmed many times since; see eg Case C-378/17 *Minister for Justice and Equality and Commissioner of the Garda Siochana* EU:C:2018:979, para 38.

[31] Case C-357/19 *Euro Box Promotions and Others* EU:C:2021:1034, para 246.

[32] ibid para 249.

Constitutional Court which had openly rejected a judgment of the Court of Justice.[33] It was also developed in writings by the President of the Court[34] and repeated in judgments after *Euro Box*.[35] There is a strange twist in the argument: in fact, the text of Article 4(2) TEU imposes a duty on the Union to respect the equality of the Member States. The argument thus uses an obligation imposed on the EU institutions as a justification for an obligation imposed on national courts.[36]

Apart from this case, in which the reference to *Costa* played a role in constructing a new dimension of the primacy doctrine, the judgment of 1964 remains very much in the background and is seldom cited.[37] More often, these days, the Court of Justice uses a standard formula that can be seen as the sedimentation of 60 years of case law following on from the *Costa* judgment:

> [I]t is settled case-law that, in accordance with the principle of the primacy of EU law, the national court called upon within the exercise of its jurisdiction to apply provisions of EU law is under a duty, where it is unable to interpret national law in compliance with the requirements of EU law, to give full effect to the requirements of EU law in the dispute brought before it, by disapplying as required, of its own motion, any national law or practice, even if adopted subsequently, that is contrary to a provision of EU law with direct effect, without it having to request or await the prior setting aside of that national rule or practice by legislative or other constitutional means.[38]

The core idea stemming from *Costa* is still reflected in the current formula, namely that there is a duty to disapply any rule of national law, even adopted subsequently, that contrasts with EU law. The additional rule, mentioned at the end of the sentence, that the national court seized with a dispute should disapply the national norm directly without waiting for other state organs to remove the norm, stems from the *Simmenthal* judgment of 1978 (see section IV above) and was applied in recent years, mainly to stop national courts from allowing the temporary application of national laws conflicting

[33] *Press release following the judgment of the German Constitutional Court of 5 May 2020*, No 58/20 of 8 May 2020, available at curia.europa.eu/jcms/upload/docs/application/pdf/2020-05/cp200058en.pdf: 'Like other authorities of the Member States, national courts are required to ensure that EU law takes full effect. That is the only way of ensuring the equality of Member States in the Union they created.' On the possible reasons prompting this new line of argument by the Court, see J Lindeboom, 'Is the Primacy of EU Law Based on the Equality of the Member States? A comment on the CJEU's Press Release Following the PSPP Judgment' (2020) 21 *German Law Journal* 1032, 1040–42.

[34] K Lenaerts, 'The Primacy of EU Law and the Principle of the Equality of the Member States before the Treaties' *Verfassungsblog* (8 October 2020); K Lenaerts, 'La primauté du droit de l'Union et l'égalité des Etats membres devant les traités' in E Dubout (ed), *L'égalité des Etats membres de l'Union européenne* (Bruylant, 2022) 35.

[35] Case C-430/21 *RS (Effets des arrets d'une cour constitutionnelle)* EU:C:2022:99, para 55.

[36] See the criticism on this point by F Weber, 'The Identity of Union Law in Primacy: Piercing Through *Euro Box promotion and others*' (2022) 7 *European Papers* 749, 765–66.

[37] It is cited, for instance, in Case C-234/17 *XC and Others* EU:C:2018:853, para 36; and in Case C-817/19 *Ligue des droits humains* EU:C:2022:491, para 293.

[38] Case C-107/23 PPU *Lin* EU:C:2023:606, para 95. Identical or almost identical wording in: *Euro Box* (n 31) para 252; *Ligue des droits humains* (n 37) para 293; Case C-205/20 *Bezirkshauptmannschaft Hartberg-Fürstenfeld* EU:C:2022:168, para 37; Joined Cases C-339/20 and C-397/20 *VD and SR* EU:C:2022:703, para 97; *RS (Effets des arrets d'une cour constitutionnelle)* (n 34) para 53; Case C-140/20 *Commissioner of An Garda Siochana* EU:C:2022:258, para 118. Of those judgments, only the last one mentions *Costa* as a key precedent.

with EU law whilst waiting for legislative action to repair the conflict (except when the ECJ itself allows for such a temporal suspension of primacy).[39]

The current primacy formula contains some important additional elements stemming from later judgments, namely the rule that the duty to disapply arises only where provisions of EU law have direct effect and the rule that the duty to disapply applies to 'any national rule or practice'.

As to the first of these two elements, the linkage between direct effect and primacy had not clearly surfaced in *Costa*. Or rather, the part of the judgment dealing with admissibility, which is where the Court formulated its primacy doctrine, did not mention direct effect, which could give the impression that the duty to disapply contrasting national laws could be triggered by any kind of binding Community law norm. However, in the merits part of the judgment, the ECJ examined, for each of the Treaty provisions invoked by Mr Costa, whether they had direct effect or not, which leads to the logical conclusion that, in the Court's view, only the ones considered to have direct effect would trigger the new duty to give precedence to Community law in the case of conflict. The linkage between direct effect and primacy was thus implicitly present already in *Costa*. Since then, it has become clear that primacy comes into play only when there is an actual conflict between two norms (a European and a national one) that are both capable of being applied by a national court to the facts of a case, that is, when the EU law provision has direct effect.

This linkage between direct effect and primacy in framing the duties of national courts was reaffirmed quite clearly by the ECJ in the fairly recent *Popławski II* judgment:

> [A] national court's obligation to disapply a provision of its national law which is contrary to a provision of EU law, if it stems from the primacy afforded to the latter provision, is nevertheless dependent on the direct effect of that provision in the dispute pending before that court. Therefore, a national court is not required, solely on the basis of EU law, to disapply a provision of its national law which is contrary to a provision of EU law if the latter provision does not have direct effect.[40]

In *Popławski II*, Dutch law was possibly incompatible with the Framework Decision on the European Arrest Warrant, but, as the Treaties expressly excluded the direct effect of framework decisions, the Dutch courts did not need to envisage the disapplication of the national law on the surrender of foreign nationals.[41] This limitation to the scope of primacy, confirmed in *Popławski II*, is, however, mitigated by the fact that the Court of Justice tends to generously recognise the direct effect of norms that do not appear, on their face, to be 'clear and unconditional', such as Article 19 TEU (on the role of national courts) and Article 325 TFEU (on the protection of the EU's financial interests). There is indeed a long-term trend in the Court's case law to loosen the direct effect test.[42]

[39] Case C-140/20 *Commissioner of An Garda Siochana* EU:C:2022:258, para 119. Underlying this case law is the problem that disapplication of national law by a court can create a legal vacuum and a problem of legal certainty, as it may not be clear, in certain situations, which other norms should apply instead of the disapplied law; see M Dougan, 'Primacy and the Remedy of Disapplication' (2019) 56 *Common Market Law Review* 1459, 1479ff.

[40] Case C-573/17 *Popławski II* EU:C:2019:530, para 68.

[41] On the circumstances of the case, see D Miasik and M Szwarc, 'Primacy and Direct Effect – Still Together: *Poplawski II*' (2021) 58 *Common Market Law Review* 571.

[42] M Bonelli, 'Growing Pains: Direct Effect, Primacy and Fundamental Rights after *Lin*' (2024) 61 *Common Market Law Review* 1045, 1061.

As for the rule, also contained in the current primacy formula, that the duty to disapply applies to 'any national rule or practice', it can be seen as building on the short passage in *Costa*, according to which Community law could not 'be overridden by domestic legal provisions, however framed',[43] although its main application was revealed in *Internationale Handelsgesellschaft* when the ECJ confirmed that European norms should be given precedence even over national *constitutional* norms (see section IV). The inclusion of 'any national *practice*' refers to the fact that national courts should not only set aside conflicting national rules, but also the case law of other national courts where that case law hinders the application of directly effective EU law norms. For example, in *Lin*, the Court of Justice imposed a duty on Romanian courts to 'disapply' judgments of the Constitutional Court and the Court of Cassation.[44]

A final important development in the life of the primacy rule is the changing significance of the term 'disapplying',[45] which is used by the ECJ to describe the duty of the national court. That term was absent from *Costa* whose final ruling rather stated that a conflicting national rule 'cannot take precedence' over Community law. This was specified in later cases as meaning that the conflicting national rule did not need to be annulled or voided but should just be 'set aside' or 'disapplied' in the particular dispute before the national court.[46] However, in the course of time the Court of Justice used the disapplication terminology to require national courts to do much more than merely 'setting aside' the conflicting national rule. In some cases, it was asked to take active steps to redraw the national legal landscape.

In the 1990 judgment *Factortame-I*,[47] the Court of Justice told the British courts to 'set aside' the unwritten constitutional norms defining their jurisdiction and their powers in relation to other state authorities. In fact, the national courts in this case were invited to assume new jurisdictional powers (namely, to offer interim protection in judicial review cases) and therefore *create* new law rather than leaving aside a national norm. This effect was even clearer in the state liability cases, particularly in *Brasserie du Pêcheur/Factortame*, where the Court of Justice held that national courts should also provide for state liability where the national legislature was responsible for the breach of Community law, whereas such liability for legislative acts was unknown to many national legal systems.[48]

In more recent years, the main way in which the Court of Justice has imposed such positive duties on the national courts is through its case law on Article 47 of the Charter of Fundamental Rights. The right to effective judicial protection of EU rights, protected by that article, has led the Court of Justice to take a close look at the concrete functioning of judicial review at the national level, requiring in some cases the creation of new

[43] The French text of the judgment states, more clearly '*un texte interne, quel qu'il soit*'.

[44] Case C-107/23 PPU *Lin* (n 38) paras 98 and 99.

[45] In the Court's working language the 'obligation to disapply a provision of national law' is worded, more elegantly, as '*l'obligation de laisser inappliquée une disposition de droit interne*' (see eg Case C-573/17 *Popławski II* (n 40) para 68).

[46] Clearly stated in Joined Cases C-10 to 22/97 *Ministero delle Finanze v IN.CO.GE. '90 and Others* EU:C:1998:498, para 21. See R Schütze, *European Constitutional Law*, 3rd edn (Oxford University Press, 2021) 200–04.

[47] Case C-213/89 *The Queen v Secretary of State for Transport, ex parte Factortame and Others* EU:C:1990:257.

[48] Cases C-46/93 and C-48/93 *Brasserie du Pêcheur v Germany and The Queen v Secretary of State for Transport, ex parte Factortame* EU:C:1996:79.

remedies or procedural rules, in order to ensure the effective enjoyment of the rights of Article 47. This happened in several cases in relation to the rights of asylum-seekers, where Article 47 was used by the Court to add positive procedural obligations beyond the ones explicitly spelled out in EU asylum legislation. For example, in *Torubarov*, the ECJ held that Article 47 required Hungarian courts to create a new remedy for the protection of asylum-seekers. It held that the referring court must be able to 'vary the decision at issue that does not comply with its previous judgment, and substitute its own decision … while disapplying the national law prohibiting it from proceeding in that way'.[49] The disapplication language is rather misleading in such cases, as the national court is required to create a new head of jurisdiction, for which it must summon a large amount of judicial creativity.[50] Also, in a number of Polish rule-of-law cases, the ECJ held that Article 47 Charter and Article 19 TEU required national courts to disapply, where necessary, the rules giving jurisdiction to 'non-independent' courts and seize a jurisdiction which national legislation did not give them.[51] In such cases, primacy is not just the usual substantive conflict norm (as in *Costa*), but rather a norm that reforms the structure of national judicial activity.

[49] Case C-556/17 *Torubarov* EU:C:2019:626, para 78.

[50] See a discussion of this recent trend in the Court's case law in M Leloup and LD Spieker, 'Rethinking Primacy's Effects: On Creating, Avoiding and Filling Legal Vacuums in the National Legal System' (2024) 61 *Common Market Law Review* 913, 940–49.

[51] Case C-585/18 *AK (Independence of the Disciplinary Chamber of the Supreme Court)* EU:C:2019:982, para 166.

3

Internationale Handelsgesellschaft and the General Principles of EU Law

TAKIS TRIDIMAS

I. Introduction

In the pantheon of judgments delivered by the European Court of Justice (ECJ), *Internationale Handelsgesellschaft*[1] occupies a distinct position. It elevated the principle of primacy to a new plain; it recognised the protection of fundamental rights as an integral part of the integration model; and it established the general principles of law as a self-standing source of constitutional doctrine. Few judgments, if any, have contributed more to the journey towards the constitutionalisation of European Union (EU) law. After explaining the judgment, this chapter discusses its implications for the protection of fundamental rights, the general principles of law, and the principle of proportionality. It then looks at its reiteration in the post-Charter era and its reception by national courts.

II. The Judgment in Context: Market Control and Constitutional Conflict

Internationale Handelsgesellschaft was decided in 1970, some 13 years after the establishment of the EEC. It came in the aftermath of two revolutionary judgments: *Van Gend en Loos*,[2] which established the doctrine of direct effect, thus challenging the nation state's monopoly to grant rights to individuals; and *Costa v ENEL*,[3] which declared primacy to be a general attribute of EU law. The political backdrop of the case was less compelling. At that time, EU law was at its infancy. In the late 1960s, the establishment of the common market was still at the planning stage and political disagreements among the Member States made decision-making in Council difficult. The EEC's achievements

[1] Case C-11/70 *Internationale Handelsgesellschaft* [1970] ECR 1125.
[2] Case C-26/62 *Van Gend en Loos* [1963] ECR 1.
[3] Case C-6/64 *Costa v ENEL* [1964] ECR 585, [1964] CMLR 425.

could be measured mostly by reference to the management of agriculture and some liberalisation in the free movement of goods.

Internationale Handelsgesellschaft involved an administrative law dispute arising in the context of the centrally controlled management of trade in agriculture. The EU regulations in issue[4] required traders who obtained licences to export or import agricultural produce to pay a deposit. If the export or import did not take place within the time specified in the licence, the deposit would be forfeited. The deposit system was intended to facilitate the operation of the intervention mechanism in cereals markets which guaranteed minimum prices to producers. The applicants had only managed a partial exportation and, as a result, had some of their deposit forfeited. They argued that forfeiture ran counter to the principles of freedom of action, economic liberty and proportionality guaranteed by Articles 2(1) and 14 of the German Basic Law (ie the Constitution). Following the Opinion of Advocate General Dutheillet de Lamothe, the ECJ made three important pronouncements: first, it stated that the validity of EU law cannot be tested by reference to national constitutional norms; secondly, it held that the EU institutions are bound to respect fundamental rights as general principles of EU law; and thirdly, it asserted that general principles of law are an autonomous source of EU law inspired but not dependent on the laws of the Member States.

The judgment was iconoclastic. First, the Court reiterated the primacy of EU law which it defended on functional grounds. Testing the validity of EU measures by reference to rules of national law would have an adverse effect on the uniformity and efficacy of EU law.[5] In the Court's eyes, the dispute raised an existential issue. It stated:[6]

> [T]he law stemming from the Treaty, an independent source of law, cannot because of its very nature be overridden by rules of national law, however framed, without being deprived of its character as Community law and without the legal basis of the Community itself being called in question. Therefore the validity of a Community measure or its effect within a Member State cannot be affected by allegations that it runs counter to either fundamental rights as formulated by the constitution of that State or the principles of a national constitutional structure.

The judgment took primacy to its outmost limits: any rule of EU law, however minor, takes precedence over any rule of national law, including the most revered dispositions of the German Basic Law, which benefit from an eternity clause.[7] The Court, however, continued:[8]

> [R]espect for fundamental rights forms an integral part of the general principles of law protected by the Court of Justice. The protection of such rights, whilst inspired by the constitutional traditions common to the Member States, must be ensured within the framework of the structure and objectives of the Community.

[4] Council Regulation No 120/67/EEC on the common organisation of the market in cereals [1967] OJ Special Edition 33; and Commission Regulation No 473/67/EEC on import and export licences [1967] OJ L204/16.

[5] Case C-11/70 *Internationale Handelsgesellschaft* (n 1) para 3.

[6] ibid.

[7] Under Art 79(3) of the German Basic Law, certain of its provisions, including those that guarantee fundamental rights, may not be amended under any procedure.

[8] Case C-11/70 *Internationale Handelsgesellschaft* (n 1) para 4.

Thus, even though EU law takes precedence even over the most precious provisions of the national constitutions, the Court reassures the Member States that the EEC Treaty shares their constitutional values and ensures ideological continuity. At the same time, it takes care to safeguard the autonomy of EU law. The national constitutional traditions provide 'inspiration' for respect of fundamental rights in the EU legal order. There their function ends. The scope and meaning of rights and the balance to be struck between them and competing interests is a matter for the Court to determine. The Court arrogates to itself important functions. Its approach, however, makes sense. The holding that the EU is bound by fundamental rights finds justification in the constitutional traditions of the Member States. As Mancini and Keeling note, it is hardly conceivable that 'the national parliaments would have ratified a Treaty which was capable of violating the fundamental tenets of their own constitutions'.[9] Once it is accepted that human rights form part of the EU legal order and bind the Union institutions, their protection must be ensured within the exigencies of the Union polity. The Union can promise to respect the same principles as those that govern the constitutional orders of the Member States, but it is difficult to see how it can promise to reach the same outcomes as those reached (or that might be reached) by national courts.

Having established that EU law protects fundamental rights, the ECJ went on to assess whether the system of deposits infringed them and gave a negative reply. The burdens imposed were not excessive in the light of the objectives of the policy.[10]

III. Building a *Corpus* of Fundamental Rights

The judgment established that fundamental rights bind the Union institutions, thus signalling that the regulation of trade by the EU and, consequently, also the construction of the internal market go hand in hand with the rule of law. Its political implications were important. First, it effected a significant transfer of powers from the courts of the Member States to the ECJ. National courts were precluded from testing the validity of EU measures vis-à-vis domestic standards of fundamental rights and, within the scope of the Treaties, had to defer to the authority of the ECJ. Secondly, the rulings strengthened the ECJ's power vis-à-vis the other EU institutions. The ECJ could now question EU action on grounds of compatibility with fundamental rights. The resonance of fundamental rights granted the Court an enormous input of legitimacy. By defending individual liberty, the ECJ could now play an important role in public discourse.[11]

The Court's call was correct. If it had refused to accept that the EU is bound by fundamental rights, national courts would have intervened to fill the resulting gap thus subordinating EU action to national constitutional standards. EU law would continuously have to yield to national law and primacy would have become a dead letter. The uniformity of EU law would also have suffered, 'lead[ing] inevitably to the

[9] GF Mancini and DT Keeling, 'Democracy and the European Court of Justice' (1994) 57 *Modern Law Review* 175, 187.

[10] Case C-11/70 *Internationale Handelsgesellschaft* (n 1) paras 5–20.

[11] JHH Weiler, 'Human Rights, Constitutionalism and Integration: Iconography and Fetishism' (2001) 3 *International Law Forum du Droit International* 228.

destruction of the unity of the Common Market and the jeopardizing of the cohesion of the Community'.[12] Without a firm grounding on the rule of law, the ECJ would have found it difficult to make the transition to the next generation of primacy cases and colonise the law of remedies. *Simmenthal, Factortame*, and *Francovich*[13] concretise the principles of primacy and direct effect. They are specific illustrations of the right to judicial protection, bred in a culture of fundamental rights which would be unable to flourish in the absence of *Internationale Handelsgesellschaft*.

The judgment was followed by *Nold*[14] and *Hauer*,[15] where EU measures were challenged as being in breach of the right to property and the freedom to trade as protected by the German Constitution. Although the challenges failed, the Court appeared more accommodating, declaring that measures which are incompatible with fundamental rights protected by the constitutions of the Member States cannot be upheld.[16] This more conciliatory approach was largely the result of the defiant reaction of the German Constitutional Court following *Internationale Handelsgesellschaft*.[17] It was a concession, but the Court was careful to retain residual control. Respect for the same rights does not mean reaching the same outcome on the facts. It is clear from *Nold* and *Hauer* that the content of a right as recognised in the EU legal order may be different from its content as recognised in the constitution of a Member State. This reflects the general position of the Court according to which, in deriving general principles of law from the national legal systems, it does not search for common denominators but makes a synthesis guided by the spirit of the EU Treaties and the requirements of EU polity. As Weiler points out, the EU is a new polity the constitutional ethos of which must give expression to a multiplicity of national traditions.[18] The frequent references to the constitutions of the Member States in *Nold* and *Hauer*, however, suggested that, in the field of fundamental rights, concepts of national law are more influential than in relation to other general principles. The reason for this is that respect for rights recognised as fundamental by the laws of the Member States provides political legitimacy and ideological grounding for the EU legal order.

Following *Nold* and *Hauer*, the ECJ began to build a *corpus* of fundamental rights. In *Wachauf*[19] and *ERT*,[20] it held that it had jurisdiction to assess the compatibility with EU fundamental rights not only of EU measures but also of national measures implementing and, more generally, falling within the scope of Union law. Those measures must also be assessed by reference to Union standards. This development exported EU standards to the national legal systems.

[12] Case 44/79 *Hauer v Land Rheinland-Pfalz* [1979] ECR 3727, para 14.

[13] Case 106/77 *Simmenthal* [1978] ECR 629; Case C-213/89 *Factortame* [1990] ECR I-2433; Joined Cases C-6 and C-9/90 *Francovich and others* [1991] ECR I-5357.

[14] Case 4/73 *Nold* [1974] ECR 491.

[15] Case 44/79 *Hauer v Land Rheinland-Pfalz* [1979] ECR 3727. See also Joined Cases 154 etc/78 and 39 etc/79 *Valsabbia v Commission* [1979] ECR I-907.

[16] Case 4/73 *Nold* (n 14) para 13; Case 44/79 *Hauer* (n 15) para 15.

[17] See below.

[18] J Weiler, 'Fundamental Rights and Fundamental Boundaries: On Standards and Values in the Protection of Human Rights' in N Neuwahl and A Rosas (eds), *The European Union and Human Rights* (Brill, 2021) 51, 66.

[19] Case C-5/88 *Wachauf* [1989] ECR 2609.

[20] Case C-260/89 [1991] ECR I-2925.

The Court's reliance on fundamental rights was criticised as utilitarian: it was not based on a genuine concern to uphold rights, but was used as an excuse to expand the ECJ's influence.[21] Whilst there is no doubt that, through its fundamental rights case law, the ECJ has increased its own power, *Internationale* should be viewed in a positive light. First, for the reasons stated above, it is difficult to see how the opposite solution could be sustained. Either the EEC Treaty remained an ordinary free trade agreement or it developed into an instrument of integration. The latter solution, which is more in line with the objectives of the Treaties, necessitated recognising respect for fundamental rights as a legal limit. Secondly, the ECJ rulings have infused a higher standard of rights protection and better governance standards both at EU and national level.

As EU law developed, the ECJ widened and deepened its fundamental rights jurisdiction. A national measure which restricts fundamental freedoms cannot be justified unless it respects also fundamental rights. It follows that a wide understanding of free movement broadens the range of national measures subject to the Court's fundamental rights control.[22] The development of Union citizenship as an independent source of rights, albeit minimal ones, has also enhanced the fundamental rights jurisdiction of the ECJ. The *Zambrano* test[23] appears to incorporate a fundamental rights enquiry: to determine whether state action deprives persons from the genuine enjoyment of their Union citizenship rights, the right to family life must be taken into account.[24]

Furthermore, the ECJ has elevated fundamental rights to core Union values accepting that their protection may take priority over free movement. *Schmidberger*[25] and *Omega*[26] are particularly instructive in this respect. In both cases, the ECJ upheld national restrictions on free movement on the ground that they sought to protect fundamental rights. The judgments promoted an integration model based on value diversity which views national constitutional standards not as being in a competitive relationship with the economic objectives of the Union but as forming part of its polity.

IV. The General Principles of EU Law: From Administrative to Constitutional Law

Internationale Handelsgesellschaft has had important repercussions not only for fundamental rights but, more generally, the development of general principles as a source law. In the early years of the European Communities, general principles were conceived as maxims of administrative law. Advocates General of the ECJ sought to cover the *lacunae* of written law by recourse to the general principles of law as they could be extrapolated from the legal systems of the Member States. Cases under the European Coal and Steel

[21] J Coppel and A O'Neill, 'The European Court of Justice: taking rights seriously?' (1992) 29 *Common Market Law Review* 669.

[22] See, for a particularly wide understanding of the free movement of services, Case C-60/00 *Carpenter v Secretary of State for the Home Department* EU:C:2002:434.

[23] Case C-34/09 *Zambrano* [2011] ECR I-1177.

[24] See Case C-133/15 *Chavez-Vilchez*, EU:C:2017:354.

[25] Case C-112/00 *Schmidberger* [2003] ECR I-5659.

[26] Case C-36/02 *Omega* [2004] ECR I-9609.

Community Treaty,[27] staff cases[28] and disputes in the field of agriculture[29] provided a fruitful ground for their development.

There was, in fact, little normative basis in the Treaties. The only express reference to general principles pertained to the non-contractual liability of the EEC and not to judicial review.[30] It was also of limited help since, traditionally, there have been wide differences among the laws of the Member States in relation to the liability of state authorities. Commonality therefore could be established only in the most abstract level. There were also two indirect references. Article 164 EEC Treaty (now Article 19(1) TEU, first subparagraph) states that the role of the Court of Justice is to ensure that, in the interpretation and application of the Treaties, the law must be observed. This provision, however, says nothing about where the law can be found. It was reasonable – indeed necessary – for the judiciary that was charged with the task of applying the law to seek to gain inspiration from the normative postures of the constituent legal systems.[31] This provided value continuity and acted as a source of judicial legitimacy. Although, in seeking to establish general principles, the ECJ did not necessarily found its inquiry expressly on Article 164 EEC Treaty,[32] the latter provides an anchor for a task that the Court inevitably had to undertake.

Another indirect reference was provided in Article 173(2) EEC Treaty (now Article 263(2) TFEU). By referring as a ground of review to the infringement of the treaty or 'any rule of law relating to its application', that provision could be taken to acknowledge judicial recourse not only to specific dispositions of written law but underlying principles that govern judicial review at national level.[33]

In truth, none of the above provisions explain fully the development of general principles as important sources of primary law. *Internationale Handelsgesellschaft* was the turning point. By binding the EU to respect unwritten fundamental rights as a quid pro quo for asserting the primacy of EU law over the national constitutions, *Internationale Handelsgesellschaft* propelled general principles to constitutional doctrine, elevating them to an integral part of the Treaties. *Internationale* marked the transition of general principles from sources of administrative law to defining pillars of constitutionality.

[27] See, eg, Case C-8/55 *Fédération Charbonnière Belgique v High Authority* [1954–56] ECR 292, 299; and Case C-19/61 *Mannesmann AG v High Authority* [1962] ECR 357, 370–71 (proportionality); Case C-14/59 *Pont-à-Mousson v High Authority* [1959] ECR 215 (equality).

[28] See, eg, Case C-32/62 *Alvis v Council* [1963] ECR 49 (rights of defence); Case C-18/63 *Wollast v EEC* [1964] ECR 97, 99 (proportionality).

[29] The earliest references to proportionality in this field are found in the Opinions of AG Gand in Joined Cases C-5, 7 and 13 to 24/66 *Kampffmeyer and others v Commission* [1967] ECR 245, 275; and AG Roemer in Case C-73/69 *Oehlmann v Hauptzollamt Münster* [1970] ECR 467, 481–83. See also Case 25/70 *Einfuhr- und Vorratsstelle v Koster* [1970] ECR 1161; Case 26/70 *Einfuhr- und Vorratsstelle v Henck* [1970] ECR 1183.

[30] See Art 215(2) EEC Treaty, which is now Art 340(2) TFEU.

[31] For an express reference to the need to gain inspiration from the solutions provided in the national laws to fill the gaps of the EEC Treaty, see Case C-7/56 and Case C-3/57 to Case C-7/57 *Algera and Others v Assemblée commune* [1957–1958] ECR I-44, 55.

[32] For an express link, see the Opinion of Warner AG in Case C-17/74 *Transocean Marine Paint Association v Commission* EU:C:1974:91.

[33] For the articulation of this argument, see P Craig, 'General Principles of Law: Treaty, Historical and Normative Foundations' in K Ziegler, P Neuvonen and V Moreno-Lax (eds), *Research Handbook on General Principles of EU Law* (Edward Elgar Press, 2022) 25–39; Oxford Legal Studies Research Paper No 46/2019, available at ssrn.com/abstract=3414315.

In the Court's conception, they derive not from any specific Treaty provision but from the nature of EU law in the light of a teleological and systematic interpretation. Their normative basis is thus inextricably linked to understanding the founding Treaties as a constitutional text. Once it is accepted that the Treaties establish a constitutional order, recourse to the general principles of law becomes inevitable to fill the empty shell of the EU's distinct constitutional space whilst ensuring value continuity and thus providing legitimacy. In a nutshell, teleology plus ex post facto acquiescence to judicial developments on the part of the Member States provide political, and ultimately legal, legitimisation of the general principles case law. These judicial developments received express treaty endorsement in the Treaty of Maastricht and now Article 6(3) TEU as amended by the Treaty of Lisbon.[34]

Following *Internationale Handelsgesellschaft*, a body of case law on general principles began to develop. This includes, among others, the protection of fundamental rights, the principle of non-discrimination, proportionality, legal certainty and the protection of legitimate expectations, and the rights of defence. The right to judicial protection lies at the apex. In relation to no other principle has the ECJ been more creative, in some cases coming dangerously closely to a *contra legem* interpretation of the Treaties, than in relation to that right.[35]

Internationale Handelsgesellschaft opened the way for the general principles of law to operate as strong forces of Europeanisation. They are constitutional in nature and rank above ordinary rules. They thus have an all-embracing binding effect. Furthermore, they have ecumenical scope. Being reflections of constitutional values, they do not apply only in specific areas of law but permeate the EU and the national legal systems and provide standards for determining the legality not only of public action but also private conduct. Moreover, they are applied not only by the ECJ, but also by national courts. Although this is also the case for written rules, general principles are in a distinct position here. Through their influence on judicial methodology, they resonate across the national legal system as a whole. Owing to their abstract nature, they foster a dialectical development of the law where national laws and EU law interchange roles as borrowers and lenders. Finally, they are characterised by hybridity in their application as, under the preliminary reference procedure, judicial outcomes are often the result of collaboration by the ECJ and the national courts. In a nutshell, general principles of law entail the convergence of national legal traditions using shared values as powerful reference points and thus nurturing a common constitutional conscience.

Despite the importance of general principles and their frequent invocation by the Court, uncertainties on some basic issues remain. There is terminological confusion. The term 'principle' or 'general principle' may refer to different categories of premises, eg rule of law principles or 'structural principles',[36] which underlie the EU legal

[34] See below, section VI.

[35] See, eg, in relation to EU measures, Case C-294/83 *Les Verts v Parliament* [1986] ECR 1339; Case C-72/15 *Rosneft* EU:C:2017:236; and, in relation to national measures, Case C-222/84 *Johnston v Chief Constable of the Royal Ulster Constabulary* [1986] ECR 1651.

[36] The term is used by M Cremona (ed), *Structural Principles in EU External Relations Law* (Bloomsbury, 2018).

system, such as the principles of autonomy or mutual trust. Somewhat paradoxically, Article 52(5) of the Charter uses the term 'principle' as the anti-thesis of rights.[37] At least for present purposes, the term 'general principle' refers to principles of law extrapolated from the common constitutional traditions of the Member States, which define the limits of power and seek to protect the individual. Thus understood, the term signifies *par excellence* the creation of constitutional doctrine. These general principles derive from the rule of law, as broadly understood in a liberal democracy, and now overlap with the EU Charter on Fundamental Rights.

The approach of the ECJ in extrapolating general principles is selective and creative. It does not look for a common denominator in the laws of the Member States, but makes a synthesis. As the Advocate General stated in *Internationale*, the fundamental principles of national legal systems[38]

> contribute to forming that philosophical, political and legal substratum common to the Member States from which through the case-law an unwritten Community law emerges, one of the essential aims of which is precisely to ensure the respect for the fundamental rights of the individual.

It appears that, to be elevated to the status of a general principle, a proposition must enjoy a degree of wide acceptance, that is, represent 'conventional morality'.[39] In *D and Sweden v Council*,[40] decided in 2001, the ECJ felt unable to equate a same-sex relationship sanctioned by national law to a marriage, but hinted that it would have been more adventurous if there had been support in the laws of the Member States.[41] Although the same facts would now be likely to be decided differently, *D and Sweden* is an example of self-restraint in the absence of crystallised national views on same-sex relations at the time that the judgment was delivered.

Nonetheless, the Court's methodology is both inconsistent and unpredictable. A prominent example is provided by *Mangold*.[42] The case concerned German law, which placed employees over the age of 52 in a less favourable position by allowing them to be employed on the basis of short-term contracts whilst employees below that age could not be so employed. The objective was to incentivise employers to reintegrate older workers in the employment market by offering them less social protection. The Framework Directive on Equality[43] prohibits, subject to certain exceptions, difference in treatment on grounds of age, but Germany had not implemented it. Since directives may not produce horizontal effect, it could not be relied upon in a dispute between private parties. Nonetheless, the Court held that the principle of equal treatment is not established by the Framework Directive itself. The Directive merely expresses that

[37] See T Tridimas, 'The general principles of EU law and the Europeanisation of national laws' (2020) 13 *Review of European Administrative Law* 5.

[38] Case C-11/70 *Internationale Handelsgesellschaft* (n 1) 1146.

[39] See JH Ely, *Democracy and Distrust* (Harvard University Press, 1980) 63, fn 97 and references provided therein.

[40] Joined Cases C-122 and C-125/99 *D and Sweden v Council* [2001] ECR I-4319.

[41] ibid paras 50–51.

[42] Case C-144/04 *Mangold v Helm* [2005] ECR I-9981.

[43] Council Directive 2000/78 establishing a general framework for equal treatment in employment and occupation [2000] OJ L303/16.

principle, its actual source being various international instruments and the constitutional traditions common to the Member States. It followed that the principle of non-discrimination on grounds of age was a general principle of EU law that could be applied in relations between private parties.[44]

This reasoning is remarkable. In the Court's rationale, the sources of the principle are to be found in the international instruments listed in the preamble to the Directive and the constitutional traditions common to the Member States. However, the preamble refers to a number of fundamental international conventions which pertain to the principle of equality before the law and the principle of equal treatment.[45] Only one of them makes express reference to age and this is only in a specific context.[46] The reference to the common constitutional traditions of the Member States appears unsubstantiated since it is not backed by any comparative analysis of national laws or case law. In fact, the constitutions of only two Member States recognised the principle at the time of the judgment.[47] The truth is that, until the very recent past, national laws were ripe with provisions creating differential treatment on grounds of age.[48] Neither the international conventions referred to in the preamble nor the constitutional traditions of the Member States point unequivocally to the derivation of a right against age discrimination in employment with a sufficiently specific ascertainable content. Whilst *Mangold* can be viewed as a bold and forward-looking judgment, its reasoning remains problematic.

Still, the reference to the common constitutional traditions in *Internationale*, and now in Article 6(3) TEU, cannot be understood as an expectation that the ECJ should conduct a thorough comparative analysis of all national laws or constitutions. In most cases, that would be as impractical as it would be unnecessary. Despite its resources, it would not be possible for the Court to do so. Even if it did, its analysis could only be superficial and it would open itself to criticism by national law experts. It is also doubtful whether such an exercise would dictate a solution. It is impossible to second guess how a national constitutional court would decide similar facts. Counting – that is looking at all national laws and trying to establish a majority – cannot be the solution. The purpose of the exercise is to provide value continuity and ultimately judicial legitimacy. Roaming into national laws can only be selective. Recourse to general principles of law is intended to anchor judicial solutions to common values rather than make EU law a prisoner of the past.

V. Proportionality

Internationale Handelsgesellschaft is also a key judgment for the development of the principle of proportionality. It firmly established the principle as a ground for review

[44] Case C-144/04 *Mangold v Helm* [2005] ECR I-9981, paras 74–75.

[45] See recital 4 to the Framework Directive.

[46] See ILO Convention No 111, which prohibits discrimination in the field of employment and occupation, Art 5(2).

[47] These were the Finnish and the Portuguese Constitutions.

[48] Age restrictions applied under many jurisdictions, eg, to access to the civil service and also to admission to practice as a lawyer.

and opened the door for its understanding as a principle of constitutional law, and not only as an attribute of administrative justice. It has since become the most oft-invoked principle in EU law and, in terms of its role in constitutional adjudication, the most influential.[49] It permeates virtually all areas of EU law and has developed into the pre-eminent balancing tool. Its appeal lies in its protean, malleable nature which enables the Court to balance conflicting rights and interests.

In contemporary EU law, proportionality fulfills three distinct but interrelated functions: it is a market integration mechanism used to determine the legality of national obstacles to the fundamental freedoms of movement; under the Charter, it is the main methodological tool for assessing whether a restriction on a fundamental right is justified;[50] and, under Article 5(4) TEU, it is, more generally, a principle of governance seeking to limit the scope and intensity of EU action for the protection of both Member States and citizens. In this respect, it goes beyond rights-review and is employed to assess whether EU action goes beyond what is necessary to achieve its objectives.[51] The underlying interests which proportionality seeks to protect in each of the above cases are different. As a result, the intensity of review may vary considerably.

Although in *Internationale Handelsgesellschaft* the ECJ upheld the proportionality of the deposit scheme, in other cases actions have been successful.[52] Proportionality acquires particular importance in the context of Article 52(1) of the Charter. Under that provision, any limitation on the exercise of Charter rights must satisfy the following conditions: it must be provided for by law; it must respect the essence of those rights and freedoms; and it must comply with the principle of proportionality. This means that limitations may be made only if they are necessary and genuinely meet objectives of general interest recognised by the Union or the need to protect the rights and freedoms of others.[53]

In practice, proportionality is by far the most important of the limiting conditions provided for in Article 52(1). The principle has been applied rigorously against both EU and national measures, especially in the field of data protection. In a series of cases, starting with *Digital Rights Ireland*,[54] the ECJ has held that the general and indiscriminate retention of traffic and location data for the purpose of combatting serious crime exceeds the limits of what is strictly necessary and cannot be justified within a

[49] For a discussion see, among others, A Stone Sweet and J Matthews, *Proportionality Balancing and Constitutional Governance: A Comparative and Global Approach* (Oxford University Press, 2019); VC Jackson and M Tushnet (eds), *Proportionality, New Frontiers, New Challenges* (Cambridge University Press, 2018); T Tridimas, *The General Principles of EU Law*, 2nd edn, (Oxford University Press, 2006) chs 3–5; P Koutrakos, N Shuibhne and P Syrpis (eds), *Exceptions from EU Free Movement Law, Derogation, Justification and Proportionality* (Hart Publishing, 2016); EJ Rivers, 'Proportionality and variable intensity of review' (2006) 65 *Cambridge Law Journal* 174.

[50] See Art 52(1) of the Charter.

[51] See, eg, Case C-62/14 *Gauweiler and Others v Deutscher Bundestag* EU:C:2015:400.

[52] See, eg, for successful challenge in the field of market regulation, Joined Cases C-453/03, C-11/04, C-12/04 and C-194/04 *ABNA & Others* [2005] ECR I-10423; Case 114/76 *Bela-Muhle v Grows-Farm* [1977] ECR 1211; Case 116/76 *Granaria* [1977] ECR 1247; Joined Cases 119 and 120/76 *Ölmühle and Becher* [1977] ECR 1269.

[53] See Art 52(1), last sentence.

[54] Joined Cases C-293/12 and C-594/12 *Digital Rights Ireland* EU:C:2014:238.

democratic society.[55] This has proved a point of tension between the ECJ and national courts who favour a less intrusive application of proportionality.[56]

VI. From General Principles to Constitutional Texts

Although the Lisbon Treaty made the EU Charter of Fundamental Rights binding, it preserved the general principles as a source of law and thus the authority of *Internationale Handelsgesellschaft*.

Article 6 TEU recognises three sources of fundamental rights: the Charter; the European Convention on Human Rights; and the constitutional traditions common to the Member States. Fundamental rights, as guaranteed by the last two, 'constitute general principles' of EU law.[57] The preservation of general principles serves to show that the Charter was not intended to make a break with the past but work in harmony with the *corpus* of existing case law.

Article 6 does not provide any guidance as to the relationship among the different sources of fundamental rights. It does not draw a priority between them nor does it differentiate between the Charter and general principles of law as to their effects.[58] Following the entry into force of the Lisbon Treaty, the primary point of reference for the protection of fundamental rights should be the Charter. This is in keeping with the intentions of the Treaty authors, which granted the Charter the same value as that of the Treaties, and also the objectives of the Charter as a document which concretises the values of the EU polity. Furthermore, viewing the Charter as the primary source of EU fundamental rights is more in keeping with national constitutional cultures which, bred in a civil law tradition, feel more comfortable with written lists of rights, however indeterminate, than case law.[59] The case law of the ECJ confirms that the Charter is now the primary point of reference.[60]

Nonetheless, the interpretation of the Charter will be informed by the general principles of law. The various sources of rights provided in Article 6 are interrelated in a way which may make it difficult to ascertain the autonomous input of each source. Notably, in *Glatzel* the Court held that the principle of non-discrimination, laid down in Article 21(1) of the Charter, is a particular expression of the principle of equal treatment

[55] See, eg, Joined Cases C-203/15 and C-698/15 *Tele2* EU:C:2016:970; Joined Cases C-511/18, C-512/18 and C-520/18 *Quadrature du Net* EU:C:2020:791; Joined Cases C-793/19 and 794/19 *Spacenet* EU:C:2022:702.

[56] See, eg, the response of the Conseil d'Etat in *French Data Network and others*, CE Ass, 21 April 2021, Req Nos 393099, 394922, 397844, 397851, 424717, 424718, FR:CEASS:2021:393099.20210421.

[57] See Art 6(3) TEU.

[58] For a more expansive analysis, see T Tridimas, 'The General Principles of Law: Who Needs Them?' (2016) 52 *Cahiers de Droit Européen* 419.

[59] An example of this is provided by the attitude of the German Federal Constitutional Court towards EU law. See, in particular, the *Honeywell* judgment of the *Bundesverfassungsgericht*, BVERFG, 2 BvR 2661/06, 6 July 2010.

[60] See, eg Joined Cases C-584/10 P, C-593/10 P and C-595/10 P *Commission et al v Kadi (Kadi II)* EU:C:2013:518; Case C-236/09, *Association Belge des Consommateurs Test-Achats* [2011] I-773; Joined Cases C-293/12 and C-594/12 *Digital Rights Ireland Ltd v Minister for Communications* EU:C:2014:238.

which is a general principle of the EU and is enshrined in Article 20 of the Charter.[61] Similarly, the Court views Article 47 of the Charter as reaffirming the general principle of effective judicial protection[62] and continues to refer as general principles of law both to fundamental rights[63] and the rights of defence.[64] Along the same lines, *HN* held that, whilst Article 41 of the Charter is addressed solely to EU bodies, the right to good administration enshrined therein is a general principle of law which binds not only EU agencies but also national authorities[65] and can be invoked against the latter even though Article 41 cannot.[66] The ECJ has thus been keen to preserve the independent normative input of general principles although their concrete added value in a specific case may not always be easy to discern. One can expect that the general principles of law will, in most cases, be used to influence and morph the interpretation of the Charter rather than establish autonomous, self-standing rights.

VII. Post-Charter Reiteration

Following the entry into force of the Lisbon Treaty, *Internationale Handelsgesellschaft* was reiterated in *Melloni*.[67] Article 53 of the Charter states as follows:

> Nothing in this Charter shall be interpreted as restricting or adversely affecting human rights and fundamental freedoms as recognised, in their respective fields of application, by Union law and international law and by international agreements to which the Union or all the Member States are party, including the European Convention for the Protection of Human Rights and Fundamental Freedoms, and by the Member States' constitutions.

Article 53 is intended to ensure compatibility between the Charter and other sources of fundamental rights. It is, however, ambiguous. What does it mean by 'in their respective fields of application'? What if there is an overlap among the respective fields of application of the various sources states therein? In *Melloni*, the Court subordinated Article 53 to the primacy of EU law. Reiterating *Internationale Handelsgesellschaft*, it held that that provision does not give general authorisation to a Member State to apply the standard of protection of fundamental rights guaranteed by its constitution when it is higher than that deriving from the Charter. Such an interpretation would undermine the primacy of EU law.[68]

[61] Case C-356/12 *Glatzel v Freistaat Bayern* EU:C:2014:350, para 43. This was reiterated in relation to the prohibition of discrimination on grounds of sexual orientation in Case C-528/13 *Léger v Ministre des Affaires sociales, de la Santé et des Droits des femmes* EU:C:2015:288, para 48.

[62] See Case C-64/16 *Associação Sindical dos Juízes Portugueses v Tribunal de Contas* EU:C:2018:117, para 35; Case C-510/11 P *Kone Oyj and Others v Commission* EU:C:2013:696, para 23.

[63] Joined Cases C-141/12 and C-372/12 *YS v Minister voor Immigratie, Integratie en Asiel* EU:C:2014:2081, para 54 and case law cited therein.

[64] Case C-166/13 *Mukarubega* EU:C:2014:2336, para 44.

[65] Case C-604/12 *HN v Minister for Justice, Equality and Law Reform* EU:C:2014:302; confirmed in Joined Cases C-141/12 and C-372/12 *YS v Minister voor Immigratie, Integratie en Asiel* EU:C:2014:2081.

[66] Case C-419/14 *WebMindLicenses* EU:C:2015:832, para 83.

[67] Case C-399/11 *Melloni* EU:C:2013:107.

[68] ibid paras 56–57.

Melloni concerned the compatibility of Article 4a of the Framework Decision on the European Arrest Warrant (EAW)[69] with the right to a fair trial. Article 4a provides that, if the person convicted *in absentia* was properly informed of the trial and chose not to appear or gave a mandate to a lawyer to defend him or her, the executing judicial authority is required to surrender that person. It cannot make his or her surrender subject to there being an opportunity for a retrial at which he or she is present in the issuing Member State. The ECJ held that Article 4a was compatible with the right to an effective remedy and the right to a hearing as provided in the Charter. It then held that that interpretation foreclosed the possibility of a Member State refusing to execute the warrant on the ground that the standard of protection of the right to a fair trial is higher under the national constitution. Such a view would run counter to the primacy of EU law.

Melloni projects an inclusive, centralised approach to the protection of fundamental rights placing the Charter at the apex of the edifice. It interpreted Article 53 as a soft conciliation clause but with little bite to restrict the interpretation of EU law by the ECJ. As the Court stated, if a Member State were allowed to make the surrender conditional upon the conviction being open to review in the issuing Member State in order to comply with fundamental rights as guaranteed by the national constitutional standards, that would cast doubt on the uniformity of the standard of protection as defined in EU law and undermine the principle of mutual recognition.

The application of national constitutional standards came again to the fore in *Taricco*[70] and *MAS*.[71] The cases concerned Italian rules pertaining to the limitation periods for the prosecution of criminal offences. In *Taricco*, the ECJ held that, to comply with the obligation of Member States to combat fraud against EU finances, a national court must disapply national rules of criminal procedure which prevented the imposition of effective penalties in cases of serious fraud. Subsequently, in *MAS*, the Italian Constitutional Court expressed doubts as to whether *Taricco* was compatible with the overriding principle of Article 25 of the Italian Constitution which requires that rules of criminal law are precise and cannot be retroactive. In its response, the ECJ held that, if the national court concluded that the obligation to disapply the provisions of the Criminal Code conflicted with the principle that offences and penalties must be defined by law, it would not be obliged to comply with that obligation. It would then be for the national legislature to take the necessary measures.[72]

A key difference from *Melloni* is that in *MAS* there was no EU legislation providing for specific standards. The ECJ allowed the national court to apply the higher constitutional standard provided by national law because there was no EU legislation governing the area. It held that the national authorities and courts remain free to apply national standards of protection of fundamental rights, on condition that the level of protection provided for by the Charter, as interpreted by the Court, and the primacy, unity and effectiveness of EU law are not thereby compromised.[73]

[69] Council Framework Decision on the European arrest warrant and the surrender procedures between Member States (2002/584/JHA) [2002] OJ L190/1.

[70] Case C-105/14 *Taricco* EU:C:2015:555.

[71] Case C-42/17 *MAS* EU:C:2017:936.

[72] ibid para 60.

[73] ibid para 47.

VIII. Reception by National Courts: The Conundrum of *Kompetenz-Kompetenz*

Internationale Handelsgeselschaft set in motion a conversation with the *Bundesverfassungsgericht* and other senior national courts as to the ultimate limits of authority.

According to the ECJ, the validity of EU law cannot be tested by reference to national law. Nor do national courts have power to determine the validity of EU law.[74] That power belongs exclusively to the ECJ. If it were otherwise, the uniform application of EU law would be prejudiced and legal certainty would suffer. National courts, on the other hand, start from a different premise. The EU is based on a transfer of sovereignty from the nation states to the Union. A national government, however, may not surrender more power than it possesses under the national constitution. Therefore to establish if the exercise of EU competence exceeds the powers surrendered to the EU, one has to look at the national constitution, of which the national supreme judiciary is the only rightful exponent. It is inevitable therefore that national courts must have the ultimate say.

Essentially, the answer to the question who has ultimate competence to define the outer limits of EU competence (*Kompetenz-Kompetenz*) receives a different answer depending on the underlying premise of one's reasoning. There is, in effect, a tacit agreement to disagree leading to a constitutional symbiosis which lies at the heart of the EU construct and makes the cooperation of the EU and the national judiciaries essential. Although it represents the fault line of the EU system, there have been only few head-on clashes.[75] Whilst the post-nation state constitutional paradigm remains unstable, there is a direct or indirect judicial dialogue through which the basic terms of the bargain morph. The threat of rebellion by the national courts provides a powerful control mechanism over the activism of the ECJ. But, at least in the overwhelming majority of cases, the conversation is disciplined, full of circumspection, and centres on boundaries rather than outcomes. Given how fluid the EU construct is, such symbiosis is a constitutional imperative. It enables the EU and the national legal orders to coexist in a state of creative disagreement.

Whilst, with limited exceptions, the judiciaries of the Member States have embraced the primacy of EU law as espoused by the ECJ, they have done so on the basis that the primacy of EU law does not flow from EU law itself but derives from, and is conditioned by, the dispositions of national law on the incorporation of EU law into domestic legal systems.[76] They reserve themselves the power to test *in extremis* the outer boundaries

[74] See Case 314/85 *Foto-Frost v Hauptzollamt Lübeck-Ost* [1987] ECR 4199; and Case C-461/03 *Gaston Schul Douane-expediteur* [2005] ECR I-10513.

[75] These include the judgment of the *Bundesverfassungsgericht* in *Weiss*, discussed below in this section; the judgment of the Czech Constitutional Court: Pl ÚS 5/12, 31 January 2012; the judgment of 6 December 2016 of the Danish Supreme Court in Case no 15/2014, which came in the aftermath of Case C-441/14, *Dansk Industri (DI), acting on behalf of Ajos A/S* EU:C:2016:278; and the unfortunate judgment of the Polish Constitutional Court (*Trybunał Konstytucyjny*) of 7 October 2021 (K 3/21), which provides for a wholesale denial of EU primacy and values.

[76] See the overview provided in the House of Lords, European Union Committee Sixth Report of Session 2003–04, 2 March 2004, Chapter 3, paras 64 et seq; and, for a comprehensive account, see, inter alia, S Griller, L Papadopoulou and R Puff, *National Constitutions and EU Integration* (Hart Publishing, 2022).

of EU competence by reference to their national constitutional principles. The path for this understanding of EU law was opened by the *Bundesverfassungsgericht*, which has been a particularly vocal interlocutor with the ECJ and has played an influential role in the development of EU law.

The German Constitutional Court found the judgment in *Internationale Handelsgeselschaft* unconvincing. It held that fundamental rights were insufficiently protected by EU law because, at that time, the Union lacked a codified catalogue of fundamental rights and also a directly elected Parliament.[77] Subsequently, in the *Second Solange* case (1986),[78] the Constitutional Court accepted that supervening developments had rendered the protection of fundamental rights at Union level sufficient. It referred to *Nold*[79] and subsequent case law, the 1977 Joint Declaration of the political institutions on human rights[80] and the European Council Declaration on Democracy of 1978.[81] The Constitutional Court accepted that it would not rule on whether an act adopted by the Union was sufficiently in conformity with the German Constitution as long as the Union continued to protect fundamental rights at an adequate level.

In subsequent cases, the Constitutional Court explained further the status of EU law under the German Constitution. The *Lisbon Treaty* case[82] evinced a more assertive approach and also a shift of emphasis. Whilst earlier judgments focused on the EU's ability to protect fundamental rights, the *Lisbon Treaty* judgment places emphasis on institutional guarantees, competence control, the principle of democracy and the need to safeguard constitutional identity.

Under the model introduced in the *Lisbon Treaty* case, as articulated in subsequent judgments,[83] the *Bundesverfassungsgericht* retains the power to review whether an act adopted by the Union institutions:

(a) is based on a 'manifest transgression of powers', that is manifestly exceeds the powers granted to the Union by the Member States (ultra vires review); or
(b) affects an area of constitutional identity which, under the German Constitution, cannot be transferred (constitutional identity review).

The Constitutional Court has since clashed with the ECJ in two cases, both pertaining to the limits of monetary policy as an exclusive EU competence and its distinction from economic policy, which remains largely within the province of the Member States. In *Gauweiler*, the tension created by a hostile preliminary reference made by the Constitutional Court[84] was defused after the latter followed the answer given

[77] See *Bundesverfassungsgericht*, judgment of 29 May 1974, [1974] 2 CMLR 551.
[78] See *Bundesverfassungsgericht*, judgment of 22 October 1986, 2 BvR 197/83, 73 BVerfGE 339, [1987] 3 CMLR 225.
[79] Case 4/73 *Nold* (n 14).
[80] [1977] OJ C103/1.
[81] EC Bull 3-1978, p 5.
[82] *Bundesverfassungsgericht*, decision of 30 June 2009, available at www.bverfg.de.
[83] See especially the *Honeywell* judgment delivered in the aftermath of *Mangold*. BVerfG, 2 BvR 2661/06, 6 July 2010, available at www.bverfg.de/entscheidungen/rs20100706_2bvr266106en.html.
[84] BVerfG, 2 BvR 2728/13, 14 January 2014, available at www.bverfg.de/en/decisions/rs20140114_2bvr272813en.html. For a discussion of the judgment, see, among others, the contributions in Special Issue, 15(2) *German Law Journal* (2014).

by the ECJ,[85] and upheld the compatibility of the ECB action with the German Constitution.[86]

A less friendly outcome was reached in *Weiss*. On a reference from the Constitutional Court, the ECJ held that the ECB's Public Sector Asset Purchase Programme (PSPP), under which the Eurosystem central banks purchased debt securities issued by Eurozone Member States, did not violate the EU Treaties.[87] But upon the return of the case to the Constitutional Court, the latter held that the PSPP was a qualified ultra vires act openly contradicting the ECJ.[88] The Constitutional Court found, in particular, that the PSPP did not satisfy the principle of proportionality. In its view, the latter requires the monetary objectives of the programme and its economic policy effects to be identified, weighted and balanced against each other. The failure of the ECB and the ECJ to do so amounted to a manifest and structurally significant excess of the competences that could permissibly be transferred to the EU pursuant to the principle of conferral under the German Constitution. The judgment was not received well by commentators, who expressed critique or even outcry, viewing it as an attack on the European Union,[89] a failure of German constitutionalism,[90] and even 'self-righteous' and 'rogue'.[91] The judgment may be criticised on several grounds. The test it proposed for distinguishing between economic and monetary policy does not take into account the interconnectedness between the two, nor is it in line with the model of the EU Treaties. It also advances a version of proportionality which is not in line with the case law of the CJEU.[92]

Following the judgment of the Constitutional Court, the ECB and the ECJ issued press releases. The former reiterated its commitment to do everything necessary within its mandate to ensure that inflation rises to levels consistent with its medium-term aim and that action taken to pursue the objective of price stability is transmitted to all parts of the economy.[93] The ECJ, without commenting specifically on the judgment, reiterated in general the binding character of its rulings and the need to ensure the uniform application of EU law in the interests of legal certainty and equality.[94]

In its judgment in *Weiss*, the Constitutional Court ordered the Bundesbank no longer to participate in purchases of bonds under the PSPP and take the steps necessary

[85] Case C-62/14 *Gauweiler and Others v Deutscher Bundestag* EU:C:2015:400.

[86] Judgment of 21 June 2016, 2 BvR 2728/13.

[87] Case C-493/17 *Weiss and Others* EU:C:2018:1000.

[88] Judgment of 5 May 2020, 2 BvR 859/15.

[89] See 'Ultra Vires? Peter Meier-Beck on the judgment of the German Constitutional Court' *D'Kart blog*, available at www.d-kart.de/en/blog/2020/05/11/ultra-vires/?fbclid=IwAR1072Y74rDHPkiGhr2TG2ElequDoUm6mdoi0U--kLjGMvWK-SiWYror0B0.

[90] P Eleftheriadis, 'The German Constitutional Court's Weiss judgment is a Failure of German Constitutionalism', available at www.eliamep.gr/en/publication/η-απόφαση-weiss-ως-αποτυχία-του-γερμανικού/ and https://verfassungsblog.de/germanys-failing-court.

[91] K Pistor, 'Germany's Constitutional Court Goes Rogue' (8 May 2020), available at www.project-syndicate.org/commentary/german-constitutional-court-ecb-ruling-may-threaten-euro-by-katharina-pistor-2020-05.

[92] See T Tridimas, 'From barking to biting: reflections on the Bundesverfassungsgericht judgment of 5 May 2020' in C Amalfitano and M Condinanzi (eds), *Paura dell'Europa: spunti di razionalizzazione* (G Giappichelli Editore, 2020) 143.

[93] See ECB press release of 9 May 2020, 'ECB takes note of German Federal Constitutional Court ruling and remains fully committed to its mandate', available at www.ecb.europa.eu/press/pr/date/2020/html/ecb.pr200505~00a09107a9.en.html.

[94] Press release No 58/20 following the judgment of the German Constitutional Court of 5 May 2020 (8 May 2020), available at curia.europa.eu/jcms/upload/docs/application/pdf/2020-05/cp200058en.pdf.

to reverse the purchases already made within three months unless the ECB issued a new decision demonstrating that the monetary policy objectives of the PSPP were not disproportionate to its effects on economic policy. The ECB did not issue a new decision but released several documents to provide further explanations of the rationale and impact of the PSPP. In response, Mr Olaf Scholz, then Finance Minister, and the Bundestag stated that these explanations satisfied the requirements of the Constitutional Court.[95] Given that the Federal Government and the Bundestag were the addressees of the judgment of the Constitutional Court, their reaction was important.

The *Weiss* dispute illustrates that the tension created by *Internationale Handelsgeselschaft* is still alive – but also shows the interdependence of the branches of government both at EU and national level. The disagreement was contained through an institutional dialogue conducted with circumspection and mutual deference. Although the ECB did not issue a new decision, as demanded by the Constitutional Court, it provided further justification and the Constitutional Court's objections are likely to have a prospective effect. The ECB's decisions in future cases are likely to be supported by a more comprehensive reasoning.[96]

IX. Conclusion

Internationale Handelsgeselschaft is one of the cornerstones of the integration bargain. It would be impossible to conceive of the EU in its current state of evolution without it. The judgment entrenched primacy, established that fundamental rights are an integral part of EU law, and elevated the general principles of law to constitutional norms. It brought proportionality to the fore, opening the way for its development to a key methodological tool in EU law adjudication. Perhaps, more importantly, by arrogating the primacy of EU law over national constitutions, it forced the national supreme courts to engage in the integration game.

[95] See at www.reuters.com/article/us-ecb-policy-germany/ecb-stimulus-plan-meets-court-requirements-german-finance-minister-idUSKBN2401OX.

[96] For an extensive discussion of the litigation, see the contributions to the ICON symposium on *Weiss* in (2021) 19 *ICON* 188.

4

Van Duyn and the Nature of Directives

SACHA PRECHAL*

I. The Historical Context

In 1987, Robert Kovar wrote 'La directive intrigue, dérange, divise. Sa singularité en est la cause.'[1] Indeed, the unique character of directives was for a long time a key source of debate. All efforts to capture it in terms of legal acts existing in international and national law seemed to fail.[2]

The most unique feature of the directive is arguably the two-stage process of norm-setting which it implies. First, the norm is laid down at the European Union (EU) level, in the content of the directive, and then on the national level. The Member State transposes the content of the directive into national law and thus turns it into a normative measure of domestic law. In the view of the Court of Justice of the European Union (CJEU), directives are *indirect* regulatory or legislative measures.[3] This also means that, in principle, directives are *indirect* sources of rights and obligations for individuals. The rights and obligations under national law find their origin in the directive. It is only after the process of transposition that these rights and obligations become fully binding for individuals within the Member States.

At the root of considerable problems and disagreement was the rather rudimentary definition of the legally binding Union law instruments set out in Article 288 TFEU. While some authors proposed to abolish the directive as an instrument of Union law, since in their view it was a failure, others considered it to be an ideal or original instrument, suitable to fulfil the functions it was designed for within the system of the TFEU.[4]

* All views expressed in this contribution are strictly personal.

[1] R Kovar, 'Observations sur l'intensité normative des directives' in F Capotorti et al (eds), *Du droit international au droit de l'intégration. Liber Amicorum Pierre Pescatore* (Nomos Verlagsgesellschaft, 1987) 359.

[2] S Prechal, *Directives in EC Law*, 2nd edn (Oxford University Press, 2005) 1, with further references.

[3] Case C-298/89 *Government of Gibraltar v Council* EU:C:1993:267, para 16. Note that the judgment dates from the pre-TFEU era. The TFEU introduced a new distinction between legislative and non-legislative acts in Arts 289 et seq. Interestingly, already in the *Van Duyn* judgment the Court qualified the directive at issue as a 'legislative act ['*un acte normatif*' in the French version] which has no automatic direct effect in its entirety'. Case 41/74 *Van Duyn v Home Office* EU:C:1974:133, para 13.

[4] See HP Ipsen, 'Richtlinien-Ergebnisse' in W Hallstein and HJ Schlochauer (eds), *Zur Integration Europas. Festschrift für Carl Friedrich Ophüls aus Anlass seines siebzigsten Geburtstages* (Verlag CF Müller, 1965) 69, with further references.

According to this definition, a directive is binding in two respects: as to the result to be achieved; and upon each Member State to which it is addressed. However, it leaves the Member States free to determine the form and methods of implementation. This definition, and in particular the unclear relationship between the result and the form and methods of implementation, gave rise to questions as to the binding nature of directives.[5] Moreover, the fact that directives are binding as to the result to be achieved could suggest that they lay down, in fairly general terms, certain objectives which are to be accomplished. In particular, in German legal writing this issue has given rise to considerable speculation as to the meaning of the term 'result'[6] *and* its implications for the content of directives.

Initially, the analyses and controversies were mainly of a theoretical and conceptual nature. Soon, however, the debate also developed a practical dimension. There are two strands to this debate, which partly overlap.

The first concentrates on the increasingly detailed content of directives, on what is perceived as improper use of the instrument (ie usually instead of regulations), the blurred distinction between directives and regulations and the neverending problems of adequate and timely implementation of directives in the Member States. The last issue raises, inter alia, intriguing questions as to the exact meaning of the term 'form and methods' and, in particular, the limits to the freedom Member States enjoy in relation to the form and methods of implementation. This freedom is limited by, on the one hand, case law of the CJEU and, on the other hand, the increasingly detailed nature of directives: the more precise and detailed the content of a directive, the less room for manoeuvre for the implementing authorities.[7]

The second strand of the debate relates to the direct effect of directives. In fact, already at a relatively early stage in the 'history' of Union law and soon after the case law of the CJEU on direct effect of Treaty provisions started to develop, a significant amount of effort was invested into considering whether directives could produce direct effect. Indeed, there were opponents as well as advocates of the direct effect of directives and other scholars taking an intermediate position. This last group allowed a sort of 'restricted direct effect', principally to maintain the distinction between regulations and directives, or so that directives could be used as a shield but not a sword. For other authors, the time was simply 'not ripe' for accepting the direct effect of directives.[8]

The principal argument against the direct effect[9] of directives was primarily based on the text of Article 288 TFEU: directives are only binding upon the Member States, which are the only addressees of a directive, and they are only binding in respect of the result to be achieved, leaving the choice of form and methods to national authorities. Therefore, any effect on individuals could only arise from the implementing measures. Furthermore, the distinction between regulations and directives made it clear that only the former are directly applicable in the Member States. A recognition of the direct effect of directives would blur the distinction between the two instruments, which would lead to legal uncertainty, affect the principle of special powers and upset the system of Union

[5] Case 14/83 *Von Colson v Land Nordrhein-Westfalen* EU:C:1984:153, para 15.

[6] Ipsen (n 4) 72–74.

[7] For a detailed discussion, see Prechal (n 2) ch 5.

[8] For an overview of the discussion, see ibid 216–19, with further references.

[9] *cf* also the observations of the Commission in Case 9/70 *Grad v Finanzamt Traunstein* EU:C:1970:78, 831–33.

acts as laid down in the Treaty.[10] An additional argument drew on the fact that directives do not have to be published. This has repercussions for equality before the law and legal certainty since the direct effect of the directive would depend on whether an individual wishing to invoke the directive was aware of its existence.

Those arguing in favour of the direct effect of directives dismissed the above-mentioned arguments as formalistic. In their view, the case law of the Court on the direct effect of Treaty provisions made it clear that it is the nature and content of the provision in question which are decisive and not the addressee of the act. They also argued that it could not simply be deduced from the fact that Article 288 TFEU defines regulations as directly applicable that directives cannot have direct effect. Indeed, paragraph 3 of that Article does not state this explicitly. Finally, they stressed that the acceptance of the direct effect of directives would both strengthen the legal protection of individuals and promote EU integration.

In 1970, in the cases of *Grad*[11] and *SACE*,[12] the Court moved in the direction of accepting the direct effect of directives. However, since both cases related to the combined effect of directives and other provisions, these judgments did not clarify the problem entirely. Clarification only came in the next case, *Van Duyn*.[13]

In any case, as was observed by Everling, the case law of the Court on the direct effect of directives was preceded by an intense debate in academic writing which more or less 'prepared the ground' for the Court's decisions.[14]

II. Facts and Judgment in *Van Duyn*

In May 1973, Ms Van Duyn, a Dutch national, flew to the UK with the intention of taking up employment as a secretary with the Church of Scientology at its college at East Grinstead. After landing at the airport, she was refused leave to enter the UK on the grounds that the Secretary of State considered it undesirable to give people affiliated with the organisation such permission. This refusal was based on policy enacted at the time by the UK Government, which considered Scientology to be socially harmful.

Ms Van Duyn then challenged this refusal before the UK High Court, arguing that it violated the free movement of workers enshrined in – then – Article 48 of the EEC Treaty as well as Article 3(1) of Directive 64/221.[15] According to the latter provision, any limitations imposed by the Member States to the free movement of workers on grounds of public policy or public security 'shall be based exclusively on the personal conduct of the individual concerned'.

[10] According to some, the direct effect of directives amounted to an 'application abusive du traité de Rome au profit d'une quasi-législation communautaire'. Foyer, quoted by U Everling, 'Zur direkten innerstaatlichen Wirkung der EG-Richtlinien: Ein Beispiel richterlicher Rechtsfortbildung auf der Basis gemeinsamer Rechtsgrundsätze' in B Börner et al (eds), *Einigkeit und Recht und Freiheit. Festschrift für Karl Carstens zum 70. Geburtstag* (Heymanns, 1984) 96.

[11] Case 9/70 *Grad* (n 9), which concerned the direct effect of decisions addressed to the Member States.

[12] Case 33/70 *SpA SACE v Finance Minister of Italy* EU:C:1970:118.

[13] Case 41/74 *Van Duyn* (n 3).

[14] Everling (n 10) 97–98.

[15] Directive 64/221/EEC of 25 February 1964 on the coordination of special measures concerning the movement and residence of foreign nationals which are justified on grounds of public policy, public security or public health, [1964] OJ 56/850.

In this context, the High Court was faced with the question of whether Article 3(1) of Directive 64/221 had 'direct effect', allowing Ms Van Duyn to directly rely on this provision to substantiate her claim regarding her entitlement to stay in the UK for work purposes. The UK Government contested this, claiming, inter alia, that, unlike regulations, directives are not directly applicable within the Member States. Having doubts in this regard, the High Court asked the CJEU to clarify this issue.

In its judgment, the CJEU held, as did Advocate General Mayras in his Opinion, that Article 3(1) of the Directive was directly effective in that it conferred rights on individuals which were enforceable by them in the courts of a Member State and which the national courts had to protect:

> If … by virtue of the provisions of Article 189 [now Article 288 TFEU] regulations are directly applicable and, consequently, may by their very nature have direct effects, it does not follow from this that other categories of acts mentioned in that Article can never have similar effects. It would be incompatible with the binding effect attributed to a directive by Article 189 to exclude, in principle, the possibility that the obligation which it imposes may be invoked by those concerned. In particular, where the Community authorities have, by directive, imposed on Member States the obligation to pursue a particular course of conduct, the useful effect of such an act would be weakened if individuals were prevented from relying on it before their national courts and if the latter were prevented from taking it into consideration as an element of Community law. Article 177 [now Article 267 TFEU], which empowers national courts to refer to the Court questions concerning the validity and interpretation of all acts of the Community institutions, without distinction, implies furthermore that these acts may be invoked by individuals in the national courts. It is necessary to examine, in every case, whether the nature, general scheme and wording of the provision in question are capable of having direct effects on the relations between Member States and individuals.[16]

According to the Court, Article 3(1) of the Directive met the test for establishing direct effect in that it laid down an unconditional obligation which, by its nature, did not require any further Community or Member State act. Legal certainty therefore required, according to the CJEU, that the persons concerned could rely on this obligation even though it was set out in a directive.

The CJEU then went on to rule that Article 48 of the EEC Treaty (now Article 45 TFEU) and Article 3(1) of Directive 64/221 in fact did allow Member States to take into account, as a matter of personal conduct of the individual concerned, this individual's association with an organisation they consider socially harmful.

III. The Reception of the Judgment

In legal writing it was observed that in *Van Duyn* the Court went further than in its judgments in *Grad* and *SACE* and accepted that both *substantive* provisions of directives and directives *standing alone* may have direct effect.[17] However, for certain national courts this was apparently not a foregone conclusion. A few years after *Van Duyn*, two

[16] Case 41/74 *Van Duyn* (n 3) para 12.

[17] ibid. According to G Bebr, *Development of Judicial Control of the European Communities* (Nijhoff, 1981) 586, this was the decisive case in this respect.

prominent domestic courts openly showed their disagreement with the CJEU's case law on the direct effect of directives. The French *Conseil d'Etat*,[18] basing itself on a strictly literal interpretation of Article 288(3) TFEU, found that it was not possible for an individual to invoke a directive with a view to challenging an administrative decision addressed to him or her. Some three years later, the German *Bundesfinanzhof*[19] held, with explicit reference to the above-mentioned decision of the *Conseil d'Etat*, that there could be no reasonable doubt that a directive was incapable of creating legal rules directly applicable in a Member State.

In Germany, the Constitutional Court brought to an end domestic controversies about the direct effect of directives in a judgment of 8 April 1987 in which it accepted the direct effect of directives.[20] An important argument in this judgment was the principle of loyalty – *Grundsatz von Treu und Glauben* – which implies that direct effect is a consequence of or even a sanction for the failure of a Member State to comply with its obligation to implement a directive correctly and in time.[21]

In France, the situation was unsatisfactory for a long time in that a review of an individual administrative decision in light of a directive was only permitted if implementing measures had already been taken.[22] Interestingly, the review of the legality of national measures implementing a directive had already been accepted by the *Conseil d'Etat* in *Cohn-Bendit*. More generally, the review of the legality, in light of EU law, of subordinate legislation such as 'règlements', or in the context of an exception of illegality has been always a rather natural way of using EU law in administrative courts. Later on, the review of the legality of legislative acts, using a directive as the standard for review, was also accepted in France.[23] However, it was only in 2009 that the *Conseil d'Etat* finally accepted in *Mme Perreux* that directives may also be relied upon against individual administrative acts, provided that the provisions invoked are unconditional and sufficiently precise.[24]

The critical reaction of the Member States, after the judgments in *Grad* and *SACE*, was not mild, especially from the German and French Governments. Next, *Van Duyn* was severely criticised by the UK, in particular in a report of the Select Committee on the European Communities of the House of Lords.[25] It was proposed, inter alia, that the

[18] *Cohn-Bendit* [1980] 1 CMLR 543.

[19] 16 July 1981, EuR 1981, 442. Subsequently, the position of the *Budesfinanzhof* was confirmed in a judgment of 25 April 1985, EuR 1985, 191.

[20] BVerfG, 8 April 1987, 2 BvR 687/85. *cf* M Hilf, 'Der Justizkoflikt um EG-Richtlinien: gelöst' (1988) *Europarecht* 1.

[21] Prechal (n 2) 221 with further references.

[22] P Cassia, 'L'invocabilité des directives communautaires devant le juge administratif: la guerre des juges n'a pas eu lieu' (2002) 1 *Revue française de droit administratif* 20, esp 30–32.

[23] For a brief overview of this case law, see, for instance, D Simon, *La directive européenne* (Dalloz, 1997) 87–90 and 95–99; and J Dutheil de la Rochère, '*Société Anonyme Rothmans International France* and *Société Anonyme Philip Morris France; Société Arizona Tobacco Products and Société Anonyme Philip Morris France,* two decisions by the *Conseil d'Etat, Assemblée* of 28 February 1992. Conclusions by Martine Laroque' (1993) 30 *Common Market Law Review* 187, 192–93 (case note).

[24] M Long et al, *Les grands arrêts de la jurisprudence administrative*, 23rd edn (Dalloz, 2021) 863; and C Charpy, 'The *Conseil d'Etat* Abandons Its *Cohn Bendit* Case-Law' (2010) 6 *European Constitutional Law Review* 123, both with a brief discussion of the jurisprudential development.

[25] *Tenth Report of the Select Committee on the European Communities: Direct Applicability of Directives* HL (1975).

Council should state explicitly whether a certain directive could produce direct effect.[26] These reactions mobilised the Legal Service of the Commission to start a discreet counteroffensive.[27]

The scholarly discussion of *Van Duyn*, which was in part welcoming of the judgment but also critical,[28] focused predominantly on two issues: the use of the term 'similar effects'; and the foundations of the direct effect of directives.

On the first issue, several authors suggested that the Court use the term 'similar effects' in order to avoid the term 'direct effect'.[29] According to some, to speak of the direct effect of directives would be inappropriate since the real issue is rather the possibility for an individual to *rely on the provision of the directive in question*.[30] It appears that for these authors direct effect meant something different from the possibility of relying on a provision. Others have however argued that this should rather be considered as a limited form of direct effect.[31] Similarly, it has been argued that by using the term 'similar effects' the Court was indicating that, in contrast to regulations which are directly applicable and will therefore as a rule have direct effect, directives do not have such direct effect 'by their very nature'. An examination of certain conditions must first take place. Despite these discussions, it was accepted that directives *can* have direct effect. However, the most important question was *in what circumstances* this might be the case.

As to the foundations of the direct effect of directives, the CJEU gave three arguments: the binding effect attributed to directives in Article 288(3) TFEU, the useful effect ('*effet utile*') of directives and an argument based on Article 267 TFEU, although this last argument disappeared quickly.[32] Not surprisingly, these arguments and the further implications of this case law have been discussed at length in legal writing.[33]

Apart from the necessity of giving an interpretation to Article 288(3) TFEU such that it will secure as far as possible the practical and effective operation of the instrument, several other arguments have been put forward in this respect in legal writing. According to some, the principal motive for the Court's acceptance of the direct effect of directives was the concern for judicial protection.[34] Another more practical

[26] *cf* in this respect the explicit statement in Art 34(2)(b) EU (the version resulting from the Treaty of Amsterdam) that framework decisions – de facto directives in the former Third Pillar – are not to entail direct effect.

[27] M Rasmussen, 'How to enforce European law? A new history of the battle over the direct effect of Directives 1958–1987' (2017) 23 *European Law Journal* 290.

[28] *cf*, for instance, M Hilf, 'Der Justizkoflikt um EG-Richtlinien: gelöst' (1988) *Europarecht* 1, 2, with further references.

[29] P Pescatore, 'The Doctrine of "Direct Effect": an Infant Disease of Community Law' (1983) 8 *European Law Review* 155, 167.

[30] P Pescatore, 'L'effet des directives communautaires: une tentative de démythification' (1980) 23 *Recueil Dalloz – Sirey* 171, 174.

[31] Everling (n 10) 106.

[32] Case 51/76 *Verbond van Nederlandse Ondernemingen v Inspecteur der Invoerrechten en Accijnzen* EU:C:1977:12.

[33] See, for instance, Bebr (n 17) 586 ff; and AJ Easson, 'The "Direct Effect" of EEC Directives' (1979) 23 *International and Comparative Law Quarterly* 319.

[34] For instance, J Mertens de Wilmars, 'Réflexion sur le système d'articulation du droit communautaire et du droit national' in *L'Europe et le droit. Mélanges en hommage à Jean Boulouis* (Dalloz, 1991) 391, 398.

consideration behind the Court's case law was the important role of citizens in contributing to the practical operation of Union law directives or to the need to combat inertia on the part of the Member States.[35]

While there was a general consensus among scholars that all these arguments constitute very important elements of the doctrine of the direct effect of directives, in the judgment in *Ratti*,[36] a new argument was put forward, which moved the rationale for direct effect from the nature of the instrument to the behaviour of the State: a Member State should not be able to rely on its own failure to implement a directive. This estoppel-like notion has been called by an eminent author the '*motif véritable*'[37] of the attitude of the Court with respect to the direct effect of directives. Many other authors and Advocates General have argued that this was indeed the quintessence of the Court's case law on the subject. However, this 'estoppel theory' has never been entirely uncontroversial.[38] In particular, scholars who advocated for the horizontal direct effect of directives often questioned the 'estoppel theory',[39] pointing out, inter alia, that the 'not able to rely on its own failure – rationale' was rather a consequence of direct effect and not its foundation.

In any case, in its case law, the Court continued to refer to this additional argument quite often. In the judgment in *Becker*,[40] in the 'pedagogic' section on 'the effect of directives in general', the Court reiterated the two first arguments from *Van Duyn* and continued by stating:

> 24. Consequently, a Member State which has not adopted the implementing measures required by the directive within the prescribed period may not plead, as against individuals, its own failure to perform the obligations which the directive entails.
>
> 25. Thus, wherever the provisions of a directive appear, as far as their subject matter is concerned, to be unconditional and sufficiently precise, those provisions may, in the absence of implementing measures adopted within the prescribed period, be relied upon as against any national provision which is incompatible with the directive or in so far as the provisions define rights which individuals are able to assert against the State.

In later cases, the Court was even more outspoken, stating that the case law on the direct effect of directives 'seeks to prevent "the State from taking advantage of its own failure to comply with Community law"'.[41]

However, as far as the legal basis of the direct effect of directives is concerned, the case law is not unequivocal. It rather presents a varied picture or a mixture of rationales. In some cases, the Court recalls the argument of the binding nature of directives only,[42]

[35] Y Galmot and J-C Bonichot, 'La Cour de Justice des Communautés européennes et la transposition des directives en droit national' (1988) 1 *Revue française de droit administratif* 1, 13.

[36] Case 148/78 *Pubblico Ministero v Ratti* EU:C:1979:110.

[37] Pescatore (n 30) 175. *cf* also Rasmussen (n 27).

[38] For a more detailed discussion, see Prechal (n 2) 220–26, with further references.

[39] For instance, G Nicolaysen, 'Keine horizontale Wirkung von Richtlinien-Bestimmungen' (1986) *Europarecht* 370; and T Tridimas, 'Horizontal effect of directives: a missed opportunity?' (1994) 19 *European Law Review* 621.

[40] Case 8/81 *Becker v Finanzamt Münster-Innenstadt* EU:C:1982:7.

[41] Case C-91/92 *Faccini Dori v Recreb Srl* EU:C:1994:292, para 22.

[42] *cf* Case C-80/86 *Kolpinghuis Nijmegen BV* EU:C:1987:431, para 8; and Case C-205/20 *NE v Bezirkshauptmannschaft Hartberg-Fürstenfeld* EU:C:2022:168, para 26.

while in other cases it is combined with the argument of effectiveness.[43] The 'estoppel-rationale' does not feature in the case law systematically, neither does another, closely related, argument which appeared in 1988, namely the obligation of cooperation laid down in Article 4(3) TEU.[44] Some other cases suggest that the legal protection of individuals is a major consideration behind the direct effect of directives.[45] Most often, however, the Court just points out that according to settled case law, unconditional and sufficiently precise provisions of a directive may be relied on before the national courts by individuals against the State where the State has failed to transpose the directive within the time limit or has transposed it incorrectly. A reference to the legal basis of the direct effect is omitted.

IV. Subsequent Developments

As indicated above, after some hesitation and debate, the direct effect of directives was generally accepted, at least in the sense that directives could be relied upon against the State. The most important development after the judgment in *Van Duyn* was the Court's finding that directives cannot directly impose obligations upon individuals. This implies, first, that directives have no horizontal direct effect; that is, the possibility for a private individual to rely on a directive against another private individual. Second, it also implies that there can be no inverse vertical direct effect of directives; that is, that provisions of directives cannot be enforced against individuals by the state. This case law started with the judgment in *Marshall I*.[46] Initially, several rationales were given for this finding, such as legal certainty and the fact that the purpose of the direct effect of directives was to preclude Member States from taking advantage of their own failure to implement directives. However, the main argument, which remains valid, was one of a constitutional nature. In *Faccini Dori*, the CJEU held that the acceptance of horizontal direct effect would mean 'to recognize a power in the Community to enact obligations for individuals with immediate effect, whereas it has competence to do so only where it is empowered to adopt regulations'.[47]

Obviously, the denial of the horizontal direct effect and inverse vertical direct effect of directives has consequences for their full effectiveness and for the protection of the rights of others. In contrast to regulations, there exists an important limitation to the validity of directives as generally binding rules in the Member States. They can directly create rights but not obligations for individuals. In order to create direct obligations, an intervention of the State is necessary. In this sense, directives may be considered as acts of general validity but of an incomplete nature.

[43] *cf* Case 8/81 *Becker* (n 40) paras 22–23; Case C-243/15 *Lesoochranárske zoskupenie VLK* v *Obvodný úrad Trenčín* EU:C:2016:838, para 44; and Case C-723/17 *Craeynest and Others v Brussels Hoofdstedelijk Gewest and Brussels Instituut voor Milieubeheer* EU:C:2019:533, paras 32 and 34.

[44] Case 190/87 *Oberkreisdirektor des Kreises, Borken v Moormann BV* EU:C:1988:424. *cf*, however, recently, Case C-723/17 *Craeynest and Others* (n 43) para 31.

[45] Case C-122/17 *Smith v Meade* EU:C:2018:631, para 37.

[46] Case 152/84 *Marshall v Southampton and South-West Hampshire Area Health Authority* EU:C:1986:84.

[47] Case C-91/92 *Faccini Dori* (n 41) para 24. Recently also Case C-122/17 *Smith* (n 45) para 42.

In order to overcome or bypass this limitation as far as possible, the CJEU has developed various techniques. These include, first, a broad interpretation of the notion of 'the State'. Indeed, the CJEU has considerably expanded the category of bodies against which directives can be relied upon. This line of case law started with *Foster*[48] and was further clarified in *Farell*.[49] According to this case law, a directive can be relied on

> against a Member State, the organs of its administration, such as decentralised authorities, or organisations or bodies which are subject to the authority or control of the State or which have been required by a Member State to perform a task in the public interest and, for that purpose, possess special powers beyond those which result from the normal rules applicable to relations between individuals.[50]

Second, in other cases, the CJEU accepted that the direct effect of directives might produce horizontal side-effects. According to this case law, an individual may make a claim based directly on a directive against a public authority, despite the fact that this may be to the detriment of another individual. Such effects will particularly occur in triangular (or multi-angular) relationships. The CJEU has explicitly admitted that, under certain circumstances, 'mere adverse repercussions on the rights of third parties' cannot prevent an individual from invoking the provisions of a directive against the Member State concerned.[51]

A third technique to obviate, as far as possible, the setbacks of the 'non-horizontal direct effect of directives' is the obligation to interpret national law in conformity with the directive at issue. This important and much debated tenet of EU law started with the judgment in *Von Colson*.[52] The jurisprudence on consistent interpretation evolved over time. Several issues needed clarification, such as what has to be interpreted in conformity with the directive, what methods of interpretation should be used, what are the limits to the obligation of consistent interpretation and what is the foundation of the obligation.

As far as the last issue is concerned, the case law oscillates. For a certain period of time the obligation to interpret national law in conformity with a directive was based on the binding nature of Article 288(3) TFEU and Article 4(3) TEU.[53] In *Pfeiffer*, the CJEU linked the obligation of consistent interpretation to the responsibility of national courts to provide effective legal protection for individuals and to ensure that Community law is fully effective.[54] In *Popławski II*, the principle of primacy was put forward as a basis.[55] The other issues were complicated to resolve. However, it was finally decided that the

[48] Case C-188/89 *Foster v British Gas* EU:C:1990:313.

[49] Case C-413/15 *Farrell v Whitty* EU:C:2017:745, paras 32–42. The problem was, in particular, whether the criteria developed in *Foster* were cumulative or alternative.

[50] Case C-122/17 *Smith* (n 45) para 45.

[51] Case C–201/02 *R (Wells) v Secretary of State for Transport, Local Government and the Regions* EU:C:2004:12.

[52] Case 14/83 *Von Colson v Land Nordrhein-Westfalen* EU:C:1984:153.

[53] ibid para 26; Case C-106/89 *Marleasing SA v La Comercial Internacional de Alimentacion SA* EU:C:1990:395, para 8.

[54] Joined Cases C-397/01 to C-403/01, *Pfeiffer v Deutsches Rotes Kreuz, Kreisverband Waldshut eV* EU:C:2004:584, para 111.

[55] Case C-573/17 *Popławski II* EU:C:2019:530, para 57.

object of consistent interpretation was not only the provisions of national law specifically introduced in order to implement the directive at issue, but the whole body of applicable law, whether anterior or posterior to the directive.[56] In addition, after some confusion,[57] it became clear that the courts may use national methods of construction. However, they must choose the most appropriate among them to achieve a result which is consistent with the directive at stake.

The case law, as it stands now, was summarised in *Popławski II* in relation to framework decisions and recently reiterated in *Thelen Technopark*[58] in relation to directives. In brief, the obligation of consistent interpretation requires that national courts interpret, to the greatest extent possible, their national law in conformity with the directive in order to achieve the result sought by it. In hearing a dispute between private individuals,[59] courts have to consider 'the whole body of rules of national law and to interpret them, so far as possible, in the light of the wording and purpose of the directive'.[60] Yet there are certain limits to this obligation. These lie in general principles of law, such as legal certainty and non-retroactivity. Similarly, the obligation of consistent interpretation cannot serve as the basis for an interpretation of national law *contra legem*. In this respect, the CJEU has clarified that a national court cannot validly claim that it is impossible for it to interpret a provision of national law in a manner that is consistent with EU law merely because that provision has consistently been interpreted in a manner that is incompatible with EU law.[61] In fact, the obligation of consistent interpretation requires national courts to change or at least not follow established case law, even that of a higher court, if the case law is incompatible with EU law.[62]

Fourth, there is the much-debated issue of the 'exclusionary effect' of directives. In these cases, a directive is used by way of a collateral challenge or, to use other terms, an exception of illegality or an incidental plea, and is relied upon in order to preclude the application of divergent national law. Simply put, this is where one private party uses the directive against another private party, often as the basis of their defence to an action based on national law, where the latter is not in conformity with the directive and thus has to be set aside. The result of such an 'exclusionary effect' is that the directive determines the legal position of the parties involved and works to the detriment of one of the parties. In scholarly writing, there was, for some time, a debate as to whether such an effect was possible in disputes between individuals, or, in general, in situations where there the relevant provisions of a directive lacked direct effect. In particular, in French

[56] For instance, Case C-106/89 *Marleasing* (n 53), para 8; and Case C-63/97 *BMW v Deenik* EU:C:1999:82, para 20.

[57] After the judgment in Case C-106/89 *Marleasing* (n 53), some authors have argued that national methods of interpretation no longer matter and that it is Community law which prescribes the methods to be used. In any case, soon after Case 14/83 *Von Colson* (n 52), it became clear that national rules of construction may be very restrictive. Therefore, it was suggested that Community law may set limits to certain methods of interpretation. For a more detailed discussion see Prechal (n 2) 193–200.

[58] *Popławski II* (n 55) paras 55 and 57; and Case C-261/20 *Thelen Technopark Berlin GmbH v MN* EU:C:2022:33, paras 26–27.

[59] Or *mutatis mutandis* in a situation in which a state authority relies on a directive against an individual.

[60] Case C-261/20 *Thelen Technopark* (n 58) para 27.

[61] Case C-684/16 *Max-Planck-Gesellschaft zur Förderung der Wissenschaften v Shimizu* EU:C:2018:874, para 60.

[62] Case C-441/14 *Dansk Industri v Estate of Karsten Eigil Rasmussen* EU:C:2016:278, para 33.

legal writing it was considered that such a setting aside was not a matter of direct effect but solely the consequence of the primacy of EU law.[63]

In its judgment in *Pfeiffer*, the CJEU made it clear and reiterated in later judgments that

> even a clear, precise and unconditional provision of a directive does not allow a national court to disapply a provision of its national law which conflicts with it, if, in doing so, an additional obligation were to be imposed on an individual.[64]

However, the CJEU also pointed out that a domestic court could not be required, *solely on the basis of EU law*, to disapply such a national provision.[65] Recently, the Court clarified this position by indicating that this finding is without prejudice to the possibility to disapply, *on the basis of domestic law*, any provision of national law which is contrary to a provision of EU law that does not have direct effect.[66]

The fifth and last mechanism[67] to attenuate the impossibility of the horizontal direct effect of directives is the horizontal direct effect of a general principle of EU law or a fundamental right in combination with a directive. This line of case law started with the judgment in *Mangold*[68] and was confirmed with greater precision in *Kücükdeveci*.[69] The CJEU found that the secondary legislation at stake – Directive 2000/78[70] – did not lay down the principle of non-discrimination on grounds of age, but only gave expression to a pre-existing general principle of equal treatment. This principle of non-discrimination on grounds of age 'as given concrete expression by Directive 2000/78, must be interpreted as precluding, national legislation [that was incompatible with that principle]'[71] and the court had to set aside the provisions of this legislation, also in disputes between individuals.[72] This 'combination-approach' – a directive giving expression to a general principle – was extensively criticised[73] and even dismissed by the Danish Supreme Court in *DI*.[74] The Højesteret refused to set aside provisions of national law that were not only contrary to Directive 2000/78 but also to the *general principle* of non-discrimination on grounds of age. According to this Supreme Court, the unwritten principle had no clear

[63] The case law of the Court was in this respect rather ambiguous for a while. *cf* M Dougan, 'When worlds collide! Competing visions of the relationship between direct effect and supremacy' (2007) 44 *Common Market Law Review* 931; and A Rigaux and D Simon, 'L'arrêt Poplawski 2: accroc limité ou ébranlement général dans la mise en oeuvre de la primauté par le juge national?' (2019) 29 *Europe* 5.

[64] Case C-261/20 *Thelen Technopark* (n 58) para 32. In Case C-573/17 *Popławski II* (n 55) paras 68–71, there was no direct effect at all as the case concerned a framework decision.

[65] Case C-122/17 *Smith* (n 45), para 49; and Case C-573/17 *Popławski II* (n 55) para 71.

[66] Case C-261/20 *Thelen Technopark* (n 58) para 33.

[67] I am leaving aside the possibility of state liability as laid down in the Joined Cases C-6/90 and C-9/90 *Francovich v Italy* EU:C:1991:428.

[68] Case C-144/04 *Mangold v Helm* EU:C:2005:709, paras 75–77.

[69] Case C-555/07 *Kücükdeveci v Swedex GmbH & Co KG* EU:C:2010:21.

[70] Directive 2000/78/EC establishing a general framework for equal treatment in employment and occupation [2000] OJ L303/16.

[71] Case C-555/07 *Kücükdeveci* (n 69) para 43.

[72] To that effect, ibid para 56.

[73] See, for instance, 'Horizontal direct effect – A law of diminishing coherence?' (2006) 43 *Common Market Law Review* 1. In Germany, the reaction was, in some corners, particularly severe. See L Gerken et al, *'Mangold' als ausbrechender Rechtsakt* (Sellier, 2009).

[74] Case C-441/14 *Dansk Industri* (n 62).

legal basis in the Treaties and was not covered by the Danish Accession Act and therefore could not override national law.[75]

In more recent case law, concerning various articles of the Charter of Fundamental Rights of the EU,[76] the consideration that a directive gives expression to a general principle/fundamental right is no longer repeated. While it is still the directive at issue that triggers the application of the Charter,[77] as far as the horizontal direct effect of a provision of the Charter is concerned, this provision must satisfy a self-standing test: the provision must be *sufficient in itself* to confer a right. If there were a need to give substance to a Charter provision while relying on a corresponding directive, the provision would not be sufficient in itself.

The various mechanisms developed to respond to the absence of the horizontal direct effect of directives led to an increasingly complex body of case law, which has been analysed and criticised *in extenso* in legal writing.[78] At the root of this is the tension between, on the one hand, the nature of directives and the balance of competences between the EU and the Member States that this instrument implies and, on the other hand, the poor compliance record of Member States and the need to protect individuals.

It is submitted that without a Treaty amendment as to the definition of directives this tension and therefore this complex case law will remain. This will be the case as long as Member States want to keep directives as instruments of Union action.[79] Paradoxically, certain regulations seem to integrate the typical characteristics of directives.[80]

[75] U Šadl and S Mair, 'Mutual Disempowerment: *Case C-441/14 Dansk Industri, acting on behalf of Ajos A/S v Estate of Karsten Eigil Rasmussen* and Case no. 15/2014 *Dansk Industri (DI) acting for Ajos A/S v The estate left by A*' (2017) 13 *European Constitutional Law Review* 347.

[76] Case C-414/16 *Egenberger v Evangelisches Werk für Diakonie und Entwicklung eV* EU:C:2018:257, paras 76–80, concerning Arts 21 and 47 of the Charter of Fundamental Rights of the European Union [2012] OJ C326/391 (CFR); Joined Cases C-569/16 and C-570/16 *Stadt Wuppertal v Bauer* EU:C:2018:871, paras 85–91, concerning Art 31(2) CFR.

[77] According to Art 51(1) CFR, the Charter is applicable in the Member States when the latter are 'implementing Union law'. This is where the directive comes in.

[78] For some examples of the critical writings, see W van Gerven, 'The Horizontal Direct Effect of Directive Provisions Revisited: The Reality of Catchwords' in D Curtin and T Heukels (eds), *The Institutional Dynamics of European Integration. Liber Amicorum Henry G Schermers* (Nijhoff, 1994) 335; F Emmert and M Pereira de Avezedo, 'L'effet horizontal des directives. La jurisprudence de la CJCE: un bateau ivre?' (1993) 3 *Revue trimestrielle de droit européen* 503; T Tridimas, 'Black, White, and Shades of Grey: Horizontality of Directives Revisited' (2001) 21 *Yearbook of European Law* 327; A Dashwood, 'From Van Duyn to Mangold via Marshall: reducing Direct Effect to Absurdity?' (2007) 9 *The Cambridge Yearbook of European Legal Studies* 81; P Craig, 'The Legal Effect of Directives: Policy, Rules and Exceptions' (2009) 34 *European Law Review* 349.

[79] See, for instance, *Edinburgh European Council*, Bull EC 12-1992, 15; the Protocol on the application of the principles of subsidiarity and proportionality to the Treaty of Amsterdam amending the Treaty on European Union, the Treaties establishing the European Communities and certain related acts [1997] OJ C340/1, para 6; and Commission of the European Communities, *European Governance: A White Paper* COM(2001) 428, 20. The framework law proposed in Art I-33 of the Treaty establishing a Constitution for Europe [2004] OJ C310/1 was, in substance, nothing other than another label for directives.

[80] A good example is Regulation (EU) 2016/679 of the European Parliament and of the Council on the protection of natural persons with regard to the processing of personal data and on the free movement of such data, and repealing Directive 95/46/EC (General Data Protection Regulation) [2016] OJ L119/1.

5

Von Colson and the Principle of 'Indirect Effect'

SARA DRAKE

I. Introduction: Historical and Doctrinal Context

From the early 1980s until the early 1990s, the European Court of Justice (ECJ) delivered a series of seminal judgments which enhanced the effective judicial protection of individuals' European Union (EU) rights before national courts. The 1984 judgment of the ECJ in *Von Colson*[1] is one of the most influential judgments of this era. It brought a new dimension to the ability of individuals to effectively protect their EU rights before national courts *independent of the principle of direct effect*.[2] For while national courts are intrinsically engaged in the task of interpreting law in accordance with domestic rules of statutory interpretation, the ECJ in *Von Colson* placed a *new* duty on national courts[3] derived directly from EU law to interpret domestic law 'as far as possible' in light of EU law.[4] This duty is often referred to as the principle of conform or consistent interpretation.[5] In English language scholarship, it is most commonly known as the principle of 'indirect effect' since EU law takes effect in the legal order *indirectly* through a judicial construction of national law rather than *directly* applying the EU provision through the doctrine of direct effect.[6]

The main contribution of *Von Colson* and the principle of indirect effect has been to act as an alternative mechanism for national courts where an individual litigant seeks

[1] Case 14/83 *Von Colson and Kamann* [1984] ECR 1891; Case 79/83 *Harz* [1984] ECR 1921.

[2] Case 26/62 *Van Gend en Loos* [1963] ECR 1. In Case 14/83 *Von Colson*, the ECJ also set down the right to an effective remedy and adequate compensation which was developed in later case law: see, eg, Case 222/84 *Johnston v Chief Constable of the Royal Ulster Constabulary* EU:C:1986.

[3] The duty applies to all national administrations: Case C-218/01 *Henkel v Deutsches Patent – und Markenamnt* [2004] ECR I-1725.

[4] The EFTA Court introduced a similar duty 20 years later in Case E-04/01 *Karlsson* [2002] EFTA Ct Rep 240, para 28.

[5] Other terms include the principle of sympathetic, harmonious, purposive, strained and EU-consistent interpretation.

[6] G Betlem and A Nollkaemper, 'Giving Effect to Public International Law and European Community Law Before Domestic Courts. A Comparative Analysis of the Practice of Consistent Interpretation' (2003) 14 *European Journal of International Law* 569.

to enforce an EU provision which is insufficiently clear, precise and unconditional to have direct effect[7] and/or where the EU rights are derived from a directive in a horizontal dispute between two private parties.[8] Although *Von Colson* pre-dates the Court's decision in *Marshall (No 1)*,[9] denying directives horizontal direct effect, having an independent means to enforce EU rights has been beneficial in policy sectors such as employment, consumer protection and intellectual property where the EU legislature enacts directives (rather than Regulations) to harmonise standards in private law and where disputes are horizontal in nature rather than vertical. The *Von Colson* mandate also plays an important role in securing the effectiveness of framework decisions[10] and general principles of EU law.[11] Forty years after its *Von Colson* judgment, the Court of Justice has arguably elevated the principle of indirect effect above the principle of direct effect and is now the preferred *primary* mechanism by which domestic courts should give effect to EU law in the national legal orders[12] with state liability the remedy of last resort.[13]

This chapter will first set out the facts and judgment in *Von Colson* (section II) before considering the judicial and academic reaction to the judgment (section III). It will move on to explore the most important follow-up judgments (section IV) before giving an overview of the reception of the principle of indirect effect by national judiciaries (section V). Finally, it concludes with some reflections on the evolution of the principle of indirect effect 40 years after its introduction by the Court of Justice and its future significance for the EU's legal order (section VI).

II. Factual Background and Judgment in *Von Colson* and *Harz*

In *Von Colson*, two female social workers brought an action against the national authority responsible for running an all-male prison claiming breach of the Equal Treatment Directive.[14] They had both applied for jobs at the prison, but two lesser qualified male candidates were recruited instead. In *Harz*, the often-overlooked sister case decided on the same day, a female graduate brought an action for sex discrimination against a private company. In both *Von Colson* and *Harz*, the claimants successfully established

[7] See Case 14/83 *Von Colson* (n 1); Case 79/83 *Harz* (n 1).

[8] In Case 79/83 *Harz* (n 1) delivered on the same day, the claimant was seeking to rely on a non-directly effective provision in a horizonal dispute between two private parties.

[9] Case 152/84 *Marshall (No 1)* [1986] ECR 723.

[10] Case C-105/3 *Criminal Proceedings against Pupino* [2005] I-ECR 5285; Case C-579/15 *Popławski I* EU:C:2017:503; Case C-573/17 *Popławski II* EU:C:2019:530. Framework decisions were enacted under the pre-Lisbon Third Pillar in accordance with Art 34(2)(b) TEU. These instruments are analogous to directives but do not have direct effect.

[11] Case C-555/07 *Kükükdeveci v Swedex GmBH & Co KG* EU:C:2010:21, para 53.

[12] Case C-282/10 *Maribel Dominguez v Centre informatique du Centre Ouest Atlantique and Préfet de la région Centre* EU:C:2012:33, para 23; Case C-573/17 *Popławski II* (n 10) para 55.

[13] Case C-441/14 *Dansk Industri (Ajos)* EU:C:2016:278.

[14] Council Directive No 76/207/EEC of 9 February 1976 on the implementation of the principle of equal treatment for men and women as regard access to employment, vocational training and promotion, and working conditions [1976] OJ L39/40.

sex discrimination had taken place. However, it was the issue of national sanctions to be imposed on the defendant and the corresponding rights available to the claimants which were at the centre of the dispute, and which gave the ECJ the opportunity to set in motion an alternative route for the national court to ensure the candidates could avail themselves of these rights. As scholars observed, the Court found a solution which avoided the 'thorny question' of whether directives could have horizontal direct effect which had emerged post-*Van Duyn*[15] and which delivered the same outcome in both cases irrespective of the legal status of the different employers.[16]

The EU provision at issue, Article 6 of the Equal Treatment Directive, states:

> Member States shall introduce into their national legal systems such measures as are necessary to enable all persons who consider themselves wronged by failure to apply the principle of equal treatment within the meaning of Articles 3, 4 and 5 to pursue their claims by judicial process after possible recourse to other competent authorities.

The German law[17] purporting to implement Article 6 of the Directive expressly limited the victim to payment of 'negative interest' based on the frustration of expectation. In effect, this entitled the victims to repayment of the expenses incurred in making the job application and attending the interview only. The claimants argued that this nominal remedy was inadequate and contravened EU law. It would not deter employers from discriminating against women and undermines the substantive right to equal treatment in the Directive itself.

The Court of Justice agreed. It recalled the obligation placed on Member States under Article 288(3) TFEU to implement the objective of a directive within their national legal system. It held:

> Although that provision leaves Member States to choose the ways and means of ensuring that the directive is implemented, that freedom does not affect the obligation imposed on all the Member States to which the directive is addressed, to adopt, in their national legal systems, all the measures necessary to ensure that *the directive is fully effective, in accordance with the objective it pursues.*[18]

Turning to the Equal Treatment Directive, the Court ruled that it was clear from the purpose of the Directive and more specifically Article 6 that

> it is impossible to establish real equality of opportunity without an appropriate system of sanctions. That follows not only from the actual purpose of the directive but more specifically from Article 6 thereof which, by granting applicants for a post who have been discriminated against recourse to the courts, acknowledges that those candidates have rights of which they may avail themselves before the courts.[19]

It acknowledged that while Article 6 does not require a *specific* sanction, 'it does entail that that sanction be such as to guarantee real and effective judicial protection. Moreover,

[15] Case 41/71 *Van Duyn v Home Office* [1974] ECR 1337; D Curtin, 'Effective Sanctions and the Equal Treatment Directive: The *Von Colson* and *Harz* cases' (1985) 22 *Common Market Law Review* 505, 506. See AJ Easson, 'The Direct Effect of EEC Directives' (1979) 28 *International and Comparative Law Quarterly* 319.

[16] A Arnull, *The European Court of Justice and its Court of Justice*, 2nd edn (Oxford University Press, 2006) 209.

[17] *Bürgerliches Gesetzbuch* (German Civil Code), para 611(a)(2).

[18] Case 14/83 *Von Colson* (n 1) para 15 (emphasis added).

[19] ibid para 22.

it must also have a real deterrent effect on the employer'.[20] The Court added that if the Member State chose 'to penalize the breach of the prohibition of discrimination by the award of compensation, that compensation must in any event be adequate in relation to the damage sustained'.[21] Since it was clear that the German implementing legislation did not meet these requirements, the Court turned to consider how this right to an effective and adequate remedy could be achieved by the national court.

The Court started by recalling the argument submitted by the German Government[22] which claimed that the directive could be effectively transposed in relation to sanctions by applying the general rules of compensation laid down in the German Civil Code. It recognised that questions concerning the interpretation of national law are a matter for the national court alone before adding a significant qualification. It held that

> the Member States' obligation arising from a directive to achieve the result envisaged by the directive and their duty under [Article 4 (3) TEU] to take all appropriate measures, whether general or particular, to ensure the fulfilment of that obligation, is binding on all authorities of Member States including, for matters within their jurisdiction, the courts. It follows that, in applying the national law and in particular the provisions of a national law specifically introduced in order to implement Directive No 76/207, national courts are required to interpret their national law in the light of the wording and the purpose of the directive in order to achieve the result referred to in the third paragraph of [Article 288 TFEU].[23]

It proceeded to add that in the absence of any unconditional and sufficiently precise obligation in relation to sanctions (that is, confirming that Article 6 did not have direct effect),

> it is for the national court to interpret and apply the legislation adopted for the implementation of the directive in conformity with the requirements of [Union] law, in so far as it is given discretion to do so under national law.[24]

Thus, it followed that the national court was under a new obligation *as a matter of EU law* to interpret national law to ensure the claimants were able to invoke their right to an effective and adequate remedy embodied in Article 6 of the Equal Treatment Directive.[25]

III. Reception History: Judicial and Academic

The initial response to the *Von Colson* judgment was mixed. Many legal scholars praised the Court's innovation in creating a new tool for the effective judicial protection of

[20] ibid para 23.
[21] ibid.
[22] Para 823(2) of the *Bürgerliches Gesetzbuch* (German Civil Code) provides for a general right to compensation. The German Government added, however, that such a remedy should be proportionate and only be available where the discrimination occurred against a better qualified candidate.
[23] Case 14/83 *Von Colson* (n 1) para 26.
[24] ibid para 28.
[25] Arnull notes that in previous case law, such as Case 111/75 *Mazzalai v Ferrovia del Renon* [1976] ECR 657, paras 10–11, the Court had only 'encouraged' national courts to interpret national law in light of directives it was attempting to implement: Arnull (n 16) 209.

individuals rights which was independent from the doctrine of direct effect.[26] However, some ambiguity in the judgment led to a debate on the nature and scope of the obligation imposed on the national courts. The main area of contention was whether the national court must only interpret national implementing legislation to comply with EU law or whether the duty extends to pre-existing national law. Advocate General Slynn in *Marshall (No 1)* expressed a preference for the narrower view of the *Von Colson* judgment, claiming that the use of the term 'in particular the provisions of a national law specifically introduced in order to implement Directive No 76/207' set out in paragraph 26 (see above) confers a duty of conform interpretation which applies only to national law adopted expressly to implement an EU directive or to fulfil a Treaty obligation to which section 2 of the European Communities Act 1972 applied.[27] In contrast, Advocate General van Gerven took a broader view, observing in *Barber*[28] that it may be difficult for a national court to discern in practice whether a particular provision of national law has been enacted to transpose a directive.[29] Equally, a national legislature may have decided in good faith that new implementing legislation was unnecessary.[30] It was not until six years later in *Marleasing*[31] that the Court finally addressed the question and confirmed that national courts should take into account pre-existing national law as well as national implementing legislation, eliminating a gap in judicial protection that had emerged for individuals who were seeking to enforce EU rights in horizontal cases.

IV. Famous Follow-Up Cases

The mandate imposed on national courts in *Von Colson* has been extensively developed by the Court of Justice through its jurisprudence over the last 40 years. Four themes can be identified in the follow-up case law and are explored below: the legal basis for the duty and its relationship with the principle of primacy (section IV.A); when the duty arises (section IV.B); the scope and strength of the duty imposed on national courts (section IV.C); and the limitations to the duty (section IV.D).

A. The Legal Basis for the Duty of Conform Interpretation

In *Von Colson*, the Court ruled that the duty of conform interpretation imposed on national courts stems from the principle of loyalty under Article 4(3) TEU read in conjunction with Article 288 TFEU, which places an obligation on Member States to

[26] D Curtin, 'Effective Sanctions and the Equal Treatment Directive: The *Von Colson* and *Harz* cases' (1985) 22 *Common Market Law Review* 505; J Steiner, 'EEC Directives: A New Route to Enforcement? (1985) 101 *Law Quarterly Review* 491, 494.

[27] See, eg, AG Slynn in *Marshall (No 1)* (n 9) 732–33. For a discussion of the reaction of the UK courts, see further J Steiner, 'Coming to terms with EEC Directives' (1990) 106 *Law Quarterly Review* 144, 148.

[28] Case C-262/88 *Barber* EU:C:1990:34.

[29] ibid 1937.

[30] Arnull (n 16) 201.

[31] Case C-106/89 *Marleasing* [1990] ECR I-4135.

transpose directives into their legal order. This pattern of reasoning was employed extensively in this era to develop new tasks and duties for national courts in their capacity as Union courts.[32]

It has also been argued that the principle of *effet utile* is implicit in the *Von Colson* judgment.[33] In the *Pfeiffer* judgment, the Court went a step further and held for the first time that the interpretative duty is 'inherent in the system of the Treaty, since it permits the national court, for matters within its jurisdiction, to ensure the full effectiveness of Community law when it determines the dispute before it'.[34] Again, this strengthening of the legal basis by referring to its inherence in the system of the Treaties follows the same approach adopted by the Court in relation to the EU remedy of state liability introduced in *Francovich*.[35]

In *Pupino*, on the basis of Article 4(3) TEU, the Court expanded the principle of indirect effect to apply to framework decisions adopted under Article 34(2)(b) of the pre-Lisbon TEU, which related to the intergovernmental third pillar of police and judicial cooperation in criminal matters.[36] The provision expressly denied framework decisions, which have the same legal characteristics as directives, direct effect. Again, the Court demonstrated its commitment to the effectiveness of EU law in the absence of direct effect.

It is worth noting that in *Von Colson*, the Court did not explicitly link the duty imposed on national courts with the principle of primacy. However, its position has now changed. In *Popławski I*, Advocate General Bot had argued that

> recognition of the principle of interpreting national law in conformity with EU law by way of the principle of loyal cooperation is necessarily predicated on the acceptance, however latent, of the primacy of EU law. How, after all, could the obligation of loyal cooperation under EU law justify the fact that the national court is required to amend the meaning of its national law in a manner in conformity with EU law if that obligation were not regarded as necessarily taking precedence over the national court's obligation to resolve the dispute in accordance with the rules of its national law?[37]

When in *Popławski II*, the dispute was referred back to the Court of Justice, it confirmed in its strongest terms to date that the duty to interpret national law to comply with EU law arises from the imperative of effectiveness of EU law *and primacy*. It held that

> in order to ensure the effectiveness of all provisions of EU law, the primacy principle requires, inter alia, national courts to interpret, to the greatest extent possible, their national law in conformity with EU law and to afford individuals the possibility of obtaining redress where their rights have been impaired by a breach of EU law attributable to a Member State.[38]

[32] J Temple Lang. 'The Duties of National Courts under Community Constitutional Law' (1997) 22 *European Law Review* 3; M Claes, *The National Courts' Mandate in the European Constitution* (Hart Publishing, 2006).

[33] See S Drake, 'Twenty years after *Von Colson*: the impact of "indirect effect" on the protection of the individual's community rights' (2005) 30 *European Law Review* 329.

[34] Case C-397/01 *Pfeiffer* EU:C:2004:584, para 114.

[35] Drake (n 33) [33].

[36] Case C-105/03 *Pupino* EU:C:2005:386, paras 42–48. See M Fletcher, 'Extending "indirect effect" to the Third Pillar: the significance of *Pupino*? (2005) 30 *European Law Review* 862–77.

[37] Opinion of AG Bot in C-579/15 *Popławski I* EU:C:2017:116, para 84.

[38] Case C-573/17 *Popławski II* (n 10) para 57.

In this case, facing clear resistance from the national court to the adoption of a conform interpretation of national law with a framework decision (which cannot have direct effect), the Court was very prescriptive in how a conform interpretation could be achieved and made it clear that existing case law or 'the fact that an interpretation of national law which is incompatible with EU law is endorsed by the Minister in no way impedes the referring court's obligation to interpret domestic law in conformity with EU law'.[39] Some commentators disagree with the Court's decision in *Popławski II* to expressly link the principle of indirect effect with primacy. Miasik and Szwarc[40] claim it would be better linked to effectiveness.

B. When does the Duty Arise?

The *Von Colson* judgment did not specify when the duty on the national courts to interpret national law in conformity with a directive arises. This is of particular importance as Member States are normally granted a two-year period to transpose a directive into their own legal order.[41] It was not until 2006 did the Grand Chamber confirm in *Adeneler*[42] that the duty arose *once the deadline for implementation of a directive had passed.* However, this must be read in conjunction with its earlier decision in *Inter-Environnement Wallonie*[43] which ruled that if a Member State transposes a directive *in advance of the deadline* for transposition, national courts are prohibited from adopting an interpretation of national law which would run contrary to the directive.

C. Clarifying the Scope of the Duty of Conform Interpretation

The most significant follow-up cases clarify the strength and scope of the interpretative mandate placed on national courts in *Von Colson*. As previously mentioned, the Court's judgment in *Marleasing*[44] is a landmark case. The ECJ unequivocally put to rest the view that the duty only applied to national implementing legislation and confirmed:

> [I]n applying national law, whether the provisions in question were adopted before or after the directive, the national court called upon to interpret it is required to do so, as far as possible, in the light of the wording and purpose of the directive in order to achieve the result pursued by the latter and thereby comply with the third paragraph of [Article 288 TFEU].[45]

In *Pfeiffer*, the Court went further, instructing national courts 'to consider national law as a whole in order to assess to what extent it may be applied so as not to produce a

[39] ibid para 95.
[40] D Miasik and M Szwarc, 'Primacy and direct effect – still together: *Popławski II*' (2021) 58 *Common Market Law Review* 571.
[41] G de Búrca, 'Giving Effect to European Community Directives' (1992) 55 *Modern Law Review* 215, 218.
[42] Case C-212/04 *Konstantinos Adeneler and Others v Ellinikos Organismos Galaktos (ELOG)* EU:C:2006:443.
[43] Case C-129/96 *Inter-Environnement Wallonie ASBL v Région Wallone* [1997] ECR I-7411.
[44] Case C-106/89 *Marleasing* (n 31).
[45] ibid para 8.

result contrary to that sought by the directive'.[46] In *Björnekulla*, the Court confirmed the duty applies, 'notwithstanding any contrary interpretation which may arise from *travaux préparatoires* for the national rule'.[47] This broad scope of the duty was confirmed in *Dominguez*, where the Court held that national courts must do

> whatever lies within their jurisdiction, taking the whole body of domestic law into consideration and applying the interpretative methods recognised by domestic law, with a view to ensuring that the directive in question is fully effective and achieving an outcome consistent with the objective pursued by it.[48]

In *Popławski II*, the Court held that a national court must interpret national law to 'the greatest extent possible'.[49]

In *Marleasing*, the fact that one party was able to rely on an EU directive to resolve a dispute with another private party (a horizontal case) contrary to the Court's interpretation of Article 288 TFEU in *Marshall (No 1)*[50] led to accusations by some scholars that the Court was 'introducing horizontal direct effect by the backdoor'.[51] However, it is argued that while this may have been the practical outcome, the principle of indirect effect is conceptually distinct since the defendant derives protection from the directive *indirectly* via national law and not *directly* from Union law as would be the case with horizontal direct effect. Moreover, in *Marleasing*, the conform interpretation allowed the defendant company to rely on the directive in its *defence* (ie as a shield). It did not lead to the imposition of a positive obligation on the other party in the sense previously referred to by the Court in *Marshall (No 1)*. The fact that the one party found themselves in a less advantageous legal position was deemed acceptable by the Court.

In subsequent case law, the Court has delivered several rulings where a conform interpretation has led to the imposition of a positive obligation on another private party in civil cases.[52] For example, the Court's judgment in *Webb*[53] required the national court to adopt a broader interpretation of national law than it had originally considered possible, which led to the imposition of *a (positive) obligation* upon the employer to comply with the principle of equal treatment and not to dismiss an employee on the grounds of pregnancy when she was a replacement for another employee on maternity leave. Save for the application of the principle of indirect effect, the employer would not have been subject to such an obligation under national law since it did not apply to such a

[46] Joined Cases C-397/01 to 403/01 *Pfeiffer* [2004] ECR I-8835, para 115.

[47] Case C-371/02 *Björnekulla* EU:C:2004:275, para 13. The Court's judgment is controversial since in some Member States, national courts regularly refer to *travaux préparatoires* to interpret national legislation. See CNK Franklin (ed), *The Effectiveness and Application of EU and EEA Law in National Courts: Principles of Consistent Interpretation* (Intersentia, 2018) 33–37.

[48] Case C-282/10 *Maribel Dominguez v Centre informatique du Centre Ouest Atlantique and Préfet de la région Centre* EU:C:2012:33, para 27.

[49] Case C-573/17 *Popławski II* (n 10), para 55.

[50] The ECJ has consistently held that according to Art 249(3) EC (now Article 288 TFEU), directives are addressed to Member States only; see, eg, Case 152/84 *Marshall (No 1)* (n 9) para 48. See also Case C-91/92 *Faccini Dori* [1994] ECR I-3325, para 20.

[51] For a summary of such views, see N Maltby, '*Marleasing*: What is all the fuss about?' (1993) 109 *Law Quarterly Review* 301.

[52] Case C-185/97 *Coote v Granada Hospitality Ltd* [1998] ECR I-5199, para 18; Case C-456/98 *Centrosteel* EU:C:2000:402; Joined Cases C-240/98 to C-244/98 *Océano Grupo* [2000] ECR I-4941, [2002] 1 CMLR 43, paras 30–32.

[53] Case C-32/93 *Webb v EMO Air Cargo* EU:C:1994:300.

dismissal. This level of legal certainty within the national legal orders appears to be acceptable for the Court in the context of civil liability.[54] For some authors, such as Craig and de Búrca, it is paradoxical for the Court to accept the legal uncertainty created for private parties by the broad degree of discretion conferred on national courts by the duty of conform interpretation, but to continue to deny directives horizontal direct effect due to concerns about inter alia legal certainty.[55]

D. Limitations on the Use of Indirect Effect

Despite the strength and breadth of the mandate of the national court under *Von Colson*, the Court has recognised two key limitations in its subsequent case law.

i. The Principle of Non-Retroactivity of Criminal Liability

Two years after *Von Colson*, the Court placed its first limit on the new duty imposed on national courts. It ruled in *Kolpinghuis*[56] that the principle of conform interpretation could not be used by a national court in a manner which infringed the principles of legal certainty and non-retroactivity in criminal law. In this case, the Dutch Public Prosecutor sought to interpret national law to comply with an *unimplemented directive* which would result in a criminal sanction being imposed by the State upon an individual which did not otherwise exist under national law.[57] Equally, in *Procura della Repubblica v X*,[58] the Court prohibited a national court from interpreting national law to comply with an *incorrectly implemented directive* where this would have resulted in criminal liability being imposed on individuals.[59] The Court reasoned that this limitation on the principle of indirect effect is a corollary of the principle of legality in the context of crime and punishment and more generally of the principle of legal certainty. This general principle can be found in the constitutional traditions common to the Member States, and is enshrined in various international treaties, in particular, Article 7 of the Convention for the Protection of Human Rights and Fundamental Freedoms.[60] It has since been included in Article 49(1) of the EU Charter of Fundamental Rights.

ii. Interpretation of National Law Contra Legem

As discussed above, national courts are subject to a strong obligation to interpret national law to conform with EU law and its scope is extremely broad. In light of this, a

[54] Betlem and Nollkaemper (n 6).
[55] P Craig and G de Búrca, *EU Law: Text, Cases and Material*, 7th edn (Oxford University Press, 2020) 258.
[56] Case 80/86 *Kolpinghuis Nijmegen* [1987] ECR 3969.
[57] Betlem and Nollkaemper (n 6) call this an inverse vertical relationship, ie, where the State wishes to impose obligations on individuals rather than an individual seeking to enforce the law against a Member State.
[58] Joined Cases C-74 & 129/95 *Procura della Repubblica v X* [1996] ECR I-6609.
[59] ibid para 24.
[60] ibid para 25. Art 7 ECHR states: 'No one shall be held guilty of any criminal offence on account of any act or omission which did not constitute a criminal offence under national or international law at the time when it was committed. Nor shall a heavier penalty be imposed than the one that was applicable at the time the criminal offence was committed.'

significant concern for national courts is whether the principle of indirect effect requires them to interpret national law *contra legem*. In *Von Colson*, the Court acknowledged that there may be limits to how far a national court can interpret national law in compliance with EU law. It states that the duty applies 'in so far as [the national court] is given discretion to do so under national law'.[61] In *Marleasing*, the Court strengthened the obligation stating that the national court must interpret national law to conform with EU law 'as far as possible, in the light of the wording and purpose of the directive'.[62] It was not until its 1993 judgment in *Wagner Miret*[63] that the Court expressly acknowledged *as a matter of EU law* that it may not always be possible for a national court to interpret national law to comply with the directive. It confirmed that the duty of conform interpretation is by no means absolute and does not require national courts to encroach on the legislature and engage in judicial law-making. In *Wagner Miret*, the Court did recognise that there may be circumstances where a conform interpretation is not possible and leave an individual without the ability to enforce their EU rights at national level. To remedy this gap, the Court held that the claimant should be entitled to bring an action for damages against the State for breach of EU law.[64] More recently, in *Kükükdeveci*, the Court held that if a conform interpretation was not possible, a national court should disapply national law conflicting with a general principle of EU law (principle of age discrimination) which has been given effect through a directive. In *Popławski II*, the Court held that if a conform interpretation is not possible as it would be *contra legem*, the national court must disapply the conflicting national law only if the EU provision has direct effect.

Nevertheless, there is some uncertainty as to where the *contra legem* limit lies and whether this limit is determined by the national court or by the Court of Justice.[65] In some recent cases, the Court has faced some resistance from the national courts which have claimed that an interpretation in conformity with EU law would be *contra legem*. In response, where the Court has disagreed, it has reinforced the strength of the interpretative obligation imposed on the national courts as a matter of EU law. In *Dansk Industri* (also known as *Ajos*),[66] the Court confirmed that the duty of the national court to adopt a conform interpretation of national law extends to changing established case law if it is based on an interpretation of national law that is incompatible with the objectives of a directive. This obligation would apply of its own motion if the precedent had been established by a higher national court.[67] In *Popławski II*,[68] the Court held that national courts are still bound to adopt a conform interpretation of national law with

[61] Case 14/83 *Von Colson* (n 1) para 28.

[62] Case C-106/89 *Marleasing* (n 31) para 8.

[63] Case C-334/92 *Wagner Miret* [1993] ECR I-6911. See also Case C-91/92 *Faccini Dori* (n 50) para 27. For further examples in the case law, see A Arnull, 'European Union law and the contra legem principle' (2022) 47 *European Law Review* 291.

[64] Case C-334/92 *Wagner Miret* (n 63); Case C-261/20 *Thelen Technopark Berlin GmbH v MN* EU:C:2022:33, paras 41–46.

[65] Arnull (n 63).

[66] Case C-441/14 *Ajos* (n 13) paras 33–34.

[67] The Danish Supreme Court infamously refused to comply with the preliminary ruling on the grounds that this would amount to a *contra legem* interpretation: see CD Tvarnø and GS Ølykke, 'Consistent Interpretation in Denmark' in Franklin (ed) (n 47) 257.

[68] Case C-573/17 *Popławski II* (n 10).

EU law even if other national authorities including the executive disagree[69] and claim the interpretation is *contra legem*.[70]

V. The Application of the Principle of Indirect Effect by National Courts: Some Comments

The *Von Colson* judgment did not attract the same level of hostility from the Member States and their senior national courts as the principles of primacy, direct effect of directives, State liability and the *Mangold* principle. First, the very nature of the *Von Colson* mandate is far less intrusive in the national legal order since it permits national judiciaries to adapt their own national interpretative methodologies to the requirements of EU law to find an effective solution.[71] The duty demonstrates respect for the autonomy of the national courts and their legal cultures.[72] Furthermore, for some national courts, the *Von Colson* mandate is similar to the interpretative obligation which exists under public international law.[73] It follows that there will be differences in how the national courts may give effect to the same provision of EU law.

Second, unlike the doctrines of primacy and direct effect, the principle of indirect effect does not usurp the legislative function.[74] The Court does not require the national court to interpret national law *contra legem*. Where this boundary lies between 'acceptable, albeit robust and creative interpretation, and the ultimate forbidden fruit: judicial legislation'[75] is not easy to determine and will differ between the Member States. For example, the Czech Constitutional Court considered itself able to interpret Article 14(4) of the Czech Constitution, which states that 'No citizen may be forced to leave his homeland' in conformity with the European Arrest Warrant.[76] In contrast, the German and Polish constitutional courts refused to adopt conform interpretations of similar provisions in their own constitutions until they had been amended.[77]

The extent to which the dividing line has come under strain is demonstrated in *Dansk Industri (Ajos)*.[78] The Court was not prepared to accept that the *contra legem* limitation applied to case law. It held that the duty to adopt a conform interpretation extends to changing well-established case law and applies to a lower court if the case law has been established by a higher court. It added that if a conform interpretation is not

[69] ibid para 79. See further Miasik and Szwarc (n 40).
[70] Case C-573/17 *Popławski II* (n 10) para 94.
[71] S Prechal, *Directives in EC Law*, 2nd edn (Oxford University Press, 2005) 180; M Brennecke, 'Hybrid Methodology for the EU Principle of Consistent Interpretation' (2017) 39 *Statute Law Review* 1.
[72] M Amstutz, 'In-Between Worlds: *Marleasing* and the Emergence of Interlegality in Legal Reasoning' (2005) 11 *European Law Journal* 766.
[73] Betlem and Nollkaemper (n 6).
[74] ibid.
[75] ibid.
[76] Judgment of 3 May 2006, case no Pl ÚS 66/04, No 434/2006 Coll.
[77] M Bobek, 'The effects of EU law in the national legal systems' in S Peers and C Barnard, *European Union Law*, 4th edn (Oxford University Press, 2023) 174; see further J Komárek, 'European Constitutionalism and the European Arrest Warrant: In Search of the Limits of "Contrapunctual Principles"' (2007) 44 *Common Market Law Review* 9.
[78] Case C-441/14 *Dansk Industri (Asos)* (n 14).

possible, the national court must disapply the conflicting national law and give effect to the general principle at issue, namely the principle of age discrimination. In response, and for the first time, the Danish Supreme Court refused to follow the Court's judgment which it considered would be *contra legem* and not foreseen in the Act on Denmark's Accession to the European. Denmark's legislature subsequently amended its national law to bring it in line with EU law.[79]

The reception of the principle of indirect effect by the national courts has evolved incrementally and at different rates.[80] A good example is the UK, where the acceptance of the principle of indirect effect has changed remarkably since the initial rejection of the *Von Colson* mandate espoused by Lord Templeman in the House of Lords judgment in *Duke v GEC Reliance*,[81] in which he stated:

> The *von Colson* case is no authority for the proposition that the German court was bound to invent a German law of adequate compensation if no such law existed and no authority for the proposition that a court of a Member State must distort the meaning of a domestic statute so as to conform with Community law which is not directly applicable.[82]

Following the *Marleasing* judgment, the UK judiciary embraced the new duty that is commonly referred to as the *Marleasing* principle. Indeed, its application can be argued to have been more far-reaching than in many of the other Member States.[83] Lord Mance had gone as far as describing the UK courts as being 'more catholic than the Pope in their understanding of this interpretative duty'.[84] Moreover, when incorporating the European Convention on Human Rights into UK law by virtue of the Human Rights Act (HRA) 1998, the interpretative obligation set in section 3 had been consciously modelled by the legislature on the *Von Colson* obligation.[85] The relationship between the two was discussed at length by the then House of Lords in its 2004 *Ghaidan v Godin-Mendoza* judgment,[86] which subsequently became the leading authority for the EU principle of consistent interpretation in the UK courts. In *Jessemey v Rowstock Ltd*,

[79] See Tvarnø and Ølykke (n 67); R Holdgaard, D Elkan and GK Schaldemose, 'From Cooperation to Collision: The ECJ's *Ajos* Ruling and the Danish Supreme Court's Refusal to Comply' (2018) 55 *Common Market Law Review* 17.

[80] For a comprehensive analysis of the application of the principle of conform interpretation in 15 EU and EEA states, see Franklin (ed) (n 47) 12.

[81] *Duke v GEC Reliance Ltd* [1988] AC 618.

[82] ibid 641. See also *Finnegan v Clowney Youth Training Ltd* [1990] 2 AC 407.

[83] For an analysis of the application of the principle of conform interpretation in the UK courts pre-Brexit, see S Drake, 'The effectiveness and application of the principle of consistent interpretation in the national courts: the UK perspective' in Franklin (ed) (n 47) 213. For a discussion of the implications of Brexit on the principle of indirect effect and legal certainty, particularly in the field of intellectual property law, see P Johnson, '"Inverted Supremacy", "Weaker Precedent" and other uncertainties brought about by the Retained EU Law (Revocation and Reform) Act 2023' (2023) 45 *European Intellectual Property Law Review* 634. See also HHJ Tindal in *E-Accounting Solutions Ltd (t/a Advancetrack) v Global Infosys Ltd (t/a GI Outsourcing)* [2023] EWHC 2038 (Ch) [106]–[116].

[84] Lord Mance, 'The Interface between national and European law' (2013) 38 *European Law Review* 437, 450.

[85] *Ghaidan v Godin-Mendoza* [2004] UKHL 30, [2004] 2 AC 557, per Lord Steyn [45]. Note that under HRA 1998, s 4, if a conform interpretation under s 3 is not possible, a declaration of incompatibility is made by the court. The legislature can then take steps to amend the law.

[86] *Ghaidan* (n 85).

the Court of Appeal referred to *Ghadain* as amounting to an 'assimilation' of the interpretative obligations set out in *Marleasing* and section 3 of the HRA 1998.[87]

Nevertheless, the UK courts are clear about the limitations that apply to the *Marleasing* principle. In *Vodafone 2*,[88] the Court of Appeal set out two key limitations. First, an interpretation must 'go with the grain of the legislation'. Second, the 'exercise of the interpretative obligation cannot require the courts to make decisions for which they are not equipped or give rise to important practical repercussions which the court is not equipped to evaluate'.[89]

VI. Concluding Remarks

The Court's judgment in *Von Colson* and the duty of conform interpretation can be safely judged to be one of the Court's constitutional success stories. Hailed as an 'ingenious'[90] solution to a 'tricky question', the principle of indirect effect has been extensively developed over the past 40 years. It has played a critical role in the development of the EU's legal order and provided a new mechanism for individuals to secure their EU rights in the absence of direct effect. More recently, the Court has employed the principle of indirect effect to guarantee the effectiveness of framework decisions and a general principle of law, namely the principle of age discrimination. Both present the Court with a constitutional dilemma as neither can be enforced using direct effect and horizontal direct effect respectively. Nevertheless, the application of the principle of indirect effect in these two contexts has come under strain with differing views on which courts should determine whether an interpretation is *contra legem*. It remains to be seen whether tensions between the Court of Justice and national courts will increase and undermine the position of the principle of indirect effect as one of the keystones of the EU's legal order.

[87] *Jessemey v Rowstock Ltd* [2014] EWCA Civ 185, per Underhill LJ [40].

[88] *Vodafone 2 v Revenue and Customs Commissioners* [2009] EWCA Civ 446 [37]–[38].

[89] See, eg, the decision of the High Court in *UK Insurance Ltd v Holden* [2016] EWHC 264, where the judge refused to interpret national law to comply with the CJEU's ruling in Case C-162/13 *Vnuk v Zavarovalnica d.d.* EU:C:2014:2146 on the scope of the EU's First Motor Insurance Directive. It is noteworthy that the EU legislation has been recast by the EU legislature removing the impact of the 'activist' ruling on the CJEU in *Vnuk*: J Marson and K Ferris, 'Changing lanes and removing rights: quashing the judicial activism of the Court of Justice through Directive 2021/2118' (2022) 47 *European Law Review* 773.

[90] Steiner (n 27) 148.

PART B

EU Competences: Vertical and Horizontal

6

The *ERTA* Case: Establishing the EU as an International Actor

MARISE CREMONA

I. Historical and Doctrinal Context

Case 22/70 *Commission v Council* (*ERTA*), decided on 31 March 1971,[1] in which the Court held that the European Economic Community (EEC) possessed the competence to conclude an international agreement in the field of transport despite the absence of an express Treaty provision to that effect, is a foundational case in the evolution of the external relations law of the European (Economic) Community and European Union (EU). It not only represents an early necessary step in defining the scope of the EU's external powers and therefore the EU's ability to act internationally; *ERTA* is still of contemporary salience, a point of reference regularly called in aid in litigation about external powers.[2] However, its claim to a place in this book as a landmark case is not limited to the field of external relations law. The ripples of its impact may be felt in the application of implied powers and pre-emption more generally,[3] in the reviewability of acts of the EU institutions[4] and – most expansively – in the conceptualisation of 'constitutional visions' of the Union.[5] The *ERTA* case may indeed be included among those cases, such as *Van Gend en Loos*[6] and *Costa v ENEL*,[7] which establish the constitutional character of the EU and its new

[1] Case 22/70 *Commission v Council (ERTA)* EU:C:1971:32; Opinion of Advocate General Dutheillet de Lamothe, 10 March 1971, EU:C:1971:23.

[2] See, eg, *Opinion 2/15* EU:C:2017:376, paras 231–34; Case C-600/14 *Germany v Council* EU:C:2017:935, para 59; Opinion of AG Ćapeta in Case C-500/20 *ÖBB-Infrastruktur* EU:C:2022:79, para 63.

[3] See, eg, Case T-240/04 *France v Commission* EU:T:2007:290, paras 35–36.

[4] See, eg, Case C-27/04 *Commission v Council* EU:C:2004:436, para 44; Joined Cases C-59/18 and C-182/18 *Italy and Comune di Milano v Council* EU:C:2022:567, para 60.

[5] L Azoulai, 'The Many Visions of Europe: Insights from the Reasoning of the European Court of Justice in External Relations Law' in M Cremona and A Thies (eds), *The European Court of Justice and External Relations Law: Constitutional Challenges* (Hart Publishing, 2014) 165; A Petti, '*ERTA* and Us: Shifting Constitutional Equilibria on the Visions of Europe' in M Cremona, C Kilpatrick and J Scott (eds), 'Using the Historical Archives of the EU to Study Cases of the CJEU' (2021) 6 *European Papers* 567.

[6] Case 26/62 *Van Gend en Loos* EU:C:1963:1; see ch 1 of this volume.

[7] Case 6/64 *Costa v ENEL* EU:C:1964:66; see ch 2 of this volume.

legal order;[8] from that perspective, scholars have pointed to the role of Pierre Pescatore as *juge rapporteur* in the case.[9]

Putting *ERTA* in its historical context is important. In the EEC's first decade, alongside the seminal case law on the new legal order, the first building blocks of the customs union and common market were being put in place. By 1970 attention was turning to the external implications of this internal integration, and *ERTA* is one (indeed, the first and most important) of a series of significant judgments during the 1970s on the scope and nature of external powers and the legal effects of the EU's early treaty-making. We may think of *Opinion 1/75* on the scope and legal nature of the common commercial policy,[10] *Opinion 1/76* developing the *ERTA* ruling on implied external powers,[11] *Haegeman* on the legal effect of treaties in the Community legal order,[12] and the first cases on the direct effect of treaties, *International Fruit Company* and *Bresciani*.[13]

These developments were not limited to case law. The circumstances of the *ERTA* case – the contention over the use of transport policy powers in the external sphere – show the development of EU external practice, moving beyond trade and association agreements and exploring the external implications of 'internal' policy-making. Transport was perhaps a natural early case, given its inherently international character (as the Court recognises in *ERTA*[14]), as indeed is fisheries conservation, another early example.[15] The pre-emption-based reasoning in *ERTA* reflects the EU's increased legislative activity in mapping out common policies as well as the nature of international governance in these policy fields. *ERTA* is also an early example (alongside *Opinion 1/75*) of a still potentially contentious phenomenon: the participation of the EU, as its activities expand, in international negotiations hitherto conducted by Member States, and the need for acceptance of the EU's role by its negotiating partners as well as its own Member States. In the pragmatic outcome of the case[16] we can see the Court's recognition of this need, as well as its insistence on the EU's international capacity and competence.

The constitutional context of *ERTA*, indeed, is the affirmation of the autonomy of the EU from its Member States, the independent capacity of its institutions to act externally and the implications this has for the Member States under the loyalty obligation. The Council, the Court insists, is not simply a gathering of Member State representatives, it is one of the 'common institutions'[17] deriving its powers and ability to bind the Member States from the Treaty. The Member States' obligation of loyalty (then Article 5 EEC Treaty,[18]

[8] A McNaughton, 'Acts of Creation: The *ERTA* Decision as a Foundation Stone of the EU Legal System' in F Nicola and B Davies (eds), *EU Law Stories* (Cambridge University Press, 2017) 135.

[9] For an illuminating account of the formation and influence of Pescatore, see V Fritz, 'Activism on and off the Bench: Pierre Pescatore and the Law of Integration' (2020) 57 *Common Market Law Review* 475.

[10] *Opinion 1/75* EU:C:1975:145; see ch 8 of this volume.

[11] *Opinion 1/76* EU:C:1977:63.

[12] Case 181/73 *Haegeman* EU:C:1974:41.

[13] Cases 21–24/72 *International Fruit Company* EU:C:1972:115; Case 87/75 *Bresciani* EU:C:1976:18.

[14] Case 22/70 *ERTA* (n 1) paras 23–27.

[15] Joined Cases 3, 4 and 6/76 *Kramer* EU:C:1976:114.

[16] T Tridimas and P Eeckhout, 'The External Competence of the Community and the Case-Law of the Court of Justice: Principle versus Pragmatism' (1994) 14 *Yearbook of European Law* 143.

[17] Case 22/70 *ERTA* (n 1) paras 52–53.

[18] Art 5 Treaty establishing the European Economic Community, 25 March 1957, available at: data.europa.eu/eli/treaty/teec/sign.

now Article 4(3) TEU[19]) operates in the external as well as internal sphere.[20] Institutionally, the *ERTA* case carries the distinction of being the first case in which the Court was asked to adjudicate directly between the Council and the Commission.[21] No doubt in part for this reason, the Court's approach to defining the nature of the Council act under challenge and the scope of its jurisdiction under what is now Article 263 TFEU has been influential in later cases involving challenge to institutional acts which do not fall within Article 288 TFEU. We can trace from *ERTA* the idea that the EU, as a Union based on the rule of law, needs to provide procedures for challenging measures which are designed to have legal effects, and that the mechanisms to ensure this may be drawn from 'the general scheme of the Treaty' and not only its express provisions.[22]

II. The Facts and Judgment in the *ERTA* Case

The *ERTA* case arose out of the negotiations for an agreement on the working conditions of the crews of vehicles engaged in international road transport. The agreement (known as the AETR, or ERTA) had a long gestation, being originally negotiated under the auspices of the UN Economic Commission for Europe; an agreement was signed in 1962 by 18 states, including all six then EEC Member States, but it did not come into force for want of sufficient ratifications. The EEC itself then started negotiations on a draft regulation, which was adopted in March 1969,[23] and in parallel negotiations started on a revised version of the ERTA. In the ERTA negotiation, the Council sought to ensure a common position of the six Member States in line with the new EEC regulation, and to this end on 20 March 1970, a few days before the meeting at which the final text of the ERTA was due to be adopted, it adopted conclusions – the act which was to be challenged by the Commission in the case under discussion. According to the record of these Council proceedings,[24] the ERTA was to be negotiated and concluded by the Member States, while 'Throughout the negotiations and at the conclusion of the agreement the Member States shall take common action, coordinating their position in accordance with the usual procedures, in close association with the Community institutions.'[25] The (rotating) Council presidency was to act as spokesperson for the Member States. The Commission, which had expressed (and minuted) disagreement with its lack of involvement in the negotiations, brought an action for annulment of these Council proceedings. In the Commission's view, the ERTA fell within the Community's powers under the Treaty provisions relating to the establishment of a common transport policy, and its negotiation and conclusion should have been governed by Article 228 EEC Treaty (now Article 218 TFEU) – essentially, negotiation by the Commission

[19] Art 4(3) TEU [2016] OJ C202/1.
[20] Case 22/70 *ERTA* (n 1) paras 20–22.
[21] A point recognised by AG Dutheillet de Lamothe, who referred to the 'curious menage' between the institutions and the 'unusual and exceptional' nature of the dispute: Opinion of the Advocate General (n 1) 284.
[22] Case 294/83 *Les Verts v Parliament* EU:C:1986:166, paras 23–24, citing Case 22/70 *ERTA*.
[23] Regulation 543/69 [1969] OJ L77/49.
[24] The term 'proceedings' is used in the case: see Case 22/70 *ERTA* (n 1) para 1.
[25] Opinion of AG Dutheillet de Lamothe (n 1) 285.

and conclusion by the Council. Meanwhile, the ERTA negotiations were successfully concluded in April 1970.

Two points may be noted before we turn to the legal issues raised by the case and the line of reasoning developed by the Court. First, the revival of the international agreement, the ERTA, was linked to the negotiation and adoption of an (internal) Community regulation on the issue. Not for the last time, the common position established by the Member States among themselves in internal legislation both spurred a broader European regulatory process and enabled the EEC to take a lead in shaping the new text. Second, the adoption of the internal act covering the same subject matter as the proposed international agreement gave rise to the need to avoid incompatibility between the two. The Council sought to achieve this both by adopting a common negotiating position and by inviting the Commission to make a proposal for the adoption of any necessary revisions to the recently adopted internal legislation. The case is thus an early example of the two-way interplay between the EU's internal legislative process and its external regulatory activity.

To a reader today, three questions appear to be at issue in the *ERTA* litigation: the admissibility of the action (the characterisation of the Council act and the scope of the Court's judicial review jurisdiction), whether the negotiation and conclusion of the ERTA fell within the competence of the Community, and – if so – whether that precludes Member State participation. The Court dealt with all these questions, but they are not neatly separated in the judgment. Not only did the Court not distinguish clearly between the existence of Community powers and their exclusive character (about which, see more below). From the start, the Court framed the question of admissibility as a question of competence: as so often in the Court's judgments, its choice of starting point is significant. The Court's framing of the whole case in terms of competence and its exercise gives its ruling a certain weight and clarity (there are no distractions from the line of argument), although it also leads to different formulations of the principles as the Court reiterates them in slightly different contexts; an early commentator found the structure of the argument 'needlessly complicated'.[26]

The relationship between the Court's judgment and the Advocate General's Opinion is particularly instructive in this case. The Court structured its approach to the case in the same way as the Advocate General, disagreed with him on the central competence issue, but then came to the same conclusion on the substance. The Advocate General's Opinion is indeed a classic example of an alternative reading of the case, a powerfully argued 'dissent'[27] which is important in displaying the arguments which the Court – characteristically – did not explicitly refute. In Dutheillet de Lamothe's view, the attribution of external powers beyond those expressly granted would threaten the principle of conferral. He argued that the reading of the Treaty ultimately adopted by the Court was a 'daring exercise in legal construction' that was, in the end, 'too audacious' for him. But the Opinion is interesting in another way too: while ultimately rejecting it, the Advocate General presented the argument which ultimately prevailed with the Court, and he did

[26] JA Winter, 'Commentary on case 22/70 Commission v Council' (1971) 8 *Common Market Law Review* 550, 554.

[27] Of course not in reality a dissent since the Opinion is written to assist the Court in its deliberations.

so in words very close to those the Court actually used.[28] It was an argument based on 'a certain Community ethic' which he rejected 'with some regret'.[29] It is as though the Advocate General was suggesting to the Court an approach which he as Advocate General could not espouse but which the Court might be 'audacious' enough to take up.

The Advocate General and the Court adopted a similar approach to the question of admissibility, but with different results. The key to the question, as the Advocate General put it, was whether the Council was acting 'as an institution of the Community', or as the 'unifying agency' of the Member States acting collectively. And in answering that question the point of departure is the issue of competence. In the words of the Court:

> The legal effect of the proceedings differs according to whether they are regarded as constituting the exercise of powers conferred on the Community, or as acknowledging a coordination by the Member States of the exercise of powers which remained vested in them. To decide on the objection of inadmissibility, therefore, it is necessary to determine first of all whether, at the date of the proceedings in question, power to negotiate and conclude the AETR was vested in the Community or in the Member States.[30]

The conclusion of the Advocate General, as we have seen, was that the conferred powers of the Community in the field of external relations could not be extended so far as to imply the power to act externally from the granting of internal competences. The contested proceedings thus could not be a Community act and were not subject to judicial review. The Court took a different view, starting its judgment with a broad statement of principle as to the Community's international capacity in general and the basis from which its external competence in specific fields may be derived.[31] Once it had determined that the Community did indeed have the power to conclude the ERTA agreement, and that the Council was therefore acting within the scope of Community powers, the Court went on to adopt a broad interpretation of its jurisdiction in actions for judicial review so as to encompass these Council 'proceedings'. In an often-cited passage, it held that Article 173 EEC Treaty (now Article 263 TFEU) was designed to ensure observance of the law and should therefore not be limited to formal regulations, directives and decisions falling within the scope of Article 189 EEC Treaty (now Article 288 TFEU): 'An action for annulment must therefore be available in the case of all measures adopted by the institutions, whatever their nature or form, which are intended to have legal effects.'[32] Again, the Court's reasoning is linked to the scope of the Community's powers: it is precisely because the Member States could not act alone in the matter of the ERTA agreement, but only within 'the framework of the common institutions',[33] that the Council proceedings could not be seen as simply a matter of voluntary coordination,

[28] 'When, through a regulation, a specific subject-matter is transferred from the national to the Community level it may be maintained that the Member States, acting either individually or collectively, may no longer validly conclude agreements with third countries relating to the same subject-matter. Thus the Community alone would be capable of concluding such agreements within the ambit of Community law.' Case 22/70 *ERTA*, Opinion of AG Dutheillet de Lamothe (n 1) 291.

[29] ibid.

[30] Case 22/70 *ERTA* (n 1) paras 4–5.

[31] On this, see further below.

[32] Case 22/70 *ERTA* (n 1) para 42. Note that Art 263 TFEU, as amended by the Maastricht Treaty, reflects this wording in referring to all 'acts … intended to produce legal effects *vis à vis* third parties'.

[33] Case 22/70 *ERTA* (n 1) para 52.

'but were designed to lay down a course of action binding on both the institutions and the Member States'.[34] They must therefore be subject to review.

The Court's discussion of competence is presented in two stages, first in the context of the initial determination of admissibility (paragraphs 6–31) and second in the context of the substantive argument (paragraphs 68–91). In the first stage, the Court assessed the capacity and competence of the Community, finding both that the Community possessed competence to conclude the ERTA and that this competence was exclusive (ie it excluded the possibility of concurrent action by the Member States). In the second stage, the Court assessed the manner in which the Council had acted in the light of its finding of competence (and, by implication, also the action of the Member States). Within these two stages the reasoning proceeds by way of four steps.

The first step is not an examination of the Treaty provisions on external relations to see whether they may cover the agreement in question. Indeed, the Court recognises at the start 'the absence of specific provisions of the Treaty relating to the negotiation and conclusion of international agreements in the sphere of transport policy'. However this absence is not the end of the story; it requires the Court to take account of the broader picture, to 'the general system of Community law in the sphere of relations with third countries'.[35] The Court, then, basing itself on the grant of legal personality to the Community in Article 210 EEC Treaty, gives a striking affirmation of its capacity to enter into international legal relations. This capacity covers the 'whole field' of Community objectives. We are left in no doubt that the Court intends this judgment as a constitutional[36] statement about the Community's ability to act internationally.

The second step in the reasoning is to assess whether the Community, given its international capacity, has competence in this specific case (the conclusion of the ERTA agreement). We need to pause here to note the two steps in the argument so far: first, the Court determines that the Community has the legal *capacity* to engage in treaty-making that goes beyond those instances expressly referred to in the Treaty; this is not however the same as the determination of *competence* ('authority' is the word used in the English translation[37]) to conclude a specific agreement. Here again, in the second step, the Court insists that we must not simply look for an express grant of external powers but must have regard to 'the whole scheme of the Treaty', since powers may be conferred 'from other provisions of the Treaty and from measures adopted, within the framework of those provisions, by the Community institutions'.[38] Indeed, the Treaty establishes a common transport policy as an explicit objective (Article 3(e) EEC Treaty), and in implementing the Treaty, 'the system of internal Community measures may not therefore be separated from that of external relations'.[39] The Court is here adopting an argument that external powers may impliedly complement internal powers in seeking to achieve an express Treaty-based competence. Again, its broad framing of the proposition, when a narrower statement would have been possible, is evidence that the judgment was intended as a fundamental ruling of principle.[40]

[34] ibid para 53.
[35] ibid para 12.
[36] Although the Court at this time would not have used the word 'constitutional'.
[37] Case 22/70 *ERTA* (n 1) para 15; in the original French the term used is '*la compétence*'.
[38] ibid.
[39] ibid para 19.
[40] Tridimas and Eeckhout (n 16) 150.

As for whether implied external powers are needed in this case, the Court relies on the fact that the transport policy provisions refer to international transport and that therefore agreements with third countries may be necessary.[41] This conclusion is then supported by the adoption of Regulation 543/69 harmonising aspects of social legislation relating to road transport: this regulation 'necessarily vested in the Community power to enter into any agreements with third countries relating to the subject-matter governed by that regulation'.[42] The overlap between the internal legislation and the ERTA means that 'the Community has been empowered to negotiate and conclude the agreement in question since the entry into force of the said regulation'.[43] In this crucial step, the Court develops its doctrine of implied external powers based on two strands of reasoning: the adoption of internal legislation (often referred to as the '*ERTA* principle'); and the need for external powers to achieve Treaty objectives (the principle of *effet utile*). Common to both strands is the complementarity between internal and external powers in achieving Community objectives.[44]

Two additional points may be noted about the Court's approach to implied powers in this line of reasoning. First, implied powers are nonetheless *conferred* powers; the Court is clear that these powers are derived directly from specific provisions of the Treaty.[45] Second, and following from this, the exercise of implied powers does not require recourse to the so-called 'flexibility clause', Article 235 EEC Treaty (now Article 352 TFEU). As the Court held a little later in its judgment, while this clause might be applied in an external context it 'confers on the Council an option' rather than an obligation.[46]

The third step of the Court's reasoning relates to the impact on Member States, the exclusivity of the implied powers. The 'common rules' adopted in the harmonising regulation, the Court goes on to rule, exclude the possibility of future external action by Member States which may impact those rules. The key statement is found in paragraph 17:

> [E]ach time the Community, with a view to implementing a common policy envisaged by the Treaty, adopts provisions laying down common rules, whatever form these may take, the Member States no longer have the right, acting individually or even collectively, to undertake obligations with third countries which affect those rules. As and when such common rules come into being, the Community alone is in a position to assume and carry out contractual obligations towards third countries affecting the whole sphere of application of the Community legal system.[47]

The statement was repeated a little later with a small change of wording:

> If [Articles 3(e) and 5 EEC Treaty] are read in conjunction, it follows that to the extent to which Community rules are promulgated for the attainment of the objectives of the Treaty,

[41] Case 22/70 *ERTA* (n 1) paras 24–27.
[42] ibid para 28.
[43] ibid para 30.
[44] A Dashwood and J Heliskoski, 'The Classic Authorities Revisited' in A Dashwood and C Hillion (eds), *The General Law of EC External Relations* (Sweet & Maxwell, 2000) 3.
[45] This point is made clearly in *Opinion 2/94* EU:C:1996:140, paras 24–25: 'That principle of conferred powers must be respected in both the internal action and the international action of the Community. The Community acts ordinarily on the basis of specific powers which, as the Court has held, are not necessarily the express consequence of specific provisions of the Treaty but may also be implied from them.'
[46] Case 22/70 *ERTA* (n 1) para 95. The distinction is also clear from *Opinion 2/94* (n 45) para 28. See also Case C-370/12 *Pringle* EU:C:2012:756, para 67, referring to Case 22/70 *ERTA*.
[47] Case 22/70 *ERTA* (n 1) para 17.

> the Member States cannot, outside the framework of the Community institutions, assume obligations which might affect those rules or alter their scope.[48]

Taking these two passages together, the basis of the Court's reasoning is the existence of a Treaty-defined common policy, its implementation by 'common rules', the need to avoid the risk that Member State action outside the Community framework may 'affect' or 'alter the scope' of the common rules, supported by the loyalty clause then found in Article 5 EEC Treaty. A little later in the judgment the point is made slightly differently:

> [T]he Community has been empowered to negotiate and conclude the agreement in question since the entry into force of [Regulation 543/69]. These Community powers exclude the possibility of concurrent powers on the part of Member States, since any steps taken outside the framework of the Community institutions would be incompatible with the unity of the Common Market and the uniform application of Community law.[49]

All three statements use a logic of pre-emption: the potential threat to the unity of the market and uniform application of Community law flows from the possibility of affecting or altering the scope of the common rules contained in the regulation which forms the basis for the Community's (exclusive) powers. The Member States are constrained once the Union has acted in a particular field.

Although in this exposition of the judgment, I have separated the Court's reasoning on the existence of the (implied) power to conclude the ERTA from its conclusions as to the exclusive nature of that power, the Court itself is not so explicit. The fact that the Commission had argued for exclusive competence meant that it was possible to treat the two issues as one.[50] This aspect of the judgment and its proper interpretation (are all external powers based on the *ERTA* reasoning by nature exclusive?) have been the subject of debate in a number of later cases.[51]

In the fourth step of its reasoning the Court addresses the demands of exclusivity and the obligation of loyalty in the specific context of the ERTA negotiations. Starting from the Treaty provisions on the adoption of a common transport policy, on the negotiation and conclusion of international agreements, and Article 116 EEC Treaty,[52] the Court outlines the powers of the institutions and the obligations on the Member States. In these passages the Court emphasises the need for the Member States to operate within the framework of the common institutions, acting 'jointly in defence of the interests of the Community'.[53] This requirement, linked to the need for the unity of the Common Market set out in the passage from paragraph 31 quoted above, will go on to form the basis of the rationale for the exclusivity of the common commercial policy developed a few years later in *Opinion 1/75*, a rationale which is not based on legislative

[48] ibid para 22.
[49] ibid paras 30–31.
[50] Dashwood and Heliskoski (n 44) 4.
[51] See, eg, *Opinion 2/91* EU:C:1993:106; *Opinion 1/94*, EU:C:1994:384; and *Opinion 1/03* EU:C:2006:81. See further section IV.
[52] According to Art 116 EEC Treaty, which has since been repealed, 'within the framework of international organizations of an economic character' the Member States were obliged to 'proceed only by common action'. As recalled above, the ERTA was originally negotiated under the auspices of the UN Economic Commission for Europe.
[53] Case 22/70 *ERTA* (n 1) para 77; see also ibid para 52.

pre-emption.[54] The *ERTA* case thus gives us the conceptual foundation for the doctrine of exclusivity more generally and not only in the context of implied powers. The Court goes on to assess the Council's action in the light of these principles, finding that the Council had in fact acted properly, with due regard to its Treaty obligations. The adoption of the regulation which triggered the Community's external power had taken place in the middle of the negotiation:

> The negotiations on the AETR are thus characterized by the fact that their origin and a considerable part of the work carried out under the auspices of the Economic Commission for Europe took place before powers were conferred on the Community as a result of Regulation No 543/69.[55]

Here, again, the characterisation of the Council proceedings is crucial. The Council, acting *qua* Council (as Community institution) and *not* as a collectivity of Member States, was able to decide that in the specific circumstances of the ERTA negotiation it was in the Community's interest that the ongoing negotiations should not be disrupted by insisting that the Community rather than the Member States should participate in the agreement.[56] The Member States would not be acting independently in concluding the ERTA; they were to act under Council authorisation, 'in the interest and on behalf of the Community' within the framework of the common institutions.[57] Thus the judgment not only establishes the doctrine of exclusivity, but also makes clear that the Council may, in circumstances of exclusivity, authorise the Member States to act on the Union's behalf.[58] In doing so the Council itself must act in the Union's interest and the Member States will be bound by the obligation of loyalty. Exclusivity is a legal construct but the Council, acting within the framework of its obligations to the Union interest – and subject to judicial review – may decide how the Union will exercise that exclusive competence in specific cases.[59]

III. The Reception of the *ERTA* Case

The judgment in *ERTA* was certainly not uncontroversial, with some sharing the Advocate General's view that it was not fully consistent with the doctrine of conferred powers.[60] Rasmussen and Sindbjerg Martinsen report that France and Germany sought to have the judgment discussed in Council in November 1970 but were rebuffed by

[54] *Opinion 1/75* (n 10); M Cremona, 'EU External Competence – Rationales for Exclusivity' in I Govaere and S Garben (eds), *The Division of Competences between the European Union and its Member States: Reflections on the Past, Present and Future* (Hart Publishing, 2017).

[55] Case 22/70 *ERTA* (n 1) para 84.

[56] ibid para 86.

[57] ibid para 90.

[58] See further M Cremona, 'Member States as Trustees of the Union Interest' in A Arnull et al (eds), *A Constitutional Order of States: Essays in European Law in Honour of Alan Dashwood* (Hart Publishing, 2011).

[59] For a recent example discussing the ability of the Council to authorise the Member States to act in a field of exclusive competence, see Case C-24/20 *Commission v Council* EU:C:2022:911.

[60] See Fritz's reference to the criticism by Jean-Pierre Puissochet (then a member of the French Conseil d'Etat and later a judge in the European Court of Justice) in *Le Monde* (27 April 1971): Fritz (n 9) 491; see also the reference to this criticism by Winter in his comment on the case: Winter (n 26) 556.

the Dutch and Luxembourg Governments.[61] Nevertheless, in terms of case law and academic commentary, the concept of implied powers as such was accepted without much fuss and was consolidated during the following decade in cases such as *Kramer*[62] and *Opinion 1/76*.[63] These and later cases built upon the *ERTA* ruling in founding implied external powers not only upon the existence of internal legislation but also on the principle of *effet utile*: the necessity of external action to achieve Treaty objectives. In a more recent formulation:

> [W]henever EU law creates for those institutions powers within its internal system for the purpose of attaining a specific objective the EU has authority to undertake international commitments necessary for the attainment of that objective even in the absence of an express provision to that effect.[64]

Although Treaty revisions in the years following the *ERTA* case added further express external powers to the Treaties (such as development policy), implied powers continued to be important in fields such as transport policy,[65] the area of freedom, security and justice,[66] and intellectual property.[67] The position changed with the major revision brought about by the Lisbon Treaty. The implied powers doctrine of *ERTA* and its line of case law was codified in the Treaties in two provisions: one relating to the existence of treaty-making powers (Article 216 TFEU); and one relating to the conditions under which such powers may become exclusive (Article 3(2) TFEU). Article 216(1) TFEU refers to express powers, the *effet ultile* rationale, and the *ERTA* rationale for implied powers.[68] As a result of these changes, rather than distinguishing between express and implied powers, it may now be more helpful to distinguish between those powers which are identified in the Treaties as expressions of its external action (such as the common commercial policy, development cooperation, association agreements and the common foreign and security policy) and those powers described as the 'external aspects of [the EU's] other policies', including environment, transport, and migration.[69] The legacy of *ERTA* is preserved in the Treaties themselves.

While the concept of implied powers as such may have been readily accepted, the debates arising out of *ERTA* have centred on the question of exclusivity. In particular,

[61] M Rasmussen and D Sindbjerg Martinsen, 'EU constitutionalisation revisited: Redressing a central assumption in European studies' (2019) 22 *European Law Journal*, 251, 263.

[62] Joined Cases 3, 4 and 6/76 *Kramer* (n 15) paras 15–45, holding that the Community had the power to adopt measures – including international agreements – to achieve objectives of fisheries conservation, while the Member States were able to exercise a 'transitional' power to act in the absence of Community action.

[63] *Opinion 1/76* (n 11) paras 3–4, affirming that in certain cases, external powers may be implied before the adoption of internal legislation.

[64] *Opinion 1/13* EU:C:2014:2303, para 67, citing *Opinion 1/03* (n 51) para 114.

[65] See, eg, Case C-600/14 *Germany v Council* (n 2).

[66] See, eg, *Opinion 1/03* (n 51); and *Opinion 1/13* (n 64).

[67] See, eg, *Opinion 3/15* EU:C:2017:114.

[68] Art 216(1) TFEU provides that 'The Union may conclude an agreement with one or more third countries or international organisations where the Treaties so provide or where the conclusion of an agreement is necessary in order to achieve, within the framework of the Union's policies, one of the objectives referred to in the Treaties, or is provided for in a legally binding Union act or is likely to affect common rules or alter their scope.' Somewhat confusingly, the *ERTA* effect (the potential effect on common rules) is referred to in both Art 216(1) and Art 3(2) TFEU; some clarification was offered in Case C-600/14 *Germany v Council* (n 2).

[69] Art 21(3) TEU. See further Cremona (n 54).

the correct application of what became known as the '*ERTA* effect' in specific instances in cases such as *Opinion 2/91*, *Opinion 1/94* and the *Open Skies* cases,[70] and the question of whether the *ERTA* basis for implied external powers necessarily involved exclusivity. We will look briefly at this case law in the next section.

The academic response to the *ERTA* judgment has of course been extensive, and the case still attracts comment and critique, not least because of its continuing relevance in the case law.[71] It was, from the first, seen as a groundbreaking judgment. Winter, writing in the *Common Market Law Review* in 1971, maintained that 'The Court's ruling … bears witness to an even more daring and dynamic approach than it took in the landmark cases *Van Gend en Loos* and *Costa v ENEL*', offering 'more than the Commission had bargained for'.[72] As he points out, prior to the *ERTA* judgment the majority of scholars took a more restrictive view of external Community competence.[73] Picking up on the fact that this was the first case litigated between the Commission and the Council, Winter saw the case in terms of the different interests represented by these institutions, the Commission arguing for the Community interest and greater Community powers, and the Council seeking to protect Member State sovereignty. In this he was prescient, as much future inter-institutional litigation (especially perhaps in the external relations field) has been seen in the same way.[74]

Later scholars have emphasised different aspects of the Court's reasoning; indeed, perhaps one feature of a 'classic' judgment (like a classic novel) is its ability to be read anew by different generations of scholarship. Here we can only briefly point to three strands in this rich scholarship. The first is more doctrinal. The Court comes close to, but does not quite espouse, an *in foro interno, in foro externo* form of parallelism,[75] and many scholars have used the case to explore the relationship between internal and external

[70] *Opinion 2/91* (n 51); *Opinion 1/94* (n 51); Case C-467/98 *Commission v Denmark (Open Skies)* EU:C:2002:625.

[71] See, eg, Winter (n 26); McNaughton (n 8); Tridimas and Eeckhout (n 16); Dashwood and Heliskoski (n 44); Petti (n 5); J Temple Lang, 'The *ERTA* Judgment and the Court's Case-Law on Competence and Conflict' (1986) 6 *Yearbook of European Law* 183; R Schütze, 'Dual federalism constitutionalized: the emergence of exclusive competences in the EC legal order' (2007) 32 *European Law Review* 3; P Eeckhout, 'Bold Constitutionalism and Beyond' in MP Maduro and L Azoulai (eds), *The Past and Future of EU Law: The Classics of EU Law Revisited on the 50th Anniversary of the Rome Treaty* (Hart Publishing, 2010); R Post, 'Constructing the European Polity' in Maduro and Azoulai (eds) ibid; I Govaere, 'Implied Powers of the EU, Limits to Political Expediency and Internationally Inspired Pragmatism: Commission v Council (*ERTA*)' in G Butler and RA Wessel (eds), *EU External Relations Law: The Cases in Context* (Hart Publishing, 2022); M Chamon, 'Implied Exclusive Powers in the ECJ's Post-Lisbon Jurisprudence: The Continued Development of the *ERTA* Doctrine' (2018) 55 *Common Market Law Review* 1101.

[72] Winter (n 26) 551.

[73] ibid 551–52, citing, among others, John J Costonis; only Jean Raux, he claims, took a more expansive view of Community powers. Interestingly, Winter includes Pescatore himself among those who, in his 1961 Hague Academy of International Law course, had taken a more restricted view; as Fritz comments, it is striking to see Pescatore, in his pre-judicial academic writing in the late 1960s plead for more extensive external powers to be granted to the Community, while recognising the rather small likelihood of the Member States agreeing to such a change: Fritz (n 10) 491.

[74] See further P Van Elsuwege, 'The Potential for Inter-Institutional Conflicts before the Court of Justice: Impact of the Lisbon Treaty' in Cremona and Thies (eds) (n 5) 115.

[75] Tridimas and Eeckhout (n 16) 151, suggest that the Court did indeed endorse the principle of parallelism, at least in the light of later cases; however, the form of parallelism to which they refer is not a 'simple' parallelism; it requires account to be taken of the specific objectives of the policy field in question, in particular the need for external action.

powers and the rationale for both external powers and their exclusivity.[76] For Dashwood and Heliskoski, for example, *ERTA* and the following cases, *Kramer*, *Opinion 1/76* and *Opinion 2/91*, establish a principle of *complementarity*, whereby the Community's external competence may be a 'necessary complement of its internal competence'.[77] For Post, the essence of the far-reaching form of loyalty which is the basis of the doctrine of exclusivity expressed in the *ERTA* case is the need to protect the process of internal decision-making, and to avoid undermining its outcomes.[78] Govaere argues along the same lines in pointing out that the reasons the Court gave for its finding of exclusivity in *ERTA* were internal (unity of the Common Market, uniformity in the application of Community law) rather than external (unity of external representation).[79]

A second strand has explored the case from the perspective of relations between the Union and its Member States, the theoretical basis for and the Court's evolving conceptions of that relation.[80] One aspect of this is the role played by the duty of loyalty.[81] Used by the Court as basis for the primacy of Union law over domestic Member State law in its judgment in *Costa v ENEL*,[82] in the *ERTA* judgment it formed a legal foundation for the doctrine of exclusivity at a time when the primacy of Union law over the Member States' international obligations towards third states had not yet been clarified.[83] As Schütze has put it, 'the demarcation of mutually exclusive spheres ... elegantly avoided the question of the normative hierarchy of the Community over the Member States being even posed *in the context of international relations*'.[84] Even in *ERTA* itself, the use of Article 5 EEC Treaty allowed the Court flexibility in assessing the conduct of the Council in the light of the specific circumstances of the negotiation.[85] And as the case law moved towards a greater acceptance of shared external competence, the duty of loyalty was to become a cornerstone of the structured relationship between Union and Member States acting to preserve unity in the external sphere.[86] The loyalty clause has proved to be a flexible instrument, supporting the Court's pragmatic solutions while ensuring the 'proper functioning' of the system of Union rules.[87]

A third strand of scholarship identifies the institutional dimension of *ERTA*, and the part it has played in establishing the EU as an international actor separate from

[76] See, eg, Dashwood and Heliskoski (n 44), Post (n 71), Schütze (n 71) and Govaere (n 71).

[77] Dashwood and Heliskoski (n 44)10.

[78] 'These cases [*ERTA* and *Open Skies*] turn precisely on how plurality within an internal agora may require unity in external affairs.' Post (n 71) 239.

[79] Govaere (n 71) 13. See also M Cremona, 'EU External Relations: Unity and Conferral of Powers' in L Azoulai (ed), *The Question of Competence in the European Union* (Oxford University Press, 2014) 65.

[80] See eg Schütze (n 71); R Schütze, 'Supremacy Without Pre-emption? The Very Slowly Emergent Doctrine of Community Pre-emption' (2006) 43 *Common Market Law Review* 1023; Eeckhout (n 71); Cremona (n 54).

[81] See, eg, E Neframi, 'The Duty of Loyalty: Rethinking its Scope Through its Application in the Field of EU External Relations' (2010) 47 *Common Market Law Review* 323.

[82] Case 6/64 *Costa v ENEL* (n 7).

[83] It was already clear that Community law must prevail over international law obligations between the Member States themselves, whether contracted prior to (Case 10/61 *Commission v Italy* EU:C:1962:2) or after (Case 26/62 *Van Gend en Loos* (n 6)) the Treaty of Rome.

[84] Schütze (n 71) 27.

[85] As Petti observes, the duty of loyalty was not referred to in the pleadings before the Court, but was introduced by the Court itself: Petti (n 5) 571.

[86] M Cremona, 'Defending the Community Interest: the Duties of Cooperation and Compliance' in M Cremona and B de Witte (eds), *EU Foreign Relations Law – Constitutional Fundamentals* (Hart Publishing, 2008).

[87] *Opinion 1/03* (n 51) para 133.

its Member States and even shaping the nature of the Union's external 'actorness'. As Winter said in 1971, the judgment 'may well augur favourably for the possibility of enhancing the Community's stature as an autonomous legal personality in the sphere of international relations'.[88] McNaughton makes a case for seeing *ERTA* as the third 'foundation stone' alongside *Van Gend en Loos* and *Costa v ENEL* in establishing the 'new legal order' independent of its Member States.[89] Both Dashwood and Heliskoski and Klabbers remark on the boldness of the Court's interpretation of Article 281 EEC Treaty as the basis for the Community's international capacity.[90] By focusing its reasoning on the concepts of capacity and competence – the 'competence prism', as Eeckhout describes it, as opposed to a primacy-oriented analysis[91] – the Court identified the basis for the institutional independence of the Union in external relations as well as recognising the importance of the inter-institutional balance of power.[92] Indeed, it can be argued that the ability to enter into international contractual relations has enabled *law* to become 'the main instrument of the Union's power in the external sphere'.[93]

IV. Subsequent Development of the Case Law

If *ERTA* is to be regarded as the third foundation stone of the new legal order, it differs from *Van Gend en Loos* and *Costa v ENEL* in one way. Those two cases have been assimilated into the fabric of EU law and are now taken for granted as part of the background; *ERTA*, in contrast is still actively cited and its meaning and application contested, even after its codification in Articles 3(2) and 216(1) TFEU. In this final section, we will outline a few strands of the post-*ERTA* case law; a number of others could certainly have been identified.

First, and most obviously, has been the case law seeking to define more precisely what is meant by the so-called '*ERTA* effect'. Shortly after *ERTA* was decided, the Court was asked in *Opinion 1/75* to determine the scope and nature of the Community's common commercial policy, and Italy and the UK argued in their submissions that the exclusivity of the common commercial policy should depend upon the existence of common rules. The Court – while not alluding to *ERTA* – was clear that the '*ERTA* effect' is not a condition of the exclusivity of the common commercial policy,[94] and indeed this distinction is preserved in Articles 3(1) and (2) TEU respectively. More often, naturally, the *ERTA* effect has arisen in the context of implied powers. Under what conditions will the EU possess implied powers, and the competence based on implied powers become

[88] Winter (n 26) 556.

[89] McNaughton (n 8) 150.

[90] J Klabbers, 'The Reception of International Law in the EU Legal Order' in R Schütze and T Tridimas (eds), *Oxford Principles of European Union Law*, vol I (Oxford University Press, 2018) 1214; Dashwood and Heliskoski (n 44) 6.

[91] Eeckhout (n 71) 219.

[92] See, eg, McNaughton (n 8); Petti (n 5); Azoulai (n 5).

[93] Azoulai (n 5) 170; see also M Cremona, 'Extending the Reach of EU Law: The EU as an International Legal Actor' in M Cremona and J Scott (eds), *EU Law Beyond EU Borders: The Extraterritorial Reach of EU Law* (Oxford University Press, 2019).

[94] *Opinion 1/75* (n 10); M Cremona and J Kukavica, 'Common Commercial Policy and the Determination of Exclusivity: Opinion 1/75' in Butler and Wessel (eds) (n 71) 53.

exclusive? In the first cases to build upon *ERTA*, in fact, the Court developed from the *effet utile* strand of reasoning what became an additional basis for implied powers which does not depend on the prior existence of internal EU legislation, but which is based on the necessity for external powers in order to achieve a Community objective.[95] *Kramer* implies that in the absence of such internal 'common rules', the Community's power would not exclude that of the Member States.[96] *Opinion 1/76* has been read (not least by the Court itself[97]) as holding that in certain circumstances – where the internal powers can only be exercised at the same time as the external power – competence may yet be exclusive as the exercise of the external power becomes necessary in order to legislate effectively in pursuance of Union objectives.[98] It is perhaps more convincing to see in *Opinion 1/76* the '*ERTA* effect' deriving from the adoption of 'common rules' externally.

Following these early cases, a number of important cases in the 1990s explored the nature and limits of the '*ERTA* effect'. *Opinion 2/91* both confirmed that implied powers were not necessarily exclusive and addressed the concept of 'common rules'. In his comment on *ERTA*, Winter had predicted that the references to common rules should not be limited to those arising from common policies such as the Common Agricultural and Transport policies, and indeed this was stated explicitly in *Opinion 2/91*.[99] It is sufficient, the Court held, if the relevant policy area is covered 'to a large extent' by common rules.[100] However the absence of any internal legislative competence led the Court to rule in *Opinion 2/94* that the Community did not have an implied competence to accede to the European Convention on Human Rights.[101] In *Opinion 1/94* and the *Open Skies* cases, the Court would not apply an exclusive Community competence to fields insufficiently covered by internal legislation,[102] nor – most significantly – where the *effet utile* of the internal competence did not require external action.[103] Given the internal focus of the Treaty provisions on the establishment of the internal market, it was not necessary (though it was certainly possible) to enter into international agreements such as the WTO agreements in the fields of services and intellectual property. The *Open Skies* cases also brought out clearly the difference between the '*ERTA* effect' leading to exclusivity, and possible substantive conflict between the international agreement and Union law. On the one hand, the *ERTA* effect does not presuppose conflict (it is designed to preclude it);[104] on the other hand, where there is no *ERTA* effect, the

[95] Joined Cases 3, 4 and 6/76 *Kramer* (n 15); *Opinion 1/76* (n 11) paras 3–4. See further Dashwood and Heliskoski (n 44), who refer to this as the principle of complementarity. For recent examples, see *Opinion 2/15* (n 2) paras 239–242; Case C-600/14 *Germany v Council* (n 2) paras 52–53.

[96] Joined Cases 3, 4 and 6/76 *Kramer* (n 15) paras 39–45.

[97] *Opinion 1/94* (n 51); Case C-467/98 *Open Skies* (n 70).

[98] In this reading it becomes an alternative (rare) route to exclusivity. For a persuasive critique of this reading, arguing that the Court's judgment in *Opinion 1/76* did not concern exclusivity but rather the existence of competence, see Dashwood and Heliskoski (n 44) 13–14. It is nevertheless an understanding which has since been re-expressed in Art 3(2) TFEU: 'The Union shall have exclusive competence for the conclusion of an international agreement when its conclusion … is necessary to enable the Union to exercise its internal competence.'

[99] Winter (n 26) 554; *Opinion 2/91* (n 51) paras 9–11.

[100] *Opinion 2/91* (n 51) para 25; *Opinion 1/03* (n 51) para 126.

[101] *Opinion 2/94* (n 45) paras 26–28. A position now altered by Art 6 TEU.

[102] *Opinion 1/94* (n 51) para 77.

[103] ibid paras 81–86.

[104] 'Member States may not enter into international commitments outside the framework of the Community institutions, even if there is no contradiction between those commitments and the common rules.' Case C-467/98 *Open Skies* (n 70) para 82.

Member State must ensure that in exercising their continuing external powers they conform to Union law.[105]

The debate around *Opinion 1/94* exposed, and did not completely resolve, different views as to the nature of implied powers: could it be argued that implied powers derived from the *ERTA* case were necessarily exclusive – and therefore that if the *ERTA* test of exclusivity were not satisfied, the Community would lack external powers altogether? In fact, *Opinion 2/91* had already made clear the distinction between the existence of implied powers and the question of exclusivity, concluding that in the field covered by the agreement in question, the Community's powers were in some respects shared and in others exclusive. *Opinion 1/03* is also significant for clarifying this issue,[106] and for attempting to reformulate the situations in which the '*ERTA* effect' will, and will not, apply.[107] Here, as in *Opinion 1/13*,[108] the Court stressed the need for a detailed examination of both the projected agreement and the internal legislation which may be affected, in order to determine whether competence is exclusive.[109]

The boundaries of the *ERTA* effect have been tested in a number of ways. It has been held to apply not only to the negotiation and conclusion of international treaties, but also in the context of decision-making bodies operating within the framework of an international organisation.[110] On the other hand, the 'common rules' which may give rise to the *ERTA* effect are rules 'adopted on the basis of' the EU Treaties (secondary legislation), and do not include the Treaty provisions themselves.[111] In coming to this conclusion in *Opinion 2/15*, the Court referred to the 'reasoning inherent in the rule' on exclusive competence, quoting from the *ERTA* case in a marked reliance on this seminal judgment from 1971 in its interpretation of the current EU Treaties. Indeed, it is striking that the Lisbon Treaty's codification of the *ERTA* case law has not rendered that case irrelevant; rather the contrary. Not only does the Court refer to Article 216(1) TFEU as being 'in line with' the *ERTA* case law,[112] and the last clause of Article 3(2) TFEU as 'corresponding to' or expressing the 'substance' of its ruling in *ERTA*;[113] it has insisted on the relevance of that evolving case law in interpreting those provisions.[114]

V. Conclusion

The *ERTA* case can certainly lay claim to being a classic judgment of EU law as well as a milestone in the evolution of EU external relations law. Its implications are perhaps less contested than they were, but are not (just) part of the fossil record of that evolution.

[105] ibid paras 122–39.

[106] On this point see more recently Case C-600/14 *Germany v Council* (n 2) paras 45–46.

[107] *Opinion 1/03* (n 51) paras 114–33.

[108] *Opinion 1/13* (n 64).

[109] For a recent restatement of this point, see *Opinion 3/15* (n 67) para 108.

[110] Case C-45/07 *Commission v Greece* EU:C:2009:81, paras 15–23; see also Case C-399/12 *Germany v Council* EU:C:2014:2258, paras 51–55.

[111] *Opinion 2/15* (n 2) paras 229–35; the Court rejected a Commission argument that exclusivity could be based on the 'common rules' contained in the Treaty provisions on capital movements.

[112] See, eg, *Opinion 2/15* (n 2) para 171.

[113] See, eg, Case C-114/12 *Commission v Council* EU:C:2014:2151, para 66; Case C-66/13 *Green Network* EU:C:2014:2399, paras 26–27; *Opinion 2/15* (n 2) para 231.

[114] Case C-114/12 *Commission v Council* (n 113) paras 66–67. On the post-Lisbon case law, see further Chamon (n 71).

The case still plays an active role in current debates over the balance between conferred and implied powers, and the incidence of exclusive external competence, in a Treaty context which differs markedly from, though reflecting, that of the *ERTA* case itself. As we have seen, the case is also credited with establishing a particular vision of the EU as an international actor, one possessing autonomous institutions correspondingly subject to the discipline of judicial review, an actor characterised by the ability to enter into legal obligations 'over the whole field' of its objectives,[115] and for which, therefore, law will become a key instrument of its foreign policy.

[115] Case 22/70 *ERTA* (n 1) para 14.

7

Tobacco Advertising and the Powers of Harmonisation

KAI PURNHAGEN*

I. Historical and Doctrinal Context

The principle of conferral (Article 5(2) TEU) stipulates that

> the Union shall act only within the limits of the competences conferred upon it by the Member States in the Treaties to attain the objectives set out therein. Competences not conferred upon the Union in the Treaties remain with the Member States.

Who is allowed to do what in the European Union's (EU's) multilevel legal order is in practice, however, not as clear-cut as a first reading of Article 5(2) of the Treaty on European Union (TEU) may make us believe. In the constitutional reality, competence norms are neither formulated in a watertight manner, nor is a rigorous application of the treaties' competence norms in line with the practical necessity of lawmaking at the EU level. This has been illustrated not least by the regulatory struggle between the Union and the Member States in response to the COVID-19 pandemic. Member States have a strong position to define their health policies in the Treaty on the Functioning of the European Union (TFEU), while the Union enjoys a strong position to protect consumer health when harmonisation concerns the free movement of goods or services. Other policies (such as consumer or environmental protection) likewise conflict with 'classic' internal market harmonisation. Attempts to resolve these conflicts generally in favour of the primacy of Union law in Article I-6 of the Treaty establishing a Constitution for Europe of 29 October 2004 were not successful because the Treaty remains unratified.[1] *Tobacco Advertising I*,[2] which concerned the first judgment to give legal guidance on how to solve the tensions on the legal limits of harmonisation of the Union law on the

* This research is funded by the Deutsche Forschungsgemeinschaft (DFG), grant agreement 465588286.

[1] See J Ziller, 'The primacy of European Union law', Policy Department for Citizens' Rights and Constitutional Affairs Directorate-General for Internal Policies of the Union PE 732.474 (July 2022) 13, available at www.europarl.europa.eu/RegData/etudes/STUD/2022/732474/IPOL_STU(2022)732474_EN.pdf.

[2] Case C-376/98 *Germany v Parliament and Council (Tobacco Advertising I)* EU:C:2000:544.

example of health and internal market policy, hence still serves as a legal guideline in this respect.

The area of health policy has been a political battleground which, through the legal responses to political action in the area, contributed to the shaping of the EU's multilevel order. On the example of health policy, important cases have determined the legal limits of the EU's competences, such as the execution of the proportionality test,[3] or the limits of the Union's competence norms as defined in the Treaties.[4] The regulation of health is a good illustration of the inherent tension concerning competences in the TFEU: Article 168 TFEU empowers the Union only to encourage, support and coordinate cooperation between the Member States in the area of public health[5] or to incentivise Member States' actions 'which have as their direct objective the protection of public health regarding tobacco',[6] excluding any harmonisation. Article 114(3) TFEU, however, requires the Commission to propose harmonisation measures in a way that they take as a base a high level of protection concerning health.[7] Achieving doctrinal coherence while reconciling these conflicting requirements is a challenging task. The leeway left by Union law provides room for lawmakers to exercise their margin of discretion and judges to reason in many possible ways based on the shaky doctrinal underpinnings. One may emphasise either the non-harmonisation requirement of Article 168 TFEU if one does not support a health measure at Union level, or the harmonisation requirement of Article 114 TFEU if one supports harmonisation.

Taking these developments into account, in this chapter I will draw on earlier research conducted by Steven Weatherill. I will endorse his claim that the *Tobacco Advertising I* judgment has become nothing more than a 'drafting guide'.[8] Going beyond his research, I will illustrate that the *Tobacco Advertising I* judgment has become a catalyst for the EU legislature to overcome its competence limitations, resulting in innovative solutions to justify harmonisation in health or other policy areas at the Union level.[9]

Despite these difficult constitutional tensions between varying yet overlapping policy areas and principles with different levels of harmonisation such as health,

[3] Case C-333/14 *The Scotch Whisky Association and Others v The Lord Advocate and The Advocate General for Scotland* EU:C:2015:845.

[4] Case C-376/98 *Tobacco Advertising I* (n 2).

[5] Art 168(2) TFEU.

[6] Art 168(5) TFEU.

[7] The Court determined in its case law that in internal market law protection of human health takes precedence over mere economic considerations (Case C-183/95 *Affish BV v Rijksdienst voor de Keuring van Vee an Vlees* EU:C:1997:373, para 43; Case C-221/10 P *Artegodan GmbH v Commission* EU:C:2012:216, para 99). The Union is obliged to 'mainstream' human health in all of its policies and activities (Arts 9, 168(1) TFEU; Article 35 Charter of Fundamental Rights of the European Union (EU CFR). Finally, scholars have argued that, if one reads these provisions and the case law jointly, a 'web of competences' may enable the Union to take health measures at Union level (KP Purnhagen et al, 'More Competences than You Knew? The Web of Health Competence for European Union Action in Response to the COVID-19 Outbreak' (2020) 11 *European Journal of Risk Regulation* 297).

[8] S Weatherill, 'The Limits of Legislative Harmonisation Ten Years after Tobacco Advertising: How the Court's Case Law has become a "Drafting Guide"' (2011) 12 *German Law Journal* 827.

[9] Elsewhere it has been noted that 'the Court has been watering down its case law': see V Delhomme, 'Internal Market as an Excuse: The Case of EU Anti-Tobacco Legislation' College of Europe Department of European Legal Studies Case Notes 02/2017, 2.

internal market regulation and solidarity, tobacco advertising was subject to early legislative action in the then European Economic Community (EEC).[10] Legislation in this area has been based on what is nowadays Article 114 TFEU, at times in combination with other provisions. For example, Article 13 of Directive 89/552/EEC[11] targeted broadcasting activities, including 'all forms of television advertising and teleshopping for cigarettes and other tobacco products'.[12] Directive 89/622/EEC[13] required all cigarette packets to carry specific health warnings. Advertising has been subject to EEC legislation, both at general level and for other specific products. Directive 84/450/EEC,[14] for example, laid down general rules for misleading and comparative advertising, and Directive 92/28/EEC[15] prescribed conditions for advertising medicinal products for human use.

At policy level, the Commission had raised in 1984 the possibility of regulating tobacco advertising.[16] The Council followed up with a resolution in 1986 promoting a Europe against Cancer programme,[17] to which the Commission responded, inter alia, with a proposal for a Council Directive based on then Article 100a EEC Treaty (now Article 114 TFEU). It sought to approximate the laws, regulations and administrative provisions of the Member States relating to the advertising of tobacco products in the press and by means of bills and posters. As a follow-up to these measures, the Commission proposed a Directive targeting tobacco advertising in the press and by means of bills and posters, as such advertising was considered to constitute a barrier to trade and distort competition. To protect younger people, all advertising for tobacco products in publications intended for people under the age of 18 was prohibited. A back-and-forth through the institutions witnessed a proposal for a complete ban, more differentiation in terms of which kind of advertising needed to be regulated and a clear formulation that the Union must take action to prevent deaths resulting from smoking.

The Commission finally submitted a proposal for a Council Directive on advertising for tobacco products on 17 May 1991. This Directive 98/43/EC[18] highlighted the

[10] See, for a full account, the summary of AG Fennelly in Case C-376/98 *Germany v Parliament and Council* EU:C:2000:324, paras 10 et seq.

[11] Council Directive 89/552/EEC of 3 October 1989 on the coordination of certain provisions laid down by law, regulation or administrative action in Member States concerning the pursuit of television broadcasting activities, [1989] OJ L298/23.

[12] AG Fennelly, Case C-376/98 *Germany v Parliament and Council* (n 10) para 10.

[13] Council Directive 89/622/EEC of 13 November 1989 on the approximation of the laws, regulations and administrative provisions of the Member States concerning the labelling of tobacco products and the prohibition of the marketing of certain types of tobacco for oral use [1989] OJ L359/1.

[14] Council Directive 84/450/EEC of 10 September 1984 relating to the approximation of the laws, regulations and administrative provisions of the Member States concerning misleading and comparative advertising [1984] OJ L250/17.

[15] Council Directive 92/28/EEC of 31 March 1992 on the advertising of medicinal products for human use [1992] OJ L113/13.

[16] AG Fennelly, Case C-376/98 *Germany v Parliament and Council* (n 10) para 14.

[17] Resolution of the Council and the Representatives of the Governments of the Member States, meeting within the Council, of 7 July 1986, on a programme of action of the European Communities against cancer [1986] OJ C184/19.

[18] Directive 98/43/EC of the European Parliament and of the Council of 6 July 1998 on the approximation of the laws, regulations and administrative provisions of the Member States relating to the advertising and sponsorship of tobacco products [1992] OJ L213/9.

interdependence between the different forms of advertising and the significant number of deaths in the Community that could be attributed to tobacco consumption. As a consequence, the Commission proposed to prohibit 'all forms of advertising of tobacco products, advertising in other areas using brands or trademarks mainly associated with tobacco, the use of other trademarks or brands for new tobacco products, and any free distribution of such products'.[19] Concerns were raised as to whether Article 100a Treaty establishing the European Community (EC) (now Article 114 TFEU) would provide sufficient basis for a Directive whose measures concern mainly the protection of public health. Those voices opted for changing the legal basis to Article 235 EC and making clearer the Directive's public health rationale. The European Parliament rejected this notion. The Council added Articles 57(2) and 66 EC as competence norms to Article 100a EC, omitted recitals which too strongly emphasised the public health character of the Directive and added several recitals which emphasised the internal market-character of the measures. The Directive was finally adopted against the votes of Germany in the Council.

II. Facts and Judgment in the Case

Germany brought an action for the annulment of Directive 98/43/EC ('the Directive'). France, Finland, the United Kingdom (UK) and the Commission were granted leave to intervene in support of the European Parliament and the Council. Germany put forward seven pleas in law. The Court narrowed down the allegations that Articles 100a, 57(2) and 66 EC do not constitute the proper legal basis for the Directive. Germany submitted that tobacco products advertising was not a cross-border activity. The design of the specific advertisements would be subject to the cultural peculiarities of each Member State. The press would be the only significant form of non-static advertising media in economic terms. Intra-community trade in such products would, however, be limited.

Germany submitted that if the measure in question would not actually contribute to the improvement of the internal market, judicial review of Article 100a EC would be rendered impossible. As advertisement at the point of sale would only account for two per cent of the tobacco industry's advertising expenditure, the Directive would constitute a total prohibition of tobacco advertising in practice. Consequently, the Directive negated the freedom to provide services in the area of tobacco advertising rather than promoting it. It followed from the case law of the Court on Articles 30 and 36 of the Treaty that Article 100a EC should be available as a legal basis only in cases where obstacles to the exercise of fundamental freedoms and distortion of competition are considerable and not only minimal. As the Court put it:

> If the Community legislature were permitted to harmonise national legislation even where there was no appreciable effect on the internal market, it could adopt directives in any area whatsoever and judicial review of the legislation's compliance with Article 100a EC would become superfluous.[20]

[19] AG Fennelly, Case C-376/98 *Germany v Parliament and Council* (n 10) para 17.
[20] Case C-376/98 *Tobacco Advertising I* (n 2) para 29.

Recourse to Article 100a EC would not be possible where the centre of gravity of a measure is focused not on promoting the internal market but on protecting public health.

The Community may not rely on Article 100a EC when the measure to be adopted only incidentally harmonises market conditions within the Community.[21] The legislative history and the content and purpose of the Directive show that the centre of gravity of the measure is public health protection. Harmonising measures in the field of public health policy are expressly prohibited by Article 129(4) first indent EC (now Article 168(5) TFEU).

The parties intervening in support relied on the existence of an internal market in the tobacco products advertising sector. They also relied on an analysis which supports a valid adoption of Article 100a EC as a competence base. Cross-border elements could be established as advertising campaigns were centralised and designed by agencies established in the Community. The choice of themes and the selection of symbols, logos and other elements were decided upon and offered at cross-border level and reached consumers in several Member States. Furthermore, identical advertising media was often offered in English and could hence be used in several Member States. Advertising via free distribution formed part of a uniformly defined advertising concept put into effect for a particular brand. Likewise, tobacco advertising in magazines available on flights and those published in one Member State but distributed in another would have a cross-border element. So too did sponsorships on cars, drivers' clothing and hoardings. Accordingly, the Directive created a uniform framework for the advertising of tobacco products in the internal market and could hence validly be adopted on the basis of Article 100a EC.

For these reasons and as witnessed by the existence of several other legislative acts with a similar emphasis as the Directive, the power conferred on the Council by Article 100a EC would not necessarily be concerned with the liberalisation of trade but rather with market regulation.

The Council dismissed the argument that recourse to Article 100a EC as a legal basis should be possible only in cases where differences in legislation give rise to appreciable obstacles to trade or appreciable distortion of competition, as it would be a competition law argument, which could not be used within the sphere of Article 100a EC. Additionally, as the Commission brought forward, existing differences in legislation would cause a real distortion of competition, as the potential profit of advertising agencies would differ according to the place where they are established or the market in which they carry on business. This could be illustrated by the level of tolerance of newspapers and magazines from other Member States and the impact on the choice of venues for events sponsored by tobacco manufacturers, for example sports events such as Formula 1 racing. Relating to different stringencies of legislation across Member States, producers and sellers of tobacco products did not enjoy the same conditions of competition. In Member States with restrictive regulation, producers and sellers could only maintain or improve their market position by price competition.

[21] Case C-70/88 *Parliament v Council* EU:C:1990:217, para 17; Case C-155/91 *Commission v Council* EU:C:1993:98, para 19; Case C-187/93 *Parliament v Council* EU:C:1994:265, para 25; and Case C-84/94 *United Kingdom v Council* EU:C:1996:431, para 45.

In the eyes of the Parliament, the Council and the Commission, health would be an incidental and subordinate or secondary objective in the wording of the Directive and hence not its centre of gravity. The main objective remained the harmonisation of Member States' legal systems; the Directive imposed a broad prohibition on tobacco advertising. The requirement of a broad prohibition derived from two sources: the obligation of Article 100a(3) EC to take as a base a high level of human health protection; and from the requirement to prevent the circumvention of the prohibition.

According to the United Kingdom of Great Britain and Northern Ireland (UK) Government, the objective of the Directive determines the correct choice of a legal basis. The objectives needed to be amendable to judicial review, as well as the aim and content of the measure. Adopting such a standard of review, the Directive would be associated mainly with the protection of human health. It would be, however, difficult to determine whether the protection of human health takes precedence over the elimination of disparities in conditions of competition and liberalisation of trade, as some of the Directive's objectives were inseparably linked to the former, others to the latter. The UK Government submitted that for a measure to be validly based on Article 100a EC, it would not be necessary to demonstrate that it has the effect of increasing the volume of cross-border trade. It would be sufficient for the measure to eliminate disparities in conditions of competition. The UK Government maintained that the Directive intended to remove distortion of competition in the advertising market and in the tobacco products market. It did so by harmonising the conditions under which manufacturers may promote their products. It also harmonised the conditions under which cultural and sports events can be sponsored by the tobacco industry. The conditions of competition between national sport teams would be affected if teams in different Member States could not receive the same subsidies from the tobacco industry, willing to sponsor sports events to counteract the association of those products with bad health. According to the UK Government, the Court previously held that a measure may be adopted with a view to anticipating the adoption of disparate national rules involving serious obstacles to trade. The situation, in which tobacco advertising is tolerated, may change in view of the evolution of stricter national regulations, resulting in a risk of increased obstacles to trade which the Directive is intended to eliminate.

According to the French Government, Article 100a EC was the valid basis for the adoption of the Directive. For secondary legislation concerning the market for pharmaceuticals,[22] where public health protection coexisted with the objective of free movement of products and the removal of distortion of competition, no point of an invalid competence norm had been raised. Furthermore, the Court made clear in cases concerning Article 129 EC that human health protection requirements are a constituent part of other Community policies, in particular the internal market policy.[23] Based

[22] Council Directive 65/65/EEC of 26 January 1965 on the approximation of provisions laid down by law, regulation or administrative action relating to proprietary medicinal products ([1965–66] OJ English Special Edition 20) to Council Directive 90/220/EEC of 23 April 1990 on the deliberate release into the environment of genetically modified organisms ([1990] OJ L117/15) and Council Directive 76/768/EEC of 27 July 1976 on the approximation of the laws of the Member States relating to cosmetic products ([1976] OJ L262/169).

[23] Case C-180/96 *United Kingdom v Commission* [1998] ECR I-2265; and Case C-269/97 *Commission v Council* [2000] ECR I-2257.

on Article 228 EC, the Commission took part in negotiations under the auspices of the World Health Organization with a view, inter alia, to concluding a protocol on the advertising of tobacco products.

The Finnish Government stated that the Directive was validly adopted on the basis of Article 100a EC. It endorsed the arguments of the Parliament, the Council and the Commission, and added that the internationalisation of that market is intensified by electronic communications, in particular advertising on the Internet and on television. It produced evidence showing that in 1996 sports programmes broadcast on the three Finnish television channels over a period of one month included four hours of advertising for such products. Furthermore, tobacco sponsorship, which would not be available to small undertakings, created inequality which was incompatible with the common market.

A. The Choice of Articles 100a, 57(2) and 66 EC as a Legal Basis and Judicial Review thereof

In its reasoning the Court first emphasised that national measures affected by the harmonisation of the Directive are to a large extent inspired by public health policy objectives. It then introduced the limiting aspect of the first indent of Article 129(4) EC (now Article 168(5) TFEU), which excludes any harmonisation of laws and regulations of the Member States designed to protect and improve human health. It clarified, however, that that provision does not mean that harmonising measures adopted on the basis of other provisions of the Treaty cannot have any impact on the protection of human health. This would be recognised by the third paragraph of Article 129(1) EC (now Article 168(1) TFEU), which provides that health requirements are to form a constituent part of the other Community's policies. At the same time, using other articles of the Treaty as a legal basis may not be used in a way to circumvent the express exclusion of harmonisation as stipulated in Article 129(4) EC (now Article 168(5) TFEU).

In its assessment, the Court first reiterated the general normative legal requirements for the assessment of the validity of the legal basis of the Directive. The Directive was based on Articles 100a, 57 (2) and 66 EC. Acts based on Article 100a (1) EC (now Article 114(1) TFEU) must have as their objective the establishment and functioning of the internal market. The internal market is characterised by the abolition, as between Member States, of all obstacles to the free movement of goods, persons, services and capital.[24] The measures to be taken in this respect need to be in accordance with the Treaty provisions.[25] Reading the provisions describing the internal market and the competence norm enabling the establishment of the internal market jointly, the measures referred to in Article 100a(1) EC (now Article 114(1) TFEU) were intended to improve the conditions for the establishment or ensuring the functioning of the internal market. This article does not vest in the Community (Union) legislature a general power

[24] Art 3(c) EC.
[25] Art 7a EC.

to regulate the internal market. The opposite interpretation would be contrary to the wording of the said provisions and be incompatible with the principle of conferral:[26]

> [A] measure adopted on the basis of Article 100a of the Treaty must genuinely have as its object the improvement of the conditions for the establishment and functioning of the internal market. If a mere finding of disparities between national rules and of the abstract risk of obstacles to the exercise of fundamental freedoms or of distortions of competition liable to result therefrom were sufficient to justify the choice of Article 100a EC as a legal basis, judicial review of compliance with the proper legal basis might be rendered nugatory. The Court would then be prevented from discharging the function entrusted to it by Article 164 of the EC Treaty [now Article 220 EC] of ensuring that the law is observed in the interpretation and application of the Treaty.[27]

The Court then pointed to its judgments in *Spain v Council*[28] and *Germany v Parliament and Council*,[29] where it specified that the Court must verify whether the measure whose validity is at issue in fact pursues the objectives stated by the Community legislature. It held in paragraph 35 of *Spain v Council* that recourse to Article 100a EC (now Article 114 TFEU) as a legal basis is possible if the aim is to prevent the emergence of future obstacles to trade resulting from multifarious development of national laws. Such obstacles must be likely, and the measure must be designed to prevent them. The Court then clarified that the judgment in *Spain v Council*, although adopted with a view of interpreting the free movement of goods, also applied to the provisions concerning the free movement of services. Public health protection can be a decisive factor in the regulatory choices to be made when adopting secondary legislation on the basis of Articles 100a, 57(2) and 66 EC, provided their prerequisites are met. Article 129(1) EC (now Article 168(1) TFEU) explicitly stipulates that health requirements are to form a constituent part of the Community's other policies and Article 100a(3) EC (now Article 114(3) TFEU) expressly requires that, in the process of harmonisation, a high level of human health protection is to be ensured.

B. Directive 98/43/EC

The Court first considered the wording of the first recitals in the preamble to the Directive to determine its objectives. In the first recital of the Directive, the Community legislature acknowledged the existence of variations in national laws concerning the advertising and sponsorship of tobacco products. It recognised that such advertising and sponsorship practices can extend beyond the borders of Member States, leading to discrepancies among regulations. These differences in advertising and sponsorship laws may create obstacles to the movement of products used for such activities, hinder the freedom to provide services in this sector, and distort competition, ultimately impacting the proper functioning of the internal market. The second recital stated that eliminating such barriers via approximation of national laws is necessary, whilst leaving leeway

[26] Art 3b EC.
[27] Case C-376/98 *Tobacco Advertising I* (n 2) para 84.
[28] Case C-350/92 *Spain v Council* EU:C:1995:237, paras 25–41.
[29] Case C-233/94 *Germany v Parliament and Council* [1997] EU:C:1997:231, paras 10–21.

to Member States to introduce their own requirements as they considered necessary to protect the health of individuals.

The Court pointed out that Article 3(1) of the Directive prohibited all forms of advertising and sponsorship of tobacco products, and Article 3(4) prohibited any free distribution with the purpose or the effect of promoting such products. This prohibition was limited to communication in business-to-consumers relationships and did not cover advertising in sales outlets or in publications published and printed in third countries which were not principally intended for the Community (now Union) market.[30] The use of the same names for tobacco products and for other products and services should also be prohibited, with exceptions.[31] Tobacco products must not bear the brand name, trade-mark, emblem or other distinctive features of any other product or service, unless the tobacco product has already been traded under that brand name, trademark, emblem or other distinctive features before that date.[32] Article 5 of the Directive gives Member States the opportunity to lay down stricter requirements concerning the advertising or sponsorship of tobacco products to protect public health. As a consequence, it would be necessary to verify whether the Directive actually contributes to eliminating obstacles to the free movement of goods and to the freedom to provide services, and to removing distortions of competition.

C. Elimination of Obstacles to the Free Movement of Goods and the Freedom to Provide Services

First, the Court emphasised that at the time of the delivery of the judgment, no obstacles existed to the importation of periodicals, magazines and newspapers which contain advertising for tobacco products. It was probable, however, that obstacles to the free movement of press products would be arising in the future due to the then emerging trend for more restrictive national rules on tobacco advertising. A Directive prohibiting the advertising of tobacco products in periodicals, magazines and newspapers could hence be adopted on the basis of Article 100a EC, taking Directive 89/552[33] as a blueprint. Article 13 of Directive 89/552 prohibited television advertising of tobacco products in order to promote the free broadcasting of television programmes. The prohibition under Article 3(1) of the Directive could not be justified by the need to eliminate obstacles to the free movement of advertising media or the freedom to provide services in the field of advertising, as it embraced many more products and services. In particular, the prohibition extended to advertising on posters, parasols, ashtrays and other articles used in hotels, restaurants and cafés, and the prohibition of advertising spots in cinemas, prohibitions which unlikely facilitated trade in the products concerned. Article 3(2) of the Directive should not be interpreted as granting unrestricted movement to products that meet the conditions specified in the Directive in one Member

[30] Art 3(5) of the Directive.
[31] Art 3(2) of the Directive.
[32] Art 3(3)(a) of the Directive.
[33] Council Directive 89/552/EEC (n 11).

State to freely circulate in other Member States, especially if those products are prohibited in those other Member States.

Member States retained the right to lay down stricter requirements concerning the advertising or sponsorship of tobacco products as they deem necessary to guarantee the health protection of individuals.[34] The Directive contained no provision ensuring the free movement of products that conform to its provisions, in contrast to other directives,[35] allowing Member States to adopt stricter measures for the protection of a general interest.

Concluding, the Community (now Union) legislature could not rely on the need to eliminate obstacles to the free movement of advertising media and the freedom to provide services in order to adopt the Directive on the basis of Articles 100a, 57(2) and 66 EC.

D. Elimination of Distortion of Competition

The Court is required to verify whether the distortion of competition which the measure purports to eliminate is appreciable.[36] Without such an assessment, the powers of the Community (now Union) legislature would remain unlimited. National laws often differ regarding the conditions under which the activities they regulate may be carried out. The differences in laws would impact directly or indirectly the conditions of competition for the undertakings concerned. For the application of Articles 100a, 57(2) and 66 EC, solely relying on the smallest distortions of competition is not compatible with the principle of conferral. As a consequence, it would be necessary to verify whether the Directive actually contributes to eliminating appreciable distortions of competition.

Advertising agencies and producers of advertising media established in Member States with fewer restrictions on tobacco advertising would be at an advantage in terms of economies of scale and increase in profits. The effects of such advantages on competition would be remote and indirect and do not constitute distortions which could be described as appreciable. They would not be comparable to the distortions of competition caused by differences in production costs.[37]

However, the differences between regulations on tobacco advertising may also give rise to appreciable distortions of competition. The fact that sponsorship is prohibited in some Member States and authorised in others gives rise to certain sports events being relocated. This may result in considerable repercussions for competition of undertakings associated with such events.

In the market for tobacco products, it is clear that the Directive is likewise not apt to eliminate appreciable distortions of competition.[38] Producers and sellers of tobacco products are obliged to resort to price competition to expand their market share in

[34] Art 5 of the Directive.

[35] See, in particular, Art 7(1) of Council Directive 90/239/EEC of 17 May 1990 on the approximation of the laws, regulations and administrative provisions of the Member States concerning the maximum tar yield of cigarettes [1990] OJ L137/36; Art 8(1) of Council Directive 89/622/EEC (n 13).

[36] Case C-300/89 *Commission v Council* EU:C:1991:244 I-02867, para 23.

[37] Case C-376/98 *Tobacco Advertising I* (n 2) para 109.

[38] ibid para 112.

Member States which have restrictive legislation. That does not constitute a distortion of competition but rather a restriction of forms of competition which applies to all economic operators in those Member States. By implementing a comprehensive ban on tobacco product advertising, the Directive would broaden the restriction on various forms of competition, thereby limiting the means through which economic operators can enter or continue operating in the market across all Member States.[39]

Concluding, the Community (now Union) legislature cannot rely on the need to eliminate distortions of competition, either in the advertising sector or in the tobacco products sector, to adopt the Directive on the basis of Articles 100a, 57(2) and 66 EC.

The Court summarised as follows:

> In view of all the foregoing considerations, a measure such as the directive cannot be adopted on the basis of Articles 100a, 57(2) and 66 of the Treaty.
>
> In those circumstances, the pleas alleging that Articles 100a, 57(2) and 66 of the Treaty do not constitute an appropriate legal basis for the Directive must be upheld. …
>
> (A) directive prohibiting certain forms of advertising and sponsorship of tobacco products could have been adopted on the basis of Article 100a EC. However, given the general nature of the prohibition of advertising and sponsorship of tobacco products laid down by the Directive, partial annulment of the Directive would entail amendment by the Court of provisions of the Directive. Such amendments are a matter for the Community legislature. It is not therefore possible for the Court to annul the Directive partially.
>
> Since the Court has upheld the pleas alleging that the choice of Articles 100a, 57(2) and 66 EC as a legal basis was inappropriate, it is unnecessary to consider the other pleas put forward by the applicant. The Directive must be annulled in its entirety.[40]

III. Reception History: Judicial and Academic

The case has been received differently in academic literature. It was widely regarded as the first of its kind to illustrate the limit of the Union's competence regimes, in particular the limits of the internal market clause Article 114 TFEU (ex-Article 100a EC). In its assessment, the literature distinguishes between three different aspects of the judgment. First, the doctrinal insights the Court provided. These are the interlinkages between Article 114 TFEU and the concepts of the internal market in Article 28(2) TFEU and Article 3(3) TEU. The amendments of these provisions have raised questions regarding the need of their dynamic interpretation, dependent on the evolutionary definition of the internal market.[41] The Court, however, was reluctant to consider these changes of the internal market concepts in the Treaties in the interpretation of Article 114 TFEU. Second, the competence tests in the judgment have been criticised for lacking teeth to effectively limit the Union's powers towards the Member States.[42] Third, these

[39] ibid para 113.

[40] 'ibid paras 114–18.

[41] I Govaere, 'Internal Market Dynamics: On Moving Targets, Shifting Contextual Factors and the Untapped Potential of Article 3(3) TEU' in S Garben and I Govaere (eds), *Internal Market 2.0* (Hart Publishing, 2020) 75, 82–85.

[42] Most famously Weatherill (n 8) 827; from a view of federal constitutionalism M Kumm, 'Constitutionalising Subsidiarity in Integrated Markets: The Case of Tobacco Regulation in the European Union' (2006) 12 *European Law Journal* 503.

developments, taken together, have resulted in using a combination of several competence norms to justify legislative harmonisation and in using the solidarity clause at EU level as a creative solution to remedy the Court's reluctance to interpret Article 114 TFEU in light of the updated internal market concept.[43] The use of the combination of competence norms has thus far not been subject to judicial review.

Regarding the connection between the principle of conferral, Article 114 TFEU and Article 3(3) TEU, the Court noted in the *Tobacco Advertising I* judgment that the principle of conferral needs to be read 'together with the "express wording" of the internal market related provisions'.[44] The aim of the harmonisation measure must be 'to prevent the emergence of future obstacles to trade resulting from multifarious development of national laws. Such obstacles must be likely and the measure must be designed to prevent them'.[45] This test has become the standard for the Court and the legislature to delineate competence in the internal market.[46] With the advancement of the social aspects in the Union, the Court has had already elaborated on the relationship between social policy and the internal market.[47] Since the coming into force of the Treaty of Lisbon, the definition of the internal market in Article 3(3) TEU has changed significantly to a more proactive wording to 'establish' the internal market,[48] and the internal market concept itself has been substantially widened.[49] Such a fundamental change in the internal market concept of Article 3(3) TEU may influence the competence test introduced in the *Tobacco Advertising I* judgment, which still relied on the old internal market concept.[50]

In other areas of EU law, specifically concerning the interpretation of the competence norm to implement the common commercial policy in Article 207 TFEU, the Court had explicitly acknowledged that 'in view of the significant development of primary law, the question of distribution of the competences of the European Union and the Member States must be examined on the basis of the Treaty now in force'.[51] Unlike in the area of external relations, such evident insights into the relationship between the evolved version of the internal market in Article 3 TEU did not resemble with the interpretation of Article 114 TFEU in the Court's case law. The Court kept referring to the classical test as stipulated in the *Tobacco Advertising I* case,[52] despite the fact that it had been noted that such a reference is difficult to reconcile with the new wording of Article 3 TEU and the 'express conferral of shared competence for the internal market in Article 4 TFEU'.[53]

[43] Purnhagen et al (n 7).
[44] Govaere (n 41) 83.
[45] Case C-376/98 *Tobacco Advertising I* (n 2) para 86.
[46] Govaere (n 41) 83.
[47] Case C-438/05 *International Transport Workers' Federation and Finnish Seaman's Union v Viking Line* EU:C:2007:772.
[48] Govaere (n 41) 83–85.
[49] K Purnhagen, 'From Supranationality to Managing Diversity: A (Re-)New(ed) Paradigm for the Establishment of the Internal Market' in Garben and Govaere (eds) (n 44) 285, 286–90; critical of R Barents, 'Constitutional Horse Trading: Some comments on the protocol on the internal market and competition' in M Bulterman et al (eds), *Views of European Law from the Mountain: Liber Amicorum for Piet Jan Slot* (Wolters Kluwer, 2009) 123.
[50] Govaere (n 41) 86.
[51] Case C-414/11 *Daiichi Sankyo* EU:C:2013:520, para 48.
[52] See, eg, the judgment Case C-547/14 *Philip Morris* EU:C:2016:325, paras 58–60.
[53] Govaere (n 41) 89.

The competence test in the judgment has been criticised for lacking teeth, and accordingly, its evolution has been identified as having little relevance when it comes to the constitutional control of the principle of conferral.[54] The adjectives and adverbs *genuinely*, *abstract*, *appreciable* and *likely*, while carrying 'immense constitutional weights',[55] have been identified as 'slippery',[56] 'a set of phrases'[57] that deliver only a low threshold as a competence test.[58] The anxiety so expressed has been confirmed by the case law subsequent to the *Tobacco Advertising I* judgment. After the entry into force of the Lisbon Treaty, the Court of Justice of the European Union (CJEU) has faced further challenges in delivering a comprehensive and coherent competence test that goes beyond the use of certain phrases and is consistently applied in its case law. This makes it, on the one hand, difficult to predict for the legislature whether the respective measure will pass the *Tobacco Advertising I* test. On the other, the 'slippery' wording provides sufficient leeway for the legislature to successfully argue around the test. As a result, after the *Tobacco Advertising I* judgment no Union measure had been declared in violation of the principle of conferral by the Court.[59] Therefore, the *Tobacco Advertising I* test has been identified as a 'drafting guide'.[60]

One could argue that the broad language of the competence test lacks a clear and well-defined threshold to control the exercise of legislative power by EU institutions. This could lead to concerns about potential overreach or 'competence creep', where the EU might exceed its delegated powers and interfere in areas better left to national or regional authorities.[61] However, the open wording may allow the EU to be a dynamic and responsive institution. It enables the EU to tackle new challenges and emerging issues that were not foreseen at the time of treaty drafting. The flexibility in the competence test has facilitated the development of EU law in various policy areas, encouraging innovation in policymaking.

Third, this encouragement to innovate manifested itself in domains beyond the scope of Article 114 TFEU. When even the broad terms employed in the *Tobacco Advertising I* judgment was considered too strict, the legislature 'innovated' by two means. The respective secondary act was based on a combination of competence norms, carefully selecting the most suitable aspects of different norms to achieve legislative harmonisation. The regulation of the food sector via the General Food Law (GFL)[62] provides an example of such an approach. The GFL is based on no less than four competence norms, which are Article 37 TEC (now Article 43 TFEU), Article 95 TEC (now Article 114 TFEU), Article 133 TEC (now Article 207 TFEU) and Article 152(4)(b) TEC (now Article 168(5) TFEU). While the Court has expressed a preference for legal acts to be based on one competence norm, which represents the predominant purpose of the

[54] Weatherill (n 8) 827.
[55] ibid 833.
[56] ibid 832.
[57] ibid 833.
[58] ibid.
[59] ibid 827.
[60] ibid.
[61] S Weatherill, 'Competence Creep and Competence Control' (2004) 23 *Yearbook of European Law* 1.
[62] Regulation (EC) No 178/2002 of the European Parliament and of the Council of 28 January 2002 laying down the general principles and requirements of food law, establishing the European Food Safety Authority and laying down procedures in matters of food safety [2002] OJ L31/1.

legal act,[63] it also accepts an act to be based on multiple competence norms, if it simultaneously pursues a number of objectives, without one being secondary or in indirect relation to the others.[64] Alternatively, EU authorities sought regulation of health-related issues beyond Article 114 or Article 168 TFEU, by invoking Articles concerning the solidarity between Member States. This has been proposed and exercised during the COVID-19 pandemic.[65] The latter approach has thus far escaped constitutional oversight by the CJEU.

Such creative solutions to overcome or 'manage' the *Tobacco Advertising I* test may be worrying from a constitutional perspective.[66] In practice, however, such innovative 'constitutional backing' of legislation prevents the need for a cumbersome Treaty change, where national parliaments would have to vote on such changes. While these solutions forego national parliaments, Member States remain involved via their voting in the Council. Whether such a foregoing of national parliaments is in line with the law is a question of national law. The division of powers in EU affairs between the executive and the legislative branch is a question of national law and is differently applied across Member States. It should be on the competent national court to determine whether such a wide interpretation of the respective competence norms would infringe their parliament's right to participate in Union legislation, depending on how much leeway the national law provides to the executive branch in European Union affairs.

IV. Famous Follow-Up Cases

The judiciary largely endorsed the judgment in follow-up cases, in particular in *ex parte BAT and Imperial Tobacco*.[67] The case concerned Directive 2001/37,[68] a measure dealing with labelling of tobacco products and tar yields. It endorsed Article 95 EC (now Article 114 TFEU) as a valid constitutional basis and dismissed Article 133 EC as non-valid, but found the latter to be a pure formal mistake and left the Directive intact. It reiterated the 'likely' test of the *Tobacco Advertising I* judgment, but made it, in its execution, de facto meaningless. When determining if disparities are 'likely', it uncritically referred to the formulation in the recitals of the Directive that found divergences and imminent divergences in national practice to occur. As a result, to pass the 'likely' test, the EU legislator only needs to choose a formulation in the recitals that without harmonisation national laws and practices would diverge.

Consequently, since the *ex parte BAT and Imperial Tobacco* judgment, the Union legislature can determine the outcome of the 'likely' test by simply choosing a smart formulation in the recitals. This interpretation makes the 'likely' test meaningless.

[63] Case C-491/01 *The Queen v Secretary of State for Health, ex parte British American Tobacco (Investments) Ltd and Imperial Tobacco Ltd* EU:C:2002:741, para 94.

[64] *Opinion 2/00* EU:C:2001:664, para 23.

[65] Purnhagen et al (n 7) 297–306.

[66] Weatherill (n 8) 827.

[67] Case C-491/01 *ex parte British American Tobacco and Imperial Tobacco* (n 63).

[68] Directive 2001/37/EC of the European Parliament and of the Council of 5 June 2001 on the approximation of the laws, regulations and administrative provisions of the Member States concerning the manufacture, presentation and sale of tobacco products [2011] OJ L194/26.

Disparities between national rules and practices are inherent to the EU's legal system. Hence, it is easy for the Union legislature to argue for the need of harmonisation, as the purpose of any legislative endeavour at the EU level is eventually harmonisation, to a varying degree. In the proceedings Member States had expressed that in the absence of Union harmonisation they would introduce national measures.[69] The avoidance of likely (future) disparities of national regulation, and only their present harmonisation, was hence the major argument to meet the 'likely' test.

This rationale was also adopted in follow-up cases. In *Swedish Match*, a case concerning a national prohibition of snus,[70] where a 'heterogenous development of that market'[71] was found to be reason enough to constitute a 'likely' obstacle, the Court endorsed a product ban based on public health concerns. This reasoning sits uneasily with the purpose of Article 114 TFEU: can a product ban facilitate the free movement of goods? It can, as follow-up cases illustrated, as closing down the market for some goods which are harmful will facilitate trust in cross-border trade of other, non-harmful goods. Whatever the EU Constitution requires (eg, protection of health or the environment, animal welfare or the protection of local cultures) becomes the decisive factor according to which competence can be applied. It is seldomly the case that a measure will benefit only one of such decisive factors without jeopardising another. Consequently, the proportionality principle should be more prominent in exercising the 'likely' test.

This was illustrated in the case *Inuit Tapiriit Kanatami*[72] concerning Directive 1007/2009,[73] which prohibited the placing on the market of seals products which did not result from hunts traditionally conducted by Inuit and other indigenous communities and contribute to their subsistence. Balancing animal welfare against the protection of local culture, the Court endorsed Article 95 EC (now Article 114 TFEU) as a correct competence norm. In *Alliance for Natural Health*,[74] a case concerning food supplements, the Court reiterated that future disparities were at the heart of the 'likely' test. It established the existence of disparities not according to the submissions of Member States, unlike in *ex parte BAT and Imperial Tobacco*. It relied on the submission of food business operators, who had complained about the legislative diversity in the EU. As a preliminary remark, the case law following *Tobacco Advertising I* expanded the Court's reasoning, rather than liming its scope of application.

This trend was confirmed in the case law when Directive 2003/33,[75] the successor of the then invalidated Directive 98/34, was subject to judicial scrutiny in *Germany v Parliament and Council (Tobacco Advertising II)*.[76] The Court reiterated the wording of the *Tobacco Advertising I* case with the difference that the cross-border element was

[69] Weatherill (n 8) 835.

[70] Tobacco sold loose or in small sachets intended to be consumed by placing between the gum and the lip.

[71] Case C-151/17 *Swedish Match AB v Secretary of State for Health* EU:C:2018:938, paras 38, 39.

[72] Case C-583/11 P *Inuit Tapiriit Kanatami et al v Parliament et al* EU:C:2013:625.

[73] Regulation (EC) No 1007/2009 of the European Parliament and of the Council of 16 September 2009 on trade in seal products [2009] OJ L286/36.

[74] Joined Cases C-154/04 and C-155/04 *Alliance for Natural Health, Nutri-Link Ltd v Secretary of State for Health* EU:C:2005:449.

[75] Directive 2003/33/EC of the European Parliament and of the Council of 26 May 2003 on the approximation of the laws, regulations and administrative provisions of the Member States relating to the advertising and sponsorship of tobacco products [2003] OJ L152/16.

[76] Case C-380/03 *Germany v Parliament and Council* EU:C:2006:772.

removed from the test and instead required that the respective measure must be intended to improve the conditions for the establishment and functioning of the internal market. In *Ireland v Parliament and Council*,[77] a case concerning Directive 2006/24,[78] the Court held that for an application of Article 95 EC it suffices to show that national practices concerning data retention vary and that these variations are likely to grow more serious over time. However, as the Court established in *Parliament v Council*,[79] this argument does not extend to such measures which are intended to harmonise the enforcement of law by public authorities.

The Court held in *Short Selling*[80] that when applying Article 114 TFEU the legislature enjoys discretion as to the most appropriate form of harmonisation. This is particularly the case where 'highly technical and special analysis'[81] must be made. In *Vodafone Ltd and Others v Secretary of State*,[82] a case concerning the 'roaming' Regulation 717/2007,[83] the Court summarised its previous case law when testing whether the Regulation was based on a valid legal basis as such:

> According to consistent case-law the object of measure adopted on the basis of Article 95(1) EC [now Article 114(1) TFEU] must genuinely be to improve the conditions for the establishment and functioning of the internal market … While a mere finding of disparities between national rules and the abstract risk of infringements of fundamental freedoms or distortion of competition is not sufficient to justify the choice of Article 95 EC [114 TFEU] as a legal basis, the Community [Union] legislature may have recourse to it in particular where there are differences between national rules which are such as to obstruct the fundamental freedoms and thus have a direct effect on the functioning of the internal market …
>
> Recourse to that provision is also possible if the aim is to prevent the emergence of such obstacles to trade resulting from the divergent development of national laws. However, the emergence of such obstacles must be likely and the measure in question must be designed to prevent them ….[84]

These paragraphs summarise the Court's competence test of Article 114 TFEU, which can still be considered valid to date. Two observations are in place: first, the Court did not take the opportunity to establish a meaningful test in such a way that there is a clear and well-defined threshold to control the exercise of legislative power by EU institutions; and second, not much is left from the Court's original dilemma to draw a valid line between the powers to harmonise the internal market and other policy areas with a diverging intensity to regulate such as the area of public health. After all, after the judgment in *Tobacco Advertising I*, EU institutions have been very careful to adopt harmonisation measures concerning 'health, consumer and environmental protection'

[77] Case C-301/06 *Ireland v Parliament and Council* EU:C:2009:68.

[78] Directive 2006/24/EC of the European Parliament and of the Council of 15 March 2006 on the retention of data generated or processed in connection with the provision of publicly available electronic communications services or of public communications networks and amending Directive 2002/58/EC [2006] OJ L105/54.

[79] Cases C-317/04 and C-318/04 *Parliament v Council* EU:C:2006:346.

[80] Case C-270/12 *UK v European Parliament and Council* EU:C:2014:18.

[81] ibid para 103.

[82] Case C-58/08 *Vodafone Ltd and Others v Secretary of State* EU:C:2010:321.

[83] Regulation (EC) No 717/2007 of the European Parliament and of the Council of 27 June 2007 on roaming on public mobile telephone networks within the Community and amending Directive 2002/21/EC (Text with EEA relevance) [2007] OJ L171/32.

[84] Case C-58/08 *Vodafone* (n 82) paras 32–33.

based on Article 114 TFEU. Rather, they found various ways to harmonise health-, consumer- and environment-related issues foregoing Article 114 TFEU.

This can be illustrated on the example of the Union's exercise of competences in the COVID-19 crisis, where the EU needed to adopt measures of public health fast and effectively; in an area of unclear competence norms. Combining different competence norms of the TFEU, the Union attracted wide-ranging competences to regulate public health. Embarking on Article 107(3)(c) and (2)(b) TFEU, for example, Member States were permitted to give state aid to key industries.[85] Scholars have noted that these approaches to health regulation in the EU fundamentally differ from controlling the Union's competence norms based on the principle of proportionality. Instead, the principle of solidarity between Member States, the Union's obligation to protect public health and the right to healthcare in the EU should have been operationalised to control the exercise of competence norms.[86] This can serve as an example of how the Union exercises its competence norms in practice, foregoing the *Tobacco Advertising I* test by first exploiting the possibilities of the rather slippery wording of the judgment, by basing legal acts on several competence norms, and by regulating via a different competence norm which had yet a diffuse doctrinal structure such as 'solidarity'.

[85] European Commission Communication, Guidelines on State aid for rescuing and restructuring non-financial undertakings in difficulty [2014] OJ C249/1; European Commission Communication, Temporary Framework for State aid measures to support the economy in the current COVID-19 outbreak, 20 March 2020, COM(2020)1863 [2020] OJ C91I/1; amended European Commission Communication, Amendment to the Temporary Framework for State aid measures to support the economy in the current COVID-19 outbreak, 3 April 2020, COM(2020)2215 final.

[86] Purnhagen et al (n 7) 297–306.

8

Opinion 1/75 and Exclusive European Union Competences

PANOS KOUTRAKOS

I. Historical and Doctrinal Context

The 1960s and early 1970s saw the introduction of the main principles that shaped the constitutional nature of the European Economic Community (EEC) legal order, namely the supremacy[1] and direct effect[2] of EEC law. During that period, the development of EEC law was firmly about the relationship of the latter with the domestic law of the Member States and, particularly, the distinct features of the nascent legal system that would ensure its effectiveness vis-à-vis recalcitrant national authorities.

The foundations of the legal order were laid gradually at a time when primary law made only a few references to external action. On the one hand, the EEC was endowed with express competence to pursue a Common Commercial Policy (CCP): Article 113 EEC Treaty (now Article 207 TFEU) provided that

> the common commercial policy shall be based on uniform principles, particularly in regard to tariff amendments, the conclusion of tariff or trade agreements, the alignment of measures of liberalisation, export policy and protective commercial measures including measures to be taken in cases of dumping or subsidies.

This competence must be viewed in the context of the establishment of the customs union at the core of the internal market and the requirement for the adoption of a common customs tariff in the relations between the Member States and third countries as a necessary component of it.[3] However, the EEC was also competent to negotiate and conclude association agreements with a third country, a union of states or an international organisation[4] and to establish cooperation with international organisations.[5]

[1] Case 6/64 *Costa v Enel* EU:C:1964:51; and Case C-11/70 *Internationale Handelsgesellschaft* EU:C:1970:114.

[2] Case 26/62 *Van Gen den Loos* EU:C:1963:1. See B de Witte, 'Direct Effect, Primacy, and the Nature of the Legal Order' in P Craig and G De Burca (eds), *The Evolution of EU Law*, 3rd edn (Oxford University Press, 2021) 187, esp 188–92. See also chs 1 and 2 of this volume.

[3] Art 9 EEC Treaty (now Art 28(1) TFEU).

[4] Art 238 EEC Treaty (now Art 218 TFEU).

[5] Arts 229–31 EEC Treaty (now Art 220(1) TFEU).

Both these legal bases made no reference to the specific objectives of these policies, referring, instead, to how the latter are to be carried out.[6]

Once the EEC had been well into its infancy, and against the dearth of primary provisions about external relations, questions about the rules governing external action started to arise. In March 1971, the Court had not only introduced the principle of implied external competence, but had also held that such competence was exclusive in cases where action by Member States would affect internal rules or alter their scope.[7] While its disjointed reasoning was underpinned by the constitutional thread that had run through the foundational case law on supremacy, the judgment broadened the scope of the EU powers in ways that were viewed in some circles as running counter to the EEC Treaty.[8]

It was at that juncture, and four and a half years after the *ERTA* judgment that the Court handed down *Opinion 1/75*,[9] in which it examined for the first time not only the scope of the EEC competence to conclude international trade agreements but also the nature of that competence. It did not do so in a policy vacuum. In terms of international law, Article XXIV:8(a) General Agreement on Tariffs and Trade (GATT 1947) defined (and still does) a customs union as 'a single customs territory' where 'substantially the same duties and other regulations of commerce are applied by each of the members of the union to the trade of territories not included in the union'. The EEC had already been active in the context of GATT negotiations, even though it had not acceded to it.

As for the nature of the Community's competence in CCP, scholarly analysis in the area had contested exclusivity on the basis of the conferral of external powers under primary law or had suggested that exclusivity was confined to the conclusion of international agreements, but did not extend to autonomous measures in the absence of common rules.[10] Even in relation to international agreements, it had been argued that exclusivity did not have to extend to all trade agreements but only to those appliable to tariffs: Everling, who later became a European Court of Justice (ECJ) judge, had suggested that, whether the uniform principles referred to in Article 113 EEC Treaty were 'to be carried into effect by truly collective proceedings or rather by concerted action of Member States remains open and is left to the discretion of the Council to decide from case to case'.[11]

[6] It is for this reason that Cremona refers to the 'absence of a *telos* in EU external policy': M Cremona, 'Structural Principles and their Role in EU External Relations Law' in M Cremona (ed), *Structural Principles in EU External Relations Law* (Hart Publishing, 2018) 3, 5.

[7] Case 22/70 *Commission v Council (ERTA)* EU:C:1971:32, para 22 (see ch 6 of this volume). See also I Govaere, 'Implied Powers of the EU, Limits to Political Expediency and Internationally Inspired Pragmatism: *Commission v Council (ERTA)*' in G Butler and R Wessel (eds), *EU External Relation Law – The Cases in Context* (Hart Publishing, 2022) 9.

[8] See the Opinion of AG Dutheillet de Lamothe, as well as the earlier analysis in P Pescatore, 'Les Relations extérieures des communautés européennes' (1961) 103/II *Recueil des Courts de l'Academie de Droit International de La Haye* 1, 97 (he subsequently reconsidered his view in 'External Relations in the Case-Law of the Court of Justice of the European Communities' (1975) 12 *Common Market Law Review* 615, fn 5).

[9] *Opinion 1/75 (re: OECD Local Cost Standard)* EU:C:1975:145.

[10] See the summary provided in PJG Kapteyn, 'The Common Commercial Policy of the European Economic Community: Delimitation of the Community's Power and the European Court of Justice's Opinion of November 11, 1975' (1976) 11 *Texas International Law Journal* 485, 492–94.

[11] U Everling, 'Legal Problems of the Common Commercial Policy in the European Economic Community' (1966–67) 4 *Common Market Law Review* 141, 150.

Three years prior to *Opinion 1/75*, it had been held in *International Fruit Company* that the Community had succeeded the Member States in the rights and obligations laid down in GATT as the Member States had transferred the relevant powers, so that the EEC 'has assumed the functions inherent in the tariff and trade policy, progressively during the transitional period and in their entirety on the expiry of that period'.[12] The judgment did not refer expressly to the exclusive competence of the EEC. However, it was couched in terms that suggest exclusivity, a point that became clearer in subsequent case law on the circumstances under which the EU may assume the rights and obligations of Member States in agreements concluded by the latter.[13]

Against this background, the significance of *Opinion 1/75* is not only about what the Court decided but also when and how it did so: *Opinion 1/75* was part of the very first cases which laid the foundations of the power of the EEC to act on the international scene and was couched in strong and uncompromising terms which, while adjusted in practice, have become a point of reference for both subsequent case law and practice.

II. Facts and Judgment

In *Opinion 1/75*, the Commission asked the Court to rule on the compatibility with the EEC Treaty of a draft Understanding on a Local Cost Standard for export credit schemes.[14] Along with other sectoral agreements (on export credits in specific aviation sectors, nuclear power plants, and telecommunications), this Understanding had been negotiated and drawn up under the auspices of the Organisation of European Economic Cooperation and Development (OECD).

In Article 112, which was subsequently repealed, the EEC Treaty provided as follows:

> Without prejudice to obligations undertaken by Member States within the framework of other international organisations, their measures to aid exports to third countries shall be progressively harmonised before the end of the transitional period to the extent necessary to ensure that competition between enterprises within the Community shall not be distorted.

The request for *Opinion 1/75* was submitted in the light of two parallel developments. On the one hand, while the transitional period had expired on 31 December 1969, the export credit systems of the Member States were still characterised by divergences. On the other hand, OECD negotiations had led to the finalisation of a draft agreement (the Understanding that was the subject matter of *Opinion 1/75*) which would introduce a common standard for financing costs incurred in the state where the buyer was established. While the Commission had proposed that the Draft Understanding be concluded

[12] Joined Cases 21–24/72 *International Fruit Company* EU:C:1972:115, para 14. This formed the origin of the so-called 'succession doctrine', the scope of which has subsequently been clarified in strict terms, including in Case C-366/10 *Air Transport Association of America and Others (ATAA)* EU:C:2011:864. See R Schütze, 'The "Succession Doctrine" and the European Union' in A Arnull et al (eds), *A Constitutional Order of States? Essays in EU Law in Honour of Alan Dashwood* (Hart Publishing, 2011) 459.

[13] See A Petti and J Scott, 'International Agreements in the EU Legal Order: *International Fruit*' in Butler and Wessel (eds) (n 7) 21, 27.

[14] The procedure on the basis of which the Court may be asked to rule on the compatibility of an envisaged agreement with EU law is laid down in Art 218 (11) TFEU. *Opinion 1/75* was the first time the Court ruled on the basis of this procedure.

solely by the EEC,[15] one of the then nine Member States disputed the existence of the EEC's competence on the matter, and two were of the view that the participation of the EEC would not exclude that of the Member States.[16]

In *Opinion 1/75*, the Court dealt with three issues. The first was the definition of an international agreement in the context of the procedure laid down in Article 228(1) EEC Treaty (now Article 218(11) TFEU): consistently with other strands of its case law,[17] the Court adopted a functional approach according to which 'any undertaking entered into by entities subject to international law which has binding force, whatever its formal designation' amounts to an agreement within the meaning of the above EEC provision.[18] Having concluded that the draft Understanding on a Local Cost Standard met that definition, it moved on to the second issue, namely whether the conclusion of the Understanding fell within the competence of the EEC pursuant to Article 113 EEC Treaty (now Article 207 TFEU) governing the CCP. The answer was affirmative: applying a broad approach, the Court held that the concept of commercial policy has 'the same content whether it is applied in the context of the international action of a State or to that of the Community' and that it

> is in fact made up by the combination and interaction of internal and external measures, without priority being taken by one over the others. Sometimes agreements are concluded in execution of a policy fixed in advance, sometimes that policy is defined by the agreements themselves.[19]

This chapter will focus on the third issue, namely the nature of the EEC's competence to conclude the Understanding.[20] The conclusion that the draft Understanding on a Local Cost Standard for export credit schemes fell within the exclusive competence of the EU was substantiated on the basis of two main arguments.

The first was the function that the CCP played for the EEC internal policies: it was designed 'in the context of the operation of the Common Market, for the defence of the common interests of the Community, within which the particular interests of the Member States must endeavour to adapt to each other'.[21] Viewed in its internal market context, the CCP was held to give rise to exclusive competence on practical grounds:[22]

> In fact, any unilateral action on the part of the Member States would lead to disparities in the conditions for the grant of export credits, calculated to distort competition between

[15] COM(1974) 2238 fin *Recommendation for a Council Decision Concerning the Community's Position within the Organisation for Economic Cooperation and Development in the Matter of a Local Costs Standard* (Brussels, 18 December 1974).

[16] This information is provided in the Commission's request for *Opinion 1/75* (p 2): while the Opinion itself makes no reference to this request, the full text, along with all other procedural documents related to *Opinion 1/75*, is now available online in the Historical Archives of the European Union (CJEU-2383, Original code: C2-02-004) at archives.eui.eu/en/files/documents/32974.pdf?d=inline. For an analysis of the whole dossier, see J Kukavica, 'The Garden Grows Lusher: Completing the Narratives on Opinion 1/75' (2021) 6 *European Papers* 621.

[17] See, for instance, the definition of an 'act' in the context of an annulment action (Case 22/70 *ERTA* (n 7) paras 41–42) or the definition of 'an emanation of the State' in the context of direct effect of directives (Case C-188/89 *Foster and Others v British Gas* EU:C:1990:313, para 20).

[18] *Opinion 1/75* (n 9) 1360.

[19] ibid 1362–63.

[20] For an analysis of the scope of the CCP, see ch 20 of this volume, as well as M Cremona, 'Defining the Scope of the Common Commercial Policy' in M Hahn and G Van der Loo (eds), *Law and Practice of the Common Commercial Policy – The First 10 years after the Treaty of Lisbon* (Brill/Nijhoff, 2020) 47.

[21] *Opinion 1/75* (n 9) 1363–64.

[22] ibid 1364.

> undertakings of the various Member States in external markets. Such distortion can be eliminated only by means of a strict uniformity of credit conditions granted to undertakings in the Community, whatever their nationality.

The second argument was about the defence of the EEC interests on the international plane: the Community's competence had to be exclusive for, otherwise,[23]

> in relations with third countries, Member States may adopt positions which differ from those which the Community intends to adopt, and would thereby distort the institutional framework, call into question the mutual trust within the Community and prevent the latter from fulfilling its task in the defence of the common interest.

The two arguments are intrinsically linked: the conception of the CCP as linked to the common market was necessary in order to protect the common interests of the Community, and unilateral external action by the Member States could have repercussions for the mutual trust within the Community.

Finally, the fact that responsibility for the financing of the mechanism in question was borne by the Member States was considered 'of little importance' regarding the transfer of competence to the Community.[24]

In *Opinion 1/75*, the exclusive nature of the EEC competence in the CCP field had two main characteristics. First, it was *a priori*: rather than flowing from the existence of internal common rules applicable to export credits, it was based on the very raison d'être of the CCP as laid down in primary law. Therefore, exclusivity in this policy context emerges as a new legal principle which flows from a policy imperative: it is inextricably linked to the existence of the CCP in primary law and is not related to pre-emption. Second, it was not affected by practical arrangements about the application of the agreement in question: whether the financing of the Understanding were to be borne by the Member States, rather than the Community, was irrelevant to the nature of the competence of the latter to conclude it pursuant to Article 113 EEC Treaty (now Article 207 TFEU).

The Court's reasoning is distinctly teleological (the wording of Article 113 EEC Treaty is only mentioned last in the relevant section of *Opinion 1/75*). The latter is, therefore, firmly in the tradition of the early constitutional case law. In this vein, the strong terms in which it is couched are striking: the internal function of the CCP is 'Quite clearly … incompatible' with the exercise of concurrent powers by the Member States which, in the field governed by the Understanding 'is impossible', while distortions of competition may be prevented 'only by strict uniformity of credit conditions'.[25] The force with which the Court sets out its reasoning is all the more remarkable in the light of the earlier part of the ruling where the scope of CCP was construed widely: in fact, the Court opined that commercial policy should have 'the same content whether it is applied in the context of the international action of a State or to that of the Community'.[26]

In construing the Community's competence in such terms, *Opinion 1/75* may appear to articulate an uncompromising approach to exclusivity and its implications for the stature of the Member States in areas that fall within the scope of CCP. However, it is

[23] ibid.
[24] ibid.
[25] ibid.
[26] ibid 1362.

not only the benefit of hindsight which questions this assumption. Whilst bolstering the foundation of exclusivity, the link between the CCP and the common market also serves to highlight the limits of the former by drawing upon practice under the latter. Indeed, the very development of the common market and the processes of establishing and managing the internal market attest to the paramount importance of observing the dividing line between Union and national competence: this line has not only been fine but has also proved to be in need of constant redefinition. In other words, to construe the CCP as the necessary adjunct to the establishment of the internal market was tantamount to implying the existence of inherent limitations to the exercise of the express competence granted to the Union.

III. Reception History: Judicial and Academic

Despite the broad and forceful terms in which *Opinion 1/75* was couched, some commentators were sceptical about the scope of the exclusive nature of the Community's competence in CCP. The question whether, in the absence of common rules, the Member States had lost their power to adopt autonomous measures was still viewed as open.[27] And yet the foundation of the competence in the very existence and raison d'être of the CPP suggests that its exclusive nature covers all aspects of the policy.

Therefore, in the light of the Court's Opinion, two questions became central not only to the EU's external relations but also to the constitutional arrangements that govern the relationship between the EEC and the Member States. The first is about the scope of the CCP: the *a priori* exclusive competence of the Community rendered the answer to this question increasingly contested. The second question is about the implications of the nature of the Community's competence: does exclusivity rule out completely Member State action in the field, or is there room for the latter and, if so, under which conditions? As the former question is beyond the scope of this chapter, the following analysis will focus on the latter.[28]

In order to address this question, let us jump ahead and see how the Member States responded to the introduction of exclusivity in the CCP at the level of primary law. Given their position as the masters of the Treaties, they may introduce exceptions. This is what they did at the Treaty of Nice by providing for shared competence in certain aspects of the CCP.[29] It is not for this chapter to analyse those provisions.[30] Suffice it to point out that the Nice amendment introduced a degree of disconcerting complexity

[27] See Kapteyn (n 10) 502; and HH Maas, 'The External Powers of the EEC with regard to Commercial Policy: Comment on Opinion 1/75' (1976) 13 *Common Market Law Review* 379, 385–87, who also saw scope for Member States powers even in the conclusion of international agreements.

[28] See ch 20 of this volume.

[29] On their interpretation, see *Opinion 1/08* EU:C:2009:739, handed down the day before the relevant provisions would become defunct and the Lisbon Treaty would enter into force. See the analysis in M Cremona, 'Balancing Union and Member State interests: Opinion 1/2008, choice of legal base and the common commercial policy under the Treaty of Lisbon' (2010) 35 *European Law Review* 679.

[30] See M Cremona, 'A Policy of Bits and Pieces? The Common Commercial Policy after Nice' (2001) 4 *Cambridge Yearbook of European Legal Studies* 61; HG Krenzler and C Pitschas, 'Progress or Stagnation? The Common Commercial Policy After Nice' (2001) 6 *EFA Review* 291; and C Hermann, 'Common Commercial Policy after Nice: Sisyphus Would Have Done a Better Job' (2002) 39 *Common Market Law Review* 7.

in functioning of the CCP; in her Opinion in Case C-13/07 *Commission v Council (Vietnam's accession to the WTO)*, Advocate General Kokott said:

> No doubt this legal position is not exactly conducive to the effective representation of Community interests in the area of external trade, particularly and precisely in the framework of the WTO. However, this disadvantage must be accepted as the Treaties stand at present.[31]

The convoluted Nice approach to exclusivity in the CCP was abandoned at Lisbon where the Treaty on the Functioning of the European Union (TFEU) codifies the conclusion of *Opinion 1/75* and in Article 3(1)(e) expressly acknowledges the exclusive nature of the Union's competence in CCP. It also confers upon the Union exclusive competence in four other areas: customs union; the establishing of the competition rules necessary for the functioning of the internal market; monetary policy for the Member States whose currency is the euro; and the conservation of marine biological resources under the common fisheries policy.[32] In most of these, the Court had already found the competence of the Community (as it then was) to be exclusive.[33] In addition to the *a priori* exclusivity of the EU's competence in the above areas, Article 3(2) TFEU also refers specifically to exclusive competence to conclude international agreements 'when its conclusion is provided for in a legislative act of the Union or is necessary to enable the Union to exercise its internal competence, or in so far as its conclusion may affect common rules or alter their scope'. An analysis of this provision and the kind of exclusivity it sets out, described by Dashwood as 'implicit or supervening',[34] is beyond the scope of this chapter.[35]

Of the small number of policy areas in which the EU is endowed expressly with exclusive competence, CCP is the only external one. In other strands of express external action, the power of the Member States either is provided for in primary law[36] or its exercise is dependent on legal and policy considerations related to the scope of the international agreement negotiated by the EU. The Common Foreign and Security Policy, in particular, is listed in Article 2(4) TEU separately and none of the other categories of competences listed in the remaining of Article 2 TEU applies to it.[37]

The codification of the EU's exclusive competence in the CCP notwithstanding, the question remains about the extent to which EU law may tolerate, sanction, or even

[31] Opinion of AG Kokott in Case C-13/07 *Commission v Council* EU:C:2009:190, para 124 (the case was removed from the register on 10 June 2010).

[32] Art 3(1)(a)–(d) TFEU.

[33] On the conservation of marine biological resources, see Joined Cases 3, 4 and 6/76, *Kramer et al* EU:C:1976:114 and Case 804/79 *Commission v UK* EU:C:1981:93; and on the customs union, see Case 41/76 *Donckerwolcke* EU:C:1976:182, paras 31–32. For the process leading to the drafting of Art 3(1) TFEU and an analysis of the provisions of the latter, see R Schütze, 'Dual federalism constitutionalised: the emergence of exclusive competences in the EC legal order' (2007) 32 *European Law Review* 3.

[34] A Dashwood, 'Mixity in the Ear of the Treaty of Lisbon' in C Hillion and P Koutrakos (eds), *Mixed Agreements Revisited: the EU and Its Member States in the World* (Hart Publishing, 2010) 351, 356 and 360.

[35] See P Koutrakos, *EU International Relations*, 2nd edn (Hart Publishing, 2015) ch 3.

[36] See Arts 208)(1), 210 and 211 TFEU, as well as Art 4(4) TFEU, about development cooperation and humanitarian aid.

[37] It has been described as a competence 'of a special nature': A Rosas, 'Mixity and the Common Commercial Policy after Opinion 1/75 – An Overview' in Hahn and Van der Loo (eds) (n 20) 27, 41. See M Cremona, 'The Position of the FSP/CSDP in the Constitutional Architecture of the EU' in S Blockmans and P Koutrakos (eds), *Research Handbook on the EU's Foreign and Security Policy* (Elgar Publishing, 2018) 5; and P Koutrakos, *The EU Common Security and Defence Policy* (Oxford University Press, 2013) 22–35.

provide for unilateral action by the Member States. The answer is affirmative and, as it emerges from a parallel development of post-*Opinion 1/75* case law and legislative initiatives, it will be set out in the following section.

IV. Famous Follow-Up Cases

Soon after *Opinion 1/75* had been handed down, a pragmatic approach to exclusivity in the CCP field emerged in the Court's case law. We may identify two strands in particular.

The first is about a practical aspect of the agreement in question: financing. Three years after it had delivered *Opinion 1/75*, the Court was asked by the Commission in *Opinion 1/78* to rule on whether the conclusion of a commodity agreement fell within the exclusive nature of the Community.[38] The request was about the International Agreement on Natural Rubber which had been negotiated in the United Nations Conference on Trade and Development (UNCTAD). Having interpreted the scope of what is now Article 207 TFEU in wide terms, the Court dealt with the mechanism set up under the Agreement about the financing of the buffer stock. The Member States had argued that, under the International Agreement on Natural Rubber, the buffer stock would be financed by public funds which, in their view, justified their participation in the conclusion of the Agreement. The Court agreed with them. It considered the financing arrangements central to the very application of the Agreement: they were 'an essential feature of the scheme for regulating the market [to be set up by the Agreement]' and, for practical reasons, they ought to determine whether the Agreement would be concluded by the Community or the Member States, depending on which would finance the Agreement.

Opinion 1/78 showed for the first time, and contrary to its conclusion in *Opinion 1/75*, that the significance of exclusivity as an *a priori* principle might not necessarily entail the conclusion of an agreement exclusively by the Community. Put differently, Member States are not necessarily precluded from concluding, along with the Community, an agreement falling within the scope of Article 207 TFEU despite the fact that their exclusion is inextricably linked to the nature of the Union's competence in that area. The pragmatism that this approach illustrates is as considerable as it is curious: given that the financing issue had been deemed irrelevant to the nature of the Community's competence and account being taken of the essential nature of exclusivity for the functioning of the common market, how could it be diluted simply because the Member States would choose to finance the application of the Agreement? The criticism levelled against this part of the ruling for 'putting the cart before the horse'[39] is correct in so far as the Court appears to strike at the very core of its construction of the CCP by undermining the principle of exclusivity in an unprincipled manner.

Cut to its bare essentials, the ruling appears to suggest that the degree of national involvement in the practical components of what is deemed central to the implementation

[38] *Opinion 1/78* EU:C:1979:224.

[39] JHH Weiler, 'The External Legal relations of Non-Unitary Actors: Mixity and the Federal Principle' in HG Schermers and D O'Keeffe (eds), *Mixed Agreements* (Kluwer, 1981) 35, 72.

and application of an international agreement should be relevant to the exercise of the express competence over the CCP. This acknowledgment of the implications of the pronounced role enjoyed by the Member States in the management of areas of activity where their competence had been transferred to the Union echoes the pronounced role that the Member States actually played in the regulation of the CCP during that period.

This parallelism between judicial construction and political reality brings us to the second strand of the case law on CCP exclusivity. When the Court handed down *Opinion 1/75*, the CCP was incomplete due to the absence of uniform rules. This state of affairs was acknowledged in post-*Opinion 1/75* case law. In *Donckerwolcke*,[40] a dispute about the legality of French law requiring that importers declare the ultimate origin of products in free circulation, it was still possible under existing EEC law for different rules to apply to products originating in a third country when they originally entered the EEC. As this disparity gave rise to the possibility of deflections of trade, the right of the Member States to deviate from the CCP was sanctioned, albeit under specific conditions.[41] This approach acknowledged the inevitable impact that the lack of progress at policy level would have for the protection of the interests of the Member States and sought to address them within a set of EEC conditions, compliance with which would ensure that national authorities would not be granted *carte blanche*.[42]

Put differently, in the absence of uniform rules that would govern trade between the EEC and the rest of the world, unilateral action by Member States was tolerated by the EEC provided that it was exercised within certain parameters set out in EEC law. Therefore, in different areas of CCP, the EU institutions showed willingness to accommodate national concerns by giving Member States time and space to adjust gradually to a uniform regulatory regime.

A case in point was the importation of cars from Japan. The 1970s saw a significant rise throughout the Community, causing alarm to national industries about its impact on labour forces and competitiveness and, ultimately, raising the prospect of significant market losses. The extent to which national industries were affected varied considerably: in 1980, for instance, Japanese firms had approximately 43 per cent of the automobile market in Greece and only 0.14 per cent in Italy. Depending on the strength of individual domestic industries, each Member State sought to resist the penetration of its market by Japanese imports pursuant to arrangements negotiated individually. These arrangements took the form of national quotas and voluntary export restraints the terms of which varied: in 1977, for instance, France imposed a limit on Japanese products of three per cent of its market, whereas Portugal only allowed the importation of 20,000 passenger cars.[43] This overtly protectionist policy was, at that time, justified in the light of the significance of domestic automobile industries for the economy of Member States.

In 1991, an agreement, entitled 'Element of Consensus', was concluded between the Commission and the Japanese Ministry of Trade and Industry. Its objective was

[40] Case 41/76 *Donckerwolcke* (n 33).

[41] ibid para 32. See also Case 52/77 *Leonce Cayrol v Giovanni Rivoira & Figli* EU:C:1977:196.

[42] On the specific authorisation requirement in other contexts, see Case 174/84 *Bulk Oil* EU:C:1986:60 (export of crude oil) and Case 59/84 *Tezi Textiel* EU:C:1986:102 (exports of textiles).

[43] See M Mason, 'Elements of Consensus: Europe's Response to the Japanese Automotive Challenge' (1994) 32 *Journal of Common Market Studies* 433, 436.

to establish the progressive and complete liberalisation of the importation of Japanese cars, off-road vehicles and light commercial vehicles by the beginning of 2000. It did so by regulating the import regime for the five most important European motor vehicle markets, namely France, Italy, Spain, Portugal and the UK, on the basis of substantially increased quotas.[44] Whilst not introducing common rules applicable immediately throughout the Community market, the Commission sought to merge a number of disparate individual national policies into a common, albeit provisionally diverse, policy negotiated and administered at Community level. Therefore, it sought to reduce the scope of diversity within the common market and render complete liberalisation a concrete objective by phasing out diversity subject to a set of EEC rules.

In substantive terms, the above episode shows how the EEC was willing to take the interests of the major national industries into account and protect them. Viewed from this angle, the agreement illustrated two broader points: exclusivity in CCP did not necessarily render national interests irrelevant, and neither did it ignore them; the exercise of exclusive competence in CCP did not necessarily entail the substitution of national concerns for an inflexible and centrally designed policy model. In political and practical terms, the negotiation and conclusion of the Elements of Consensus might not have been possible had it not been for the gradual evolution of the CCP: the acknowledgment of national concerns by the Union's Community's institutions and the sanctioning of the ensuing policies by the EU judiciary had created the political environment necessary both for the Commission to step in and seek to address national concerns within a common framework and for the Member States to entrust the defence of their interests to the EU's executive. In other words, the implied acknowledgement by the Court in the 1970s and early 1980s that neither was the CCP a genuinely common policy nor was the Union exclusive competence truly exclusive was central to the development of that policy. Viewed from this angle, the contribution of the Court of Justice to the development of EU international relations was no less significant than that underpinning the establishment of the single market pursuant to its construction of the principles of free movement.

It follows from the above that, in addition to its introduction regarding the CCP, the Court has been pivotal to the management of exclusivity in so far as it sanctioned the exercise of power by domestic authorities under EU law conditions. The remainder of this section will explore this aspect of exclusivity by focusing on two areas of CCP: bilateral investment treaties (BITs) and transport.

As far as the former is concerned, the Lisbon Treaty brought foreign direct investment (FDI) within the scope of the EU's exclusive CCP competence, and the Court held that BITs that Member States had concluded with third countries prior to their accession to the EU contained provisions that were contrary to EU law.[45] However, the

[44] See BT Hanson, 'What Happened to Fortress Europe? External Trade Policy Liberalization in the European Union' (1998) 52 *International Organization* 55, 74–80; Mason (n 43); and CRA Swaak, *European Community Law and the Automobile Industry* (Kluwer, 1999) 187–204.

[45] See Case C-249/06 *Commission v Sweden* EU:C:2009:119; Case C-205/06 *Commission v Austria* EU:C:2009:118; Case C-118/07 *Commission v Finland* EU:C:2009:715. See the analysis in E Denza, 'Bilateral Investment Treaties and EU Rules on Free Transfer-Comment on *Commission v Austria, Commission v Sweden*, and *Commission v Finland*' (2010) 35 *European Law Review* 263; P Koutrakos, 'Annotation on Case C-205/06, Commission v Austria, judgment of the Court (Grand Chamber) of 3 March 2009, not yet

replacement of the rights and obligations laid down in more than 1,200 BITs concluded by Member States by EU rules was dependent upon the adoption of the latter, which itself was dependent on the development of an investment policy by the EU institutions. Put differently, it would take time for the EU to decide how to exercise its exclusive FDI competence and it would not be sensible for the Member States to abandon their existing arrangements in a policy vacuum. It was for this policy reason that, in 2012, the EU adopted Regulation 1219/2012 which provides for the maintenance in force and amendment of existing, as well as the negotiation and conclusion of new BITs by Member States under certain conditions.[46]

The Regulation establishes a procedural framework which is controlled by the Commission and revolves around two procedures dealing with the authorisation of existing agreements and the amendment of existing or the conclusion of new agreements. The authorisation of existing BITs is granted following their notification by all the Member States to the Commission. Such authorisation is granted without prejudice to either the Union's competence in the area[47] or any other EU law obligations of the Member States.[48] The Commission reviews the agreements in order to ascertain whether they are compatible with EU law, or overlap with an agreement which the Union negotiates, or constitute an obstacle to the development and implementation of the Union's investment policy.

On the other hand, the authorisation to amend existing or conclude new BIT follows a notification by the Member State concerned (covering the provisions to be addressed in the negotiations, the objectives of the negotiations and any other relevant information) at least five months prior to the commencement of the negotiations. This information is disseminated to the other Member States and, within three months, the Commission decides whether to authorise the opening of formal negotiations. Such an assessment depends on whether the opening of negotiations would be in conflict with EU law, whether it would be superfluous in the light of imminent negotiations of an EU agreement, whether it is inconsistent with the EU's principles and objectives for external action, or constitute a serious obstacle to the negotiation or conclusion of BITs with third countries by the EU. All BITs notified to the Commission are published annually.[49]

The interactions between the Member States and the Commission that Regulation 1219/2012 provides are of considerable intensity and scope. It refers not only to the opening of negotiations, and the signing and conclusion of BITs, but also the application of such agreements. For instance, in the process of the negotiation of a BIT, the Commission may require that the Member State include any appropriate clauses and participate in the negotiations. As for the application of the agreement, Member States are required to keep the Commission informed without undue delay of all meetings under existing BITs and may even have to take a particular position set by the

reported; Case C-249/06, Commission v Sweden, judgment of the Court (Grand Chamber) of 3 March 2009, not yet reported' (2009) 46 *Common Market Law Review* 2059; and L Lonardo, 'Potential Incompatibility of International Agreements Concluded by Member States before Accession: *Commission v Austria, Commission v Sweden* and *Commission v Finland*' in Butler and Wessel (eds) (n 7) 599.

[46] Regulation 1219/2012 establishing transitional arrangements for bilateral investment agreements between Member States and third countries [2012] OJ L351/40.

[47] ibid, recital 3 of preamble and Art 1.

[48] ibid Art 3.

[49] For the most recent list, see [2023] OJ C150/1.

Commission. Similarly, any dispute about the application of a BIT must be notified to the Commission, which may even go as far as to require that it participate in any settlement procedure. Its agreement would also be required prior to the activation of any dispute settlement mechanisms included in the BIT by the Member State concerned.

The transitional arrangements about the BITs concluded by Member States illustrate a pragmatic approach to the exercise of the EU's exclusive CCP competence. Not only does the existence of the latter not have to rule out unilateral action by the Member States, but it may render it part of a procedural framework governed by EU law within which the Commission may even become intrusive in all phases of the negotiation, conclusion and application of BITs concluded by Member States.[50]

This choice of conditioning the EU's exclusive competence on the basis of a proceduralised set of rules is not confined to policy fields in which the EU is endowed with an express external competence. In order to illustrate this point, we shall focus, by way of example, on international aviation.[51] After a series of judgments finding certain aspects of Open Skies Agreements concluded by Member States with the United States to fall within EU exclusive and others within shared competence,[52] the EU adopted Regulation 847/2004/EC on the negotiation and implementation of air service agreements between Member States and third countries.[53] This measure established a system of cooperation between the Commission and Member States aiming at the coordination of negotiations with third countries, the achievement of a harmonised approach in the implementation and application of air services agreements, and the verification of their compliance with Union law.

Rather than dealing with an area where the Member States had ceased to enjoy any competence (as was the case with Regulation 1219/2012), Regulation 847/2004 authorises Member States to act in areas where their competence may coincide partly with that of the Union.[54] It sets out a framework of constant interaction

[50] This aspect of the CCP must be viewed alongside the gradual development of the EU's FDI policy through negotiations with third countries (eg EU–Singapore Investment Protection Agreement [2018] OJ L279/3, investment protection chapter in the Comprehensive Economic and Trade Agreement with Canada [2017] OJ L11/23, and the EU–China Comprehensive Agreement on Investment, finalised in 2020 but now moribund).

[51] For other examples, see Regulation 662/2009 establishing a procedure for the negotiation and conclusion of agreements between Member States and third countries on particular matters concerning the law applicable to contractual and non-contractual obligations [2009] OJ L200/25; and Regulation 664/2009 stablishing a procedure for the negotiation and conclusion of agreements between Member States and third countries concerning jurisdiction, recognition and enforcement of judgments and decisions in matrimonial matters, matters of parental responsibility and matters relating to maintenance obligations, and the law applicable to matters relating to maintenance obligation [2009] OJ L200/46. Both measures were adopted following *Opinion 1/03 (Lugano Convention)* EU:C:2006/81, where the Court had held that the Union had exclusive competence on matters affecting rules set out in the Brussels I Regulation, in particular regarding jurisdiction and the recognition and enforcement of judgments in civil and commercial matters.

[52] Case C-467/98 *Commission v Denmark* EU:C:2002:625; Case C-468/98 *Commission v Sweden* EU:C:2002:626; Case C-469/98 *Commission v Finland* EU:C:2002:627; Case C-471/98 *Commission v Belgium* EU:C:2002:628; Case C-472/98 *Commission v Luxembourg* EU:C:2002:629; Case C-475/98 *Commission v Austria* EU:C:2002:630; Case C-476/98 *Commission v Germany* EU:C:2002:631. In addition, the Court ruled in Case C-466/98 *Commission v UK* [2002] ECR I-9427. Its conclusions were reaffirmed in Case C-523/04 *Commission v Netherlands* EU:C:2007:244.

[53] Regulation 847/2004/EC on the negotiation and implementation of air service agreements between Member States and third countries [2004] OJ L157/7.

[54] Following the judgments set out in n 52 above, the Commission also argued that the Union's exclusive competence also extends to a range of other issues which may be addressed in bilateral air services agreements, including safety issues, commercial opportunities, customs duties, taxes and (user) charges, restrictions on

between the Commission and the Member State negotiating an air services agreement in which the latter are under certain substantive and procedural obligations. In terms of the former, Member States must include in their negotiations any relevant standard clauses, developed and laid down jointly between Member States and the Commission, and are prohibited from introducing more restrictive arrangements regarding the number of Union air carriers designated to provide services.[55] In terms of procedural duties, a Member State must notify its intention to enter into negotiations at least one calendar month prior to the commencement of formal negotiations (or, due to exceptional circumstances, as soon as possible) to the Commission which disseminates it to the other Member States for comments. It is for the Commission to ascertain whether the negotiations 'are likely to undermine the objectives' of EU negotiations with the third country underway, and/or lead to an agreement which is incompatible with EU law.[56]

The scope and intensity of the duties which Regulation 847/2004 imposes on Member States are considerable. For instance, a Member State may not enter into negotiations unless it has agreed to include any relevant standard clauses. Indeed, once these have been incorporated in the Agreement, that Member State 'shall be authorised' to conclude it, 'provided that this does not harm the object and purpose of the Community transport policy'.[57]

While the two measures outlined in this section have different subject matter and objectives, they also have a number of features that shed light on the EU's approach to exclusivity in EU external relations. First, both Regulations 1219/2012 and 847/2004 aim to achieve their different objectives by setting out a set of rules and procedures which are based on the constant interaction between the Commission and the national authorities of individual Member States (and, in certain cases, the authorities of the other Member States too). Second, they constitute the response of the Union's legislature to the assessment of the Court of Justice as to how competence should be distributed in the Union's constitutional order, while the case law of the Court itself also responds to the absence of common rules adopted by the EU decision-maker. Third, both sets of rules and procedures draw upon the duty of cooperation. Regulation 847/2004, for instance, states in its preamble that 'It is essential to ensure that a Member State conducting negotiations takes account of Community law, broader Community interests and ongoing Community negotiations.'[58]

This analysis illustrates an understanding of exclusivity that differs from the terms in which it was first introduced in CCP in *Opinion 1/75*. The uncompromising implications of the transfer of competence from the Member States to the EU, which was based on the teleological interpretation of CCP, has gradually given way to a subtler construction of exclusivity. The latter does not only acknowledge a role for the Member States, but it may even rely upon them in order to deal with policy issues that the EU competence alone may not address effectively. This chapter has showed that the pragmatic

aircraft for environmental reasons: COM(2002) 649 final *Communication on the consequences of the Court judgments of 5 November 2002 for European air transport policy* (Brussels, 19 November 2002) at 7–8.

[55] Regulation 847/2004/EC (n 53), Arts 1(1) and 3.

[56] ibid, Art 1(4).

[57] ibid, Art 4(2)).

[58] ibid, para (8). See also Regulation 1219/2012 (n 46), Art 6.

understanding of exclusivity was not confined to the case law or policy-making: it was shared by the Court and the EU's legislature. In fact, the interactions of these two actors in the area suggest a shift from the question of the nature of the EU's competence (determined robustly in *Opinion 1/75*) to that of its exercise. This shift enables the EU to address specific policy imperatives on the basis of practical and mutual acceptable arrangements. For the EU and its Member States, moving away from the theology of exclusivity to the effectiveness of practice can only be a good thing.

9

The *Working Time* Case and the Death of Subsidiarity

GARETH DAVIES

I. Introduction

The *Working Time* case involved a challenge by the United Kingdom (UK) to a new directive regulating aspects of working time.[1] At that time – the early 1990s – the UK was committed to a labour market model which involved high flexibility and limited constraints, whereas most continental European countries were taking a more paternalistic and regulated approach.[2] The UK felt that it was being forced into a mode of regulation that it did not want, and that did not suit its economic approach at that time. It felt also that it was perfectly capable of regulating working time and conditions itself, had no objection to other Member States doing the same, and failed to see that there was any persuasive need for harmonisation.[3] The essence of its objection was thus a subsidiarity claim: this matter can be better regulated by the Member States, and not by the EU. It did not in fact make subsidiarity central to its legal arguments before the Court, but philosophically its position is best expressed in subsidiarity terms – this belongs properly to us, not to you.

In the judgment the Court did therefore address subsidiarity, albeit quite briefly.[4] In doing so, it made a choice to formulate it, to understand it, in a particular way, that would have fateful consequences. For what it did was no less than to kill subsidiarity as a meaningful element of EU law. It gave the principle an interpretation that would ensure that it would have no effect in any of the situations in which it might be applied. In the years since, with its customary loyalty to its first interpretations, it has stuck to its guns, and maintained its *Working Time* understanding of what subsidiarity is, with indeed the consequence that subsidiarity has never had any legal impact.[5] As the Court, and

[1] Case C-84/94 *UK v Council (Working Time)* EU:C:1996:431.

[2] E Ellis, 'Case C-84/94 United Kingdom of Great Britain and Northern Ireland v Council' (1997) 34 *Common Market Law Review* 1049.

[3] ibid.

[4] Case C-84/94 *Working Time* (n 1) paras 46–47 and 54–55.

[5] See, eg, D Burbidge, 'The Inherently Political Nature of Subsidiarity' (2017) 62 *The American Journal of Jurisprudence* 143; F Fabbrini, 'The Principle of Subsidiarity' in T Tridimas and R Schütze (eds), *Oxford Principles of EU Law* (Oxford University Press, 2018) 221; G Davies, 'Subsidiarity: the Wrong Principle, in the Wrong Place, at the Wrong Time' (2006) 43 *Common Market Law Review* 63; *cf* T Horsley, 'Subsidiarity

now the Commission, read it, it is a hollowed-out, dead-in-the-water principle without effects.

It might have been different. The interpretation that the Court took is close to the text.[6] However, generally, if a particular interpretation of a legal rule leads to it being ineffective by its own lights, unable to achieve the goals for which it has been adopted, that is a reason to consider alternatives, and this is even more true in EU law, where effectiveness is the single most dominant interpretative principle in the canon.[7] It is thus a little mysterious, and somewhat disappointing, that it was discarded when subsidiarity came to be read.

This chapter will examine how this emasculation of subsidiarity came about, why the Court's interpretation in *Working Time* was regrettable, what alternative paths it could have taken, and why those paths are ultimately more loyal to the idea of subsidiarity. It will also place the death of subsidiarity in a wider context: that of a consistent judicial and institutional aversion to admitting that EU law involves conflicts that are not always resolvable. However positive European integration may be, it still has costs, and there is a legal reluctance to admit, name and measure those costs, with the consequences that it is hard to see when they may be so high that they should be avoided: that a measure which the EU appears to have the legal power to do should nevertheless be left well alone.

II. The Context of the *Working Time* Case

A. Subsidiarity and the EU

Subsidiarity was inserted into the Treaties in 1992, with the hope that it would be an important tool for the management and control of ever-growing EU competences. However, the truth is that subsidiarity is not really suited to the EU. It comes from contexts where multiple layers of government may be concerned to achieve the same goals, and provides some normative guidance on which layer has the best claim to policy ownership: who should be entrusted with the task of achieving that goal.[8] However, in the EU the problem is typically that different layers of government have *differing* goals, but the means that they employ for these overlap.[9] The question then is which goal should prevail in the specific situation.[10] Conflicts arise because the EU's pursuit

and the Court of Justice: Missing Pieces in the Subsidiarity Jigsaw?' (2012) 50 *Journal of Common Market Studies* 267.

[6] See Art 5 TEU; Protocol to the Treaty of Amsterdam on the Application of the Principles of Subsidiarity and Proportionality [1997] OJ C340/105; Davies (n 5).

[7] E Herlin-Karnell, 'Effectiveness and Constitutional Limits in European Criminal Law' (2014) 5 *New Journal of European Criminal Law* 267.

[8] T Latimer, 'The principle of subsidiarity: A democratic reinterpretation' (2018) 25 *Constellations* 586. See also A Estella, *The EU Principle of Subsidiarity and its Critique* (Oxford University Press, 2002).

[9] Latimer (n 8); Davies (n 5).

[10] Latimer (n 8); Davies (n 5); R Schütze, *From Dual to Co-operative Federalism* (Oxford University Press, 2009) 533–35; G Taylor, 'Germany: A slow death for subsidiarity?' (2009) 7 *International Journal of Constitutional Law* 139.

of its policy imperatives constrains and obstructs the ability of the Member States to pursue theirs. That is a rather different problem than the one subsidiarity was historically applied to. From its beginning in EU law, it was given a task that it would struggle to complete.

In particular, this is because the EU is to a very large extent concerned with harmonisation – the creation of uniformity. It is this drive which impacts, sometimes distressingly, on many national policies. A local policy goal, utilising some nationally specific legal structure, then conflicts with the European goal of uniform law. Traditional subsidiarity has never been about the drive to harmonise, and to transplant it to this situation requires a little effort; an effort which the Court chose not to make.[11] It could be argued, if one wanted to be generous, that it was loyal to the text, but not to the idea. On the other hand, the text is ambiguous enough that there is little need to divorce it from the idea it expresses. Hence it is probably more accurate to say just that the Court decided to throw subsidiarity out.

B. The *Working Time* Directive

Directive 93/104/EC, concerning certain aspects of the organisation of working time, was adopted on the basis of Article 118a(1) and (2) of the EC Treaty, part of the social policy chapter, which provided:

1. Member States shall pay particular attention to encouraging improvements, especially in the working environment, as regards the health and safety of workers, and shall set as their objective the harmonization of conditions in this area, while maintaining the improvements made.
2. In order to help achieve the objective laid down in the first paragraph, the Council, acting in accordance with the procedure referred to in Article 189c and after consulting the Economic and Social Committee, shall adopt by means of directives, minimum requirements for gradual implementation, having regard to the conditions and technical rules obtaining in each of the Member States.

EU law often compares favourably with national law regarding transparency and clarity. Many Treaty articles, directives and regulations are relatively simple to understand and avoid the self-referential complexity that is certainly typical of British law, and no doubt of the law of many other states. However, Article 118a stands out, by comparison with other legal bases, for its internal incoherence. The linguistically unhappy and relatively meaningless first phrase of Article 118a(1) ('shall pay particular attention') is quickly revealed to be essentially superfluous. It is Article 118a(2) which contains the actual legal base. It is a clumsy legal base, cross-referring to paragraph (1), but it is not ambiguous. It allows for just one thing: directives laying down harmonised minimum health and safety standards. The requirement to 'pay particular attention' has no role in this legal base, and, it would seem, no legal consequences, for it is not precise enough to have direct effect.

[11] Öberg has though: see J Öberg, 'Subsidiarity as a Limit to the Exercise of EU Competences' (2017) 36 *Yearbook of European Law* 391.

But if the objective of harmonisation is the meat of Article 118a, it is meat with a funny flavour, for it is an objective allocated not to the Union, but also to the Member States themselves.[12] Independently of the Article 118a(2) competence to harmonise, the Member States are also supposed to be trying to harmonise on their own. Article 118a thus appears to imagine a process of voluntary, organic convergence of standards, helped along by a bit of legislation now and then. Presumably, if Article 118a(1) is to have any meaning, the powers in Article 118a(2) are only to be employed in situations where divergence between national standards is so significant and enduring that the Member States must be considered to have failed. The essentially residual and facilitative competence in Article 118a(2) is nevertheless noteworthy, because it is generally the position of the Court that the one thing which Member States cannot do is harmonise, that requiring by definition EU action.[13] Article 118a(1) appears to be asking the impossible.

It is also not stated in Article 118a why harmonisation might be desired. On the face of it, the objective of the article appears to be to raise standards for workers, and to make those standards common. That sounds sympathetic enough, but it is not the task of the EU to do things just because they are sympathetic. Why must these be harmonised? Why are health and safety standards a matter for the EU and not for the Member States? Purely because otherwise Member States might make the 'wrong' choices? Or is this the pursuit of uniformity for its own sake? Either would raise troubling constitutional questions – for which subsidiarity would be the right frame. It is the essence of subsidiarity that the EU should only take over policy where there is some advantage to central action. Article 118a cannot be read in the light of subsidiarity without considering what that advantage is.

The obvious answer is to do with preventing distortions of competition. It is accepted that harmonisation is appropriate in circumstances where differences between the Member States might cause (sufficiently serious) externality-type problems.[14] Those could be the normative political problems that arise when national communities diverge too much in their values, but typically they are more concrete economic ones. In an internal market, differing working conditions could indeed become a distortion of competition, and Member States might perhaps be pressured into a race to the bottom by the fear that raising their standards would drive away businesses. Although Article 118a presents as social policy it looks just as much like an internal market legal base.[15]

This is what the directive itself also implies. In its preamble it refers to the need to create an internal market with high standards, implicitly acknowledging that without harmonisation those standards might be driven down below what national populations

[12] See Art 118a(1) above.

[13] See Case C-151/17 *Swedish Match* EU:C:2018:938; Case C-547/14 *Philip Morris* EU:C:2016:325; Case C-508/13 *Estonia v Parliament and Council* EU:C:2015:403; Case C-58/08 *Vodafone* EU:C:2010:321; C-154/04 *Alliance for Natural Health* EU:C:2005:449; Case C-491/01 *British American Tobacco* EU:C:2002:741; Case C-84/94 *UK v Council (Working Time)* EU:C:1996:431; Case C-377/98 *Netherlands v Parliament and Council (Biotechnology directive)* EU:C:2001:523. See also AG Fennelly in Case C-376/98 *Germany v Parliament and Council (Tobacco Advertising)* EU:C:2000:544.

[14] Öberg (n 11); R Van den Bergh, 'The Subsidiarity Principle in European Community Law: Some Insights from Law and Economics' (1994) 1 *Maastricht Journal of European and Comparative Law* 337.

[15] *cf Opinion 2/91* EU:C:1993:106.

would prefer. The aim is not to overrule local preferences, but to give those preferences a chance to survive in the market.

III. Facts and Judgment

It is in this context that the Court was asked to consider, inter alia, whether the directive violated the principle of subsidiarity, in the context of an action for annulment brought by the UK. It is this aspect of the case that has had consequences for the law and the development of the EU which continue today.

In EU law the principle of subsidiarity is expressed in Article 5(3) TEU:

> 3. Under the principle of subsidiarity, in areas which do not fall within its exclusive competence, the Union shall act only if and in so far as the objectives of the proposed action cannot be sufficiently achieved by the Member States, either at central level or at regional and local level, but can rather, by reason of the scale or effects of the proposed action, be better achieved at Union level.

It is thus applicable to shared competences, which include both social policy (Article 118a EC) and the internal market.

In the judgment the Court wastes few words on subsidiarity.[16] It simply notes that once the Council has decided that harmonisation is necessary, this presupposes Community action, since only the Community can harmonise. Implicitly, the question whether the Member States could sufficiently achieve the goals of this directive, or whether they are better achieved by the Community is answered by the fact that the goal is harmonisation: only the Community can achieve that.

If subsidiarity is indeed no more than the question of which level can achieve the goals of the directive, and the goal is indeed no more than harmonisation, then there is no criticism to be made of this reasoning. It is watertight.

The case law since has maintained this approach.[17] Although in more recent cases the Court recognises that a Union measure may have two goals, not just harmonisation, and that the other one – public health, for example, or the safety of workers – might be better achieved by the Member States, the fact that allowing them to do this would create diversity justifies the Union action.[18] In substance, the objective of harmonisation is what determines the appropriate level of action, and the other objectives must simply tag along – they are essentially irrelevant to the subsidiarity consideration. The Court simply finds that since there is an argument for harmonisation, and the Member States cannot harmonise, that ends the matter. Subsidiarity, in its EU form, simply has no grip on the situation. It is entirely toothless against harmonisation measures.[19]

This is however somewhat problematic, since harmonisation measures are precisely what subsidiarity is intended in the Treaty to apply to. It applies to shared competences,

[16] Case C-84/94 *Working Time* (n 1) paras 46–47.

[17] Davies (n 5); see also n 18 below.

[18] Case C-151/17 *Swedish Match* (n 13); Case C-547/14 *Philip Morris* (n 13); Case C-508/13 *Estonia v Parliament and Council* (n 13); Case C-58/08 *Vodafone* (n 13).

[19] P van Nuffel, '*Working Time Directive* (UK v Council)' (1996–97) 3 *Columbia Journal of European Law* 298; AG Toth, 'The Principle of Subsidiarity in the Maastricht Treaty' (1992) 29 *Common Market Law Review* 1079.

such as the internal market, social policy and the environment, and the goals of these policies are achieved by harmonisation, and if not by harmonisation then typically by coordination, or other action which is inherently central, and to which the same form of reasoning would apply. A court ought to scratch its collective head if its chosen interpretation of a principle means that it is absolutely ineffective in the context where the legislator has made it applicable.[20]

It has also had consequences for the so-called 'subsidiarity control mechanism', whereby national parliaments may raise objections to Union measures on grounds of subsidiarity and proportionality.[21] The Commission, as one would expect, cut and pastes the Court's approach to subsidiarity.[22] With a challenge to the so-called Monti II Regulation on the right to strike, it noted that the need was to harmonise and therefore considered legal subsidiarity arguments unfounded.[23] With a challenge to the establishment of a European Public Prosecutor's Office, it noted that the whole point of the regulation in question was to establish a capacity for Union action, and so it was rather hopeless to argue that Member States could achieve this alone.[24] Where national parliaments objected to the Posted Workers Directive it rejected their case because the point was to harmonise.[25] Subsidiarity loses again.

The core subsidiarity question is thus why the Union is acting. Were the Union to act purely for the purposes of health, the environment, safety, the prevention of crime, or some other good cause, subsidiarity could be applied, because these are goals which the Member States might conceivably also be able to achieve. However, as soon as the Union phrases its goals in more European terms – that it wishes to establish a European framework for policy X, or strengthen the Union's capacity to support policy Y, or create a common standard in the Member States regarding policy Z – then this Euro-speak works as a trump card: subsidiarity is a priori excluded, because the goal is now something that can only be pursued by the EU.[26]

Some of the Union's competences are not structured purely in terms of such Euro-goals: if the Union simply legislates for the purposes of protecting the environment or workers, subsidiarity ought still to be a meaningful constraint. However, even within these competences, as the *Working Time* case shows, much action will be taken precisely to achieve something at European level, or to achieve uniformity or coordination, and then subsidiarity will de facto not apply. Moreover, other competences, notably the internal market legal bases, are exclusively to be used for the primary purposes of

[20] Öberg (n 11).

[21] Protocol on Subsidiarity and Proportionality (n 6); P Kiiver, *The Early Warning System for the Principle of Subsidiarity. Constitutional Theory and Empirical Reality* (Routledge, 2012); F Fabbrini and K Granat, 'Yellow Card but No Foul: The Role of the National Parliaments Under the Subsidiarity Protocol and the Commission Proposal for a EU Regulation on the Right to Strike' (2013) 50 *Common Market Law Review* 115; G Davies, 'The post-Laeken division of competences' (2003) 28 *European Law Review* 686.

[22] Commission Communication, COM(2013) 851 final, 27 November 2013; G Davies, 'The post-Laeken division of competences' (2003) 28 *European Law Review* 686.

[23] Although there was a political impact. See Fabbrini (n 5); K Borońska-Hryniewiecka, 'Beyond Legislative Veto Power: The Transformative Effects of the Early Warning System for Subsidiarity Control Ten Years Down the Line' (2021) 58 *Política y Sociedad* e71934, 1; I Cooper, 'National parliaments in the democratic politics of the EU: The subsidiarity early warning mechanism, 2009–2017' (2019) 17 *Comparative European Politics* 919.

[24] Commission Communication, COM(2013) 851 final, 27 November 2013.

[25] See Borońska-Hryniewiecka (n 23).

[26] van Nuffel (n 19).

creating uniformity, coordination, or free movement.[27] Subsidiarity, as the Court interprets it, and contrary to Article 5 TEU, simply does not apply to the internal market.[28] The Treaties include subsidiarity as a matter of doctrine, but then exclude it by the working of law.

It may be said that this problem is because subsidiarity is already integrated into the Treaties – the Union's powers are largely confined to doing things where it adds value because of its scale and nature. Since the things that it does are largely the things that only it can do, it is logical that there should be no discussion about whether the Member States could do them better, or even sufficiently. On this view, as long as the Court properly polices competence, and ensures that there is a legal base for Union action, it is quite proper that subsidiarity is superfluous.[29]

However, this analysis is unsatisfying, for Union action does impinge, often dramatically, on the things that Member States do and have traditionally done, and sometimes the merits – whether functional, economic, political or social – of doing things locally will outweigh the advantages for Union policies of having commonality.[30] One cannot simply trust the legislator to make this judgment, not because the legislator is dishonest, but because the idea of a Union of conferred powers entails that the proper limits of Union action are policed by law and not just politics. The balance between central and local is certainly an element of those proper limits, so where is the principle to play this role? Something has to do it.

In *Working Time* the Court suggests it might be proportionality.[31] It argues that subsidiarity is about whether something should be done, and proportionality about whether what has been done is the right thing. Yet it understands proportionality in that case – and in almost all others – to be confined to whether the measure efficiently and effectively achieves the goals it sets.[32] Balancing the merits of central versus decentral action could, in theory, be a part of proportionality,[33] but it almost never is.

In truth, such balancing falls into a gap between the steps in the Court's reasoning. In considering whether there is a need for action, it is enough to show that a Euro-reason exists. There is no need to consider whether it is outweighed by local considerations. Balancing does not yet arise. Then, having established that this Euro-reason is there, the Court moves to policing the action that has been taken, but it assesses it purely in terms of its relationship to that Euro-goal. Since the need for Union action has been established, the only issue is whether the need is being satisfactorily met. The question of balancing has been surpassed.

It seems as if EU law does not want to weigh the merits of local versus central action. The Court has found a linguistic legal pathway to ensure that this does not occur. Yet examining subsidiarity more carefully suggests that this balancing is at its heart. To avoid it, is to pay lip-service to subsidiarity while violating its principled core.

[27] Case C-376/98 *Germany v Parliament and Council (Tobacco Advertising)* (n 13).

[28] Toth (n 19). But see Horsley (n 5).

[29] Horsley (n 5). See similarly Case C-264/18 *PM* EU:C:2019:472; Case C-151/17 *Swedish Match* (n 13); Case C-547/14 *Philip Morris* (n 13); Fabbrini (n 5).

[30] A Follesdal, 'Subsidiarity' (1998) 6 *Journal of Political Philosophy* 231; Van den Bergh (n 14).

[31] Case C-84/94 *Working Time* (n 1) para 47. See also Case C-626/14 *Poland v Parliament* EU:C:2020:1000.

[32] Following Art 5 TEU: Protocol on Subsidiarity and Proportionality (n 6).

[33] Schütze (n 10) 263.

IV. Critique: The Path not Taken

A. The Meaning of Subsidiarity

While the origins of subsidiarity are traditionally traced to Catholic thinking,[34] its ideas are present in other philosophical traditions.[35] Aristotle is sometimes mentioned as a source of foundational subsidiarity thinking, about the nature of the freedoms that humans need, while Protestant philosophy and the writings of the French thinker Proudhon also contain subsidiarity-like ideas. An invaluable discussion of these is present in Jonasson's work, *The Political Uses of Subsidiarity*, upon which the following paragraphs draw heavily.[36]

Although there are differences of nuance in the different subsidiarity traditions, the core of all of them is a resistance to high-level authoritarianism.[37] The normative foundation of subsidiarity is a belief that that there is a natural order of society, and that certain kinds of functions belong most properly at certain levels, typically the family, or the community, and should not be taken away from them by higher powers. Above all, and in all traditions, subsidiarity is a principle of resistance: it is a principle standing in the way of the higher-level power that wishes to take over functions or exercise authority over functions carried out by a lower level. It has, necessarily, a touch of the subversive to it, being an obstacle to the freedom of those who have climbed to the highest positions in society, and a protector of the freedoms of those who have not.[38]

The substance of the normative claim that functions 'belong' at a certain level is typically somewhat vague.[39] It is not however primarily a question of economics or efficiency.[40] The thriving literature on subsidiarity as a principle allocating functions to the level that can perform them most efficiently is a response to the EU's bastardised version of the principle,[41] but does not reflect subsidiarity's origins.[42] Rather, subsidiarity has its origins in ideas about how human beings need to live, and the need for autonomy, community, and control over one's living space.[43] It also has an element of moral hazard-type thinking – the feeling that responsibility at a lower level encourages good behaviour, whereas once the higher level, perhaps the state, takes over a function, the citizens feel more distant from it, and cease to accept their responsibility to make it

[34] M Evans, 'The Principle of Subsidiarity in European Union Law: Some Comparisons with Catholic Social Teaching' (2013) 3 *Solidarity: The Journal of Catholic Social Thought and Secular Ethics* Article 5.

[35] RF Jonasson, *The Political Uses of Subsidiarity: From Thomas Aquinas to Thomas Courchene* (National Library of Canada/Bibliothèque nationale du Canada, 2002); P Rinderle, 'The Political Philosophy of European Subsidiarity' in G Walzenbach and R Alleweldt (eds), *Varieties of European Subsidiarity. A Multidisciplinary Approach* (E-International Relations Publishing, 2021) 18; Follesdal (n 30).

[36] Jonasson (n 35).

[37] ibid; Burbidge (n 5).

[38] Jonasson (n 35); Burbidge (n 4).

[39] Burbidge (n 5).

[40] Jonasson (n 35); JM Finnis, 'Subsidiarity's Roots and History: Some Observations' (2016) 61 *American Journal of Jurisprudence* 133; G de Búrca, 'The Principle of Subsidiarity and the Court of Justice as an Institutional Actor' (1998) 36 *Journal of Common Market Studies* 217.

[41] Described in Schütze (n 10) 250 as a 'textual failure'. See, for expression of this failure, Commission of the European Communities 'Communication on the Principle of Subsidiarity' (1992) 10 *EC Bulletin* 2.2.1.

[42] Finnis (n 40); Jonasson (n 35); Evans (n 34).

[43] Jonasson (n 35); Evans (n 34).

work well and justly.[44] Local responsibility creates good citizens: respect for subsidiarity is seen as a part of the European Christian Democratic tradition, if not only that.[45] Subsidiarity, despite being inherently liberal in its resistance to over-collectivisation, can also be understood as a balance to individualism, seeking to maintain responsibility to the community at a local, and therefore meaningful, level.[46] It is, in spirit, liberal communitarianism, treating the social embeddedness of individuals as part of their own, and wider society's, best interests.[47] It recognises that the further power moves from the local, the more that citizens are enabled to distance themselves from local problems and pursue a self-oriented and self-interested path in life. In this light, subsidiarity seems a perfectly appropriate constitutional counter-balance to the individualising, market-oriented, and emancipatory tendencies of the EU.

In discussions of subsidiarity, both in law and political science, there tends to be a great deal of talk about abstract formulations and not very many examples of what it means in practice. The two examples that recur repeatedly are the welfare state, and care for the poor.[48] The Catholic Church's expression of subsidiarity took place in the context of concern that both left- and right-wing secular governments would seek to displace the family and the local community as those with responsibility for care. They might be partly motivated by a sense that the state could do these things better, but the Church's fear was that they would also be using these policies to attract the loyalty of the citizen, and to weaken the hold of the Church, and indeed the father, over society.[49] For who need bow to their authority, if their protection is no longer needed? Institutional self-interest and now-archaic patriarchy are here bound up with a moral conviction that if individuals feel there is a mother-state that will take care of them then they will become decadent and irresponsible, and the foundations of a good and moral society will crumble. The modern reader, probably even the Christian Democrat, will have little sympathy with some of these motivations, but the sense that freedoms and responsibilities should be bound together and made concrete on a level where the input and participation of the individual is meaningful, is still timely. There is hardly any social policy issue today where it would not be claimed that change should be 'bottom-up' and communities should have meaningful influence over decisions affecting them. The more the world globalises, the louder the calls for local communities to be able to shape their own lives. Subsidiarity is about this.[50]

The example of welfare shows that the competition between levels which subsidiarity mediates, is competition to carry out or control a certain function. The definition of that

[44] Jonasson (n 35).

[45] ibid.

[46] Burbidge (n 5); P de Hert, 'Division of Competences between National and European Levels with Regards to Justice and Home Affairs' in J Apap (ed), *EU Justice & Home Affairs* (Edward Elgar, 2004) 55; M Cahill, 'Theorising Subsidiarity: Towards an Ontology-Sensitive Approach' (2017) 15 *International Journal of Constitutional Law* 201.

[47] See A Etzioni, *Happiness is the Wrong Metric: A Liberal Communitarian Response to Populism* (Springer Open, 2018) 131, including the profoundly relevant remark that 'If one seeks to reduce populism, violence, prejudice, and xenophobia, then communities must be nurtured as they change, rather than be overridden.'

[48] Jonasson (n 35). Although see Cahill (n 46) for some nice hypotheticals.

[49] Jonasson (n 35).

[50] M Cahill, 'Sovereignty, Liberalism and the Intelligibility of Attraction to Subsidiarity' (2016) 61 *American Journal of Jurisprudence* 119.

function plays hardly any role in the literature on subsidiarity, because it is assumed not to be an important part of the debate. The question is not 'what do you mean by care for the poor', but 'who should be responsible for it?'

By contrast, the EU has adopted a corrupted definition of subsidiarity, which actually has little connection to the philosophical subsidiarity from which it claims to derive.[51] For the EU does not ask 'who should own this function', but 'who can best achieve the objectives of the higher level', a radically different question which, in its assumption that the goals of the higher level are not up for discussion, pre-empts the very issue which is subsidiarity's essence.[52] It is, on the face of it, utterly misleading to use the word 'subsidiarity' to describe the rule in Article 5 TEU. The EU makes the higher-level goals part of the definition of the function for which there is competition, essentially distorting the playing field before the game starts.

Rather, in subsidiarity, the goals of the higher level are among the reasons that it may put forward why it, contrary to the default presumption that lower is better, should nevertheless take control of the function. Against this, the lower level may put forward other reasons why control should stay local. The meaning and importance of the function in question for each level is part of their normative claim to own it.[53]

Thus the Working Time Directive was a directive to protect workers.[54] The subsidiarity question is which level should best be responsible for this function. The Member State arguments for control will rest on claims about local differences, culture, responsiveness, and so on. The EU arguments will rest on the need for a shared framework, for normative, integrationist and economic reasons. Subsidiarity insists that it is for the EU to prove its case, and for Member State control to be the default. Assessing subsidiarity should be about weighing advantages and disadvantages within this frame, whereas in practice in EU law it is enough to show an advantage to central action: the downsides, or the advantages of decentral control, are ignored.[55]

One reason for the EU's incoherent definition of subsidiarity may be that it was influenced by German constitutional thinking, which appears to have been equally confused.[56] It was commonly supposed that subsidiarity was present in German law, and yet the Constitution gave a default priority to national purposes in a similar way to the EU. In an article in *ICON* in 2006, Taylor noted critically the ineffectiveness of subsidiarity in German law, remarking in a follow-up article that 'one cannot, after all, have a justiciable principle that produces the same answer (in this case, favorable to the federation) no matter what the input'.[57] That comment could be perfectly transplanted to the EU. And yet, it is in itself a reason for the Court of Justice to take a different approach. No court should interpret a principle so that it fails to achieve its own purpose, and

[51] Schütze (n 10) 250.

[52] European Commission (n 41); Art 5 TEU.

[53] Latimer (n 8).

[54] Council Directive 93/104/EC of 23 November 1993 concerning certain aspects of the organization of working time [1993] OJ L307/18, recital 19; Case C-84/94 *Working Time* (n 1) para 47; *Opinion 2/91* (n 15).

[55] See, for examples of this approach, Case C-151/17 *Swedish Match* (n 13); Case C-547/14 *Philip Morris* (n 13); Case C-508/13 *Estonia v Parliament and Council* (n 13); Case C-58/08 *Vodafone* (n 13); Case C-154/04 *Alliance for Natural Health* (n 13); Case C-491/01 *British American Tobacco* (n 13).

[56] G Taylor, 'Germany: The subsidiarity principle' (2006) 4 *International Journal of Constitutional Law* 115.

[57] G Taylor, 'Germany: A slow death for subsidiarity?' (2009) 7 *International Journal of Constitutional Law* 139, 146.

indeed fails to achieve any purpose at all, unless the text is so strict that an alternative is impossible and the legislator's right to make pointless law is conceded.

In Germany, things did change: in that same follow-up article Taylor went on to note that a change had taken place, describing how the Federal Constitutional Court had woken up to the need for meaningful subsidiarity review, and had begun to engage in critical and substantive review of whether national uniformity – the trump card played by the Federal Government when overruling the regions – was really necessary in the specific case, and whether the measure really achieved it to a degree justifying its impact.[58] Subsidiarity came to life! The question for EU lawyers is whether there is space for the Court of Justice to do something similar in EU law. Could it read Article 5 TEU so that it performs a meaningful constitutional balancing function?

B. Alternative Interpretations of EU 'Subsidiarity'

The remarkable step that the Court took in *Working Time* was to assume that the goal of the directive was to harmonise. In doing that, it ended the conversation. By contrast, if one reads Article 118a, the legal base, in a moderately holistic and purposive way, one can equally argue that the goal of the article is to protect workers, and the goal of harmonisation is to contribute to this. If one reads the preamble to the directive itself, one could be in no possible doubt that its fundamental purpose is to improve the protection of the health and safety of workers, and harmonisation is the means to this end, not the end in itself. The Court's suggestion that the purpose of the directive was to harmonise may indicate an insight into the motivations and psychology of the Commission and Parliament, but it is not a persuasive reading of the directive itself.

Had it followed the directive, it would have found that the purpose of that measure was to protect workers, and subsidiarity would then have required it to consider whether this could be better done by the Union or the Member States. The relative values of excluding regulatory competition and preventing national parliaments from taking the wrong decisions, on the one side, and creating locally accepted law that is adapted to cultural and economic conditions, on the other, could have been weighed. The right question would have been asked, and the debate would have been opened up.

However, it has to be admitted that in some sense many directives do have uniformity, or harmonisation, as their goal, even if they do not state this as such. The Working Time Directive may not be the most powerful example, but measures adopted as part of the internal market often standardise in order to promote free movement, and it is hard to deny that it is the uniformity they create which is the point. They may not even raise standards, on the whole, but in making them common they create a working market.

Fortunately, Article 5 TEU refers to 'objectives' in the plural. A measure may serve more than one purpose.[59] Taking the article seriously implies unpacking these as carefully as possible. It may be suggested that uniformity or harmonisation as such should not be seen as a legitimate objective: it is not an end in itself. Rather, it can be an essential means to creating free movement, or undistorted competition, or a common

[58] ibid.

[59] Case C-151/17 *Swedish Match* (n 13); Case C-547/14 *Philip Morris* (n 13); Case C-508/13 *Estonia v Parliament and Council* (n 13).

European identity, or preventing a race to the bottom. These Euro-objectives are the ones that should be considered. However, alongside them there is always at least one other, more traditional objective. The standardisation of products also aims to protect safety or health or quality, for example. Each level can try to show that its added value with respect to one or more of the objectives is more significant than the added value of the other level with respect to others. The language of Article 5 TEU subsidiarity can thus be reconciled with its purpose and history.

This would of course be an intensely political form of judicial review.[60] That is quite right. Subsidiarity is an inherently normative, value-drenched concept.[61] The ideas upon which it is built, about a natural order of society, and the proper nature of communities and individual needs and responsibilities, are extremely contestable.[62] One is tempted to say that if the Member States do not want politics and values to be part of adjudication they should not have put subsidiarity in the Treaty.

In any case, politically sensitive policy judgments are hardly new to the Court, and it has the same range of techniques available to it as does any other constitutional tribunal. It can defer, it can do light review, and above all, it can give great weight to process.[63] Indeed, it has been suggested that substantive subsidiarity review would be just too political, and that review should be purely procedural.[64] Whether or not one needs to go that far, it would surely not be unreasonable to insist that the Commission do two things. One, it could provide reasons why it is necessary to address the particular competitive, or free movement, or other issue in question, and show the urgency of this, and show how its measure effectively addresses the matter.[65] It would not be enough to just make an abstract claim that competition is being distorted by differences, but it should provide evidence that the degree and type of harmonisation proposed would make a meaningful difference – for sometimes making a few things the same achieves little, if lots of other things remain different. Two, it could address the particular merits of local control of the policy, whether cultural, economic or functional,[66] and show why it considers that the loss of that local control would not be of great significance – perhaps there is wide discretion remaining, or perhaps it is a policy field where there is a great pan-EU consensus on values and methods, and efficiency is the prevailing lodestar, which efficiency could be maintained post-harmonisation. Whatever the arguments, it could show that it had considered them seriously, and where relevant quantitatively and empirically, so that subsidiarity had been genuinely addressed, and not merely dismissed by a reference to the need for Union action. It is the second element that is

[60] GA Bermann, 'Taking Subsidiarity Seriously: Federalism in the European Community and the United States' (1994) 94 *Columbia Law Review* 331; P Syrpis, 'Theorising the relationship between the judiciary and the legislature in the EU internal market' in P Syrpis (ed), *The Judiciary, the Legislature and the EU Internal Market* (Cambridge University Press, 2012) 3.

[61] Burbidge (n 5).

[62] eg, S Walby, 'Gender in the crisis and remaking of Europe: re-gendering subsidiarity' (2018) 1 *European Journal of Politics and Gender* 307; Finnis (n 40).

[63] de Búrca (n 40).

[64] Öberg (n 11).

[65] de Búrca (n 40); Öberg (n 11); DZ Cass, 'The word that saves Maastricht? The Principle of Subsidiarity and the division of powers within the European Community' (1992) 29 *Common Market Law Review* 1107; van Nuffel (n 19).

[66] See E Herlin-Karnell, 'Subsidiarity in the Area of EU Justice and Home Affairs Law – A Lost Cause?' (2009) 15 *European Law Journal* 351; de Hert (n 46).

primarily missing from the law, and the combination of the two that would create the balancing process which is genuine subsidiarity.

It is tempting to think, reviewing this suggestion, that in practice the Union would still win most of its cases. If Member States commit to creating a market and to integrating, they must surely accept that the needs of this process weigh heavily in the scales. The default preference for the lower order that is subsidiarity's signature is not removed by the nature of the Treaties, but it is put in a challenging context.

On the other hand, in the absence of a thorough discussion of the merits of action at each level, it is hard to know how important, effective, and desirable Union action really is. We have become used to harmonisation as a conversation-killer, and we are not used to thinking in subsidiarity terms within EU law.

In any case, whichever side wins, there is a merit to voicing what is at stake.[67] EU law is profoundly disruptive, and its legitimacy is constantly questioned. It can hardly abandon its own agenda, but one thing that its institutions can do is recognise the nature of their own actions, and the values and interests that are being affected, and give those values and interests due voice. The claim that arrogation of powers to a higher level is necessary is more plausible, and the arrogation itself is more legitimate, if the consequences of that move are transparently taken into account.

V. The Legacy of *Working Time*: Scholarly Reception and Subsequent Cases

As the discussion above implies, the Court has not changed its position since *Working Time*. There has been a steady trickle of cases over the years where subsidiarity has been raised, but in each of them it has proved ineffective and irrelevant, for the reasons already outlined: it has no grip on measures which only the EU can take.[68] As a consequence, *Working Time* has been important, but not as the source of a new line of case law. Rather, its legacy is an absence, a gap in the law on competence control.

That is reflected in the dialogue between the Court and national constitutional courts. The case law of these, notably the German Federal Constitutional Court, on the limits to EU law as they see it, has been of growing importance and much discussed.[69] Prima facie, and certainly 30 years ago, one might have expected subsidiarity to be one of the central concepts put to work. Rather, we see the FCC speaking over the years of human rights, democracy, primacy and proportionality, but not of subsidiarity.[70] *Working Time* quite effectively knocked this ball off the field.

[67] C Taylor, 'The Politics of Recognition' in A Gutmann (ed), *Multiculturalism: Examining the Politics of Recognition* (Princeton University Press, 1994) 25.

[68] See n 17 above.

[69] See, eg, M Kumm, 'The Jurisprudence of Constitutional Conflict: Constitutional Supremacy in Europe before and after the Constitutional Treaty' (2005) 11 *European Law Journal* 262; A Albi, 'Supremacy of EC Law in the New Member States' (2007) 3 *European Journal of Constitutional Law* 25; P Craig, 'The ECJ and Ultra Vires Action: A Conceptual Analysis' (2011) 48 *Common Market Law Review* 395; A Bobic, *The Jurisprudence of Constitutional Conflict in the European Union* (Oxford University Press, 2022).

[70] See discussions in n 69 above.

Something similar, but a little more complex, can be said about scholarly reactions to *Working Time*. There has been regular criticism of subsidiarity's relative weakness, but at the same time this has been accepted: it has been seen rather as a weakness inherent to the concept, than as a result of a choice by the Court.[71] Only a very few scholars suggested that subsidiarity might have a meaning more substantial and important than the one the Court gave it.[72] As a result, subsidiarity has been on the sidelines of legal discussion of EU competences, and the same issues that concern the FCC have been at the centre.[73]

Yet *Working Time* has also had a positive scholarly legacy. This is in the considerable literature claiming that EU law denies politics, and excludes conflicts, treating as objective and technocratic what is actually contestable, political, and in need of more legitimation than a judgment written with the familiar tone of deductive inevitability can confer.[74] Many have argued that the internal market, the home of the harmonisation that subsidiarity so fails to address, should be a place for contestation and balance, but has been turned by the Court into a venue for pseudo-objective marginalisation of national concerns.[75] Whether one agrees with this critique or not, the balancing that is missed could have taken place within subsidiarity. The Court's choice not to allow this balancing to enter the law echoes today both in the speed with which integration has moved, and the intensity of the social and political backlash that is being experienced in some Member States.

VI. Conclusion

The case law of the Court of Justice, just as the policy documents of the European Commission, shows a consistent reluctance to admit that integration has its costs.[76]

[71] Davies (n 5); T Schilling, 'A New Dimension of Subsidiarity: Subsidiarity as a Rule and a Principle' (1994) 14 *Yearbook of European Law* 203; N Emiliou, 'Subsidiarity: An Effective Barrier Against the Enterprises of Ambition?' (1992) 17 *European Law Review* 383; LC Backer, 'Harmonization, Subsidiarity and Cultural Difference: An Essay on the Dynamics of Opposition within Federative and International Legal Systems' (1996) 4 *Tulsa Journal of Comparative and International Law* 185; N Bernard, 'The Future of European Economic law in the Light of the Principle of Subsidiarity' (1996) 33 *Common Market Law Review* 633.

[72] R Schütze, 'Subsidiarity after Lisbon: Reinforcing the Safeguards of Liberalism?' (2009) 68 *Cambridge Law Journal* 525, esp 532–35; M Cahill, 'Theorizing subsidiarity: Towards an ontology-sensitive approach' (2017) 15 *International Journal of Constitutional Law* 201; Öberg (n 11).

[73] Schütze (n 72).

[74] C Joerges, 'Reconceptualizing the supremacy of European law: A plea for a supranational conflict of laws' in B Kohler-Koch, and B Rittberger (eds), *Debating the democratic legitimacy of the European Union* (Rowman and Littlefield, 2007) 311; D Chalmers, 'The European Redistributive State and a European Law of Struggle' (2012) 18 *European Law Journal* 667; M Dani, 'Rehabilitating Social Conflicts in European Public Law' (2012) 18 *European Law Journal* 621; F De Witte, 'Transnational Solidarity and the Mediation of Conflicts of Justice in Europe' (2012) 18 *European Law Journal* 694; M Everson and C Joerges, 'Reconfiguring the Politics–Law Relationship in the Integration Project through Conflicts–Law Constitutionalism' (2012) 18 *European Law Journal* 644; D Grimm, 'The Democratic Costs of Constitutionalisation: The European Case' (2015) 21 *European Law Journal* 460; G Davies, 'Democracy and Legitimacy in the Shadow of Purposive Competence' (2015) 21 *European Law Journal* 2.

[75] See n 74.

[76] G Davies, 'Internal Market Adjudication and the Quality of Life in Europe' EUI Department of Law Research Paper No 2014/07.

In free movement law it recognises some, if not all, of the interests at stake, but likes to maintain that those interests can be reconciled with free movement, rather than admitting that actually – *Cassis de Dijon* and consumer protection, for example – one is being subordinated to the other.[77] Joerges has noted that the heart of EU law is 'norm collisions' while many others have highlighted the way it frames, limits and steers politics in democratically important ways.[78] Yet the legal texts themselves all read quite peacefully, as if the decisions of the Court or legislature are just the exercise of objective, inevitable, well-informed common sense, not value-laden and contestable choices.

Subsidiarity is about loss. It proclaims that local control is a good in itself, and that taking away that control does harm. It may be that the harm is justified by a greater good, but the principle demands that this balance be made, and carefully, for the things that subsidiarity claims to be at stake are not just minor efficiencies, but the conditions for human happiness and virtue.

The Court in *Working Time* decided to ignore this, and reduce subsidiarity to a formula that would have no legal consequences for the Union. It was encouraged by a bizarre formulation in the Treaty, perhaps an attempt to adapt an old principle to a novel context of purposive integration, but one that seemed to define the nature of the competition between levels in a way that meant the Union would always win. However, there are alternatives, and this chapter has tried to show them. Subsidiarity can be read, without doing violence to its text, in a way that makes it effective, and allows it to achieve the purpose for which it exists, and presumably – one does not want to be too cynical – for which it was inserted into Union law.

It would not just be the correction of an unfortunate and long-lasting legal error to do so, but also a sign of legal maturity. Contrary to the wording of the TEU, union cannot be ever-closer.[79] It is then no longer union but annihilation of the self. Integration must have its limits. There is certainly a long way to go before this point is reached, but it is arguable that integration is far enough advanced that in individual cases it is becoming increasingly relevant to ask whether the added value really justifies the loss. The Union legislature obviously thought it was, or it would not have adopted the legislation in question. However, the Union is a creature of law, so it is for the Court to check whether it had sufficient reason to take this stance. Contra the reasoning in *Working Time* and every subsidiarity case that has followed it since, subsidiarity should be the name for this process of control.

[77] ibid; Case 120/78 *Cassis de Dijon* EU:C:1979:42.
[78] Joerges (n 74).
[79] Art 1 TEU.

10

Chernobyl and the Inter-Institutional Balance

JOANA MENDES*

I. History and Doctrinal Content: A Matter of Institutional Balance and of Judicial Protection

In 1990, when the Court issued its *Chernobyl* judgment, the standing rules in actions of annulment were still the ones that the Treaties of Rome had defined in 1957.[1] Direct action before the Court was available to a select group of privileged applicants – the Member States, the Council and the Commission – and to natural and legal persons against decisions addressed to them or of individual or direct concern to them.[2] The original lack of capacity of the Parliament to sue and be sued went hand-in-hand with its weak powers in the original institutional set-up.[3] It thus reflected the deeply executive nature of the European Communities. Yet the continued absence of the Parliament from Article 173 of the Treaty establishing the European Economic Community (EEC Treaty) and Article 146 of the Treaty establishing the European Atomic Energy Community (Euratom Treaty) contrasted with the enhanced powers it had been given in the Single European Act in 1986.

The immediate significance of the judgment in *Chernobyl* lies here: it granted standing to the Parliament in actions of annulment, even if limited to instances where it sought 'to safeguard its prerogatives' and grounded 'only on submissions alleging their infringement'.[4] The Court thus created an intermediate category of 'semi-privileged applicants' in actions of annulment. Shortly after *Chernobyl*, the Treaty incorporated this limited standing of the Parliament in the 1992 revision of Article 173, which also extended such conditional standing to the European Central Bank (ECB). In the

* I am grateful for the research assistance of Pavlina Hubková.

[1] Case C-70/88 *Parliament v Council* EU:C:1990:217 ('*Chernobyl*'), para 27.

[2] Treaty Establishing the European Economic Community, 25 March 1957, Art 173 at 129, available at eur-lex.europa.eu/legal-content/FR/TXT/PDF/?uri=CELEX:11957E/TXT.

[3] Opinion of AG Van Gerven of 30 November 1989, Case C-70/88 *Parliament v Council* EU:C:1989:604, para 3.

[4] Case C-70/88 *Chernobyl* (n 1) para 27.

Amsterdam revision of 1999, the Court of Auditors would join this group of semi-privileged applicants.

But if *Chernobyl* was a matter of legal protection, institutional balance was what made that result possible. In the absence of any written norm and faced with a 'procedural gap' that prevented the Court from protecting the Parliament's institutional prerogatives,[5] the Court considered that the principle of institutional balance required the recognition of a legal remedy in case of breaches that impinged on the prerogatives of the institutions as established in the Treaty.[6] *Chernobyl* would become known because of the role it gave to the principle of institutional balance: it was not only the foundation of the Parliament's standing, but also a means to enable the Court to change that balance, despite the voices that insisted that the Court was merely spelling out the institutional balance as it resulted from the Treaties. It thus seemed to give this principle a 'dynamic character',[7] even if with hindsight *Chernobyl* was the single instance in which the Court resorted to this principle as a means to 'supplement' the text of the Treaties.[8]

A. Institutional Balance before *Chernobyl*

Institutional balance had become a principle of EU law in *Meroni*.[9] Based on the article of the Treaty establishing the European Coal and Steel Community (ECSC Treaty) that defined the binding character of the objectives of the Community on the institutions, within the framework of their respective attributions and in the common interest, the Court considered that this norm reflected the 'balance of powers which is characteristic of the institutional structure of the Community' and held it to be 'a fundamental guarantee granted by the Treaty in particular to the undertakings and associations of undertakings to which it applies'.[10] As Jacqué later noted, this element of protection of legal persons subsided in the subsequent judgments.[11] It was mostly relevant in judgments involving only the institutions – an aspect that *Chernobyl* confirmed.[12] Before *Chernobyl*, that was notably the case in *Köster*,[13] where the Court had framed the legality of the controls over comitology committees as a question of institutional balance, and in *Roquette Frères*.[14] Here, the Court had equated the Parliament's consultation in the legislative procedure to 'an essential factor in the institutional balance intended by the Treaty,' which 'although limited, … reflects at Community level the fundamental democratic principle that the peoples should take part in the exercise of power through the intermediary of a representative assembly.'[15]

[5] ibid para 26.
[6] ibid paras 21–23.
[7] J-P Jacqué, 'The Principle of Institutional Balance' (2004) 41 *Common Market Law Review* 383, 386.
[8] B de Witte, 'The Role of the Court of Justice in Shaping the Institutional Balance in the EU' in J Mendes and I Venzke (eds), *Allocating Authority: Who Should Do What in European and International Law?* (Hart Publishing, 2018) 148.
[9] Case 9/56 *Meroni v High Authority* EU:C:1958:7.
[10] ibid 152.
[11] Jacqué (n 7) 385–86.
[12] Case C-301/02 P *Tralli v European Central Bank* EU:C:2005:306, para 46.
[13] Case 25/70 *Köster* EU:C:1970:115.
[14] Case C-138/79 *Roquette Frères v Council* EU:C:1980:249.
[15] *Köster* (n 13) para 4; *Roquette Frères* (n 14) para 33.

As will be seen in more detail below, institutional balance has been termed a constitutional law principle and has been invoked to establish both the constitutional parallels between the EU law and national constitutional law, on the one hand, and the specificity of the Union, on the other. In *Chernobyl*, specifically, the principle of institutional balance stressed the distinctive character of EU law, since at stake was, in essence, the ability of the Parliament to act judicially to protect its prerogatives, an odd element for political parliamentary institutions. As Advocate General van Gerven wrote in his Opinion,

> the choice made in the Treaties of having the scope of powers subject to review also by the courts, even when the legislature [at the time, the Council] is affected thereby, is a choice which departs from that adopted in more than a few Member States – especially those where there is no federal structure.[16]

B. The Parliament at the Court: A Politically Delicate Issue

Chernobyl must be understood against the legal background of two judgments that immediately preceded it, both issued after the adoption of the Single European Act: *Les Verts*[17] and *Comitology*.[18] In *Les Verts*, rule of law arguments had supported the judicial recognition of the Parliament's capacity to be sued, despite Article 173 EEC Treaty's continued exclusion of the Parliament from the group of privileged applicants. The Court anchored this result in the necessity of subjecting acts 'intended to have legal effects vis-à-vis third parties' to judicial review, and added one of its most famous proclamations: the Community is 'based on the rule of law, inasmuch as neither its Member States nor its institutions can avoid a review of the question whether the measures adopted by them are in conformity with the basic constitutional charter, the Treaty'.[19] In *Comitology*, on the contrary, the Court had blocked the Parliament's attempt to have standing in an action for annulment on rather peremptory grounds: 'the applicable provisions, as they stand at present, do not enable the Court to recognize the capacity of the European Parliament to bring an action for annulment'.[20]

The contrast between the position the Court had assumed in *Les Verts* – drawing on a general principle in the absence of a written Treaty norm and against the wording of the Treaty norm – and the position it took in *Comitology* was noted by many commentators at the time.[21] Both judgments had been issued just after the Single European Act

[16] Opinion of AG Van Gerven in Case C-70/88 *Parliament v Council* (n 3) para 3.

[17] Case C-294/83 *Les Verts v Parliament* EU:C:1986:166.

[18] Case C-302/87 *Parliament v Council* EU:C:1988:461 ('*Comitology*').

[19] Case C-294/83 *Les Verts* (n 17) paras 25, 23.

[20] Case C-302/87 *Comitology* (n 18) para 28. The *Comitology* judgment was issued roughly seven months after the Parliament registered its application for *Chernobyl* (4 March 1988).

[21] For a strong critique of *Comitology*, based on the constitutional role of the Court of Justice, see G Bebr, 'Case C-70/88, *European Parliament v Council*, Judgment of the Court of Justice of 22 May 1990' (1991) 28 *Common Market Law Review* 663. For a more sober analysis, see J-P Jacqué, 'La légitimation active du Parlement européen ou il n'était pas nécessaire d'espérer pour entreprendre' (1990) 26 *Revue Trimestrielle de Droit Européen* 620 (the references below are to the paragraphs of the article, as indicated in its electronic version); and M Condinanzi, 'Il ruolo del Parlamento europeo nel contenzioso comunitario. Una nuova pronuncia della Corte di giustizia' (1991) *Rivista italiana di diritto pubblico comunitario* 127, 134 (pointing out 'an evident logical contradiction').

(*Les Verts* a few months after the Treaty revision had been signed, *Comitology* two and a half years later) but only in *Comitology* did the Court explicitly invoke the contrast between the unchanged wording of Article 173 EEC Treaty and the revised Parliament's enhanced powers as one reason to deny granting the Parliament powers to defend judicially its institutional prerogatives.[22]

The matter was politically rather delicate: in the revision of 1986 the Council had refused to approve a proposal by the Commission to include the Parliament in the group of privileged applicants.[23] The sign that the Treaty revision had given seemed clear: at the very least there was no unanimity among the Member States to support the inclusion of the Parliament in the group of privileged applicants. While that had not prevented the Court from mitigating this blockage in *Les Verts*, the same Court had been unwilling to take a step further in *Comitology*. As a result, it struck a balance between respecting the Treaties and ensuring legal protection for the Parliament's prerogatives that satisfied neither the Commission nor the Parliament. According to *Comitology*, the Commission had the duty to protect the prerogatives of the Parliament, which was contrary to the Parliament's autonomy of decision-making and placed the Commission in an impossible position when, in a case such as this, it did not support the Parliament in substance.[24]

Comitology stood out as an apparent exception to the Court's consistent jurisprudence of building 'an adequate and coherent system of legal protection',[25] and to the 'tendency to extend the Parliament's right to bring actions', while respecting the 'principle of restrictive attribution of judicial powers'.[26] Before *Les Verts*, the Court had recognised the Parliament's capacity to bring an action for failure to act, its general right to intervene before the Court (ie not dependent on proof of interest in the result of the case), the Court's ability to ask the Parliament to provide information in direct actions and in preliminary reference procedures.[27] Before still, measures of the Parliament had been the object of references for preliminary ruling, both of interpretation and validity.[28]

Chernobyl, at the end, provided a legal solution to a deeply political issue. The judicial recognition of the Parliament's *locus standi* in actions for annulment would mean a self-attribution of review powers by the Court, following the presumed lack of agreement between the Member States to amend Article 173 EEC Treaty. One option out of the conundrum was a principle-based position; namely, the Court could draw on the adequacy and coherence of the system of legal protection, as in *Les Verts*. That was the path that Advocate General van Gerven set in his Opinion: limited attribution of judicial powers was justified as 'an inalienable task of the courts'.[29] Institutional balance – be it by 'establishing (or [by] re-establishing)' it – in the opinion of the Advocate General,

[22] Case C-302/87 *Comitology* (n 18) para 26.

[23] Opinion of AG Van Gerven in Case C-70/88 *Parliament v Council* (n 3) para 5.

[24] 'Report for the Hearing', Case C-70/88 *Parliament v Council* [1986] ECR I-2042 ('*Chernobyl* Hearing Report') I-2049, I-2051 (para 3). Obviously, having refused to change the proposal following the opinion of the Parliament, the Commission could not support its position in Court, a point which the Parliament used to argue the existence of 'a legal vacuum': ibid I-2050.

[25] Opinion of AG Van Gerven in Case C-70/88 *Parliament v Council* (n 3) para 5.

[26] ibid para 4.

[27] See, respectively, Case 13/83 *Parliament v Council* EU:C:1985:220; Case C-138/79 *Roquette Frères* (n 14); Case 149/85 *Wybot v Faure* EU:C:1986:310.

[28] Opinion of AG Van Gerven in Case C-70/88 *Parliament v Council* (n 3).

[29] ibid para 6.

was '*not* the province of the courts'.[30] As is well known, this was not the path the Court followed.

II. Facts and Judgment

A. An Institutional Play of Catch-Up

One year after the Chernobyl nuclear accident, the Commission, concerned about the contamination of foodstuffs and of feedingstuffs, submitted to the Council a proposal to adopt a regulation setting maximum permitted levels of radioactive contamination, to apply also to 'any other case of radiological emergency'.[31] The proposal would enable the Commission to adjust those levels, in line with 'the latest scientific advice' and international regulatory practice, 'to the circumstances of any particular nuclear accident' or emergency, and ban from circulation within the internal market foodstuffs and feedingstuffs in breach of the defined levels.[32] At stake was the protection of the health of the population, the reassurance of the public, and the unity of the internal market, as to 'avoid deflections of trade within the Community'.[33] The legal basis chosen was Article 31 Euratom, which stipulated that basic standards for the protection of the health of the general public and workers against the dangers arising from ionising radiation (envisaged in Article 30 Euratom) are, first, 'worked out' by the Commission, subsequent to the opinion of a group of Member States' scientific experts and the opinion of Economic and Social Committee, and, second, are established by the Council, after consultation of the Parliament.[34]

The facts of the case point to a clear marginalisation of the Parliament during this process and document a strong political reaction against that marginalisation. The Parliament was officially informed of the proposed regulation only through the Council's request of consultation. Yet, in the immediate aftermath of the nuclear accident, it had been rather swift in requesting 'the competent Community authorities to protect the health of the general public by setting, on a uniform basis, the maximum radiation limits applicable to foodstuffs'.[35] In a resolution adopted by an impressive majority (232 votes to two, with nine abstentions), the Parliament disputed the appropriateness of the legal basis that the Commission had chosen.[36] In its view, the contested

[30] ibid.

[31] Council Regulation (Euratom) No 3954/87 of 22 December 1987 laying down maximum permitted levels of radioactive contamination of foodstuffs and of feedingstuffs following a nuclear accident or any other case of radiological emergency [1987] OJ L371/11, Preamble, Arts 1 and 2.

[32] ibid, Preamble.

[33] ibid.

[34] These provisions remain in force: see Consolidated Version of the Treaty Establishing the European Atomic Energy Community [2012] OJ C327/1.

[35] *Chernobyl* Hearing Report (n 24) I-2043, para 4 (referring to European Parliament resolutions adopted on 15 May 1986 and 11 September 1986).

[36] Resolution on the legal basis for the proposal from the Commission of the European Communities for a Council regulation (Euratom) laying down maximum permitted radioactivity levels for foodstuffs, feedingstuffs and drinking water in the case of abnormal levels of radioactivity or of a nuclear accident [1987] OJ C305/1, 33.

regulation should be adopted on the basis of Article 100a EEC Treaty, the clause on the harmonisation of the internal market which provided for the cooperation procedure for the adoption of Community acts. The Parliament requested the Commission to revise its proposal accordingly. Two weeks later, it voted in favour of the amendments to the Commission's proposal, including an amendment to the legal basis. This resolution, too, was approved by an absolute majority.[37]

The Commission, however, kept Article 31 Euratom as the legal basis of the regulation, prompting the Parliament to adopt a strong restatement of its position. Before the Christmas break of 1987, the Parliament passed yet another resolution (again adopted by a very strong majority of 348 votes to 26, with nine abstentions) entitled 'Legislative resolution (cooperation procedure)'.[38] It rejected the Commission proposal and, procedurally, it instructed the President of the Parliament to 'forward [that] legislative resolution to the Council and Commission as Parliament's opinion'.[39] But, two days previously, the Council had reached an agreement on the original Commission's proposal. Taking 'note' of the Parliament's opinion, the Council adopted Regulation No 3954/87 just in time for the Christmas closure.

The matter, naturally, ended up in Court. The Council, supported by the Commission and by the UK, contested that the Parliament had standing to bring the action of annulment, given the wording of Article 173 EEC Treaty. Admissibility on grounds of standing became the only issue of the judicial dispute.

B. Behind Legal Protection: A Dispute on the Role of the Parliament

Institutional balance came forcefully in the Council's argumentation before the Court. Two years before *Chernobyl* was brought to Court, *Les Verts* had recognised the Parliament's capacity to be sued in actions of annulment, and the Council's argumentation was, naturally, directed at disentangling standing from the case law that had, until then, strengthened the Parliament's position as a litigant. In the Council's view, standing would be not only in breach of the Treaty's system of remedies. Granting standing to the Parliament was contrary the principle of institutional balance (understood as 'accordance with legal rules'), as it would place the Parliament 'in direct competition' with the Commission as guardian of the Treaties. It would, then, 'split in two' the power of 'political review'.[40] The Council recalled that the Parliament was not the legislature. That was the role of the Council. If recognised, the ability to sue the Council would give the Parliament the ability to intervene in the legislative procedure in addition to the opportunities enshrined in the Treaties.[41] The Council saw, therefore, a direct link between

[37] *Chernobyl* Hearing Report (n 24) I-2044 (quoting the October 1987 Resolution on Legal Basis (n 36)).

[38] ibid I-2045 (quoting Legislative Resolution (Cooperation procedure) embodying the opinion of the European Parliament on the proposal from the Commission of the European Communities to the Council for a regulation laying down maximum permitted radioactivity levels for foodstuffs, feedingstuffs and drinking water in the case of abnormal levels of radioactivity or of nuclear accident [1988] OJ C13/61).

[39] ibid.

[40] *Chernobyl* Hearing Report (n 24) I-2048.

[41] While this is not stated as such, it seems implicit in the Council's line of argumentation.

the possibility of the Parliament to trigger judicial review in actions of annulment and the change that such judicial recognition would mean in the institutional balance set by the Treaty.[42] *Comitology* supported its plea. Issued while *Chernobyl* was pending, that judgment had explicitly rejected the Parliament's argument that institutional balance required a parallelism between legal remedies (action for annulment and action for failure to act) and between the capacity to be sued and capacity to sue.[43]

The Parliament, in turn, argued that the Court in *Comitology* had recognised the Parliament as 'a political institution equipped with the power of political review'.[44] Unlike the Council, the Parliament attached the label 'political review' to the 'right to participate in the legislative procedure'.[45] The Parliament did not fail to notice that, while being 'an eminently political institution' that must 'defend its prerogatives by political means', it was nevertheless obliged to defend them judicially, unlike national parliaments.[46] In the circumstances of *Chernobyl*, the Parliament had been precluded from enforcing its institutional prerogatives of participation in the legislative procedure. The Commission, who, according to *Comitology*, had 'the responsibility for ensuring that the Parliament's prerogatives are respected and for bringing for that purpose such actions for annulment as might prove to be necessary', had not supported the Parliament in this specific case.[47] The circumstances underlying *Chernobyl*, therefore, showed, in the Parliament's view, that the 'concept of a complete system of legal remedies' required a recognition of its ability to bring an action of annulment.[48] Only then would the existing 'legal vacuum' be closed.[49]

C. Legal Protection Rather than Institutional Balance?

The facts of the case made legal protection a compelling argument. The Court started by stating the obvious: under the Treaty, the Parliament did not have the right to bring an action for annulment.[50] Yet, unlike the position it had taken in *Les Verts* – where the Court had found no obstacle in the exclusion of the Parliament from Article 173 EEC Treaty to recognise its ability to be sued – the Court now considered that the letter of the Treaty was *not* an obstacle that it could overcome. As we shall see below, this premise was consequential.

[42] *Chernobyl* Hearing Report (n 24) I-2048.

[43] Opinion of AG Van Gerven in Case C-70/88 *Parliament v Council* (n 3) para 9 (mentioning only the latter point).

[44] *Chernobyl* Hearing Report (n 24) I-2048–I-2049.

[45] The Parliament's argument was the following: 'in [*Comitology*] the Court stated that the European Parliament was a political institution equipped with powers of political review, that is to say its motion of censure *and* its right to participate in the legislative procedure' (emphasis added). Indeed, the Court in *Comitology* specifically stated that 'As is apparent from Articles 143 and 144 the European Parliament is empowered … to exercise political control over the Commission … and … to censure the Commission, where necessary, if the latter should fail properly to discharge that task.' *Comitology* (n 18) para 12. Aside from the power of censure (Art 144 EEC Treaty), those norms only referred to the Parliament's competence to discuss the Commission's annual report (Art 143 EEC Treaty).

[46] *Chernobyl* Hearing Report (n 24) I-2049.

[47] Case C-302/87 *Comitology* (n 18) para 27; and Case C-70/88 *Chernobyl* (n 1) para 6.

[48] *Chernobyl* Hearing Report (n 24) I-2051.

[49] Case C-70/88 *Chernobyl* (n 1) para 8.

[50] ibid paras 12–14 (the later aspect had been analysed by the Council in its submissions).

In essence, the facts in *Chernobyl* required that the Court revise the position it had adopted in *Comitology*. It was clear that the various legal remedies available to the Parliament to defend its prerogatives could 'prove to be ineffective or uncertain'; manifestly, they were not sufficient to guarantee 'with certainty and in all circumstances' that judicial review could ensure respect of those prerogatives.[51] The action for failure to act would be of no avail when, as in this case, an act had been adopted. The Parliament could not rely on other litigants bringing a preliminary reference on validity or an action of annulment. In particular, the protection by the Commission, which the Court had invoked in *Comitology*, could clash with the Commission's position on the legislative procedure. The Court could not oblige the Commission to bring proceedings that were not in its own interest.[52]

The Court was clearly convinced by the case that the Parliament had mounted to show the existence of 'a legal vacuum', as, without standing, 'the choice of legal basis could not be challenged and the Parliament could not ensure that its own institutional prerogatives were respected'.[53] The matter was, like in *Les Verts*, a matter of rule of law, of securing 'a complete system of legal remedies'. Advocate General Van Gerven had forcefully made the point:

> The essential question which has arisen with perfect clarity in this case is … this: should the Parliament be offered less extensive legal protection than that enjoyed by individuals … whenever it is necessary to safeguard through the courts own rights, powers or prerogatives?[54]

By using a broad definition of legal protection – as covering rights, powers and prerogatives – the Advocate General had established a direct comparison between the Parliament and individuals; he noted also that Les Verts was a political party (hence, with 'a public law vocation') that had not claimed 'subjective rights', but electoral funds.[55] Yet, if it was clear that the Parliament needed to be released of its position of 'tutelage' under the Commission,[56] the Court reached that result without even mentioning *Les Verts*.

D. The 'Apotheosis' of Institutional Balance

The Court was convinced by the correction that the Advocate General asked for, but not by its reasoning. In the absence of a written norm that could support the standing of the Parliament, institutional balance was the foundation on which it justified the need to enable the Parliament to protect its prerogatives in an action for annulment. *Chernobyl* ended up meaning

> the restoration, not to say the apotheosis, of the concept of 'institutional balance' as a benchmark in identifying the legal obligations governing relationships between the institutions in the decision-making process, and in defining the Court's own role in settling disputes in this area.[57]

[51] ibid paras 16, 20.
[52] ibid paras 17–19, where the Court rejects the position it had defended in Case C-302/87 *Comitology* (n 18) para 27.
[53] *Chernobyl* Hearing Report (n 24) I-2050.
[54] Opinion of AG Van Gerven in Case C-70/88 *Parliament v Council* (n 3) para 9.
[55] ibid paras 6–12.
[56] ibid para 12; J-C Bonichot, 'Note', *Recueil Dalloz Sirey – Jurisprudence* (1990) 446, 447.
[57] K Bradley, 'Sense and Sensibility: *Parliament v Council* Continued' (1991) 16 *European Law Review* 245, 254.

That 'apotheosis' was made possible by three main steps: the prerogatives of the Parliament are 'one of the elements of institutional balance';[58] observance of this balance requires that 'it should be possible to penalize' any breaches thereof through remedies that are 'suited' to the result sought by the Parliament, and can be deployed in 'a certain and effective manner';[59] this is a duty of the Court.[60] Having framed the problem in these terms, the Court could argue that the lack of written support for the Court to deploy this role was 'a procedural gap' – and no longer, as in *Comitology*, a choice of the Member States – which could not 'prevail over the fundamental interest in the maintenance and observance of the institutional balance'.[61] As one commentator pointed out, the adjective 'procedural' minimised the importance that the Court attributed to what it characterised as a silence of the Treaty in the same paragraph where it stressed the importance of institutional balance.[62] Still, the absence of the Parliament from Article 173 EEC Treaty and Article 146 Euratom was meaningful. Given the grounds of the judgment, the Parliament's ability to bring an action of annulment would be admissible on conditional grounds: only to safeguard the prerogatives of the Parliament and only based on submissions alleging their infringement.[63]

The Court thus took one step back from its constitutional-like reading of the Treaty, of which *Les Verts* remains a hallmark, while still taking an important step in the Community institutional evolution. By relying on a procedural lacuna and on its duty that the 'law be observed',[64] the Court took the cue that the some of the Member States reportedly had left it: develop the law, as needed, also by settling a point – the standing rights of the Parliament – on which the Member States had not been able to reach an agreement.[65]

III. Academic Reception

Most of the judgments that drew directly on *Chernobyl* were either occupied with refining the conditional aspect of the Parliament's standing or involved legal bases disputes, which had been the background of *Chernobyl*. Yet the relatively modest references to *Chernobyl* in subsequent case law contrast with the academic reception of the judgment. Most academics greeted *Chernobyl* with enthusiasm. Some stressed its constitutional significance, more because of the role that the Court itself had assumed in shaping the EU's institutional balance in a 'dynamic way' than of what the standing of the Parliament could mean for the transformation of the EU institutional set up in support of a more democratic Community. A few, more soberly, preferred to stick to a limited

[58] Case C-70/88 *Chernobyl* (n 1) para 21.
[59] ibid paras 22, 23, 25.
[60] ibid paras 23, 25.
[61] ibid para 26.
[62] V Constantinesco, 'Chronique de jurisprudence de la Cour de justice des Communautés européennes. Institutions et ordre juridique communautaire' (1991) *Journal du Droit International* 451, 454.
[63] Case C-70/88 *Chernobyl* (n 1) para 27.
[64] See Bradley (n 57) 251.
[65] Opinion of AG Van Gerven in Case C-70/88 *Parliament v Council* (n 3) para 5, fn 16 (citing a declaration by then-Commission President, Jacques Delors, on the lack of unanimity of the Council on the Commission's proposal to extend standing of the Parliament during the revision of the Treaties in 1985).

legal-dogmatic analysis and emphasised the technical relevance of the judgment in two respects: the explication of the traits of the principle of institutional balance; and the creation of a new category of semi-privileged litigants. They pointed out that, as significant as the judgment was, the Court had remained within the boundaries of its judicial role and respected the will that the Member States had expressed in the Treaty. Others, still, emphasised the political significance of the judgment, in articulation with the legal novelty of standing, and assessed it in view of the possible contribution of the judgment to the democratic legitimacy of the Union (then Community). These three positions will be presented next.

A. One View: A Further Step in the Construction of a 'Constitutional Order'

Influential academics in the French legal world saw *Chernobyl* as a sign that the Court was assuming a role akin to that of a domestic constitutional court.[66] For some, this was the main contribution of this judgment. Jacqué was adamant: 'the judgment is of capital importance since the Court, at the cost of a 'creative interpretation', recognises itself as the guardian of the *Community constitutional order* and confirms its function as a *constitutional court*'.[67] The constitutional reading of the judgment was shared by Bradley, at the time member of the Legal Service of the European Parliament. He praised the Court for protecting the prerogative of the Parliament, correcting its 'defective or incomplete' reasoning in *Comitology* and for being responsive to 'the desirability of an extensive view of its own duties as constitutional arbiter',[68] noting that the Court had 'returned to the *spirit* of *Les Verts*'.[69] Still in the constitutional vein, the rather emphatic – if not fervent – terms by Gerhard Bebr, contrast with the mostly cautious constitutional reading of the judgment of other commentators. Writing in his capacity as former legal advisor to the Commission and member of the journal's advisory board, he took the constitutional role of the Court as a premise and not as a consequence of the judgment, welcoming *Chernobyl* as reflecting 'a sense of constitutional realism and responsibility sorely missed in *Comitology*'.[70] He rejected *Comitology* as a 'precipitated, unreflected ruling' where 'the Court largely abdicated … its mission as a Community constitutional court' and 'unfortunately failed to demonstrate boldness and vision it had shown in instances crucial for the development of the Community legal order in the absence of any explicit, formal Treaty provision'.[71] This reasoning begged the unanswered question of when it is that the lack of Treaty provision means a lacuna.

The constitutional role of the Court was shared even by scholars whose analyses of *Chernobyl* did not turn on a constitutional argument, but stressed the relevance that

[66] Constantinesco (n 62) 455.
[67] Jacqué (n 21) para 12 (emphasis added).
[68] Bradley (n 57) 245.
[69] ibid, 250 (emphasis added).
[70] Bebr (n 21) 676.
[71] ibid 666 (in the footnote he drew the parallelism with 'supremacy', direct effect, and fundamental rights' protection; the qualification of *Comitology* as 'precipitated, unreflected' can be found ibid 667).

the judgment gave to institutional balance.[72] Yet the authors who took this position simply identified the constitutional character of the judgment in the fact that the Court arbitrates inter-institutional conflicts, through the principle of institutional balance. The relative position of the Court while filling in what the Court identified as a lacuna (following, in part, the Parliament), on the one hand, and of the Member States, who had recently refused a proposal to include the Parliament in Article 173 EEC Treaty, on the other, did not weigh in on their characterisation of the judgment as 'constitutional'.[73]

It was the preeminence that the Court gave to the principle – as a justification for the recognition of a limited standing that must prevail over a 'procedural gap' – that led Constantinesco and Jacqué to attach the label 'constitutional' to the principle. For Constantinesco, the Court expressed in *Chernobyl* 'a coherent overall vision of the Community's institutional order and of its structuring principles', specifically of the principle of institutional balance that it 'established as a "constitutional principle"'.[74] While the inverted commas still denote a certain reservation over the use of 'constitutional' attribute, Constantinesco did not hesitate to conclude that the principle thereby became the expression of separation of powers at the EU level.[75] Jacqué, in turn, while noting the due differences between separation of powers and institutional balance, concluded that the *Chernobyl* invited 'a reflection on the constitutional principles of EU law', which 'the Court will carry out at the rhythm of the cases that it will receive'.[76]

By labelling these developments 'constitutional', and drawing the parallels with separation of powers, these academics were stressing an evolution that '[seemed] to lead Communities increasingly towards techniques of national law'.[77] But they were also agents in slowly opening the way for the 'theoretical schemes' that would in the future shape an institutional system which, in essence, was still largely a product of institutional practice.[78] Yet the explicit analogy between institutional balance and separation of powers was far from unanimous. Separation of powers was also mentioned to deny any analogy with institutional balance. Boulois argued forcefully in his handbook that 'the division of powers characteristic of the Community's institutional system is not … a modality of such a separation and cannot become one for the reason that the institutions do not derive from the same legitimacy'.[79] This was the reason that, in his view, rendered the legal protection of the scope of competences so crucial.

[72] M Thill, 'Jurisprudence récente de la Cour concernant le Parlement européen' (1994) 1 *Tendances actuelles et évolution de la jurisprudence de la Cour de justice des Communautés européennes: suivi annuel* (Ed Institut européen d'administration publique – Maastricht) 1, 10 (*Chernobyl* 'underlines forcefully – if it were still necessary – that the Court … has the nature of a constitutional Court'); Bonichot (n 56) 448 ('the Court is increasingly asserting itself as the Communities' Supreme Court').

[73] This point is, however, noted, in very different terms by Jacqué (n 21, para 13), on the one hand, who speculates whether the Court had realised that the 'silence of certain Member States' during the 1985 intergovernmental conference meant that they thought that the question would be settled by the Court; and Bebr (n 21) 679–80, on the other, for whom, 'the fundamental requirement of the rule of law had to prevail in this instance over the inertia of the Member States'.

[74] Constantinesco (n 62) 453.

[75] ibid 454.

[76] Jacqué (n 21) para 21.

[77] Constaninesco (n 62) 455.

[78] Contrasting the Community system to internal constitutional law, see C Blumann and L Dubois, *Droit Institutionnel de l'Union Européenne* (Litec, 2004) 123.

[79] J Boulois, *Droit Institutionnel de l'Union Européenne*, 5th edn (Montchrestien, 1995) 143–44.

Those who resisted the too easy likening of institutional balance to separation of powers preferred to point out the specific traits of institutional balance and the contribution of *Chernobyl* in this regard. The Court had identified the 'substantive content' of the principle: it simply meant that 'each institution must respect the competences of the others, and that breaches of the rule imposing such respect must be open to judicial sanction'.[80] Yet, while this was affirmed explicitly for the first time in *Chernobyl*, this content was hardly noteworthy. Bradley associated this notion of institutional balance to the principles of conferred powers and rule of law, which he identified as 'respectively … the political and the jurisdictional elements' of institutional balance.[81] The mandate that the Treaty defined for the Court – 'to ensure that the law is observed' – invoked explicitly in the judgment, enabled the Court 'to take account of structural considerations' and, hence, to create 'new means of recourse'.[82] Not going this far, Jacqué noted that the institutional balance is composed of a series of specific balances, expressed in the legal bases, which depend on the interests at stake, that the Court must preserve.[83] He stressed the dynamic side of the principle, which enabled the institutions, through loyal cooperation, to mutually adjust their relationships within the powers assigned by the Treaty.[84] Nevertheless, Jacqué pointed out the limits of the Court as *guardian* of the institutional balance, and attached this dynamism to the role of the other institutions.[85] Bradley also invoked this dynamic character and noted its clear consequence: 'far from being an "empty formula"', institutional balance has 'both allowed, and defined the limits of, a significant development in the Community's institutional structure'.[86] The Court's 'creative' reliance on the principle of institutional balance was evident. At the same time, the Court itself claimed to be bound by the 'balance created by the Treaties' and saw its duty as ensuring that 'the provisions of the Treaties concerning the institutional balance *are fully applied*'.[87] Manifestly, the line between, on the one hand, preserving the institutional balance – a task that Advocate General van Gerven considered to be outside of the purview of the courts – and, on the other, changing it is a very fluid one. More accurately, Blumann and Dubois indicated the 'constant tension between the need of changing and the need of preserving the existing order', a tension which institutional balance reflects.[88]

[80] Bradley (n 57) 255.
[81] ibid 255–56.
[82] ibid 256.
[83] Jacqué (n 21), para 17.
[84] Jacqué (n 21), para 20. The characterisation of institutional balance as having a passive and an active component appears to come from Constantinesco, 'Les institutions. Présentation Géneral' in JCL Europe, Fasc 200, JCL Droit international, fasc 161-10, cited by C Schmitter, 'Equilibre Institutionnel, Principe de l'–' in A Barav and C Philip (eds), *Dictionnaire Juridique des Communautés Européennes* (Presses Universitaires de France, 1993) 473, 475.
[85] Jacqué (n 21), paras 19, 20. See also J-P Jacqué, *Droit institutionnel de l'Union européenne* (Dalloz, 2001) 180, who characterised *Chernobyl* as an instance of this dynamism without however discussing whether the Court *had changed* the institutional balance defined in the Treaty.
[86] Bradley (n 57) 255. *Chernobyl* was another instance of 'the dynamic, and indeed creative, reliance by the Court on the concept of institutional balance'.
[87] Case C-70/88 *Chernobyl* (n 1) paras 21, 25 (emphasis added).
[88] Blumann and Dubois (n 78) 126.

B. Another View: The Parliament as a Litigant in a Reversal of Jurisprudence

While the commentaries cited so far indicate the constitutional leaning of some of the doctrine, this was not a uniform reading of the judgment. The analysis of Chambault in the *Revue du Marché Comum* is illustrative of a different stance. Chambault's general approach was that the judgment represented 'a reversal of case law, but one that [was] both limited and strongly reasoned'.[89] He noted the passages where the Court stressed the importance of the institutional balance established by the Treaty as evidence that the Court *did not* arrogate to itself the power to modify the institutional balance of the Treaty, but instead *acted to improve* that balance.[90] He argued that the principle of institutional balance needed to be sanctioned by the Court because of the judicial powers assigned to it by Treaty. The novelty of *Chernobyl* lay, then, on the recognition that each institution must have 'a legal remedy, among those laid down in the Treaties' that is certain and effective.[91] The conditional recognition of the Parliament's standing meant, he argued, that the Court refused to be a 'regulator of a dynamic institutional balance, as can be the diplomatic conference of the Member States'.[92] The Court thereby had taken distance from the arguments of the Parliament that, in previous cases, had sought the recognition of institutional balance as equality among the institutions.[93] And yet he concluded that the judgment was the culmination of an evolution of over a decade that had solidified the standing status of the Parliament.

Chambault further identified the elements of institutional balance that, in his view, *Chernobyl* had stabilised: institutional balance has a conventional origin (each institution must act within the competences defined in the constitutive treaties), and it evolves if the Treaties change; it presupposes a separation of powers between the institutions that is legally established and its breach must be judicially sanctioned; because such control must be effective, procedural breaches must be filled.[94] In his analysis, *Chernobyl* boiled down to a contribution to the legal-dogmatic construction of the principle of institutional balance, a contribution that also reflected the Court's constant search for the agreement of the Member States. In short, a legal solution to a deeply political matter.

Without this detail of analysis, the handbooks of the 1990s and early 2000s stuck largely to the technical aspect of the standing of the Parliament before the Court. While the relevance that they gave to *Chernobyl* varied, there is little or no echo of the constitutional role of the Court or any constitutional characterisation of the principle of

[89] J-F Chambault, 'L'ouverture du recours en annulation au Parlement européen: aboutissement et cohérence d'une décennie de jurisprudence' (1991) 343 *Revue du Marché Commun* 40. Similarly, Bonichot (n 56) 446; and Condinanzi, who stresses that *Comitology* is not 'espressamente rinegata' and that the Court in *Chernobyl* only considered that the solution there adopted was not sufficient in all instances (Condinanzi (n 21) 135).

[90] Case C-70/88 *Chernobyl* (n 1) paras 21, 25 (see n 87); Chambault (n 89) 43.

[91] Chambault (n 89) 43.

[92] ibid 47.

[93] Similarly, Thill (n 72) 9–10.

[94] Chambault (n 89) 41.

institutional balance. Most recognised – even if to different degrees – the fundamental importance that the judgment had for the institutional position of the Parliament.[95] But *Chernobyl* appeared also as just one step in the process of progressively defining the content of the principle, without any particular emphasis.[96] In some, the significance of the judgment for the evolution of the EU institutional system is fully absent. *Chernobyl* is then either cited in sections dealing with the action for annulment, losing any constitutional veneer under the categorisation of applicants in actions of annulment;[97] or treated as a matter of choice of legal basis, being then just one judgment among others.[98] Others still, mostly ignored the judgment.[99]

C. An Intermediate Position: The Political Stakes of an Important Institutional Development

By contrast, the significance of *Chernobyl* to the institutional role of the Parliament in the evolution of EU law and its political stakes were stressed by the English handbook authors, without losing sight of the judgment's dictum on standing. Craig and de Búrca noted the strategic use that the Parliament made of its litigation rights and placed *Chernobyl* in this line of institutional evolution.[100] They indicated too how the Parliament used the position it acquired in *Chernobyl* to advance litigation on legal bases and secure its procedural rights in the legislative process.[101] They noted also the judicial recognition of the Parliament's 'democratic credentials' in the *Isoglucose* cases,[102] but did not see the overall reinforcement of the Parliament, in particular since the Single European Act, as necessarily '[rendering] the Community or the Union a considerably more democratic organization'.[103]

This was the point that Jo Shaw highlighted. Her premise was the importance of each institution's role 'in relation to questions of democracy, legitimacy and institutional efficiency'.[104] Against this background, she took *Chernobyl* as evidence of the Court's contribution to secure institutional balance through policing the correct use of legal bases – a type of legal dispute that, as she noted, is 'intensely political'.[105] *Chernobyl*

[95] Implicit only in G Isaac and M Blanquet, *Droit communautaire général*, 8th edn (Colin, 2001) 288, who mention that the *Chernobyl* solution was taken up in subsequent revisions of the EEC Treaty.

[96] Jacqué, *Droit institutionnel de l'Union européenne* (n 85) 177–80. In some cases, those sections omit *Chernobyl* from their accounts: Boulois (n 79)143–44.

[97] P Manin, *Les Communautés Européennes. L'Union européenne. Droit Institutionnel*, 3rd edn (Pedone, 1997) 378; PJ Slot, 'Le role du juge et du législateur dans le développement de droit communautaire et du Droit des États membres' in PJ Slot and W Van Gerven (eds), *Droit Européen* (Pedone, 1998) 44; and to, a large extent, Isaac and Blanquet (n 95).

[98] J Rideau, *Droit Institutionnel de l'Union et des Communautés Européennes* (LGJD, 1999) 139.

[99] Boulois (n 79) does not mention *Chernobyl* in his section on institutional balance (ibid 143–44), neither does Paolo Mengozzi in his section on standing in action for annulment, referring only to the Treaty: P Mengozzi, *Il Diritto Communitario e dell'Unione Europea* (CEDAM, 1997) 207.

[100] P Craig and G de Búrca, *EC Law: Text, Cases, & Materials* (Oxford University Press, 1995) 65–68. Equally noted by Jacqué (n 21) and Bradley (n 57) 245 and fn 16. On the risks that the Parliament would use its newly found right inappropriately, see Bradley (n 57) 253; Bonichot (n 56) 449.

[101] Craig and de Búrca (n 100) 68–69.

[102] Case C-138/79 *Roquette Frères* (n 14) and Case C-139/79, *Maizena v Council* EU:C:1980:250.

[103] Craig and de Búrca (n 100) 57, 65–67.

[104] J Shaw, *Law of the European Union*, 2nd edn (Palgrave, 1996).

[105] ibid 70 and 175.

was 'the logical conclusion to the process of recognition of the Parliament in the institutional structure of the EU begun in the *Isogluclose* cases'.[106] The conditional standing it recognised to the Parliament was, importantly, 'a change of heart by the Court' that foreshadowed the Treaty revision of Article 173.[107] More emphatically, Mancini and Keeling noted the contribution of *Chernobyl* to strengthening the democratic legitimacy of the Community's 'system of checks and balances'.[108]

With these exceptions, the possible significance of *Chernobyl* to strengthen democracy in the Community and in the Union was mostly absent from the academic analyses. It appeared only in passing in a couple of commentaries. Condinanzi noted that, by 'interpreting the Treaties in an evolutive sense', the Court contributed to 'ensure, beyond the letter of the norm, respect for fundamental principles of the Community legal order, among which feature prominently the *democratic model* of the rule of law [*stato di diritto*]'.[109] This was illustrative of the views on democracy in the Union that envisaged it from a Westminster-type point of view.[110] In his analysis, the judgment narrowed the distance between the democratic legitimacy of the Parliament and its powers under the Treaty, even if placing a parliament in the need to resort to a court to defend its prerogatives remained questionable.[111] Bradley, on the other hand, mentioned democracy to point out the limits of the Parliament's conditional standing. Since standing was granted as a matter of legal protection, he asked whether the Parliament would be 'unable to argue before the Court that a legislative measure infringes the Treaty or constitutes a violation of the fundamental rights of the *citizen (and voter)*'. Such possibility could be in reach but was highly unlikely: while 'the Court may reach findings on such matters proprio motu', the Parliament had 'only exceptionally [resorted] to judicial proceedings to protect interests other than its own' and was unlikely to deviate from that practice.[112] Pushing 'democratization through law' did not seem to be on the agenda, at least not as a result of *Chernobyl*.[113]

IV. Judicial Reception: The Faded Legal Component of a Political Principle

A. *Chernobyl*'s First Decade

The judgments issued in the immediate aftermath of *Chernobyl* contrast with the 'grand' constitutional readings, while confirming the importance of the judgment in securing the Parliament's position in the institutional balance established by the Treaties.

[106] ibid 175.
[107] ibid 320.
[108] G Mancini and D Keeling, 'Democracy and the European Court of Justice' (1994) 57 *Modern Law Review* 175, 181.
[109] Condinanzi (n 21) 136, emphasis added.
[110] G Majone, 'Europe's "Democratic Deficit": The Question of Standards' (1998) 4 *European Law Journal* 5.
[111] Condinanzi (n 21) 137.
[112] Bradley (n 57) 252–53, emphasis added.
[113] The term is from A Caiola and F Nicola, 'Defending Democracy Through Law: The Establishment pf the Legal Service of the European Parliament' (2023) 46 *Fordham International Law* 1.

They mostly gave the Court the opportunity to solidify the path it had opened in that judgment.

In two judgments, the Court pushed back against the attempts of the UK and of the Council to limit the range of actions where the Parliament would have standing. In a legal-basis dispute, it rejected summarily the UK's argument that the Parliament's right of action would arise only if the Commission disagreed with the Parliament on the legal appraisal of the Parliament's prerogatives.[114] In another instance, ruling on the Parliament's right to be consulted, the Court rejected the Council's claim that the Parliament's standing was limited to 'cases where the balance of the Treaty system risks being disturbed or there is a substantial infringement of the Parliament's basic prerogatives', while implying that *Chernobyl* was limited to legal basis disputes in cooperation procedures. In both cases, the Court reiterated the criteria set in *Chernobyl*.

Subsequent case law indicates that the main task that *Chernobyl* left to the Court was to delimit the precise scope of *Chernobyl*, that is, which parliamentary prerogatives justified standing under the judgment's criteria.[115] A case pertaining to the Parliament's right to be consulted in the adoption of the Community's financial regulation, decided in 1994, confirmed that its right to participate in the legislative procedures was one of such prerogatives.[116] Because standing was conditional, the Court specified that the Parliament needed to indicate 'in an appropriate manner the substance of the prerogative to be safeguarded and how that prerogative [was] allegedly infringed'.[117] In that same case, the Court strengthened the institutional importance of the Parliament by referring to the passages of the *Isoglucose* cases where the right to participate in the legislative procedure – in need of judicial protection – was characterised as the limited expression at the Community level of the principle of democracy.[118] Nevertheless, it was clear that the Parliament's right to participate in the legislative procedure depended strictly on there being a Treaty norm that secured the Parliament's involvement, no matter the democratic relevance of the matters that may be decided without involving the Parliament.[119] Later on, the Court maintained this position: despite the step that it had taken in *Chernobyl*, on the grounds of a political and legal principle (institutional balance), its reliance on the principle of democracy would not trump choices clearly expressed in the Treaty.[120]

[114] Case C-295/90 *Parliament v Council* EU:C:1992:294, paras 8–9 (annulment of the student's residence directive).

[115] Jacqué (n 21) para 20; Chambault (n 89) 47; Thill (n 72) 10; Craig and de Búrca (n 100) 454 (citing Bradley (n 57)).

[116] Case C-316/91 *Parliament v Council* EU:C:1994:76, paras 11, 19 (Lomé Convention). See also Case C-58/94 *Netherlands v Council* EU:C:1996:171.

[117] Case C-316/91 (n 114) para 13; Case C-156/93 *Parliament v Commission* EU:C:1995:238, paras 10, 11, 13; Case C-303/94 *Parliament v Council* EU:C:1996:238, para 17; Case C-189/97 *Parliament v Council* EU:C:1999:366, para 13.

[118] Case C-316/91 (n 116) para 17. See also Case C-300/89 *Commission v Council* EU:C:1991:244, paras 20–21 (annulling the Titanium Dioxide Directive also on the grounds of breach of prerrogatives of the Parliament due to the use of the wring legal basis).

[119] Case C-58/94 (n 116) paras 32, 37, 41 (access to documents, granted at the time through the decisions of the institutions based on their power of internal organisation).

[120] Case C-130/10 *Parliament v Council* EU:C:2012:472, paras 80–82 (on the Common Foreign Security Policy).

Legal-basis disputes during the 1990s, though not always decided to the advantage of the Parliament, confirmed the position that the Parliament had acquired with *Chernobyl*.[121] Thus, the Parliament's right to participate in legislative procedures required, specifically, that the Parliament be reconsulted where pertinent to secure that it had a substantive say on the final content of the acts.[122] Yet, as successive Treaty revisions solidified the participation of the Parliament in legislative procedures, and in particular with the extension of the co-decision procedures, legal-basis disputes largely subsided. In this regard, the Treaties fundamentally changed the 'system for distributing powers among the different Community institutions'.[123] This is the essence of institutional balance, making it largely a self-referential principle deprived of autonomous content.[124]

B. Institutional Balance as a Static and Political Principle

The principle reappeared again in the late 2000s, but, naturally, the element of legal protection following *Chernobyl* that had been so important in solidifying the institutional position of the Parliament had lost its relevance. The constitutional relevance of institutional balance as a principle that could push for, or endorse, Treaty changes – the 'dynamic' character that had enabled the Court to 'supplement the Treaty' – clearly subsided. *Chernobyl* remained a single instance thereof.[125]

The principle now supported the Court in refining aspects of the distribution of powers between the institutions and in preserving the Treaty system against what could become important disruptions. Thus, in *Parliament v Council* (list of safe countries of origin), institutional balance strengthened the argument that the institutions cannot define, in secondary provisions, decision-making procedures that amend the procedure defined in the Treaty: such practice would undermine a principle that 'requires that each of the institutions must exercise its powers with due regard for the powers of the other institutions'.[126] In a consistent line of case law, the Court resorted to institutional balance to deny standing to the governments of regions or other local authorities within Member States, in the capacity of 'Member States'.[127]

In many cases, institutional balance was either a preliminary point in the Court's reasoning or an ancillary aspect of the institutions' assigned competences, to signify 'a

[121] Case C-187/93 *Parliament v Council* EU:C:1994:265, para 16.

[122] Case C-65/90 *Parliament v Council* EU:C:1992:325, paras 11–14; Case C-388/92 *Parliament v Council* EU:C:1994:213, paras 10, 19 (transport).

[123] Case C-70/88 *Chernobyl* (n 1) para 21.

[124] Case C-316/91 (n 116) para 11; De Witte (n 8) 144. Chamon identifies an autonomous content in this self-referential character: it indicates the principle's systemic protection function (M Chamon, *The European Parliament and Delegated Legislation: An Institutional Balance Perspective* (Hart Publishing, 2022) 2–3).

[125] De Witte (n 8).

[126] Case C-133/06 *Parliament v Council* EU:C:2008:257, paras 53–57. Similarly, and more recently, Case C-275/20 *Commission v Council* EU:C:2022:142 (on the extension of the period of entitlement for audiovisual co-productions as provided for in Art 5 of the Protocol on Cultural Cooperation to the Free Trade Agreement between the European Union and its Member States, of the one part, and the Republic of Korea).

[127] Case C-452/98 *Nederlandse Antillen v Council* EU:C:2001:623, para 50; Case C-417/04 P *Regione Siciliana v Commission* EU:C:2006:282, para 21.

system allocating powers among the EU institutions', without having any specific bearing on the outcome of the judgment.[128] But there were important exceptions, where the principle of institutional balance was a basis to entrench the Treaty's allocation of powers, in view of the general functions of the institutions. Two cases stand out: *Macro-financial Assistance* and *EPSU*.

In *Macro-financial Assistance*, the Council, supported by several Member States, contested the Commission's withdrawal of a legislative proposal on the grounds that, in doing so, the Commission had exceeded its Treaty powers and, consequently, had undermined the institutional balance.[129] No such powers are conferred on the Commission, so they claimed, in the conditions in which it had withdrawn its proposal. The Court drew on several Treaty provisions to conclude that the Commission had that power, subject to providing reasons for the withdrawal that both the institutions and the Court could ascertain.[130] Short of such reasons, withdrawal would amount to a veto right which would indeed be contrary to institutional balance. In this case, the grounds the Commission had invoked were such as to justify the withdrawal and that much sufficed to comply with the principle of institutional balance.[131] Unlike the *Isoglucose* cases, the principle of democracy – invoked by the claimants – had no bearing on the dispute. Considering the power of the Commission to withdraw a proposal as 'inseparable' from the right of initiative, the Court summarily stated that '*there can be no question*, in this instance, of an infringement of [the principle of democracy laid down in] Article 10(1) and (2) TEU'.[132]

The Court took a similar position, in very different circumstances, in *EPSU v Commission*.[133] The protection of the Commission's right of initiative meant, in this case, that, contrary to the appellant's claims, the Commission can refuse to submit to the Council a proposal for a decision implementing an agreement concluded between management and labour under the European social dialogue provisions. The Court invoked Article 17(2) TEU in support of this conclusion, arguing that it 'reflects the principle of institutional balance, characteristic of the institutional structure of the European Union'.[134] In this case, this reliance on the general provision of Article 17(2) TEU, in combination with institutional balance, enabled the Court to go against the letter of the Treaty.[135] If in *Macro-financial Assistance* a reading of institutional balance

[128] See, respectively, Case C-539/09 *Commission v Germany* EU:C:2011:733, paras 56–57 (a case opposing the Commission to Germany over the latter's objection to an audit by the Court of Auditors, where the Court concluded that Germany had breached its duties to collaborate with the Court of Auditors); and Case C-660/13 *Council v Commission* EU:C:2016:616, paras 31, 33–38 and 40–46 (Swiss Financial Contribution), in which the Court held that the Commission needed to secure the Council's approval prior to signing an addendum to the memorandum of understanding with Switzerland on the latter's contribution to the EU budget.

[129] Case C-409/13 *Council v Commission* EU:C:2015:217 ('*Macro-financial Assistance*').

[130] ibid paras 67, 70–78.

[131] ibid paras 85–94.

[132] ibid para 96. Institutional balance served a similar function in *Puppinck*, preserving the Commission's power of initiative against the binding character of a successfully registered ECI: Case C-418/18 P, *Puppinck v Commission* EU:C:2019:1113, para 65.

[133] Case C-928/19 P *EPSU v Commission* EU:C:2021:656.

[134] ibid, para 48.

[135] According to Art 155(2) TFEU, 'agreements concluded at Union level shall be implemented … by a Council decision on a proposal from the Commission'.

in isolation from the principle of democracy precluded a change that was defensible in the post-Lisbon context,[136] in *EPSU* it hindered the specificity of the European social dialogue, and its democratic function that the Court had upheld in the past.[137]

V. Conclusion

Chernobyl was undoubtedly a landmark judgment in the 1990s. Standing in actions of annulment was more than just a means of ensuring the legal protection of an institution whose prerogatives should – from a liberal-constitutional perspective – be protected by political means. It reinforced the position of the Parliament in the institutional system of the Treaty through a contortionist reasoning: the principle of institutional balance – purportedly followed only insofar as defined in the Treaty – enabled the Court to give the Parliament what the silence of the Treaty had denied it. The legal technique of a 'procedural gap' overcame the Member States disagreement on the role that of the Parliament in the EU set-up.

Many greeted the audacity of the judgment that, in line with *Les Verts*, marked the evolution of EU law towards a 'constitutional order'. Yet *Chernobyl* was the only instance in which the Court used the principle of institutional balance to 'supplement' the institutional balance that the Treaty had enshrined.[138] The judicial activism that some had feared, and that others unmistakably attributed to *Chernobyl*,[139] did not ensue. Neither did the empowerment of the Parliament following *Chernobyl* mean that the principle had the vocation of protecting democracy, as had also been argued. In different ways, both the judgments in *Macro-financial Assistance* and in *EPSU* confirm the dissociation between the two principles.

Chernobyl is part of the history of EU law. The contrast between the most emphatic academic analyses and its judicial reception, however, tells a story of the limits both of EU constitutional thinking (in particular, of the misplaced analogy between institutional balance and separation of powers) and of legal-dogmatic constructions too prone to identify the content of a principle that can be, in reality, very thin and easily shifted by judicial practice.

[136] See further D Ritleng, 'Does the European Court of Justice take democracy seriously? Some thoughts about the Macro-Financial Assistance case' (2016) 53 *Common Market Law Review* 11.

[137] P Carré and M Steiert, 'Social Europe without Social Dialogue: Decision of the Court of Justice of the European Union in C-928/19 P European Federation of Public Service Unions' (2022) 18 *European Constitutional Law Review* 315. See Case T-135/96 *Union Européenne de l'artisanat et des petites et moyennes entreprises (UEAPME)* EU:T:1998:128.

[138] De Witte (n 8).

[139] On judicial activism, see Bradley (n 57) 257, replying to such concerns. See also D Chalmers, *European Union Law – Law and EU Government*, vol 1 (Ashgate, 1998) 327.

PART C

Judicial Architecture within the Union

11

Plaumann: The Narrow Gateway to Direct Judicial Review

ALBERTINA ALBORS-LLORENS

I. Introduction: Historical and Doctrinal Context

One of the arguments used by the Court of Justice of the European Union (CJEU or 'the Court') in its seminal decision in *Van Gend en Loos* to reach the conclusion that the (then) Community constituted 'a new legal order of international law'[1] whose subjects were not only the Member States but also their nationals, was that the Treaties had established a set of 'institutions endowed with sovereign rights, the exercise of which affects Member States and also their citizens'.[2] It followed, therefore, that if the Union institutions had the power to impose obligations on natural and legal persons, then the Treaties should also provide for a complete system of judicial protection against potentially unlawful acts of those institutions. Accordingly, the European Economic Community Treaty (EEC) put in place such a system, reflected today in the Treaty on the Functioning of the European Union (TFEU), offering a combination of direct and indirect procedural avenues to the EU judiciary that could be used to challenge illegal acts[3] and omissions[4] of the Union institutions, to remedy the consequences of these illegal acts or omissions[5] and to protect the interests of applicants and other parties while one of the main direct actions was pending before the CJEU.[6] In this composite

[1] Case 26/62 *Van Gend en Loos v Nederlandse Administratie der Belastingen* EU:C:1963:1, 12.

[2] ibid.

[3] The direct actions that can be brought by natural and legal persons to challenge the legality of legally binding acts of the Union institutions are the action for annulment (Art 263 TFEU) and the plea of illegality (Art 277 TFEU) – though the latter can only be brought if another direct action, which typically will be an action for annulment, is already pending before the Court. The indirect mechanism to challenge those acts is provided by the possibility of a national court making a preliminary reference on validity to the Court (Art 267 TFEU) in relation to an allegedly illegal EU act that is at stake in proceedings pending before a national court.

[4] The action for a failure act provides a direct avenue before the Court to challenge unlawful omissions of the Union institutions (Art 265 TFEU).

[5] The action for damages allows private parties to claim for compensation directly before the Union judicature for damage or loss suffered because of illegal Union acts (Arts 268 and 340(2) TFEU).

[6] Arts 278 and 279 TFEU, respectively, provide for negative and positive interim relief, that is provisional legal protection for private applicants, while one of the main direct actions – either an action for annulment, a plea of illegality, an action for a failure to act or an action for damages – is pending before the Court.

of judicial remedies, the action for annulment – now set out in Article 263 TFEU – has always occupied a central position because it is the most direct and expedient route for the judicial review of unlawful legally binding acts of the Union institutions.

While private parties were included in the list of applicants who could bring an action for annulment against a Union act, the second paragraph of (as it was then) Article 173 EEC Treaty set out obscure – and, as it turned out, formidable – conditions of standing for such an application to be admissible. In the initial formulation of these conditions that was reflected in that provision,[7] private parties who were not the addressees[8] of a Union act had to overcome three obstacles to prove they had *locus standi*. Thus, they had to show that the act was, in substance, a decision – either addressed to another person or in the form of a regulation – and that they were both directly and individually concerned by it. The Treaty was silent as to how these conditions were to be construed and it fell to the Court to breathe life into them. In *Plaumann*,[9] the Court explained, for the first time, what it meant for a non-addressee to be individually concerned by a Union act. As we shall see, the choice made by the Court in that decision by providing a very restrictive interpretation of the notion of individual concern, was to have a profound effect on the prospects of private parties when challenging acts of the Union institutions.

Those initial standing conditions were somewhat softened over the years both through the interpretative work of the CJEU and through of the Lisbon Treaty amendments. The former eventually led to the dispensation from the requirement that the act challenged had to be *in substance* a decision, a change now reflected in the letter of Article 263(4) TFEU.[10] This meant that *all* legally binding Union acts, and not only decisions, could be subject to annulment proceedings brought by natural or legal persons if these could demonstrate that they were directly and individually concerned by them.[11] The latter provided an additional set of less rigorous standing conditions applicable to the challenge of a certain type of acts: *regulatory* acts. These conditions constitute now the so-called 'Lisbon test' which, crucially, does not prescribe the satisfaction of the requirement of individual concern. Instead, a private applicant must demonstrate that the act in question is a regulatory act, that they are directly concerned by it and that the act in question does not entail implementing measures.

It came as no surprise that, following the entry into force of the Lisbon Treaty, private applicants endeavoured to prove standing based on the 'Lisbon test' rather than on the

[7] This wording was then also later reflected in Art 230(4) European Community Treaty (EC).

[8] Addressees of a Union act have always had automatic standing under the Treaty to challenge such an act.

[9] Case 25/62 *Plaumann v Commission* EU:C:1963:17.

[10] After a long period of uncertainty and inconsistency in the case law, the Court clarified, in an anti-dumping case (Case C-358/89 *Extramet v Council* EU:C:1991:214, para 14) that private parties could challenge true regulations so long as they fulfilled the tests of direct and individual concern. The same conclusion followed soon afterwards in *Codorníu*, in the case law concerning the organisation of agricultural markets (Case C-309/89 *Codorníu v Council* EU:C:1994:197, para 19); and in relation to the challenge of directives (Case T-135/96 *Union Européenne de l'artisanat et des petites et moyennes entreprises (UEAPME) v Council* EU:T:1998:128, paras 67–69). See the excellent and comprehensive study of this line of case law by A Arnull, 'Private Applicants and the Action for Annulment since *Codorníu*' (2001) 38 *Common Market Law Review* 1, 20–23 and 51.

[11] The Lisbon Treaty finally amended Art 263(4) TFEU to reflect this development, and now this provision refers to 'acts' in general and not just decisions. See also Case C-583/11P *Inuit Tapiriit Kanatami and Others v European Parliament and Council* EU:C:2013:625, para 56.

longstanding and 'general' standing test centred on the notions of direct and individual concern, which remained in the Treaty. However, while the Lisbon test is, by nature, less restrictive than the general standing test, private applicants have been frequently unable to fulfil its conditions, the most notable examples being those cases when they have tried to challenge EU legislative acts – which are not regulatory acts[12] – or acts that require further implementing measures either at EU or national level.[13] As a result, the general standing test has continued to be routinely applied on a residual basis in those situations. In this context, the Court has weathered storms of criticism and has tenaciously upheld to this day the original interpretation of the notion of individual concern formulated in *Plaumann*.

Plaumann is a landmark case in the history of EU law because it set the tone for a controversial line of case law and shaped the expectations of private applicants – the so-called non-privileged applicants – in the direct challenge of Union acts. This chapter will explore the background to that case, the reasoning deployed by the Court, its reception in academic and judicial circles and the multiple effects of the decision. These have ranged from those referring to the specific interpretation of the test of individual concern – including the departure from the rigid construction of individual concern adopted in *Plaumann* in several exceptional cases – to the broader implications of that case on the Union's abiding objective to provide a system of judicial protection without any gaps.

II. The Facts of and Background to *Plaumann* and the Opinion of the Advocate General

The facts underpinning *Plaumann* seemed, at first sight, rather uninspiring. However, they were to yield an early textbook example of the use of a panoply of direct actions before the Court by a private applicant and provide a first opportunity for the Court to elucidate the meaning of some of the standing conditions applicable to private parties in the context of the action for annulment. In July 1962, Plaumann & Co, a German importer of fruits, brought annulment proceedings before the Court against a Commission decision addressed to Germany that had refused to authorise this Member State to suspend partially the custom duty set out in the Common Customs Tariff for the importation of clementines from third countries into the EU. In the same set of proceedings, the applicant also brought an action for damages against the Commission. Finally, Plaumann also made two consecutive applications for interim relief[14] shortly after it had brought these two main actions.

[12] Case T-18/10 *Inuit Tapiriit Kanatami v European Parliament and Council* EU:T:2011:419, para 56.

[13] Case C-274/12P *Telefónica v Commission* EU:C:2013:852, paras 27–39.

[14] Both applications for interim relief were unsuccessful. The first Order of the Court, delivered on 31 August 1962, dismissed the first application for interim measures on the basis that the urgency and necessity of the measure requested had not been sufficiently established (see Case 25/62R *Plaumann v Commission* EU:C:1962:32, 125). A second Order of the Court of 21 December 1962 dismissed the second application for interim relief on the basis that it had not been proved that there was a high likelihood that the applicant would suffer serious damage (Case 25/62R *Plaumann v Commission* EU:C:1962:50, 128).

The case raised several legal issues which concerned principally the action for annulment, although some referred to the action for damages. In relation to the action for annulment three main points emerged, all of which focused on the admissibility of the action and, specifically, on the construction of the original standing conditions applicable to non-privileged applicants set out then by Article 173(2) EEC Treaty. The first two centred on the type of acts that could be challenged by private applicants. At the time, this provision allowed non-addressees to challenge decisions addressed to 'another person'. Given that the Commission decision at stake in *Plaumann* was addressed to Germany, the Commission had posited that a Member State could not constitute 'another person' within the meaning of Article 173(2) EEC Treaty. Furthermore, the Commission had also contended that, although the act had been labelled as a decision, it was, in substance, a general act of a legislative nature and hence would appear to fall outside of the scope of challenge by private parties under the contemporary formulation of the *locus standi* conditions in the Treaty. As seen above, this seemed to require that the act being challenged by a private party should be substantively a decision, that is an individual act. The third issue, which would become the core one and the reason why the case was – and remains – so significant, referred to the interpretation of the notion of individual concern.

The judgment of the Court was preceded by the Opinion of Advocate General Roemer,[15] delivered on 28 May 1963, whose conclusion that the action for annulment should be dismissed as inadmissible was later mirrored later by the judgment of the Court. However, the reasoning employed by the Advocate General, while similar in some key points, was by no means identical to the one ultimately espoused by the Court. Thus, Advocate General Roemer rejected the suggestion that a decision addressed to a Member State could not be challenged by private applicants on the basis that this would attribute to 'the authors of the Treaty an intention to narrow down the right of action to an excessive degree'.[16] He had more sympathy for the argument that the Commission decision in question could be, in substance, a measure of a legislative character and hence potentially excluded from challenge by private parties. By implication, this meant that the *true* legal nature of an EU act being challenged might have to be examined in all cases[17] – and therefore not only where the act had been labelled as a regulation, but also where the act took the form of a decision – with a view to ascertaining that the act was, truly and in nature, an individual act. He predicted that *Plaumann* would provide an opportunity for the Court to address this point,[18] as indeed turned out to be the case.

Advocate General Roemer's observations were particularly salient in relation to his proposed interpretation of the concept of individual concern. He submitted that Plaumann was not individually concerned because it was a member of an 'abstractly defined group of all those who wished to import clementines during the period in question'.[19] Importantly, he observed that the class to which the applicant belonged was 'not ascertainable at the time of issue of the decision'.[20] This construction of the notion

[15] Case 25/62 *Plaumann v Commission* (Opinion of the Advocate General at EU:C:1963:7).
[16] ibid 113.
[17] ibid 113–14.
[18] ibid 114.
[19] ibid 116.
[20] ibid.

of individual concern requiring a private applicant to be a member of a group of people that was ascertainable before the contested EU act was adopted showed a certain affinity with the 'closed category' test that the Court would regularly use later as a tool to determine individual concern. Crucially, however, Mr Roemer did not go as far as to suggest that the class should be 'fixed' before the measure entered into force. This seems an important difference, with the construction eventually adopted by the Court in the cases following *Plaumann*. Thus, the Court would go on to hold that standing would be reserved for those members of a group of people that was 'fixed' before a measure entered into force, thereby encapsulating in its interpretation an element of retroactivity. By contrast, this did not seem a necessary component of the Advocate General's construction, which simply required the possibility of determination of the members of the group.

III. The Judgment of the Court

The judgment of the Court was remarkable in its terseness, particularly considering its seminal importance in determining the circumstances in which a private applicant would satisfy the standing conditions formulated in the Treaty. However, the Court still addressed all three points concerning the admissibility of the action for annulment outlined above.

First, the Court, like its Advocate General, concluded that the expression 'a decision addressed to another person' in Article 173 EEC Treaty should be interpreted broadly to include a decision addressed to a Member State. The Court justified this approach by observing that the 'words and natural meaning of this provision justify the broadest interpretation' and that 'provisions of the Treaty regarding the right of interested parties to bring an action must not be interpreted restrictively'.[21] Given that the Treaty was silent on that point, the Court surmised that a limitation in the meaning of that expression could not be assumed. The judgment therefore seemed start promisingly by suggesting that the Court would be prepared to interpret generously the standing conditions imbued in the original standing test.

Second, the Court did not look beyond the form of the contested decision to consider the legal effects that it created. Instead, it relied on what is today Article 288 TFEU to hold that decisions are characterised by the limited number of persons to whom they are addressed. Given that the Commission decision was addressed to Germany, the measure was to be regarded as a decision 'referring to a particular person and binding on them alone'.[22] The Court therefore did not examine whether, despite the decision being addressed to a Member State, it could have a general character in substance, or in other words whether it constituted a 'disguised' regulation. In short, while the reasoning of the Court was brief, its effect was clear. In interpreting the standing conditions in Article 173 EEC, the Court would consider whether an act adopted in the form of a

[21] Case 25/62 *Plaumann* (n 9) 106–07.
[22] ibid 107.

regulation could be, in nature, a decision – as indeed suggested by the Treaty[23] – but, conversely, it would not contest that an act adopted in the guise of a decision – and thus formally addressed to a Member State or a natural or legal person – was anything other than a 'genuine' decision in substance. This second finding seemed to reinforce the conclusion that the Court was prepared to interpret the *locus standi* conditions in Article 173 EEC Treaty and fill the lacunae left in the Treaty in the spirit of facilitating the access of private parties to the judicial review of EU acts.

Third, the Court was faced with the task of defining the meaning of the notion of 'individual concern' in Article 173 EEC Treaty. It was at this point that the liberal approach permeating the earlier paragraphs of the judgment ended abruptly. The Court provided its famous formulation of individual concern and one which would be repeated thereafter in a multitude of cases and never amended. Thus, it held that non-addressees would be individually concerned if a decision

> affects them by reason of certain attributes or by reason of circumstances in which they are differentiated from all other persons and by virtue of these factors distinguishes them individually just as in the case of the person addressed.[24]

It was clear at this juncture that the Court was going to require a very high degree of individualisation for a non-addressee to satisfy the condition of being individually concerned. In particular, this formula required the applicant to be in a position akin to the addressee of the measure. Its full effect became evident when the Court next applied it to the facts of the case. Thus, the Court held that Plaumann was not individually concerned because it was affected by the Commission decision 'as an importer of clementines, that is to say, by a commercial activity which may at any time be practised by any person'.[25] In other words, and in practical terms, the reason why Plaumann failed to demonstrate individual concern was that it belonged to an 'open category' of people – that is, that of importers of clementines – which could be joined (at least in theory) by other natural or legal persons *after* the measure entered into force. Essentially, therefore, the Court determined that the pursuit of an economic activity – which was moreover likely to be adversely affected by the EU act, as was the case of Plaumann's – was not in itself sufficient to meet the condition of individual concern. After the Court held that Plaumann was not individually concerned, it dismissed the action for annulment as inadmissible, having explained earlier in the judgment that there would be no need to consider whether the applicant was directly concerned if individual concern was not met since the two conditions were cumulative.[26]

[23] This led to the application of the so-called 'abstract terminology test' to ascertain whether acts that had been labelled as regulations were, in fact, 'disguised' decisions. The test was extremely difficult to satisfy in practice, creating another obstacle in the access of natural and legal persons to the action for annulment (see Joined Cases 789 and 790/79 *Calpak v Commission* EU:C:1980:159, para 9). Furthermore, the case law on this point was not entirely consistent and, in some cases, the Court skipped this test in annulment proceedings brought against regulations and only considered whether the applicants were directly and individually concerned (see Case 100/74 *CAM v Commission* EU:C:1975:152, para 19). On the draconian combination of this test and the condition of individual concern and its effect on the chances of private parties to overcome the admissibility stage in annulment proceedings, see A Arnull, 'Private Applicants and the Action for Annulment under Article 173 of the EC Treaty' (1995) 32 *Common Market Law Review* 7, 20–24, 25–40 and 44–49.

[24] Case 25/62 *Plaumann* (n 9) 107.

[25] ibid.

[26] Case 25/62 *Plaumann* (n 9) 107.

The Court did not explicitly state in the case that the applicant would have to belong to a group of people that was fixed and ascertainable before the measure entered in force – what became known later as the 'closed category' test. However, this was the clear implication of the approach followed in *Plaumann* and consistent with the blueprint for individual concern which required a successful applicant to be as individually distinguished as the addressee of the act. Proof of this is that the Court did so soon afterwards in *Toepfer*,[27] decided only two years after *Plaumann*. There, the Court found that a group of private applicants who had applied for import licences before a Commission decision had been adopted were individually concerned since the 'number and identity of these importers had already become fixed and ascertainable' *before* the contested decision had been passed.[28] Other cases followed suit and membership of a limited or 'closed class' of people emerged[29] – and has remained[30] – as the consistent standard to satisfy the *Plaumann* formulation of individual concern and the main reason why interested private parties have so frequently failed to discharge the general test of standing.

Next, the Court turned its attention to the action for damages. The main legal issue arising on the claim for compensation submitted by the applicant was the relationship between the action for annulment and the action for damages. On this, the Court seemed also to take a very strict approach and held that an action for damages arising as result of an unlawful Union act could not be brought unless this measure had first been annulled.[31] The reasoning used by the Court was that, otherwise, an action for damages would be used, in fact, to set aside a Union act that had not been annulled. Practically, this meant that an action for damages was not to be considered as an independent remedy[32] that could be brought in parallel with an action for annulment – as Plaumann had done – or on its own before the Court. Rather, only *after* a Union act had been annulled – presumably through an action for annulment or declared invalid through a preliminary ruling on validity – or a failure to act declared unlawful could an action for damages be litigated. On this basis, the Court went on to dismiss the action for damages as unfounded. This finding of the Court did not seem to have a firm basis on the letter of the Treaty, which has never suggested the subordination of the action for damages to the action for annulment. Further, it failed to appreciate the different purposes – compensatory and declaratory respectively – of these two actions. However, this aspect of the judgment was short-lived. Only eight years later, in *Lütticke*,[33] the Court reversed this approach by confirming – in the context of proceedings where an applicant had brought an action for damages before the Court following from an allegedly illegal failure to act of the Commission which had not been contested by means of an

[27] Joined Cases 106/63 and 107/63 *Toepfer v Commission* EU:C:1965:65.

[28] ibid 411.

[29] See, among many others, Case 62/70 *Bock v Commission* EU:C:1971:108, para 10; Case 97/85 *Deutsche Lebensmittelwerke v Commission* EU:C:1987:243, para 11, which referred to a 'closed circle of persons'; and Case C-321/95P *Stichting Greenpeace Council v Commission* EU:C:1998:1530, para 12.

[30] For more recent examples, see Case C-132/12P *Stichting Woonpunt v Commission* EU:C:2014:100, para 57, referring to the applicants as belonging to a 'closed circle of operators' (ibid para 62); Case C-133/12P *Stichting Woonlinie v Commission* EU:C:2014:105, using the same expression at para 49; and Case T-330/18 *Carvalho v European Parliament and Council* EU:T:2019:324, para 45.

[31] Case 25/62 *Plaumann* (n 9) 108.

[32] See further K Lenaerts, I Maselis and K Gutman, *EU Procedural Law* (Oxford University Press, 2014) 488–89.

[33] Case 4/69 *Lütticke v Commission* EU:C:1971:40, para 6.

Article 265 TFEU action – that the action for damages constituted an independent form of action.[34]

IV. The Significance and Impact of *Plaumann*

The significance of *Plaumann* cannot be overstated. As we have seen, some of the findings in the judgment have been superseded by later developments. Thus, the general standing test currently embodied in Article 263(4) TFEU allows private applicants to challenge other types of legally binding acts – and not just decisions – and actions for damages can be brought independently from an action for annulment. However, the formulation of the notion of individual concern and its practical application in the form of the closed category test have remained resolutely entrenched in the case law with their ripple effect felt to this day. The next sections will aim to explore the range of these implications.

A. The Application of the Closed Category Test

In the years following the decision in *Plaumann*, as the full impact of the application of the individual concern formula began to unfold, commentators highlighted that this construction severely restricted the access to judicial review for private parties.[35] The first point of criticism was the realisation, distilled from the few situations where individual concern was found in those early years, that the closed category test presupposed an element of retroactivity.[36] Only those applicants that were able to demonstrate not only that they belonged to an ascertainable group of people but also that they had taken a certain course of action *before* the EU act was adopted would appear to be individually concerned. Such a course of action distinguished them, not only from the public in general but also from those other applicants whose interests were also adversely affected by the measure in question. It was through the pursuit of this specific course of action in

[34] This approach remained thereafter in the case law. See, eg, Case 197/80 *Ludwigshafener Walzmühle Erling v Council and Commission* EU:C:1981:311, para 4; Case T-178/98 *Fresh Marine Company v Commission* EU:T:2000:240, para 45; Case C-234/02P *European Ombudsman v Lamberts* EU:C:2004:174, para 59; Case T-341/07 *Sison v Council* EU:T:2011:687, para 32.

[35] See, inter alia, A Barav, 'Direct and Individual Concern: An Almost Insurmountable Barrier to the Admissibility of Individual Appeal to the EEC Court' (1974) 11 *Common Market Law Review* 191; H Rasmussen, 'Why is Article 173 Interpreted against Private Plaintiffs?' (1980) 5 *European Law Review* 112; C Harlow, 'Towards a Theory of Access for the European Court of Justice' (1992) 12 *Yearbook of European Law* 213; GF Mancini and DT Keeling, 'Democracy and the Court of Justice' (1994) 57 *Modern Law Review* 175, 188–89; P Craig, 'Standing, Rights and the Structure of Legal Argument' (2003) 9 *European Public Law* 493; J Usher, 'Direct and Individual Concern: An Effective Remedy or a Conventional Solution?' (2003) 28 *European Law Review* 57; R Schütze, *European Constitutional Law*, 3rd edn (Oxford University Press, 2021) 370.

[36] Barav (n 35) 196–98. For a case which highlighted the element of retroactivity imbued in the closed class test, see Case 191/88 *Co-Frutta v Commission* EU:C:1989:134, para 23. See also P Craig, 'Legality, Standing and Substantive Review in Community Law' (1992) 14 *Oxford Journal of Legal Studies* 507, 509. See, more recently and in the same vein, P Craig and G de Búrca, *EU Law: Text, Cases and Materials*, 7th edn (Oxford University Press, 2020) 571.

the past that membership of the class became 'fixed' in addition to being 'ascertainable' – the latter simply implying the possibility of being determined. Looking at the early case law, examples of such a course of action would include having applied for import licences[37] or export refunds[38] *before* the contested act had been adopted.

The rigidity of this construction, the arbitrary results to which it led and its disengagement from economic reality soon became evident. If a private applicant belonged to a group of traders with little realistic prospect of enlargement after the measure was adopted – or was even the only one in that group[39] – which in all likelihood would be adversely affected by the EU act, individual concern would not be satisfied so long as the category of those affected remained theoretically open. Everything seemed to turn on furnishing proof of the existence of a course of action taken *before* the EU act was adopted. While it was clear that applicants who happened to have applied for import licences or export refunds before a contested measure was adopted could demonstrate an adverse effect of it on their interests, it was equally clear that the interests of other operators[40] – or allegedly even their fundamental rights[41] – might have also been adversely impacted by that EU measure. That these applicants would be unable to satisfy the condition of individual concern – and hence deprived from access to the action for annulment – purely on the basis that they could not demonstrate engagement on a fortuitous course of action before the measure was adopted seemed deeply problematic.[42]

B. The Development of the Case Law on Individual Concern and Legal Uncertainty

Aside from the conceptual and practical criticisms that could be levelled to the 'closed category' test, the ulterior development of the case law emerging from the *Plaumann* decision has also yielded a degree of legal uncertainty for private parties. This is due to two main reasons. First, because in a small number of exceptional cases and some

[37] See Joined Cases 106/63 and 107/63 *Toepfer* (n 27); Case 62/70 *Bock* (n 29); and Case 41/70 *International Fruit Company v Commission* EU:C:1971:53).

[38] Case 100/74 *CAM* (n 23).

[39] Case 38/64 *Getreide-Import Gesellschaft v Commission* EU:C:1965:35, 208; Case C-231/82 *Spijker Kwasten BV v Commission* EU:C:1983:220, para 10.

[40] See Case 10/68 *Società Eridania Zuccherifici Nazionali and others v Commission* EU:C:1969:66, paras 6–7, where the applicants in the action for annulment were a small group of sugar undertakings who challenged a decision of the Commission granting aid from the European Agriculture Guidance and Guarantee Fund to three of their competitors for the enlargement of their sugar refineries. There, the Court essentially took the view that the mere existence of a competitive relationship between the beneficiaries of the measure and the applicants was not sufficient to determine individual concern.

[41] See Case 40/64 *Sgarlata v Commission* EU:C: 1965:36, which provides an early example of a private applicant making the argument that the interpretation of the notion of individual concern and application of the closed category test was likely to deprive them from a remedy, a result incompatible with the general principles of law governing EU law (at p. 227). This argument has been played much more frequently in later case law with little success (ie Case C-345/00 P *FNAB and Others v Council* EU:C:2001:270, para 40.

[42] AG Roemer suggested in Case 10/68 *Società Eridania Zuccherifici Nazionali* (n 40), a case decided a few years after *Plaumann*, that the Court should adopt a less strict interpretation of the notion of individual concern based on the impact of the measure on the applicants and dispensing with the element of retroactivity (see his Opinion at EU:C:1969:50, 492 and the comments made on this point by Barav (n 35) 197).

specific areas in the case law, the Court of Justice has adopted a more liberal approach and has departed from the traditional 'closed category' test when appraising the standing of private applicants. Second, because, by contrast, in a handful of decisions, the Court has suggested a construction of individual concern that, while based on the 'closed category' test, has appeared to be even more demanding than it.

To the first category belong the decisions of the Court in *Les Verts v European Parliament*[43] and *Codorníu*,[44] and a consistent line of case law in the fields of competition, state aid and anti-dumping proceedings. In *Les Verts*,[45] the private applicant was a new political party not yet represented in the European Parliament that brought annulment proceedings against a decision adopted by this EU institution allocating financial help to political parties already present in the European Parliament in preparation for the forthcoming European elections. It was clear that the applicant – which was not one of the addressees of the decision – was not a member of a closed category of people. However, after recognising that the action concerned a situation which had 'never come before the Court',[46] the Court surmised that upholding the traditional interpretation of individual concern in that case would not only create an unjustified discrimination between political groupings, but would lead to a denial of justice.[47] On this basis, and after determining that the applicants were directly concerned, the Court effectively set aside the application of the test of individual concern and recognised that the applicants had standing.

In *Codorníu*,[48] a Spanish manufacturer of sparkling wine challenged a Council regulation that reserved the use of the description '*crémant*' to certain sparkling wines produced in France and Luxembourg. The basis for the challenge was that Codorníu held a trademark since 1924 that it used to designate its wines and that included 'crémant'. The effect of that regulation was to prevent Codorníu from using that term. The judgment of the Court on the point of individual concern was brief, but also novel and significant. While the Court repeated the *Plaumann* formula, it did not go on to consider Codorníu to be part of a 'closed circle' of operators. Instead, the emphasis was placed on the fact that the Regulation *prevented* Codorníu from using its trademark.[49] Intriguingly, such reasoning suggested a new way to satisfy the high threshold of individualisation inherent in the *Plaumann* formula: it hinted that Codorníu might have been individually concerned because of the damaging impact of the regulation on its rights, rather than on the basis more formalistic and retroactive parameters imposed by the closed category test.

However, later case law was to demonstrate soon enough that the *Codorníu* decision was indeed exceptional and that the promise that it showed was unlikely to be fulfilled in other cases. Thus, the Court began to refer to the finding in *Codorníu* as a separate construction, explaining that, in that case, the applicant had been found to be

[43] Case 294/83 *Parti écologiste 'Les Verts' v European Parliament* EU:C:1986:166.
[44] Case C-309/89 *Codorníu* (n 10).
[45] Case C-294/83 *Les Verts* (n 43).
[46] ibid para 35.
[47] ibid para 36.
[48] Case C-309/89 *Codorníu* (n 10).
[49] ibid paras 21–22.

individually concerned because the EU act in question had affected its 'specific right'.[50] Unsurprisingly, other private applicants tried in numerous cases thereafter to invoke this argument, positing that some of their rights, such as ownership[51] or even intellectual property rights,[52] had been affected by an EU measure. However, in doing so they had very limited success.[53] Today, the *Codorníu* construction remains an oddity in the case law, the reasons for its exceptionality seemingly based on the severity of the interference on the rights of the applicant. It would appear that, only where the effect of an EU measure is to *prevent* an applicant from using or *deprive* them from an exclusive right – as opposed to simply limiting or affecting the use of that right – would that construction be satisfied.[54]

Finally, and in addition to these specific decisions, the case law in three areas – competition, state aid and anti-dumping proceedings – has consistently shown a more relaxed construction of the test of individual concern.[55] All these specialised fields of EU law have in common the fact that procedural regulations govern the administrative proceedings conducted by an EU institution – mostly by the EU Commission, but also the Council in the field of anti-dumping – that lead to the adoption of EU legally binding acts.[56] Those regulations crucially give some interested private parties certain rights of participation and procedural guarantees. From early in the case law, the Court took the view that, if a private applicant had participated in those administrative proceedings leading to the adoption of the contested EU measure – for example, by submitting a complaint to the Commission or observations in the course of the investigation – they would then have standing to bring an action for annulment against that act. In those

[50] See Case C-10/95P *Asociación Española de Empresas de la Carne (Asocarne) v Council* EU:C:1995:406, para 43.

[51] See Case C-362/06 P *Sahlstedt and Others v Commission* EU:C:2009:243, paras 32–36; and Case T-291/04 *Enviro Tech Europe Ltd and Enviro Tech International, Inc v Commission* EU:T:2011:760, para 116.

[52] Case C-113/05P *European Federation for Cosmetic Ingredients (EFfCI) v Council* EU:C:2006:222, paras 46–47.

[53] A case that showed some affinity with the decision in *Codorníu*, even though the Court did not directly allude to it, was Case C-125/06P *Commission v Infront* EU:C:2008:159, where the Court found the applicants to be individually concerned on the basis that the relevant EU decision retrospectively altered broadcasting rights acquired by the applicants before the measure was adopted. AG Bot in his Opinion, however, did highlight the parallels with the *Codorníu* decision (EU:C:2007:611) at para 102.

[54] See, eg, Case T-213/02 *SNF v Commission* EU:T:2004:255, paras 65–71, where the applicant had complained about the effect of the contested directive on their patented processes. The Court distinguished that case from *Codorníu* by stating that the effect of the contested regulation on Codorníu had been to *deprive* them from the use of their trademark, whereas in the instant case the effect of the contested directive was to *limit* the use of those processes. See also, in the same vein, Case C-483/07P *Galileo Lebensmittel v Commission* EU:C:2009:95, para 45; and Case T-483/07P *Beul v European Parliament and Council* EU:T:2015:907, para 48.

[55] See, for instance, in competition law, Case 26/76 *Metro v Commission* EU:C:1977:1670; Case 169/84 *Cofaz v Commission* EU:C:1986:42 in state aid law; and Case 264/82 *Timex Corporation v Council and Commission* EU:C:1985:119 in anti-dumping law. See further, Arnull (n 23) 30–33; Craig and de Búrca (n 36) 573–75; and LW Gormley, 'Judicial Review in EC and EU law: Some Architectural Malfunctions and Design Improvements?' (2017) 23 *Cambridge Yearbook of European Legal Studies* 167, 175. For a detailed examination of the application of the concept of individual concern in these specialised fields, see Lenaerts, Maselis and Gutman (n 32) 337–54.

[56] See, eg, Council Regulation (EC) No 1/2003 of 16 December 2002 on the implementation of the rules on competition laid down in Articles 81 and 82 EC [2003] OJ L1/1.

cases, the Court seldom referred to the *Plaumann* formula[57] – or, for that matter, to the traditional construction of direct concern. It simply recognised standing to those applicants on the basis that those rights to participation implicitly reflected a legitimate interest deserving of legal protection.

In some cases, the Court went even further, like in *Extramet*,[58] an anti-dumping case where the applicant had participated in the proceedings leading to the adoption of the contested regulation and could have easily satisfied the parameters described above.[59] However, the Court found the applicant to be individually concerned because it was the largest importer of calcium metal into the EU and because its economic activity was seriously affected by the regulation.[60] While the Court moved quickly to limit the potential effect of this decision in later case law,[61] the decision in *Extramet*, like the one in *Codorníu*, intimated another foray into a construction of individual concern based on adverse effect on the economic interests or rights of an applicant.

In the second category, where the Court adopted a construction of individual concern that was based on the 'closed category test', but which seemed to require an additional component, we find decisions such as those in *Piraiki-Patraiki*[62] and *Sofrimport*.[63] These cases were characterised by a common pattern in that they involved two measures. First, a higher-ranking EU law provision or measure[64] that had imposed an obligation on an EU institution (generally the EU Commission), when adopting certain legally binding acts derived from that provision or measure, to take into account the situation of a group of economic operators that had engaged in a particular course of action. Second, the measure contested in the annulment proceedings in the course of whose adoption the relevant EU institution failed to observe that duty imposed by the hierarchically superior measure towards those operators. In these cases, the Court seemed to find the applicants individually concerned on the basis that they belonged to a closed group of people – singled out because they had performed a particular course of action before the contested measure was adopted[65] – *and* because they enjoyed the special legal protection granted by the hierarchically superior measure that enabled them to enforce its observance.[66] At the time, leading commentators[67] recognised that this ultimately led to an even more restrictive interpretation of individual concern because of what appeared to be the cumulative nature of the requirements.[68] While there were some

[57] See, eg, Case 26/76 *Metro* (n 55), one of the first competition cases dealing with this issue, where the *Plaumann* formula was not even mentioned.

[58] Case C-358/89 *Extramet* (n 10).

[59] ibid para 12.

[60] ibid para 17.

[61] Case T-598/97 *British Shoe Corporation Footwear Supplies v Council* EU:T:2002:52, para 50.

[62] Case 11/82 *Piraiki-Patraiki v Commission* EU:C:1985:18.

[63] Case C-152/88 *Sofrimport v Commission* EU:C:1990:259.

[64] In Case 11/82 *Piraiki-Patraiki* (n 62), this was Art 130(1) of the Act of Accession of Greece to the European Union; and in Case C-152/88 *Sofrimport* (n 63), this was a 'parent' Council regulation that set out the conditions and framework within which the EU Commission could impose protective measures in the market of fruit and vegetables.

[65] In Case 11/82 *Piraiki-Patraiki* (n 62), the applicants had pending contracts when the Commission decision was adopted; and in Case C-152/88 *Sofrimport* (n 63), the applicants had goods in transit to the EU when the contested Commission regulations imposing restriction on importation were adopted.

[66] See Case 11/82 *Piraiki-Patraiki* (n 62) paras 24–31; and Case C-152/88 *Sofrimport* (n 63) paras 11–12.

[67] See Arnull (n 10) 34–40.

[68] It became clear that, where the Court applied this construction, it regarded the two elements as cumulative. See Case T-60/96 *Merck v Commission* EU:T:1997:81, paras 58–60; Case T-489/93 *Unifruit*

isolated indications that this construction might supersede the pure 'closed category' test derived from *Plaumann*,[69] the Court continued to deploy the latter in the majority of cases.[70] In more recent years, the *Piraiki-Patraiki* and *Sofrimport* interpretation of individual concern seems to have been infrequent, with some decisions implying that the essential element in those cases was the membership of a closed category of people or, in other words, the classical *Plaumann* formulation.[71]

This section has attempted to illustrate not only that the *Plaumann* construction of individual concern generated several conceptual difficulties, but also that the evolution of the case law led to a degree of inconsistency and hence of legal uncertainty for private applicants. It is therefore unsurprising that calls for reform of the test continued to be voiced not only in the academic literature but also from within the Court itself. The next section will explore these, and the impact of the changes brought about by the new 'Lisbon test'.

C. Calls for Reform and the Effect of the Lisbon Treaty Amendments

While, as we have seen, the original formulation of the condition of individual concern in *Plaumann* was the subject of longstanding criticism in the academic literature, two of the most high-profile suggestions for its reformulation came from within the Court itself. The first took the form of the landmark Opinion delivered in 2002 by Advocate General Jacobs,[72] at the time the longest serving Advocate General in the Court, in *Unión de Pequeños Agricultores (UPA) v Council*.[73] This was a case where the traditional application of the test of individual concern would clearly render the action for annulment inadmissible given that the applicants were members of an open category of people and did not seem to satisfy any of the special constructions of individual concern considered above. Furthermore, it was a case where recourse to the indirect avenue to challenge the legality of the contested regulation through the instigation of proceedings before the national courts which could lead to a preliminary reference on validity under Article 267 TFEU seemed very uncertain, not to say impossible.[74] This, in turn raised the important issue – regularly invoked before the Court – of a potential denial of justice, a result incompatible with a Union governed by the rule of law.

Advocate General Jacobs demonstrated that the alternative avenue provided by a preliminary reference on validity – to which the Court had frequently directed applicants

Hellas v Commission EU:T:1994:297, para 25; and Case C-451/98 *Antillean Rice Mills v Council* EU:C:2001:622, paras 61–62.

[69] See Case C-209/94 *Buralux v Council* EU:C:1996:54, paras 33–34; and the Order of the President of the Court in the context of interim proceedings in Case C-300/00P(R) *Federación de Cofradías de Pescadores de Guipúzcoa* v *Council* EU:C:2000:567, para 46.

[70] See, for instance, Case T-585/93 *Greenpeace Council (Greenpeace International) and others v Commission* EU:T:1995:147, paras 53–54.

[71] Case T-560/17 *Fortischem v European Parliament and Council* EU:T:2018:764, para 55.

[72] Case C-50/00P *Unión de Pequeños Agricultores v Council* EU:C:2002:197, Opinion of AG Jacobs.

[73] Case C-50/00P *Unión de Pequeños Agricultores v Council* EU:C:2002:462, Judgment of the Court.

[74] Case C-50/00P *UPA* (n 72) Opinion of AG Jacobs, para 43.

unable to satisfy the strictures of the 'closed category' test[75] – was not only less advantageous from a procedural point of view but also, crucially, sometimes unavailable to private parties.[76] This was his platform to advise a departure from the *Plaumann* formulation of individual concern as the only reliable course of action to secure a complete system of judicial protection for private parties. He explained that 'there are no compelling reasons to read into that notion a requirement that an individual applicant seeking to challenge a general measure must be differentiated from all others affected by it in the same way as an addressee'.[77] Instead, he suggested a new construction of individual concern where a private applicant would satisfy that condition if, by reason of their particular circumstances, the contested measure 'has or it is liable to have substantial adverse effect' on their interests.[78] This represented a shift towards a test based on the real or likely impact of a measure on an applicant's interests in contrast to the formalistic and somewhat arbitrary 'closed category' test.

The second call for reform came only a few weeks later – before the Court had the opportunity to deliver its judgment in *UPA* – when the General Court also proposed a relaxation of the test of individual concern in *Jégo-Quéré*.[79] While the formula advanced by the General Court was more restrictive than that suggested by Advocate General Jacobs in *UPA*,[80] both constructions momentously advocated a move away from the 'closed category' test as the practical template to determine individual concern.

The Court, however, in its judgment in *UPA*,[81] declined to follow those leads. The judgment was terse but it implicitly engaged with the argument that a gap in the system of judicial protection could arise if the preliminary ruling avenue were unavailable, by suggesting that it was also the responsibility of the Member States to have a system of legal remedies that would generally ensure the existence of a comprehensive system of judicial protection.[82] In this context, this meant that national courts should interpret procedural rules in a way that would allow private applicants to plead the invalidity of Union acts before national courts so as to enable the triggering of a preliminary reference on validity.[83] On the point of the relaxation of the test of individual concern, the Court did not pay heed to the advice given by its Advocate General in *UPA* or by the General Court in *Jégo-Quéré*. Thus, it posited that the Court could not 'set aside'

[75] See, eg, Case C-209/94 *Buralux* (n 69) paras 35–36; Case T-87/92 *Kruidvat v Commission* EU:T:1996:191, para 75.

[76] See Case C-50/00P *UPA* (n 72), Opinion of AG Jacobs, paras 36–49.

[77] ibid para 59.

[78] ibid para 60. The detachment of the *Plaumann* formula from the damaging effect that an EU act may have on certain applicants – who do not belong to a closed category of people – had emerged in the earlier case law. See, eg, the Order of the General Court in Case T-585/93 *Greenpeace* (n 70) paras 49–58, rejecting the argument that individual concern should be based on the harmful impact of a Union act on the applicants' interests. AG Jacobs' Opinion in Case C-50/00P *UPA* provided a systematic and thorough examination as to why a test based of a substantial adverse effect on an applicant's interests might be a better mechanism to ensure complete judicial protection.

[79] Case T-177/01 *Jégo-Quéré v Commission* [2002] ECR II-2365.

[80] Thus, the General Court in *Jégo-Quéré* (ibid) suggested that an applicant would be individually concerned if the contested Union act affects their 'legal position, in a manner which is both definite and immediate, by restricting his rights or by imposing obligations' on them (para 51). For a comparison between this test and the one suggested by AG Jacobs in Case C-50/00P *UPA*, see T Tridimas and S Poli, '*Locus Standi* of Individuals under Article 230(4): The Return of Euridice?' in A Arnull, P Eeckhout, and T Tridimas (eds), *Continuity and Change in EU Law: Essays in Honour of Sir Francis Jacobs* (Oxford University Press, 2008) 71, 79–81.

[81] Case C-50/00P *UPA* (n 73).

[82] ibid para 41.

[83] ibid para 42.

the condition of individual concern provided in the Treaty without exceeding the limits of its jurisdiction and that it would be for the Member States to amend the Treaty if a change in the standing conditions applicable under (then) Article 234 EC were deemed to be necessary.[84] While the evident counterargument to this conclusion is that it was the Court itself that had given meaning to the notion of individual concern in *Plaumann* and the subsequent case law, the message emerging from the judgment was that the Court would not contemplate a change in that traditional interpretation.[85]

Apart from the continuing adherence to the *Plaumann* interpretation of individual concern, the judgment of the Court in *UPA* was noteworthy because it appealed directly to the responsibility of the Member States in two different ways. First, by highlighting the collaborative duty of the Member States in ensuring a system of judicial protection without any gaps through enabling the availability of proceedings before national courts where the invalidity of a Union act could be pleaded. Second, by clarifying that any changes to the standing conditions pertaining to the action for annulment would have to come through the normal procedures for the revision of the Treaties, which require unanimous approval and ratification by the Member States.

A few years later, the steer given by the Court when outlining the possibility of Treaty revision bore fruit. As we saw in section I above, the Treaty of Lisbon ushered in an additional test of standing in Article 263 TFEU. This test applies to the challenge of the so-called 'regulatory acts, later defined by the Court as acts of 'general application apart from legislative acts'.[86] By default, this meant non-legislative acts of general application.[87] In relation to these, the new test of standing does not include the condition of individual concern, but rather the conditions of direct concern and that the contested act should not entail implementing measures. In relation to the latter, the Court has given a very broad meaning to the term 'implementing measures', thereby redirecting many challenges either to the rigours of the general standing test or the indirect mechanisms of review.[88]

While an extensive study of the way in which the Court has interpreted the conditions in the new Lisbon test is outside the scope of this chapter,[89] it suffices to say that the

[84] ibid paras 44–45.

[85] This has been consistently borne out in later case law. See, eg, Case T-95/06 *Federación de Cooperativas Agrarias de la Comunidad Valenciana v Community Plant Variety Office (CPVO)* EU:T:2008:25, para 116; Case T-18/10 *Inuit Tapiriit Kanatami* (n 11) paras 97–98.

[86] See Case T-18/10 *Inuit Tapiriit Kanatami* (n 12) para 56 and the judgment of the Court on appeal in Case T-18/10 *Inuit Tapiriit Kanatami* (n 11) paras 50–61. For the choices faced in giving definition to this term, see S Balthasar, '*Locus Standi* for Challenges to Regulatory Acts by Private Applicants: The New Article 263(4) TFEU' (2010) 35 *European Law Review* 542; and Schütze (n 35) 373.

[87] The criteria for determining the general or individual in nature of an act have not been always entirely straightforward (ie see Case T-262/10 *Microban v Commission* EU:T:2011:623, paras 20–25; and compare with Case C-33/14P *Mory v Commission* EU:C:2015:609, para 92). Both cases involved decisions addressed to Member States, but while the former was thought to constitute an act of general application, the latter was held to be individual in character.

[88] For the interpretation of the notion of implementing measures in this context, see Case C-274/12P *Telefónica v Commission* (n 13) paras 27–39; and Case C-132/12P *Stichting Woonpunt* (n 30) paras 50–53.

[89] On this point, see, among others, Balthasar (n 86); C Werkmeister, S Potters and J Traut, 'Regulatory Acts within Article 263(4) TFEU: A Dissonant Extension of *Locus Standi* for Private Applicants' (2010–11) 13 *Cambridge Yearbook of European Legal Studies* 311; A Albors-Llorens, 'Remedies against the EU Institutions after Lisbon: An Era of Opportunity?' (2012) 71 *Cambridge Law Journal* 507; S Peers and M Costa, 'Judicial Review of EU Acts after the Treaty of Lisbon' (2012) 8 *European Constitutional Law Review* 82.

Plaumann construction of individual concern continues to be applied in those situations where the applicants do not satisfy the standing conditions in the Lisbon test. There, the general test of standing – based on the conditions of direct and individual concern – is regularly used with a residual nature.[90] Consequently, the prospect of securing the admissibility of an action for annulment against potentially illegal legislative acts – or even regulatory acts that entail implementing measures at national level – remains uncertain, with many applicants having to turn to the indirect review of legality through the national courts, an avenue which is, as Advocate General Jacobs demonstrated in *UPA*, less advantageous and certain than annulment proceedings.

V. Concluding Remarks

More than 60 years later, *Plaumann* remains a landmark case in the history of EU law. In recent years, high-profile decisions have confirmed its acute relevance and apparent immutability. One such decision was that delivered in *Inuit Tapiriit Kanatami*,[91] one of the first in this area after the entry into force of the Lisbon Treaty. There, in a situation where the applicants did not satisfy the parameters of the new Lisbon test of standing, the Court refused to reframe the *Plaumann* construction of individual concern and confirmed that this would continue to apply in those cases where the general test of standing was deployed.[92] Another was the judgment in the *People's Climate Case*,[93] where the Court firmly refused to adapt the settled case law even on the face of the argument that the contested act in question could potentially infringe the fundamental human rights of the applicants.[94] While both this argument and the reaction of the Court are not new,[95] the outcome of this case and of the *Inuit Tapiriit Kanatami* litigation underlines the deeply seated reluctance of the Court to relax the original interpretation of individual concern given in *Plaumann*.

We have seen how, in *UPA*, there had been a concern that a failure to fulfil the demanding closed category test could lead in certain situations to a denial of justice, something that is at odds with the need to ensure a complete system of judicial remedies against illegal action of the Union institutions and with the requirements of Article 47 of the Charter. While the new Lisbon test has certainly closed some of these gaps,[96] it has not closed all of them and therefore it is suggested that this argument endures. If we imagine a fictitious repetition of the – admittedly rather unusual – *UPA* set of facts, where a private applicant wishes to challenge a Union legislative act which does not

[90] The general test of standing has been applied in numerous decisions post-Lisbon. See, eg, Case T-18/10 *Inuit Tapiriit Kanatami* (n 12) para 92; *Stichting Woonpunt* (n 30) para 57; Case C-297/20 *Sabo v European Parliament and Council* EU:C:2021:24, paras 31–34.

[91] Case T-18/10 *Inuit Tapiriit Kanatami* (n 11).

[92] ibid paras 70–72.

[93] Case T-330/18 *Carvalho* (n 30); and, on appeal, Case C-565/19 P *Carvalho and Others v European Parliament and Council* EU:C:2021:252.

[94] Case C-565/19P *Carvalho* (n 93) paras 69–79.

[95] See n 41.

[96] See, for instance, the decision in Case T-262/10 *Microban* (n 87) for an applicant that managed to satisfy the Lisbon test in a case where they would have been unlikely to satisfy the test of individual concern.

necessitate of any other EU or national measures of implementation and in relation to which proceedings at national level seem inviable, a lack of effective judicial protection could still arise.[97] Post-Lisbon, the Court has addressed this point by alluding to the joint responsibility of the Members States to ensure a comprehensive system of judicial protection – as it had hinted in *UPA* – supporting its conclusion on a primary source of EU law, namely, the second subparagraph of Article 19(1) TEU.[98]

Aside from the implications that the use of the *Plaumann* interpretation of individual concern may have in securing a comprehensive system of judicial protection, the conceptual and practical difficulties surrounding the application of the closed category test remain unresolved. Contrary to what the Court implies regularly, it is not clear that the Treaty itself binds the Court to adopt such a narrow interpretation of that condition. In relation to more unspoken considerations, it is not clear either that a more liberal approach based on the proof of substantial adverse effect on the interests of the applicants – suggested by Advocate General Jacobs – would necessarily have a dramatic impact either on the workload of the Court[99] or on the viability of Union acts. However, the steadfast observance of that interpretation by the Court suggests that the narrow gateway to direct judicial review in EU law in relation to challenges brought by private applicants will remain in place.

[97] However, see the Opinion of AG Kokott in Case T-18/10 *Inuit Tapiriit Kanatami* (n 11) EU:C:2013:21, paras 115–123, arguing that, following the entry into force of the Lisbon Treaty, a comprehensive set of legal remedies does exist and explaining how it can be used to avoid any gaps in the system of judicial protection. On this point, see also A Kornezov, 'Shaping the new Architecture of the EU System of Judicial Remedies' (2014) 39 *European Law Review* 251.

[98] *Inuit Tapiriit Kanatami* (n 11) paras 99–107. For another case, where the applicants argued that, in order to trigger proceedings before the national court to plead the invalidity of the contested EU act they would have to break the law – a result incompatible with the requirements of Art 47 of the Charter – see Case C-467/17P *Società Agricola Taboga Leandro v European Parliament and Council* EU:C:2017:916 (available in French and Italian), paras 26–30.

[99] On the argument that case management should not take priority over the requirements emanating from the Rule of Law, see A Arnull, 'Judicial Review in EU Law' in A Arnull and D Chalmers (eds), *The Oxford Handbook of EU Law* (Oxford University Press, 2015) 376, 401. Further, the recent dramatic increase in the number of judges in the General Court – which has jurisdiction to deal with actions for annulment brought by private parties – suggests that the capacity of the Union judiciary in this area has been significantly strengthened.

12

CILFIT and the Doctrine of *Acte Clair*

ALEXANDER KORNEZOV*

I. Historical and Doctrinal Context

Back in 2016, I wrote that the *acte clair* doctrine, introduced into European Union (EU) law by the Court of Justice of the European Union (CJEU or 'the Court') in its landmark *CILFIT* judgment,[1] was one of those rare issues on which almost everyone agrees to disagree.[2] In fact, this statement was as true then as it was in 1982, when the *CILFIT* judgment was delivered. Today, the topic still haunts Europe's brightest legal minds. Indeed, from its very inception, the *acte clair* doctrine sparked a persistent and robust debate within the CJEU itself and beyond. Over the past four decades, it has been met concurrently with scepticism,[3] disapproval[4] and full support.[5] In 2021, the CJEU sought to put the matter to bed once and for all in its Grand Chamber judgment in *Consorzio*.[6]

Article 267 of the Treaty on the Functioning of the European Union (TFEU), whose content has essentially remained the same since the very creation of the European Economic Community (EEC), confers jurisdiction on the Court to give preliminary rulings concerning both the interpretation of the Treaties and acts of the institutions, bodies, offices or agencies of the Union and the validity of those acts, on a reference by a national jurisdiction. Under the third paragraph of that article, when a question about the interpretation of EU law is raised in a pending case before a national court or tribunal against whose decisions there is no judicial remedy under national law, that court or

* All views expressed are strictly personal. I would like to thank Doyin Lawunmi for her help with drafting the present chapter.

[1] Case 283/81 *CILFIT and Others* EU:C:1982:335.

[2] A Kornezov, 'The New Format of the *acte clair* doctrine and its consequences' (2016) 53 *Common Market Law Review* 1317.

[3] For instance, AG Wahl noted in his Opinion in Joined Cases C-72/14 and C-197/14 *X and van Dijk* EU:C:2015:319, point 62, that 'coming across a true "*acte clair*" situation would, at best, seem just as likely as encountering a unicorn'.

[4] In his Opinion in Case 283/81 *CILFIT and Others* EU:C:1982:267, 3437, point 4, AG Capotorti argued that the *acte clair* theory had far reaching consequences insofar as its effect was, in substance, to deprive the third paragraph of Art 267 of any meaning.

[5] GF Mancini and DT Keeling, 'From *CILFIT* to ERT: The Constitutional Challenge Facing the European Court' (1991) 11 *Yearbook of European Law* 1, 5.

[6] Case C-561/19 *Consorzio Italian Management and Catania Multiservizi* EU:C:2021:799.

tribunal is *obliged* to make a preliminary reference to the Court. The *acte clair* doctrine is, in essence, a judge-made exception to that obligation.

Before delving further into the matter, it is important to understand that the preliminary reference procedure has, for all intents and purposes, constitutional status in EU law. It is the darling of the Court. Most of its landmark judgments have indeed been rendered under this procedure. It has always been the centrepiece of the EU legal order due to its objective, which is to secure the uniform interpretation of EU law, as well as its full effect and autonomy.[7] While uniformity is important in any legal order, it is paramount in the system of European integration, because, put simply, divergences in the interpretation of EU law at national level could quickly degenerate into discrimination between the Member States, their citizens and undertakings. Such divergences, if unchecked, could threaten the very foundations of the EU. This explains the extraordinary vigilance with which the CJEU has always sought to preserve and enhance its dialogue with national courts, anchored in the preliminary reference procedure.

Supreme courts, or more generally courts of last instance,[8] have a special role to play in that dialogue: ultimately, they are the guardians of the uniformity of the law at national level. It is thus no surprise that the founding fathers of the Treaties decided that such national courts or tribunals must be under an obligation to make a preliminary reference to the CJEU. The treaties provide for no exception to this obligation. The founding fathers had thus most probably never thought of an *acte clair* exception to this obligation or anything of the kind, or, if they had, they must have rejected the idea.

However, in its 1982 judgment in *CILFIT*, it was the CJEU who carved out an exception to that obligation, which came to be known as the *acte clair* doctrine or the *acte clair* exception.

II. *CILFIT* – Facts and Judgment

Wool, a commodity that has been significant in European trade since the Middle Ages, was at the origins of the dispute in *CILFIT*. To recap briefly, the case concerned an action between wool importers and the Italian Ministry of Health relating to the payment of a fixed health inspection levy in respect of wool imported from outside the (then) EEC. The applicants argued, in essence, that imported wool fell within the scope of the rules governing the common organisation of agricultural markets. Accordingly, the relevant Community legislation prohibited the Italian authorities from levying any charge having an effect equivalent to a customs duty on imported animal products. The Italian authorities submitted that wool was not covered by the Community legislation at issue and therefore it was not subject to the rules on common organisation of agricultural markets. In the context of the domestic proceedings, the applicants considered that a question concerning the interpretation of the relevant Community legislation arose. Contrary to that view, the Italian Government argued that the answer to the question of interpretation of the Community rules was so obvious as to rule out the

[7] *Opinion 2/13 (Accession of the European Union to the ECHR)* EU:C:2014:2454, para 176.
[8] For ease of reference, I use both terms interchangeably.

possibility of there being any interpretative doubt. It considered that there was no need for the national court to make a preliminary reference to the Court of Justice. Given the conflicting arguments, the Italian Corte Suprema di Cassazione referred a question for a preliminary ruling to the Court under Article 267 TFEU[9] asking, in essence, whether it could consider itself free from the obligation to refer a question on the interpretation of EU law to the CJEU, if it thought that there was no 'reasonable interpretative doubt' as to the meaning of the applicable EU rule.

In his Opinion, Advocate General Capotorti set out a number of forceful arguments against the introduction of an *acte clair* doctrine into EU law. He started by defining the concept of *acte clair*, the concise meaning of which is that if a provision is unequivocal, there is no need to interpret it. He then explained that the doctrine had emerged within the French legal system, which entrusted the interpretation of international treaties exclusively to the executive and merely allowed the courts to apply them. In that context, in order to restrict the role of the executive and its interference with judicial activity, the French courts developed the aforementioned doctrine, which allowed them to retain power to determine whether or not genuine difficulties of interpretation existed. However, according to the Advocate General, that situation was not comparable to the division of tasks of national courts of last instance and the CJEU under Article 267 TFEU.

In his analysis, the Advocate General relied on the distinction between the wording of the second paragraph of that provision and the express language of the third paragraph of Article 267 TFEU, which imposes an obligation on the courts specified therein, to refer questions concerning the interpretation of EU law to the CJEU. Next, he emphasised that the objective of the obligation to refer is to ensure certainty and the uniform interpretation and application of EU law throughout the Member States, as well as to prevent divergent case law from being established at national level. Last, the Advocate General drew attention to practical difficulties inherent to the doctrine of *acte clair* in the context of EU law. First, he pointed out that a provision that is truly *acte clair* was merely an ostensible proposition, because it is only through interpretation that it is possible to ascertain whether a provision's meaning is obscure or clear. Second, he warned that the *acte clair* doctrine could be applied in an 'anomalous' manner, pointing to instances where the French Conseil d'Etat had ruled on questions of the interpretation of EU law that were in sharp contrast to well-established CJEU case law. Third, the obligation to refer was further supported by the unique technical and formal characteristics of EU law – the different language versions, novelty of content and terminology, the different methods of interpretation of the CJEU and national courts. Thus, in his view, the third paragraph of Article 267 TFEU left the national courts of last instance 'no margin of discretion in applying it'.

In its judgment, the Court did not follow its Advocate General. In essence, the Court introduced three exceptions to the obligation of supreme courts to refer, as follows: first, where the question of interpretation of EU law raised before them is irrelevant, that is to say, if the answer to that question, regardless of what it may be, cannot affect the outcome of the case at issue; second, where the provision of EU law in question has

[9] Art 177 of the EEC Treaty was the relevant provision at the time of the *CILFIT* judgment. However, I shall refer in this text to Art 267 TFEU, which is the present incarnation of that provision.

already been interpreted by the Court; and, third, where the national court concerned is convinced that the correct application of EU law is so obvious as to leave no scope for any reasonable doubt as to the manner in which the question raised is to be resolved. While the first two exceptions were never contentious,[10] the third one – for which *acte clair* is often used as shorthand – needed further qualification.

In that regard, the Court set out to establish a set of strict conditions that had to be met in order for the *acte clair* exception to apply. To that end, the Court emphasised that the national court of last instance must be convinced that the matter is equally obvious to the courts of the other Member States as well as to the CJEU. Recourse to that exception must be assessed 'on the basis of the characteristic features of EU law and the particular difficulties to which its interpretation gives rise'. To this end, the following three specific elements must be taken into consideration: (1) the interpretation of a provision of EU law involves a comparison of the different language versions, which are all equally authentic; (2) the peculiar terminology used in EU law and the fact that legal concepts do not necessarily have the same meaning in that system and in national law; and (3) each EU legal provision in question must be placed in its context and interpreted in the light of EU law as a whole, regard being had to the objectives thereof and to the state of evolution at the date on which the provision in question is to be applied.[11]

The principal message of the *CILFIT* judgment was thus twofold: on the one hand, national supreme courts were given the possibility to dispense with the obligation to refer, while, on the other hand, that possibility was made subject to a number of stringent conditions.

Placed back in its historical and legal context in 1982, the judgment could be viewed as being both radical and conservative. It was radical, in so far as the Court dared to carve out a judge-made exception to primary EU law, the wording of which made no room for exceptions: this was a clear nod to national supreme courts. But it was also conservative, as that 'nod' came with many strings attached.

This overall message made perfect sense in 1982. At that time, EU law was still very much a work in progress. In particular, the preliminary reference mechanism was not yet deeply embedded within national legal systems. Against that background, the Court felt that while indeed national supreme courts could be entrusted with dealing with the most obvious EU-related cases, their newly acquired prerogative had to be circumscribed. The stakes were high. The Court had to make sure that the risk to the uniform interpretation of EU law was limited from the outset. Moreover, given their central role within national legal systems, the Court also had to ensure that national supreme courts would continue to refer the bulk of their EU-related cases. After all, they have always been the privileged interlocutor of the Court.

Besides, put bluntly, lawyers can easily come up with a decent argument as to why a given legal rule is clear beyond reasonable doubt. If that were to be enough to trump the obligation of supreme courts to refer to the CJEU, then the very kernel of the preliminary reference edifice could be at risk. Indeed, what may be a legal conundrum to a German lawyer might as well appear crystal-clear to an Irish jurist.

[10] I will therefore not discuss these two exceptions, nor preliminary references on the *validity* of EU law which follow different rules and logic and which are not concerned by the *acte clair* doctrine and the *CILFIT* judgment.

[11] Case 283/81 *CILFIT* (n 1) paras 16–20.

This explains why the conditions to which the *acte clair* doctrine was subjected were worded in a rather strict manner. Taken literally, they give the impression that the *acte clair* exception could apply only to a trickle of the most obvious cases in which a preliminary reference would have been practically a waste of time and resources, given the absolute clarity of the applicable legal norm. Thus, on the face of it, national courts of last instance were required to perform a quasi-impossible exercise: ensure that the matter is equally obvious to the courts of the other Member States as well as to the CJEU (how could they?); compare all the language versions of the EU norm (24 at the time of writing); examine whether the same legal term has different meanings under EU law and national law, etc. This is how *CILFIT* came to be known for its rigour.

Upon close inspection, however, one discovers another, less well-known feature of *CILFIT*: its subjectivity. Indeed, *CILFIT*'s infamous condition – that the national court of last instance must be '*convinced*' that the correct application of EU law is so obvious as to leave no scope for any reasonable doubt and that the matter is equally obvious to the courts of the other Member States and to the CJEU – is inherently subjective. The Court did not state that the case law of the courts of the other Member States should be examined objectively and that, in case of discrepancy, the matter should not be considered to be *acte clair*. Rather, what matters is the national court's *own conviction* that something should also be obvious to the other courts. As Advocate General Stix-Hackl noted, since the national court cannot realistically engage in imagining the workings of the minds of other judges, it can ultimately only rely on its own judgment.[12] After all, conviction in that context is a synonym for belief, which by its very nature can only be subjective.[13]

It is this combination of rigour and subjectivity that has ultimately generated a great deal of confusion about how the conditions are to be understood and applied.

III. Reception History: Judicial and Academic

The *acte clair* exception has sparked debate in the legal community ever since. Some have endorsed it, while others have criticised it, albeit for different reasons.

At one end of the spectrum were those who argued that no such exception is warranted in EU law at all,[14] much as Advocate General Capotorti did in his Opinion in *CILFIT* 11 years later. At the other end of the spectrum were those who considered that the *CILFIT* conditions are not only strict, but unfulfillable,[15] making recourse to the *CILFIT* waiver almost impossible.[16] This has led a number of illustrious jurists to advocate a more pragmatic reading of the judgment, which, in their view, should be understood as setting out nothing more than common sense guidance. Thus, the

[12] Opinion of AG Stix-Hackl in Case C-495/03 *Intermodal Transports* EU:C:2005:215, point 94.

[13] ibid points 92, 93 and 100. See also Opinion of AG Tizzano in Case C-99/00 *Lyckeskog* EU:C:2002:108, points 71 and 72, where he observes that the *CILFIT* criteria give national courts of last instance 'a substantial measure of discretion'.

[14] P Pescatore, 'L'interprétation du droit communautaire et la doctrine de l'acte clair' (1971) 33–34 *Bulletin de l'association des juristes européens* 49.

[15] H Rasmussen, 'The European Court's *acte clair* strategy in *CILFIT*' (1984) 9 *European Law Review* 242.

[16] K Lenaerts, I Maselis and K Gutman, *EU Procedural Law* (Oxford University Press, 2014) 100–01; Mancini and Keeling (n 5) 3; Rasmussen (n 15) 258.

CILFIT criteria should not be taken verbatim, but rather as guidance or a 'tool kit' designed to help national courts of last instance evaluate the clarity of the EU rule at issue.[17] Rasmussen posited that the Court should develop a '*CILFIT II*', which would return the initiative to 'the judges of the Member States, trusting them to solve on their own far more questions of interpretation of Community law, including those which are not straightforward'.[18] In contrast, Craig has endorsed *CILFIT*, questioning whether a radical liberalisation would serve a meaningful purpose.[19]

The Court was itself divided over the issue. In the following years, proposals to reconsider the *acte clair* doctrine were not short in coming forward. In 1997 Advocate General Jacobs suggested a radical overhaul by maintaining the obligation to make a reference only where the question is of 'general interest'.[20] In 2005, Advocate General Ruiz Jarabo Colomer called for amending the *CILFIT* case law with a view to enabling the CJEU to focus on questions of 'general importance'.[21] By contrast, Advocate General Tizzano supported the *CILFIT* orthodoxy, warning against exposing the doctrine to an even higher degree of subjectivity and discretion.[22]

In legal practice, the *acte clair* exception has, in fact, led a double life. From an EU point of view, the rigour of *CILFIT* meant that, while, in theory, supreme courts could indeed legitimately abstain from referring an EU matter to the CJEU on the basis of the *acte clair* doctrine, it was in practice a very narrow filter through which only a few cases could escape the Court's jurisdiction. However, as the volume of substantive EU law increased dramatically through the years, and, with it, the Court's case load, it became apparent that applying the *CILFIT* criteria to the letter would lead to significant delays within the national systems as well as a potential overload for the Court.

Simultaneously, at national level, the *acte clair* exception took on a life of its own. National courts of last instance often applied it as a convenient waiver from the obligation to refer to Luxembourg.[23] The *CILFIT* conditions, if examined at all, frequently received only lip service.[24] There were two main reasons for that. On the one hand, these were seen as being impossible to fulfil and, ultimately, as the CJEU said it itself, it came down to the national court's own conviction of what is clear and what is not. On the other hand, the lack of effective legal remedies against violations of the obligation to

[17] Opinion of AG Wahl in Joined Cases C-72/14 and C-197/14 *X and van Dijk* (n 3) point 67. See also D Edward, '*CILFIT* and *Foto-Frost* in their historical and procedural context' in M Maduro and L Azoulai (eds), *The Past and Future of EU Law* (Hart Publishing, 2010) 173, 179; J-C Masclet, 'Vers la fin d'une controverse? La Cour de justice tempère l'obligation de renvoi préjudiciel en interprétation faite aux juridictions européenne (Art 177, al 3, CEE)' (1983) 26 *Revue de Marché Commun et de l'Union européenne* 363; T Tridimas, 'Knocking on heaven's door: Fragmentation, efficiency and defiance in the preliminary reference procedure' (2003) 40 *Common Market Law Review* 9.

[18] H Rasmussen, 'Remedying the crumbling EC judicial system' (2000) 37 *Common Market Law Review* 1071, 1109.

[19] P Craig, 'The classics of EU law revisited: *CILFIT* and *Foto-Frost*' in Maduro and Azoulai (eds) (n 17) 185, 188–89.

[20] Opinion of AG Jacobs in Case C-338/95 *Wiener* EU:C:1997:352, point 50.

[21] Opinion of AG Ruiz Jarabo Colomer in Case C-461/03 *Gaston Schul* EU:C:2005:415, points 58–59.

[22] Opinion of AG Tizzano in Case C-99/00 *Lyckeskog* (n 13) point 71.

[23] N Fenger and M Broberg, 'Finding light in the darkness: On the actual application of the *acte clair* doctrine' (2011) 30 *Yearbook of European Law* 180.

[24] M Broberg, '*Acte clair* revisited: Adapting *acte clair* to the demands of the times' (2008) 45 *Common Market Law Review* 1383, 1384–86.

refer made that obligation – and with it the misuse and abuse of the *acte clair* exception – practically unenforceable.[25]

IV. Famous Follow-Up Cases

In its subsequent case law, the Court sought to clarify the *acte clair* exception. After some hesitation in its post-*CILFIT* case law, the Court revisited the matter in its 2021 Grand Chamber judgment in *Consorzio*.[26]

A. From *CILFIT* to *Consorzio*

In a first stroke of judgments delivered on the same date in 2015, in Joined Cases C-72/14 and C-197/14 *X and van Dijk*[27] and in Case C-160/14, *Ferreira da Silva e Brito*,[28] the CJEU seemed set on course to relax the conditions under which the *acte clair* exception could be triggered.

In *van Dijk*, the Netherlands Hoge Raad asked whether it could consider a legal issue to be *acte clair*, despite the fact that a lower court had requested a preliminary ruling in a similar case concerning that same legal issue. The Hoge Raad pointed out that, in its view, the meaning of the applicable EU rule was obvious beyond reasonable doubt and that therefore it considered itself to be under no obligation to make a preliminary reference. However, it wondered whether it had to wait for the CJEU's reply to the lower court's reference before giving judgment itself, and whether it was precluded from relying on the *acte clair* exception following the lower court's reference.

In *Ferreira da Silva e Brito*, a first instance Portuguese court asked the CJEU whether the Portuguese Supremo Tribunal de Justiça had breached the third paragraph of Article 267 TFEU by erroneously invoking the *acte clair* exception in litigation where the lower courts adjudicating on the case had rendered contradictory decisions. This question was raised in an action for damages caused by a judgment of the *Supremo Tribunal de Justiça*, which was allegedly contrary to EU law.

In *X* and *van Dijk*, the CJEU ruled in essence that a national court of last instance is not required to make a reference to the Court on the sole ground that a lower national court, in a case similar to the one before it and involving the same legal issue, had referred a question to Luxembourg for a preliminary ruling; nor is it required to wait until an answer to that question had been given. In reaching its decision, the Court referred to the 'criteria laid down in *CILFIT*' only fleetingly without, however insisting on them.

In *Ferreira da Silva e Brito*, the CJEU observed that the fact that other national courts have given contradictory decisions is not in itself a conclusive factor capable of triggering the obligation to refer, set out in the third paragraph of Article 267 TFEU. Thus, a

[25] See Kornezov (n 2) 1331.
[26] Case C-561/19 *Consorzio* (n 6).
[27] Joined Cases C-72/14 et C-197/14 *X et van Dijk* EU:C:2015:564.
[28] Case C-160/14 *Ferreira da Silva e Brito e.a.* EU:C:2015:565.

court of last instance may take the view that, although lower courts have interpreted a provision of EU law in a particular way, the interpretation that it proposes to give to that provision, which differs from the construction espoused by the lower courts, is so obvious that there is no reasonable doubt. In its reasoning, the CJEU again refrained from insisting on the *CILFIT* conditions. Thus, no mention was made of the condition that the national court must be 'convinced' that the courts of other Member States as well as the Court of Justice would interpret the contested provision in exactly the same way. The conditions relating to the language comparison, the EU specific terminology and the need to place every provision of EU law in its context and interpret it in the light of EU law as a whole, regard being had to the objectives thereof and to the state of evolution of that law, were omitted altogether.

Admittedly, the Court could have done otherwise. In *Ferreira da Silva e Brito*, the Portuguese Supremo Tribunal de Justiça had concluded that there was 'no material doubt as to the interpretation of the rules', without however examining whether the *CILFIT* conditions were fulfilled. In *van Dijk*, there was no indication either that the Netherlands Hoge Raad had specifically checked whether those conditions were met. Thus, the Court could have easily found that both supreme courts had failed to conduct a proper *acte clair* analysis. Yet the Court chose a different path. By not insisting on the specific *CILFIT* criteria the Court created the impression that they were not mandatory.

The main feature of both judgments is the strong emphasis which the Court placed on the 'sole responsibility' of the national courts of last instance to determine 'alone' and 'independently' whether the meaning of a legal provision is obvious beyond reasonable doubt. Thus, the mere fact that a lower court had made a reference to the Court on the same legal issue did not preclude a national court of last instance from concluding that the issue was *acte clair*, nor was it obliged to wait for the Court's reply. Likewise, the sole fact that other national courts have espoused different interpretations of the applicable EU rule did not necessarily mean that the matter was not *acte clair*. While these facts were to be taken into account, they were not in themselves decisive.

Both judgments were interpreted in the literature as bestowing a large margin of discretion on national courts of last instance as to the circumstances under which they are obliged to make a reference for a preliminary ruling.[29]

However, within a year, in its judgment of 26 July 2016, in *Association France Nature Environment*,[30] the Court seemed intent on retracting the liberalised version of the *acte clair* doctrine advanced in *X and van Dijk* and *Ferreira da Silva e Brito*.

The case concerned a request for a preliminary ruling from the French Conseil d'Etat, where the applicant argued in substance that certain national provisions infringed EU environmental legislation. In the domestic proceedings, the Conseil d'Etat had ruled that those national provisions were indeed contrary to EU law. Nevertheless, it sought to ascertain, in essence, whether a national court can annul with retroactive effect certain provisions of national law which incorrectly transpose a directive or whether it can temporarily maintain the unlawful provisions in force until the error is corrected by the legislator. In that regard, the Conseil d'Etat wondered

[29] Kornezov (n 2) 1323–29; M Broberg and N Fenger, 'If you love somebody set them free: on the Court of Justice's revision of the *acte clair* doctrine' (2022) 59 *Common Market Law Review* 711, 718.

[30] Case C-379/15 *Association France Nature Environnement* EU:C:2016:603.

whether it was under an obligation to refer the matter to the CJEU or whether it could consider it *acte clair*.

In contrast to the two judgments in *X and van Dijk* and *Ferreira da Silva e Brito*, the Court expressly reiterated the *acte clair* orthodoxy as set out in *CILFIT*, including the three well-known conditions expounded in that judgment.[31] It also used wording suggesting a return to a stricter version of *CILFIT*. Thus, a national court of last resort must make a reference to the Court of Justice for a preliminary ruling when it has the '*slightest* doubt as regards the interpretation or correct application of EU law'.[32] In addition, the national court must establish '*in detail*' that there is no such doubt.[33] Even if that renewed rigour could be explained at least in part by the particular circumstances of the case (namely, maintaining the effects of a national law which violates EU law amounts to undermining the primacy of the latter over conflicting domestic provisions), the steer back to a more orthodox expression of the *acte clair* doctrine could not go unnoticed.

Two years later, in an extraordinary case, by all counts, the Court confirmed once again the *CILFIT* orthodoxy and found explicitly that the French Conseil d'Etat had breached its obligation to refer under the third paragraph of Article 267 TFEU. Case C-416/17 *Commission v France* was exceptional because it was the first case ever in which the Commission decided to file an infringement action against a Member State alleging that a final judgment rendered by its supreme jurisdiction had breached not only substantive EU law but also the third paragraph of Article 267 TFEU.[34]

After recalling that a Member State's failure to fulfil obligations may, in principle, be established under Article 258 TFEU whatever the agency of that State whose action or inaction is the cause of the failure to fulfil its obligations, even in the case of a constitutionally independent institution, the CJEU observed that the obligation of national courts of last instance to make a reference laid down in the third paragraph of Article 267 TFEU where a question of the interpretation of the Treaties is raised is intended in particular to prevent a body of national case law that is not in accordance with the rules of EU law from being established in any of the Member States.[35] It then emphasised that in its existing case law, it had not addressed the question adjudicated by the French Conseil d'Etat and that, on substance, the latter's judgment infringed EU law, as interpreted by the Court. Therefore, the Conseil d'Etat had also breached its obligation to refer since it could not rely on the *acte clair* exception.

[31] ibid paras 48–50.

[32] ibid para 51.

[33] ibid paras 52, 53 and point 2 of the operative part (emphasis added).

[34] In 2004, the Commission initiated infringement proceedings against Sweden, arguing that Swedish courts of last instance systematically failed to comply with the obligation to make a reference; see the Commission's reasoned opinion 2003/2161 of 12 October 2004, C(2004) 3899. The case was however settled and never reached the Court. For more details, see M Schmauch, 'Lack of preliminary references as an infringement of Article 234 EC?' (2005) 11 *European Law Reporter* 445. Furthermore, in its judgment of 12 November 2009, Case C-154/08 *Commission v Spain* EU:C:2009:695, not published, the Court found that the Spanish Tribunal Supremo, who was a tribunal of last instance, had not made a reference under Art 267, third para, TFEU. However, the Commission's infringement action covered only the substantive infringement of EU law and it did not extend to an alleged breach of the obligation to refer, which prevented the Court from adjudicating on the matter (see paras 34, 64 and 65).

[35] Case C-416/17 *Commission v France (Advance payment)* EU:C:2018:811, paras 105–07, 109.

These four decisions caused some perplexity. While the overall message stemming from *X and van Dijk* and *Ferreira da Silva e Brito* seemed to suggest a course towards the relaxation of the *CILFIT* conditions, the subsequent judgments in *Association France Nature* and *Commission v France* indicated that the orthodoxy set out in *CILFIT* should prevail and that any discretion afforded to national courts resulting from the *acte clair* exception was relatively narrow.

Accordingly, the situation was ripe for clarification. The Court seized that opportunity by sending Case C-561/19 *Consorzio Italian Management and Catania Multiservizi*, ('*Consorzio*') to its Grand Chamber in a clear sign that it intended to settle the matter once and for all.

B. *Consorzio*

The facts giving rise to the *Consorzio* case date back to a 2017 preliminary reference from the Italian Consiglio di Stato in a case concerning a public contract for the supply of services relating to the cleaning, inter alia, of Italian railway stations. By a judgment of 19 April 2018,[36] the Court stated, in substance, that Directive 2004/17[37] must be interpreted as not precluding national rules which do not provide for periodic price review after a contract has been awarded in the sectors covered by that directive.

The parties to the national proceedings then asked the national court to refer other questions concerning the interpretation of EU law to the CJEU in the same case. The referring court took the view that some of those questions had been answered in the first judgment of 19 April 2018, but others were raised for the first time. It considered that it was obliged to make a further reference to the CJEU. The referring court therefore sought to ascertain whether a national court of last instance must bring before the CJEU a question concerning the interpretation of EU law, where that question is put to it by a party at an advanced stage of the proceedings, such as where the case had already been set down for judgment or even where a reference for a preliminary ruling had been made previously in that case.

Even though the national court did not formulate its question in terms of the *acte clair* exception, nor did it question the *CILFIT* criteria, both the Court and its Advocate General took the opportunity to revisit this highly contentious topic.

In his Opinion, Advocate General Bobek proposed a total overhaul of *CILFIT*. In a nutshell, his view was that the duty to refer should exist only where three cumulative criteria were met. First, a general issue of interpretation of EU law must be raised. Second, the provision at issue may be reasonably interpreted in more than one possible way. Third, the interpretation of EU law cannot be inferred from existing CJEU case law. That system would be bolstered by an obligation on national courts of last instance to provide a statement of reasons in cases where the decision is not to refer.

[36] Case C-152/17 *Consorzio Italian Management and Catania Multiservizi* EU:C:2018:264.

[37] Directive 2004/17 of the European Parliament and of the Council of 31 March 2004 coordinating the procurement procedures of entities operating in the water, energy, transport and postal services sectors, [2004] OJ L 134/1.

Crucially, the Advocate General underpinned his analysis with two fundamental points. First, he argued cogently that a distinction had to be made between the *interpretation* and the *application* of EU law. In his view, uniformity for the purposes of Article 267 TFEU is not aimed at single results in individual cases, but at the 'level of legal rules to be applied'. Thus, the *acte clair* exception could be invoked only with regard to the *interpretation* of EU law. Second, he considered that *CILFIT* was problematic not only in terms of its 'feasibility', but that it was also 'mistakenly conceptualised', because it was based on the absence of subjective doubts regarding the correct application of EU law. He advocated that the focus of the duty to refer must change, from there being no *subjective* reasonable doubt as to the correct *application* of EU law in respect of the outcome of the *specific* case, to there being an *objective* divergence detected in the *case law* at the national level thereby threatening the uniform *interpretation* of EU law within the EU.[38]

In its judgment, the Grand Chamber did not endorse the proposed overhaul. In essence, it confirmed the *CILFIT* orthodoxy, while rendering it more pragmatic and more workable. Nevertheless, the Court took on some of the ideas of its Advocate General, which it inscribed in its revisited *CILFIT* formula.

Let us start with what the Court did not do. It is clear that the Court did not overturn *CILFIT*. On the contrary, it repeated the orthodoxy, faithfully listing all of the *CILFIT* criteria without exception.[39] *Consorzio* can thus be seen, largely, as a confirmation of *CILFIT* 40 years later. Given that the judgment was delivered by the Grand Chamber, one can safely assume that *CILFIT* is here to stay.

However, the Court also redrafted some essential parts of *CILFIT*, adding new elements, which aim at rendering the *acte clair* doctrine more pragmatic and easier to apply.

First, it added an important twist to the existing *CILFIT* formula. While citing the latter, it replaced the term 'application', used in *CILFIT* and the subsequent case law, with 'interpretation'. Thus, according to the Court in *Consorzio*, national courts of last instance are under a duty to refer unless 'the correct *interpretation* of EU law is so obvious as to leave no scope for any reasonable doubt'.[40] This is a welcome and correct clarification. While indeed the distinction between 'application' and 'interpretation' of the law may be difficult to make in practice, that distinction is particularly relevant, even crucial, in the preliminary reference mechanism. Indeed, Article 267 TFEU gives the Court jurisdiction to 'interpret' EU law, not to apply it in a given case pending before a national court. In principle, within the system for preliminary references, which is based upon cooperation and dialogue between the CJEU and national courts, specific tasks are attributed to the two main protagonists. Thus, the CJEU provides guidance on the *interpretation* of EU law requested by national courts in order to determine disputes

[38] Opinion of AG Bobek in Case C-561/19 *Consorzio Italian Management and Catania Multiservizi* EU:C:2021:291, points 129 and 133.

[39] Case C-152/17 *Consorzio* (n 6) paras 39–46.

[40] ibid paras 39, 66 and the operative part. The devil is truly in the detail: when the CJEU delivered its *Consorzio* judgment, the English and Danish language versions referred to the 'application' rather than the 'interpretation' of EU law. A rather important slip! Subsequently, those two language versions of the text were corrected, and now refer to the 'interpretation' of EU law. See Broberg and Fenger (n 29) 735.

of which they are seised, whilst national courts, in their capacity as arbiters of fact and domestic law, bear responsibility for the correct *application* of that law.[41]

This represents a significant albeit understated shift in the *acte clair* doctrine, which clearly echoes Advocate General Bobek's reflections on the matter. Thus, if a supreme court has doubts about the correct application of EU law in a given case, it would not be under an obligation to refer, if it is of the view that the meaning (or interpretation) of the EU rule as such is clear beyond reasonable doubt. Only time will tell if that change will produce meaningful results.

It is a pity that the Court chose not to explain the reasons for which it decided to modify the *CILFIT* formula. In fact, one could be forgiven for not even noticing the change. The Court simply replaced one word for another, while still citing *CILFIT*, without any explanation whatsoever. One can thus speculate that, in the Court's view, that change was evident and self-explanatory.

Second, in an equally understated fashion, the Court operated one further change to the *CILFIT* formula. It stated that the national court of last instance must be convinced that the matter would be equally obvious to the other courts or tribunals 'of last instance' of the Member States and to the Court of Justice. The addition 'of last instance' is new. The Court thus rendered that formula more pragmatic and more workable.

Third, the Court repeated the three *CILFIT* conditions, while clarifying the one pertaining to the linguistic verification of the wording of the EU rule in question. It observed that while a national court or tribunal of last instance cannot be required to examine each of the language versions of the provision in question, the fact remains that it must bear in mind those divergences between the various language versions of that provision of which it is aware, in particular when those divergences are set out by the parties and are verified.[42] This is a welcome and long-awaited clarification. In 1982, when *CILFIT* was decided, there were seven official languages while, at the time of the *Consorzio* judgment, there were 24! A verified linguistic review by national courts is thus today much less realistic than it was in 1982. The Court's judgment implicitly acknowledges past criticism of this condition and the current reality of a significantly larger Union. This is yet another pragmatic and workable solution.

The CJEU then repeated the other two *CILFIT* criteria without further ado.

Fourth, a palpable shift towards objectivity can also be detected between the lines. Thus, the Court stated that the *CILFIT* criteria, as modified, served to 'help' a national court or tribunal of last instance to examine whether there were 'circumstances' capable of giving rise to any reasonable doubt as to the correct interpretation of EU law.[43] To this end, where the national court or tribunal of last instance is made aware of the existence of diverging lines of case law – among the courts of a Member State or between the courts of different Member States – concerning the interpretation of a provision of EU law applicable to the dispute in the main proceedings, that court or tribunal must be 'particularly vigilant' in its assessment of whether or

[41] *Opinion 1/09 (Agreement creating a Unified Patent Litigation System)* of 8 March 2011, EU:C:2011:123, para 84.

[42] *Consorzio* (n 6) para 44.

[43] ibid para 47.

not there is any reasonable doubt as to the correct interpretation of the provision of EU law at issue. In so doing, it must have regard, inter alia, to the objective pursued by the preliminary ruling procedure which is to secure uniform interpretation of EU law.[44]

The existence of diverging lines of case law among the courts of the same Member State or of different Member States is therefore an important factor that supreme courts must take into account when deciding whether they are under an obligation to refer. This is clearly an objective factor of great significance. The fact that supreme courts must be 'particularly vigilant' in such circumstances is a strong indication that the *acte clair* exception would only rarely apply when there are diverging lines of case law at the national level. Yet, here again, the Court added a pragmatic twist by specifying that that 'particular vigilance' must be exercised when the national courts of last instance in question 'is made aware' of such divergence. There is therefore no obligation as such to examine *ex officio* the jurisprudence, especially that of other Member States, every time an EU matter is before that court. It will mostly be for the parties to adduce evidence to that end. This is objectivism and pragmatism at its best.[45]

Finally, the CJEU added another – new – condition for the *acte clair* exception to apply: the national court of last instance must state reasons for which it had concluded that the matter before it was *acte clair*. This development echoes the case law of the European Court of Human Rights, which has already held that failure to state reasons as to why a court of last instance of a Member State considers itself not to be under an obligation to refer a preliminary question to the CJEU may amount to a breach of Article 6(1) of the ECHR.[46] It is submitted that this is another step in the right direction, as has been argued both by Advocate General Bobek[47] and academia.[48] It makes accountability and enforcement easier as it helps to detect violations of Article 267, third paragraph, TFEU.

We thus come to our final query: does *Consorzio* liberalise the *acte clair* doctrine or does it represent a return to orthodoxy? Arguably, neither of those contentions correctly sums up the CJEU's judgment. It is in essence a pragmatic reinstatement of *CILFIT* with some careful fine-tuning.

V. Concluding Remarks

In *Consorzio*, the CJEU draws a line: the *acte clair* doctrine is to remain a feature of EU law rendering that case the new reference point regarding the interpretation of the third paragraph of Article 267 TFEU. However, there may yet be further twists to the plot of this particular story.

[44] ibid para 49.

[45] It is also another implicit nod to the Advocate General who argued in favour of more objectivity. In the same vein, see Kornezov (n 2); Opinion of AG Tizzano in Case C-99/00 *Lyckeskog* (n 13) point 65.

[46] See, eg, *Somorjai v Hungary*, no 60934/13, § 57, 28 August 2018.

[47] Opinion of AG Bobek in *Consorzio* (n 38), points 50 and 51.

[48] Kornezov (n 2) 1338; Broberg (n 24) 1394–95.

At the systematic level, the lack of effective legal remedies in EU law[49] against infringements of the obligation to refer, and, hence, against the misapplication of the *acte clair* exception, remains a problem. While, in theory, two remedies can be envisaged, none of them is sufficiently effective. First, in principle, an individual or an undertaking can bring an action at national level for damages caused by a judgment of a national supreme court which is contrary to EU law. However, this remedy is a white elephant as far as 'pure' breaches of the obligation to refer are concerned.[50] Indeed, as EU law currently stands, the mere breach of the obligation to refer under Article 267 TFEU does not trigger the non-contractual liability of the State, since two of the three conditions for establishing liability[51] cannot be met: first, because, according to the case law, the third paragraph of Article 267 does not confer rights on individuals;[52] and, second, there would normally be no direct causal link between the breach of the obligation to refer as such and the damage caused (the latter would normally be the direct cause of the breach of a substantive EU rule).[53]

The other available remedy is infringement proceedings under Article 258 TFEU. However, the Commission – which is the only party empowered to bring such proceedings – has been traditionally very reluctant to use this mechanism in the context of a perceived breach of the third paragraph of Article 267 TFEU. That unwillingness may be due to numerous factors, including a disinclination on the part of the Commission, as the Union's executive, to interfere with what is essentially a dialogue between courts. The concern that infringement proceedings could become a back-door mechanism to 'quash' final judgments of national courts of last instance, thus undermining the principle of *res judicata*, is another reason capable of explaining the Commission's reluctance. *Commission v France* is an isolated example of an infringement action for failure to refer under the third paragraph of Article 267 TFEU, which shows that that remedy may be effective, if put into practice. That case remains, however, an exception.

I have argued that these remedies should be revisited with a view to enabling a more effective enforcement of the obligation to refer. Several specific changes can be envisaged in that regard.[54] The *Consorzio* judgment is helpful in this context, in so far as it requires national supreme courts to state reasons when they decide not to refer. That

[49] There could also be remedies at the national level in some Member States. However, they apply only in certain Member States, and therefore differ according to the relevant national jurisdiction. Moreover, such national remedies are not regulated by EU law. Likewise, the ECHR also provides a remedy where individual rights are invoked, as mentioned above, but naturally that remedy is not governed by EU law. As I have argued elsewhere, EU law must provide for effective remedies against violation of EU law: Kornezov (n 2) 1333–41.

[50] ibid 1318 and 1331.

[51] As is well known, Case C-224/01 *Köbler* EU:C:2003:513, para 51 establishes three conditions for holding the State liable for breaches of EU law: the infringement concerns a rule intended to confer rights on individuals; the breach is sufficiently serious or manifest; and existence of a direct causal link between the breach and the damage.

[52] Case C-261/95 *Palmisani* EU:C:1997:351, para 31.

[53] See G Anagnostaras, 'Erroneous judgments and the prospect of damages: The scope of the principle of governmental liability for judicial breaches' (2006) 31 *European Law Review* 735.

[54] Kornezov (n 2) 1333–41; see also T Tridimas, 'State liability for judicial acts: Remedies unlimited?' in P Demaret, I Govaere and D Hanf (eds), *European Legal Dynamics* (European Interuniversity Press, 2007) 147, 155–56.

obligation will certainly facilitate monitoring and detecting possible violations of the *acte clair* exception. Nevertheless, the problem of the ineffectiveness of the available EU legal remedies should be addressed sooner than later. Indeed, any legal obligation risks becoming nothing more than wishful thinking, if it is essentially unenforceable. Wasn't that the real problem of the *CILFIT* doctrine in the first place?

As long as that problem remains unresolved, *acte clair* will continue to haunt Europe's legal minds.

13

Factortame and Interim Measures before National Courts

JASPER KROMMENDIJK

I. Introduction: Historical and Doctrinal Context

Factortame I was part of one of the 'longest-running judicial soap operas' in the European Union (EU)'s history.[1] Litigation by Spanish fishing vessels in the United Kingdom (UK) resulted in three judgments of the European Court of Justice (ECJ), of which two have had a lasting impact on EU law. *Factortame I* involved the power of national courts to grant interim relief.[2] In *Factortame II*, the ECJ answered the questions of the UK High Court and determined that the disputed UK act (the Merchant Shipping Act 1988) breached EU law, more specially, the freedom of establishment.[3] Almost five years later, the ECJ accepted in *Factortame III* that the *Francovich* principle of Member State liability for damage caused to individuals through breaches of EU law also applied to acts or omissions of the Member State's legislature.[4]

Factortame I and *III* belong to the classics of EU institutional law, and generations of students have been taught about them. *Factortame I* is one of the most significant 'constitutional' cases of the ECJ signifying the evolvement of the EU legal order.[5] It belongs to an era in ECJ jurisprudence which was marked by a weakening of procedural autonomy and considerable interference with national remedies aimed at enhancing

[1] P Oliver, 'Case C-46/93 and C-48/93, Brasserie du Pêcheur v. Germany, and The Queen v. Secretary of State for Transport ex parte Factortame, [1996] ECR I-1029' (1997) 34 *Common Market Law Review* 635, 635–58.

[2] Case C-213/89 *The Queen v Secretary of State for Transport, ex parte Factortame* EU:C:1990:257 ('*Factortame I*').

[3] Case C-221/89 *The Queen v Secretary of State for Transport, ex parte Factortame* EU:C:1991:320 ('*Factortame II*').

[4] Joined Cases C-46/93 and C-48/93 *Brasserie du pêcheur v Bundesrepublik Deutschland and The Queen/Secretary of State for Transport, ex parte Factortame and Others* EU:C:1996:79 ('*Factortame III*'); H Toner, 'Thinking the unthinkable? State liability for judicial acts after *Factortame (III)*' (1997) 17 *Yearbook of European Law* 165; P Craig, 'The EU, the Member States and damages liability' in M Heidemann (ed), *The Transformation of Private Law – Principles of Contract and Tort as European and International Law* (Springer 2024) 811.

[5] L Papadias, 'Interim protection under Community law before the national courts. The right to a judge with jurisdiction to grant interim relief' (1994) 21 *Legal Issues of Economic Integration* 153, 170.

the effectiveness of EU law.[6] *Factortame I* is frequently grouped together with other judgments such as *Johnston*,[7] *Heylens*,[8] *Marshall II*,[9] *Francovich*[10] and *Emmott*[11] that emphasise effective judicial protection.[12] This series of cases followed a more conservative period in which the ECJ exercised restraint towards national procedural law as evidenced by *Rewe* and the notion of national procedural autonomy.[13]

As discussed later in this chapter, the rationale of interim measures is beyond doubt from the perspective of the effectiveness of EU law and the principle of effective judicial protection.[14] Interim relief ensures that the protection of EU rights is not merely illusory. Without interim relief as a remedy, the substantive EU law rights cannot be guaranteed at all times: *ubi ius, ibi remedium*.[15] Without interim relief, proper operation of the (decentralised) enforcement mechanisms of EU law would also be endangered. One author aptly notes that direct effect would be 'only a beautiful fairy tale' without the possibility of interim measures.[16]

After discussing the facts and judgment in the case (section II), this chapter focuses on the popular, judicial and academic reception of the judgment (section III). The last section focuses on important ECJ follow-up judgments (section IV.A) and analyses those judgments from the perspective of national procedural autonomy and *Rewe* (section IV.B). To analyse the actual impact of *Factortame* and subsequent judgments, section IV.C studies the way in which Dutch courts have dealt with interim relief in relation to EU law. The chapter concludes with some critical reflections on the approach of the ECJ towards interim relief.

II. Case Facts and Judgment

The questions of the House of Lords in *Factortame I* arose during proceedings initiated by 95 fishing vessel companies incorporated under the laws of the UK and the directors and shareholders of those companies, most of whom were Spanish nationals. Of those 95 vessels, 53 were originally registered in Spain and flew the Spanish flag, but on various dates since 1980, they were listed in the British register. The remaining 42 vessels had always been registered in the UK, but were purchased by the companies after 1983.

[6] M Taborowksi, 'Case C-432/05 *Unibet* – Some practical remarks on effective judicial protection' (2008) 14 *Columbia Journal of European Law* 621; Papadias (n 5) 190–91.

[7] Case 222/84 *Johnston v Chief Constable of the Royal Ulster Constabulary* EU:C:1986:206.

[8] Case 222/86 *Unectef v Heylens* EU:C:1987:442.

[9] Case C-271/91 *Marshall v Southampton and South West Hampshire Area Health Authority* EU:C:1993:335.

[10] Joined Cases C-6/90 and C-9/90 *Francovich and Bonifaci v Italy* EU:C:1991:428.

[11] Case C-208/90 *Theresa Emmott v Minister for Social Welfare and Attorney General* EU:C:1991:333.

[12] Papadias (n 5) 181; HG Schermers, 'Case note Joined Cases C-143/88 and C-92/89, Zuckerfabrik Süderdithmarschen and Zuckerfabrik Soest' (1992) 29 *Common Market Law Review* 133, 137.

[13] Case 33/76 *Rewe-Zentralfinanz and Rewe-Zentral* EU:C:1976:188; A Arnull, 'Case C-432/05, *Unibet (London) Ltd and Unibet (International) Ltd v Justitiekanslern*, judgment of the Grand Chamber of 13 March 2007' (2007) 44 *Common Market Law Review* 1763, 1763–64.

[14] 'Effective judicial protection and interim protection are indissoluble concepts' Papadias (n 5) 164.

[15] AM Collins, 'The availability of interim relief in national courts to uphold community law rights' (1992) 1 *Irish Journal of European Law* 60; Craig (n 4).

[16] EA Garcia, 'Is Europe ready for the administrative law remedial revolution? Litigation before national courts of the EEC Member States and interim relief' (1990) 42 *Administrative Law Review* 181, 211.

The companies challenged the Merchant Shipping Act 1988 and the Merchant Shipping (Registration of Fishing Vessels) Regulations 1988 (SI 1988/1926). This legislative package considerably changed the registration system to stop the practice of quota hopping. According to the UK Government, its fishing quotas were 'plundered' by vessels flying the British flag but lacking any genuine link with the UK. The 1988 Act required all vessels to be recorded in the new register, including those catalogued under the previous 1894 Act. Section 14 of the 1988 Act imposed a nationality requirement, restricting registration to British-owned vessels that were managed from within the UK by a 'qualified person or company'; a 'qualified person' referred to a British citizen residing in the UK, and a 'qualified company' meant one incorporated in the UK with at least 75 per cent of its shares being owned by one or more qualified persons or companies and at least 75 per cent of its directors being qualified persons. As a result of this legislative change, the 95 vessels, including Factortame Ltd, could no longer be registered and started judicial proceedings challenging the conformity of the 1998 Act with EU law while requesting interim relief.

While the Divisional Court of Queen's Bench Division ordered such interim relief, the Court of Appeal held that UK courts had no power to suspend, by way of interim relief, the application of Acts of Parliament. In fact, there were two obstacles: (a) the presumption of the validity of parliamentary acts; and (b) the lack of jurisdiction or the existence of a rule excluding interim relief against the Crown due to immunity of the Crown.[17] These complications led the House of Lords to refer two questions to the ECJ: first, whether English courts were obliged or had the power, under Community law, to grant an interim injunction against the Crown and, second, what criteria were to be applied in deciding whether or not to grant such interim protection of the rights claimed. While the case was pending in Luxembourg, the European Commission also started infringement proceedings.[18] Five months after the reference was made by the House of Lords, the ECJ accepted the Commission's request for an interim order requiring the UK to suspend the application of the nationality requirements.[19]

In its judgment on the merits, the ECJ reformulated the first question of the House of Lords: are national courts required to disapply a rule of national law that constitutes 'the sole obstacle' precluding the national court from granting interim relief?[20] It answered this question in the affirmative in no less than six paragraphs. In its judgment, the ECJ started with a citation of its earlier pronouncement of the principle of supremacy in *Simmenthal*.[21] It subsequently referred to the principle of loyal and sincere cooperation (currently) in Article 4(3) TEU and underscored the need to ensure legal protection that persons derive from the direct effect of EU law.[22] With another reference to *Simmenthal*, the ECJ reiterated that it

> also held that any provision of a national legal system and any legislative, administrative or judicial practice which might impair the effectiveness of Community law by withholding from

[17] AG Toth, 'Case C-213/89, *Regina v. Secretary of State for Transport, ex parte Factortame Limited and Others*, Judgment of the Court of 19 June 1990' (1990) 27 *Common Market Law Review* 573, 584.

[18] Case C-246/89 *Commission of the European Communities v United Kingdom of Great Britain and Northern Ireland* EU:C:1991:375.

[19] Case 246/89 R *Commission v United Kingdom* EU:C:1989:368.

[20] Case C-213/89 *Factortame I* (n 2) para 17.

[21] ibid para 18.

[22] Case 106/77 *Amministrazione delle finanze dello Stato v Simmenthal SpA* EU:C:1978:49, paras 18–19.

> the national court having jurisdiction to apply such law the power to do everything necessary at the moment of its application to set aside national legislative provisions which might prevent, even temporarily, Community rules from having full force and effect are incompatible with those requirements, which are the very essence of Community law.

The ECJ pointed to two arguments to support its affirmative response. First, the full effectiveness of EU law would be impaired if interim relief to protect rights under EU law was impossible. Second, the effectiveness of the preliminary ruling system of Article 267 TFEU would be undermined if a national court stayed the proceedings pending the reply of the ECJ after a reference without being able to grant interim relief before a final judgment. The ECJ did not address the second question about the criteria for granting interim protection.

III. Reception History: Popular, Judicial and Academic

As with most landmark constitutional cases, *Factortame I* has met with different reactions. In the UK, popular press and some politicians were outright critical, while (EU law) academics have been largely supportive of the ECJ's judgment, despite some criticism around the level of generality of the judgment.

The 'anti-Community hysteria' following the ECJ judgment is aptly described by Toth. He enumerates the dramatic newspaper headlines following the judgment from Luxembourg: 'EC "rewrites" British constitution', 'UK courts empowered to overrule Parliament' and 'EC power over UK law'.[23] Eurosceptic Members of Parliament lamented that the ECJ had overridden the sovereignty of the British people by setting aside the British constitution. As argued below, while these reactions were overdone, especially from an EU law perspective, they nonetheless show that the judgment occupies an important position in the UK's legal landscape and in its relationship with the EU. Albeit that this frenzy was short-lived, it has had an impact on judges. It also perplexed many UK lawyers and judges.[24] Lord Bingham qualified the granting of interim relief by the Divisional Court as a 'constitutional enormity'.[25] One (former) UK Supreme Court judge interviewed in 2020 still referred to *Factortame I* and the perceived implication that the EU legal system is 'stronger than our own'.[26]

The legal turmoil is surprising from an EU law perspective, since *Factortame I* was clearly built on the well-established case law of the ECJ without treading novel legal paths.[27] According to Toth, the outcome was implicit in three fundamental principles of EU law: the principle of supremacy requiring national courts to set aside national legislation breaching EU law; the principle of effective judicial protection; and the *Rewe*

[23] Toth (n 17) 582.

[24] S Douglas-Scott, 'The *Factortame* case. Fishing in troubled waters?' (1992) 2 *The King's College Law Journal* 7, 12.

[25] NP Gravells, 'Disapplying an Act of Parliament pending a preliminary ruling: 'constitutional enormity or Community law right' [1989] *Public Law* 568.

[26] J Krommendijk, *National courts and preliminary references to the Court of Justice* (Edward Elgar, 2021) 91.

[27] Toth (n 17) 583. *cf* 'the general principles … already provide a reasonably safe answer'. A Barav, 'Enforcement of community rights in the national courts: The case for jurisdiction to grant an interim relief' (1989) 26 *Common Market Law Review* 369, 372.

requirements of effectiveness and equivalence.[28] Lord Bridge also labelled the suggestion that *Factortame I* was 'a novel and dangerous invasion by a Community institution of the sovereignty of the United Kingdom Parliament' a 'misconception'.[29]

What explains the screaming headlines and the shock? Some commentators construed a story in which the blame is primarily on the narrow-minded Euroscepticism of UK courts. Gravells, for example, notes that 'the reasoning of the Court of Appeal and the House of Lords was characterised by a disappointing retreat into parochialism'.[30] Related are comments that downplay the implications of *Factortame I*. Toth argues that the ECJ judgment did not increase the powers of courts to the detriment of Parliament, because UK courts had already accepted the possibility to *definitively* disapply an Act of Parliament on the basis of section 2 of the European Communities Act 1972.[31] *Temporarily* suspending the operation of an act is, in his view, a less impactful power.[32] In addition, when courts disapply Acts of Parliament, they simply comply with the 'command' given by the Parliament in its 1972 Act accepting the principle of supremacy of EU law.[33]

Both views disguise that – at least from a UK perspective – the fury was not entirely without foundation. Barav, for example, contests Toth's 'fallacious' argument on the grounds that when definitively disapplying an act, a conflict is actually found to exist, whereas it is only alleged at the moment when (temporary) interim relief is granted (or not).[34] This explanation reflects the position of Lord Bingham, who strongly adheres to the notion that 'a statute remains inviolable unless or until it is shown to be incompatible with the higher law of the Community'.[35] The foregoing illustrates that the major problem for UK judges was that they viewed the *Factortame* litigation as a conflict between a clear and undoubted provision of national law with claimed but unproven rights under EU law.[36] Douglas-Scott points to the '(perhaps subconscious) mental block suffered by our judiciary, inclining them to presume the validity of national legislation … where there is really only doubt'.[37]

Another related explanation of the tensions is the indeterminacy of EU law and the judgment of the ECJ being 'long on principle and short of specifics'.[38] In order to truly understand the UK difficulties, rather than to ridicule them, it is thus important to go beyond simplifications pointing to parochialism or Euroscepticism and examine the reasoning of the ECJ more closely. Critical views are also not entirely without merit considering the way in which the ECJ answered the questions of the House of Lords. The ECJ reformulated one question of the House of Lords, while dodging another. By

[28] Note, however, that the last two principles were not explicitly alluded to by the ECJ, as discussed in section IV.B. Toth (n 17) 584.

[29] *Factortame Ltd, R (On the Application of) v Secretary of State for Transport* [1990] UKHL 13.

[30] Gravells (n 25) 568.

[31] Toth (n 17) 584–85.

[32] *cf* Hodgson J in the Divisional Court, *R v Secretary of State for Transport, ex parte Factortame Limited and Others* [1989] 2 CMLR 353.

[33] Douglas-Scott (n 24) 7.

[34] Barav (n 27) 374.

[35] Gravells (n 25) 568.

[36] Lord Donaldson in *R* (n 32), 396; Douglas-Scott (n 24) 15.

[37] Douglas-Scott (n 24) 16–17.

[38] Papadias (n 5) 166. *cf* Douglas-Scott (n 24) 16.

reformulating the first question, it significantly simplified and thereby did not answer fully the questions of the House of Lords.[39] Papadias contrasts the House of Lords' questions of 'a conspicuous clarity and every word carefully chosen' with the ECJ's failure to answer an explicit and pertinent question.[40] First, the problem was not so much the existence of a UK rule preventing interim relief, but the complete absence of jurisdiction for courts to do so.[41] The ECJ changed the scope of the questions by framing it as a supremacy matter.[42] In doing so, the ECJ also implied that the House of Lords appeared to be prepared to grant interim relief.[43] Through reformulating the questions, the ECJ also seemed to assume that jurisdiction to grant interim relief actually existed.[44] Per Lord Donaldson, 'the ruling by the European Court is based upon a misunderstanding of English law and to that extent may be mistaken'.[45] Papadias criticises the ECJ for failing to engage with the obstacle for the House of Lords, the principle of the presumption of the validity of parliamentary acts, although he acknowledges that the ECJ judgment might be read as implicitly rejecting the absolute nature of this presumption.[46]

Second, the ECJ simply dodged the second question of the House of Lords as to the criteria to be applied in deciding whether or not to grant interim protection of the rights claimed.[47] The European Commission too suggested the ECJ to lay down such criteria.[48] The ECJ, however, did not specify the nature of relief and the measures that could be ordered, nor the specific criteria for national courts.[49] Even though the complete silence of Luxembourg in relation to the second question can be questioned from the perspective of the dialogical set-up of the preliminary reference procedure,[50] EU law academics and UK lawyers alike have been generally appreciative of the implied margin for national courts. The ECJ's reluctance to delve into the specificities of the remedy reflects its approach to previous cases involving national remedies: leaving the particulars to the referring national court.[51] Scholars generally note with approval that the ECJ shows respect for and confidence in national courts.[52] Lord Bridge thus determined in the House of Lords' follow-up judgment that 'the judgment of the European Court of Justice does not fetter our discretion to determine whether an appropriate case for the grant of interim relief has been made out'.[53] The ECJ rightly considers implicitly

[39] Toth (n 17) 581.
[40] Papadias (n 5) 171, 177.
[41] Toth (n 17) 586.
[42] Papadias (n 5) 171.
[43] Rather, the House of Lords left this in the middle and noted that there are serious arguments both for and against the existence of the rights claimed, while mentioning that the parties would suffer irremediable damage unless given such interim protection. *cf* Lord Bridge in *Factortame* (n 29).
[44] *cf* R Joliet, 'Protection juridictionnelle provisoire et droit communautaire' (1992) *Rivista di diritto europea* 253; Papadias (n 5) 176.
[45] Lord Donaldson, 'Can the Judiciary control Acts of Parliament?' (1991) 25 *The Law Teacher* 4, 7–8.
[46] Papadias (n 5) 174.
[47] ibid 173.
[48] Collins (n 15) 72.
[49] Toth (n 17) 585.
[50] eg Krommendijk (n 26) 121–23.
[51] eg Case 79/83 *Harz* on the absence of damages for abuse of confidence in German law. Case 79/83 *Dorit Harz v Deutsche Tradax GmbH* EU:C:1984:155; Garcia (n 16) 217.
[52] Collins (n 15) 72. More critically, however, D Simon and A Barav, 'Le droit Communautaire et la suspension provisoire des mesures nationales. Les enjeux de l'affaire *Factortame*' (1990) *Revue du Marché Commun* 591.
[53] Lord Bridge in *Factortame* (n 29).

that the types of interim relief (ie order to stay, injunctions, interlocutory proceedings) are national legislative choices.[54] National procedural rules are obviously subject to *Rewe* requirements (see section IV.B).[55] Nonetheless, the natural consequence of this reticence is that conditions diverge across EU Member States.

The above analysis shows that while there is quite a wide variety of views on the ECJ's statement of principle with respect to interim relief, there is more consensus in relation to the Court's handling of the reference and its reasoning in *Factortame I*. This gives to the question of what the House of Lords eventually decided. Despite the shock and the partly justified criticism, the House of Lords fully complied with the ECJ in its follow-up judgment and decided that relief should be granted. In doing so, the House disapplied UK law in two different ways.[56] First, it disapplied the old common law rule precluding courts from granting interim relief against the Crown. Second, it disapplied temporarily the contested provisions of the Merchant Shipping Act 1988, which were claimed (and later found in *Factortame II*) to be in violation of EU law. Interestingly, the House did not refer to the principle of supremacy, which played an important role in the ECJ judgment.[57] It further did not raise any of the aforementioned objections to the judgment of the ECJ, as the earlier quote of Lord Bridge also shows.[58] With the absence of any guidance from Luxembourg regarding the conditions, the House applied criteria that are used by most national courts within the EU, as also discussed in the Opinion of Advocate General Tesauro. These criteria included the risk of severe and irrecoverable damage (*periculum in mora*) and the existence of a prima facie case (*fumus boni iuris*), as well as the balance of inconvenience whereby it weighed the interests of the applicants with the defendant.[59] Shortly after, the House of Lords also granted interim injunctions against the Crown in a situation not regulated by EU law.[60] The rather obedient and subsequent progressive approach of the House of Lords thus stands in sharp contrast with the initial political and media frenzy that arose shortly after the ECJ's judgment in *Factortame I*.

IV. Famous Follow-Up Cases

Factortame I left quite a few matters unresolved, including the conditions for interim relief and the question of whether there is also a positive duty to provide interim relief.[61] The ECJ accepted such a duty in *Siples* and *Unibet*, as discussed later in this section. With respect to the conditions, the ECJ has continued to leave the same margin to national courts, except for *Zuckerfabrik/Atlanta Fruchthandelgesellschaft* cases involving

[54] Garcia (n 16) 219; Papadias (n 5) 175.
[55] Papadias (n 5) 189.
[56] W van Gerven, 'Bridging the gap between Community and national laws: Towards a principle of homogeneity in the field of legal remedies' (1995) 32 *Common Market Law Review* 679.
[57] I Maher, 'National courts as European community courts' (1994) 14 *Legal Studies* 226.
[58] Douglas-Scott (n 24) 14.
[59] AG Tesauro in Case C-213/89 *The Queen v Secretary of State for Transport, ex parte Factortame* EU:C:1990:216, paras 23, 31 and 33.
[60] *M v Home Office* [1993] UKHL 5 (27 July 1993).
[61] *cf* in favour S Prechal, *Directives in EC law* (Oxford University Press, 2005) 131, 169.

the invalidity of EU law. Section IV.A below discusses the evolution of the case law of the ECJ on interim measures since *Factortame I*. Section IV.B subsequently focuses specifically on the ECJ's case law on the *Rewe* principles of equivalence and effectiveness. Finally, section IV.C concludes with a critical reflection on this jurisprudence following an analysis of interim relief provided by Dutch courts.

A. The ECJ Case Law on Interim Measures after *Factortame I*

Less than a year after *Factortame I*, the ECJ was confronted with questions on interim relief in two German cases contesting the validity of an EU Regulation introducing a higher levy in the sugar sector. More specifically, the *Zuckerfabrik* case dealt with the suspension of the enforcement of national provisions based on a Regulation challenged before the national court. Contrary to *Factortame I*, the ECJ provided uniform conditions for national courts to suspend the enforcement of a national measure implementing an EU measure. It held that such suspension

> may be granted by a national court only if that court entertains serious doubts as to the validity of the Community measure and, should the question of the validity of the contested measure not already have been brought before the Court of Justice, itself refers that question to the Court of Justice, if there is urgency and a threat of serious and irreparable damage to the applicant and if the national court takes due account of the Community's interests.[62]

The different approach in *Zuckerfabrik* stems from the fact that the validity of EU law instead of national law is at stake.[63] Hence, the ECJ pointed to the need for uniformity in all Member States. Another consideration is the alignment of the conditions of *Zuckerfabrik* situations with conditions for interim relief in actions for annulment before the ECJ itself on the basis of Article 279 TFEU.[64] These conditions are quite stringent and difficult to fulfil.[65] This is not surprising considering the ECJ's interest in preserving the uniform application of EU law. If national courts were to suspend the operation of national measures implementing alleged invalid EU law instruments all too easily, this would lead to differences in the application of EU law. In *Atlanta Fruchthandelgesellschaft*, the ECJ further clarified the *Zuckerfabrik* conditions.[66] It also determined that interim measures could go beyond 'mere' suspension of enforcement of a national administrative measure and also take the form of a positive order setting or regulation of the disputed legal positions or relationships for the benefit of individuals.[67] In subsequent cases, the ECJ underlined that the decision to provide interim relief in

[62] Joined Cases C-143/88 and C-92/89 *Zuckerfabrik Süderdithmarschen AG v Hauptzollamt Itzehoe and Zuckerfabrik Soest GmbH v Hauptzollamt Paderborn* EU:C:1991:65, paras 26–27; Papadias (n 5) 181.

[63] See Arts 160–166, and esp Art 160(3), of the Rules of Procedure; *cf* Case C-432/05 *Unibet* EU:C:2007:163, para 79; Collins (n 15) 80.

[64] See Arts 160–166 of the Rules of Procedure; Joined Cases C-143/88 and C-92/89 *Zuckerfabrik* (n 62) para 20.

[65] Papadias (n 5) 182; *cf* Case C-68/95 *T Port v Bundesanstalt für Landwirtschaft und Ernährung* EU:C:1996:452.

[66] Case C-465/93 *Atlanta Fruchthandelsgesellschaft and Others (I) v Bundesamt für Ernährung und Forstwirtschaft* EU:C:1995:369, paras 32–51.

[67] ibid paras 26–30.

Zuckerfabrik situations can only be made by (independent) national courts and not administrative authorities.[68] It also determined that national courts are not obliged to provide an opportunity to express views to the EU institution that adopted the act whose validity is in doubt.[69]

The ECJ has not fundamentally changed or expanded its case law in relation to *Factortame* situations in which the conformity of national law with EU law is at stake. The major innovation is the acceptance of a positive duty to provide for interim relief. In *Siples*, the ECJ held in unequivocal terms with reference to *Factortame* that national courts 'must be in a position to grant interim relief in order to ensure the full effectiveness of the judgment to be given on the existence of the rights claimed under Community law'.[70] With this positive obligation, the ECJ went further than in *Factortame I*, where it 'only' held that a national rule precluding the national court from granting interim relief should be disapplied.[71]

Unibet is another landmark case[72] involving the conformity of the Swedish law on lotteries with the freedom to provide services. Unibet sought the temporary suspension of the advertising ban. In *Unibet*, the ECJ finally answered the question that it left unaddressed in *Factortame I*. It clarified that in *Factortame* situations, the criteria to be applied would be governed by national law.[73] The ECJ contrasted this with *Zuckerfabrik* situations in which national provisions are based on an EU Regulation that is challenged before the national court. In such cases, it is the ECJ that enjoys exclusive jurisdiction to declare EU measures invalid, thereby necessitating uniform criteria.[74] In situations as in *Factortame* and *Unibet* regarding the validity of national measures, the final word can be left to national courts. The only limitations to national procedural law are the *Rewe* principles of equivalence and effectiveness (for further discussion, see section IV.B).

The ECJ, however, went one step further than in *Siples* in one respect. It decided that the suspension of national law was a remedy that should be available in all EU Member States. The national court '*must* be able to grant the interim relief sought'.[75] EU law thus requires interim relief instead of only providing a mandate to do so.[76] While the ECJ based interim relief on the principle of loyalty and effectiveness in *Factortame*, the principle of effective legal protection played a central role in *Unibet*. The ECJ furthermore made clear that no interim relief would be required in the context of an application that is inadmissible under national law, provided that EU law does not call into question such inadmissibility.[77] When it is uncertain whether the application is admissible, national courts are required to provide for such relief.[78] The ECJ did not follow Unibet's

[68] Joined Cases C-453/03, C-11/04, C-12/04 and C-194/04 *ABNA and others* EU:C:2005:741.
[69] Case C-334/95 *Krüger v Hauptzollamt Hamburg-Jonas* EU:C:1997:378, paras 45–46.
[70] Case C-226/99 *Siples* EU:C:2001:14, para 19. *cf* Case C-432/05 *Unibet* (n 63) para 67.
[71] *cf* Taborowski (n 6) 643.
[72] Taborowski (n 6) 646.
[73] Case C-432/05 *Unibet* (n 63) paras 79–80. *cf* AG Tesauro in *Factortame* (n 59).
[74] *cf* AG Sharpston in Case C-432/05 *Unibet* EU:C:2006:755, para 93.
[75] Case C-432/05 *Unibet* (n 63) para 76.
[76] Taborowski (n 6) 644.
[77] Case C-432/05 *Unibet* (n 63) para 73.
[78] ibid para 72.

claim that there was an absolute and almost automatic right to interim measures as soon as there was an EU law element. Unibet's attempts to present its case as a Swedish version of *Factortame I* thus failed.[79]

Apart from *Zuckerfabrik* and the additional clarifications in *Siples* and *Unibet*, the case law of the ECJ on interim relief before national courts has not developed a great deal. A *Curia* search of the ECJ's case law explicitly citing *Factortame I* yielded 17 judgments in relation to interim relief.[80] In several of those cases, the ECJ and/or national court merely brought up the possibility of interim relief in a specific legal area. The ECJ, for instance, sided with the referring Hungarian court in *FMS* when it confirmed the possibility to grant interim relief in relation to the Reception Conditions Directive 2013/33 in the form of ordering a financial allowance enabling applicants for international protection to house themselves or housing in kind (outside the transit zone).[81] The ECJ also underlined in *Oliva* the possibility for national courts to order relief in the form of a declaration that a term in a consumer contract is unfair out of their own motion in an individual action pending final judgment in an ongoing collective action.[82] It also raised the possibility of relief in the form of ordering suspension of the implementation of a customs authority decision – in this case a notice to recover customs duties and VAT on imports (*Siples* and *Kofisa Italia*).[83] In *Križan*, the ECJ held that members of the public have the right to request courts to order interim measures to prevent pollution through a temporary suspension of the disputed permit for a landfill site.[84] It also underlined the legally binding nature of interim measures in its Grand Chamber judgment on the appointment of Polish Supreme Court judges, holding that the effectiveness of the preliminary ruling system is impaired when public authorities disregard such measures.[85] Interestingly, the ECJ also used the possibility of national interim relief in case of urgent disputes as justification for dismissing requests to determine the references under the expedited procedure in Article 105 of the Rules of Procedure.[86]

The preceding analysis suggests that interim relief does not play a prominent role in the EU legal order. This hypothesis is tested in section IV.C, after an examination of the relationship between interim relief and *Rewe* effectiveness in IV.B.

[79] AG Sharpston discussed the difference between both cases. Unibet's application for interim measures (an order that it has the right pending final judgment to take specified marketing measures despite the advertising ban) does not correspond to the main relief sought (damages). What's more, there was no need to 'preserve' damages because of the expectation that the Swedish authorities would pay if the final judgment orders them to do so. By contrast, Factortame and the other fishing companies' principal claim in both the main and interim relief was disapplication of UK legislation. See AG Sharpston in Case C-432/05 *Unibet* (n 74) paras 62, 76–79; and Taborowski (n 6) 645.

[80] Search performed on 6 March 2022 with 'C-213/89' and 'interim'. Another six judgments cited *Factortame I* more generally in relation to the principle of supremacy, in conjunction with *Simmenthal*: Case C-336/14 *Ince* EU:C:2016:72; Case C-112/13 *A* EU:C:2014:2195; Joined Cases C-188/10 and C-188/10 *Melki and Abdeli* EU:C:2010:363, [2010] I-5667; Case C-435/06 *C* EU:C:2007:714, [2007] I-10141; Case C-298/04 *Murgolo* EU:C:2006:461; Case C-443/03 *Leffler* EU:C:2005:665.

[81] Joined Cases C-924/19 PPU and C-925/19 PPU *Országos Idegenrendeszeti Főigazgatóság Dél-alföldi Regionális Igazgatóság (FMS)* EU:C:2020:367, paras 295–298.

[82] Case C-568/14 *Fernández Oliva* EU:C:2016:828.

[83] Case C-226/99 *Siples* (n 70), paras 15–20; Case C-1/99 *Kofisa Italia* EU:C:2001:10, paras 44–49.

[84] Case C-416/10 *Križan and others* EU:C:2013:8, paras 105–10.

[85] Case C-487/19 *WŻ* EU:C:2021:798, para 142.

[86] Case C-14/21 *Sea Watch* EU:C:C:2021:149, para 33.

B. Interim Relief and *Rewe*-Effectiveness

The previous analysis raises the question as to how *Factortame* relates to the ECJ's case law on national procedural autonomy and *Rewe*, especially because the ECJ has left the actual criteria for national courts and legislatures to decide. The ECJ has held in *Rewe* and subsequent cases that, in the absence of EU rules governing the matter, it is for each Member State, in accordance with the principle of the procedural autonomy, to lay down the detailed rules of administrative and judicial procedures governing actions for safeguarding rights which individuals derive from EU law. Those detailed procedural rules must, however, be no less favourable than those governing similar domestic actions (principle of equivalence) and must not render practically impossible or excessively difficult the exercise of rights conferred by EU law (principle of effectiveness).

There has been quite extensive discussion in the literature as to how *Rewe*-effectiveness relates to the principle of effective judicial protection (PEJP), as laid down in Article 47 of the Charter of Fundamental Rights.[87] There are several differences between *Rewe*-effectiveness and the PEPJ, at least on paper.[88] *Rewe*-effectiveness is formulated negatively (ie precluding national procedural rules), because of its instrumental rationale (ie the enforcement of EU law) and subject to a – for Member States less intrusive – contextual procedural rule of reason test. The PEPJ, by contrast, works as a standard entailing positive (procedural) obligations possibly giving rise to new remedies and national powers because of its fundamental rights rationale as well as a stricter (proportionality) test based on the Charter. *Rewe*-effectiveness and the PEJP should also be distinguished from the broader notion of (full) effectiveness of EU law (*effet utile*), which could be said to comprise both the PEJP and *Rewe*-effectiveness.[89]

As discussed before, in *Factortame* the ECJ does only mention (full) effectiveness of EU law in *Simmenthal* terms, with only a rather implicit allusion to the PEJP when it determined that national courts must 'ensure the legal protection which persons derive from the direct effect of provisions of Community law'.[90] The limited engagement with national procedural autonomy and its limiting principles illustrates the ECJ's substantial interference with national remedies aimed at enhancing the effectiveness of EU law. The introduction to this chapter already referred to several other (older) judgments in which the ECJ adopted a similar approach, including *Johnston*, *Heylens*, *Marshall II*, *Francovich* and *Emmott*.

The post-*Factortame* case law on interim measures shows a mixed picture in relation to the application of the three effectiveness principles. *Zuckerfabrik* and *Atlanta* only refer to full effectiveness, which is not surprising considering that it laid down uniform conditions for interim relief when the validity of EU law is at stake.[91] In the customs cases of *Siples* and *Kofisa*, the ECJ coupled references to full effectiveness with reliance

[87] S Prechal and R Widdershoven, 'Redefining the relationship between "Rewe-effectiveness" and effective judicial protection' (2011) 4 *Review of European Administrative Law* 31; J Krommendijk, 'Is there light on the horizon? The distinction between "Rewe effectiveness" and the principle of effective judicial protection in Article 47 of the Charter after Orizzonte' (2016) 53 *Common Market Law Review* 1395.

[88] For an extensive analysis, see Krommendijk (n 87).

[89] eg Case C-61/14 *Orizzonte Salute* EU:C:2015:655, paras 50 and 69.

[90] Case C-213/89 *Factortame I* (n 2) paras 19 and 20–22.

[91] Joined Cases C-143/88 and C-92/89 *Zuckerfabrik* (n 62) paras 19 and 30–31; Case C-465/93 *Atlanta Fruchthandelsgesellschaft* (n 66) paras 23 and 42–43.

on the PEJP in conjunction with Articles 6 and 13 ECHR.[92] In the Hungarian reception conditions case of *FMS*, the ECJ invoked in quite strong terms the PEJP and full effectiveness together with the principle of primacy.[93]

In several more recent cases, the ECJ took the procedural autonomy perspective as a starting point. Within this category of cases there is also variance in the room for manoeuvre of national courts. In the consumer case of *Oliva*, the ECJ analysed Spanish procedural rules in the light of the *Rewe*-principles and concluded that the procedural system is not compatible with *Rewe*-effectiveness.[94] In the environmental case of *Križan*, the ECJ referred to the 'discretion' of Member States subject to the *Rewe*-principles but left the analysis to the referring court.[95] In *Unibet*, the ECJ opted for a middle way. Even though it held that it 'is a matter for the national court to establish' whether Swedish procedural rules satisfy the *Rewe*-principles, it provided quite detailed instructions and indications suggesting these rules to be in conformity.[96] Interestingly, the ECJ mentioned both the *Rewe*-principles and the PEJP at the same time, seemingly treating *Rewe*-effectiveness as an aspect or sub-principle of the PEJP.[97]

The analysis of the case law on interim measures from a *Rewe* perspective thus leads to the same conclusion as earlier more comprehensive studies on *Rewe*-effectiveness. That is to say, the approach of the ECJ is inconsistent and difficult to predict, even though a trend to an increasing reliance on the PEJP and the Charter has been observed.[98] Three observations can be made. First, it seems that the older judgments on interim relief primarily opt for the full effectiveness paradigm, while the ECJ has been more mindful of national procedural autonomy in some recent cases (*Unibet*, *Križan* and *Oliva*). This reliance on national courts and national procedural law fits in a broader trend. Arnull describes, in this regard, how the ECJ once again became slightly more reticent and cautious from the mid-1990s.[99] The ECJ has reiterated in several cases that the national court 'is best placed to assess' to grant 'adequate interim measures to guarantee the full effectiveness of the decision that it itself is called upon to make'.[100] Second, Article 47 of the Charter has so far played a relatively limited role in the case law on interim measures in comparison with other cases dealing with national procedural rules, especially in the area of migration law.[101] This can possibly be attributed to the fact that most cases predate the entry into force of the Charter in December 2009 and/or deal with issues that are far removed from fundamental rights, such as betting, consumer law and environmental law. This relates to a third observation that the ECJ seems more likely to opt for

[92] Case C-226/99 *Siples* (n 70) paras 17 and 19–20; Case C-1/99 *Kofisa Italia* (n 83) paras 46 and 48–49.

[93] Joined Cases C-924/19 PPU and C-925/19 PPU *FMS* (n 81), paras 138–46, 289–91, 297 and 299.

[94] Case C-568/14 *Fernández Oliva* EU:C:2016:828, paras 29–37.

[95] This is as such in conformity with the division of tasks between the ECJ and national courts considering that the former interprets EU law while the referring court is responsible for the subsequent application to the case before it. Case C-416/10 *Križan and others* (n 84) para 106.

[96] Case C-432/05 *Unibet* (n 63) para 65.

[97] ibid paras 42–43. *cf* Case C-268/06 *Impact* EU:C:2008:223, para 48.

[98] Krommendijk (n 87); M Eliantonio and E Muir, 'The principle of effectiveness: under strain?' (2019) 12 *Review of European Administrative Law* 255.

[99] The ECJ did so after 'overreaching' itself in *Emmott*, a case about time limits. eg Case C-188/95 *Fantask and Others v Industriministeriet* EU:C:1997:580; Arnull (n 13) 1765. *cf* P Craig and G de Búrca, *EU Law. Text, cases and material*, 7th edn (Oxford University Press, 2020) 273 and 277.

[100] Case C-14/21 *Sea Watch* (n 86); *cf* Case 186/01 *Dory* EU:C:2001:563.

[101] eg Case C-194/19 *HA* EU:C:2021:270; Case C-403/16 *El Hassani* EU:C:2017:960.

an interventionist logic on the basis of primacy, full effectiveness and the PEPJ in cases involving (important) fundamental rights, as illustrated by the Hungarian *FMS* case. Another recent example of the latter is the decision of the Grand Chamber that national courts are required to *ex officio* review whether detention of an illegally staying foreign national or asylum-seeker is still lawful. The ECJ put Articles 6 and 47 of the Charter at the forefront, while Advocate General Richard de la Tour and the referring Dutch courts approached the case from the perspective of national procedural autonomy.[102]

C. Interim Measures in Relation to EU Law in the Netherlands

Factortame I was considerably less controversial in Member States outside the UK, including the Netherlands. This can be partly explained by the fact that the possibility of interim relief existed already in most Member States.[103] The analysis of quite circumscribed body of ECJ case law in section IV.A suggests that interim relief only plays a limited role before national courts. One may thus wonder what the practical importance of interim relief in relation to EU law is. In order to answer this question, a study has been conducted on an EU Member State in which EU law plays a considerable role and in which national courts are generally eager to apply EU law.[104] Moreover, the purpose of this analysis was also to determine the conditions applied by Dutch courts and to examine the cases in which interim relief was indeed adopted. While conducting an exhaustive analysis of all cases is nearly impossible, only a handful of cases across a period of 30 years were found on the basis of various methodological approaches.[105]

Dutch courts have generally been quite reluctant to adopt interim relief on the basis of EU law in *Factortame* situations. The Dutch Supreme Court, which is the country's highest court in civil, criminal and tax law, has adopted quite a high threshold. For example, it decided against interim measures in a case regarding a tax exemption for air passengers for environmental purposes. It sided with the Court of Appeal, which had determined that a legislative provision could only be set aside in interlocutory proceedings if such a provision was 'unmistakably' (*onmiskenbaar*) incompatible with provisions of EU law that have direct effect.[106] The Supreme Court also rejected interim relief in relation to an import ban of beef heads, because this case also did not meet the

[102] Joined Cases C-704/20 and C 39/21 *CBX* EU:C:2022:858.

[103] In the Netherlands, Art 8:81 Awb relates to decisions of administrative authorities, while Art 223 Rv can be used in relation to legislative measures by the civil law interim relief judge. Dutch procedural rules are also less stringent than the *Zuckerfabrik/Atlanta* requirements. R Ortlep and RJGM Widdershoven, 'VI. Rechtsbescherming' in S Prechal and RJGM Widdershoven (eds), *Inleiding tot het Europees Bestuursrecht* (Ars Aequi Libri, 2017) 427.

[104] M Rasmussen and DS Martinsen, 'EU constitutionalisation revisited: Redressing a central assumption in European studies' (2019) 25 *European Law Journal* 251, 264–65.

[105] Two approaches were used. First, two prominent Dutch sources were used that discuss EU law cases before national courts dealing with interim relief. This includes Ortlep and Widdershoven (n 103) as well as the 'Kroniek Europees staats- en bestuursrecht' in the *Nederlands Tijdschrift Bestuursrecht* that includes a paragraph on interim relief ('voorlopige voorziening'). Second, a case law search of rechtspraak.nl was performed with the search terms *Factortame* (68 results) and *Zuckerfabrik* (30 results).

[106] This criterion stems from HR 1 July 1983, NJ 1984, 360. In this case both courts held that the exemption is not unmistakably a measure of state aid in the sense of Art 87(1) EC (currently Art 107(1) TFEU). HR 4 September 2009, NL:HR:2009:BI3451, paras 4.1, 4.6.4.

threshold.[107] One might wonder whether the 'unmistakably incompatible' requirement is too severe and in conformity with the *Rewe* effectiveness or the principle of effective legal protection principles.[108] Several observers are of the opinion that there is no problem. They hold that in some cases not involving EU law, the Supreme Court found the criterion to be satisfied.[109] Hence it is difficult to argue that this criterion makes the exercise of rights conferred by the EU legal order 'impossible in practice or excessively difficult'.[110] A comparison of the approach of the Supreme Court with the ECJ's case law on interim measures also leads to a mixed picture. The 'unmistakable' criterion appears more stringent than the ECJ's condition of an existence of a prima facie case.[111] Nonetheless, the (other) criteria for interim relief before the ECJ are more restrictive, especially the requirement of urgency and irreparable damage.[112]

The Administrative Section of the Council of State, one of the three highest Dutch administrative courts, has also been generally reluctant to impose interim measures, especially considering the far-ranging effects of such decisions.[113] While the Dutch Supreme Court focuses on the likelihood of a breach of EU law ('unmistakably incompatible'), the Council primarily considers the consequences of the alleged breach, requiring those to be 'irreversible'. The Council has mainly been confronted with requests for interim relief in environmental cases and required almost certain (and irreparable) environmental damage.[114] The Council, for example, decided against interim measures when requesting a preliminary ruling on the widening of a motorway and the consequent increase in nitrogen deposits on Natura 2000 sites in the light of the Habitats Directive.[115] The Council held, mentioning Article 4(3) TEU, but without reference to ECJ case law, that it was not convinced that the loss of quality following the increase in nitrogen deposits would be irreversible.[116] In a subsequent nitrogen case, the Council only adopted interim measures, after an initial refusal,[117] when it was evident

[107] HR 12 May 2000, NL:HR:2000:AA5775, para 3.7.

[108] Former AG to the Supreme Court Mok noted that this criterion is undetermined and used as a magic formula. He argued that it was rather similar to the *acte clair* requirement ('so obvious as to leave no scope for any reasonable doubt'). AG Mok in HR 14 April 1989, NL:PHR:1989:AD5725 (*Harmonisatiewet*), para 3.4; LAD Keus, 'De toverformule van de onmiskenbare onverbindendheid en buitenwerkingstelling van wetgeving wegens strijd met supranationaal recht' in DC Buijs and others (eds), *Mok-aria; opstellen aangeboden aan Prof. Mr M.R. Mok ter gelegenheid van zijn 70ste verjaardag* (Kluwer, 2002) 118.

[109] AG Wattel in NL:PHR:2009:BI3451, para 5.6; Keus (n 108) 121.

[110] Schutgens in *JB* 2009/229; Keus (n 108) 121.

[111] According to the ECJ, the condition is satisfied when there is a major legal or factual disagreement whose resolution is not immediately obvious, so that the action is not prima facie without reasonable substance. eg Case C-441/17 R *Commission v Poland (Białowieża Forest)* EU:C:2017:877, para 31.

[112] Keus (n 108) 121.

[113] Since December 2016, the *voorzieningenrechter* (judge hearing applications for interim measures) of the Council has been more willing than before to order that an alien will not be deported before a decision has been made on his appeal. This change of practice stemmed from the judgment of the European Court of Human Rights (ECtHR) concluding that the absence of automatic suspensory effect means that appeal before the Council of State in cases with an alleged violation of Art 3 ECHR does not constitute an effective remedy. ECtHR 5 July 2016, *AM v the Netherlands* CE:ECHR:2016:0705JUD002909409.

[114] ABRvS 13 October 2009, NL:RVS:2009:BK0772, para 2.5; ABRvS 14 October 1992, NL:RVS:1992:AN3461.

[115] Case C-521/12 *Briels and others* EU:C:2014:330.

[116] It was not persuaded that deposits in one area may slightly accelerate the loss of quality already occurring there. Without explicating, the Council pointed to the balancing of interests involved. ABRvS 7 December 2012, NL:RVS:2012:BY2504, para 93. See earlier ABRvS 9 December 2011, NL:RVS:2011:BU7894.

[117] With reference to Art 4(3) TEU, the Council examined the need to adopt interim measures without, however, referring to criteria in an explicit or structured way. It reiterated that the mere fact that a reference

that the consequences were indeed irreversible. It ordered the suspension of specific permits when it turned out that the dairy farm activities did indeed use more than 60 per cent of the available nitrogen deposits activities.[118] One might wonder whether the high threshold of irreversible consequences in environmental law cases, requiring near certainty, is in line with the precautionary principle.[119]

The Central Appeals Tribunal, the highest administrative court in social security cases, has employed a similarly reluctant approach mirroring the 'unmistakably incompatible' criterion applied by the Supreme Court. For example, it decided against providing social assistance benefits by way of interim relief in relation to several of the applicants, which led to the *Chavez Vilchez* judgment of the ECJ.[120] This case dealt, in short, with the rights of residence of third-country nationals with a child who was an EU citizen. The Tribunal held – quite surprisingly – that because of this reference, it could not consider in its balancing of interests the (im)probability that the disputed court judgment would be annulled, thereby implying a provisional opinion on the dispute.[121] It could merely consider whether the decision not to order such benefits would lead to irreversible consequences in the light of the objectives of EU citizenship. Although the Tribunal acknowledged the difficult situation of a mother-and-daughter duo with limited financial means, it held that the alleged psychological damage for the daughter was insufficiently substantiated. It also noted that recovery of the publicly funded benefits in case the judgment were to stand under appeal was 'virtually illusory'.[122] After the ECJ rendered its judgment, the Tribunal did order interim relief, because the immigration authority expected that the mother would be granted a residence permit on the basis of *Chavez Vilchez*, as well as the right to social assistance benefits. Hence, the Tribunal considered it highly likely that the judgment under appeal would not be upheld and held that the interests of the family outweighed the limited risk of non-restitution in case the judgment was upheld.[123]

This overview illustrates the reluctance of the highest Dutch courts to grant interim relief. The rationale of the restrictive position of courts is the far-ranging nature of interim relief. First-instance interlocutory judges of district courts seem slightly more willing to order interim measures, especially when the consequences are rather minimal. In two pharmaceutical cases[124] and a real estate case[125] the consequence mainly

for a preliminary ruling was made did not mean that an application for interim relief should automatically be granted. The Council considered that there was a certain buffer. ABRvS 17 May 2017, NL:RVS:2017:1259, paras 29.2 and 7.

[118] ABRvS 9 March 2018, NL:RVS:2018:795.

[119] With reference to the precautionary principle, the ECJ itself adopted interim measures in an infringement procedure started by the Commission against Poland suspending the logging of centuries-old trees in the Białowieska forest. Case C-441/17 R *Poland (Białowieża Forest)* (n 111) para 42.

[120] CRvB 16 March 2015, NL:CRVB:2015:665; CRvB 1 September 2016, NL:CRVB:2016:3287 (see also: 3279 and 3286); Case C-133/15 *Chavez-Vilchez and others* EU:C:2017:354.

[121] CRvB 1 September 2016, NL:CRVB:2016:3287, paras 4.2–4.3.

[122] CRvB 1 September 2016, NL:CRVB:2016:3287, paras 4.3–4.8.

[123] CRvB 30 June 2017, NL:CRVB:2017:2422.

[124] Courts suspended the ban on marketing unregistered pharmaceutical products and thus 'tolerated' anthroposophic medicinal products. Gh Den Haag 27 May 2004, NL:GHSGR:2004:AP0196, para 8; HR 27 January 2006, NL:HR:2006:AU5271; Case C-84/06 *Antroposana and Others* EU:C:2007:535. With respect to the order to maintain the registration of medicine Yewtaxan, ABRvS 22 May 1998, nr. K01.98.0155.

[125] ABRvS 2 April 2012, NL:RVS:2012:BW1539.

consisted of a delay in the application of legislation or a court decision – in other words, the mere prolonging of the existing status quo.

The reluctance of courts is also visible in *Zuckerfabrik* situations in which the validity of EU law is at stake. In these cases, national courts apply uniform EU criteria. Most requests to adopt interim measures have been rejected.[126] Courts primarily adopt a high threshold for the criterion of 'serious doubts as to the validity', especially when the EU legislature has a broad discretion and requires complex assessments and political, economic and social choices.[127] The legality of an EU measure is only at stake when the measure is manifestly inappropriate or disproportionate.[128] Two cases were found in which interim relief was provided: while in *ABNA* the court was proven right in adopting interim relief, this was not necessarily the case in *Affish*. The latter case marked the first time a Dutch court suspended national implementing measures of Commission Decision 95/119 concerning certain protective measures with regard to fishery products originating in Japan.[129]

The Dutch Trade and Industry Appeals Tribunal (CBb), one of the three highest administrative courts in socio-economic administrative law, applied all criteria in a structured way and noted, for instance, that there were 'serious doubts' about the validity of the blanket ban on all fish from the whole of Japan, as well as the unavoidable bankruptcy of the importing Dutch company.[130] Interestingly, the UK Queen's Bench Division was more reluctant and did not order interim measures in a similar case, perhaps not surprisingly, considering the tensions following *Factortame* (discussed above). The Bench required an 'apparent disproportionality' of the Commission decision with a view on the interest of the EU.[131] The ECJ eventually declared the decision as valid. This case thus illustrates that the Bench's reluctance was in a way justified, while the CBb was perhaps too focused on judicial protection.

There was more unanimity among national courts in *ABNA*. Courts in several EU Member States had already suspended implementing measures and referred questions to the ECJ in relation to Directive 2002/2/EC[132] on the circulation of compound

[126] Ortlep and Widdershoven (n 103) 427. The CBb rejected interim measures in *Emesa* because the Aruban sugar company had also challenged the commission decision rejecting the application for import licences. For the final judgment, see Case T-44/98 *Emesa Sugar v Commission* EU:T:2001:280. CBb 12 February 1998, JB 1998/119, para 5.3. The Court of Appeal The Hague rejected suspension of legislation implementation with explicit reference to the *Zuckerfabrik* conditions, because Privacy First had not made it 'sufficiently plausible' that disclosure of the data posed a risk of serious damage. Gh Den Haag 16 November 2021, NL:GHDHA:2021:2176, para 3.13.

[127] The Council of State decided against interim measures in *Willems*, in which it referred questions about Regulation 2252/2004 on standards for security features and biometrics in passports and travel documents and the requirement to take fingerprints and store them in passports [2004] OJ L385. ABRvS 5 December 2013, NL:RVS:2013:2311, paras 2.3–4; Joined Cases C-446/12 to C-449/12 *Willems and others* EU:C:2015:238; ABRvS 3 December 2012, NL:RVS:2012:BY5838, para 2.3.

[128] Joined Cases C-453/03, C-11/04, C-12/04 and C-194/04 *ABNA* (n 68) para 69; see Gh 's Gravenshage 6 December 2007, NL:GHSGR:2007:BB9593 *(Nevedi)*, paras 6 and 12; *cf* CBb 22 September 2008, NL:CBB:2008:BF3951, para 5.4.

[129] Case C-183/95 *Affish v Rijksdienst voor de keuring van Vee en Vlees* EU:C:1997:373.

[130] CBb 24 May 1995, NL:CBB:1995:ZG0367, paras 6.1–6.8.

[131] *The Queens v Secretary of State, ex parte MacRae Seafoods* (12 June 1995) as discussed in Ortlep and Widdershoven (n 103) 428.

[132] Directive 2002/2/EC of the European Parliament and of the Council of 28 January 2002 amending Council Directive 79/373/EEC on the circulation of compound feedingstuffs and repealing Commission Directive 91/357/EEC [2002] OJ L63/23.

feeding stuffs. The Directive required companies to indicate the exact percentages by weight of the feed materials contained in feeding stuffs. Affected companies complained about violations of the right to property and the proportionality principle. The affected Dutch company argued that without suspension, Dutch companies would be placed at a significant disadvantage compared to foreign competitors, because they injected secret and substantial know-how about the composition of compound feeding stuffs into the market.[133] This was also reason for the district court The Hague to suspend implementation of measures. Without explicitly applying or mentioning the *Zuckerfabrik* criteria and the substantive reasoning therein, the court heeded the request of the company – and was proven right. The Grand Chamber of the ECJ eventually determined that a provision of the Directive indeed violated the proportionality principle.[134]

V. Concluding Critical Reflections

The discussion so far points to three ideas. The first is common to both *Factortame* and *Zuckerfabrik* situations, namely the difficulty to obtain interim relief in practice.[135] The Merchant Shipping Act 1988 that played a central role in *Factortame* has so far been the only Act of Parliament to be disapplied by UK courts.[136] Interim relief on the basis of EU law thus seems largely a theoretical possibility, also in the Netherlands.[137] This is especially so in Member States with a strong presumption of constitutionality coupled with a limited tradition of judicial review of parliamentary acts, including the UK and perhaps also Scandinavian countries.[138] The question is whether the findings in this chapter for the Netherlands (and the UK) also hold true for other EU Member States. There is currently a lack of research on the practical impact of interim relief on the basis of EU law. In this regard, the meagre attention paid in the FIDE 2021 country reports on national courts and the enforcement of EU law illustrates the limited role of interim relief.[139]

A second comment stemming from the *Factortame* approach is that the ECJ allows for considerable differences among EU Member States in terms of the nature of relief and the criteria applied. The implication is that there is notable diversity among EU Member States in terms of the level of judicial and interim protection for individuals, as well as the uniform application of EU law.[140] Arnull fiercely criticises the ECJ for not

[133] Rb 's-Gravenhage 22 April 2004, NL:RBSGR:2004:AR5136 (*Nevedi*), paras 2 and 3.1.

[134] This relates to the requirement in Art 1(1)(b) of Directive 2002/2 to indicate, at a customer's request, the exact composition of a feeding stuff. Joined Cases C-453/03, C-11/04, C-12/04 and C-194/04 *ABNA* (n 68) para 85.

[135] Taborowski (n 6) 647.

[136] J Marson, H Alissa and K Ferris, 'Resolving the Inconsistency Between National and EU Motor Insurance Law. Was Factortame the Solution Nobody Sought?' (2021) 22 *German Law Journal* 122, 138.

[137] Similar scepticism as to the opaqueness of EU law remedies has been voiced in relation to state liability: ibid; Garcia (n 16) 192.

[138] M Wind, 'The Nordics, the EU and the reluctance towards supranational judicial review' (2010) 48 *Journal of Common Market Studies*, 1039.

[139] M Botman and J Langer, *National Courts and the Enforcement of EU Law: The Pivotal Role of National Courts in the EU Legal Order* (Eleven, 2021).

[140] Taborowski (n 6) 645; Arnull (n 13) 1778; M Dougan, 'The vicissitudes of life at the coalface: Remedies and procedures for enforcing Union law before the national courts' in P Craig and G de Búrca (eds), *The Evolution of EU Law*, 2nd edn (Oxford University Press, 2011).

providing uniform conditions in *Factortame* and *Unibet* situations and thereby departing from *Zuckerfabrik*.[141] He attributes this to the increased sensitivity of the ECJ to national procedural autonomy.[142] Apart from differences in the effectiveness of EU law, the lack of EU-wide conditions leads to uncertainty regarding the exact possibilities of national courts.[143] One might wonder whether the entry into force of the Charter of Fundamental Rights in 2009 and the growing importance of Article 47 might be a reason for the ECJ to change its emphasis on national procedural autonomy and resulting objections to uniform criteria.[144] The last time the ECJ dealt with – and rejected – such uniform criteria was in *Unibet* in 2007.

A third observation relates to the more uniform approach in relation to *Zuckerfabrik* cases involving the invalidity of EU law measures. This approach is also not free from criticism. While the conditions are uniform and provided by the ECJ, they are applied in a decentralised way by national courts. Ortlep and Widdershoven wonder whether this decentralised system is still desirable, because of its complexity and the concurrence of similar proceedings in different Member States, as in *ABNA* involving similar references of four courts from three different EU Member States.[145] They also lament the divergences across EU Member States. The *Affish* case regarding Japanese fish illustrates that courts have taken different approaches while applying the same criteria. The fact that courts in other Member States have suspended national implementation of measures and asked for a preliminary reference does not in itself justify interim measures, as the Dutch Supreme Court also determined.[146] Differences among EU courts are even more challenging in *Zuckerfabrik* cases than in *Factortame* situations. They can distort competition when companies enjoy competitive advantages in Member States through benefitting from suspension of bans on their economic activities.

Altogether, these critical reflections illustrate that the last word on interim relief has certainly not be said, even though the practical value of interim relief in relation to EU law is (still) rather limited. The future will reveal whether the ECJ dares to adopt a new *Factortame* judgment in which it takes the bold step of providing (uniform) criteria with a view of strengthening effective legal protection and the effectiveness of EU law. One should, however, not be so naive as to believe that such adoption would automatically remove differences across EU Member States, especially as the different applications of the uniform *Zuckerfabrik* criteria in *Affish* show otherwise.

[141] Arnull (n 13) 1778.
[142] ibid 1780; Joined Cases C-222/05 to C-225/05 *Van der Weerd and others* EU:C:2007:318.
[143] Taborowski (n 6) 647.
[144] Krommendijk (n 87).
[145] Ortlep and Widdershoven (n 103) 430.
[146] Gh 's Gravenshage 6 December 2007, NL:GHSGR:2007:BB9593 *(Nevedi)*, para 13; upheld in cassation by HR 13 November 2009, NL:HR:2009:BJ8329.

14

Francovich and the Liability of States

ROBERTO CARANTA

I. Individuals and Undertakings: Instruments and Protagonists of EU Law

What has become the European Union (EU) never had, and essentially still lacks, an army, a police force or a sizeable bureaucracy proportionate to its 447 million inhabitants. The majority of EU rules are implemented and enforced by administrations in the Member States and often require transposition by the Member States as a first step towards becoming the applied law of the land.

The seminal judgment in *van Gend en Loos* made the EU a new kind of legal order.[1] Since then, the Court of Justice – one of the engines of EU integration together with the Commission – has developed a number of doctrines shaping a legal order in which individuals and undertaking are both instrumental and protagonists in making sure that EU law is applied against the Member States.

During the first two decades following *van Gen den Loos*, one might have seen the role of legal and natural persons as instrumental to the effectiveness of then EEC law. *Effet utile* and *primauté* were the watchwords that mobilised vigilant individuals and undertakings. However:

> The limits of indirect effect and direct effect in the case of Directives were apparent by the early 1990s. Neither protected against flagrant violations of EU law by Member States where these either passed no legislation to transpose a Directive or had legislation in place which explicitly contradicted it.[2]

State liability may be considered as the third building block of decentralised enforcement of EU law alongside primacy and direct effects.[3] However, a Member State liability is much more than that. 'Rights' and even 'subjective rights' were mentioned early on in the case law of the Court of Justice. But they were not centre stage. Even in the first *Factortame* judgment,[4] which brought effective judicial protection to new heights,

[1] Case 26/62 *Van Gend en Loos* [1963] ECR 1.

[2] D Chalmers, G Davies and G Monti, *European Union Law*, 4th edn (Cambridge University Press, 2019) at 314.

[3] TA Börzel and P Sabatier, 'Enforcement and compliance' in C Harlow, P Leino and G della Cananea (eds), *Research Handbook on EU Administrative Law* (Edward Elgar, 2017) 241 at 247 ff.

[4] Case C-213/89 *Factortame I* EU:C:1990:257.

'rights' are mentioned only once in the Court's reasoning, to reinforce the effectiveness of EU law.[5] For legal technical reasons, which will be clarified later, holders of 'rights' became instead protagonists in *Francovich*.[6]

II. *Francovich*: The Facts, the Opinion of Advocate General Mischo and the Judgment

Throughout the 1980s, Italy was often significantly behind the curve regarding the implementation of directives. This was also the case with Directive 80/987/EEC[7] relating to the protection of employees in the event of the insolvency of the employer. As one of its recitals indicated, rules were needed to guarantee payment of employees' outstanding claims. Under Article 11, the Member States were required to implement the directive by 23 October 1983. Italy did not, as the Court of Justice found in 1989.[8]

Pending implementation, proceedings were brought in Vicenza by Mr Francovich and in Bassano del Grappa by Ms Bonifaci and 33 others. The competent local first instance courts sent identical questions to the Court of Justice asking whether the directive could be considered as having direct effect so that the Member State concerned could be asked to pay the benefits foreseen under EEC law. In case this were not so, the referring courts asked if private individuals were entitled 'to claim reparation of the loss and damage sustained in relation to provisions to which that right does not apply'.

The first question was answered in the negative.[9] Suffice to say that the requirement that establishes that the relevant provisions are 'are unconditional and sufficiently precise' was defeated by the facts that those provisions 'do not identify the person liable to provide the guarantee'.[10]

The issue of Member State liability for breaches of what has since become EU law was unavoidable. This question left many uneasy, including the Commission. As Advocate General Mischo recalled,

> the Commission was at pain to stress that it did not propose that in this case the Court should rule on the general question whether the failure to implement a directive which does not have direct effects may give rise to an action for damages.[11]

[5] ibid para 21; see the seminal analysis by W van Gerven, 'Bridging the Gap between Community and National Laws: Towards a Principle of Homogeneity in the Field of Legal Remedies?' (1995) 33 *Common Market Law Review* 507.

[6] See also the analysis by S Prechal, 'Article 19 TEU and National Courts. A New Role for the Principle of Effective Judicial Protection?' in M Bonelli, M Eliantonio and G Gentile (eds), *Article 47 of the EU Charter and Effective Judicial Protection*, vol 1: *The Court of Justice's Perspective* (Hart Publishing, 2022) 11, esp at 22 (and fn 71 for reference to Case C-213/89 *Factortame I*); see also T Lock, 'Is Private Enforcement of EU Law through State Liability a Myth? Assessment 20 Years after Francovich' (2012) 49 *Common Market Law Review* 1702, and, stressing that rights and values – including equality – deserve a larger role in the discussion about remedies, M Dougan, *National Remedies before the Court of Justice* (Hart Publishing, 2004) esp 68 ff.

[7] Council Directive 80/987/EEC of 20 October 1980 on the approximation of the laws of the Member States relating to the protection of employees in the event of the insolvency of their employer [1980] OJ L283/23.

[8] Case 22/87 *Commission v Italy* EU:C:1991:428.

[9] Joined Cases 6/90 and 9/90 *Francovich and Bonifaci v Italy* EU:C:1991:428, paras 25 et seq.

[10] ibid para 26.

[11] ibid para 34.

However, in his view, there was 'no escaping the need to decide once and for all, that is to say independently of the particular circumstances, whether Member States can incur liability for failure to implement a directive'.[12]

Advocate General Mischo argued that, while it is for the Member States to designate the competent courts and lay down the procedural conditions appliable to actions brought to vindicate rights that find their source in EU law, that protection must be 'effective' to ensure both the 'effectiveness of Community law' and the 'effective protection of the rights which individuals derive from Community law'.[13] More specifically, he then drew an analogy pertaining to the long-standing case law concerning the recovery of sums unduly paid on the basis of national rules inconsistent with EU law.[14] Through such an analogy, Advocate General Mischo came to conclude that 'the possible compensation of an individual for loss or damage suffered as a result of the breach of a provision of Community law with direct effect has its foundation in the Community legal order itself'.[15]

Advocate General Mischo went on to clarify the dicta in some precedents that had been invoked by the Member States. He showed how those pronouncements – while referring to the procedural autonomy of the Member States as to the procedural setup of remedies – never accepted a situation in which it would have been 'impossible in practice to exercise the rights' conferred on individuals by EU law.[16]

In any case, he argued that, since the then recent judgment *Factortame*, there can no longer

> be any doubt that in certain cases that Community law may itself directly confer on national judicial authorities the necessary powers in order to ensure effective judicial protection of those rights, even where similar powers do not exist in national law.[17]

Relying next on *Zuckerfabrik Süderdithmarschen and Zuckerfabrik Soest*,[18] Advocate General Mischo argued that 'Community law may even lay down the conditions governing the exercise of the jurisdiction which it thus confers on national courts'.[19] The need for uniformity, or at least coherence, in the remedies provided to individuals at both EU and national level prompted him to analyse the Treaty and the case on the liability of EU institutions to lay down the essential conditions for liability. Those conditions include illegality, a manifest and serious breach – at least in so far the wrongdoer enjoys 'wide discretion' – of a rule intended for the protection of the individual, a causal link and actual damage.[20] No such discretion being given to the Member States as to the duty to implement directives, and no doubt being possible that Directive 80/987/EEC aims

[12] ibid para 35.

[13] Joined Cases 6/90 and 9/90 *Francovich and Bonifaci v Italy* EU:C:1991:221, paras 38 et seq; Case 179/84 *Bozzetti v Invernizzi* EU:C:1985:306; Case C-213/89 *Factortame I* EU:C:1990:257 and Case 106/77 *Amministrazione delle Finanze dello Stato v Simmenthal* EU:C:1978:49 are referred to.

[14] Joined Cases C-6/90 and C-9/90 *Francovich* (n 13) paras 40 et seq; see also para 51.

[15] ibid para 42.

[16] ibid paras 44 et seq.

[17] ibid para 53.

[18] Joined Cases C-143/88 and C-92/89 *Zuckerfabrik Süderdithmarschen and Zuckerfabrik Soest* [1991] ECR 1-415.

[19] Joined Cases C-6/90 and C-9/90 *Francovich* (n 13) para 54.

[20] ibid paras 65 et seq.

at protecting workers, national formal and procedural rules may be followed, provided that they are no less favourable than those relating to similar claims under national law and that they do not render the exercise of EU rights virtually impossible.[21]

As a final salvo, he strongly stated that

> the scope of the reasoning which I have proposed in order to deal with that question goes beyond the particular features of this case. It is applicable to all infringements of Community law committed in the past by the Member States, whether these are infringements of provisions of the Treaty, of regulations or of directives with or without direct effect.[22]

Because of the wide repercussions of such liability, the Advocate General proposed to prospectively limit the effects of the judgment.[23]

In essence, the Court of Justice followed its Advocate General. The Court too held that

> the issue of the existence and scope of a State's liability for loss and damage resulting from breach of its obligations under Community law … must be considered in the light of the general system of the Treaty and its fundamental principles.[24]

Once the approach from highest EU constitutional viewpoint is taken, the first references from the Court of Justice naturally were made to *van Gend en Loos* and *Costa v ENEL*.[25] Relying on the two judgments, whose analyses open this book, the Court thus indicated that:

> It should be borne in mind at the outset that the EEC Treaty has created its own legal system, which is integrated into the legal systems of the Member States and which their courts are bound to apply. The subjects of that legal system are not only the Member States but also their nationals. Just as it imposes burdens on individuals, Community law is also intended to give rise to rights which become part of their legal patrimony. Those rights arise not only where they are expressly granted by the Treaty but also by virtue of obligations which the Treaty imposes in a clearly defined manner both on individuals and on the Member States and the Community institutions.[26]

Simmenthal[27] and *Factortame*,[28] two other landmark judgments, are recalled immediately thereafter to stress that it is the task of national courts to ensure that EU rules 'take full effect' and the rights conferred on individuals are protected.[29]

According to the Court:

> The full effectiveness of Community rules would be impaired and the protection of the rights which they grant would be weakened if individuals were unable to obtain redress when their rights are infringed by a breach of Community law for which a Member State can be held responsible.[30]

[21] ibid para 78; Case 199/82 *San Giorgio* [1983] ECR 3595, para 12 is referred to.
[22] Joined Cases C-6/90 and C-9/90 *Francovich* (n 13) para 85; see also ibid para 2.
[23] ibid paras 86 et seq.
[24] Joined Cases C-6/90 and C-9/90 *Francovich* (n 9) paras 29 et seq.
[25] Case 6/64 *Costa v ENEL* [1964] ECR 585.
[26] Joined Cases C-6/90 and C-9/90 *Francovich* (n 9) para 31.
[27] Case 106/77 *Amministrazione delle Finanze dello Stato v Simmenthal* [1978] ECR 629.
[28] Case C-213/89 *Factortame* [1990] ECR 1-2433.
[29] Joined Cases C-6/90 and C-9/90 *Francovich* (n 9) para 32.
[30] ibid para 33.

It is worth remarking that from this perspective, liability serves both the *effet utile* of EU law and the effective judicial protection of EU rights. In both cases, liability is 'particularly indispensable' where Member States' action is required to implement EU rules.[31] Consequently, the 'the principle whereby a State must be liable for loss and damage caused to individuals as a result of breaches of Community law for which the State can be held responsible is inherent in the system of the Treaty'.[32] The conclusion is buttressed by reference to the principle of sincere cooperation (now Article 4(3) TEU), which requires the Member States to nullify the consequences of breaches of EU law.[33]

As to the conditions for such liability, the starting point is 'the conditions under which that liability gives rise to a right to reparation depend on the nature of the breach of Community law giving rise to the loss and damage'.[34] In case the breach consists of the non- or mis-implementation of a directive, three conditions must be fulfilled: (a) the directive should 'entail the grant of rights to individuals'; (b) the directive should make it possible 'to identify the content of those rights'; and (c) a causal link between the breach and the harm.[35]

Those conditions are sufficient to give rise to liability. Absent secondary EU rules, it is up to the laws of the Member States to 'designate the competent courts and lay down the detailed procedural rules' for damages actions.[36] Still, in line with the indications from the *San Giorgio* case,[37] those rules 'must not be less favourable than those relating to similar domestic claims and must not be so framed as to make it virtually impossible or excessively difficult to obtain reparation'.[38]

Finally, the Court of Justice is ready to direct the referring courts, holding that the first two conditions for liability are given on the facts of the case.[39]

Francovich significantly raised the costs for the Member States and their institutions breaching EU law, providing a remedy for the natural and legal persons, thereby strengthening the effectiveness of EU law.

These results were achieved thanks to references by two first instance monocratic judges (*pretori*) from deep in the provinces of Italy, more specifically Veneto. The references did not come from Venice, but respectively from Vicenza, a small town unproportionally beautified by the local architectural genius – no one less than Andrea Palladio – and from Bassano del Grappa, an even smaller town known for its wooden bridge on which thousands of soldiers marched to their death during WWI and – in a lighter but not unconnected theme – as being the seat of some of the oldest and best schnapps (*grappa* in Italian) distilleries. Italian first instance judges greatly contributed to the development of EU law providing the Court of Justice with ammunitions to design the law of a 'new legal order of international law for the benefit of which the states have limited their sovereign rights'.[40] A *pretore* in Susa, yet again a small alpine

[31] ibid para 34.
[32] ibid para 35; see also para 37.
[33] ibid para 36; Case 6/60 *Humblet v Belgium* [1960] ECR 559 is referred to by analogy.
[34] Joined Cases C-6/90 and C-9/90 *Francovich* (n 9) para 38.
[35] ibid para 40.
[36] ibid para 42.
[37] Case 199/82 *San Giorgio* (n 21).
[38] Joined Cases C-6/90 and C-9/90 *Francovich* (n 9) para 43.
[39] ibid para 45.
[40] Case 26/62 *van Gend en Loos* (n 1).

town, triggered the *Simmenthal* judgment, while the President of the first instance court in Trento, a bigger alpine town, raised the questions that the Court of Justice answered in *San Giorgio*.[41] The judges were not alone. What could be read as coordinated test cases were launched by Claudio Mondin, Aldo Campesan and Alberto dal Ferro of the Vicenza, then all in their 30s but punching well above the weight of their small firms.[42]

III. Reception History: Judicial and Academic

Francovich had a powerful impact not just on EU law, but on the way different actors in the legal arena saw each other. In most Member States, directives are implemented through legislation. Those Member States might now be liable because of omissions by their Parliaments. Together with *Factortame*, *Francovich* put a nail into the coffin of Parliamentary sovereignty cherished by the UK and elsewhere.

Before delving into the reactions triggered by *Francovich*, a short historical note is needed to recall that Mr Francovich never benefited from the judgment that secured him a relevant place in the pantheon of EU law. Italy finally implemented Directive 80/967/EEC and extended retroactively the same benefits as reparation of the harm suffered by the belated implementation. Mr Francovich had been working for a SME and under Italian law SMEs were not subject to insolvency proceedings. In a second preliminary reference (*Francovich II*), the Court of Justice held that indeed the EU legislature had pursued a partial harmonisation of the matter and had expressly limited the scope of the directive so that it cannot be relied upon 'by employees whose contract of employment or employment relationship is with an employer who cannot', under the applicable national provisions, 'be subject to proceedings to satisfy collectively the claims of creditors'.[43]

Ms Bonifaci and others were luckier, as the Court of Justice, to which the case had been referred again, read the different options for calculating the benefits in Directive 80/987/EEC in such a way that the employees' claim could not be frustrated by the unusually long time then required in Italy to come to an official finding of bankruptcy.[44] Echoing *Bonifaci*, in *Maso*, the Court of Justice held that, 'in making good the loss or damage sustained by employees as a result of the belated transposition of the Directive, a Member State is entitled to apply retroactively to such employees belatedly adopted implementing measures'.[45] 'Retroactive and proper application in full of the measures implementing the Directive' will normally provide sufficient redress for breaches of EU law, but those harmed might 'establish the existence of complementary loss sustained on account of the fact that they were unable to benefit at the appropriate time from the financial advantages guaranteed by the Directive'.[46] Finally, in *Palmisani*,

[41] Case 199/82 *San Giorgio* (n 20).

[42] See at www.studiolegalemondin.it; www.studiolegalevis.it/soci/avv-aldo-campesan; and www.dfalex.eu/it/lo-studio-legale-associato-dfa/alberto-dal-ferro-avvocato-cassazionista.

[43] Case C-479/93, *Francovich v Italy* EU:C:1995:372, paras 19 et seq.

[44] Joined Cases C-94/95 and C-95/95, *Bonifaci and Others* and *Berto and Others* EU:C:1997:348; see also Case C-373/95 *Maso* EU:C:1997:353.

[45] Case C-373/95 *Maso* (n 44) para 47.

[46] ibid paras 39 et seq.

the Court of Justice held that a one-year deadline as of the entry into force of the legislation implementing Directive 80/967/EEC to bring damages actions in Italy did not make judicial protection impossible or excessively difficult.[47]

It is worth noting that all the judgments in the *Francovich* and *Bonifaci* saga, with the exception of *Francovich II*, were decided after Member State liability was codified in *Brasserie du Pêcheur and Factortame* five years later (see section IV). In those fraught years, *Francovich* was only briefly referred to in *Marshall* – the well-known sex discrimination case – and with merely oblique effects on issues of liability and compensation.[48] In *Marshall*, the Court relied upon *Francovich* to hold that the fact that a Member State may choose among several possible means of achieving the objectives of a directive 'does not exclude the possibility for individuals of enforcing before national courts rights whose content can be determined sufficiently precisely on the basis of the provisions of the directive alone'.[49] On this basis, the Court went on holding that a person injured as a result of a discriminatory dismissal may rely on EU law 'to set aside a national provision which imposes limits on the amount of compensation recoverable by way of reparation'.[50]

Francovich was commented upon far and wide in the literature, including by some of the lawyers who had brough the case.[51] With the benefit of hindsight, the reception of *Francovich* among most academic commentators was decidedly positive. Chalmers, Davies and Monti recall that 'Most academic commentators welcomed the decision on the ground that it would lead to better enforcement of EU law and greater citizen empowerment.'[52] However, the authors also recall the 'wise, cautionary words' by Carol Harlow, who criticised recourse to damages action which would in most cases benefits business and cost not just the public purse but welfare spending and its beneficiaries.[53]

IV. After *Francovich*

Many Member States were tempted to think that *Francovich* was a one-off judgment, a last resort remedy to discipline a notoriously recalcitrant and morose Member State. They were in for a shock. Five years after the ruling, a few judgments were delivered on the same day or at short distance, *Brasserie du Pêcheur and Factortame* being the leading one.[54]

After a most detailed analysis of the case law up to and including *Francovich*, in *Brasserie du Pêcheur and Factortame*, Advocate General Tesauro strongly concluded that

[47] Case C-261/95 *Palmisani* EU:C:1997:351.
[48] Case C-271/91 *Marshall* EU:C:1993:335.
[49] ibid para 37.
[50] ibid para 38.
[51] A Campesan and A Dal Ferro, 'La responsabilità dello Stato per la violazioni degli obblighi ad esso incombenti in forza del diritto comunitario alla luce della sentenza *Francovich*' (1992) *Rivista di diritto Europeo* 2.
[52] Chalmers, Davies and Monti (n 2) 315.
[53] See C Harlow, '*Francovich* and the Problem of the Disobedient State' (1996) 2 *European Law Journal* 199, 210 ff.
[54] Joined Cases C-46/93 and C-48/93 *Brasserie du Pêcheur and Factortame* EU:C:1996:79.

> far from being a moment of eccentricity in the case-law of the Court, *Francovich* was completely consistent with and a logical extension of a value which has been upheld on several occasions without question in Luxembourg: effectiveness of Community provisions and hence complete judicial protection.[55]

He argued that liability must a fortiori arise in case of breach of EU provisions having direct effect.[56] He also concluded that 'in view of the specific nature of the Community legal system considered as a whole, it is completely irrelevant whether the unlawful act or omission is attributable to the legislature or to the executive'.[57]

Following the Opinion, the Court of Justice affirmed *Francovich* in the strongest words, holding that 'the full effectiveness of Community law would be impaired if individuals were unable to obtain redress when their rights were infringed by a breach of Community law'.[58]

Further, the Court of Justice rejected the contention by the German Government that a remedy in damages could be created only by legislation and that 'for such a right to be recognized by judicial decision would be incompatible with the allocation of powers as between the Community institutions and the Member States and with the institutional balance established by the Treaty'.[59] The Court retorted that 'the existence and extent of State liability for damage ensuing as a result of a breach of obligations incumbent on the State by virtue of Community law are questions of Treaty interpretation which fall within the jurisdiction of the Court'.[60] That answer represents a high point for courts in a centuries-old spar on who makes the law.[61] The conclusion was that

> the principle of State liability for loss and damage caused to individuals as a result of breaches of Community law for which it can be held responsible is inherent in the system of the Treaty. It follows that that principle holds good for any case in which a Member State breaches Community law, whatever be the organ of the State whose act or omission was responsible for the breach.[62]

Having cemented a principle, the Court, once more following the Opinion of its Advocate General, laid down the necessary and sufficient conditions for liability. Reasoning by analogy on the Treaty provision and related case law on the liability of EU institutions,[63] the Court somewhat reworded *Francovich* by holding that liability is engaged when three conditions are met:

> [T]he rule of law infringed must be intended to confer rights on individuals; the breach must be sufficiently serious; and there must be a direct causal link between the breach of the obligation resting on the State and the damage sustained by the injured parties.[64]

[55] Joined Cases C-46/93 and C-48/93 *Brasserie du Pêcheur and Factortame* EU:C:1995:407 para 32.
[56] ibid paras 25 et seq.
[57] ibid para 42.
[58] Joined Cases C-46/93 and C-48/93 *Brasserie du Pêcheur and Factortame* (n 54) para 20.
[59] ibid para 24.
[60] ibid para 25.
[61] On which see RC van Caenegem, *Judges, Legislators & Professors. Chapters in European Legal History* (Cambridge University Press, 1987).
[62] Joined Cases C-46/93 and C-48/93 *Brasserie du Pêcheur and Factortame* (n 54) paras 31 et seq.
[63] ibid para 42.
[64] ibid para 51.

Compared to *Francovich*, the new element is the requirement of a sufficient serious breach. This avoids the risks of a wide exposure to damages linked to the choice of a strict liability regime.[65] The Court of Justice recalled that the wide discretion available to the institutions concerning legislative measures involving choices of economic policy justifies a rather restrictive case law on the liability of those institutions.[66] However, 'the national legislature – like the Community institutions – does not systematically have a wide discretion when it acts in a field governed by Community law'; on the contrary, EU law must often be read as reducing the margins of discretion of the Member States.[67] The margins of discretion are therefore one of the elements to be considered in assessing whether a breach is 'grave and manifest'. Other elements include the clarity and precision of the rule breached, the intentional or involuntary character of the action or omission, whether any error of law was excusable or inexcusable, and the position taken by EU institutions contributing to the breach or, on the contrary, having already denounced it, for instance through an infringement decision or judgment.[68]

Provided that liability arises as a matter of EU law when the three above conditions are met, damages actions are regulated under domestic law, which must be consistent with the equivalence and effectiveness principles already spelt out in *San Giorgio*.[69]

Francovich, *Brasserie du Pêcheur and Factortame* have been followed by the EU courts in many cases. Here we cannot but focus on the essential characteristics of Member States' liability for breach of EU law.

The first question is whose actions may make a Member State liable. *Brasserie du Pêcheur and Factortame* indicated it to be irrelevant what body had breached EU law, and indeed legislators and parliaments were fair game in *Francovich*.[70] In *Dillenkofer*, decided a few months after *Brasserie du Pêcheur and Factortame*, the Court of Justice clarified that the requirement as to the manifest and serious breach was already implied in *Francovich* since 'failure to take any measure to transpose a directive in order to achieve the result it prescribes within the period laid down for that purpose constitutes per se a serious breach'.[71] Finding Member States liable for actions of omissions of government or other administrative organs plainly follows from *a majori* reasoning.[72]

Based on Montesquieu tripartition, what was still open was the liability of the Member States for judicial errors. Such an eventuality was upheld in *Köbler*.[73] In breach of EU law, Professor Köbler had been denied the seniority he could claim because of previous service in Germany. The denial was upheld all the way up to the Austrian Supreme Administrative Court. The Court of Justice repeated that 'the principle of liability on the part of a Member State for damage caused to individuals as a result of breaches of Community law for which the State is responsible is inherent in the system

[65] See P Craig, 'Francovich, Remedies and the Scope of Damages Liability' (1993) 109 *Law Quarterly Review* 620.

[66] Joined Cases C-46/93 and C-48/93 *Brasserie du Pêcheur and Factortame* (n 54) paras 43 et seq.

[67] ibid para 46.

[68] ibid paras 57 et seq.

[69] ibid para 67.

[70] ibid paras 31 et seq.

[71] Joined Cases C-178/94, C-179/94, C-188/94, C-189/94 and C-190/94 *Dillenkofer et al* EU:C:1996:375, para 29.

[72] Case C-5/94 *Hedley Lomas (Ireland) Ltd* EU:C:1996:205.

[73] Case C-224/01 *Gerhard Köbler v Republik Österreich* EU:C:2003:513.

of the Treaty' and that 'that principle applies to any case in which a Member State breaches Community law, whichever is the authority of the Member State whose act or omission was responsible for the breach'.[74]

The Court stressed the specific role of last instance national courts, which are generally under a duty to refer questions under Article 234 TFEU.[75] The Court further denied that such liability could undermine the independence and authority of the judiciary.[76] The Court was however ready to accept the specificities of the judicial function when considering the conditions governing that liability holding that 'State liability for an infringement of Community law by a decision of a national court adjudicating at last instance can be incurred only in the exceptional case where the court has manifestly infringed the applicable law'.[77]

Köbler was affirmed in *Traghetti del Mediterraneo*,[78] while the difficulty to find a last instance court liable for breaches of EU law is epitomised by *Milena Tomášová*.[79]

The second group of questions concerns the three requirements for liability. Finding that EU confers rights has been normally straightforward.[80] Since *van Gen den Loos*, conferring rights to individuals, be they natural – or more often than not – legal persons, has been a great part of what makes the EU special. A case in point is the example of *Presidenza del Consiglio dei Ministri*.[81] BV, a resident in Italy, was victim of violent sexual crimes in late 2005. At the time, Italy had not yet implemented Directive 2004/80/EC[82] relating to compensation for crime victims and specifically Article 12(2), providing for the establishment of a scheme on compensation to victims of violent intentional crimes. BV sued the Italian Government for damages from the late implementation of the directive. Pending the judicial proceedings, BV was offered €4,800 based on a 2016 law that, albeit belatedly, implemented the directive and provided for a retroactive extension of the 'benefits' foreseen therein. The obvious difficulty in her case was that Directive 2004/80/EC was a measure to facilitate free movement of people, and the Court of Justice had previously held that the directive 'regulates only cross-border situations, by ensuring that the victim of a violent intentional crime committed in a Member State other than that of their habitual residence will be compensated by the Member State in which the crime was committed'.[83] While not reconsidering whether the provisions in the first chapter of Directive 2004/80/EC cover cross-border situations only, the Court of Justice held that the setting up of a compensation scheme was a different matter altogether. The directive ensures third Member States residents' access to the compensation schemes active in the Member State within whose territory they

[74] ibid paras 30 et seq.

[75] ibid paras 35 et seq.

[76] ibid paras 41 et seq.

[77] ibid para 53; see also Case C–620/17 *Hochtief Solutions AG Magyarországi Fióktelepe* EU:C:2019:630, para 41.

[78] Case C-173/03 *Traghetti del Mediterraneo SpA, in liquidation v Italy* EU:C:2006:391.

[79] Case C-168/15 *Milena Tomášová* EU:C:2016:602.

[80] For a theoretical analysis, P Aalto, *Public Liability in EU Law* (Hart Publishing, 2011) esp 162 ff.

[81] Case C-129/19 *Presidenza del Consiglio dei Ministri* EU:C:2020:566.

[82] Council Directive 2004/80/EC of 29 April 2004 relating to compensation to crime victims [2004] OJ L261/15.

[83] eg, Case C-601/14 *Commission v Italy* EU:C:2016:759, paras 45 and 48–50.

suffered violence. For this to be possible, Article 12(2) had to be read as imposing upon each Member State the establishment of such a scheme, open to their residents and – by virtue of the directive – to non-residents.[84] In conclusion, the directive also confers the right to obtain fair and appropriate compensation to victims who reside habitually in the territory of that Member State.[85]

Unsurprisingly, the Court also concluded that 'a fixed rate of EUR 4 800 for the compensation of a victim of sexual violence does not appear, at first sight, to correspond to "fair and appropriate compensation" as required under Article 12(1)'.[86]

Reading *Presidenza del Consiglio dei Ministri*, one cannot but to pay tribute to the ingenuity of the judges sitting in Luxembourg. Against all odds, they managed to find a right where the protection of the law was demanded by basic moral standards, thus extending the remit of EU law to purely internal situations without, however, disavowing less forthcoming precedents. This is EU law at its best, following in the footsteps of *van Gen den Loos*. Denying the existence of a right is simply self-defeating for EU law.

To date, the Court has denied the existence of such a right only twice. The first case was *Paul*.[87] Having lost their money, Mr Paul and others claimed compensation for the belated transposition by Germany – again – of Directive 94/19/EEC[88] on deposit-guarantee schemes and for defective supervision on the bank they were customers of. According to the Court of Justice, the directive grants depositors a right of action against the deposit-guarantee scheme and requires the competent authority to make sure that the credit institution in which they make their deposits belongs to a deposit-guarantee scheme. This is in order to ensure protection of their right to compensation in the event that their deposits are unavailable, but 'does not confer on depositors a right to have the competent authorities take supervisory measures in their interest'.[89]

Moreover, Directives 77/780/EEC, 89/299/EEC and 89/646/EEC,[90] in so far as they contain rules on the supervision of credit institutions, aim only to achieve

> the essential harmonisation necessary and sufficient to secure the mutual recognition of authorisations and of prudential supervision systems, making possible the granting of a single licence recognised throughout the Community and the application of the principle of home Member State prudential supervision.[91]

To this end, liability towards depositors of the supervisory authorities in case of shortcomings in the supervision over banking institutions is neither expressly foreseen nor

[84] Case C-129/19 *Presidenza del Consiglio dei Ministri* (n 81) paras 39–51.

[85] ibid para 55.

[86] ibid para 68.

[87] Case C-222/02 *Paul and others* EU:C:2004:606.

[88] Directive 94/19/EC of the European Parliament and of the Council of 30 May 1994 on deposit-guarantee schemes [1994] OJ L135/5.

[89] ibid paras 26 et seq; Recital 24 of the Directive is also referred to.

[90] First Council Directive 77/780/EEC of 12 December 1977 on the coordination of the laws, regulations and administrative provisions relating to the taking up and pursuit of the business of credit institutions [1977] OJ L322/30; Council Directive 89/299/EEC of 17 April 1989 on the own funds of credit institutions [1989] OJ L124/16; Second Council Directive 89/646/EEC of 15 December 1989 on the coordination of laws, regulations and administrative provisions relating to the taking up and pursuit of the business of credit institutions and amending Directive 77/780/EEC [1989] OJ L386/1.

[91] Case C-222/02 *Paul* (n 87) para 37.

necessary.[92] Further, considering that forms of (limited) protection for depositors are instead foreseen, in the end the relevant provisions 'cannot be interpreted as meaning that they confer rights on depositors in the event that their deposits are unavailable as a result of defective supervision on the part of the competent national authorities'.[93]

The Court of Justice refrained from extending the protection of depositors offered by EU law beyond the limits foreseen by the deposit-guarantee scheme. The financial impacts of a different interpretation might have been in the mind of the justices in Luxembourg, but reference to the 'complexity'[94] inherent in banking supervision might have been easily accommodated under the second condition of a manifest and serious breach, thus, reasonably limiting any financial impact from the judgment.

A more difficult case is *Ministre de la Transition écologique and Premier ministre (Responsabilité de l'Etat pour la pollution de l'air)*.[95] Arguing that he had been suffering from worsening health problems since 2003, JP seised the French courts asking for an injunction against the competent Prefect to take measures to comply with the limit values under Directive 2008/50/EU[96] on ambient air quality and cleaner air for Europe. In addition, JP sought compensation for the various heads of damages which he attributed to air pollution, assessed at €21 million.

In Advocate General Kokott's view, 'direct applicability provides a significant indication that rights are to be conferred, because, in that case, the content of the right conferred can be identified, which is a condition of entitlement to compensation'.[97] The Advocate General reached a nuanced conclusion. She contended that the Member States were not under a directly enforceable obligation to comply with the limit values, but were required

> to take measures to reduce the duration of the exceedance to a minimum on the basis of a balance between the conflicting interests. That second … is sufficiently clear only with regard to a breach of the limits of the discretion existing in that respect.[98]

Moreover, under Article 23 of Directive 2008/50/EU, they were under 'a clear *independent* obligation to establish air quality plans, which is triggered by the infringement of limit values'.[99]

Advocate General Kokott subsequently addressed the objectives of the relevant EU provisions.[100] In her Opinion, limit values are fixed to avoid, prevent or reduce harmful effects on health and/or the environment.[101] The case law on the relevant directive has already held that they confer rights to be judicially protected.[102] The same case law is relied on to dismiss the argument of some Member States that the objective of health protection 'is intended to relate solely to the protection of the general public', as

[92] ibid paras 41 and 43.
[93] ibid para 46.
[94] ibid para 44.
[95] Case C-61/21 *Ministre de la Transition écologique* EU:C:2022:1015.
[96] Directive 2008/50/EC of the European Parliament and of the Council of 21 May 2008 on ambient air quality and cleaner air for Europe [2008] OJ L152/1.
[97] Case C-61/21 *Ministre de la Transition écologique* EU:C:2022:359, para 34.
[98] ibid para 54.
[99] ibid paras 66 et seq.
[100] ibid para 72.
[101] ibid para 74.
[102] ibid para 76.

the interest in health is instead 'highly personal and thus individual in nature'.[103] This contention leads her to distinguish the case at hand from *Paul and Others*. The latter concerned EU harmonisation rules adopted in the interest of the internal market. On the contrary, air pollution rules are adopted based 'on the EU's environmental competence and therefore, in accordance with Article 191 TFEU, necessarily aim at a high level of protection with regard to human health'.[104]

Finally, Advocate General Kokott spoke to the question of whether EU law 'really intend to confer on a scarcely delimitable group of persons potentially affected a right to a certain quality of ambient air, infringement of which could give rise to entitlement to compensation'.[105] The staggering number of infringement cases makes it possible to foresee a large number of claims for compensation which could place a considerable burden on the national courts. Still, this is taken to show 'the importance of adequate air quality'.[106] In any case, according to the Advocate General, those directly affected will mostly be 'certain groups who live or work in particularly polluted areas. Those groups often consist of people of low socio-economic status, who are particularly reliant on judicial protection.[107] This allows her to consider it to be

> incorrect to assume, together with Ireland and the Republic of Poland, that the rules on ambient air quality serve exclusively to protect the general public. Although ambient air quality must be protected in general, the specific problems arise in specific places and affect specific, identifiable groups of people. Therefore, only persons who are directly concerned by an exceedance of the limit values or the risk of an exceedance can rely on Article 23(1) of Directive 2008/50.[108]

The Court of Justice instead denied that the relevant provisions granted a right to the EU's citizens. Having recalled the cases laying down both the principle of and the requirements for the liability of the Member States, the Court recalled the case law under which 'direct effect is neither necessary ... nor sufficient in itself' to meet the first condition for State liability.[109]

The Court was ready to concede that the relevant EU provisions 'lay down fairly clear and precise obligations as to the result to be achieved by Member States'.[110] However, relying on Article 1 and 'in particular' Recital 2 of Directive 2008/50/EU, the Court held that those obligations pursue 'a general objective of protecting human health and the environment as a whole'.[111] Considered that the provisions concerned 'do not contain any express conferral of rights on individuals', the Court galloped to the conclusion that it cannot be inferred from those provisions with a general objective that

> individuals or categories of individuals are, in the present case, implicitly granted, by reason of those obligations, rights the breach of which would be capable of giving rise to a Member State's liability for loss and damage caused to individuals.[112]

[103] ibid para 77.
[104] ibid para 87.
[105] ibid para 95.
[106] ibid para 98.
[107] ibid para 100.
[108] ibid para 101.
[109] Case C-61/21 *Ministre de la Transition écologique* (n 97) para 47.
[110] ibid para 54.
[111] ibid para 55.
[112] ibid para 56.

Coming to the second requirement for liability, the finding of a manifest and serious breach very much depends on the discretion left under EU to the alleged wrongdoer. In *Hedley Lomas*, decided on the same day as *Brasserie du Pêcheur and Factortame*, concerning ministerial refusals to issue licences for the export of live animals for slaughter to Spain, the Court of Justice held that as the Minister 'was not called upon to make any legislative choices and had only considerably reduced, or even no, discretion, the mere infringement of Community law may be sufficient to establish the existence of a sufficiently serious breach'.[113]

In *British Telecommunications*,[114] a wide discretion was instead acknowledged to Member States when transposing – possibly incorrectly – a directive into national law based on 'the concern to ensure that the exercise of legislative functions is not hindered by the prospect of actions for damages whenever the general interest requires the institutions or Member States to adopt measures which may adversely affect individual interests'.[115] On the facts of the case, the Court of Justice acknowledged that the relevant EU law provision was 'imprecisely worded and was reasonably capable of bearing … the interpretation given to it by the United Kingdom in good faith and on the basis of arguments which are not entirely devoid of substance',[116] and that no guidance had been provided to the Member States either by the Commission of by the Court itself.[117]

Together, *Hedley Lomas* and *British Telecommunications* very much clarified the 'manifest and serious breach' requirement, creating a two-tiered system in which the latter is either assumed or to be proved based on the residual discretion of the alleged wrongdoer.[118] Arguably, one might rather see shades of discretion;[119] however, the width of discretion, if any, is central to the need or at least the difficulties in finding a manifest and serious breach.[120]

Only serious breaches are relevant in case of breaches of EU due to judicial errors.[121] In many cases, the Court of Justice has repeated that breaches persistent after one or more judgments by the Court itself – in infringement procedures but also in preliminary reference proceedings – are to be considered manifest and serious, as these judgments dissipate uncertainties about the content of the Member States' obligations and thus eliminate the margins of manoeuvre of state authorities.[122]

A recurring question has been whether the requirement about the seriousness of the breach was the same as a requirement of fault (intent or at least negligence). In *Brasserie du Pêcheur and Factortame*, the Court of Justice answered an explicit question from the German *Bundesgerichthof*, indicating that, 'certain objective and subjective factors connected with the concept of fault' in this or that Member State 'may well be relevant

[113] Case C-5/94 *Hedley Lomas* (n 72) para 29.
[114] Case C-392/93 *British Telecommunications plc* EU:C:1996:131.
[115] ibid para 49.
[116] ibid para 43.
[117] ibid paras 44 et seq.
[118] A Ward, *Judicial Review and the Rights of Private Parties in EC Law* (Oxford University Press, 2000) 99.
[119] Dougan (n 6) 244 ff.
[120] See also the analysis by C Hilson, 'The role of discretion in EC law on non-contractual liability' (2005) 42 *Common Market Law Review* 677.
[121] Case C-224/01 *Köbler* (n 73) para 53.
[122] eg, Case C-429/09 *Fuß II* EU:C:2010:717, paras 55 et seq.

for the purpose of determining whether or not a given breach of Community law is serious'. However, liability cannot be made dependent

> upon a condition based on any concept of fault going beyond that of a sufficiently serious breach of Community law. Imposition of such a supplementary condition would be tantamount to calling in question the right to reparation founded on the Community legal order.[123]

Still the question resurfaced in *Fuß I*.[124] Mr Fuß, a fire fighter, had been many hours in excess of working time foreseen by Directive 93/104/EC[125] concerning certain aspects of the organisation of working time, as amended by Directive 2000/34/EC[126] and Directive 2003/88/EC.[127] He requested his weekly working time not to exceed the maximum average limit of 48 hours and claimed reparation for unlawfully worked overtime. The Court of Justice quickly acknowledged that the relevant provisions 'constitutes a rule of EU social law of particular importance from which every worker must benefit'.[128] Since the case law of the Court had already clarified the content of the obligations flowing from EU law, the Court of Justice held the breach by the employer to be manifest and serious.[129] Concerning fault, the Court held that, since a qualified breach had already been established, an additional condition which would have 'made the right to reparation for an infringement of EU law dependent on proof of a specific form of fault, such as intentional fault or negligence, by the employer' would restrict the right to damages and would be inconsistent with EU law.[130]

The Court of Justice has seldom been questioned about causation and – to some extent – damages. The former issue has mostly been left to the national court to resolve.[131] Concerning the latter, the Court has consistently held that reparation for loss or damage caused to individuals as a result of breaches of EU law 'must be commensurate with the loss or damage sustained so as to ensure the effective protection for their rights'.[132] In *Hochtief Solutions*, the Court held that a national rule excluding the damages from an infringement of a rule of EU law by a decision of a last instance court the costs incurred by one party (as a result of that decision) 'may render it, in practice, excessively difficult or even impossible to obtain adequate compensation for the harm suffered by that party'.[133] In *Fuß II*, the Court held that the grant of additional time in

[123] Joined Cases C-46/93 and C-48/93 *Brasserie du Pêcheur and Factortame* (n 54) paras 78 et seq.

[124] Case C-429/09 *Fuß II* (n 122).

[125] Council Directive 93/104/EC of 23 November 1993 concerning certain aspects of the organization of working time [1993] OJ L307/18.

[126] Directive 2000/34/EC of the European Parliament and of the Council of 22 June 2000 amending Council Directive 93/104/EC concerning certain aspects of the organisation of working time to cover sectors and activities excluded from that Directive [2000] OJ L195/41.

[127] Directive 2003/88/EC of the European Parliament and of the Council of 4 November 2003 concerning certain aspects of the organisation of working time [2003] OJ L299/9.

[128] ibid para 33; see also ibid paras 49 et seq; the direct effect of the relevant provisions had already been established in Case C-243/09 *Fuß I* EU:C:2010:609.

[129] Case C-429/09 *Fuß II* (n 122) paras 54 et seq.

[130] ibid para 68.

[131] A Koukiadaki, 'Remedies and Sanctions in EU Labour Law' in Z Rasnača et al (eds), *Effective Enforcement of EU Labor* Law (Hart Publishing, 2022) 35, 53; but see Case C-319/96 *Brinkmann Tabakfabriken GmbH v Skatteministeriet* EU:C:1998:429.

[132] Joined Cases C-46/93 and C-48/93 *Brasserie du Pêcheur and Factortame* (n 54) para 82.

[133] Case C–620/17 *Hochtief Solutions AG Magyarországi Fióktelepe* EU:C:2019:630, para 47.

lieu of a financial payment might make it impossible or excessively difficult to obtain such reparation.[134]

Finally, a last issue concerns the margins left to the procedural autonomy of the Member States. As the Court of Justice confirmed in *Köbler*, it is a power, but also a duty incumbent on the Member States to designate the Court competent to hear damages claims.[135] A notably interesting application of the limits posed by the principle of effectiveness to the autonomy of the Member States is provided by *Fuß II*.[136] The Court of Justice held that, while it is generally for the Member States to lay down the procedure, possibly providing for an appeal as a condition precedent to judicial review, such a requirement breached the principle of effective judicial protection in a case in which the employer had declared that it would have taken retaliatory measures against workers who would have asked for the respect of their rights.[137]

There is no perfect correspondence between which rules – EU or national – regulate which aspect of Member States liability and the competence to adjudicate on this or that aspect. Generally speaking, the Court of Justice is the one deciding on the existence of a right. In 'easy' cases it has often enough indicated whether the breach is manifest, serious or not, and seldomly given indications on causality. All other aspects are adjudicated by national courts, subject to the review of the Court of Justice concerning whether domestic rules are consistent with the principle of effective judicial protection.[138] Still, what is valuable is the kind of cooperation created by the *Francovich* case law.[139]

V. Conclusions: Rights are Central, but whose Rights?

As Sacha Prechal wrote, 'state liability for breaches of EU law, as laid down in … *Francovich*, is a culmination of the case law on effective judicial protection'.[140] The principle has now been enshrined in Article 19 TEU and right to effective judicial protection in Article 47 of the EU Charter of Fundamental Rights.[141]

Research on England and Germany 20 years after *Francovich* showed that the number of claims has been limited.[142] Yet the situation is different in Member States traditionally generous concerning liability claims, such as France. In Italy, *Francovich* contributed to the change of decades old doctrine making the Member State responsible, a change that was perceived by most as long overdue. Still, liability rules in the Member States remain much at variance.[143] Overall, it would seem that *Francovich*

[134] Case C-429/09 *Fuß II* (n 122) para 95.

[135] Case C-224/01 *Köbler* (n 73) paras 45 et seq.

[136] Case C-429/09 *Fuß II* (n 122).

[137] ibid paras79 et seq.

[138] See also Ward (n 118) 81 and 108 ff; T Tridimas, 'Liability for Breach of Community Law: Growing Up and Mellowing Down?' in D Fairgrieve, M Andenas and J Bell (eds), *Tort Liability of Public Authorities in Comparative Perspective* (BIICL, 2002) 180.

[139] A Biondi, 'In Praise of *Francovich*' in M Poiares Maduro and L Azoulai (eds), *The Past and Future of EU Law* (Hart Publishing, 2010) 417.

[140] Prechal (n 6) 14, fn 18.

[141] M Bonelli, M Eliantonio and G Gentile, 'Conclusions' in Bonelli et al (eds) (n 6) and the chapters included therein.

[142] Lock (n 6) 1675.

[143] See the chapters in G della Canenea and R Caranta (eds), *Tort Liability of Public Authorities in European Laws* (Oxford University Press, 2020).

has increased the protection of those holding rights based on EU law, thus, somewhat contributing to the effectiveness of EU law. As it is normally the case with liability, both deterrence and compensation are at play.[144]

The doctrinal developments following *Francovich* have spilled over to the matter of liability of EU institutions following *Bergaderm*.[145] Provisions on Member States liability have been included in sectoral legislation. Prior to *Francovich*, damages were foreseen alongside interim relief and annulment as remedies to be offered in public procurement litigation.[146] These days liability has become a private enforcement tool of choice, even working against private parties, as in the case with competition law[147] and, but not without difficulties, State aids.[148]

However, in *Ministre de la Transition écologique*, the Court of Justice has hit the brakes on Member States' liability. The case concerned environmental protection, an area in which the case law had instead been characterised by a creative attitude in recognising rights.[149] In *Wells*, the Court had opened the possibility of a claim for damages against a public authority having granted consent for mining operations in breach of EU rules requiring prior environmental assessment.[150] Admittedly, the judgment, which does not refer to the case law on Member States' liability, is somewhat ambiguous, as it leaves it to

> the national court to determine whether it is possible under domestic law for a consent already granted to be revoked or suspended in order to subject the project in question to an assessment of its environmental effects ... or alternatively, if the individual so agrees, whether it is possible for the latter to claim compensation for the harm suffered.[151]

And yet a few paragraphs earlier, the Court had clearly indicated that the Member State is 'likewise required to make good any harm caused by the failure to carry out an environmental impact assessment'.[152]

The Court could have easily held that emission limits protect *both* the general interest *and* individual rights. No logical reason precludes such possibility.[153] True, the costs from liability for breaches of emission limits might have been staggering for (delinquent) Member States. This argument was already raised against *Francovich* and the early liability cases.[154] The Opinion of the Advocate General Kokott was lukewarm at

[144] P Craig, 'Once More Unto the Breach: The Community, the State and Damages Liability' (1997) 113 *Law Quarterly Review* 85.

[145] Case C-352/98 P *Bergaderm* EU:C:2000:361; see Aalto (n 79).

[146] See R Caranta, 'Article 47 of the EU Charter of Fundamental Rights in the Field of Public Procurement: Time to Take the Charter Seriously?' in Bonelli et al (eds) (n 6) 2013.

[147] See P Kirst, *The Impact of the Damages Directive on the Enforcement of EU Competition Law* (Edward Elgar, 2021).

[148] F Pastor-Merchante, *The Role of Competitors in the Enforcement of State Aid Law* (Hart Publishing, 2017) 75 ff.

[149] L Krämer, 'Article 47 of the Charter and Effective Judicial Protection in Environmental Matters: The Need to Grant Civil Society the Right to Defend the Environment' in Bonelli et al (eds) (n 6) 204.

[150] Case C-201/02 *Wells* EU:C:2004:12.

[151] ibid para 69.

[152] ibid para 66; see also Á Ryall, *Effective Judicial Protection and the Environmental Impact Assessment Directive in Ireland* (Hart Publishing, 2009) 187 ff.

[153] R Caranta, 'Governmental Liability after *Francovich*' (1993) 52 *Cambridge Law Journal* 284.

[154] eg, Harlow (n 53) 214 f.

best in mitigating concerns about litigation and costs based on the second and third requirements for liability.[155]

Critics of *Francovich* lamented that it might be used to compensate (pure) economic losses of business going to the detriment of social welfare.[156] Still, *Ministre de la Transition écologique* was not about business interests, it concerned human health and climate. It is hoped that the judgment stays confined within the narrow borders of that case. If not, it will mean that the EU regime of liability of the Member States will be useless in – and *Francovich* will be unfit for – addressing the most pressing challenges faced by the EU and the global community at large.

[155] Case C-61/21 *Ministre de la Transition écologique* (n 97) para 106 et seq.
[156] See the strong pleading by Harlow (n 53) 202 ff.

15

Associação Sindical dos Juízes Portugueses and Judicial Independence

MICHAL OVÁDEK AND LAURENT PECH

I. Introduction

While the rule of law situation in Hungary and Poland is not explicitly mentioned in the Court of Justice's ruling in *Associação Sindical dos Juízes Portugueses* (*ASJP*),[1] this judgment was (correctly) understood as the Court's (implicit) answer to the process of rule of backsliding which has characterised these two countries.[2]

The President of the Court of Justice of the European Union (CJEU), Koen Lenaerts, has since recognised in extra-judicial interventions the seminal nature of *ASJP*, which he described as a judgment of the same order as '*Van Gend en Loos*, *Costa/ENEL*, *Simmenthal* or *ERTA*',[3] and confirmed that the Court was well aware that the *ASJP* ruling amounted to a 'constitutional moment'.[4] By contrast, there has been no acknowledgment that the Court's reasoning in *ASJP* was directly motivated with the view of addressing the deliberate and sustained attacks on judicial independence witnessed first in Hungary and subsequently in Poland. However, President Lenaerts has publicly and repeatedly warned about the existential threat 'authoritarian tendencies at national level'[5] represent for the EU and its legal order since *ASJP* was delivered.

With the rule of law situation continuing to steadily deteriorate, coupled with an increasingly open and deliberate disregard for the rule of law-related rulings of both the CJEU and the European Court of Human Rights (ECtHR), the Court's ruling in *ASJP* has been abundantly relied upon by national judges seeking to defend their judicial independence.[6] Another crucial consequence of *ASJP* has been to push an arguably reluctant European Commission into action.

[1] Case C-64/16 *Associação Sindical dos Juízes Portugueses* EU:C:2018:117.

[2] See L Pech and KL Scheppele, 'Illiberalism Within: Rule of Law Backsliding in the EU' (2017) 19 *Cambridge Yearbook of European Legal Studies* 3.

[3] Quoted by A von Bogdandy and LD Spieker, 'Transformative Constitutionalism in Luxembourg: How the Court can support democratic transitions' (2023) 29 *The Columbia Journal of European Law* 65, 72.

[4] ibid.

[5] K Lenaerts, 'On Checks and Balances: The Rule of Law Within the EU' (2023) 29 *The Columbia Journal of European Law* 25, 63.

[6] See L Pech, *The European Court of Justice's jurisdiction over national judiciary-related measures*, Study requested by the AFCO Committee of the European Parliament, PE 747.368, April 2023.

Even if judicial safeguards might not rescue national democracy,[7] the far-reaching impact the *ASJP* ruling has had on EU law and politics to date – from empowering national judges and leading to Commission enforcement followed by the use of national captured bodies to prevent compliance with CJEU judgments and orders – has been one of the most important turning points in European integration in the twenty-first century.

II. Historical and Doctrinal Context

This section traces the origins of the *ASJP* case by briefly outlining the background to the dispute and the domestic proceedings which led the Portuguese Supreme Administrative Court to submit a request for a preliminary ruling.

A. Background to the Dispute

The roots of the *ASJP* case find themselves in the era of austerity that came in the aftermath of the 2007–08 financial and subsequent eurozone crises. High levels of sovereign debt were at the time identified as key threats to the stability of the eurozone. Servicing this debt became unsustainable for a number of countries in southern Europe around 2010–13 in the face of rising bond yields stemming from increased perception of risk of these countries defaulting on their debt obligations. Portugal was among the countries that requested a bailout, which was negotiated by the Portuguese Government with the European Commission, European Central Bank and International Monetary Fund (the 'Troika') in May 2011.

In exchange for the €78 billion bailout package, Portugal committed to adopting austerity measures as set out in three memoranda of understanding. Public servants earning above €1,500 per month – which included judges – were to have their salaries reduced at the outset by between 3.5 and 10 per cent. In 2014, the monthly earnings threshold above which public sector workers were subject to pay cuts was lowered to €675, which meant that at some point during the austerity period, the wages of virtually all state employees were affected in one way or another.

B. Domestic Proceedings

Public sector pay cuts were challenged each year by national parliamentarians before the Portuguese Constitutional Court, with the Court gradually turning against austerity measures in a more forceful way.[8] In 2012, the previous year's salary cuts were

[7] M Blauberger and RD Kelemen, 'Can courts rescue national democracy? Judicial safeguards against democratic backsliding in the EU' (2017) 24 *Journal of European Public Policy* 321; M Ovádek, 'The rule of law in the EU: many ways forward but only one way to stand still?' (2018) 40 *Journal of European Integration* 495.

[8] M Canotilho, T Violante and R Lanceiro, 'Austerity measures under judicial scrutiny: the Portuguese constitutional case-law' (2015) 11 *European Constitutional Law Review* 155.

supplemented by a reduction in holiday pay. This additional measure was considered unconstitutional by the Court, though the effects of the ruling were to be only applied from 2013. The same conclusion was reached by the Court in 2013, but this time without any postponement of the effects. In 2014, pay cuts were expanded to cover public sector wages above €675 per month with the range of cuts oscillating from 2.5 per cent to 12 per cent. This was deemed excessive by the Court and the cuts were annulled as of May 2014 when the ruling was handed down. The Government readopted the 2011 wage reduction formula in September 2014, legislating also for subsequent years and foreseeing a gradual restoration of full wages in 2018. The Constitutional Court once again declared the measure unconstitutional, leaving in place only the cuts for 2014 and 2015.

These constitutional challenges notwithstanding, the Trade Union of Portuguese Judges (ASJP) was of the view that the situation of judges differed from that of the rest of the public sector employees.[9] In short, the ASJP leadership took the position that the Government violated the principle of judicial independence when it imposed severe pay cuts on judges. While this was ASJP's principled legal position, it was also adopted in response to disquiet among members regarding the economic impact of the cuts. Rather than calling for a strike, ASJP sought to first prioritise discussions with parliamentarians and government officials. In the absence of any positive outcome, ASJP subsequently explored legal avenues.

ASJP originally asked the Portuguese Prosecutor General and Ombudsman to bring an action on behalf of the judges before the Constitutional Court, alleging a violation of Article 203 of the Portuguese Constitution, which protects the principle of judicial independence. Unlike ordinary judges, the Prosecutor General and the Ombudsman have privileged access to the Constitutional Court. Likely due to the party-political alignment of these two offices with the Government at the time, ASJP's efforts in this regard bore no fruit. The Constitutional Court presented an obvious avenue for testing ASJP's legal claim not only because it already ruled on austerity-related measures, but also because a similar case was successfully pursued in Italy in 2012.[10]

In the absence of breakthrough on this front, ASJP came up with an alternative litigation strategy. ASJP asked two law professors – Alessandra Silveira and Pedro Madeira Froufe of the University of Minho in Braga – to look into the EU law dimension of their case. The document prepared by the professors then fed into a legal submission for Portuguese national courts that aimed to have a preliminary question referred to the CJEU. The crux of the European law aspect of the submission – which formed the minority of the legal claims put forward – centred on the salary reduction violating the principle of judicial independence as protected by Article 19(1) TEU[11] and Article 47 of the Charter.

ASJP initiated three cases before different national courts, but the only one to gain traction within a reasonable time was the lawsuit lodged with the Supreme

[9] This part draws on interviews with judges who were active in the ASJP. See M Ovádek, 'The making of landmark rulings in the European Union: the case of national judicial independence' (2022) 30 *Journal of European Public Policy* 1119.

[10] Italian Constitutional Court, Decision 223/2012 of 8 October 2012.

[11] Consolidated Version of the Treaty on European Union [2016] OJ C202/13.

Administrative Court. The submission by the ASJP contained the proposed formulation of a preliminary reference to the CJEU regarding a possible violation of Articles 19(1) TEU and 47 of the Charter. The case was made so as to facilitate the referral, and on 5 February 2016 the Supreme Administrative Court obliged and referred virtually verbatim the preliminary question prepared by ASJP.

III. The *ASJP* Ruling: The Court of Justice's Answer to National Rule of Law Backsliding

Before turning to the Court's handling of the *ASJP* preliminary reference, the state of EU law regarding judicial independence will be outlined below.

A. Judicial Independence in the CJEU Case Law Pre-*ASJP*

Prior to *ASJP*, one could distinguish between two main situations in which the principle was applied by the CJEU. First, the CJEU developed the principle of judicial independence in its case law concerning the broader principle of effective judicial protection, especially before the latter was largely subsumed by Article 47 of the Charter.[12] In the most important pre-Charter and *ASJP* case – *Wilson*[13] – the CJEU had to decide whether an appeal procedure for lawyers refused registration in Luxembourg was sufficiently effective, in particular in light of concerns over the independence of the appeals' body. As recently summarised by the CJEU President himself (who was the *judge rapporteur* in *Wilson*):

> [T]he concept of judicial independence, as developed in the seminal Wilson judgment, has both an internal and an external component. Internally, judicial independence is intended to ensure a level playing field for the parties to proceedings and for their competing interests … Externally, judicial independence draws the dividing line between the political process and the courts. Courts must be shielded from any external influence or pressure that might jeopardise the independent judgement of their members as regards proceedings before them.[14]

Subsequently to *Wilson*, the entry into force of the Lisbon Treaty represented a major milestone as the EU Charter, including Article 47 on the right to an effective remedy and to a fair trial, gained legally binding force. The Charter did not however fundamentally alter the legal situation existing prior to the Lisbon Treaty as regards judicial independence. Indeed, Article 47 of the Charter merely reflected Articles 6(1) and 13 of the European Convention on Human Rights (ECHR) and the pre-Lisbon CJEU case law on the right to an effective remedy before a Court and the right to a fair hearing.

[12] See L Pech, 'Right to an independent and impartial tribunal previously established by law', Article 47 EU Charter entry, section VIII, in S Peers et al (eds), *The EU Charter of Fundamental Rights. A Commentary*, 2nd edn (Hart Publishing, 2021) 1339.

[13] Case C-506/04 *Wilson* EU:C:2006:587. For further analysis, see A-L Hinds and L Pech, 'When the Public Interest Masks Lawyers' Interests' (2007) 14 *Irish Journal of European Law* 161.

[14] Lenaerts (n 5) 30.

Furthermore, the Charter explicitly provided that Member States are bound by the Charter 'only when they are implementing Union law'.[15]

The restriction on the scope of application of the Charter was and remains a fundamental element of the EU's quasi-federal political system.[16] The Member States made the conscious choice in the drafting of the Charter that federal (EU-level) rights could not be applied – to oversimplify – in the absence of domestic EU law implementation. By and large, the CJEU's case law kept close to this fundamental bargain. For each case that marginally moved the needle towards a broader scope of the Charter, there was another that would make it clear that the Court was serious about respecting the limits of Article 51(1) of the Charter.[17]

One may for instance mention the set of cases where the CJEU declined jurisdiction to address national austerity measures on the ground that a sufficient connection did *not* exist between the contested domestic and EU law.[18] Professor Barnard understood the Court's reluctance to consider these cases as stemming from the existential threat the debt crisis posed to the Economic and Monetary Union and traditional national prerogatives over social policy.[19] The CJEU's approach began to gradually change once the worst of the eurozone crisis was in the rear-view mirror, coinciding with the appointment of Koen Lenaerts as CJEU President.[20] A good example is the case of *Florescu*,[21] in which the Court held itself competent to rule on an austerity-related memorandum of understanding (MoU) between Romania and the EU, thereby triggering the applicability of the Charter.[22] While it is not our intention to suggest this is a critical factor to understand *ASJP*, it is nonetheless worth noting that President Lenaerts happened to be *juge rapporteur* in the *Wilson* case and, prior to this, a *référendaire* for Judge René Joliet, who was *juge rapporteur* in the previous seminal rule of law judgment known as *Les Verts*.[23]

[15] Art 51(1) of the Charter.

[16] See X Groussot, L Pech and GT Petursson, 'The Reach of EU Fundamental Rights on Member State Action after Lisbon' in S de Vries, U Bernitz and S Weatherhill (eds), *The Protection of Fundamental Rights in the EU after Lisbon* (Hart Publishing, 2013) 97.

[17] See M Ovádek, 'Le champ d'application de la Charte des droits fondamentaux de l'Union européenne et les États members' (2017) 10 *Journal des Tribunaux-Droit Européen* 386; M Ovádek, 'Un-Chartered Territory and Formal Links in EU Law' in W Benedek et al (eds), *European Yearbook on Human Rights* (NWV, 2017) 213.

[18] See Cases C-434/11 *Corpul Naţional al Poliţiştilor v Ministerul Administraţiei şi Internelor (MAI) and Others* EU:C:2011:830; C-128/12 *Sindicato dos Bancários do Norte and Others v BPN – Banco Português de Negócios SA* EU:C:2013:149; C-134/12 *Corpul Naţional al Poliţiştilor – Biroul Executiv Central (în numele şi în interesul membrilor săi – funcţionari publici cu statut special – poliţişti din cadrul IPJ Tulcea) v Ministerul Administraţiei şi Internelor and Others* EU:C:2012:288; C-264/12 *Sindicato Nacional dos Profissionais de Seguros e Afins v Fidelidade Mundial – Companhia de Seguros* SA EU:C:2014:2036; C-369/12 *Corpul Naţional al Poliţiştilor – Biroul Executiv Central, reprezentant al reclamanţilor Chiţea Constantin şi alţii v Ministerul Administraţiei şi Internelor and Others* EU:C:2012:725; C-665/13 *Sindicato Nacional dos Profissionais de Seguros e Afins v Via Directa – Companhia de Seguros SA* EU:C:2014:2327.

[19] C Barnard, 'The Charter in time of crisis: a case study of dismissal' in N Countouris and M Freedland (eds), *Resocialising Europe in a Time of Crisis* (Cambridge University Press, 2013) 250. See also C Kilpatrick, 'Are the Bailouts Immune to EU Social Challenge Because They Are Not EU Law?' (2014) 10 *European Constitutional Law Review* 393.

[20] Joined Cases C-8/15 P to C-10/15 P *Ledra Advertising and Others* EU:C:2016:701.

[21] Case C-258/14 *Florescu and Others* EU:C:2017:448.

[22] P Dermine and M Markakis, 'Bailouts, the legal status of Memoranda of Understanding, and the scope of application of the EU Charter: Florescu' (2018) 55 *Common Market Law Review* 643.

[23] Case 294/83 *Parti écologiste 'Les Verts' v European Parliament* EU:C:1986:166.

At the same time, the CJEU began to change tack on austerity cases, and democratic and rule of law backsliding emerged and gained strength within the EU. In the face of increasingly sustained and systemic violations of EU rule of law principles, in particular judicial independence in Hungary and Poland, the major legal problem until 2018 and the clarification provided by the Court in the *ASJP* judgment, has been the Commission's narrow understanding of the scope of application of the infringement procedure:

> Action taken by the Commission to launch infringement procedures, based on Article 258 TFEU, has proven to be an important instrument in addressing certain rule of law concerns. But infringement procedures can be launched by the Commission only where these concerns constitute, at the same time, a breach of a specific provision of EU law.[24]

In the same Communication, the Commission justified this stance with reference to Article 51 of the Charter and noted that while it is 'determined to use all the means at its disposal to ensure that the Charter is fully respected by the Member States', the Commission can only do so 'vis-à-vis Member State "only when they are implementing EU law" as set out explicitly in Article 51 of the Charter'.[25] This explains why, for instance, the Commission attempted to defend judicial independence via an indirect route in Case C-286/12.[26] Faced with the retroactive lowering of the retirement age of Hungarian judges in 2011, which meant that judges who reasonably expected to continue working until the age of 70 were abruptly forced to retire at the age of 62 with immediate effect,[27] the Commission did launch a successful infringement action. However, the Commission did *not* invoke judicial independence but instead raised a violation of Council Directive 2000/78 establishing a general framework for equal treatment in employment and occupation. While the Court agreed and found a violation of the Directive as Orbán's compulsory retirement scheme gave rise to a difference in treatment on grounds of age which is not proportionate, the Commission's enforcement action 'changed absolutely nothing in the troubling situation on the ground'.[28]

Similarly, the preliminary ruling procedure was not a viable avenue to defend judicial independence prior to *ASJP*. Indeed, in line with the situation regarding infringement actions, the legally binding nature of the EU Charter post-Lisbon Treaty did *not* expand the preliminary ruling jurisdiction of the CJEU. As outlined by the Court itself:

> [T]he provisions of the Charter are addressed to the Member States only when they are implementing EU law. While the circumstances of such implementation can vary, it must nevertheless be clearly and unequivocally apparent from the request for a preliminary ruling that a rule of EU law other than the Charter is applicable to the case in the main proceedings. Since the Court has no jurisdiction to give a preliminary ruling where a legal situation does

[24] Communication from the Commission, *A new EU Framework to strengthen the Rule of Law*, COM(2014) 158 final/2, 19 March 2014, 5.

[25] ibid, 5, fn 14.

[26] Case C-286/12 *Commission v Hungary* EU:C:2012:687.

[27] This resulted in the removal and replacement of about 8% of the 2,900 ordinary court judges, more than 50% of Appeal Court presidents and 27% of Supreme Court judges. See P Bárd and L Pech, 'How to build and consolidate a partly free pseudo democracy by constitutional means in three steps' in P. Bárd and L. Pech, *La formation des régimes autoritaires* (Presses universitaires juridiques de Poitiers, forthcoming).

[28] KL Scheppele, D Kochenov and B Grabowska-Moroz, 'EU Values Are Law, after All' (2021) 39 *Yearbook of European Law* 3, 42.

> not come within the scope of EU law, any provisions of the Charter that may be relied upon by the referring court or tribunal cannot, of themselves, form the basis for such jurisdiction.[29]

The traditional understanding of the jurisdictional limits of both the infringement and preliminary ruling procedures proved particularly problematic in an era of increasing 'authoritarian tendencies'[30] and 'authoritarian drifts'[31] at EU Member State level as many national measures seeking to undermine judicial independence in a systemic manner could be deemed, for the most part, to fall *outside* the scope of EU law traditionally understood.

As will be further outlined below, the CJEU addressed this problem in 2018 by holding that the principle of effective judicial protection laid down in the second subparagraph of Article 19(1) TEU includes a directly effective obligation to guarantee judicial independence at Member State level and has a scope of application 'broader than the rest of EU law'.[32]

B. Operationalisation of the Second Subparagraph of Article 19(1) TEU in *ASJP*

Prior to the Court's judgment in *ASJP*, a number of scholars had called on the Commission to operationalise Article 2 TEU by connecting it to other provisions of the TEU, such as Articles 4(3) and 19(1) TEU, and use the latter provision to build infringement cases against Member States when they engage in the systemic undermining of judicial independence.[33] In 2016, building up on the scholarship of Professor Scheppele, Professor Kochenov and one of the present authors argued for the combined use of these Treaty provisions so as to enable the Court's review of *national* breaches of the rule of law *beyond* the areas covered by the EU's acquis strictly understood.[34]

However, the Commission proved reluctant to rely on the second subparagraph of Article 19(1) TEU even in the face of Poland's rule of law crisis worsening, with the *ASJP* case providing a perfect illustration of the Commission's position. Indeed, in this case, both the Portuguese Government and the Commission objected to the Court's jurisdiction and the admissibility of the questions submitted by the referring court.

One may find the Commission's stance particularly puzzling. At the time *ASJP* was pending before the Court, the Commission was already embroiled in a gradually

[29] CJEU, Recommendations to national courts and tribunals in relation to the initiation of preliminary ruling proceedings [2019] OJ C380/1, para 10 (emphasis in original).

[30] Lenaerts (n 5) 33.

[31] ibid 52.

[32] M Bonelli, 'Infringement Actions 2.0: How to Protect EU Values before the Court of Justice' (2022) 18 *European Constitutional Law Review* 30, 36.

[33] European Parliament Research Service, *An EU mechanism on democracy, the rule of law and fundamental rights*, Annex I (study by L Pech et al at the request of the Impact Assessment Unit), PE 579.328, April 2016, 198.

[34] D Kochenov and L Pech, 'Better late than never? On the European Commission's Rule of Law Framework and its First activation' (2016) 54 *Journal of Common Market Studies* 1062, 1065. See also C Hillion, 'Overseeing the Rule of Law in the EU: Legal mandate and means' in C Closa and D Kochenov (eds), *Reinforcing Rule of Law Oversight in the European Union* (Cambridge University Press, 2016) 59; KL Scheppele, 'Enforcing the Basic Principles of EU Law through Systemic Infringement Actions' in Closa and Kochenov (eds) ibid 105.

escalating conflict with Poland and could have benefited from the Court developing a justiciable judicial independence doctrine. Yet, signalling a lack of strategic foresight, the Commission treated the case as merely another austerity dispute that ought to be rejected by the Court as inadmissible. One may note in passing that this lack of strategic vision was not unique to the Commission. Indeed, despite being assigned to the Grand Chamber, the case drew little attention prior to the Court's ruling, including from national governments with a record of violating judicial independence. Among the Member States, only the Portuguese Government filed an observation but it is customary for the state from which a case is referred to do so.[35]

Be that as it may, the plea of inadmissibility centred on the question whether the Portuguese Government was implementing EU law within the meaning of Article 51 of the Charter. Both Portugal and the Commission considered the link between the austerity measures and EU law to be insufficient to satisfy this requirement with the consequence that the Court would not have jurisdiction. Neither the Commission nor Portugal thought about distinguishing the scope of application of Article 47 of the Charter from the scope of Article 19(1) TEU.[36]

By contrast, Advocate General Saugmandsgaard Øe was of the opinion that the Court had jurisdiction to provide an interpretation of both Article 19(1) TEU and Article 47 of the Charter. In relation to the former, the Advocate General submitted that the principle of effective judicial protection binds Member States 'when the national courts are likely to exercise their judicial activity in areas covered by EU law, and therefore to act as European judges', which 'may be the case of the judges affected by the legislation at issue in the main proceedings, in so far as they may be required to settle disputes falling within the scope of EU law'.[37] In relation to Article 47 of the Charter, the Advocate General submitted that this provision would also be applicable as the Portuguese legislation may be understood as implementing EU law within the meaning of Article 51 of the Charter.

As regards substance, the Advocate General's main conclusions were more unorthodox. The purpose of the second subparagraph of Article 19(1) TEU was presented as 'primarily procedural in nature'.[38] As for the concept of effective judicial protection, it was not to be confused with the principle of judicial independence.[39] According to the Advocate General, the second subparagraph of Article 19(1) TEU cannot therefore be interpreted as enshrining 'a general principle of EU law according to which the independence of judges sitting in all the courts of the Member States should be guaranteed'.[40] Advocate General Saugmandsgaard Øe reached this conclusion by unusually and unpersuasively distinguishing between the right to effective judicial protection and judicial independence. Be that as it may, the Advocate General identified what would be the key point of principle to be adjudicated by the Court which, as will now be outlined,

[35] Member States are notified of all preliminary questions referred to the ECJ by national courts. The average number of Member State submissions per Grand Chamber preliminary ruling was 3.71 in 2017.

[36] The Commission also considered the preliminary reference to be insufficiently precise.

[37] Opinion of AG Saugmandsgaard Øe delivered on 18 May 2017 in Case C-64/16 *ASJP* EU:C:2017:395, para 41.

[38] ibid para. 63.

[39] ibid paras 64 and 66.

[40] ibid para 67.

rejected the Advocate General's substantive reasoning while building on his point that the scope of application of Article 19(1) TEU is *not* constrained by Article 51 CFR as is Article 47 CFR.

Before addressing the substance of the case, the Court quickly disposed of the inadmissibility points raised by the Commission and the Portuguese Government. In brief, the Court found that it had been provided with sufficient information to enable it 'to understand the reasons why the referring court seeks an interpretation of the second subparagraph of Article 19(1) TEU and Article 47 of the Charter for the needs of the main proceedings'.[41] The Court did not further address the issue of whether it has jurisdiction in the admissibility part of its judgment. Instead, the Court moved on the substance of the referred questions to address the respective scope of application of the second subparagraph of Article 19(1) TEU and Article 47 CFR. In doing so, the Court indirectly clarified why it has jurisdiction to answer questions relating to these two provisions.

In this respect, the most crucial aspect of the judgment concerns the material scope of the second subparagraph of Article 19(1) TEU. According to the Court, that provision relates to the fields covered by Union law, '*irrespective* of whether the Member States are implementing Union law, within the meaning of Article 51(1) of the Charter'.[42] In other words, the scope of application of the EU principle of effective judicial protection under the second subparagraph of Article 19(1) TEU is broader than the scope of application of the EU right to an effective remedy and to a fair trial under Article 47 of the Charter. Indeed, the second subparagraph of Article 19(1) TEU covers any national court or tribunal within the meaning of EU law which may rule as a court or tribunal on questions concerning the application or interpretation of EU law. Any such court must meet the EU requirements of effective judicial protection such as judicial independence.

In the present instance, as the Portuguese Court of Auditors may rule, as a court or tribunal within the meaning of EU law, on questions concerning the application or interpretation of EU law, it follows that 'the Member State concerned must ensure that that court meets the requirements essential to effective judicial protection, in accordance with the second subparagraph of Article 19(1) TEU'.[43]

The practical, if not far-reaching, consequence of the Court's interpretation is that private parties have since been able to directly rely upon the second subparagraph of Article 19(1) TEU to directly challenge, in the context of domestic proceedings, national measures or practices on account of their (alleged) violation of the EU requirements of effective judicial protection. Indeed, while the Court only initially implicitly recognised that the second subparagraph of Article 19(1) TEU has direct effect, the Court has since explicitly confirmed that this provision 'imposes on the Member States a clear and precise obligation as to the result to be achieved that is not subject to any condition as regards the independence which must characterise the courts called upon to interpret and apply EU law'.[44] As will be further detailed in section IV, another crucial consequence of the *ASJP* judgment is that it also finally convinced the Commission to launch

[41] Case C-64/16 *ASJP* (n 1) para 21.
[42] ibid para 29 (emphasis added).
[43] ibid para 40.
[44] Case C-824/18 *AB et al (Appointment of judges to the Supreme Court – Actions)* EU:C:2021:153, para 146.

infringement actions directly on the basis of Article 19(1) TEU, which the Commission did soon afterwards.

As regards the immediate outcome of *ASJP*, as has been the case in the past when the Court takes a decisive leap forward in its doctrine, the application of the new interpretation to the dispute was restrained. The Court found, in essence, in favour of the Portuguese Government and its ability to impose general salary cuts across the civil service, including the judiciary. The broad nature of the austerity measures was highlighted by the Court as an important factor when weighing up whether a government intervention impacting the judiciary should be understood as violating the principle of judicial independence. In the circumstances of the case, the Court deemed it not to be so. In other words, Article 19(1) TEU does *not* 'preclude general salary-reduction measures … linked to requirements to eliminate an excessive budget deficit and to an EU financial assistance programme, from being applied to the members of the Tribunal de Contas'.[45]

Underlining the principled dimension of the *ASJP* case was the fact that by the time of the Court's ruling, the domestic dispute over salaries was largely over. Most salary cuts were gradually reversed as Portugal exited the bailout and macroeconomic conditions improved. In contrast, the impact of the *ASJP* decision on the protection of judicial independence at Member State level has been extremely significant and long-lasting.

IV. Reception

In the first casebook dedicated to the CJEU rule of law case law published in 2021, one of the present authors writing with Professor Kochenov referred to the *ASJP* ruling 'as belonging to the Pantheon of ECJ rulings, on a par with *Van Gend en Loos* and *Costa*'.[46] This is not simply the view from academia, but the view from the Court itself, with CJEU President Lenaerts for instance stating extra-judicially in 2019 that *ASJP* 'has the same significance as cases like *Van Gend en Loos*, *Costa/ENEL*, *Simmenthal* or *ERTA* – it's a judgment of the same order and we were absolutely aware of that constitutional moment'.[47]

The potential significance of the *ASJP* ruling was immediately recognised by scholars. On 28 February 2018, the day after the ruling, the *Verfassungsblog* published a post by one of the present authors which accurately foresaw the impact of the decision in the broader EU rule of law crisis:

> [T]he CJEU is sending a signal to Poland (and others) and preparing for future engagement with what could possibly be independent Polish courts … when it comes to judicial independence and effective protection, the EU cannot stop at the traditional limits posed by the material criterion which normally delineates the respective spheres of EU and national law.[48]

On 13 March 2018, Professor Platon and one of the present authors also published a post which presented *ASJP* as 'the most important judgment since *Les Verts* as regards

[45] Case C-64/16 *ASJP* (n 1) para 52.

[46] L Pech and D Kochenov, *Respect for the Rule of Law in the Case Law of the European Court of Justice: A Casebook Overview of Key Judgments since the Portuguese Judges Case*, SIEPS Report (2021) 12.

[47] Quoted by von Bogdandy and Spieker (n 3) 72.

[48] M Ovádek, 'Has the CJEU just Reconfigured the EU Constitutional Order?' *VerfBlog* (28 February 2018) available at verfassungsblog.de/has-the-cjeu-just-reconfigured-the-eu-constitutional-order.

the principle of the rule of law in the EU legal system' and a ruling which 'comes close to being the EU equivalent of the US Supreme Court case of *Gitlow*' and must be understood as a 'shot across the Polish bows'.[49] The same post stressed that by making Article 19(1) a standalone provision, the Court had 'drastically increased the number of situations where litigants (for instance, a trade union representing judges) may challenge national measures which undermine judicial independence'.[50] In their subsequent article for *Common Market Law Review*, the judgment was characterised as 'nothing short of ground-breaking' as regards the meaning and scope of the principle of the rule of law in EU law while further expanding on their earlier comparison to the US Supreme Court case of *Gitlow*,[51] where it was established that the federal Bill of Rights applied to state law even when purely state competences were being exercised.[52] Professors Bonelli and Claes similarly connected *ASJP* with the situation in Poland while summarising the importance of the Court's ruling as follows: 'it is now evident that while Member States are still largely free to organise their judiciaries in accordance with domestic preferences, they do so under the supervision of the Court of Justice'.[53]

Looking beyond the immediate legal impact of *ASJP*, similarly to the analysis of Pech and Platon, Krajewski understood this ruling as a not-so-subliminal message addressed to the Commission to encourage it to become more proactive in the defence of the rule of law.[54] Most observers of the EU's rule of law crisis have long considered the Commission to be acting in a too little, too late fashion[55] and it fell to the Court in *ASJP* to make the decisive breakthrough. In the words of Van Elsuwege and Gremmelprez, 'the Court is increasingly discovering the potential of Article 2 TEU, in conjunction with Article 19(1) TEU' in the wake of the rule of-law crisis in Poland and Hungary especially.[56]

In this context, there is ample evidence of growing worries within the Court in relation to the existential threat which worsening and spreading rule of law backsliding represents for the EU legal order. To quote President Lenaerts again, the EU's 'foundations as a Union based on the rule of law are under threat and that the very survival of the European project in its current form is at stake'.[57] One may also refer to the academic article published by the CJEU President dedicated to the Court's rule of law case law in

[49] L Pech and S Platon, 'Rule of Law backsliding in the EU: The Court of Justice to the rescue?' *EU Law Analysis* (13 March 2018) available at eulawanalysis.blogspot.com/2018/03/rule-of-law-backsliding-in-eu-court-of.html.

[50] ibid.

[51] *Gitlow v New York*, 268 US 652 (1925).

[52] L Pech and S Platon, 'Judicial independence under threat: The Court of Justice to the rescue in the ASJP case' (2018) 55 *Common Market Law Review* 1827, 1827.

[53] M Bonelli and M Claes, 'Judicial serendipity: how Portuguese judges came to the rescue of the Polish judiciary' (2018) 14 *European Constitutional Law Review* 622, 643.

[54] M Krajewski, 'Associação Sindical dos Juízes Portugueses: The Court of Justice and Athena's Dilemma' (2018) 3 *European Papers* 395.

[55] See, most recently, KL Scheppele, 'The Treaties Without a Guardian: The European Commission and the Rule of Law' (2023) 29 *The Columbia Journal of European Law* 93, 99: '[I]t's not that the Commission did nothing as the rule of law crisis intensified. Instead of bringing infringement actions, it spent much of its energy inventing new tools to cope with the crisis … But while the Commission was doing this, it left its most effective tool – infringement procedures – underutilized.'

[56] P Van Elsuwege and F Gremmelprez, 'Protecting the Rule of Law in the EU Legal Order: A Constitutional Role for the Court of Justice' (2020) 16 *European Constitutional Law Review* 8.

[57] K Lenaerts, 'Constitutional relationships between legal orders and courts within the European Union', FIDE 2021, XXIX FIDE Congress in The Hague, 4 November 2021, Congress Proceedings, Eleven, vol 4, 2022, 155.

which, quite stinkingly, he repeatedly warned of the dangers of the current authoritarian tendencies and drifts as they 'call into question the effectiveness of Articles 2, 19(1) and 49 TEU'.[58]

Before looking at the broader impact of *ASJP* and rapid development of the Court's rule of law-related case law, one may note that this ruling was not universally welcomed. Some, for instance, deplored the Court's alleged 'dubious legal grounding' on the grounds that 'the independence of national courts is mentioned nowhere in the text of Article 19 TEU, nor was judicial independence previously conceptualised by the CJEU as being an element of the obligation under Article 19 to ensure equivalent domestic remedies'.[59] However, this critique failed to take account of the fact that Article 19(1) TEU has been *deliberately* inserted in EU primary law by the Member States to reinforce the Court of Justice's case law on the right to effective judicial protection which the Court has always and logically interpreted as necessarily requiring access to national *independent* courts. Indeed, 'independence is not an ancillary matter but an essential characteristic of courts'.[60] One may also add in passing that Poland's own constitution does not mention judicial independence, yet not even current Polish authorities would argue that judicial independence is not a legal principle which underlies the Polish legal order as a whole.

Be that as it may, captured and/or irregularly composed courts of last resorts in countries subject or previously subject to rule of law backsliding have also – unsurprisingly – deplored the Court's ruling in *ASJP*. To give a single example, the body masquerading as Poland's Constitutional Tribunal, in an *irregular* bench formation,[61] held that various provisions of EU primary law were allegedly incompatible with Poland's Constitution, including Article 19(1) TEU as interpreted by the Court in *ASJP* and subsequent case law.[62] This development eventually led the Commission to launch an infringement action against Poland based inter alia on Article 19(1) TEU, as will be detailed in section V.[63]

V. Impact

Five years after the *ASJP* judgment, the case law of the Court of Justice has firmly established that the second subparagraph of Article 19(1) TEU imposes a number of obligations, including a *general* and *justiciable* obligation on every Member State to *guarantee* and *maintain* the independence of any national courts which may be called upon to rule on questions relating to the application or interpretation of EU law.

[58] Lenaerts (n 5) 52.

[59] M Dawson, 'How can EU law respond to populism?' (2020) 40 *Oxford Journal of Legal Studies* 183, 211.

[60] Opinion of AG Stix-Hackl delivered on 11 May 2006 in Case C-506/04 *Wilson* EU:C:2006:311, para 55.

[61] As per the judgment of the ECtHR in *Xero Flor*. See *Xero Flor w Polsce sp. z o.o. v. Poland* App no 4907/18 (ECtHR, 7 May 2021). For further analysis, see M Szwed, 'The Polish Constitutional Tribunal Crisis from the Perspective of the European Convention on Human Rights' (2022) 18 *European Constitutional Law Review* 132.

[62] Case no K 3/21. For further analysis, see F Zoll et al, *Primacy of EU law and jurisprudence of Polish Constitutional Tribunal*, Study requested by the JURI committee of the European Parliament, PE 732.475, June 2022.

[63] Section V borrows from Pech (n 6).

To justify the wide scope of application of Article 19(1) TEU, the CJEU President, writing extra-judicially, has fittingly emphasised that

> any undue interference with the independence of national judges triggers a domino effect by undermining mutual trust and the uniform application of Union law and thus directly threatens the rule of law in the EU as a whole. Such attacks on the judiciary in one Member State cannot therefore be brushed aside as being 'no one else's business'. On the contrary, due to the essential nature of judicial independence in the EU legal order, they are 'everyone's business'.[64]

Post-*ASJP*, Article 19(1) TEU has become the main vehicle through which national judiciary-related measures raising judicial independence issues have been brought to the Court of Justice's attention, primarily via national requests for a preliminary ruling. Within the five-year period which followed *ASJP*, more than 50 national requests for a preliminary ruling raising questions directly related to the potential incompatibility of national measures with the principle of effective judicial protection have been lodged with the Court. Most of these national requests originate from Polish and Romanian courts. There have also been two important requests from Maltese and Hungarian courts in addition to multiple requests relating to Poland's rule of law crisis originating from Dutch, German and Irish courts in cases connected to surrender requests under the European Arrest Warrant issued by Polish bodies.[65]

In contrast, while the new interpretation of Article 19(1) TEU was swiftly relied upon by the Commission, the Commission has made an extremely parsimonious use of its infringement powers with a total of five infringement actions based on Article 19(1) TEU lodged with the Court since 2018, all of them in relation to the systemic violations of the EU rule of law requirements organised by Polish authorities. In other words, this means less than one infringement action per year and only in relation to systemic attacks targeting Polish courts since *ASJP* notwithstanding the open disregard of the Court of Justice's rule of law judgments in countries such as Hungary and Romania, coupled with systemic attempts, largely successful, to undermine the functioning of the preliminary ruling procedure.[66] Adding insult to injury, by acting 'too little, too late', the EU has de facto externalised Poland's rule of law crisis to the ECtHR.[67]

To date, within the framework of the infringement procedure, the Court has reviewed the following national measures and practices in light of Article 19(1) TEU and found multiple violations of this provision in every infringement case decided to date:

- Polish legislation concerning the lowering of the retirement age of judges of a Supreme Court and grating the President of the country the power to authorise

[64] K Lenaerts, 'The Rule of Law and the Constitutional Identity of the European Union', speech delivered by the president of the CJEU on 17 February 2023 at the conference organised by the Bulgarian Association for European Law in Sofia, published on 5 March 2023, available at evropeiskipravenpregled.eu/the-rule-of-law-and-the-constitutional-identity-of-the-european-union.

[65] For references and analysis, see Pech and Kochenov (n 45); and Pech (n 6).

[66] On the Commission's infringement (in)action and the broader factors at play, see Scheppele (n 54); and RD Kelemen and T Pavone, 'Where Have all the Guardians Gone?' (2023) 75 *World Politics* 779.

[67] See L Pech, P Wachowiec and D Mazur, 'Poland's Rule of Law Breakdown: A Five-Year Assessment of EU's (In)Action' (2021) 13 *Hague Journal on the Rule Law* 1. As of 6 July 2023, there were close to 400 applications pending before the ECtHR relating to Poland's rule of law crisis, with more to be expected as these applications mostly relate to changes made to the organisation of Poland's judiciary under laws that mainly entered into force in 2017 and 2018. More than 150 of these applications have been communicated with the EctHR

affected judges to continue in active judicial service beyond the new retirement age on a case-by-case basis.[68]

- Polish legislation establishing a different retirement age for men and women who are judges or public prosecutors and the lowering of the retirement age of judges of the ordinary courts and public prosecutors while conferring on the Minister for Justice the power to extend the period of active service of those judges.[69]
- Polish legislation establishing a disciplinary regime for judges which, inter alia, established a new disciplinary chamber; allows the content of judicial decisions adopted by judges of the ordinary courts to be classified as a disciplinary offence; and makes it possible to trigger disciplinary proceedings for submitting requests for a preliminary ruling to the Court of Justice.[70]
- Polish legislation (informally known as 'muzzle law') which, inter alia, limits or excludes the possibility for a national court to ensure that individuals claiming rights under EU law have access to an independent and impartial tribunal previously established by law.[71]

The fifth and last infringement action to date in relation to Poland's rule of law crisis and based, inter alia, on the second subparagraph of Article 19(1) TEU, was first launched in December 2021 with a referral to the Court of Justice announced in February 2023.[72] This action will offer the Court the opportunity to review for the first time not merely legislative measures but also the irregular composition of Poland's (captured) constitutional court, its lack of independence as well as its decisions which, inter alia, denied the binding effect of any interim measures of the Court of Justice when they seek to guarantee the effective judicial review by an independent and impartial tribunal established by law.

Space precludes a comprehensive overview of all the preliminary ruling cases where the Court held that it had jurisdiction to interpret the second subparagraph of Article 19(1) TEU and answer judicial independence related questions. Among the most important preliminary rulings judgments issued in the five-year post *ASJP* period, one may mention:

- The Court's judgment of 19 November 2019 in Joined Cases C-585/18, C-624/18 et C-625/18, *AK ea (Independence of the disciplinary chamber of the Supreme Court)*: The referring court must ascertain whether Poland's Disciplinary Chamber is

having decided a total of 12 applications on the merits to date. In addition, the Court has received a total of 60 requests for interim measures from Polish judges in 29 cases concerning the disciplinary and waiving of judicial immunity cases against them and granted these requests in 17 cases. See ECtHR, 'Non-compliance with interim measure in Polish judiciary cases', Press release, ECHR 053 (2023), 16 February 2023; 'Multiple violations in case concerning disciplinary regime for judges in Poland', Press release, ECHR 212 (2023), 6 July 2023.

[68] Case C-619/18 *Commission v Poland (Independence of the Supreme Court)* EU:C:2019:531.

[69] Case C-192/18 *Commission v Poland (Independence of ordinary courts)* EU:C:2019:924.

[70] Case C-791/19 *Commission v Poland (Disciplinary Regime of Judges)* EU:C:2021:596.

[71] Case C-204/21 *Commission v Poland (Independence and private life of judges)* EU:C:2023:442.

[72] European Commission, 'The European Commission decides to refer POLAND to the Court of Justice of the European Union for violations of EU law by its Constitutional Tribunal', Press release, IP/23/842, 15 February 2023.

independent in cases where both Article 47 of the Charter and Article 19(1) were applicable in order to decide whether it has jurisdiction to rule on relevant cases involving Supreme Court judges.[73]

- The Court's judgment of 2 March 2021 in Case C-824/18, *AB et al (Appointment of judges to the Supreme Court – Actions)*: Successive amendments to the Polish Law on the National Council of the Judiciary are liable to infringe Article 19(1) TEU as they have the effect of removing effective judicial review of that council's decisions proposing to the Polish President candidates for the office of Supreme Court judge.[74]
- The Court's judgment of 20 April 2021 in Case C-896/19, *Repubblika*: Article 19(1) TEU does not preclude national provisions which confer on the Prime Minister a decisive power in the process for appointing judges while providing for the involvement of an independent body but precludes any measure which brings about a regression in the protection of the rule of law and in particular, judicial independence.[75]
- The Court's judgment of 6 October 2021 in Case C-487/19, *WŻ.(Chamber of Extraordinary Control and Public Affairs of the Supreme Court – Appointment)*: Transfers without consent of a judge are liable to infringe Article 19(1) TEU and an order adopted by a judge must be declared null and void if that judge was appointed in clear breach of fundamental rules governing the judicial system concerned.[76]
- The Court's judgment of 21 December 2021 in Joined Cases C-357/19, C-379/19, C-547/19, C-811/19 and C-840/19, *Euro Box Promotion*: Article 19(1) TEU along with other provisions of EU law preclude national courts from being bound by the case law of a national constitutional court when this case law is contrary to EU judicial independence requirements and preclude national judges from being subject to disciplinary proceedings if they do so.[77]
- The Court's judgment of 22 February 2022 in Case C-430/21, *RS (Effects of a constitutional court rulings)*: Article 19(1) TEU along with other provisions of EU law preclude national rules or practices which prevent national ordinary courts from assessing the compatibility with EU law of national legislation which the constitutional court of the relevant Member State has found to be consistent with a national constitutional provision providing for the primacy of EU law.[78]

The rise in the quantity and prominence of Article 19(1) TEU case law happened so quickly after *ASJP* that even some within the Court worried where it might lead. For instance, in his Opinion of 23 September 2020 in the *Romanian Judges I* preliminary ruling case, Advocate General Bobek warned of 'gates which are too open' due to the 'apparently limitless, reach of the second subparagraph of Article 19(1) TEU'.[79]

[73] EU:C:2019:982.
[74] EU:C:2021:153.
[75] EU:C:2021:31.
[76] EU:C:2021:798.
[77] EU:C:2022:200.
[78] EU:C:2022:99.
[79] Joined Cases C-83/19, C-127/19 and C-195/19 *Romanian Judges I* EU:C:2020:746, para 222.

The subsequent development of the case law indicates, however, that this fear was misplaced.

To quote the CJEU President, while the second subparagraph of Article 19(1) TEU aims to protect 'the independence of Member State courts at all times',[80] this does not mean that, on the one hand, national courts may in any dispute pending before them raise Article 19(1) TEU questions and, on the other hand, that the scope of Article 19(1) TEU is boundless.

As regards the former, national courts may only refer Article 19(1)-related questions where there is a connecting factor between the disputes pending before the referring courts and the second subparagraph of Article 19(1) TEU. As regards the latter, in examining the compatibility of national measures relating, for instance, to judicial appointments or the disciplinary regime applicable to judges with Article 19(1) TEU, 'the Court of Justice does not seek to redesign national judiciaries' but 'limits itself to examining whether rules that concern the organization and functioning of national courts'[81] comply with fundamental principles of EU law such as the principle of judicial independence, which are themselves enshrined in ECHR law and in the national law of each of the EU Member States.

VI. Conclusion

For the present authors, the EU and its legal order would cease to exist if compliance with Article 2 TEU values such as the rule of law – a value which, as the Court has repeatedly stressed since *ASJP*, is given concrete expression in Article 19(1) TEU – could be reduced to an obligation a candidate State must meet in order to accede to the EU but could disregard following its accession. Viewed in this light, the Court of Justice's interpretation of the second subparagraph of Article 19(1) TEU as a provision 'of both a constitutional and procedural nature, compliance with which must, moreover, be guaranteed across all the substantive areas of application of EU law and before all national courts seised of cases falling within those areas',[82] may be viewed as compelling if not imperative.

While the significance of *ASJP* lies firmly in the rule-of-law realm, the case offers broader lessons into the making of landmark rulings by the CJEU. First, seemingly mundane but suitably framed cases arriving from the national level can acquire much wider importance in the hands of the Court. The impact *ASJP* has had on European integration has been far beyond the expectations of the Portuguese judges initiating the domestic litigation. At the same time, the case reveals the potential effect of innovative legal drafting and influence of EU law academics for doctrinal change.

Second, *ASJP* is a testament that landmark cases offering bold interpretive moves are – somewhat counterintuitively given recent populist backlash against independent

[80] Lenaerts (n 63).
[81] K Lenaerts, 'New Horizons for the Rule of Law Within the EU' (2020) 21 *German Law Journal* 29, 33.
[82] Case C-204/21 *Commission v Poland (Independence and private life of judges)* (n 70) para 268.

courts and European integration – still capable of garnering nearly unequivocal support from the Member States. Rather than protesting a judge-led creation of a general and justiciable obligation to respect national judicial independence, the Member States codified it in the EU's Rule of Law Conditionality Regulation.[83] Conversely, the CJEU is unlikely to issue similarly transformative judgments in more contentious areas of EU law. The permissive consensus[84] surrounding the issue of judicial independence in the EU caught Poland and Hungary off-guard. As long as this permissive consensus holds, it should act as a deterrent for other governments in the future.

[83] Regulation 2020/2092 of the European Parliament and of the Council of 16 December 2020 on a general regime of conditionality for the protection of the Union budget [2020] OJ L433/1. For further analysis, see L Pech 'The rule of law as a well-established and well-defined principle of EU Law' (2022) 14 *Hague Journal on the Rule of Law* 107.

[84] M Blauberger and DS Martinsen, 'The Court of Justice in times of politicisation: "law as a mask and shield" revisited' (2020) 27 *Journal of European Public Policy* 382, 387.

PART D

Fundamental Rights and the Union Legal Order

16

Nold and the Sources of EU Fundamental Rights

SIONAIDH DOUGLAS-SCOTT

I. Historical and Doctrinal Context

Notwithstanding the somewhat majestic claim of the present Article 2 of the Treaty on European Union (TEU) that the European Union (EU) is 'founded' on the value of respect for human rights, human rights were not a pressing concern in the early European Economic Community (EEC) (as it then was) and the original treaties establishing the three European Communities contained no catalogue of fundamental human rights. The reasons for this lack of attention are embedded in the EU's history. The Treaty establishing the European Economic Community (EEC Treaty) started out as an economic treaty, of limited ambitions, with the aim of creating a common market. It was originally modest in nature, partly no doubt because of the failure of the draft Political and Defence Union treaties[1] due to the refusal of General de Gaulle to countenance perceived attacks on French national sovereignty. There were no sections on fundamental rights because the EEC founders (nor those of the European Coal and Steel Community (ECSC) or Euratom) did not think this relevant to a treaty with mainly economic aspirations. The European Convention on Fundamental Rights (ECHR) was also, of course, already in existence, and probably thought sufficient to operate as a 'Bill of Rights' for Europe. Although during the drafting process of the EEC Treaty the German delegation had proposed a human rights 'reservation clause', as an attempted constraint on the way the new Community would exercise its conferred powers, this was rejected, apparently due to the fear that it might be applied by Member States to frustrate Community objectives.[2]

The fact that fundamental rights were not a pressing concern in the early EEC may be gleaned from the very little space allotted to this subject in earlier textbooks.[3]

[1] In which human rights had a prominent role: E Stein and G Vining, 'Citizen Access to Judicial Review of Administrative Action in a Transnational and Federal Context' in F Jacobs (ed), *European Law and the Individual* (North Holland, 1976).

[2] See M Zuleeg, 'Fundamental Rights and the Law of the European Communities' (1971) 8 *Common Market Law Review* 446; G de Búrca, 'The Evolution of EU Human Rights Law' in P Craig and G de Búrca (eds), *The Evolution of EU Law*, 3rd edn (Oxford University Press, 2020) 480.

[3] Even by 1989, JG Kapteyn and P Verloren, *Introduction to the Law of the European Communities*, 2nd edn (Kluwer, 1989) devoted just four pages out of 900.

However, the EU has gone beyond being a common market, now encompassing a much greater range of activities, particularly in the area of freedom, security and justice,[4] which includes visas, asylum and criminal law – matters with obvious relevance for human rights.

Nonetheless, in spite of the EU's increased competences, it was only in December 2000 that the EU proclaimed its own (then non-binding) Charter of Fundamental Rights, and only with the coming into force of the Treaty of Lisbon on 1 December 2009 that this Charter became legally binding.[5] Therefore, for most of its history, the EU possessed no Charter of Rights. However, this does not mean that fundamental rights were ignored. For over 40 years, fundamental rights have had a recognised status in the EU as 'general principles of law', a status confirmed by successive versions of Article 6 TEU.[6] And there is of course Article 2 TEU's assertion of the foundation of the EU on respect for human rights, which is backed up by a sanctions procedure, in Article 7 TEU, whereby an EU State's membership rights may be suspended if it engages in 'a serious and persistent breach … of values mentioned in Article 2'.

Given the absence of any EU Bill of Rights until 2000, protection of fundamental rights for the first 40 years of European integration developed through the case law of the European Court of Justice. This resulted in a system in which litigation played a large role in the development, profile and enforcement of fundamental rights.[7]

Although in early cases (the so-called 'sins of youth')[8] the Court of Justice rejected any applications based on alleged breach of fundamental rights by Community institutions, by the 1960s the German and Italian courts[9] were beginning to express concern at the possible erosion of fundamental rights entrenched in their national Constitutions, given that it had already been established in *van Gend* and *Costa* that directly effective EEC law took priority over conflicting domestic provisions.[10] It became increasingly clear that a shift in attitude was required by the Court of Justice to assure Member States that fundamental rights could be adequately protected by Community law. In a famous trilogy of rulings – *Stauder*, *Internationale Handelsgesellschaft* and *Nold*[11] – the

[4] For which see now Title V TFEU.

[5] Now affirmed in Art 6(1) TEU: 'The Union recognises the rights, freedoms and principles set out in the Charter of Fundamental Rights of the European Union of 7 December 2000, as adapted at Strasbourg, on 12 December 2007, which shall have the same legal value as the Treaties.'

[6] Art 6(3) TEU now states that 'Fundamental rights, as guaranteed by the European Convention for the Protection of Human Rights and Fundamental Freedoms and as they result from the constitutional traditions common to the Member States, shall constitute general principles of the Union's law.'

[7] In some of its earliest case law, the Court of Justice stated that 'the vigilance of individuals concerned to protect their rights amounts to an effective supervision in addition to the supervision entrusted to … the Commission and member States': Case 16/62 *Van Gend en Loos* [1/963] ECR 1.

[8] See, eg, Case 1/58 *Stork* v *High Authority* [1959] ECR 17; and Case 40/64 *Sgarlata* v *Commission* [1965] ECR 215, in which the Court refused to allow Community law to be overridden by a plea based on national fundamental rights.

[9] These jurisdictions placed particular emphasis on observance of fundamental rights, given their past history.

[10] Case 26/62 *van Gend en Loos* (n 7); Case 6/64 *Costa v Enel* [1964] ECR 585.

[11] Case 29/69 *Stauder v City of Ulm* [1969] ECR 419; Case C-11/70 *Internationale Handelsgesellschaft* [1970] ECR 1125; Case 4/73 *Nold* [1974] ECR 491.

ECJ attempted to demonstrate that. *Nold* will be examined in greater detail below, but a brief explanation of *Stauder* and *Handelsgesellschaft* will be given here, to set the scene.

In the *Stauder* case (1969), which concerned vouchers for reduced-price butter, a pensioner in Ulm objected to having to reveal his name on the basis that this violated his dignity, a fundamental right under German law. He therefore asked the ECJ to declare the offending EEC Regulation null and void. The ECJ held that the provision in question could not be interpreted as requiring the identification of beneficiaries by name, and therefore contained 'nothing capable of infringing the fundamental rights enshrined in the general principles of Community law and protected by the Court'.[12] Thus, the doctrine of fundamental rights found its first mention in EU law. (And, somewhat ironically, an applicant who did not wish his name to be revealed, became famous in Community law, for that very reason.)

This matter was revisited the next year in the *Internationale Handelsgesellschaft* case, where the applicants claimed that the forfeiture system required under EEC Council Regulation 120/67 was a violation of their basic rights under German law, namely, the freedom of action, of economic liberty and proportionality. On the one hand, the ECJ expressly rejected the review of European law according to national constitutional rights:

> Recourse to the legal rules or concepts of national law in order to judge the validity of measures adopted by the institutions of the Community would have an adverse effect on the uniformity and efficacy of Community law. The validity of such measures can only be assessed in the light of Community law.[13]

However, the Court also suggested that Community law itself might protect these very same fundamental rights:

> In fact respect for human rights forms an integral part of the general principles of Community law protected by the Court of Justice. The protection of such rights, whilst inspired by the constitutional traditions common to member states, must be ensured within the framework of the structure and objectives of the Community.[14]

After examining the grounds of infringement alleged, the ECJ concluded that there had been no infringement, as the restriction on the freedom to trade was not disproportionate to the interest which the deposit system sought to advance.

II. Facts and Judgment in the *Nold* Case

The decision in the *Nold* case not only completed the trio of groundbreaking fundamental rights cases, but was also the first case in which the ECJ made a reference (albeit *indirect*) to the ECHR.

[12] Stauder (n 11) 425.
[13] Case C-11/70 *Handelsgesellschaft* (n 11) para 3.
[14] ibid para 4.

A. Facts

Nold (a limited partnership under German law) was a direct wholesaler of Ruhr coal who sought the annulment of Commission Decision of 21 December 1972 (taken under the European Coal and Steel Community (ECSC) Treaty) authorising new terms of business for Ruhrkohle AG, the company that had been formed by the merger of the Ruhr Basin coal-mining companies. This Decision set out the conditions to be met by wholesalers like Nold who wished to be directly supplied by Ruhrkohle AG. One such condition required the wholesaler to enter a two-year contract to buy at least 6,000 metric tons of coal per year from Ruhrkohle. This was much more restrictive than previous conditions and greatly exceeded Nold's annual sales, making it impossible for Nold to continue as a directly supplied wholesaler of coal.

Nold's challenge was actually brought under the ECSC Treaty, although by this stage the institutions of the three treaties had been merged. Nold challenged the measure in the ECJ, arguing that the Commission Decision was inadequately reasoned, discriminated between Community dealers, and that it violated fundamental rights, including the right of property guaranteed by the German Constitution. It is this last argument with which we are concerned here. More specifically, Nold argued that the Commission Decision interfered with its vested proprietary right to be a coal wholesaler which it had enjoyed for more than 100 years, with the effect of excluding it from the coal trade – an act equivalent to expropriation because it deprived it of 'actual possession'. Nold also argued that other rights, including the freedom of economic action, as well as the principle of proportionality, were infringed by the Decision, and also relied on international treaties, including in particular the ECHR and the Protocol to that Convention of 20 March 1952.

The Commission countered that it was not for the Court of Justice to interpret and apply domestic laws, even fundamental rights in domestic constitutions. Moreover, it argued, the ECSC Treaty contained no general principle of law, written or unwritten, guaranteeing the maintenance of acquired positions.

B. Judgment

Although this judgment is a landmark case for the Court's acknowledgement of fundamental rights, Nold did not succeed in getting the Commission Decision annulled. In its judgment of 14 May 1974, the Court of Justice found both that the Decision was adequately reasoned and that no discrimination had occurred. But it is the fundamental rights aspects of the judgment with which we are here concerned. The Court not only reasserted that 'fundamental rights form an integral part of the general principles of law, the observance of which it ensures', but also explained that:

> In safeguarding these rights, the Court is bound to draw inspiration from constitutional traditions common to the member States, and it cannot therefore uphold measures which are incompatible with fundamental rights recognized and protected by the Constitutions of those States.[15]

[15] Case 4/73 *Nold* (n 11) para 13.

Significantly, it went on to state that:

> Similarly, international treaties for the protection of human rights on which the member States have collaborated or of which they are signatories, can supply guidelines which should be followed within the framework of Community law.[16]

However, ultimately, Nold failed to convince the Court. The Court held that there had been no violation of fundamental rights in this case because property rights are not absolute but are 'subject to certain limits justified by the overall objectives pursued by the Community, on condition that the substance of these rights is left untouched'.[17] The Court added that 'The disadvantages claimed by the applicant are in fact the result of economic change and not of the contested Decision.'[18] Indeed, Advocate General Trabucchi, who wrote the Opinion in *Nold*, cited four German cases in support of his conclusion that Community law, like Member State systems, only protected the essential content of property rights.[19]

C. Assessment

A few comments are appropriate here. First, this litigation is typical of cases from the earlier years of the European Communities. In fact, Nold was a well-known litigator to Community institutions, and, as expressed in Advocate General Trabucchi's Opinion, 'The applicant undertaking … has in the past obtained, by repeated actions before this Court, the annulment of several decisions of the High Authority'.[20] The subject matter of this earlier case law, even when it concerned fundamental rights, reflects the centre of gravity of the Communities in those days. *Stauder* concerned measures (free butter) to manage the butter mountain which had accrued under the EEC Common Agricultural Policy (CAP). *Handelsgesellschaft* was also provoked by CAP measures – in this case rules on grain exports. And *Nold* reflected the ECSC reorganisation of the markets in coal. The applicants – at least *Nold* and *Handelsgesellschaft* were not what we might think of as typical human rights applicants – rather than being individuals or groups of persons, were agricultural or industrial companies or partnerships.

Second, all three of these cases – *Stauder, Handelsgesellschaft, Nold* – were brought by German litigants who relied on rights protected under the German Constitution. There was already vigorous debate about the intersection of fundamental rights and Community law in Germany, if not in most of the other initial Member States (with the exception of Italy). We shall return to this point.

Third, although these three cases established an important fundamental rights jurisdiction for the Community, in none of these cases did the Court find that the applicant's

[16] ibid.

[17] ibid 14.

[18] ibid para 15.

[19] The four cases were: 13 B Verf GE 226; 17 B Verf GE 172; 28 B Verf GE 104; NJW (1968) 293 (*Bundesgerichtshof*).

[20] Nold was also a party to Joined Cases 36, 37, 38 and 40/59 *Comptoirs de vente du charbon de la Ruhr: 'Geitling', 'Mausegatt' Entreprise I Nold KG* [1960] ECR 857, in which an unsuccessful plea based on fundamental rights was made.

rights had actually been violated, nor did it nullify the Community measure in question. This somewhat pyrrhic outcome is relatively typical for these earlier cases.

Fourth, this is the first time that the ECHR is mentioned in the European Court's case law, even if somewhat obliquely. Indeed, France had ratified the European Convention only a few days before the *Nold* judgment was given. This gives the ECJ a concrete source on which to draw for fundamental rights. The applicant had specifically mentioned the ECHR in its submissions, but the Court only refers to 'international treaties' in its judgment. Notably, however, the Court referred not to *ratified* but to *signed* treaties, as well as to treaties on which the Community's Member States have *collaborated* – broadening the reference, but also leaving it vague, as indeed does its reference to these treaties being able to 'supply guidelines which should be followed within the framework of Community law'. The Court did not explain why reference could be made to such treaties. Nor, however, and contrary to some fears at the time, did this reference mean that the ECHR became directly applicable or binding in EEC law.[21] Nonetheless, it signalled the start of the long and sometimes tortuous relationship between the EEC/EU and ECHR – a relationship which will be considered in following sections of this chapter.

III. Reception History: Judicial and Academic

Therefore, one may summarise the evolution of the Court of Justice's case law on fundamental rights by 1974 thus. Although, before 1969, fundamental rights were treated as outwith the Court's jurisdiction, or otherwise immaterial to the dispute, by the 1969 *Stauder* judgment the Court recognised that Community law must guarantee protection of fundamental rights enshrined in general principles of law; in the 1970 *Handelsgesellschaft* case, it declared that the protection of fundamental rights must be inspired by the constitutional traditions common to the Member States; and in *Nold*, it affirmed these two earlier rulings and added that international treaties for the protection of human rights can supply guidelines which should be followed within the framework of Community law.

Notably, however, the *Nold* judgment created some uncertainty. The concept of general principles of law is quite vague and reference to 'the constitutional traditions common to the Member States' left it unclear whether it was necessary for *all* Member States to recognise a right before it was accepted by the Court, in which case the standard for fundamental rights in the EU would be rather low. For quite some time, there was a debate as to whether the Community took a maximalist or minimalist approach[22] to fundamental rights derived from national constitutional standards, a debate that has now subsided since the Charter became binding and a first source of reference for the Court. It was also unclear what was intended by the words 'inspiration' and 'guidelines' in the context of international treaties.

[21] See WR Edeson and F Wooldridge, 'European Community Law and Fundamental Human Rights: Some Recent Decisions of the European Court and of National Courts' (1976) 3 *Legal Issues of Economic Integration* 1, 30–31. See further n 73 below.

[22] See, eg, L Besselink, 'Entrapped by the Maximum Standard: On Fundamental Rights, Pluralism and Subsidiarity in the European Union' (1998) 35 *Common Market Law Review*, 629.

Nonetheless, the implications of these judgments were significant. Notably, they brought about a transfer of judicial power. The ECJ asserted for itself the review of Community measures according to Community fundamental rights standards, thus averting the risk of subverting the supremacy of Community law to national constitutional standards. Second, we may add the Court's fundamental rights doctrine to its earlier groundbreaking doctrines of direct effect and supremacy of Community law, neither of which finds explicit basis in the treaties. For Brun-Otto Bryde, former judge at the German Constitutional Court, 'The introduction of fundamental rights was also a logical conclusion from other steps the Court had undertaken to transform the international law treaty system of the Rome treaties into a novel legal order.'[23] And Takis Tridimas put it this way: 'While *Van Gend en Loos* and *Costa v ENEL* defined the "*essential conditions*"[24] of Community law, in incorporating fundamental rights into the Treaty', the Court 'completed its content'.[25] Tridimas also added that by providing a firm grounding for the rule of law in its fundamental rights cases, the ECJ was able 'to make the transition to the third-generation primacy cases and colonise the law of remedies'.[26] Furthermore, as de Búrca writes, 'In this way a position close to that which was rejected during the drafting of the EEC Treaty was eventually accepted by the Court of Justice, even without an express reservation clause in the Treaty.'[27]

However, there is a strong line of argument that contends that the Court did this, not because of any great love for the noble ideas of human rights, but for rather more cynical motives – because it feared that if it did not, some Member State courts, particularly the Constitutional courts of Germany and Italy, would refuse to accord supremacy to Community law if they found it violated fundamental rights in their own constitutions. Therefore, to avoid that, the European Court identified a respect for fundamental rights taking the form of general principles of law within the Community legal order itself. The late Judge Mancini, writing in 1989, summed up the position the ECJ had achieved in relation to fundamental rights in the following way: 'Reading an unwritten Bill of Rights into Community law is indeed the most striking contribution the Court has made to the development of a Constitution for Europe.' But he continued by qualifying it by saying 'this statement was forced on the Court by the outside, by the German and, later, the Italian Constitutional courts'.[28] And, in describing the European Court's resolution, Joseph Weiler has written 'the surface language of the Court is … the language of human rights. The deep structure is all about supremacy'.[29] Coppell and O'Neill, in their sceptical account, wrote 'In response to [the] threat of national courts, … the [ECJ] discovered that the protection of fundamental rights was indeed a general principle of

[23] B-O Bryde, 'The ECJ's Fundamental Rights Jurisprudence – A Milestone in Transnational Constitutionalism' in M Poiares Maduro and L Azoulai (eds), *The Past and Future of EU Law* (Hart Publishing, 2010) 119.

[24] The term is from P Pescatore, *L'Ordre Juridique des Communautés Européennes* (Presses Universitaires de Liège, 1975) 227.

[25] T Tridimas, 'Primacy, Fundamental Rights and the Search for Legitimacy' in Maduro and Azoulai (eds) (n 23) 100.

[26] ibid.

[27] de Búrca (n 2) 489.

[28] F Mancini, 'The Making of a Constitution for Europe' (1989) 26 *Common Market Law Review* 595.

[29] J Weiler, 'Eurocracy and Distrust' (1986) 61 *Washington Law Review* 1103, 1119.

[EEC] law.'[30] More generally, the complaint is that the Court is guilty of a judicial activism redolent of a *gouvernement des juges.*[31]

This approach renders the Court's embrace of fundamental rights a far more cynical exercise. But was this actually the case? In a 2019 article, Fabbrini and Delledonne reconsidered this 'simplistic understanding',[32] pointing out that the case law of the ECJ recognising fundamental rights as general principles of EU law pre-dated high-profile Member State case law antagonistic to EC supremacy, such as *Solange I*.[33] Their article also noted the weak mechanisms for fundamental rights protection in founding members other than Italy and Germany. As a result, they concluded that

> the rise of an EU human rights jurisprudence should be seen as the result of a transnational development consisting of greater sensitivity towards human rights at all levels of government – and not of a supranational response to national pressures.[34]

However, their reassessment has been contested.[35] First, regarding chronology, even if some prominent national responses came later, there was already a vigorous debate in 1960s Germany over the issue of Community supremacy and fundamental rights.[36] Indeed, the Constitutional courts in Italy and West Germany had already questioned the supremacy of Community law on human rights grounds in 1965 and 1967, prior to the higher profile *Solange I* and *Frontini* cases.[37] And it is surely no coincidence that the first major cases on fundamental rights in the Court of Justice were brought by German litigants. There is also evidence predating the *Stauder* case of 1969, which suggests the European Court's (or at least members of the Court) awareness of the threat posed to Community supremacy by national courts and standards. Pierre Pescatore (one of the European Court judges in *Nold*) assessed this national debate as 'threatening' to supremacy in his influential 1968 article, written when he was already a judge at the Court of Justice.[38]

But the motivation for recognising fundamental rights surely goes beyond the need to protect European integration from national attacks. Elsewhere, law was mobilising in

[30] J Coppel and A O'Neill, 'The European Court of Justice: Taking Rights Seriously' (1992) 29 *Common Market Law Review* 669, 689; see also J Weiler and N Lockhart, '"Taking Rights Seriously" Seriously: The European Court and its Fundamental Rights jurisprudence' – part I (1995) 32 *Common Market Law Review* 51; part II (1995) 32 *Common Market Law Review* 579.

[31] See generally on judicial activism in the ECJ, H Rasmussen, *On Law and Policy in the European Court of Justice: A Comparative Study in Judicial Policymaking* (Nijhoff, 1986) 399.

[32] G Delledonne and F Fabbrini, 'The founding myth of European human rights law: revisiting the role of national courts in the rise of EU human rights jurisprudence' (2019) 44 *European Law Review* 178.

[33] This case law is discussed in section IV.

[34] Delledonne and Fabbrini (n 32) 178.

[35] By, eg, W Phelan, 'The Role of the German and Italian Constitutional Courts in the rise of EU Human Rights Jurisprudence: A Response to Delledonne & Fabbrini' (2020) TRiSS Working Papers.

[36] See, eg, B Davies, *Resisting the European Court of Justice: West Germany's confrontation with European law, 1949–1979* (Cambridge University Press, 2012); HP Ipsen, *Europäisches Gemeinschaftsrecht* (Mohr, 1972) 716.

[37] According to Phelan, 'The fundamental rights aspects of the 1965 *San Michele* judgment of the Italian Constitutional Court and the 1967 *EEC Regulations* judgment of the German Constitutional Court are less well-known than those in the 1973 *Frontini* and 1974 *Solange I* judgments but they are regularly mentioned in accounts of the national reception of EU law in Italy and Germany.' Phelan (n 35) 19.

[38] P Pescatore, 'Les droits de l'homme et l'integration Europeenne' (1968) *Cahiers de droit européen*, 629, 636. Also P Pescatore, 'Fundamental Rights and Freedoms in the system of the European Communities' (1970) 18 *American Journal of Comparative Law* 343.

favour of human rights – for example, by the late 1960s, the UN had promulgated two human rights Covenants. De Búrca notes that

> already some years before the ECJ's decision in *Stauder*, the President of the Commission had been arguing openly for an understanding of fundamental human rights as part of the 'general principles' of EC law, which although autonomous in source from national constitutions, nevertheless took into account the common legal conceptions of the Member States.[39]

Pescatore, in the same 1968 article that recognised the threat posed to supremacy, also claimed that the EEC already had its own unwritten catalogue of fundamental rights.[40] Indeed, in much earlier litigation brought by *Nold*, Advocate General Roemer (also the Advocate General in *Stauder*), although he dismissed Nold's appeal to German constitutional rights, did not exclude 'having regard to fundamental legal principles which are also to be found in the provisions of national constitutions'.[41] Nevertheless, whatever the motivation, Bryde suggests that 'there is a certain dialectical justice in the fact that those who tried to derail the constitutionalisation of Europe mobilising fundamental rights as an argument moved the Court to a further step of constitutionalisation'.[42]

In any case, the Court's case law acknowledging fundamental rights issues continued to evolve, and was supported and entrenched by the Community's political institutions, initially in the Common Declaration by the Parliament, Council and Commission of 1977,[43] subsequently in Article 6(2) TEU, which officially affirmed the Court's formulation on fundamental rights, stating that the Union is bound by fundamental rights as guaranteed by the ECHR and as they result from the constitutional traditions common to the Member States. The original mandate of the Cologne European Council for drafting the 2000 Charter of Fundamental Rights was the codification of the Court's jurisprudence (although the Charter as concluded exceeded this mandate). Indeed, since the Treaty of Lisbon, the Charter now constitutes the first point of reference for fundamental rights norms in EU law, as a binding document rather than as a source of inspiration.[44] The transformation of the Charter into a legally binding document with primary law status, and the extension of the Court's jurisdiction in areas such as asylum, immigration and criminal matters, has increased the Court's profile in the fundamental rights field. And although in principle, at the national level, EU fundamental rights apply only when EU law more generally is applicable,[45] this limitation has been reduced in importance by the ever-increasing scope of EU law.

According to Bryde, 'The importance of the court's reference to the ECHR in *Nold* can hardly be overstated', adding that 'Because it draws on both the national Constitutions and the European Convention on Human Rights, the Court holds a strategic position in the enterprise of harmonising the European human rights system.'[46] In 1968, in his

[39] De Búrca (n 2) 489, citing W Hallstein, *Discussions on the Dehousse Report*, 79 Proceedings of the European Parliament (French edn, 1965) 218–22.

[40] Pescatore (n 38) 636.

[41] Case 18/57 *Nold KG v High Authority* [1959] ECR 41, 73–74.

[42] Bryde (n 23) 122.

[43] [1977] OJ C103.

[44] See, eg, further confirmation of this in Case C-272/09 P *KME* [2011] ECR I-12789.

[45] See Art 51(1) Charter: 'The provisions of this Charter are addressed to the institutions and bodies of the Union with due regard for the principle of subsidiarity and to the Member States only when they are implementing Union law', which has been elaborated in case law.

[46] Bryde (n 23) 126, 127.

article in the *Cahiers de Droit European*, Pierre Pescatore had rejected the prospect of the inspiration of Community law by the ECHR because France had not then ratified the Convention. But he also noted that things would change when France did so, arguing that in that case, the Court could, and should, be inspired by the contents of the ECHR.[47] Indeed, Pescatore was the Juge Rapporteur in the *Nold* case, in which he took the same approach as in his earlier article.

From *Nold* onwards, references to the ECHR increased. In *Rutili*, the Court referred explicitly to the ECHR.[48] In 1989, the ECHR was cited as having a 'particular significance'.[49] Between 1975 and 1998 the ECHR was cited in over 70 judgments of the Luxembourg Court. Yet citation of Strasbourg *case law* in Luxembourg took some time, commencing in the late 1980s with the Opinions of Advocates General, and only occurring as late as 1996 in the case of the Court of Justice itself. Indeed, the ECJ's first reference in *P v S*[50] was made, somewhat ironically, after it had denied, in its Opinion *2/94*,[51] that the EU had the competence, as the treaties then stood, to accede to the ECHR.

The growth of the EU into a feasible polity in its own right, with a substantial fundamental rights jurisprudence, raises the issue of its external accountability. The most obvious source of this would be the ECHR. Accession to, or a close official relationship with, the ECHR has long been on the agenda, although never achieved.[52] (Indeed, the ECHR was to be incorporated as an integral part of the (failed) European Political Community (EPC) treaty in the 1950s, and the EPC draft treaty also included a procedure (Article 46) for the ECJ to renounce jurisdiction to the ECtHR. Nothing of course came of this.) There are many perceived advantages in EU accession to the ECHR. All Member States of the EU are already contracting parties to the ECHR. A formal linking of the EU and ECHR could be seen as underlining EU concern with human rights, and also eliminate charges of double standards, based on the criticism that whereas the EU requires all of its Member States to be members of the ECHR, it is not itself a member. It would also minimise the danger of conflicting rulings emanating from the ECJ, and ECtHRs, given that they could now rule on virtually identical issues.

However, the CJEU concluded in *Opinion 2/94* that,[53] under the existing treaty provisions, there was no competence for what was then the Community to accede to the ECHR. So the two institutions continued on their separate ways. However, as amended by Lisbon, Article 6(2) TEU now places an obligation on the EU to accede to the ECHR. This, however, has not happened and subsequent developments are considered in the last section.

[47] Pescatore (n 38) 649–50.
[48] Case 36/75 *Rutili* [1975] ECR 1219, discussed in section IV.
[49] Cases 46/87 and 227/88 *Hoechst v Commission* [1989] ECR 2859, para 13.
[50] Case C-13/94 *P v S* [1996] ECR I-2143.
[51] *Opinion 2/94* [1996] ECR I-1759.
[52] For example, the Commission issued a Memorandum in April 1979 on 'The Communities becoming a signatory of the European Convention on Human Rights' (*Bulletin of the European Communities*, supplement, 2/79).
[53] *Opinion 2/94* (n 51).

IV. Famous Follow-Up Cases (Including National Supreme Courts)

In subsequent cases, the ECJ expanded its case law on fundamental rights, applying them across diverse subject matter, extending beyond the commercial and agricultural, which had tended to concern its earlier case law. In *Rutili*, the Court expanded on its *Nold* reasoning and, for the first time, explicitly referred to specific provisions of the ECHR. Not only did the Court expressly refer to the ECHR in *Rutili*, but it also considered fundamental rights in the context of Member State action – in this case state action restricting the free movement of workers under Community law on grounds of public policy. The ECJ held that the scope of the public policy derogations was a matter for Community law, and that the limits of Member State action under EC law were parallel to provisions in Articles 8–11 of the ECHR.[54]

Therefore, in *Rutili*, not only did the ECJ expressly invoke specific provisions in the ECHR, but it applied them, not to acts of Community institutions, but to an act of a Member State derogating from Community freedoms, thus indicating a willingness to police the boundaries of Community law. Other cases followed,[55] which established an incremental expansion of Member State action which could be subject to fundamental rights scrutiny by the ECJ.

More recently, in several areas, the Court's application of fundamental rights has been disappointing. These include the refugee crisis[56] and Eurocrisis. In particular, the European Court does not seem to have acted as an effective counterbalance to Eurozone measures applied to sensitive domestic fields of social policy. Given that the Court has been willing to hear arguments concerning the Charter in cases of other sorts, it is hard to see why the Charter should be seen as inoperable in cases arising out of EU measures on the financial and economic crisis.[57] In contrast, other courts and supervisory bodies within the framework of the Council of Europe and the ILO appear to have acted more progressively.[58]

A. National Supreme Courts

There has also been an on-and-off backlash to ECJ fundamental rights jurisprudence from national constitutional courts. Following *Handelsgesellschaft*, which had come

[54] Case 36/75 *Rutili* [1975] ECR 1219.

[55] eg, Case 5/88 *Wachauf* [1989] ECR 2609; Case C-260/89 *ERT* [1991] ECR I-2925.

[56] eg, L Heschl, A Stankovic, C Strohal and S Kieber, 'The Decline of Fundamental Rights in CJEU Jurisprudence after the 2015 "Refugee Crisis"' [2018] *European Yearbook on Human Rights* 103.

[57] See further C Barnard, 'The Silence of the Charter: Social Rights and the Court of Justice' in S de Vries, U Bernitz and S Weatherill, *The EU Charter of Fundamental Rights as a Binding Instrument* (Hart Publishing, 2015) 174; also C Kilpatrick, 'Are the Bailouts Immune to EU social challenge because they are not EU Law?' (2014) 10 *European Constitutional Law Review* 393; J Fraczyk, 'EU Fundamental Rights and the Financial Crisis' in S Douglas Scott and N Hatzis (eds), *Research Handbook on EU Law and Human Rights* (Elgar, 2017) 468; and S Douglas Scott and N Hatzis 'EU Law and Social Rights' in Douglas Scott and Hatzis (eds) ibid 492.

[58] See, eg, *Demir and Baykara v Turkey* [2008] ECHR 1345; *Enerji Yapi-Yol Sen v Turkey* [2009] ECHR 2251.

by means of a preliminary reference from the German courts, the case went on to the German Constitutional Court, and that Court gave its famous judgment, otherwise known as *Solange I* (in fact just a few days after the *Nold* decision of the ECJ, which the German Court disregarded). In *Solange I*, the German Constitutional Court stated that, while it recognised that the Community constituted an independent legal order derived from autonomous sources of law, it, however, suspected that effective protection of fundamental rights had not been assured with sufficient certainty within the EEC, at least at that stage of the integration process, since the Community contained no formal catalogue of fundamental rights. The German Court therefore considered itself competent, so long as these conditions were not satisfied, to check whether Community law was compatible with fundamental rights enshrined in the Constitution.[59] Furthermore, in *Frontini*, decided in 1974, the Italian Constitutional Court stated that that it would ensure that EEC norms could not undermine the fundamental rights set out in the Italian Constitution.[60] Although the German Constitutional Court moderated its approach in *Solange II*,[61] subsequent national supreme court judgments, such as the German *Maastricht* case, the Danish *Maastricht* case and *Thoburn*[62] (decided when the UK was still in the EU) illustrated that domestic courts remained willing to derive the primacy of EU law from their national constitutions and to maintain the jurisdiction to assess the boundaries of EU law.

Indeed, given the expansion of EU competence, the scope for fundamental rights issues constantly grows, and it is to be expected that national courts will keep a watchful eye on this. For example, the German Constitutional Court's 2009 judgment on the compatibility of the Lisbon Treaty with German law[63] maintains and elucidates the earlier theory of conditional acceptance of EU law established by the German Court in its *Solange I*, *Solange II* and *Maastricht* judgments, according to which Germany only accepts the supremacy of EU law 'so long' as EU law guarantees the fundamental rights laid down in the German Basic Law.

All of this indicates that national courts will continue to reaffirm their own role in policing the observance of fundamental rights in the EU, thus ensuring that somewhat complex structures of fundamental rights protection in the EU will continue.

B. Relations with the ECHR Again

The *Nold* case was the first acknowledged indication of a relationship between the EU and ECHR. This brings us back to the EU's possible accession to the ECHR, which might seem a logical conclusion to the *Nold* case. EU accession is dealt with in another chapter of this collection, so this account will be brief, but because it concerns important case

[59] The *Solange* decision is reported at [1974] 2 CMLR 540. Notably there was a strong dissent, which found EEC fundamental rights protection to be adequate: para 55 of the dissenting judgment.

[60] No 183/1973 *Frontini* [1974] 2 CMLR 372.

[61] BVerfGE 73, 339.

[62] *Brunner* [1994] 1 CMLR 57; *Norup Carlsen v the Prime Minister* [1999] 3 CMLR 854; *Thoburn v Sunderland City Council* [2002] EWHC 195.

[63] Federal Constitutional Court, 30 June 2009, Entscheidungen des Bundesverfassungsgerichts, 210 (FRG) 67.

law illustrating the ECJ's approach to fundamental rights, it is nonetheless discussed here.

As stated, Article 6(2) of the TEU has been amended to provide a legal basis for EU accession, reading as follows:

> The Union shall accede to the European Convention for the Protection of Human Rights and Fundamental Freedoms. Such accession shall not affect the Union's competences as defined in the Treaties.

The ECHR has also been amended, and a new Article 59(2) makes provision for the accession of the EU. EU institutions prepared an Accession Agreement and the ECJ was asked to provide its Opinion under Article 218(11) TFEU, on the compatibility of the ECHR accession agreement with the EU treaties. EU accession would have conferred official jurisdiction on the Strasbourg Court over EU acts, making it possible for claimants to challenge EU acts in the Court of Human Rights. However, and notably, despite the fact that the three major EU institutions, as well as the EU's 28 Member States, submitted at the Court hearing that the draft Accession Agreement was compatible with EU law, the ECJ concluded, to the great surprise of many, that it was not.[64] Indeed, it found so many obstacles to the agreement that it has now rendered accession very difficult, if not impossible.

The Court's judgment considered some complex points of EU and ECHR law, which will not be considered here, but what was striking was that it overall amounted to a robust declaration of the autonomy of EU law. Indeed, the word 'autonomy' is used 17 times in the Opinion, including in a section entitled, 'The specific characteristics and the autonomy of EU law'. The CJEU's insistence on autonomy has an air of a claim to sovereignty, more traditionally associated with Westphalian concepts of the state, and out of keeping with the CJEU's insistence in *Opinion 2/13* that the EU is not a state. Indeed, the Opinion is open to the criticism that it can be read as the expression of a fear that the CJEU could be displaced from its constitutional position as apex court of the EU.[65] The Court's Opinion is pervaded with statements on autonomy, and most particularly with concern for its own prerogatives as ultimate determinant of the EU legal order, rather than any abiding concern with human rights.

Therefore, EU accession to the ECHR seems unlikely any time soon. In its place, what remains is the indirect control of the ECtHR over the EU, by means of the 'Bosphorus presumption'. This derives from the ECtHR *Bosphorus Airways* judgment, which stipulates that if an international legal organisation

> protect(s) fundamental rights … in a manner which can be considered at least equivalent to that for which the Convention provides,' then 'the presumption will be that a state has not departed from the requirements of the Convention when it does no more than implement legal obligations flowing from its membership of the organisation'.[66] However, 'such [a] presumption can be rebutted … [if] the protection of Convention rights was manifestly deficient.[67]

[64] *Opinion 2/13* [of 18 December 2014] [2014] ECR 2454. AG Kokott, in an Opinion delivered on 13 June 2014, had also found the agreement compatible with EU law, albeit in highly qualified terms.

[65] See, eg, A O'Neill, 'Opinion 2/13 on EU Accession to the ECHR: The CJEU as Humpty Dumpty' *Eutopia Law Blog* (18 December 2014).

[66] *Bosphorus Hava Yollari Turizm Ve Ticaret Anonim Sirketi v Ireland* (2006) 42 EHRR 1, paras 155–56.

[67] ibid paras 155–56.

As one of the concurring judgments[68] stressed in *Bosphorus*, 'manifestly deficient' is a low threshold to set, suggesting that the Strasbourg Court does not want to get involved unless outrageous breaches of human rights are at issue – an approach which is deferential to Luxembourg. Nonetheless, the Strasbourg Court has continued to exercise this indirect jurisdiction, including since *Opinion 2/13*.[69]

It is clear, then, that EU accession to the ECHR is now by no means inevitable. Instead, the EU has achieved an 'autonomous' system of protection of fundamental rights through the Charter and the case law of the Court. Indeed, the Court's concern for the autonomy of Community law is traceable back to its earliest days, as Weiler noted, in highlighting this concern in the early *Stork* case.[70] Recent years have seen the Luxembourg Court increasingly and more assuredly rely on Charter jurisprudence, and also, notably, become much more assertive about the autonomy of EU law both from the ECHR, and from international law more generally.[71] Indeed the Luxembourg Court has been criticised for its rare references to other international human rights treaties.[72]

Notably, since Lisbon, when the Charter became binding, the Luxembourg Court has increasingly identified it as the source of rights in EU law, rather than the ECHR.[73] The ECJ has made clear that the ECHR 'does not constitute, as long as the European Union has not acceded to it, a legal instrument which has been formally incorporated into EU law'.[74] Although the Court has paid heed to Article 52(3)[75] Charter – which declares that rights in the Charter which correspond to rights guaranteed by the ECHR are to have the same meaning and scope of as those laid down by the European Convention – and taken account of relevant Strasbourg case law in interpreting provisions of the EU Charter of Rights,[76] as de Burca notes,

> This practice has however been uneven, with reference to Strasbourg case law being made in certain kinds of cases, for example with reference to Article 3 of the ECHR and Article 4 of the Charter on inhuman or degrading treatment in the context of transfer of refugees and

[68] ibid, Joint Concurring Opinion of Judge Ress at para 113.

[69] eg, judgment in *Avotiņš v Latvia*, App No 17502/07 (ECtHR Grand Chamber, 23 May 2016); also App no 21055/11 *Pirozzi v Belgium* (2018); and App no 44460/16 *O Sullivan McCarthy v Ireland* (2018); also P Gragl, 'An Olive Branch from Strasbourg? Interpreting the European Court of Human Rights' Resurrection of *Bosphorus* and Reaction to *Opinion 2/13* in the *Avotiņš* Case' (2017) 13 *European Constitutional Law Review* 551.

[70] 'The Court in … *Stork*, clearly affirms the notions of separation and autonomy': Weiler (n 29) 1114.

[71] See K Ziegler, 'Autonomy: From Myth to Reality – or Hubris on a Tightrope? EU Law, Human Rights and International Law' in Douglas Scott and Hatzis (eds) (n 57).

[72] eg O De Schutter, *The Future of Europe: International Human Rights in European Integration* (UN Human Rights Regional Office for Europe, 2020).

[73] See G de Búrca, 'After the EU Charter of Fundamental Rights: The Court of Justice as a Human Rights Adjudicator?' (2013) 20 *Maastricht Journal of European and Comparative Law* 168; J Krommendijk, 'The Use of ECtHR Case Law by the CJEU after Lisbon: The View of the Luxembourg Insiders' (2015) 22 *Maastricht Journal of European and Comparative Law* 812.

[74] See Case C-601/15 PPU *JN v Staatssecretaris van Veiligheid en Justitie*, EU:C:2016:84 para 45; Case C-524/15 *Menci*, EU:C:2018:197 para 22.

[75] Art 52(3) of the Charter provides: 'In so far as this Charter contains rights which correspond to rights guaranteed by the Convention for the Protection of Human Rights and Fundamental Freedoms, the meaning and scope of those rights shall be the same as those laid down by the said Convention. This provision shall not prevent Union law providing more extensive protection.'

[76] eg Case C-562/13 *Centre public d'action sociale d'Ottignies-Louvain-La-Neuve* EU:C:2014:2453; Case C-353/16 *MP v Secretary of State for the Home Department* EU:C:2018:276; Case C-688/18 *Spetsializirana prokuratura* EU:C:2020:94; Case C-752/18 *Deutsche Umwelthilfe* EU:C:2019:1114.

> asylum-seekers, or surrender under the European Arrest Warrant ... but not in others where it might have provided guidance.[77]

She concludes that even Article 52(3) Charter 'has been carefully interpreted so as to protect the autonomy of EU law and the exclusive jurisdiction of the Court of Justice to interpret EU law'.[78]

V. Conclusion

Have the aspirations of the *Nold* judgment been fulfilled?

On the positive side, in spite of *Opinion 2/13*, good relations exist between the ECJ and ECtHRs, which generally defer to each other – mainly because it is in their interests to maintain good relations. The relationship is one of comity and dialogue, given that no formal, official relationship exists between the two courts. Strasbourg judgments continue to provide inspiration for the EU, 50 years after the *Nold* judgment. Furthermore, it could be said that protection of fundamental rights in the EU has actually increased, given that the ECJ has now actually annulled some EU acts[79] – an action which did not occur in the first 50 years of Community history.

However, on the other side of the balance sheet, fundamental rights protection in the EU can seem unsatisfactory – especially in the fields of asylum, immigration, and justice and home affairs, in which a balance has often been struck in favour of security over justice, while other EU laws which were swiftly adopted, such as the European Arrest Warrant, have been attacked by national constitutional courts as violating constitutional human rights.[80] Furthermore, although the EU possesses an infringement procedure, under Article 7 TEU, whereby offending states may be suspended or ejected from the EU for, inter alia, breaches of fundamental rights, this has not prevented authoritarian states, such as Hungary and Poland, from undermining the rule of law and human rights within their territories.

So there is still room for improvement. Of course, it is the case that – unlike the ECtHR – the ECJ was not designed as a human rights court, and the EU's preferred use of the term 'fundamental', rather than 'human' rights, is no doubt an illustration of this. Nonetheless, the history of the growth of respect for fundamental rights in the EU, as illustrated by the *Nold* case, highlights the tensions and ambiguities in the EU's claim to respect fundamental rights.

[77] De Búrca (n 2) 498. Also AG Kokott (extra-judicially), 'The relevance of the case-law of the Human Rights Court in Strasbourg for the jurisprudence of the Court of Justice after the Opinion on accession of the EU to the Human Rights Convention' (2015); and for a view from Strasbourg: D Spielmann, 'The Judicial Dialogue between the European Court of Justice and the European Court of Human Rights or How to Remain Good Neighbours after the Opinion 2/13' (27 March 2017).

[78] de Búrca (n 2) 497.

[79] eg Joined Cases C-293/12 and C-594/12 *Digital Rights Ireland* [2014] ECR I-238.

[80] Decision of the German Constitutional Court, 18 July 2005, 2 BvR 2236/04.

17

Åkerberg Fransson and the Question of Incorporation

DANIEL SARMIENTO

The judgment in *Åkerberg Fransson*[1] sits rightly in the pantheon of leading cases of the Court of Justice in the field of fundamental rights. The ruling settles the crucial matter of the scope of application of EU fundamental rights in the Member States, while also setting out the basis for a federal-like approach towards the implementation of EU law and fundamental rights protection. To make it more unique, the Court of Justice delivered its judgment in 2013, shortly after the Charter of Fundamental Rights of the EU had entered into force.[2] The ruling in *Åkerberg Fransson* was delivered against a backdrop of three decades of fundamental rights case law, reformulated in 2009 by a new written text of primary law (the Charter) which, according to some authors, nothing had changed, whilst for others it represented a departure from past precedent. The Court of Justice therefore had the task of settling the question of whether the Charter had innovated in *federalising* or *de-federalising* the protection of fundamental rights in that EU, or whether it had simply codified past case law on the matter.

It is in this specific context that the Court of Justice settled the 'incorporation' question in a post-Charter context, with the aim of providing long-term guidance while simultaneously accommodating its doctrine with past pre-Charter precedent. The balance reached by the Court of Justice is one in which the rules on the scope of application of EU fundamental rights are interpreted expansively, whilst the rules on the levels of protection provide flexibility and space for national supreme and constitutional courts. While the first immediate reactions of some national jurisdictions did not indicate high degrees of satisfaction with the outcome, a consensus among Europe's highest courts has gradually emerged in the field of fundamental rights. Overall, *Åkerberg Fransson* is now accepted and implemented throughout the Member States and, 10 years after its delivery, it can be said that the doctrine of incorporation, as resolved in the *Åkerberg Fransson* case, is now part and parcel of the main pillars of EU law.

[1] Case C-617/10 *Åkerberg Fransson* EU:C:2013:105.

[2] The Charter entered into force on 1 December 2009, as a result of the entry into force of the Lisbon Treaty. Although the Charter is not part of the text of the Treaties as amended by the Lisbon Treaty, Art 6 TEU refers to the Charter and confers on it the same legal value as the Treaties. The Charter is published, in its amended version, in the *Official Journal* ([2016] OJ C202/391).

I. Historical and Doctrinal Context

The question of incorporation draws its roots in US constitutionalism. It refers to the enforcement of the Bill of Rights to the Federal Government as well as to the states. Prior to the enactment of the Fourteenth Amendment, the Supreme Court declined to apply the Bill of Rights to the states, limiting its role to the actions of the Federal Government.[3] It was not until following the ratification of the Fourteenth Amendment, in 1868, that the Supreme Court changed its approach and ruled that the Due Process Clause prohibits the states from depriving their citizens of certain privileges and protections contained in the Bill of Rights.[4] Although not all the provisions of the Bill of Rights have been confirmed to apply to the states, at the present time the broad majority of rights are enforceable at both federal and state level.[5]

The evolution of fundamental rights in the EU raised different challenges at first. The main problem was not linked to the federal question, but to the very existence of fundamental rights in the Community legal order of the 1960s and 1970s. The matter was linked to what Piet Eeckhout defined as 'the federal question',[6] inasmuch most Member States already had in their legal orders complete and robust schemes of fundamental rights protection, in addition to the external control performed by the European Convention of Human Rights (ECHR). The absence of any reference to fundamental rights in the Community treaties of the time raised a different matter, more closely linked to the *inception* of such rights in the Community legal order, and whether such inception had been agreed and accepted by the Member States. The Court of Justice ruled on the matter in several seminal cases, starting with *Stauder*[7] and robustly reaffirmed in *Internationale Handelsgesellschaft*[8] and *Nold*,[9] where it was stated that fundamental rights were to be recognised and understood in the Community legal system as general principles of Community law, with the ability to override all acts of national law, including constitutional provisions.[10] The Court of Justice thus solved the issue of the existence of fundamental rights in the Community legal order, and it did it in a way that preserved the uniformity of Community law, so that national fundamental rights could not be instrumentalised to fragment the overall unity of Community law. Although the

[3] See, inter alia, *Barron v Baltimore*, 32 US (7 Pet) 243 (1833).

[4] In the 1925 case of *Gitlow v New York*, 268 US 652, 666 (1925), the US Supreme Court stated the following: 'For present purposes we may and do assume that freedom of speech and of the press – which are protected by the First Amendment from abridgment by Congress – are among the fundamental personal rights and "liberties" protected by the due process clause of the Fourteenth Amendment from impairment by the States.'

[5] The doctrine of 'selective incorporation' of the Bill of Rights has been embraced by the US Supreme Court. To date, the Court has declined to apply to the states the Fifth Amendment's right to a grand jury indictment, and the Seventh Amendment's guarantee of a jury trial in civil cases in which the amount in controversy exceeds twenty dollars. The Court has yet to decide whether the states must comply with the Third Amendment's limitations on quartering troops in homes.

[6] P Eeckhout, 'The EU Charter of Fundamental Rights and the Federal Question' (2002) 39 *Common Market Law Review*.

[7] Case C-29/69 *Stauder v Stadt Ulm* EU:C:1969:57.

[8] Case C-11/70 *Internationale Handelsgesellschaft mbH v Einfuhr- und Vorratsstelle für Getreide und Futtermittel* EU:C:1970:114.

[9] Case C-4/73 *Nold KG v Commission* EU:C:1974:51.

[10] T Tridimas, *The General Principles of EU Law*, 2nd edn (Oxford University Press, 2007).

'federal question' was not explicitly addressed in these early judgments, its implications for the distribution of powers between the EU and its Member States were undeniable.[11]

The next step in the evolution of the case law emerged in the *Wachauf* case,[12] a ruling of the Court of Justice in which the question of incorporation appeared more crudely, raising the issue of the 'agency situation'. The questions raised in the specific case concerned the position that Member States were left in, from the standpoint of fundamental rights protection, when implementing EU law. If a Member State implements a regulation, do the implementing national acts come under the review of EU fundamental rights, or under the scrutiny of national fundamental rights? The question touches the very root of the question of incorporation, and it was answered by the Court of Justice in terms that maximised the scope of EU fundamental rights when implemented by the Member States. According to the *Wachauf* ruling, Member States are under a duty to respect EU fundamental rights when they implement EU law, whether the EU provision is contained in primary or secondary law.[13] Rather surprisingly, the ruling in *Wachauf* was delivered by a chamber of three judges, as proof that the matter did not appear to raise any new principled question of law.[14] However, the answer and its effects were certainly new and principled, as the following developments happened to prove.

The scope of the *Wachauf* judgment had to be refined in the following years. In *Booker Aquaculture*,[15] the Court of Justice was confronted with the question of whether *Wachauf* also applied to the transposition and implementation of a Directive, to which the Court replied in the affirmative.[16] In *Schmidberger*,[17] the issue of fundamental rights compliance appeared when Member States invoked justifications to free movement rules. If a Member State relied on the freedom of assembly to restrict the free movement of goods, was the fundamental right applicable to the case a *national* right or an *EU* right? The Court of Justice confirmed the latter option, thus expanding even further the uniforming role of EU fundamental rights in the national legal orders. Furthermore, in *ERT*,[18] the Court of Justice took the matter a further step when it confirmed that justifications to restrictions of free movement rules shall be in compliance with EU fundamental rights. The combination of *Schmidberger* and *ERT* put the Member States under a hard look of EU law every time a restriction to free movement comes under the

[11] K Alter, *Establishing the Supremacy of European Law: The Making of an International Rule of Law in Europe* (Oxford University Press, 2001).

[12] Case C-5/88 *Wachauf v Bundesamt für Ernährung und Forstwirtschaft* EU:C:1989:321.

[13] '[I]t must be observed that Community rules which, upon the expiry of the lease, had the effect of depriving the lessee, without compensation, of the fruits of his labour and of his investments in the tenanted holding would be incompatible with the requirements of the protection of fundamental rights in the Community legal order. Since those requirements are also binding on the Member States when they implement Community rules, the Member States must, as far as possible, apply those rules in accordance with those requirements' (ibid para 19).

[14] F Jacobs, 'Wachauf and the Protection of Fundamental Rights in EC Law' in M Poiares Maduro and L Azoulai, *The Past and Future of EU Law. The Classics of EU Law Revisited on the 50th Anniversary of the Rome Treaty* (Hart Publishing, 2010).

[15] Case C-20/00 *Booker Aquaculture and Hydro Seafood* EU:C:2003:397.

[16] B De Witte, 'The past and future of the European Court of Justice in the protection of human rights' in P Alston (ed), *The EU and Human Rights* (Oxford University Press, 1999).

[17] Case C-12/00 *Schmidberger* EU:C:2003:333.

[18] Case C-260/89 *ERT v DEP* EU:C:1991:254.

radar of an EU fundamental right. The overall effect of this evolving case law was a full incorporation doctrine, wide in scope and federal in spirit. The fact that it was developed by the Court of Justice on the basis of unwritten general principles of EU law, and mostly acquiesced by the Member States and its highest courts, makes the construction even more remarkable.

In the year 2000 a Convention was instituted to draft a Charter of fundamental rights of the EU.[19] The result of the works of this first Convention, shortly followed by a second Convention focused on the broader and more ambitious project of drafting a Constitutional Treaty, was an exhaustive bill of rights including social rights, as well as rights in the field of the environment, protection of minors, disabled persons, personal data, etc.[20] The Charter that ensued from the first Convention included a set of horizontal provisions that codified the case law of the Court, particularly on the matter of incorporation. Article 51(1) provided that the rights and principled in the Charter were addressed to the Union and the Member States 'only when they are implementing Union law'. A set of Explanations were added to the Charter with the aim of providing guidance in the interpretation of its provisions, and when referring to Article 51(1) they simply pointed at the case law of the Court of Justice rendered to date.[21] When the Charter was subtly reviewed during the works of the second Convention and the IGC that led to the Constitutional Treaty and eventually to the Lisbon Treaty, the question of incorporation of EU fundamental rights remained unaltered.

However, several authors noticed a certain nuance in the drafting of Article 51(1), which contrasted with the formulations of prior case law. When referring to the duty of Member States to comply with the Charter as addressees of its provisions, commentators highlighted the fact that the rule now included the term 'only'. On top of that, the Explanations referred to the case law of the Court of Justice and explicitly quoted the cases of *Wachauf* and *ERT*, but also of *Angonese*,[22] a ruling in which the Luxembourg court nuanced its approach and recognised some Member State leeway in certain contexts with looser links with EU law. In sum, the Lisbon Treaty, which introduced the Charter as a binding text of EU primary law, was perhaps not merely incorporating

[19] G De Búrca, 'The Drafting of the EU Charter of Fundamental Rights' (2001) 26 *European Law Review* 126.

[20] See G Braibant, *La Charte des droits fondamentaux de l'Union européenne* (Seuil, 2001); and Lord Goldsmith, 'A Charter of Rights, Freedoms and Principles' (2001) 38 *Common Market Law Review*.

[21] The only reference in the Explanations to the issue of incorporation is the following: 'As regards the Member States, it follows unambiguously from the case-law of the Court of Justice that the requirement to respect fundamental rights defined in the context of the Union is only binding on the Member States when they act in the scope of Union law (judgment of 13 July 1989, Case 5/88 *Wachauf* [1989] ECR 2609; judgment of 18 June 1991, Case C-260/89 *ERT* [1991] ECR I-2925; judgment of 18 December 1997, Case C-309/96 *Annibaldi* [1997] ECR I-7493). The Court of Justice confirmed this case law in the following terms: "In addition, it should be remembered that the requirements flowing from the protection of fundamental rights in the Community legal order are also binding on Member States when they implement Community rules …" (judgment of 13 April 2000, Case C-292/97 [2000] ECR I-2737, para 37 of the grounds). Of course this rule, as enshrined in this Charter, applies to the central authorities as well as to regional or local bodies, and to public organisations, when they are implementing Union law'. On the role of the Explanations, see J Ziller, 'Le fabuleux destin des Explications relatives à la Charte des droits fondamentaux de l'Union européenne' in *Chemins d'Europe. Mélanges en l'honneur de Jean-Paul Jacqué* (Dalloz, 2010).

[22] Case C-281/98 *Angonese* EU:C:2000:296.

the prior case law, but it could appear to be smoothening some of its most aggressive edges, in an attempt to balance out what could be seen as a too-invasive and federalist approach towards the question of incorporation in the pre-Lisbon case law.

Two years after the entry into force of the Charter, the case of *Åkerberg Fransson* reached the Court of Justice, being called to solve this delicate matter and to decide if the Charter (and the Member States when ratifying the Lisbon Treaty) intended indeed to clip the wings of the previous case law, or whether it left things untouched. That was the challenge that the Court of Justice faced, in a case that would shape the scope of EU fundamental rights for decades to come.

II. Facts and Judgment

The facts of the case in *Åkerberg Fransson* were straightforward: a self-employed fisherman, Mr Åkerberg Fransson, was subject to a tax inspection and, subsequently, the tax authorities imposed on him an administrative penalty. The authorities ruled that Mr Åkerberg Fransson had breached his VAT and income tax obligations. Following the imposition of the administrative penalty, criminal proceedings were instituted by the prosecutor's office. In Sweden it was possible to open criminal proceedings following the imposition of an administrative penalty based on the same facts in cases of tax fraud. The Swedish Supreme Court had settled this matter in a well-established case law, considering that the double punishment did not constitute a violation of the principle of *ne bis in idem*. In fact, several Member States had introduced Reservations and/or Declarations to Protocol No 7 to the ECHR (on the 'Right not to be tried or punished twice') to reaffirm the power of their authorities to impose a duality of penalties, including in the case of tax fraud.[23]

EU law seemed rather distant to the case. Income tax is not harmonised under EU law, and VAT, which was governed at the time of the relevant facts by Directive 2006/112/EC[24] and covers a broad variety of aspects of this indirect tax, had no rules on administrative or criminal sanctions, and indeed no coordination between the two. The point of connection between the facts of the case and EU law appeared to be found at that time in Article 273 of Directive 2006/112/EC, which included a vague mandate to Member States, so that they

> may impose other obligations which they deem necessary to ensure the correct collection of VAT and to prevent evasion, subject to the requirement of equal treatment as between domestic transactions and transactions carried out between Member States by taxable persons.

[23] Protocol No 7 to the ECHR has still not been ratified by Germany, Belgium, the Netherlands and the UK. Among the Member States which have ratified the protocol, France lodged a reservation to Art 4, restricting its application solely to criminal offences. At the time of signature, Germany, Austria, Italy and Portugal lodged a number of declarations leading to the same situation: restriction of the scope of Art 4 of Protocol No 7 so that the protection under that provision applies only to double punishment in respect of criminal offences, within the meaning laid down in national law.

[24] Council Directive 2006/112/EC of 28 November 2006 on the common system of value added tax [2006] OJ L347/1.

Another possible point of connection could be found in the fact that VAT comprises one of the EU's own resources and is therefore subject to specific rules on their protection by the Member States, as stated in Article 325 TFEU. However, none of these provisions gave any particular indication as to how to solve the coordination between administrative and criminal proceedings and penalties in a case of VAT fraud in a Member State, and the implications of this matter in the fundamental right enshrined in Article 50 of the Charter.

Considering the settled nature of the matter under Swedish law, the local district court hearing the criminal case of Mr Åkerberg Fransson referred the matter to the Court of Justice, questioning whether Article 50 of the Charter, which precludes double incrimination in criminal proceedings, applied to the facts of the case. In addition to the question of applicability, the referring court also raised several questions regarding the status of Protocol No 7 of the ECHR in the case at hand, but also as to the role of the Swedish Supreme Court's case law on fundamental rights protection and its implementation of Strasbourg judgments. This comment will only focus on the incorporation question, but the reader can deduce that the case was no simple task for the Court of Justice to handle.

The Advocate General delivered a cautious Opinion on the point of incorporation. Advocate General Cruz Villalón, a former President of the Spanish Constitutional Court, took the matter as a point of fundamental importance for the distribution of tasks between the Union and the Member States, but most particularly for the allocation of powers between Europe's highest courts.[25] His analysis was reacting to the many concerns arising from some national courts on the risks of over-expansiveness in the Court of Justice's case law, in a field that had traditionally been the terrain of national supreme and constitutional courts. In some cases, such courts are mostly, if not uniquely, devoted to the protection of fundamental rights. If the Court of Justice was to continuously expand the scope of application of EU fundamental rights, what role would be left for national high courts in an area of law that is vital for the protection of citizens and, in some cases, touches closely the national identity of the Member States? As a result, he proposed that the Court of Justice should depart from its previous case law and approach the matter in a different light, focusing on a two-step test, in which, first, a determination 'of the different situations in which the transfer from the Member States to the Union of responsibility for guaranteeing fundamental rights is primarily likely to be justified',[26] and second, 'an appraisal of the specific circumstances of each case [which allows for] a final, definitive adjudication regarding the allocation of responsibility for guaranteeing the fundamental rights to either the Union or the Member States'.[27]

The Court of Justice did not follow its Advocate General and it embraced the opposite view, one which could be associated with a 'fusion thesis', according to which EU and national fundamental rights coexist, subject to conflict rules in which, once EU law

[25] Opinion of AG Cruz Villalón, in *Åkerberg Fransson* EU:C:2012:340, points 25–46.
[26] ibid point 46.
[27] ibid.

applies, it deploys its primacy.[28] According to the Court of Justice, following its previous and settled case law, any situation of implementation of EU law by the Member States brings about the full impact of the Charter and its fundamental rights. In the words of the Court of Justice at paragraph 21 of the judgment in *Åkerberg Fransson*:

> Since the fundamental rights guaranteed by the Charter must therefore be complied with where national legislation falls within the scope of European Union law, situations cannot exist which are covered in that way by European Union law without those fundamental rights being applicable. The applicability of European Union law entails applicability of the fundamental rights guaranteed by the Charter.[29]

In sum, the judgment in *Åkerberg Fransson* confirmed the previous and expansive approach towards the question of incorporation, sidelining the commentators who had spotted subtle nuances in the wording of Article 51(1) of the Charter that would have justified (in their view) a restrictive turn in the case law. But this decision cannot be considered in isolation. On the very same day, the Court of Justice delivered another landmark ruling in the case of *Melloni*, a preliminary reference made by the Spanish Constitutional Court on the level of protection between EU and national fundamental rights and the interpretation of Article 53 of the Charter.[30] When interpreting this provision, the Court of Justice approached the matter in a balanced way, stating that in situations not completely determined by Union law, national courts were to decide on the level of protection applicable to a concrete case. This flexible approach was subject to two provisos: first, if the Charter conferred a higher level of protection it would override national standards; and second, the national standard would always to be conditioned to the 'effectiveness, unity and autonomy' of EU law.[31] This combined approach allowed the Court of Justice to expand the scope of EU fundamental rights as far as possible, but keeping a margin of manoeuvre for national high courts to set domestic standards within a composite European panoply of rights.

The way in which the Court of Justice ruled in both judgments, rendered on the same day, also provides an additional indication of the subtle balance that it attempted to reach. Article 50 of the Charter would be applicable to the facts of the case, but the terms in which it was interpreted left plenty of space to the national court to interpret it in a way that could balance the stance of the Swedish Supreme Court with the terms of the ECHR's case law. In its judgment in *Åkerberg Fransson*, the Court of Justice stated:

> It is for the referring court to determine, in the light of those criteria, whether the combining of tax penalties and criminal penalties that is provided for by national law should be examined in relation to the national standards …, which could lead it, as the case may be, to regard their combination as contrary to those standards, as long as the remaining penalties are effective, proportionate and dissuasive.[32]

[28] D Thym, 'Separation versus Fusion – or how to accommodate national autonomy and the Charter? Diverging visions of the German Constitutional Court and the European Court of Justice' (2013) 9 *European Constitutional Law Review* 391.

[29] Case C-617/10 *Åkerberg Fransson* (n 1) para 21.

[30] Case C-399/11 *Melloni* EU:C:2013:107.

[31] ibid para 60.

[32] Case C-617/10 *Åkerberg Fransson* (n 1) para 36.

In sum, *Åkerberg Fransson* confirms an expansive interpretation of the scope of application of EU fundamental rights when Member States implement EU law, but this expansive approach is combined with a careful balance between national fundamental rights protection in areas in which Member States act within discretional EU rules, together with a cautious interpretation of the levels of protection of EU fundamental rights, particularly when there is no clear consensus among the domestic legal orders. The 'fusion thesis' triumphed, and EU and national fundamental were called to coexist simultaneously in areas covered by EU law, but the price of coexistence is one of careful balancing acts, highly dependent on the willingness of national high courts to accept the terms of coexistence.

III. Reception of the Judgment: Judicial and Academic

The judgment in *Åkerberg Fransson* had two contrasting receptions, in line with the division that the Court of Justice also portrayed between the ruling and the Advocate General's Opinion. Some authors criticised the expansive interpretation of Article 51(1) of the Charter and the reductionist impact that the ruling would have on the autonomy of national supreme and constitutional courts. Voices were particularly critical in Germany,[33] where a growing concern over the Court of Justice's federalist case law had been brewing for several years, particularly since the early 2000s following the judgment in the case of *Mangold*.[34] It should also be said that most critical voices came from constitutional scholars, while, in the field of EU scholarship, the judgment was received as a mere confirmation of past orthodoxy, as nothing too revolutionary nor creative, considering the state of the case law prior to the entry into force of the Charter. EU law scholars focused more closely (and critically) on the case law on standards of protection and the balance introduced in *Melloni*, which was considered too restrictive by many authors.[35] The 'breathing space' provided by the Court of Justice, despite all the careful balancing acts, was considered to be insufficient to ensure national autonomy and, in particular, constitutional developments in the national case law. To a certain extent, it was not the question of incorporation that concerned the more critical scholars, but the insufficient space to think that EU law left for supreme and constitutional courts.

[33] See, eg, J Vogel, 'Radu – Melloni – Akerberg Fransson: »Staatsstreich« in Luxemburg?' 4/2013 *Strafverteidiger*, Editorial, I. An overview of some of the critical reactions in Germany is provided by OJ Gstrein and S Zeitzmann, 'Die 'Akerberg Fransson'-Entscheidung des EuGH – "Ne bis in idem" als Webgereiter für einen effektiven Grundrechtsschutz in der EU?' (2013) 16 *Zeitschrift für Europarechtliche Studien* 239, 254–57.

[34] See J-H Bauer and C Arnold, 'Auf *Junk* folgt *Mangold* – Europarecht verdrängt deutsches Arbeitsrecht' (2006) 59 *Neue Juristische Wochenschrift* 6, 8–10; and L Gerken et al, *'Mangold' als ausbrechender Rechtsakt* (Sellier European Law Publishers, 2009) 17–35. Not so blunt is M Schmidt, 'The Principle of Non-discrimination in Respect of Age: Dimensions of the ECJ's *Mangold* Judgment' (2006) 7 *German Law Journal* 505, who nonetheless criticised (ibid 520) the 'sibylline character' of the Court's reasoning.

[35] See A Torres López, 'Melloni in three acts: From dialogue to monologue' (2014) 10 *European Constitutional Law Review* 308; L Besselink, 'The parameters of constitutional dialogue after Melloni' (2014) 4 *European Law Review* 531; C Safferling, 'Der EuGH, die Grundrechtecharta und nationales Recht: Die Fälle *Åkerberg Fransson* und *Melloni*' (2014) 34 *Neue Zeitschrift für Strafrecht* 545; or D Thym, 'Die Reichweite der EU-Grundrechte-Charta – Zu viel Grundrechtsschutz?' (2013) 32 *Neue Zeitschrift für Verwaltungsrecht* 889.

The reception in the judicial field reflected similar tensions to those that appeared in academia. However, the passage of time has contributed to diffuse the divergence of views, while a gradual consensus has emerged in several significant jurisdictions. This evolution provides an optimistic outlook of the long-term sustainability of *Åkerberg Fransson* and a federalised arrangement of fundamental rights protection in the EU.

The first reaction to *Åkerberg Fransson* came from the German Constitutional Court, shortly after the Luxembourg ruling was delivered, in which it tacitly rejected an expansive interpretation of Article 51(1) of the Charter.[36] Thus, a conceptual distinction emerged that allowed the German Constitutional Court to ignore the expansive interpretation of Article 51(1) and act as if the ruling was confined to the specificities of a VAT case only. The second reaction came from the referring court in the *Melloni* case, the Spanish Constitutional Court, when having to rule on the specific case brought by Mr Melloni following the judgment of the Court of Justice. Whilst the Spanish Constitutional Court came to the same conclusion of the Court of Justice on the merits of the case, the former was eager to highlight that the ruling coming from Luxembourg was 'of great use' to solve the case, but not binding in any way. Ignoring the reasoning of the *Melloni* judgment, the Spanish Constitutional Court tacitly rejected the authority of the Court of Justice and sent a mixed signal that could not hide the irritation felt by the referring constitutional court.[37] The third and final sign that confirmed that *Åkerberg Fransson* would not be easily interiorised by the national judicial sphere came again from the German Constitutional Court in the *European Arrest Warrant case*,[38] where it openly rejected the 'fusion thesis' and refused to apply the balancing exercise followed in *Melloni* in the interpretation of Article 53 of the Charter. In the view of the German Constitutional Court, even in situations fully determined by Union law, such a framework '[does] not relieve German authorities or courts of their obligation to ensure that the principles of Art 1 sec 1 GG are complied with in the context of extraditions executing a European arrest warrant'.[39]

[36] See the judgment in the anti-terrorist data retention case of 24 April 2013 1BvR 1215/07, hardly two months after the judgment in *Akerberg Fransson* was delivered, at para 91. According to the German Federal Constitutional Court, the *Akerberg Fransson* judgment 'must not be interpreted in such a way that it would obviously be judged as an ultra vires act or would jeopardise the protection and enforcement of the fundamental rights of the Member States in a way (Art 23.1 sentence 1 GG) in such a way that this would call into question the identity of the constitutional order established by the Basic Law. In this respect, the decision must not be understood and applied in a way according to which every factual reference of a regulation to the merely abstract scope of application of Union law or purely actual effects on it suffice for the Member States to be bound by the fundamental rights of the European Union laid down in the Charter of Fundamental Rights' (unofficial translation).

[37] 'These preliminary issues have been replied in the Judgment of the Court (Gran Chamber) of 26 February 2013, C-399/11, Melloni. This response will be of great use when determining the content of a right to a process with full guarantees (Article 24.2 of the Spanish Constitution) deploying ad extra effects.' (judgment of the Spanish Constitutional Court of 13 February 2014, 26/2014, para 2, official translation).

[38] Judgment of 16 December 2015, 2 BV 2735/14.

[39] At para 83, the German Federal Constitutional Court continued by adding the following: 'Rather, [the German authorities] must ensure that in executing the Framework Decision on the European arrest warrant and the Act on International Cooperation in Criminal Matters, the minimum guarantees of the rights of the accused required by Art. 1 sec. 1 GG will also be observed in the requesting Member State, or – where this is impossible – refrain from extraditing the person concerned. To this extent, the principle of mutual trust that governs extraditions within Europe is limited by human dignity guaranteed under Art. 1 sec. 1 GG. It is to this extent, as well, that the court is under a constitutional obligation to conduct the investigations mentioned above' (official translation).

In parallel, another line of case law, more nuanced and cooperative, began to emerge. It started in Austria, where its Constitutional Court, the *doyen* of constitutional jurisdictions in Europe, issued a landmark ruling in which it confirmed the Charter's position within the Austrian legal order as a constitutional parameter of interpretation, subject to the Court's jurisdiction in cooperation with the Court of Justice. This ruling provided a constructive reaction to the ruling in *Åkerberg Fransson*, according to which Constitutional Courts would not simply interpret national fundamental rights in the 'space' allocated to them, but also would become involved in the interpretation of EU fundamental rights. This willingness was signalled shortly after by the Italian Constitutional Court in a line of case law that attempted to centralise the preliminary references to Luxembourg within its jurisdiction, with the aim of providing uniform interpretations of EU law throughout the Italian legal order and centralising the dialogue with the Court of Justice.[40] This first approach was shortly followed by a partial reconsideration to avoid undermining the autonomy of lower instance courts to refer cases to the Court of Justice, but the message of active cooperation in the interpretation of the Charter was clearly enounced.[41]

The ultimate step in the development of the cooperative approach, in which national high courts assume the role of interpreters and active collaborators of the EU legal order, arrived in the 'right to be forgotten' rulings of the German Constitutional Court.[42] In a notable turn of events, the same jurisdiction that was rejecting the 'fusion thesis' seemed to suddenly embrace the opposite view with open enthusiasm. In the two referred judgments, the German Constitutional Court came to terms with its duties as interpreter of fundamental rights in a European composite system, stating that in cases fully determined by EU law it would declare itself with jurisdiction to review state activity in light of the Charter. In other words, the parameter of review of the German Constitutional Court in situations fully determined by EU law will be the Charter, and not the *Grundgesetz*, and it is for this court to interpret the Charter and apply the standard of protection therein.[43] The 'fusion thesis' is taken to the point of becoming a 'replacement thesis', but only in situations fully determined by EU law in which there is no room for national discretion.

The follow-up to *Åkerberg Fransson* shows that the European framework on fundamental rights is gradually becoming a more habitable judicial environment, in which national supreme and constitutional courts refuse to 'chose' between EU and national fundamental rights, and instead opt to implement the Charter and actively cooperate with the Court of Justice in designing the scope and meaning of the text's provisions. In this sense, no other national constitutional court has mastered the art of constructive judicial dialogue as finely as the Italian Constitutional Court. From 2016 to 2023, this

[40] Decision 269/2017 of the Italian Constitutional Court.

[41] Order 182/2020 of the Italian Constitutional Court. See N Lazzerini, 'Dual Preliminarity Within the Scope of the EU Charter of Fundamental Rights in the Light of Order 182/2020 of the Italian Constitutional Court' *European Papers*, 25 November 2020.

[42] Judgments of 6 November 2019 (1 BvR 276/17 and 1 BvR 16/13). On both rulings, see (2020) 21 *German Law Journal*, special issue.

[43] D Burchardt, 'Backlash against the Court of Justice of the EU? The Recent Jurisprudence of the German Constitutional Court on EU Fundamental Rights as a Standard of Review' (March 2020) *German Law Journal* 1.

court referred to the Court of Justice five preliminary references on issues concerning the protection of fundamental rights.[44] In the case of *MAS*, the Italian Court convinced its European counterpart to reverse a prior ruling which had had a serious impact in the protection of individuals having been acquitted in criminal proceedings due to the reduction of time limitations under national law. In a follow-up case the Italian Court once again convinced the Court of Justice to fine-tune its case law, this time on the right to remain silent of physical persons in administrative sanctions proceedings. In another case the issue of non-enforcement of arrest warrants was discussed, in circumstances that could affect the dignity of the person concerned due to poor health. Once again, the Court of Justice bowed to the protection of fundamental rights that the Italian Constitutional Court considered most appropriate to solve the case at hand.

The dialogue that is currently taking place between these two courts is good proof of how the *Åkerberg Fransson/Melloni* doctrine can be an appropriate framework to stimulate a judicial dialogue among Europe's highest courts, in a constructive fashion that contributes to enhance the protection of fundamental rights, while at the same time it provides room for accommodation among the Member States and their highest courts. As it was explained, not all supreme and constitutional courts operate in the same framework, but the reality is that the overall rationale of *Åkerberg Fransson/Melloni* is generally accepted, in a sign that the Court of Justice's gamble to maximise the scope of Union law in this sensitive field has paid off.

IV. Follow-Up Cases

The success underlying the *Åkerberg Fransson/Melloni* case law should also be seen in the light of the Court of Justice's cautious development of the two rulings, in particular of the *Åkerberg Fransson* doctrine. While it is generally accepted that *Åkerberg Fransson* introduces a broad incorporation test, the reality is more nuanced when seen in a temporal perspective, particularly focusing on the follow-up case law of the Court of Justice. It is true that *Åkerberg Fransson* has expanded the scope of application of the Charter to many situations covered by Union law, but the case law also confirms that the Court has been strict in rejecting cases which showed insufficient links with Union law. The post-*Åkerberg Fransson* case law is nowhere near an all-expansive approach towards the Charter's scope of application, as it will be now explained.

Shortly after the judgment in *Åkerberg Fransson* was delivered, the Court found an opportunity to provide further guidance in a case that was, once again, on the fringes of Union law. In *Torralbo Marcos*,[45] a reference from a Spanish court, the issue of applicability of the Charter arose in the context of an insolvency proceeding in which the applicant was charged with payment of court fees in the course of an appeal. The substance of the case had no apparent connection with Union law, but success for the applicant could have paved the way in the long run to benefits covered by the Wages

[44] Case C-42/17, *MAS MB* EU:C:2017:936; Case C-481/19 *Consob* EU:C:2021:84; Case C-350/20 *INPS* EU:C:2021:659; Case C-699/21 *EDL* EU:C:2023:295; and Case C-700/21 *OG* EU:C:2023:444.

[45] Case C-265/13 *Torralbo Marcos* EU:C:2014:187.

Guarantee Fund, as provided in Directive 2008/94.[46] The Court of Justice considered that the connection between the substance of the case (insolvency proceedings) and the questions of the specific dispute (court fees in appeal) bore too loose a connection with the Union rules on access to the Wages Guarantee Fund. As a result, the matter under dispute was considered not be within the scope of application of Union law and, consequently, the Charter did not apply to the case. In the words of the Court of Justice:

> The fact that, by the steps he has taken, Mr Torralbo Marcos is seeking, according to the statements of the referring court, to obtain such a declaration of insolvency in order to benefit from the Fogasa's intervention in accordance with Article 3 of Directive 2008/94 is not sufficient to allow the view to be taken that the situation at issue in the main proceedings, at their present stage, falls within the scope of the directive and, consequently, of European Union law.[47]

In a more discreet format, through the issuance of reasoned orders, some of them pursuant to Article 99 of the Rules of Procedure, the Court has been ruling on a wide variety of cases with hardly a link with Union law, confirming the Charter's exclusion from a considerable number of situations. The list is long, as good proof of the Court's willingness to set boundaries to the expansive interpretation of Article 51(1) that *Åkerberg Fransson* enshrined.[48] However, a close reading of the orders confirms that the rationale of the incorporation doctrine remains the same. In all the cases on which the Court refused to rule, the lack of connection with Union law was evident. This evolution in the case law is not a sign of retreat from the *Åkerberg Fransson* judgment; rather the contrary. However, some cases emerge in which there appear to be signs of retreat from the original stance of 2013. The most telling of those apparent retreats is the case of *TSN*.

In *TSN*, an important question on the applicability of the Charter arose in a situation of higher social protection voluntarily chosen by a Member State.[49] The case law had interpreted Directive 2003/88/EC (the Working Time Directive) in light of Article 31(2) of the Charter, coming to the conclusion that a refusal in national law to carry over annual leave as a result of illness was in breach of the Union law. The issue in TSN concerned the specific situation of a worker subject to national provisions that went beyond the Working Time Directive, as a result of the 'minimum harmonization' that Article 153 TFEU provides, allowing Member States to provide higher levels of social protection. As a result, in a situation not strictly covered by the Working Time Directive, but by the additional protection granted by the Member State when implementing the Directive, the question as to the applicability of the Charter was raised. In a rather surprising turn, the Court of Justice rejected that such a case was covered by Union law, thus refusing to provide Charter protection to the worker. According to the Court, the case of 'social directives' with minimum social standards are different from the situation

> in which an act of the Union gives the Member States the freedom to choose between various methods of implementation or grants them a margin of discretion which is an integral part of

[46] Directive 2008/94/EC of the European Parliament and of the Council of 22 October 2008 on the protection of employees in the event of the insolvency of their employer [2008] OJ L283/36.

[47] Case C-265/13 *Torralbo Marcos* (n 44) para 40.

[48] See, inter alia, the Orders in C-498/12 *Pedone* EU:C:2013:76; Case C-499/12 *Genile* EU:C:2013:77; Case C-555/12 *Loreti and Others* EU:C:2013:174; Case C-73/13, *T* EU:C:2013:299; Case C-488/12 *Nagy and Others* EU:C:2013:703; Case C-224/13 *Lorrai* EU:C:2013:750; and Case C-614/12 *Dutka and Sajtos* EU:C:2014:30.

[49] Case C-609/17 *TSN* EU:C:2019:981.

> the regime established by that act, and from the situation in which such an act authorises the adoption, by the Member States, of specific measures intended to contribute to the achievement of the objective of that act.[50]

The impact of *TSN* could be rather broad, considering the large number of minimum harmonisation directives in the current Union legal order. However, the Court's careful reasoning in the judgment points to a more cautious approach, specifically confined to the field of social policy, an area in which the Treaties provide high levels of competence protection to the Member States. There are no signs in the case law that the same result would apply to a national legislation providing additional protection, for example, to an undertaking in the context of a directive enacted under Article 49 TFEU. In fact, the *TSN* ruling coexists with a number of rulings in which the Court has been willing to tilt the balance in hard cases towards an expansive interpretation of Article 51(1) of the Charter, as evidence of the continuous equilibrium that the case law searches in this terrain.

A revealing example of the impact of *Åkerberg Fransson* can be seen in the evolution of the case law concerning the financial assistance programmes introduced in the midst of the 2007–12 financial crisis. At first, the Court was firm in rejecting any link of the conditionality imposed on some Member States through the Memoranda of Understanding with Union law. In *Sindacato dos Bancários do Norte* it was made clear, through an order, that such cases were well beyond the remit of Union law, even though most of the provisions under review had been approved in the Council.[51] This strict approach was confirmed in *Pringle*, when the Court of Justice rejected the application of the Charter to situations in which the Member States decided to enter into an agreement to create the European Stability Mechanism.[52] However, in *Florescu* the Court of Justice changed course, highlighting the obvious links between the measures enacted in the Council on the basis of Regulation 332/2002 and the implementing acts undertaken by the Member States subject to the programmes.[53] This change of approach was complemented in *Ledra Advertising*, with the confirmation of the Charter's applicability to the Union's institutions when implementing financial assistance programmes, as was the case of the Commission's decision to endorse and sign a Memorandum of Understanding.[54]

In *Berlioz*, the question of the transnational implementation of the Charter arose, in the specific situation of a request of information in tax matters to the Luxembourg authorities issued by the French tax authorities. In the absence of a complete response by the addressee (Berlioz Investments), the Luxembourg authorities imposed a fine on Berlioz.[55] In proceedings in the Luxembourg courts, Berlioz questioned not only the fine imposed on it, but also the relevance of the information requested by the French tax authorities. As a result, the Court of Justice found itself in the delicate position of ensuring access to justice to Berlioz in Luxembourg courts (pursuant to Article 47 of the Charter) and at the same time ensuring the effectiveness of the tax cooperation

[50] ibid para 50.
[51] Case C-128/12 *Sindicato dos Bancários do Norte and Others* EU:C:2013:149.
[52] Case C-370/12 *Pringle* EU:C:2012:756, paras 180–181.
[53] Case C-258/14 *Forescu and others* EU:C:2017:448.
[54] Case C-8/15 P *Ledra Advertising v Commission and ECB* EU:C:2016:701, para 59.
[55] Case C-682/15 *Berlioz Investment Fund* EU:C:2017:373.

mechanism enshrined in Directive 2011/16. In its ruling the Court confirmed that the Charter applied in such a case, to the extent that the Luxembourg authorities (and courts) had a duty not only to verify the procedural correctness of the request of information referred from another Member State, but also its substantive legality. However, when it comes to review the substantive legality, the Court was careful to point to the fact that such review should be 'limited'. Nevertheless, *Berlioz* introduced a transnational dimension to the Charter's scope, allowing courts in one Member State to review the legality of decisions from another Member State, in order to ensure the fundamental right to an effective legal remedy enshrined in the Charter. This line of reasoning expanded into other areas of mutual recognition and it is now a standard position as a result of other rulings, as in the cases of *Aranyosi*,[56] *Puig Gordi*[57] and others.

The missing piece of the puzzle of Article 51(1) concerns the implementation of the Charter by private parties. This matter was not addressed in *Åkerberg Fransson*, but it raises the always delicate issue of 'horizontal effect' of fundamental rights, and the extent to which individuals are addressees of the obligations derived from such rights.[58] The matter was solved on a case-by-case basis, starting with the landmark *Defrenne* case in the context of the prohibition of discrimination on the grounds of sex,[59] followed by a very contested (and now settled) case law extending the scope of Defrenne to discriminations on the grounds of age in situations 'given expression' by a directive.[60] The entry into force of the Charter raised the question of how did Article 51(1) impact the previous case law on the horizontal effect of fundamental rights, to which the Advocates General of the Court of Justice made diverging proposals.[61] Eventually the issue was addressed by the Court of Justice following a similar approach to the pre-Charter case law, confirming that a case-by-case analysis could ensue in the confirmation of a horizontal effect of a fundamental right.

This conclusion was indirectly outlined at first in the case of *Association de Médiation Sociale*,[62] but it was confirmed in several rulings concerning the fundamental right to annual paid leave and freedom of religion: *Bauer* and *Cresco Investigations*.[63] In the second case, the horizontal effect of the fundamental right was reinforced by the interplay with the fundamental right to an effective legal remedy, provided in Article 47 of the Charter.[64] This approach shows that the Court of Justice has not embraced a bold approach towards the enforcement of fundamental rights by private parties, but rather a subtle and careful individualised analysis, in line with past case law and with the practice of the majority of national high courts dealing with this matter.[65]

[56] Case C-404/15 *Aranyosi and Căldăraru* EU:C:2016:198.

[57] Case C-158/21 *Puig Gordi and others* EU:C:2023:57.

[58] See E Frantziou, *The Horizontal Effect of Fundamental Rights in the European Union. A Constitutional Analysis* (Oxford University Press, 2019).

[59] Case C-43/75 *Defrenne II* EU:C:1976:56.

[60] See Case C-144/04 *Mangold* EU:C:2005:709; Case C-411/05 *Palacios de la Villa* EU:C:2007:604; and Case C-555/07 *Kücükdeveci* EU:C:2010:21.

[61] See the Opinion of AG Trstenjak in Case C-282/10 *Dominguez* EU:C:2011:559; and the Opinion of AG Cruz Villalón in Case C-176/12 *Association de médiation sociale* EU:C:2013:491.

[62] Case C-176/12 *Association de médiation sociale* EU:C:2014:2, paras 44–50, specifically referring to Art 27 of the Charter, but not ruling on the matter more generally.

[63] Case C-569/16 *Bauer* EU:C:2018:871.

[64] Case C-193/17 *Cresco Investigation* EU:C:2019:43.

[65] See the Opinion of AG Cruz Villalón in *Association de mediation sociale* (n 60) points 36–42.

In sum, the current state and degree of acceptance of the *Åkerberg Fransson* case law is the result of a continuous balancing act. The Court of Justice combines an orthodox interpretation of the limits of applicability of Union law, together with specific but expansive decisions. The underlying rationale of the case law appears to combine the goal of ensuring an effective protection of fundamental rights with the protection of spheres of competence of the Member States. The result might not always be pleasing for the national authorities, but the truth is that the balancing act has managed to consolidate the interpretation of Article 51(1) of the Charter 10 years after the enactment of the judgment in *Åkerberg Fransson*.

V. Conclusion

The judgment in *Åkerberg Fransson* reflects the EU's evolutive process of constitutional development. Changes never happen bluntly in the EU, they are always the result of a maturing process in which significant amounts of dialogue, discrepancy, empathy, and trial and error are involved. The EU's doctrine of incorporation of fundamental rights is the result of that process, starting in the late 1960s through the development of general principles of EC law, followed by a subtle but relentless process of incorporation of EU fundamental rights into the national legal orders. The entry into force of the Charter and the Court's ruling in *Åkerberg Fransson*, no matter how relevant and symbolic they may be, are a reaffirmation of a trend that began three decades earlier. The success of the EU legal order to keep the doctrine of incorporation functional and accepted by all the stakeholders will depend on the balances reached by the Court, ensuring effective enforcement of EU law, while simultaneously guaranteeing a 'space to think' for national supreme and constitutional courts in the field of fundamental rights, an area deeply attached to values and, in some cases, the national identity of some or all the Member States. The gradual acceptance of the *Åkerberg Fransson* judgment is a sign of the success of the Court's efforts, but nothing is written in the stars, and the future will probably demand further balancing acts from the judges in the Kirchberg. In their ability to preserve and fine-tune the exact and right balance will depend the long-term success of *Åkerberg Fransson* and of the doctrine of incorporation in EU law.

18

Bauer and Broßonn: Affirming the Horizontal Effect of the EU Charter of Fundamental Rights

ELENI FRANTZIOU

I. Introduction

Can the EU Charter of fundamental rights be invoked in disputes between private parties? This constitutional question was at the heart of the seminal ruling of the Court of Justice of the European Union (CJEU) in *Bauer*.[1] This chapter analyses the key features of the *Bauer* ruling, which it posits as the crystallisation of the CJEU's understanding of the horizontal effect of fundamental rights, presenting a clearer methodology for both direct and indirect effect in this field than previously developed in its case law. The chapter is structured as follows. Section II explains the significance of the constitutional question mentioned above by highlighting the terse legal context of horizontal direct effect in the field of EU fundamental rights before the *Bauer* judgment. The chapter then unpacks the judgment itself in section III, before considering in section IV its key contribution, as this can be gleaned from the academic literature and judicial discourse on the topic. Finally, before concluding, section V underlines the significance of *Bauer* and of the broader family of cases that it exemplifies, by showing how it has shaped subsequent case law, both at the EU level and at the national level.

II. Historical and Doctrinal Context

The Court's finding in *Marshall* that 'a directive may not of itself impose obligations on an individual and that a provision of a directive may not be relied upon as such against such a person'[2] has been a topic of significant controversy amongst

[1] Joined Cases C-569/16 and C-570/16 *Stadt Wuppertal and Volker Willmeroth als Inhaber der TWI Technische Wartung und Instandsetzung Volker Willmeroth eK v Maria Elisabeth Bauer and Martina Broßonn* EU:C:2018:871.

[2] Case C-271/91 *Marshall v Southampton and South-West Hampshire Area Health Authority (Teaching)* EU:C:1986:84, para 48.

EU lawyers – a controversy which only deepened upon the entry into force of the EU Charter of Fundamental Rights.

Starting from its early fundamental rights case law, in *Defrenne II*, the Court had pioneered an understanding of rights derived from EU law as cutting across the traditional legal divide between the public and private spheres. To be fully effective, EU rights had to be guaranteed not only vis-à-vis Member States, but also in relations between private persons.[3] In *Marshall*, the Court limited this approach by distinguishing directives (including in the field of fundamental rights) from other binding elements of EU law. This choice was founded upon various arguments that it is not the purpose of this chapter to examine in detail, including the fact that directives were addressed to specific states and were not, at the time of the *Marshall* ruling, easily accessible by persons other than their addressees. The Court's continued insistence upon this principle over the years despite several calls for reform[4] led to the adoption of often unpredictable exceptions that were met with nearly universal criticism.[5]

In its *Mangold* judgment,[6] the Court held that, notwithstanding the non-horizontality of directives, certain general principles of EU law, such as non-discrimination, were still capable of generating horizontal direct effect, even if the legislation giving 'specific expression' to them was a directive. This finding led to substantial legitimacy challenges[7] and bids to 'stop the European Court of Justice' from what was perceived to be a course of overt activism and unpredictability.[8] As a *Common Market Law Review* editorial put it at the time, horizontal direct effect was fast becoming 'a law of diminishing coherence'.[9]

The entry into binding force of the Charter of Fundamental Rights was an opportunity to set the record straight. In one of the first cases post-dating the entry into force of the Charter, *Kücükdeveci*, the Court emphatically reaffirmed *Mangold*, showing that provisions of the Charter such as non-discrimination, enshrined in Article 21 thereof, would seamlessly succeed the general principles of EU law that pre-existed them.[10]

[3] Case 43/75 *Defrenne v Sabena* [1976] EU:C:1976:56, para 39.

[4] See, eg, Opinion of AG Lenz in Case C-91/92, *Faccini Dori v Recreb Srl* [1994] ECR I-03325, paras 50–57; Opinion of AG Jacobs in Case C-316/93 *Vaneetvel* EU:C:1994:32, paras 30–31. In the academic commentary, see PP Craig, 'Directives, Direct Effect, Indirect Effect and the Construction of National Legislation' (1997) 22 *European Law Review* 519; T Tridimas, 'Horizontal Direct Effect of Directives: A Missed Opportunity?' (1994) 19 *European Law Review* 621; D Kinley, 'Direct Effect of Directives: Stuck on Vertical Hold' (1995) 1 *European Public Law* 79; R Mastroianni, 'On the Distinction Between Vertical and Horizontal Effects of Community Directives: What Role for the Principle of Equality?' (1995) 5 *European Public Law* 417; T Tridimas, 'Black White and Shades of Grey: Horizontality of Directives Revisited' (2002) 21 *Yearbook of European Law* 327.

[5] See n 4 above for examples of this criticism. A notable exception in the commentary is M Dougan, 'In defence of Mangold' in A Arnull et al (eds), *A Constitutional Order of States? Essays in EU Law in Honour of Alan Dashwood* (Hart Publishing, 2011).

[6] Case C-144/04, *Mangold v Helm* ECR I-9981, discussed further in ch 3 of this volume.

[7] German Constitutional Court 6 July 2010, *Honeywell* – BVerfGE 126 (Az: 2 BvR 2661/06). For a detailed discussion, see M Payandeh, 'Constitutional Review of EU Law after Honeywell: Contextualising the Relationship between the German Constitutional Court and the European Court of Justice' (2011) 48 *Common Market Law Review* 9; C Möllers, 'German Federal Constitutional Court: Constitutional Ultra Vires Review of European Acts Only Under Exceptional Circumstances; Decision of 6 July 2010, 2 BvR 2661/06, Honeywell' (2011) 7 *European Constitutional Law Review* 161.

[8] R Herzog and L Gerken, 'Stop the European Court of Justice' *EU Observer* (10 September 2008), available at euobserver.com/opinion/26714.

[9] Editorial comments, 'Horizontal Direct Effect – A Law of Diminishing Coherence?' (2006) 43 *Common Market Law Review* 1, 1.

[10] Case C-555/07, *Kücükdeveci v Swedex GmbH* [2010] ECR I-365.

However, it was not clear whether the status of general principles would apply *across* the Charter, thus giving all of its provisions the benefit of the *Mangold* exception. A nearly decade-long debate about the horizontal direct effect of the Charter thereby emerged.[11] Supporters of a cautious approach pointed to the problems of the *Mangold* ruling and the text of Article 51(1) of the Charter, which is addressed to Member States and Union institutions. They argued that the principle of horizontality should not be extended to its substantive provisions or, at least, that it should not be extended to provisions that would not otherwise be recognised as general principles.[12] This doubt was strongest with regard to the employment rights listed in the Charter's Solidarity chapter, which had not previously been understood as general principles, as well as provisions considered to be aspirational principles (many of which are also part of the Solidarity chapter).[13] Others advocated a more expansive approach, founded upon the coherent and effective application of fundamental rights to all legal disputes, against the state and private actors alike.[14]

Initially, the cautious approach appeared to take hold. In *Association de Médiation Sociale*, the Court found that the *Mangold* exception did not apply to provisions such as information and consultation within the undertaking, enshrined in Article 27 of the Charter.[15] The difference between such provisions and rights such as Article 21 was thought to be that the latter type of rights was invocable as such (in the sense of being self-executing) whereas the former was not. However, this finding led to considerable confusion about the status of different provisions of the Charter and a fear, as Advocate General Bot tellingly put it in *Bauer*, that the Charter's social rights would start to be viewed as 'a mere entreaty' by actors central to their application (private employers).[16] Following the Advocate General's assessment, in its judgment in *Bauer*, the Court's Grand Chamber finally put this debate to rest, in favour of the broader interpretation.

Bauer was the last of a promising bundle of 2018 rulings, including *Egenberger*, *IR* and *Max Planck*, which set the fundamental rights enshrined in the Charter apart from

[11] An overview is provided in the Opinion of AG Bot in Joined Cases C–569/16 *Stadt Wuppertal v Maria Elisabeth Bauer* and C-570/16 *Volker Willmeroth als Inhaber der TWI Technische Wartung und Instandsetzung Volker Willmeroth eK v Martina Broßonn* EU:C:2018:337 ('*Bauer* Opinion') paras 77–78; see further E Frantziou, *The Horizontal Effect of Fundamental Rights in the European Union: A Constitutional Analysis* (Oxford University Press, 2019) ch 4.

[12] The most significant challenge to the horizontal effect of the Charter was mounted by AG Trstenjak in her Opinion in *Dominguez*, a case which concerned the same right (paid annual leave): Opinion of AG Trstenjak in Case C-282/10 *Dominguez v Centre Informatique du Centre Ouest Atlantique and Préfet de la Région Centre* EU:C:2011:559 ('*Dominguez* Opinion') paras 80–83; see also C Ladenburger, 'FIDE Conference 2012 Institutional Report' (2012) XXV FIDE Congress, Tallinn, 30 May–2 June 2012, 34–35.

[13] *Dominguez* Opinion (n 12) paras 128–35.

[14] AG Cruz Villalón had powerfully advocated this approach, especially in his Opinions in *Prigge* and *Association de médiation sociale*, which were not followed by the Court: Opinion of AG Cruz Villalón in Case C-447/09 *Prigge and Others v Deutsche Lufthansa* EU:C:2011:321; Opinion of AG Cruz Villalón in Case C-176/12 *Association de médiation sociale v Union locale des syndicats CGT* EU:C:2013:491. See further D Leczykiewicz, 'Horizontal Application of the Charter of Fundamental Rights' (2013) 38 *European Law Review* 479; E Frantziou, 'The Horizontal Effect of the Charter of Fundamental Rights of the EU: Rediscovering the Reasons for Horizontality' (2015) 21 *European Law Journal* 657.

[15] Case C-176/12, *Association de Médiation Sociale (AMS) v Union Locale des Syndicats CGT Hichem Laboubi Union Départementale CGT des Bouches-du-Rhône Confédération Générale du Travail (CGT)* EU:C:2014:2. See also Case C-282/10 *Dominguez v Centre Informatique du Centre Ouest Atlantique and Préfet de la Région Centre* EU:C:2012:33.

[16] *Bauer* Opinion (n 11) para 57.

prior rules on horizontality[17] and affirmed that the Charter of Fundamental Rights is, in principle, capable of producing horizontal direct effect in its entirety.[18] Moreover, *Bauer* is an especially significant part of this broader set of rulings, because it brings the earlier case law together and clarifies its breadth within the field of EU fundamental rights jurisprudence where the above-mentioned debate was most readily manifested: the social rights enshrined in the Charter's Solidarity chapter (in this case, the right to paid annual leave protected in Article 31(2) thereof).

III. Facts and Judgment

A. Facts

The *Bauer* case concerned two separate disputes, which were joined by the Court for reasons of doctrinal coherence. The first, Case C-569/16 *Bauer*, was a dispute between Stadt Wuppertal and Mrs Maria Elisabeth Bauer. The second, Case C-570/16 *Broßonn*, concerned a dispute between Mr Volker Willmeroth, the owner of a private company, and Mrs Martina Broßonn. The reason the cases were joined was that the legal claims were identical in both cases: Stadt Wuppertal and Mr Willmeroth had been the last employers of the late husbands of Mrs Bauer and Mrs Broßonn, respectively. Both had refused to pay the claimants an allowance in lieu of annual leave not taken by their spouses before their death. The two widows were claiming that they were entitled to this payment, under Article 7(4) of the revised *Bundesurlaubsgesetz* (Federal law on leave; BUrlG), which provides for payment in lieu of leave in case of termination of the employment relationship, and Article 1922(1) of the *Bürgerliches Gesetzbuch* (Civil Code; BGB), which provides that the estate of a deceased person passes in whole to their heirs. Their claim at the EU level rested upon Article 7 of Directive 2003/88,[19] which provides:

> 1. Member States shall take the measures necessary to ensure that every worker is entitled to paid annual leave of at least four weeks in accordance with the conditions for entitlement to, and granting of, such leave laid down by national legislation and/or practice.
>
> 2. The minimum period of paid annual leave may not be replaced by an allowance in lieu, except where the employment relationship is terminated.

Both claimants argued that, read in the light of Article 31(2) of the Charter, which provides that 'every worker has the right to limitation of maximum working hours, to daily and weekly rest periods and to an annual period of paid leave', annual leave

[17] Case C-414/16, *Egenberger v Evangelisches Werk für Diakonie und Entwicklung eV* EU:C:2018:257; Case C-68/17 *IR v JQ*, EU:C:2018:696; Case C-684/16 *Max-Planck-Gesellschaft zur Förderung der Wissenschaften eV v Tetsuji Shimizu* EU:C:2018:874.

[18] K Lenaerts, 'Limits on Limitations: The Essence of Fundamental Rights in the EU' (2019) 20 *German Law Journal* 779, fn 70.

[19] Directive 2003/88/EC of the European Parliament and of the Council of 4 November 2003 concerning certain aspects of the organisation of working time [2003] OJ L299/9.

should be understood as an inalienable fundamental right, which precluded an understanding of death as distinct from termination and, therefore, meant that the annual leave entitlement should be compensated for. The only difference between the two cases was that Mrs Bauer's claim was against a state employer, who was directly bound to observe both the Directive and the Charter, whereas Mrs Broßonn's case was against a private employer, who benefited from the non-horizontality of directives. As such, Ms Broßonn needed the Charter right to lend direct effect to her claim, in line with *Mangold/Kücükdeveci*. The joining of the two cases was thus particularly apt, as it showcased the main justice paradox to which the non-horizontality of directives gives rise, which is to place in a remedially very different position two similarly situated persons.

B. Opinion of Advocate General Bot

As noted earlier, the judgment was clearly influenced by the elaborate Opinion that preceded it. Maintaining a position he has consistently defended since *Kücükdeveci*,[20] Advocate General Bot invited the Court to reconsider case law such as *AMS* and *King*, and to confirm, once and for all, that the social rights enshrined in the Charter had a status equally fundamental to its other provisions.[21] The Advocate General also made a remarkable effort to reconcile *Kücükdeveci* with *AMS*, and explained that he had never intended his Opinion in *Kücükdeveci* to be read as if Charter provisions could only have horizontal direct effect when further expressed in directives. On the contrary, it was the constitutional character of the Charter that had led to the finding in *Kücükdeveci*, which therefore did not depend on 'further expression' in a directive at all.[22] In other words, the non-horizontality of directives was immaterial to Charter provisions because direct effect stemmed from the fundamental rights themselves and did not *depend* on the secondary legislation. Advocate General Bot also took care to distinguish *Bauer* from *AMS*. Unlike Article 27, which is conditional upon 'national laws and practices', the Advocate General argued that Article 31 was clearly mandatory and specific enough to be relied upon in itself – this finding not being dependent on whether a dispute was between private parties as opposed to between a private party and the state.[23] Relying extensively on *Defrenne II*, the Advocate General urged the Court to treat the Charter in the same way as the Treaties, thus affirming its constitutional, fully mandatory status. Like provisions of the Treaty, then, rights which are sufficiently clear and unconditional should be considered horizontally applicable *as such*, removing any remaining doubt regarding the need for further implementation of these rights in secondary legislation.[24]

[20] See Opinion of AG Bot in Case C-555/07, *Kücükdeveci v Swedex GmbH* [2010] ECR I-365; Opinion of AG Bot in Case C-441/14 *Dansk Industri (DI) v Estate of Karsten Eigil Rasmussen* EU:C:2015:776.

[21] *Bauer* Opinion (n 11) para 57, citing Case C-214/16 *King* EU:C:2017:914, para 32.

[22] *Bauer* Opinion (n 11) paras 74–76.

[23] ibid paras 79–81.

[24] ibid para 76.

C. Judgment

In a detailed and methodical ruling, the Court's Grand Chamber agreed with the Advocate General. First, the Court analysed the content of the right to paid annual leave carefully and explained that the proviso limiting payment in lieu of leave to cases of termination was intended to ensure the meaningfulness of this right during employment (so that employers do not coerce their employees not to take leave) as well as after the end of the employment relationship (by monetising its value, and thus facilitating compensation).[25] As the reason for termination was immaterial, it was unreasonable to exclude death – an unfortunate but not unusual reason for the termination of an employment relationship – from the range of options triggering payment in lieu of leave not taken.[26] Annual leave, the Court reasoned, has a clearly measurable pecuniary dimension, which cannot dissipate upon the death of an employee, as it has been accumulated during his or her employment, and must therefore be passed on to their heirs.[27]

Having thus set out the meaning of the right to paid annual leave, the Court also followed the Advocate General's suggestion to revise overcomplicated distinctions between different rights in EU law, some of which had explicitly achieved the status of general principles, whereas social rights were mostly classified as 'particularly important', thus creating substantial and 'unnecessary ambiguity' in the case law.[28] In this regard, the Court found that

> the right to paid annual leave, as a principle of EU social law, is not only particularly important, but is also expressly laid down in Article 31(2) of the Charter, which Article 6(1) TEU recognises as having the same legal value as the Treaties.[29]

It was, therefore, the constitutional status of this provision, and not its designation as a 'general' or 'particularly important' principle of EU law, that led the Court to its answer to the first question. Leaving the Directive aside entirely, the Court found that Article 31(2) of the Charter in itself limited the Member States' discretion to retroactively remove the enjoyment of the right, for example by prohibiting payment in lieu after a person's death.[30] In turn, national law and other aspects of EU law, including the Directive, should be interpreted in accordance with that core obligation.

But does it necessarily follow from saying that Article 31 has a fundamental status that this right is also capable of producing a remedy for the deceased's heirs in a private dispute? In EU law, it is now safe to answer this question affirmatively. In this regard, as expected, the Court firstly affirmed the possibility of reliance on directives against the state only.[31] It thus swiftly found that the state employer in Mrs Bauer's case was liable to pay compensation to her, before turning to the more complicated question raised by Mrs Broßonn's circumstances. In analysing Mrs Broßonn's case, the Court clearly

[25] Case C-569/16 *Bauer* (n 1) paras 42–43.
[26] ibid para 46.
[27] ibid para 48.
[28] L Pech, 'Between Judicial Minimalism and Avoidance: The Court of Justice's Sidestepping of Fundamental Constitutional Issues in *Römer* and *Dominguez*' (2012) 49 *Common Market Law Review* 1841, 1857.
[29] Case C-569/16 *Bauer* (n 1) para 51.
[30] ibid paras 61–63.
[31] ibid paras 70–72.

reaffirmed the non-horizontality of directives, even when these are clear, precise and unconditional.[32] Mrs Broßonn could not have relied upon the Directive in a dispute with her late husband's employer in a field not governed by the Charter or another provision of the Treaties. However, the existence of a self-executing Charter right did permit Mrs Broßonn to rely on that right directly in her dispute with Mr Willmeroth and to thereby acquire compensation for the breach of Article 31, in exactly the same way as Mrs Bauer.

To reach this finding, the Court first turned to the scope of the Charter and resolved authoritatively the above-referenced debate regarding its ability to produce horizontal direct effect, by using precisely the reasoning that it had employed to establish the horizontal direct effect of Treaty provisions 42 years earlier, in *Defrenne II*, that is, by highlighting that the fact that certain provisions are addressed to Member States does not necessarily preclude them from creating obligations for other actors, who are not explicitly mentioned:

> [A]lthough Article 51(1) of the Charter states that the provisions thereof are addressed to the institutions, bodies, offices and agencies of the European Union with due regard for the principle of subsidiarity and to the Member States only when they are implementing EU law, Article 51(1) does not, however, address the question whether those individuals may, where appropriate, be directly required to comply with certain provisions of the Charter and cannot, accordingly, be interpreted as meaning that it would systematically preclude such a possibility.[33]

Bauer thus unequivocally affirmed the horizontality not just of a particular provision of the Charter, as other cases had done before it, but of *any* of its provisions as a matter of constitutional principle and regardless of their formal designation or place within the Charter. As in *Defrenne*, though, after having proclaimed the availability of horizontal direct effect in theory, the Court went on to elaborate a series of more specific conditions that had to be met before establishing it in practice. It thus turned to the nature of Article 31(2) of the Charter and examined its characteristics. On this point, too, the Court followed the Advocate General's approach, finding that Article 31(2) was both mandatory and specific enough to be relied upon as such. As the Court put it:

> The right to a period of paid annual leave, affirmed for every worker by Article 31(2) of the Charter, is thus, as regards its very existence, both mandatory and unconditional in nature, the unconditional nature not needing to be given concrete expression by the provisions of EU or national law, which are only required to specify the exact duration of annual leave and, where appropriate, certain conditions for the exercise of that right.[34]

Finally, the ruling affirmed the Court's earlier approach, clearest in cases such as *Dansk Industri*[35] and *Egenberger*, of not necessarily harmonising the remedial stage of the litigation at the national level. Whereas it confirmed that the direct effect of fundamental rights was available in private relationships subject to the above conditions as a matter of EU law, unlike in *Mangold* and *Kücükdeveci*, the Court did not immediately

[32] ibid para 77.
[33] ibid para 87.
[34] ibid para 85.
[35] Case C-441/14, *Dansk Industri (DI) v Estate of Karsten Eigil Rasmussen*, EU:C:2016:278, paras 29–35.

associate it with the disapplication of national law. Rather, the Court allowed national courts the possibility of shaping the full effectiveness of the right through *any* appropriate remedial means, including disapplication through direct effect if necessary, but also through reinterpretation of the legislative framework (indirect effect) if that possibility was envisaged by national law.[36] Indeed, while the omission of an explicit reference to disapplication at the end of the ruling might be easy to overlook, read in the light of the cases and Opinions that preceded it, including perhaps the rejection of the *Mangold* doctrine by the Danish Supreme Court in *Dansk Industri*,[37] the judgment appeared to make a careful procedural adjustment to the operation of the case law on horizontal direct effect, by recognising a distinction between direct effect and disapplication.

Where, then, does *Bauer* leave us in respect of the horizontal effect of fundamental rights in the EU? First, the Charter is capable of producing indirect and direct horizontal effect in principle because, in line with Article 6(1) TEU, it has 'the same legal value as the Treaties'. National courts should thus strive to interpret national law in the light of any materially relevant provision of the Charter. Second, if an interpretation of national law in conformity with the right is impossible and the right in question is mandatory and unconditional (its 'unconditional nature not needing to be given concrete expression by the provisions of EU or national law'),[38] national courts must ensure that a remedy is offered within the dispute in question, including – but not necessarily limited to – disapplication. Failing that, state liability in damages may be claimed.

IV. Reception History: Judicial and Academic

It is possible to credit the *Bauer* ruling with three significant contributions to fundamental rights law in the EU: it affirmed the status of the Charter's social rights as binding; it settled the question of the Charter's horizontality in principle and by reference to its most controversial set of provisions (those found in the Solidarity title); and it clarified important aspects of the operation of the doctrine of horizontal direct effect. In turn, the ruling has been very positively received in the legal commentary, both by proponents of the broader interpretation of the Charter's addressees (of which it is emblematic) and by scholars who welcomed the clarity that it added to a historically terse area of EU doctrine and litigation.[39]

[36] Case C-569/16 *Bauer* (n 1) paras 90–91.

[37] Danish Supreme Court 6 December 2016, Case no 15/2014, *DI acting for Ajos A/S v The Estate left by A*. For an analysis of this case, see MR Madsen, HP Olsen and U Šadl, 'Competing Supremacies and Clashing Institutional Rationalities: the Danish Supreme Court's Decision in the *Ajos* Case and the National Limits of Judicial Cooperation' (2017) 23 *European Law Journal* 140; S Klinge, 'Dialogue or Disobedience between the European Court of Justice and the Danish Constitutional Court? The Danish Supreme Court Challenges the Mangold-Principle' *EU Law Analysis Blog*, (13 December 2016), available at http://eulawanalysis.blogspot.com/2016/12/dialogue-or-disobedience-between.html. See also the German Constitutional Court's judgment in *Honeywell* (n 7) para 61.

[38] Case C-569/16 *Bauer* (n 1) para 85.

[39] eg, D Leczykiewicz, 'The Judgment in Bauer and the Effect of the EU Charter of Fundamental Rights in Horizontal Situations' (2020) 16 *European Review of Contract Law* 323; E Muir, 'The Horizontal Effects of Charter Rights Given Expression to in EU Legislation, from *Mangold* to *Bauer*' (2019) 12 *Review of European Administrative Law* 185; MA Panascì 'The right to paid annual leave as an EU fundamental social right.

As Sarmiento has noted, in definitively revising the Court's approach to the horizontal effect of the Charter, *Bauer* confines the earlier ruling in *AMS* to its well-deserved 'isolated corner' of EU law,[40] thus addressing at least in part the extensive criticism that had followed that ruling.[41] More specifically, in *Bauer* the Court confirmed that the fundamental social rights enshrined in the Charter have a normative core – what the Court's President has termed an 'essence' or 'hard nucleus' – which cannot be alienated as a result of public *or* private action, and is therefore applicable in all disputes falling within the scope of EU law.[42] As such, while *Bauer* does not overrule *AMS*, it clarifies that all fundamental rights should be taken into account in the interpretation of national law before even considering their ability to produce direct effect and, in this sense, suggests that the Charter's provisions are indivisible in their constitutional status, even if they are not always directly effective.

In this sense, the Court in *Bauer* reveals a more nuanced understanding of the overall relationship between fundamental rights and private law than earlier case law had suggested. It recognises horizontal effect in two ways, rather than solely through direct effect. First, all rights can radiate, because of their constitutional status, across the EU legal order, thus giving rise to a soft form of horizontality or 'radiating effect', that is, indirect horizontal effect or consistent interpretation, before the need for a more drastic form of horizontality is considered.[43] Second, provisions of the Charter which are clear and unconditional may *also* be relied upon directly. In this regard, taking the view of direct effect that had been developed by the reporting judge in her academic capacity,[44] *Bauer* clarifies that the direct effect of EU law refers to its invocability as such in a dispute before national courts and not necessarily to the way in which it is ultimately applied at the national level. In cases involving the state, of course, invoking the right and having it applied do not need to be treated as separate issues, in line with the primacy principle. Yet, in horizontal disputes, the Court's traditional approach of associating invocability and application had been a point of procedural contestation for domestic courts, as shown in cases such as in *Honeywell* and *Dansk Industri*.[45]

Comment on Bauer et al: Joined Cases C-569/16 and C-570/16 *Stadt Wuppertal v Maria Elisabeth Bauer and Volker Willmeroth v Martina Broßonn*, EU:C:2018:871' (2019) 26 *Maastricht Journal of European and Comparative Law* 441; E Frantziou, '(Most of) the Charter of Fundamental Rights is Horizontally Applicable: ECJ 6 November 2018, Joined Cases C-569/16 and C-570/16, *Bauer et al*' (2019) 15(2) *European Constitutional Law Review* 306.

[40] D Sarmiento, 'Sharpening the Teeth of EU Social Fundamental Rights: Comment on *Bauer*', *Despite Our Differences* (8 November 2018), available at despiteourdifferencesblog.wordpress.com/2018/11/08/sharpening-the-teeth-of-eu-social-fundamental-rights-a-comment-on-bauer.

[41] See, eg, N Lazzerini, '(Some of) the fundamental rights granted by the Charter may be a source of obligations for private parties: *AMS*' (2014) 51 *Common Market Law Review* 907; E Frantziou, 'Case C-176/12 *Association de Médiation Sociale*: Some Reflections on the Horizontal Effect of the Charter and the Reach of Fundamental Employment Rights in the European Union' (2014) 10 *European Constitutional Law Review* 332; S Platon, «L'invocabilité horizontale des normes de droit de l'Union européenne: un pas sur place, un pas en avant, deux pas en arrière (CJUE, grande chambre, 15 janv 2014, aff C-176/12)» (2015) *Revue de l'Union européenne* 33.

[42] Lenaerts (n 18) 781.

[43] See, on the 'radiating effect of fundamental rights', R Alexy, *A Theory of Constitutional Rights* (tr J Rivers) (Oxford University Press, 2002) 355.

[44] See, eg, S Prechal, 'Does Direct Effect Still Matter?' (2000) 37 *Common Market Law Review* 1047; and, more recently, S Prechal, 'Horizontal direct effect of the Charter of Fundamental Rights of the EU' (2020) 66 *Revista de Derecho Comunitario Europeo* 407.

[45] *Honeywell* (n 7); and Case C-441/14 *Dansk Industri* (n 35).

Different legal systems have historically incorporated fundamental rights into horizontal disputes in a variety of ways – for example, by imposing an obligation through a more extensive reading-in of the relevant right, by requiring the state to step in to protect the victim of a violation, and only rarely by directly placing a constitutional duty on a private actor.[46] By contrast, since consistent interpretation already forms part of the first step in the EU approach to horizontality, the typical response once EU direct effect was established would be to require the disapplication of the national law and the direct application of the relevant EU right, even though individuals did not necessarily draw an additional benefit from doing so: a use of indirect effect in lieu of direct effect usually does not raise concerns about effectiveness, as already explained in longstanding commentary on the topic, including by Drake, Lenaerts and Corthaut.[47]

Bauer now suggests that, *as long as* the remedies used are outcome-neutral,[48] that is, they do not place the aggrieved party at a disadvantage or leave them without redress simply because of settled structures of national law, the constitutional complexity of horizontality in the field of fundamental rights at the national level may be accommodated within EU discourse. This may mean, for example, that once the possibility of direct effect has been established, national courts may employ other means of giving effect to the right provided they achieve the same result for the applicant, such as using a 'supercharged' indirect effect principle that revises the relevant legislation, rather than disapplying it altogether.

This approach fits into a series of cases offering more detailed guidance regarding the horizontal direct effect of the Charter, including *Egenberger* and *IR*.[49] The clarifications of the EU horizontal direct effect doctrine provided in *Bauer* are significant, as they permit – for the first time – an overarching understanding of horizontal effect (both direct and indirect) as a structural feature of fundamental rights adjudication in the EU, rather than as a subset of the direct effect doctrine alone.[50] But *Bauer* is an especially important aspect of this broader case law because of its specific subject matter. As suggested earlier, the heart of the debate for the Court had never been whether provisions of the Charter that previously enjoyed (or almost certainly would have enjoyed) horizontal direct effect as general principles of EU law under the *Mangold/Kücükdeveci* exception would also enjoy such effects under the Charter, but whether this extended to the Charter as a whole, at least in principle. The Grand Chamber's judgment in *Bauer* answers this question affirmatively, showing beyond any doubt that the inclusion of a right within the Charter can be a sufficient reason for horizontal effect when a case

[46] Frantziou (n 11) ch 2. The history and contestability of the doctrine of horizontality in Germany, in particular, is explained in further detail in A Colombi Ciacchi, 'The Direct Horizontal Effect of EU Fundamental Rights: ECJ 17 April 2018, Case C-414/16, *Vera Egenberger v Evangelisches Werk für Diakonie und Entwicklung eV* and ECJ 11 September 2018, Case C-68/17, *IR v JQ*' (2019) 15 *European Constitutional Law Review* 292, 303–04.

[47] K Lenaerts and T Corthaut, 'Of birds and hedges: the role of primacy in invoking norms of EU law' (2006) 31 *European Law Review* 287, 293; S Drake, 'Twenty Years After Von Colson: The Impact of "Indirect Effect" on the Protection of the Individual's Community Rights' (2005) 30 *European Law Review* 329.

[48] E Engle, 'Third Party Effect of Fundamental Rights (*Drittwirkung*)' (2009) 5 *Hanse Law Review* 165, 169–70.

[49] See further Colombi Ciacchi (n 46).

[50] E Frantziou, 'The Horizontal Effect of the Charter: Towards an Understanding of Horizontality as a Structural Constitutional Principle' (2020) 23 *Cambridge Yearbook of European Legal Studies* 208.

falls within the scope of EU law – an approach consonant with the broader view of the Charter's scope, expressed in significant parts of the academic literature, including by members of the Court writing extra-judicially.[51]

Nevertheless, the *Bauer* ruling is not without problems. The Court's appeal to the differences between rights such as information and consultation within the undertaking and rights such as paid annual leave may become more problematic than it might initially appear. Whereas, unlike Article 31, Article 27 defers to national laws and practices, placing an acute emphasis on that distinction raises questions. If conditionality upon national laws and practices is the reason why certain provisions of the Charter are not directly effective, then the radiating effect to which the Court appeals as the first step of its analysis may matter very little in practice for these rights. Where a right is conditional upon national laws and practices, the obligation in the light of which national law should be interpreted itself logically depends on what national law provides. In turn, the affirmation of social rights in *Bauer* may not help much in areas where the core obligation is defined by reference to national law.

This limitation applies to provisions across different parts of the Charter and not just those found in the Solidarity chapter. For example, Article 9 (the right to marry and found a family), Article 10(2) (the right to conscientious objection), Article 14(3) (aspects of the right to education), and Article 16 (the freedom to conduct a business) might all be rendered ineffective in horizontal disputes, if references to national laws and practices were taken to be the only criterion determinative of their conditionality. In reality, though, conditionality is likely to operate as a particular hurdle for the Solidarity title, within which Article 31 is exceptional in *not* deferring to national laws and practices, rather than in doing so. The only other provisions in the Solidarity title that do not include a conditionality statement are Articles 29 (access to a placement service), 37 (environmental protection), and 38 (consumer protection). Are these provisions – the last two being clearly considered 'principles' within the Charter's Explanations[52] – any more mandatory or unconditional than, say, Articles 27 or 28, respectively enshrining the rights to be informed and consulted in the workplace and to collective bargaining and action?

The above reflections suggest that the problem of conditionality remains unresolved, and that identifying the 'essence'[53] of protected rights which are conditional upon national laws and practices may not be straightforward. Telling apart the core from the peripheral aspects of the right is always likely to be the subject of internal debate within the Court and can, as Tridimas and Gentile argue through an analysis of both national

[51] See further K Lenaerts, 'Exploring the Limits of the EU Charter of Fundamental Rights' (2012) 8 *European Constitutional Law Review* 375, 376; see also K Lenaerts and J Gutiérrez-Fons, 'The Constitutional Allocation of Powers and General Principles of EU Law' (2010) 47 *Common Market Law Review* 1629, 1656 ff.

[52] Explanations Relating to the Charter of Fundamental Rights [2007] OJ C303/17, 27–28. On the distinction between rights and principles, see T Lock, 'Rights and Principles in the EU Charter of Fundamental Rights' (2019) 56 *Common Market Law Review* 1201; Lord Goldsmith QC, 'A Charter of Rights, Freedoms and Principles' (2001) 38 *Common Market Law Review* 1201; J Krommendijk, 'Principled Silence or Mere Silence on Principles? The Role of the EU Charter's Principles in the Case Law of the Court of Justice' (2015) 11 *European Constitutional Law Review* 321; S Peers and S Prechal, 'Article 52: Scope and Interpretation of Rights and Principles' in S Peers et al (eds), *The EU Charter of Fundamental Rights: A Commentary* (Beck/Hart Publishing, 2014) para 52.190.

[53] Lenaerts (n 18).

and CJEU uses of that concept, lead to unreliable judgments.[54] This concern becomes particularly strong once we zoom out of the *Bauer* case in order to assess the significance of references to national laws and practices in the Court's broader case law. For example, does *Bauer* succeed in reconciling cases like *AMS*, which concerned Article 27, with earlier cases like *Alemo-Herron*, which concerned Article 16 on the freedom to conduct a business?[55] While both of these provisions referred to national laws and practices, the former succumbed to a full limitation of direct and indirect effect, whereas the Court in *Alemo-Herron* required that a collective agreement be read in the light of Article 16. In turn, if the Court does not always take references to national laws and practices to be determinative of the absence of a core EU obligation, as the *Alemo-Herron* judgment suggests, what other criteria are relevant in making this determination?

It follows that, whereas *Bauer* stands neatly alongside *Egenberger* and *IR* in clarifying the relevance of *Mangold*, its scope becomes far more uncertain within the EU case law on employment rights.[56] Unfortunately, as is further discussed in section V, the Court has not yet resolved questions about the invocability as such of other important but conditionally framed provisions of the Charter, such as Articles 16 and 28, which could shed further light upon the ways in which they may bind private actors in the future, as well as upon how the core or essential content of these provisions may be identified.

V. Famous Follow-Up Cases (Including National Supreme Courts)

The significance of the *Bauer* ruling is evident from the frequent reliance placed upon this case before both the Court of Justice and national courts. In less than five years, *Bauer* has been mentioned in at least 30 judgments,[57] several of which have relied upon it extensively. More specifically, *Bauer* has principally influenced the case law in three areas.

First, *Bauer* has of course been used in the specific context of pensions and employment benefits, being consistently referred to in subsequent rulings in this field.[58] Secondly, some of the most well-known cases that mention *Bauer* have followed shortly after the ruling, largely confirming and extending its findings regarding horizontal direct effect. For example, in *Max Planck* (delivered on the same day as *Bauer*) and *CCOO*,

[54] T Tridimas and G Gentile, 'The Essence of Rights: An Unreliable Boundary?' (2019) 20 *German Law Journal* 794.

[55] Case C-426/11 *Alemo-Herron and Others v Parkwood Leisure Ltd* EU:C:2013:521. Substantial critiques have been made of the use of this provision in the Union. See notably J Prassl, 'Freedom of Contract as a General Principle of EU Law? Transfers of Undertakings and the Protection of Employer Rights in EU Labour Law (Case C-426/11 *Alemo-Herron v Parkwood Leisure*)' (2013) 42 *Industrial Law Journal* 434; S Weatherill, 'Use and Abuse of the EU's Charter of Fundamental Rights: On the Improper Veneration of "Freedom of Contract"' (2014) 10 *European Review of Contract Law* 157.

[56] See, most notably, Case C-438/05, *The International Transport Workers' Federation and The Finnish Seamen's Union v Viking Line ABP and OÜ Viking Line Eesti* [2007] ECR I-10779; see also Case C-341/05, *Laval Un Partneri Ltd v Svenska Byggnadsarbetareförbundet, Svenska Byggnadsarbetareförbundets Avdelning 1, Byggettan and Svenska Elektrikerförbundet* [2007] ECR I-11767.

[57] Based on a term-specific search of the case number on the Court's database on curia.eu.

[58] See, eg, Case C-244/20, *INSS (Pension de veuvage fondée sur le concubinage)* EU:C:2021:854.

the Court reached very similar findings as in *Bauer*, with *CCOO* addressing a different aspect of Article 31 (working time).[59] In *Cresco Investigation*, the *Bauer* methodology of starting from indirect effect and moving to direct effect (if necessary including disapplication), was confirmed more widely, being employed also in the context of Article 21 of the Charter.[60] The Court refused to accept the Advocate General's suggestion that state liability be integrated into the Court's analysis to avoid unnecessary costs for private persons.[61] And, finally, in *Thelen Technopark*, the Court affirmed that the principles set out in *Bauer* did not in fact extend beyond the Charter, thus highlighting that the non-horizontality of directives remains valid in other contexts.[62]

A third strand of EU cases in which *Bauer* has been influential concerns the constitutional status of the Charter, more generally. In *TSN*, the Court highlighted that the distinction made in *Bauer* between provisions that are conditional upon national laws and practices was valid, employing it to distinguish a situation in which Article 28 of the Charter was affected, yet where its core content was not compromised.[63] In *Popławski*, the Court relied on the *Bauer* method outside of the specific context of horizontal effect, as authority for the principle that, even where a provision of EU law is not directly effective (in that case a Framework Decision), national courts were under an obligation to take into account, in its interpretation, the fundamental rights protected in the Charter.[64]

At the national level, too, *Bauer* has not gone unnoticed. In addition to cases in which it has led to a judgment by the Court, *Bauer* has formed the basis of interesting preliminary references which were settled or not ultimately answered, including on the horizontal direct effect of Article 16 and the implications of conditionality upon national laws and practices.[65] This shows that the nuances of the case have been appreciated by national courts and that they are likely to become the subject of considerable attention as the case law develops. Similarly, *Bauer* has been relied upon in decisions of numerous national courts. For example, the French *Cour de Cassation* recently decided that a 12-month limitation to the carry-over period for annual leave was compatible with the ruling and did not compromise the core of the right to annual leave.[66] The First Hall of the Maltese Civil Court (Constitutional Jurisdiction) relied extensively on *Bauer* before establishing the lack of horizontal direct effect of Article 34 of the EU Charter of Fundamental Rights (the right to social assistance).[67] The Court of Appeal (England and Wales) relied on *Bauer* in high-profile cases concerning the calculation of pensionable benefits (*Hughes*) and claims for annual leave not taken before termination of the employment relationship (*Pimlico Plumbers*).[68] Last but not least, it will be interesting to

[59] Case C-684/16 *Max-Planck* (n 17); Case C-55/18 *CCOO* EU:C:2019:402.
[60] Case C-193/17 *Cresco Investigation v Markus Achatzi* EU:C:2019:43.
[61] Opinion of AG Bobek in Case C-193/17, *Cresco*, ibid, EU:C:2018:614, paras 173–85.
[62] Case C-261/20 *Thelen Technopark* EU:C:2022:33.
[63] Joined Cases C-609/17 and C-610/17 *Terveys- ja sosiaalialan neuvottelujärjestö* ('*TSN*') EU:C:2018:223.
[64] Case C-573/17 *Popławski* EU:C:2019:530.
[65] See, eg, Case C-366/19 *Bosolar v CHEZ* EU:C:2021:944.
[66] Ruling No 997 FS-B of 15 September 2021, Appeal No R 20-16.010.
[67] 95/2018 *MH*, 15 February 2019.
[68] *Secretary of State for Work and Pensions & Anor v Hughes & Ors* [2021] EWCA Civ 1093; *Smith v Pimlico Plumbers Ltd* (Rev1) [2022] EWCA Civ 70.

see whether and, if so, to what extent, the clarifications and adaptations of the horizontal direct effect doctrine made in *Bauer* will feature in the constitutional complaint against *Egenberger*,[69] which is pending before the Second Senate of the German Constitutional Court at the time of writing.

VI. Conclusion

In *Bauer*, the Court of Justice confirmed that Charter provisions which are mandatory and unconditional are horizontal, with or without further expression in secondary legislation. In light of this ruling, it may be time we stopped teaching the *Mangold* saga as an exception to the non-horizontality of directives and entirely reversed our analysis. The constitutional norm now appears to be that the Charter of Fundamental Rights is horizontally applicable, at least indirectly and, in many cases, directly as well. There is a limited exception to this basic premise, stemming from the *Marshall* rule, which is that direct horizontal effect must be rooted in primary law and not in a directive. In turn, Charter provisions which are not concrete enough because they are conditional upon national laws and practices will not enjoy direct effect in horizontal relations if they are only further expressed in a directive, but they could still enjoy some indirect effect therein. Thus, while the non-horizontality of directives is still good law and can have a negative impact on the protection of some fundamental rights in the European Union, cases like *Bauer* significantly limit the scope of this principle and, crucially, do so outside the field of non-discrimination, where the majority of earlier cases have been placed.

[69] BVerfG – 2 BvR 934/19.

19

Kadi I and *Kadi II*: Fundamental Rights and Judicial Protection

CHRISTINA ECKES*

I. Introduction

The *Kadi* cases[1] illustrate deep intrinsic tensions between fundamental constitutional characteristics of European Union (EU) law: on the one hand, the autonomy of the EU legal order and, on the other, its openness to international law. They also demonstrate why the EU as a non-state actor can only adopt state-like measures, such as targeted sanctions, if it is willing and able to protect fundamental rights within its legal order.

In 2005, the then Court of First Instance (now called the General Court) delivered the first *Kadi* case. It endorsed a situation in which individuals identified by the United Nations Security Council (UNSC; the Security Council) Sanctions Committee were targeted by directly applicable EU sanctions without full access to justice. The bank accounts of the designated individuals were frozen. They could no longer travel to or from the EU. Three years later, in September 2008, the Court of Justice annulled on appeal large parts of this decision (*Kadi I appeal*).[2] By contrast with the General Court, the Court of Justice held that all EU acts, including those giving effect to UNSC resolutions, had to comply with EU law, in particular the rights of access to justice and property as they are protected by the general principles of EU law.[3] However, after

* This chapter draws on some of my previous work, including C Eckes, *EU Counter-Terrorist Policies and Fundamental Rights: The Case of Individual Sanctions* (Oxford University Press, 2009); C Eckes, 'International Sanctions against Individuals: A Test Case for the Resilience of the European Union's Constitutional Foundations' (2009) 15 *European Public Law* 351; C Eckes, 'The Role of Judges Confronted with Norms from Different Origins: The Case of Counter-Terrorist Sanctions' in KE Jorgensen and KV Laatikainen (eds), *Routledge Handbook on the European Union and International Institutions* (Routledge, 2012) 171; C Eckes, 'EU restrictive measures against natural and legal persons: From counterterrorist to third country sanctions' (2014) 51 *Common Market Law Review* 869; C Eckes, 'The Autonomy of EU Law vis-à-vis International Law: Kadi I and II' in G Butler and RA Wessel (eds), *EU External Relations Law: The Cases in Context* (Hart Publishing, 2022) 523.

[1] Case T-315/01 *Kadi v Council and Commission (Kadi I)* EU:T:2005:332; Joined Cases C-402/05 and C-415/05 *Kadi and Al Barakaat International Foundation v Council and Commission* (*Kadi I appeal*). EU:C:2008:461; Case T-85/09 *Kadi v Commission (Kadi II)* [2010] EU:T:2010:418; Joined Cases C-584/10 P, C-593/10 P and C-595/10 P *Commission v Kadi* (*Kadi II appeal*) EU:C:2013:518.

[2] C-415/05 *Kadi I appeal* (n 1).

[3] ibid paras 283–85, 335, 355.

Mr Kadi won on appeal, he remained both listed by the UN and subject to EU sanctions giving effect to this listing. The Council had adopted the new sanctions in a slightly revised procedure. In response Mr Kadi brought a second action for annulment. Both the General Court (2010) and, on appeal, the Court of Justice (2013), confirmed the Court's position in *Kadi I* and annulled the sanctions for a second time.

The *Kadi* cases are landmark cases for the protection of fundamental rights in the EU legal order. They are also key cases confirming the autonomy of the EU legal order vis-à-vis international law. Advocate General Maduro referred in his Opinion in the *Kadi I appeal* to the EU legal order as a 'municipal legal order'[4] and argued that the Court must 'first and foremost, ... preserve the constitutional framework of the [EU] Treat[ies]'.[5] At the same time, he famously stated that '[T]his does not mean ... that the [Union]'s legal order and the international legal order pass by each other like ships in the night.'[6] The Court of Justice followed this position in less literary terms.

This chapter is structured as follows. Section II sets out the historical and doctrinal context of the *Kadi* cases.[7] Section III turns to the facts and judgments.[8] Section IV discusses their reception history. Section V sketches relevant follow-up cases.

II. Historical and Doctrinal Context

A. A Short History of Sanctions in the UN and the EU

About two years before the 9/11 attacks on US territory, the UNSC adopted Resolution 1267.[9] This Resolution marks the starting point of the United Nations' (UN) practice of sanctioning private individuals as terrorist suspects.[10] Following the lead of the UN, the EU has adopted sanctions (restrictive measures) against natural and legal persons (targeted sanctions) for more than 20 years. They have become a cornerstone of European Common Foreign and Security Policy (CFSP) and are certainly the most litigated aspect of CFSP.

Particularly in the earlier years, the EU courts have repeatedly struck down different types of EU sanctions for infringing procedural safeguards of those listed. The *Kadi* cases are the first and most well-known to successfully challenge sanctions giving effect to UN listings. In response, the EU institutions have significantly reformed their listing procedures in order to meet the requirements set out by the EU courts. In addition, several cases have been brought before national courts.[11] In the context of counter-terrorist

[4] ibid, Opinion of AG Maduro, paras 21–22.
[5] ibid, Opinion of AG Maduro, para 24.
[6] ibid, Opinion of AG Maduro, para 22.
[7] Section II draws on Eckes, 'EU restrictive measures against natural and legal persons' (n *) paras 2.3.1, 2.4.1; and Eckes, *EU Counter-Terrorist Policies and Fundamental Rights* (n *) ch 1.
[8] Section III draws on Eckes, 'The autonomy of EU Law vis-à-vis International Law' (n *) para 4.1.
[9] UNSC Resolution 1267 (15 October 1999) S/RES/1267.
[10] See, in particular, ibid, para 4b.
[11] See, eg, in the UK only: *R (Bredenkamp) v Secretary of State for Foreign and Commonwealth Affairs* [2012] EWHC 3297 (Admin), [2013] 2 CMLR 10; *R (El-Maghraby and El Gazaerly) v HM Treasury and Foreign and Commonwealth Office* [2012] EWHC 674 (Admin); *R (Europäisch-Iranische Handelsbank) v Secretary of*

sanctions, both national and international courts have, in addition to annulments, established, in certain circumstances, a duty of states to work in the UN context towards delisting and supported judicial review of compliance with that duty.[12]

UN sanctions regimes are adopted by the Security Council as resolutions under Chapter VII of the UN Charter. This entails that the situation in the targeted country – in the case of Al Qaida sanctions 'international terrorism' – is classified as falling under the Security Council's primary responsibility of maintaining international peace and security. It also means that, pursuant to Article 103 of the UN Charter, Security Council sanctions resolutions benefit from primacy over international agreements.

In the context of targeted sanctions, the Security Council resolutions created committees, which are mandated to draw up lists of natural and legal persons that fall under the respective regime.[13] Sanctions committees are specialised fora, comprised of representatives of the same countries that are represented in the Security Council, that offer an efficient decision-making structure for listing requests and exemptions. For counter-terrorist sanctions, a 'Monitoring Team' has, since 2004, evaluated the compliance of UN Member States and makes suggestions aimed at improving the effectiveness of the system.[14]

The EU is competent to give effect to UN sanctions and routinely does so for the EU Member States, who are without exception members of the UN.[15] Article 215 TFEU remains in practice the legal basis for all restrictive measures.[16] The provision foresees a two-tier procedure, which first requires a CFSP instrument containing the political decision to adopt these sanctions and then a regulation containing the actual operational measures. Since the entry into force of the Lisbon Treaty, Article 275(2) TFEU gives the EU courts the mandate to review 'the legality of decisions providing for restrictive measures against natural or legal persons adopted by the Council on the basis of Chapter 2 of Title V [TFEU]'.[17] This is an exception to the general rule that the CFSP generally does not fall within the scope of jurisdiction of the EU Courts. Article 275(2) TFEU makes no distinction as to the EU or UN origin of the sanctions.

State for Foreign and Commonwealth Affairs CO/10718/2012. See also for other issues: *Bank Melli and Persia International Bank v Shere Shipping and others* [2013] EWHC 2321 (Comm); *Bank Mellat v HM Treasury (No 1)* [2013] UKSC 38, [2013] 4 All ER 495, on appeal from *Bank Mellat v HM Treasury (No 1)* [2011] EWCA Civ 1, [2012] QB 101. See section V below.

[12] *Nada v Switzerland* App No 10593/08 (ECtHR, 12 September 2012); *Sayadi and Vinck* (22 October 2008) 1472/2006 (UN Human Rights Committee); *Youssef Mustapha Nada v Staatssekretariat für Wirtschaft* [2007] 1A.45/2007 (Swiss Supreme Court).

[13] See for the *Kadi*-type sanctions: Security Council Committee pursuant to UNSC Resolution 1267 (n 9); UNSC Resolution 1989 (17 June 2011) S/RES/1989; UNSC Resolution 2253 (17 December 2015) S/RES/2253, concerning Islamic State in Iraq and the Levant (Da'esh), Al-Qaida and associated individuals, groups, undertakings and entities.

[14] See, for the Monitoring Team's mandate, www.un.org/securitycouncil/sanctions/1267/monitoring-team/work-and-mandate.

[15] M Cremona, 'EC Competence, "Smart Sanctions", and the Kadi Case' (2009) 28 *Yearbook of European Law* 559; Eckes, *EU Counter-Terrorist Policies* (n *) ch 2.

[16] Case C-130/10 *Parliament v Council* EU:C:2012:472. See also C Eckes, 'EU Counter-Terrorist Sanctions against Individuals: Problems and Perils' (2012) 17 *European Foreign Affairs Review* 113, 113–32.

[17] The review extends to both the TFEU (former Community) instrument and the CFSP decision (adopted under the TEU); see Art 275(2) TFEU.

B. Constitutional Principles Challenged by Targeted Sanctions

Targeted sanctions are used to pursue (foreign) policy goals. Their use has steeply increased over time. However, they have also pushed boundaries of established EU constitutional principles. The *Kadi* cases are exemplary cases in that they brought the inherent constitutional tensions within the EU to the fore with unprecedented clarity. The intensity of the struggle is also reflected in the great amount of litigation before the EU courts that followed them. As mentioned above, the two core constitutional issues at stake are the protection of fundamental rights within the EU and the autonomy of EU law.

The autonomy of EU law is an essential feature of the EU legal order in its self-conception as construed by the Court of Justice. This autonomy allows the Court to approach international law as a domestic legal order.[18] If EU law were directly dependent in its validity on national and international law, the Court would no longer be in the position to filter and determine the precise effects of national and international law within the EU legal order. The same is true for the interpretation of EU law. While EU law in numerous ways relies on and refers to national and international law, the monopoly of interpretation over EU law allows the Court of Justice to keep other legal norms at arm's length. In other words, it is the Court of Justice that decides what constitutes 'the constitutional traditions common to the Member States' within the meaning of Article 6(3) TEU and which Charter rights 'correspond to rights guaranteed by the' ECHR.[19]

Consequently, if national law could directly determine the validity or content of EU law, the latter would no longer enjoy the same effectiveness vis-à-vis national law. If international law could directly determine the validity or content of EU law, the latter could no longer take a dualist position and as a result it would no longer be able to protect individual rights in cases like *Kadi*. This is the position of the Court, most visibly in *Kadi* and, later, in *Opinion 2/13*.[20]

However, the autonomy of EU law does not take away from the fact that the EU is legally committed to comply with and give effect to international law.[21] Usually, the EU courts resolve tensions between Union law and international law by interpreting the former in the light of the latter (consistent interpretation) and so avoid open conflict between the two.[22] In the *Kadi* cases, however, the peculiar set of facts excluded solving the tension by means of consistent interpretation. Member States' obligations under the UN Charter were so specific (freeze specific assets of singled out individuals) that the possibility of consistent interpretation did not exist.[23] The Court had to choose to either allow the Union to give effect to these very specific obligations, even if they breached fundamental rights (as the General Court did), or to annul the measures and bring Member States in the situation that they fail to comply with their obligations under the UN Charter.

[18] C Eckes, 'The autonomy of the EU legal order' (2020) 4 *Europe and the World: A law review* 1.

[19] Art 52(3) Charter of Fundamental Rights.

[20] *Opinion 2/13* EU:C:2014:2454, regarding EU accession to the ECHR.

[21] See notably Art 3(5) TEU.

[22] See, eg, Case C-310/06 *FTS International BV v Belastingdienst* EU:C:2007:456. See also M Bronckers, 'From "Direct Effect" to "Muted Dialogue": Recent Developments in the European Courts' Case-law on the WTO and Beyond' (2008) 11 *Journal of International Economic Law* 885.

[23] Eckes, *EU Counter-Terrorist Policies and Fundamental Rights* (n *) 247 ff.

III. Facts and Judgment in the Case

A. Facts and Judgment

At a day's notice, Mr Kadi found all his financial funds within the EU frozen, first by Regulation 467/2001,[24] and then by Regulation 881/2002 (contested in *Kadi I*).[25] Mr Kadi is an international businessman of Saudi Arabian citizenship. The freezing of his assets was ordered without any limitation in time or quantity, and, above all, the Regulation did not provide him, or anyone else sanctioned, with the possibility to be heard and argue that they were innocent. Mr Kadi asserted that he had never been involved in terrorism, nor financially supported terrorism in any form.[26]

Mr Kadi was sanctioned because he was listed by the UN as a terrorist (suspect). Following the attacks on the US embassies in Nairobi and Dar-e-Salaam in 1998, the UNSC had, in a series of resolutions,[27] requested the Taliban regime in Afghanistan to extradite Osama bin Laden to close all terrorist training camps and to cease providing sanctuary for terrorists on its territory. After the Taliban ignored these requests, the UNSC unanimously approved Resolution 1267,[28] reinforcing those requests and calling, amongst other things, upon all states to freeze all financial and economic resources, either directly belonging to the Taliban, or from which they might benefit in any way.

The resolution further established a Sanctions Committee,[29] whose composition is identical to that of the Security Council and tasked it to manage and monitor the implementation of the sanctions imposed by Resolution 1267. One year later, Resolution 1333 was adopted as a response to the Taliban's continuous failure to respond to the demands of the Security Council.[30] This resolution instructed the Sanctions Committee to maintain an updated list of individuals and entities designated as associated with Osama bin Laden. On 19 October 2001, the Sanctions Committee included Mr Kadi's name and city of origin on its list.[31]

[24] Council Regulation 467/2001/EC of 6 March 2001 prohibiting the export of certain goods and services to Afghanistan, strengthening the flight ban and extending the freeze of funds and other financial resources in respect of the Taliban of Afghanistan, and repealing Regulation 337/2000/EC [2001] OJ L67/1.

[25] Council Regulation 881/2002/EC of 27 May 2002 imposing certain specific restrictive measures directed against certain persons and entities associated with Usama bin Laden, the Al-Qaida network and the Taliban, and repealing Council Regulation 467/2001/EC [2002] OJ L139/9.

[26] The summary of facts and judgment leans on Eckes, 'The Autonomy of EU Law vis-à-vis International Law' (n *) para 2; Eckes, 'The Role of Judges' (n *), section 'The case of Kadi'.

[27] UNSC Resolution 1189 (13 August 1998) S/RES/1189; UNSC Resolution 1193 (28 August 1998) S/RES/1193; UNSC Resolution 1214 (8 December 1998) S/RES/1214.

[28] UNSC Resolution 1267 (n 9).

[29] Now called Security Council Committee pursuant to UNSC Resolutions 1267 (n 9), 1989 (n 13) and 2253 (n 13), concerning Islamic State in Iraq and the Levant (Da'esh), Al-Qaida and associated individuals, groups, undertakings and entities.

[30] UNSC Resolution 1333 (19 December 2000) S/RES/1333.

[31] However, seven days earlier (12 October 2001) the Office of the Coordinator for Counterterrorism of the US Government designated Mr Kadi as a new person on the Comprehensive List of Terrorists and Groups Identified Under Executive Order 13224 (the President Executive Order on Terrorist Financing of 23 September 2001). One cannot fight off the impression that the listing took place on the initiative of the United States.

Taking the view that action by the Union was necessary to comply with these Security Council resolutions, the Council adopted a series of legal instruments,[32] including on 27 May 2002 Common Position 2002/402/CFSP and Regulation 881/2002. Both instruments contain an annex listing Mr Kadi's name and further details identifying him. Mr Kadi brought an action for annulment of the Regulation,[33] arguing that the Council acted ultra vires in adopting the sanctions and that the measures further infringed Article 249 EC (now Article 288 TFEU) and breached his fundamental rights.[34]

The then Court of First Instance (CFI) (now the General Court) dismissed Mr Kadi's application for annulment on 21 September 2005. The CFI found that it did not have full jurisdiction to review the Council regulation because of the prevailing force of the underlying Security Council resolutions. It held that its competence was limited to review the Council regulation in the light of *jus cogens*[35] to then conclude that the regulation complied with that standard. Mr Kadi appealed to the Court of Justice.

On 3 September 2008, the Court of Justice set aside the CFI's judgment. It confirmed that the European legal order is autonomous in that no norm of international law can change the competence division under the European treaties. The Court exercised full judicial review and annulled the Council regulation in so far as it concerns Mr Kadi for breaching his right to judicial protection, his rights to be heard and his right to respect for property. Mr Kadi powerfully argued:

> So long as the law of the [UN] offers no adequate protection for those whose claim that their fundamental rights have been infringed, there must be a review of the measures adopted by the Community in order to give effect to resolutions of the Security Council.[36]

The Court agreed and referred to a fundamental element of the 'Union of law', namely the protection of constitutional guarantees under EU law from interference from the outside.[37] It confirmed that no international law obligations – not even UN Security Council resolutions under Chapter VII – can justify blatant fundamental rights violations within the EU legal order.

One of the main points of criticism was that, at no point had the Court been in the position to exercise a meaningful judicial review, because it simply had no access to the relevant information.[38] The Court gave the political institutions three months to reform the sanctioning system before the regulation became void. After certain adaptations – such as issuing of a statement of reasons and notifying the applicant – the Council and

[32] See, for an overview of the instruments and actions brought against them, I Tappeiner, 'The Fight Against Terrorism: The Lists and the Gaps' (2005) 1 *Utrecht Law Review* 97.

[33] Initially against Regulation 467/2001 (n 24), then redirected to Regulation No 881/2002 (n 25), repealing the former.

[34] In particular their right to a fair hearing, their right to respect for property and their right to effective judicial review.

[35] *Jus cogens* means 'compelling law'; it refers to a body of peremptory principles or norms from which no derogation is permitted. See also Art 53 of the Vienna Convention on the Law of Treaties (Vienna, 23 May 1969).

[36] C-415/05 *Kadi I appeal* (n 1) para 256.

[37] ibid paras 285, 316.

[38] Case T-315/01 *Kadi I* (n 1) para 351.

the Commission relisted Mr Kadi.[39] In response, Mr Kadi brought a second application for annulment before the General Court.

On 30 September 2010, the General Court gave a ruling whose main theme could be described as: 'We do what you want – *under protest*!' The General Court boldly criticised the Court of Justice, arguing that once the inherent competence of the Security Council was accepted, judicial 'review would encroach on the Security Council's prerogatives' and that

> a review of the legality of a Community act which merely implements, at Community level, a resolution affording no latitude in that respect necessarily amounts to a review, in the light of the rules and principles of the Community legal order, of the legality of the resolution thereby implemented.[40]

This clearly contradicts the Court of Justice position that judicial review by the EU courts is limited to the legality of *EU* law and does not extend to the underlying UN resolution.[41]

The General Court further concluded that

> the Court of Justice thus seems to have regarded the constitutional framework created by the EC Treaty as a wholly autonomous legal order, not subject to the higher rules of international law – in this case the law deriving from the Charter of the United Nations.[42]

The difference in view is obvious. While the Court of Justice had treated the EU legal order as autonomous and denied any hierarchical relationship between EU and international law, the General Court insisted on the hierarchical superiority of the UN Charter over the European Treaties. In the end, and after making clear that it was *not* bound by the points of law, the General Court applied the Court of Justice decision in *Kadi I*,[43] and hence EU standards of procedural and judicial protection, and concluded that it had to annul the regulation.

Importantly, the General Court developed in *Kadi II* that the applicable standard of review is the same as for EU autonomous sanctions regimes.[44] This means that even though the political institutions enjoy broad discretion concerning the assessment of the appropriateness of the listings,[45] it is for the Court to 'establish whether the evidence is factually accurate, reliable and consistent', as well as 'whether that evidence contains all the relevant information to be taken into account in order to assess the situation and whether it is capable of substantiating the conclusions drawn from it'.[46] While exceptions might be conceivable on whether and what evidence is communicated to parties,[47]

[39] Entry 22 in Commission Regulation 36/2011 of 18 January 2011 amending for the 143rd time Council Regulation 881/2002/EC imposing certain specific restrictive measures directed against certain persons and entities associated with Usama bin Laden, the Al-Qaida network and the Taliban [2011] L 14/11.

[40] Case T-85/09 *Kadi II* (n 1) paras 114 and 116.

[41] Case T-315/01 *Kadi I* (n 1) paras 286 et seq.

[42] Case T-85/09 *Kadi II* (n 1) para 119 (emphasis added).

[43] ibid para 112.

[44] Case T-85/09 *Kadi II* (n 1) para 139.

[45] ibid para 141.

[46] ibid para 142.

[47] ibid para 147.

it is not possible to rely on evidence that is not communicated to the Court.[48] On appeal, the Court of Justice confirmed the General Court's ruling and position on evidence (*Kadi II appeal*).

B. Analysis

The relationship between the '[EU] legal order', on the one hand, and the 'international legal order under the [UN]',[49] on the other, is the issue on which the General Court and the Court of Justice disagreed most essentially. It is also the greatest point of criticism by legal scholars, particularly international legal scholars, against the Court of Justice's ruling in the *Kadi I appeal*. More importantly, this point remains one of the EU's challenges as a non-state actor in international relations.[50]

i. Hierarchy of Norms

The General Court found that Union acts implementing obligations under the UN Charter fell as a matter of principle outside of the scope of its jurisdiction. It took what could be characterised as a monist perspective and conferred on Security Council resolutions a supra-constitutional status in relation to EU law. Security Council resolutions are in this view capable of justifying departure from EU primary law, including the general principles of Union law, or, at least, excluding judicial review considering these principles.

The Court of Justice, by contrast, stayed firmly within the logic of EU law. On the one hand, the Court's ruling in *Kadi I* can be seen 'an act of civil disobedience to international law'; on the other, it is 'loyal to the principles which underpin international law', namely fundamental rights.[51] The Court started from a dualist perspective and proposed in *Kadi I* to rank the UN Charter, including obligations under Chapter VII of the UN Charter (if they were binding on the Union), the same way as any other international agreements. They 'would occupy' a rank between primary and secondary EU law.[52] By contrast, the Court granted a special status to the 'very foundations' of the EU legal order as expressed in Article 6(1) TEU.[53] In other words, while the General Court gave obligations under the UN Charter primacy putting forward an actor-based argument, that is because of the status of the Security Council, the Court of Justice vested human rights and the rule of law with a supra-constitutional status, ranking above EU primary law, based on their *content* rather than the status of their author.

[48] ibid para 145.
[49] C-415/05 *Kadi I appeal* (n 1) para 249.
[50] Section III.B draws on Eckes, 'The Autonomy of EU law vis-à-vis International Law' (n *) para 4.
[51] T Isiksel, 'Fundamental rights in the EU after Kadi and Al Barakaat' (2010) 16 *European Law Journal* 551, 563.
[52] C-415/05 *Kadi I appeal* (n 1) para 305. See also Eckes, 'International Sanctions against Individuals' (n *) 366–67.
[53] C-415/05 *Kadi I appeal* (n 1) paras 303–04.

ii. Autonomy in its Beginnings

The *Kadi I appeal* is one of the first clear expressions of the Court's autonomy conception as protecting the Union's *core substantive values*. In *Kadi*, the protection of fundamental rights and judicial protection became intertwined with the autonomy of the EU legal order. The autonomy of the EU legal order from international law is in *Kadi* for the first time understood as a necessary precondition for the Union to be in the position to ensure that individuals enjoy in practice the constitutional guarantees under EU law. Only by declaring the EU legal order autonomous could the Court submit the actions of the EU institutions to fundamental rights review. However, the Court arguably went further than protecting Mr Kadi's fundamental rights. It examined and commented in detail on the UN listing procedure.[54] The Court's conception of autonomy as a normative shield hence also has *reflective* effects carrying beyond the EU legal order. The Court examined the Security Council's actions considering generally accepted rights of the defence of individuals and strongly criticised the UN procedure. This could either be read as potentially undermining the work of the UNSC, or as a legitimacy check that led to or at least strengthened demands for reform of a peculiar procedure, in which the perhaps highest political body in the world directly declares individual persons to be terrorist (suspects).

Many years after the *Kadi I appeal*, it is not easy to demonstrate that the Court's pushback harmed the UN peace and security system or the EU's credibility within that system. What can be shown is that, in 2009, the UN established the office of an Ombudsperson to offer those sanctioned at least some possibility of being heard and having their case examined.[55] The Ombudsperson can collect and evaluate the information which associates and disassociates any listed person with terrorism. This of course depends on the willingness of countries to supply the Ombudsperson with the relevant information. Originally, the he or she was not bound by a specific judicial standard in his or her evaluation. The Ombudsperson defined the standard of review that he or she applies as 'whether there is sufficient information to provide a reasonable and credible basis for the listing'.[56] Many considered the establishment of the position of the Ombudsperson as related to the Court's pushback and the difficulties of the Member States after *Kadi I* to give effect to the UN counter-terrorist sanctions.

iii. Fundamental Rights between Primacy and Pluralism: So Long as – Logics

While asserting the role of a single international actor, the Union remains, internally and externally, a complex and compound structure in which numerous actors participate and struggle for visibility. Power is shared between the EU institutions and the Member States, as well as national institutions, all of whom are sometimes subordinated to each other and sometimes act as equals, but who ultimately have different, and (to a

[54] See, in particular,: ibid paras 323–25.
[55] See at www.un.org/securitycouncil/ombudsperson. The office was established by UNSC 1904 (2009).
[56] Office of the Ombudsperson of the Security Council's 1267 Committee, 'Approach and Standard' (UNSC web page) at www.un.org/securitycouncil/ombudsperson/approach-and-standard.

certain extent) independent, legal foundations and practical preferences.[57] The normative frictions between the different actors have traditionally been most visible between the Court of Justice and national constitutional courts.

Individual sanctions combine two factors that have led to the outburst of usually well-contained normative frictions between the different actors. First, the combination of international, EU and national rules with overlapping personal, material and territorial scope is unique. Individual sanctions are exceptional in that nearly identical rules that directly restrict the rights of specific individuals are adopted at all three levels.

The 'so long as' terminology used by Mr Kadi,[58] mentioned above, raises an argument parallel to the position of national constitutional courts vis-à-vis the primacy of EU law. The 'so long as' doctrine as originally developed by the German Federal Constitutional Court (GFCC)[59] could be crudely summarised as follows: so long as the Court sufficiently protects fundamental rights, the GFCC will not step in to review EU law and rulings of the Court. Since the GFCC's early judgments that coined this phrase, the GFCC has continuously confirmed this line and even explicitly agreed to exercise jurisdiction in response to an alleged individual infringement, rather than only a structural lowering of the fundamental rights protection offered by the Court.[60]

The 'so long as' parallel between *Kadi* and the case law of the GFCC has been used to support diametrically opposed conclusions. On the one hand, it can be argued that if the Court of Justice had failed to protect fundamental rights from external interference, as the General Court did in *Kadi I*, this would likely have led national constitutional courts to challenge the primacy of EU law in order to ensure an acceptable fundamental rights protection within their own legal order. National (constitutional) courts are autonomous judicial actors within the EU with whose position the Court of Justice needs to reckon. The Court of Justice does not have hierarchical jurisdiction over their actions and cannot repeal their rulings. It must ensure their cooperation with other means. It is also fair to say that the pressure by national courts on the Court of Justice has again intensified in the years following the *Kadi I* appeal.[61]

On the other hand, the Court's 'so long as' logic vis-à-vis international law has been criticised for being seemingly contradictory. The Court of Justice demands national courts in its settled case law to accept the primacy of EU law and so stifles pluralism, while at the same time refusing to defer to 'supreme' obligations under the UN Charter.[62] It was feared that this would give national courts a(n additional) argument to reject the

[57] C Eckes, 'Disciplining Member States: EU Loyalty in External Relations' (2020) 22 *Cambridge Yearbook of European Legal Studies* 85.

[58] C-415/05 *Kadi I appeal* (n 1) para 256.

[59] BVerfGE 37, 271, of 29 May 1974 (*Solange I*) (German Federal Constitutional Court); BVerfGE 73, 339, 2 BvR 197/83, of 22 Oct 1986 (*Solange II*) (German Federal Constitutional Court).

[60] BVerfGE, 2 BvR 2735/14, of 15 December 2015 (*Solange III*) (German Federal Constitutional Court). The facts were similar to the decision in Case C-399/11 *Melloni v Ministerio Fiscal* EU:C:2013:107 at the European Court of Justice.

[61] *Slovakian Pension Case*, Pl ÚS 5/12 of 31 January 2012 (Czech Republic Constitutional Court) holding (*Landtová* C-399/09) ultra vires; *Ajos Case*, nr 15/2014 of 6 December 2016 (Danish Supreme Court), holding (*Dansk Industri* C-441/14) ultra vires; BVerfG, 2 BvR 2728/13, of 21 June 2016 (*OMT Judgment*) (German Federal Constitutional Court); BVerfG, 2 BvR 859/14, of 5 May 2020 (*PSPP*) (German Federal Constitutional Court); Case K 3/21 of 7 October 2021 (Polish Constitutional Tribunal).

[62] 'Supreme' because of Art 103 of the Charter of the United Nations (San Francisco, 26 June 1945).

primacy of EU law. Indeed, the GFCC referred in its 2009 Treaty of Lisbon decision to the *Kadi I appeal* and argued that the Court of Justice took a view 'similar' to its own by placing 'the assertion of its own identity as the legal community above the commitment that is otherwise respected'.[63]

Despite certain communalities, it is possible and convincing to distinguish the Court's position in the *Kadi I* appeal, denying Security Council resolutions effects within the EU legal order, from the GFCC's 'so long as' logic, threatening to deny effects of EU law within Germany. Both courts are concerned with the effects of legal norms originating outside their own legal order. However, while the EU is committed to being a Union of law, offering review by an independent judiciary considering widely recognised fundamental rights, the Security Council's sanctions practices result in a blatant disregard of the fundamental rights. They directly deprive individuals of their rights without offering, even after the introduction of the Ombudsperson, basic procedural rights, or review by an independent judge, who is in the position to annul the measures in question. The Court of Justice hence reasonably took in the *Kadi I* appeal the position of the GFCC in its first 'so long as' decision, when the GFCC still structurally reviewed EU law because at the time the EU did not yet offer an adequate (judicial) protection of fundamental rights. This is now different. Therefore, the GFCC's use of the *Kadi I* appeal to justify reviewing EU law seems unconvincing.

iv. Judicial Review as a Form of Normalisation and Judicialisation of CFSP

Foreign policy is traditionally the realm of (executive) politics rather than law. The political nature of foreign policy decisions is preserved by either formally limiting the jurisdiction of courts,[64] or by judicial self-restraint. This is in the US context referred to as the 'political question doctrine'.[65]

One core issue in *Kadi I* was whether the EU courts had jurisdiction to review the EU's sanctions measures. The Council, the Commission and the United Kingdom contended that EU sanctions giving effect to UN lists of terrorist suspects do not lend themselves to judicial review.[66] Advocate General Maduro, in his Opinion in the *Kadi I appeal*, opined that it is 'untenable' that 'even the most humble degree of judicial interference would be inappropriate'.[67] He argued that despite the high importance of maintaining international peace and security, it is 'the duty of the courts to assess the lawfulness of measures that may conflict with other interests that are equally important' (such as human rights).[68] The Court agreed.

The contested measures in *Kadi* were EU regulations rather than CFSP decisions. However, the listings in these EU regulations were identical to the listings in CFSP

[63] BVerfGE 123, 267, of 30 June 2009 (*Lisbon Treaty decision*) (German Federal Constitutional Court) para 340.
[64] Art 275(1) TFEU.
[65] See T Franck, *Political Questions/Judicial Answers* (Princeton University Press, 1992); G Butler, 'In Search of the Political Question Doctrine in EU Law' (2018) 45 *Legal Issues of Economic Integration* 329.
[66] See C-415/05 *Kadi I appeal* (n 1), Opinion of AG Maduro, para 33.
[67] ibid, Opinion of AG Maduro, para 34.
[68] ibid, Opinion of AG Maduro, para 34.

decisions that formed, pursuant to ex-Article 301 EEC Treaty (now Article 215 TFEU), the basis for the adoption of the former. By reviewing specific listings in EU regulations that are identical to those in CFSP decisions, the *Kadi* cases have also indirectly contributed to expanding judicial review into CFSP and so normalising this policy area.[69]

In general, individual sanctions were the trigger for introducing a specific exception to the exceptional exclusion of CFSP from the Court's jurisdiction. Since the entry into force of the Treaty of Lisbon, Article 275(2) TFEU establishes the jurisdiction of the Court over individual sanctions adopted in CFSP decisions. In October 2020, the Court continued to normalise the CFSP in the context of individual sanctions by accepting jurisdiction for actions for damages for wrongful listings.[70]

Generally, the assertion by the Court of jurisdiction over matters of foreign policy in general and individual sanctions in particular forms part of a broader trend towards the judicialisation and legalisation of foreign policy that we can witness more broadly. On the one hand, this trend contributes to protecting fundamental rights and avoiding arbitrariness. On the other hand, it may result in an overreach of law into the terrain of pure politics that may undermine the former's relevance and ability in framing politics. However, individual sanctions single out identified persons as terrorist suspects. Such specific measures cannot benefit from a limitation of judicial review over general foreign policy.

IV. Reception History: Judicial and Academic

A. Judicial Reception

i. *Autonomy of EU Law after* Kadi

Six years after *Kadi*, the Court of Justice issued *Opinion 2/13* on the EU's accession to the European Convention on Human Rights (ECHR). *Opinion 2/13* confirmed the Court's position that the autonomy of EU law is central to the functioning of the EU legal order.[71] However, there is one core difference between the *Kadi* cases and *Opinion 2/13*, namely what they mean for fundamental rights protection. In the former cases, the EU infringed fundamental rights by giving effect to an international legal obligation of the Member States, and the Court stepped in and upheld these rights. In the latter case, the Court made it all but impossible for the EU to submit to a widely recognised external mechanism of fundamental rights protection (the ECHR). At the same time, *Opinion 2/13* directly flows from and further develops the autonomy conception as

[69] See, on the normalisation of CFSP more broadly, C Eckes, 'Common Foreign and Security Policy: The Consequences of the Court's Extended Jurisdiction' (2016) 22 *European Law Journal* 492; R Wessel, 'Common Foreign, Security and Defence Policy' in R Wessel and J Larik (eds), *EU External Relations Law: Text, Cases and Materials* (Hart Publishing, 2020).

[70] Case C-134/19 *Bank Refah Kargaran v Council* EU:C:2020:793; C Eckes, 'Constitutionalising the EU Foreign and Security Policy: The ECJ accepts jurisdiction over claims for damages under the Common Foreign and Security Policy (CFSP)' *Verfassungsblog* (18 October 2020), available at www.verfassungsblog.de/constitutionalising-the-eu-foreign-and-security-policy.

[71] *Opinion 2/13* (n 20).

the Court had set it out in the *Kadi I* appeal, arguably already based on earlier cases.[72] The autonomy of EU law vis-à-vis international law remains a priority of the Court of Justice. This may be expected to remain this way, considering the relevance of autonomy for the functioning of the EU legal order, explained above.

ii. Reaction of the General Court

Kadi II demonstrated the problems arising from the extended powers of the judiciary. It was the tone rather than the outcome of the *Kadi II* ruling that raised questions as to the role and influence of the individual judge in shaping the legal discourse and the outcome of the case. The same judge acted as the *juge rapporteur* both when the CFI ruled on *Kadi I* and when the General Court ruled on *Kadi II*. In between, the Court of Justice had set aside the CFI's ruling in *Kadi I*. In *Kadi II*, the General Court goes far in criticising the Court of Justice.

The acridity of the General Court's criticism is exceptional. This may be due to, on the one hand, deep disagreement on substance and, on the other, disappointment in the lower court's powerless position. *Kadi II* stands in clear contrast with the earlier cases of *Othman* and *Al Faqih*.[73] Both concerned individual sanctions giving effect to UN lists and both were decided after the *Kadi I* appeal decision, but before *Kadi II*. The difference between *Kadi II* on the one hand and *Othman* and *Al Faqih* on the other is that the former case concerned sanctions adopted under the listing procedure reformed *after* 3 September 2008, the day the Court of Justice decided the appeal in *Kadi I*. To put it mildly: rulings in which the personality of the judge is expressed with such clarity do not contribute to the authority of legal reasoning, which after all is an important source of judicial authority.[74]

iii. Foundational Reference

The *Kadi I* appeal is a landmark decision which has been decisive for numerous sanctions-related cases since 2008.[75] Yet it has also regularly been referred to in foundational constitutional rulings. First, the *Kadi I* appeal forms a foundational part of the consistent line of decisions confirming that 'an international agreement cannot affect

[72] See, eg, *Opinion 1/91* EU:C:1991:490.

[73] Case T-318/01 *Othman v Council and Commission* EU:T:2009:187; Joined Cases T-135/06, T-136/06, T-137/06 and T-138/06 *Al-Faqih et al v Council* EU:T:2010:412. Other cases on sanctions giving effect to UN lists (decided between CFI, *Kadi I* and Court of Justice, *Kadi I*): Case T-49/04 *Hassan v Council and Commission* EU:T:2006:201; Case T-253/02 *Ayadi v Council* EU:T:2006:200.

[74] R Dworkin, 'The Judge's New Role: Should Personal Conviction Count?' (2003) 1 *Journal of International Criminal Justice* 4, 4.

[75] CJEU: Case C-239/12 P *Abdulrahim v Council and Commission* EU:C:2013:331; Case C-130/10 *Parliament v Council* (n 16); Case C-340/08 *M and Others v Her Majesty's Treasury* EU:C:2010:232; Case C-403/06 P *Ayadi v Council* EU:C:2009:496; Case C-399/06 P *Hassan and Ayadi v Council and Commission* EU:C:2009:748. General Court: Case T-248/13 *Al-Ghabra v Commission* EU:T:2016:721; Case T-134/11 *Al-Faqih and Others v Commission* EU:T:2015:812; Case T-306/10 *Yusef v Commission* EU:T:2014:141; Case T-527/09 RENV *Ayadi v Commission* EU:T:2015:205; Case T-127/09 RENV *Abdulrahim v Council and Commission* EU:T:2015:4; Case T-49/07 *Fahas v Council* EU:T:2010:499; *Al-Faqih* (n 73).

the allocation of powers fixed by the Treaties or, consequently, the autonomy of the EU legal system'.[76] However, beyond this, the *Kadi I* appeal is cited as establishing fundamental rights as 'the very foundations of the European Union legal order' that rank above EU primary law. This aspect has informed the Court of Justice's reasoning, but has been less discussed in the literature. The *Wightman* case concerning the Article 50 TFEU procedure in the context of Brexit is an example of where this reasoning has been considered.[77]

B. Academic Reception

The importance of the *Kadi* cases can hardly be overstated. This is reflected in the avalanche of scholarly writings on *Kadi* and its constitutional intricacies,[78] as well as the very diverging academic reception.[79]

The General Court was criticised for taking the role of a world court when it evaluated sanctions in the light of *jus cogens* in *Kadi I* in 2005.[80] However, the Court of Justice decision in *Kadi I* (2008) equally received criticism, above all from international legal scholars, warning about the fragmentation of international law and accusing the Court of Justice of establishing an exceptionalism of EU law that other international legal actors do not claim, cannot claim, and should not accept.[81] It was portrayed as undermining the UN system for protecting international peace and security.[82] Some critically compared it with the European Court of Human Rights' (ECtHR) ruling in *Nada*.[83] Others, by contrast, argued that 'Kadi is best understood as an act of civil disobedience prompted by the UN Security Council's misapplication of foundational principles of the international order'.[84] Again, others found 'that the Court indicated a possible opening to allow for precedence of Security Council measures, if sufficient safeguards for human rights are created'.[85]

[76] Case C-284/16 *Slowakische Republik v Achmea BV* EU:C:2017:699, Opinion of AG Wathelet, para 102.

[77] Case C-621/18 *Wightman et al v Secretary of State for Exiting the European Union* EU:C:2018:999, para 62.

[78] K Ziegler, 'Strengthening the Rule of Law, But Fragmenting International Law: The Kadi Decision of the ECJ from the Perspective of Human Rights' (2009) 9 *Human Rights Law Review* 288; P Eeckhout, 'The Growing Influence of European Union Law' (2011) 33 *Fordham International Law Journal* 1490; G de Búrca, 'The European Court of Justice and the International Legal Order after Kadi' (2010) 51 *Harvard International Law Journal* 1; J d'Aspremont and F Dopagne, 'Two Constitutionalisms in Europe: Pursuing an Articulation of the European and International Legal Orders' (2009) 69 *Heidelberg Journal of International Law* 939; Eckes (n *).

[79] See, eg, RA Wessel, 'The Kadi Case: Towards a More Substantive Hierarchy in International Law' (2008) 5 *International Organizations Law Review* 323.

[80] C Eckes, 'Judicial Review of European Anti-Terrorism Measures – The Yusuf and Kadi Judgments of the Court of First Instance' (2008) 14 *European Law Journal* 74, 88.

[81] Ziegler (n 78); de Búrca (n 78); d'Aspremont and Dopagne (n 78).

[82] Ziegler (n 78); de Búrca (n 78); d'Aspremont and Dopagne (n 78).

[83] E de Wet, 'From Kadi to Nada: Judicial Techniques Favouring Human Rights over United Nations Security Council Sanctions' (2013) 12 *Chinese Journal of International Law* 787.

[84] Isiksel (n 51).

[85] J Kokott and C Sobotta, 'The Kadi Case – Constitutional Core Values and International Law – Finding the Balance?' (2012) 23 *The European Journal of International Law* 1015.

For its *Kadi II* in 2013, the Court of Justice was criticised for sticking to the same position, not engaging sufficiently with the UN context, and not giving enough credit for the improvements made. However, from a rule of law perspective many reservations remain and it is unclear how the EU courts could appreciate the improvements in the UN context if the procedural guarantees are still not sufficient and most likely never will be. Critically, in a different way, *Kadi* and *Nada* have been identified of part of a black-listing practice and its contestations that together inscribe the principles of pre-emption into the international juridical order.[86]

While the issue of EU competence has been settled by the Lisbon Treaty,[87] Kadi has raised fundamental conceptual questions concerning the validity, the rank and the effects of international law within the EU legal order, which continue to require the Court of Justice to strike a balance between autonomy and openness.[88] Arguably, the discussion of whether the Court's conception of the autonomy of the EU legal order threatens the EU's ability to pursue a leading role in promoting the international rule of law and multilateralism for international relations continues since *Kadi.* Opinion *2/13* and *Opinion 1/17* have again raised concerns about the EU's relationship with international law.[89]

V. Famous Follow-Up Cases (Including National Supreme Courts)

Besides the many cases in Luxembourg that followed *Kadi*, courts in different national and international jurisdictions were confronted with challenges of *Kadi*-type sanctions, that is, implementation of UN counter-terrorist listings.[90] All of these cases concern

[86] M de Goede, 'Blacklisting and the ban: Contesting targeted sanctions in Europe' (2011) 42 *Security Dialogue* 499.

[87] Cremona (n 15); Eckes, *EU Counter-Terrorist Policies* (n *) ch 2.

[88] S Besson, 'European Legal Pluralism after Kadi' (2009) 5 *European Constitutional Law Review* 237; K Lenaerts, 'The Kadi Saga and the Rule of Law within the EU' (2014) 67 *SMU Law Review* 707.

[89] *Opinion 2/13* (n 20); and *Opinion 1/17* EU:C:2019:341.

[90] Examples of cases decided by national courts: UK: *Bank Mellat v HM Treasury (No 1)* [2011] EWCA Civ 1, [2012] QB 101; *Bank Mellat v HM (No 1)* [2013] UKSC 38, [2013] 4 All ER 495; *Bank Melli and Persia International Bank v Shere Shipping and others* [2013] EWHC 2321 (Comm); *R (Bredenkamp) v Secretary of State for Foreign and Commonwealth Affairs* [2012] EWHC 3297 (Admin), [2013] 2 CMLR 10; *R (El-Maghraby and El Gazaerly) v HM Treasury and Foreign and Commonwealth Office* [2012] EWHC 674 (Admin); *R (Europäisch-Iranische Handelsbank) v Secretary of State for Foreign and Commonwealth Affairs* CO/10718/2012. Switzerland: *Youssef Mustapha Nada v Staatssekretariat für Wirtschaft* [2007] 1A.45/2007 (Swiss Supreme Court). Canada: *Abousfian Abdelrazik v Minister of Foreign Affairs and Attorney General of Canada, 2009 FC 580*, 4 June 2009, available at decisions.fct-cf.gc.ca/en/2009/2009fc580/2009fc580.pdf. ECtHR: *Nada v Switzerland* (n 12); *Al-Dulimi & Montana Management Inc v Switzerland* [2013] ECHR 1173. UN Human Rights Committee: *Sayadi and Vinck* (22 October 2008) 1472/2006. CJEU: Case T-134/11 *Al-Faqih and Others v Commission* EU:T:2015:812; Case T-248/13 *Al-Ghabra v Commission* EU:T:2016:721; Case T-253/02 *Ayadi v Council* EU:T:2006:200; Case C-403/06 P *Ayadi v Council* EU:C:2009:496; Case T-527/09 RENV *Ayadi v Commission* EU:T:2015:205; Case C-134/19 *Bank Refah Kargaran v Council* EU:C:2020:793; Case C–310/06 *FTS International BV v Belastingdienst* EU:C:2007:456; Case T-49/04 *Hassan v Council and Commission* EU:T:2006:201; C-399/06 P *Hassan and Ayadi v Council and Commission* EU:C:2009:748; Case C-340/08 *M and Others v Her Majesty's Treasury* EU:C:2010:232; Case T-318/01 *Othman v Council and Commission* EU:T:2009:187; Case C-130/10 *Parliament v Council* EU:C:2012:472; Case T-228/02 *People's Mojahedin Organization v*

different legal contexts, that is national law, and the UN Charter, and often also the ECHR and EU law. Three cases have attracted particular attention – I will discuss them in chronological order.

Domestic sanctions under UN Security Council Resolution 1267, just as in *Kadi*, were challenged outside of Europe in *Abdelrazik v Canada* (2009).[91] The Canadian Federal Court offered the applicants an effective remedy. It grounded its ruling in the principles of effectiveness and common sense, and implicitly provided a justification for the breach of international law. The literature criticises the Canadian Federal Court for 'interpreting away' the obligations of Canada under the UN Charter, potentially forcing upon the state a breach of its international obligations.[92]

In the UK, many *Kadi*-type cases emerged, with the UK Supreme Court's decision in *Ahmed* of 2010 remaining the most prominent.[93] In *Ahmed*, the UK Supreme Court did not follow the Court of Justice's reasoning in *Kadi* but distinguished it by pointing at the exceptional position of the EU, which is not a member of the UN.[94] Implicitly, it also rejected in *Ahmed* the primacy of EU law. The UK Supreme Court concluded that;

> For the time being we must proceed on the basis that article 103 [of the UN Charter] leaves no room for any exception, and that the [ECHR] rights fall into the category of obligations under an international agreement over which obligations under the Charter must prevail.[95]

The ECtHR dealt with *Kadi*-type sanctions in *Nada v Switzerland* (2012).[96] In the decision challenged before the ECtHR, the Swiss Federal Court had largely followed the General Court's earlier ruling in the case of *Kadi I*, accepting the primacy of Security Council resolutions to permeate the domestic legal order.[97] The ECtHR found such a conflict of norms between the ECHR and Switzerland's obligations under the UN Charter to exist;[98] yet it did not find it necessary to decide upon this conflict, simply ruling that Switzerland had acted in violation of the right to freedom of movement by not doing all it could to adapt the implementation of the sanction, as far as possible, to the specific circumstances of Mr Nada.[99]

Council and UK (PMOI I) EU:T:2006:384; Case T-256/07 *People's Mojahedin Organization of Iran v Council (PMOI II)* EU:T:2008:461; Case T-284/08 *People's Mojahedin Organization of Iran v Council (PMOI III)* EU:T:2008:593; Case T-306/10 *Yusef v Commission* EU:T:2014:141.

[91] Canadian Federal Court, *Abousfian Abdelrazik* (n 90).

[92] A Tzanakopolous, 'United Nations Sanctions in Domestic Courts: From Interpretation to Defiance in Abdelrazik v Canada' (2010) 8 *Journal of International Criminal Justice* 249.

[93] *HM Treasury v Mohammed Jabar Ahmed and ors (FC); HM Treasury v Mohammed al-Ghabra (FC); R (on the application of Hani El Sayed SabaeiYoussef) v HM Treasury* [2010] UKSC 2. See C Eckes and S Hollenberg, 'Reconciling Different Legal Spheres in Theory and Practice: Pluralism and Constitutionalism in the Cases of Al-Jedda, Ahmed and Nada' (2013) 20 *Maastricht Journal of European and Comparative Law* 220.

[94] UKSC, *HM Treasury v Ahmed* (n 93) para 71.

[95] ibid para 74.

[96] ECtHR, *Nada v Switzerland* (n 12).

[97] See for the *Nada* decision of the Swiss Supreme Court, J Reich, 'Due process and sanctions targeted against individuals pursuant to resolution 1267 (1999)' (2008) 33 *Yale Journal of International Law* 505.

[98] Agreeing that there is a conflict and discussing different ways of dealing with it, S Hollenberg, 'The diverging approaches of the European Court of Human Rights in the cases of Nada and Al-Dulimi' (2015) 64 *International and Comparative Law Quarterly* 445.

[99] Comparing the reconciliation techniques of the Court of Justice in *Kadi* and the ECtHR in *Nada*, de Wet (n 83).

20

Opinion 2/13 and Accession to the ECHR

TOBIAS LOCK

I. Introduction

Opinion 2/13, handed down just before Christmas 2014, is a landmark decision in both European Union (EU) human rights law and EU external relations law.[1] It showed that the EU's rhetorical commitment to international human rights protection is not necessarily matched by action: *Opinion 2/13* was the second time the Court of Justice put the brakes on the EU's ambition to become a party to the European Convention on Human Rights (ECHR) for reasons rooted in the EU's constitutional set-up. Having comprehensively assessed the fairly elaborate ECHR Draft Accession Agreement (DAA), the CJEU provided the yardstick for any future attempt at accession: the constitutional hurdles identified will have to be taken for any reworked DAA to pass muster. The Opinion is also a landmark judgment in the wider field of EU external relations. By clarifying and strengthening the principle of the autonomy of the EU legal order, the Court reiterated the legal limits governing the EU's ability to integrate into the wider international order at a time when EU external relations and EU treaty-making are becoming increasingly important.

II. Historical and Doctrinal Context

A. The History of EU Accession to the ECHR

Opinion 2/13 was not the first time the Court of Justice was asked to rule on the compatibility of EU accession to the ECHR with the Treaties. In *Opinion 2/94* the Council sought the Court's view on whether accession of the (then) European Communities to the ECHR would be compatible with the EC Treaty.[2] As is the case with all EU action, EU external action is governed by the principle of conferred powers. At the time of

[1] *Opinion 2/13 (Accession of the European Union to the European Convention for the Protection of Human Rights and Fundamental Freedoms)* EU:C:2014:2454.

[2] *Opinion 2/94 (Accession to the ECHR)* EU:C:1996:140.

Opinion 2/94 the Treaties did not contain an express competence clause empowering the EU to become a party to the ECHR. There was also no implied power that could be derived from an express legislative competence, so that the argument revolved around whether the gap-filling competence laid down in what is now Article 352 TFEU (then Article 235 TEC) could be employed. The Court's (literally) short answer was that it could not. In a first step the Court reiterated that the EU Treaties – including the gap-filling competence – did not confer *Kompetenz-Kompetenz*, that is, a power for the EU to extend its own competences. In the Court's words 'Article [352] cannot be used as a basis for the adoption of provisions whose effect would, in substance, be to amend the Treaty without following the procedure which it provides for that purpose.'[3] In a second step the Court concluded that accession to the ECHR 'would be of constitutional significance' as it would result in a substantial change in how human rights are protected in the EU by entering the EU into a distinct international institutional system and by integrating all of the provisions of the ECHR into EU law.[4]

The Lisbon Treaty brought the necessary Treaty change. Article 6(2) TEU – enacted alongside the Charter of Fundamental Rights as part of a 'fundamental rights package' – contains an express competence: 'The Union shall accede to the European Convention for the Protection of Human Rights and Fundamental Freedoms. Such accession shall not affect the Union's competences as defined in the Treaties.' It is complemented by Protocol No 8 to the Lisbon Treaty, which provides further detail on the EU's constitutional constraints. Any accession treaty must preserve the 'special characteristics of the Union and Union law'[5] with particular regard to the participation of the EU in the control bodies of the ECHR, viz the European Court of Human Rights (ECtHR) first and foremost, and 'the mechanisms necessary to ensure that proceedings by non-Member States and individual applications are correctly addressed to Member States and/or the Union as appropriate', which hints at the need for an arrangement like the co-respondent mechanism discussed below. Furthermore, the Protocol reiterates the principle of conferred powers and stipulates in essence that the Member States' responsibilities under the ECHR should not be extended due to accession. Finally, the Protocol reiterates the Court's exclusive jurisdiction over matters of Union law in disputes between Member States enshrined in Article 344 TFEU.

In addition to Treaty change at EU level, the ECHR needed to become open to EU membership, which happened with the entry into force of Protocol 14 in 2011. It added Article 59(2) ECHR, which says that the 'European Union may accede to this Convention.'[6]

B. Why Accession?

Three broad arguments are typically advanced in favour of the EU's accession to the ECHR.

[3] ibid para 30.
[4] ibid paras 34–35.
[5] This concern is also reflected in Declaration No 2 to the Lisbon Treaty.
[6] Quoted in n 1.

First, an external scrutiny argument emphasises the need for any legal system that protects fundamental rights to be open to independent external review applying international human rights standards. Apart from the symbolic value of accession, it ensures that the minimum human rights standards defined in the Convention are guaranteed and any systemic biases counteracted,[7] for example, in the EU's case, a potential bias towards market integration.

Second, a consistency argument voices the concern that in the absence of accession it would be difficult to avoid inconsistencies between ECtHR and CJEU case law.[8] Given that the substance of EU fundamental rights protection has its origin in the ECHR[9] and the EU Charter of Fundamental Rights builds on it,[10] consistency is a desirable outcome. This goes hand in hand with an integrationist rationale, which maintains that there is a collective responsibility for protecting fundamental rights in Europe shared between the EU and the Council of Europe, which in the absence of accession might unravel.[11]

Third, an attribution argument holds that accession would close existing gaps in the protection against EU acts and, even where no gap exists, it would lead to a more appropriate allocation of responsibility for ECHR violations rooted in EU law.[12] This argument alludes to the ECtHR's case law on Member State responsibility for such violations, which goes back to the *Matthews* case.[13] The ECtHR held that in the absence of EU membership of the ECHR,

> [EU] acts as such cannot be challenged before the Court because the [EU] is not a Contracting Party. The Convention does not exclude the transfer of competences to international organisations provided that Convention rights continue to be 'secured'. Member States' responsibility therefore continues even after such a transfer.[14]

This means that in the event that a violation of the ECHR is shown, a Member State is found to have been in breach of the ECHR. The problem with this is that the Member State concerned is typically not in a position to unilaterally remedy the violation as the violation is found in EU law. Accession would change this as the EU could then be a respondent[15] before the ECtHR and be held responsible for its own failings.

The rule in *Matthews* has been subject to two modifications. The first came with the *Bosphorus* case, where the ECtHR introduced a rebuttable presumption of Convention

[7] See, eg, E Spaventa, 'A Very Fearful Court? The Protection of Fundamental Rights in the European Union after Opinion 2/13' (2015) 22 *Maastricht Journal of European and Comparative Law* 35, 38; Editorial Comments, 'The EU's Accession to the ECHR – a "NO" from the ECJ!' (2015) 52 *Common Market Law Review* 1, 4.

[8] See, eg, in relation to EU competition law, A Andreangeli, 'Competition Law and the Opinion 2.13 on the Accession of the EU to the European Convention on Human Rights: Back to Square one?' (2015) 6 *Journal of European Competition Law and Practice* 583, 585.

[9] Starting with Case 4/73 *Nold* EU:C:1974:51 and extended to the ECtHR's case law since Case C-13/94 *P v S and Cornwall County Council* EU:C:1996:170.

[10] See notably Art 52(3) CFR, which stipulates that ECHR standards are minimum requirements where CFR rights correspond to rights found in the ECHR.

[11] See, eg, J Callewaert, 'Do we still need Article 6(2) TEU? Considerations on the absence of EU accession to the ECHR and its consequences' (2018) 55 *Common Market Law Review* 1685, 1688.

[12] Spaventa (n 6) 41–42; Editorial Comments (n 6) 4.

[13] *Matthews v United Kingdom* (1999) 28 EHRR 361.

[14] ibid para 32.

[15] Or co-respondent, on which see below.

compliance for member states of international organisations that provide equivalent protection of fundamental rights to what the Convention requires, something the EU does.[16] The presumption is premised on the further condition that the Member State 'does no more than implement legal obligations flowing from its membership of the organisation', that is, if it has no discretion and is acting on the basis of secondary EU law.[17] The presumption can only be rebutted if 'in the circumstances of a particular case, it is considered that the protection of Convention rights was manifestly deficient'.[18] The second exception can be found in the *Connolly* case – arising from a dispute between an EU civil servant and the EU – where the ECtHR held that the conduct of an EU institution could not be attributed to any Member State because there had been no Member State involvement in the matter at any point.[19] Accession by the EU to the ECHR would certainly close the *Connolly* gap in accountability and would call into the question the maintenance of the *Bosphorus* presumption.

C. How Accession would Unfold

Article 218(6) TFEU presupposes that EU accession to the ECHR happens by way of an international agreement, whereas ordinarily parties wishing to sign up to the ECHR simply ratify it. This shows that EU accession to the ECHR is less straightforward in that it will require specific arrangements for the EU. These specific arrangements are necessary because – unlike federations like Belgium, Austria or Germany, where powers are shared between different levels of government – the EU will be a party alongside the Member States. This necessitates rules on the attribution of conduct and on the division of responsibility between the two, notably where an EU Member State acts on the basis of EU law and where it is therefore not evident whether an ECHR infringement is the fault of the EU or the Member State or both and which entity is best able to provide a remedy for the breach.

The constitutional difficulty with this lies in the autonomy of the EU legal order. Long-established as far as the internal relationship between Member States and the EU is concerned – the 'independent source of law' in *Costa v ENEL* is '*une source autonome*' in the French language version[20] – the autonomy of the EU legal order came to prominence in EU external relations law with *Opinion 1/91*.[21] That Opinion was concerned with the powers given to the EEA court, which the Court of Justice considered to violate the autonomy of the EU legal order and its own exclusive jurisdiction concerning the interpretation and validity of EU law found in what is now Article 19(1) TEU and Article 344 TFEU. The Court held in essence that no international court must be given jurisdiction to decide on the distribution of competences between the EU and its Member States.[22] It further held that no international court must be given jurisdiction

[16] *Bosphorus v Ireland* (2005) 42 EHRR 1, para 155.
[17] ibid paras 156–57.
[18] ibid; this has happened only once so far in *Bivolaru et Moldovan v France* App nos 40324/16 and 12623/17 (ECtHR, 25 March 2021).
[19] *Connolly v 15 Member States of the EU* App no 73274/01 (ECtHR, 9 December 2009).
[20] Case 6/64 *Costa v ENEL* EU:C:1964:66.
[21] *Opinion 1/91 (Agreement on the European Economic Area)* EU:C:1991:490.
[22] ibid paras 34–36.

to interpret the substantive rules of EU law in a manner that is binding on the EU or its Member States.[23] And finally, that no EU agreement may give new powers to the EU instructions – including the Court itself – which would otherwise require a treaty amendment.[24]

III. Background and Decision of the CJEU

A. Key Features of the Draft Accession Agreement

The Court of Justice examined the compatibility of the DAA with the Treaties following a request by the European Commission according to Article 218(11) TFEU. The Court identified several reasons why the DAA was not compatible with the Treaties, all of which centred on the autonomy principle. In a first step, this section therefore presents the key features of the DAA before outlining the Court of Justice's view in a second step.

Apart from numerous technical issues – such as budget contributions, procedure before the Committee of Ministers – the DAA pursued the overall aim of accommodating the EU – a supranational organisation, all of whose members would individually remain parties to the ECHR – as a party to the ECHR.

The central question confronting the negotiators was how to ensure that an individual application brought before the ECtHR alleging a violation of the ECHR by an EU institution or by EU law is addressed to the correct party – that is the EU or the Member States, depending on who is capable of providing an effective remedy against the violation – whilst respecting the autonomy of the EU legal order and whilst avoiding 'gaps in the participation, accountability and enforceability in the [ECHR] system'.[25]

The negotiators appeared to have two basic scenarios in mind when drafting the relevant Article 3 DAA. The first is based on a scenario like in *Bosphorus*, where an EU regulation is applied by a Member State, and is allegedly in violation of the ECHR. While from the perspective of the victim of the violation the Member State has acted, only the EU can remedy the violation. The second consists of a situation where an EU institution allegedly violates the Convention, but the violation is rooted in EU primary law, which only the Member States can amend.

The DAA therefore featured a rule of attribution in Article 1(4), which says that

> an act, measure or omission of organs of a member State of the European Union or of persons acting on its behalf shall be attributed to that State, even if such act, measure or omission occurs when the State implements the law of the European Union ….

Hence whenever a Member State acts, the conduct is attributed to it. In rare cases where only an EU institution is involved – such as staffing disputes like *Connolly* or competition proceedings – the conduct is attributed to the EU.

[23] ibid paras 39–46.
[24] ibid paras 58–61.
[25] Draft Explanatory Report to the Agreement on the Accession of the European Union to the Convention for the Protection of Human Rights and Fundamental Freedoms (47+1(2013)008rev2), para 39.

This rule of attribution was then coupled with the so-called co-respondent mechanism, which would operate in two situations. First, where the conduct is initially attributed to a Member State,

> the [EU] may become a co-respondent to the proceedings in respect of an alleged violation notified by the Court if it appears that such allegation calls into question the compatibility with the rights at issue defined in the Convention … notably where that violation could have been avoided only by disregarding an obligation under European Union law.[26]

Second, where the conduct is initially attributed to the EU, the Member States

> may become co-respondents to the proceedings in respect of an alleged violation notified by the Court if it appears that such allegation calls into question the compatibility with the rights at issue defined in the [ECHR] of a provision of the Treaty on European Union, the Treaty on the Functioning of the European Union or any other provision having the same legal value pursuant to those instruments, notably where that violation could have been avoided only by disregarding an obligation under those instruments.[27]

Article 3(5) DAA set out two procedures by which a party may become co-respondent: either by accepting an invitation from the ECtHR or upon its request. In the latter case, the ECtHR would seek the views of all parties and on that basis assess whether 'in light of the reasons given … it is plausible that the conditions … are met'.

According to Article 3(7) DAA, the general rule would then be that the co-respondents would be jointly responsible, that is, in each situation the conundrum faced by the negotiators would be resolved in a way that both the party that had committed the violation vis-à-vis the applicant and the party that is actually in a position to remedy the violation would be jointly held responsible. How precisely that joint responsibility would be managed – including the question of who would have to pay just compensation if so ordered by the ECtHR – would be the subject of EU internal rules. Article 3(7) DAA contained an important exception, however, for situations where the ECtHR, 'on the basis of the reasons given by the respondent and the co-respondent, and having sought the views of the applicant, decides that only one of them be held responsible'.

The first variety of the co-respondent mechanism – where conduct is attributed to a Member State and the EU becomes co-respondent – results in a further issue: what if the Court of Justice was never involved in the case, notably because the national court dealing with the matter in the respondent Member State did not refer any questions as to the validity or interpretation of EU law to the CJEU according to Article 267 TFEU? If the ECtHR were to decide on a violation of the Convention rooted in EU law without the CJEU's involvement, this would arguably be contrary to the subsidiary character proceedings before the ECtHR are supposed to have.[28] The solution in the DAA is the prior involvement mechanism found in Article 3(6) DAA:

> In proceedings to which the [EU] is a co-respondent, if the [CJEU] has not yet assessed the compatibility with the rights at issue defined in the [ECHR] of the provision of [EU] law as

[26] Article 3(2) DAA.
[27] Article 3(3) DAA.
[28] See the Joint Communication from the Presidents of the European Court of Human Rights and the Court of Justice of the European Union, available at curia.europa.eu/jcms/jcms/P_72317.

> under paragraph 2 of this article, sufficient time shall be afforded for the Court of Justice of the European Union to make such an assessment, and thereafter for the parties to make observations to the Court. …

The precise procedure for prior involvement would be subject to internal EU rules.

B. The Opinion of the Court

In *Opinion 2/13* the Court held that the DAA was not compatible with the Treaties. The Court identified a number of flaws in the DAA. These mostly related to the DAA not respecting the specific characteristics, viz the autonomy of the EU legal order and in particular the constitutional role of the Court of Justice itself.

In a first step, the Court of Justice found that the DAA lacked a number of coordinating provisions. The first of these concerned the relationship between Article 53 ECHR and Article 53 of the EU Charter of Fundamental Rights (CFR) as construed by the Court of Justice. Article 53 ECHR says that the Convention does not limit or derogate from the human rights in the laws of the parties to the ECHR or under any other agreement to which they are parties. This clause therefore provides that the ECHR requires a minimum of human rights protection, but does not stand in the way of better protection.[29] On the face of it Article 53 CFR says much the same, that is, that nothing in the 'Charter shall be interpreted as restricting or adversely affecting human rights and fundamental freedoms as recognised, in their respective fields of application, by Union law'. The crucial difference for the Court, however, was that it had held in *Melloni* that Member States may not provide higher standards of fundamental rights protection when acting within the scope of EU law if 'the primacy, unity and effectiveness of EU law' are compromised.[30] Thus in *Opinion 2/13* the Court required that the DAA should include a coordinating provision making it clear that the power of the Member States to provide a higher level of protection reserved by Article 53 ECHR is restricted by EU law requirements where Member States are acting in the scope of EU law.[31]

The second missing coordinating provision related to the principle of mutual trust, which governs the area of freedom, security and justice (AFSJ), and which the Court – for the first time – expressly considered to be of fundamental importance in EU law.[32] The principle of mutual trust requires that Member States 'consider all the other Member States to be complying with EU law and particularly with the fundamental rights recognised by EU law'.[33] Hence an argument before a national court that, for example, a European arrest warrant was adopted by another Member State in a way that is contrary to the Charter, cannot be accepted on the basis of mutual trust. Instead, the EU system of fundamental rights protection requires that a challenge to such a Member State measure must be brought in the issuing Member State.

[29] *National Union of Rail, Maritime and Transport Workers v the United Kingdom* [2014] ECHR 366, Opinion of Judge Wojtyczek, para 3.
[30] Case C-399/11 *Stefano Melloni v Ministerio Fiscal* EU:C:2013:107, para 60.
[31] *Opinion 2/13* (n 1) paras 187–90.
[32] ibid para 191.
[33] ibid para 191.

This is based on the premise that all Member States share the values of the EU – laid down in Article 2 TEU – and therefore protect fundamental rights sufficiently well for this not to be detrimental to the individual concerned. According to the Court of Justice, EU accession to the ECHR would imperil the operation of the principle of mutual trust if it enabled precisely such challenges to be brought on the basis of the ECHR because this would mean that a Member State could be held responsible under the ECHR for not having reviewed the compatibility with the Convention of an AFSJ measure – such as a European arrest warrant – issued by another Member State. Hence the CJEU held that in the absence of a provision in the DAA preventing this from happening, the DAA would 'upset the underlying balance of the EU and undermine the autonomy of EU law'.[34]

The final missing coordinating provision concerned Protocol No 16 to the ECHR, which had entered into force since the DAA had been finalised. Protocol No 16 contains a mechanism by which highest courts of the parties to the ECHR can request an advisory opinion from the ECtHR 'on questions of principle relating to the interpretation or application of the rights and freedoms defined in the Convention'. The Protocol – which is optional and has been opted into by nine EU Member States thus far[35] – is evidently modelled on the preliminary reference procedure found in Article 267 TFEU, from which it differs in two key respects: first, it is limited to highest courts; and, second, advisory opinions by the ECtHR are not binding. The Court of Justice's concern in respect of Protocol No 16 – to which the EU was not going to accede – was a perceived danger that it could be used to undermine the preliminary reference procedure. The Court was concerned that a highest court of a Member State might choose to refer a case to the ECtHR instead of the CJEU, where a question of the interpretation of an ECHR right that corresponds to a right in the CFR is concerned. Such a move – if the case was in the scope of EU law – would evidently be contrary to the duty of highest national courts to refer such matters to the CJEU, spelled out in Article 267(3) TFEU. Hence the Court held that in the absence of a provision coordinating the relationship between Protocol No 16 and Article 267 TFEU, the DAA was liable 'adversely to affect the autonomy and effectiveness of the latter procedure' and thus the Treaties.

The Court went on to hold that the DAA also infringed its own exclusive jurisdiction protected by Article 344 TFEU because Article 33 ECHR would continue to allow the EU and Member States to bring inter-party applications against each other. However, where such an inter-party case came within the scope of EU law, this would be contrary to Article 344 TFEU, which grants the Court of Justice an exclusive jurisdiction over the interpretation and validity of EU law. Hence the 'very existence of such a possibility undermines' Article 344 TFEU, so that such scenarios would need to be expressly excluded from the ECtHR's jurisdiction under Article 33 ECHR.[36]

The Court subsequently examined the co-respondent mechanism, which it considered to suffer from three flaws. First, the procedure for designating the co-respondent contained in Article 3(5) DAA gave the ECtHR the option of rejecting a request of a Member State or the EU to become co-respondent where the reasons given for such

[34] ibid para 194.
[35] Estonia, Finland, France, Greece, Lithuania, Luxembourg, Netherlands, Slovakia, Slovenia.
[36] *Opinion 2/13* (n 1) paras 201–14.

a request did not meet a plausibility threshold. This would – according to the CJEU – raise questions of the division of competences between the EU and its Member States, which the ECtHR would be given jurisdiction to determine. This, however, would be contrary to the autonomy of the EU legal order as such matters are the exclusive domain of the CJEU.[37] The second and third flaws are found in Article 3(7) DAA. It is recalled that that provision contains the rule that co-respondents are jointly responsible for a violation of the Convention. The CJEU took issue with the fact that the DAA did not expressly account for a situation where a Member State may have made a reservation to the ECHR and could not normally be held responsible. Given that Article 2 of Protocol No 8 expressly required that Member State reservations be respected, it held that the lack of an express provision to that effect would not be compatible with the Treaties. The third flaw is closely connected to the first. Article 3(7) DAA provided that exceptionally the ECtHR can find that the co-respondents should not be found jointly responsible 'on the basis of reasons given by the respondent and he co-respondent'. According to the CJEU, this would grant the ECtHR jurisdiction to decide on the division of competences between the EU and its Member States, which was contrary to the exclusive jurisdiction of the CJEU on this matter.[38]

The Court then examined the prior involvement mechanism, which was – again – not fully compatible with the demands of the Treaties. It identified two issues in this regard: first, it took issue with the requirement in Article 3(6) DAA that the prior involvement of the CJEU should only happen where the CJEU had not yet assessed the fundamental rights compatibility of the act or omission that is the subject of the complaint. In the eyes of the CJEU this would require the ECtHR to interpret the case law of the CJEU, which would be incompatible with the Treaties.[39] Second, the CJEU considered the prior involvement mechanism to be tailored too narrowly as it was confined to questions of the compatibility of EU law with Convention rights, but did not extend to questions of interpretation of EU law. According to the CJEU, this would circumvent the CJEU's exclusive jurisdiction to interpret EU primary and secondary law, so that the DAA would need to be amended in this regard to be compatible with the Treaties.[40]

The final deficiency in the DAA concerned the ECtHR's potential jurisdiction over matters concerning the Common Foreign and Security Policy (CFSP), which the DAA did not engage with at all. The issue lay in the CJEU's own limited jurisdiction over CFSP matters, which results from Article 24(1) TEU and Article 275(1) TFEU. These provisions exclude the CJEU's jurisdiction over CFSP matters with the exception of cases concerning the delineation of CFSP competences from 'ordinary' external relations competences – Article 40 TEU – as well as annulment proceedings concerning restrictive measures, viz sanctions. The DAA did not contain a provision mirroring this restriction. This would have resulted in the ECtHR potentially being competent to decide CFSP cases, over which the CJEU would not have had jurisdiction. A potential example would be cases concerning EU missions under the Common Security and Defence Policy. According to the CJEU, 'Such a situation would effectively entrust the

[37] ibid paras 223–25.
[38] ibid paras 231–35.
[39] ibid para 239.
[40] ibid para 247.

judicial review of those acts, actions or omissions on part of the EU exclusively to a non-EU body',[41] even though the Court admitted that any such review would be limited to compliance with the ECHR. The Court then pointed out that such jurisdiction cannot exclusively be conferred on a non-EU court and was thus contrary to the Treaties.[42]

Opinion 2/13 thus had the practical implication that the EU could not accede to the ECHR on the basis of the DAA.

IV. The Advocate General's Contrasting View and Academic Reception

The academic reaction to *Opinion 2/13* was on the whole negative,[43] although some authors expressed some sympathy for the Court's reasoning.[44] Before addressing the main lines of criticism expressed in academic commentary, it is worth pointing out that Advocate General Kokott had expressed a more accession-friendly view.[45] While she too concluded that the DAA could not be ratified unamended, her objections were confined to a number of technical issues, notably the 'plausibility' assessment as part of the co-respondent mechanism; the need to ensure that a prior involvement of the CJEU would also happen in cases raising questions over the interpretation of EU law as well as stricter conditions for the ECtHR to dispense with a prior involvement; the question of Member State reservations and the deviation from the rule of joint responsibility of the co-respondents. By contrast, the Advocate General did not share the CJEU's other concerns, including the most fundamental ones relating to the CFSP and mutual trust. As for the former, the Advocate General concluded that accession could be effected without first granting the CJEU powers to review all CFSP measures given that individuals already enjoy effective legal protection from national courts in such cases.[46]

[41] ibid para 255.

[42] ibid para 256.

[43] See, eg, B de Witte and Š Imamović, 'Opinion 2/13 on accession to the ECHR: defending the EU legal order against a foreign human rights court' (2015) 40 *European Law Review* 683; Spaventa (n 6); S Lambrecht, 'The sting is in the tail: CJEU Opinion 2/13 objects to draft agreement on accession of the EU to the European Convention on Human Rights' [2015] *European Human Rights Law Review* 185; Andreangeli (n 7); J Odermatt, 'A Giant Step Backwards – Opinion 2/13 on the EU's Accession to the European Convention on Human Rights' (2015) 47 *New York University Journal of International Law and Politics* 783; B Pirker and S Reitemeyer, 'Between Discursive and Exclusive Autonomy – Opinion 2/13, the Protection of Fundamental Rights and the Autonomy of EU Law' (2015) 17 *Cambridge Yearbook of European Legal Studies* 168; T Lock, 'The future of the European Union's accession to the European Convention on Human Rights after Opinion 2/13: is it still possible and is it still desirable?' (2015) 11 *European Constitutional Law Review* 239; G Butler, 'The Ultimate Stumbling Block: The Common Foreign and Security Policy, and Accession of the European Union to the European Convention on Human Rights' (2016) 39 *Dublin University Law Journal* 229; SØ Johansen, 'The Reinterpretation of TFEU Article 344 in Opinion 2/13 and Its Potential Consequences' (2015) 16 *German Law Journal* 169; RA Wessel and A Łazowski, 'When Caveats Turn into Locks: Opinion 2/13 on Accession of the European Union to the ECHR' (2015) 16 *German Law Journal* 179.

[44] D Halberstam, '"It's the Autonomy, Stupid!" A Modest Defense of Opinion 2/13 on EU Accession to the European Convention on Human Rights' (2015) 16 *German Law Journal* 105; C Krenn, 'Autonomy and Effectiveness as Common Concerns: A Path to ECHR Accession after Opinion 2/13' (2015) 16 *German Law Journal* 147.

[45] *Opinion 2/13 (View of Advocate General Kokott)* EU:C:2014:2475.

[46] ibid paras 82–103.

The latter issue the Advocate General did not mention. Furthermore, she did not share the CJEU's concerns regarding its exclusive jurisdiction laid down in Article 344 TFEU by rightly noting that a clause in the accession agreement divesting the ECtHR of jurisdiction in such cases would not only be highly uncommon in international law practice, but would also not be strictly necessary given the option for the Commission to initiate infringement proceedings in such cases.[47] Finally, the Advocate General considered there to be no issue arising from Protocol No 16 either as Article 267(3) TFEU contains a clear duty on courts of last instance to refer cases to the CJEU.[48] The Advocate General did not mention the Article 53 problem identified by the Court.

The academic criticism of *Opinion 2/13* can be divided into three categories: a doctrinal criticism concerning both the CJEU's understanding and application of EU law and the law of the ECHR; a criticism that the CJEU has shifted the goalposts by tightening its own standards of review; and a criticism that the Opinion was bad judicial politics.

As far as the various issues identified by the CJEU are concerned, academic commentary oscillated between puzzlement – notably where the need to coordinate the two Articles 53 is concerned – and some degree of sympathy – mostly in relation to the technicalities of the co-respondent and prior involvement mechanisms – and allegations of selfishness – notably concerning the CFSP and mutual trust issues.

As far as the need to coordinate Article 53 CFR and Article 53 ECHR is at issue, commentators almost unanimously expressed their puzzlement. This is chiefly due to a doctrinal misunderstanding on part of the CJEU of the import of Article 53 ECHR,[49] which merely aims to assert the subsidiary character of the ECHR as requiring only a basic standard of protection, which the Member State and EU are free to exceed. In a similar vein, it was argued the perceived difficulties with Protocol No 16 should not have been raised at all given that it is an issue that arises independently of accession.[50] Given the national courts' discretion whether to refer a case or not under Protocol No 16 ECHR, the issue would appear to be moot.[51] Others, however, argue that the CJEU was not wrong to raise this issue given that after accession the ECHR would have been an 'integral part of EU law'[52] so that an interpretation by the ECtHR of the ECHR would amount to an interpretation of EU law,[53] at least so far as the case was in the scope of EU law. This latter argument, however, ignores the fact that an interpretation by the ECtHR under Protocol No 16 would, first, not absolve a national court from its duty to refer the case to the CJEU; and, second, would not be binding on the national court.

The CJEU's issues with the technicalities of the co-respondent and prior involvement mechanisms were on the whole considered to be more persuasive,[54] even though some commentators accuse the CJEU of being overly stringent here,[55] and of adopting

[47] ibid paras 115–18.
[48] ibid para 141.
[49] Lambrecht (n 39) 186.
[50] de Witte and Imamović (n 39) 696; Lambrecht (n 39) 188.
[51] Spaventa (n 6) 47.
[52] Case 181/73 *Haegeman v Belgium* EU:C:1974:41.
[53] Halberstam (n 40) 121.
[54] eg de Witte and Imamović (n 39) 694.
[55] Lambrecht (n 39) 190–91.

a methodologically flawed understanding of the autonomy of the EU legal order.[56] It should be recalled that according to the CJEU's case law up until *Opinion 2/13*, the autonomy of EU law required that no other court but the CJEU be given jurisdiction to rule on the interpretation of EU law, including the division of competences between EU and Member States, in a way that would be binding on the EU or its Member States. Before this background the CJEU's argument about the 'plausibility' test which the ECtHR was to carry out if a co-respondent request would have been made makes some sense. However, the Opinion ignores the fact that the negotiators deliberately included a plausibility review as a very low standard of review, which one could argue does not go much further than allowing the ECtHR to sift out abuses of the co-respondent mechanism, which is a power any court – national or international – typically has.

The ECtHR's power to allocate responsibility to only one co-respondent was more problematic and the CJEU rightly did not accept this; the same goes for the questions around prior involvement, notably the power of the ECtHR to review whether a prior involvement has happened or not. However, as far as respect for Member State reservations is concerned, the CJEU was again overly strict. After all, the co-respondent can never be forced to join proceedings so that reservations would have been highly unlikely to ever have any import in practice.[57] The CJEU's defence of its exclusive jurisdiction laid down in Article 344 TFEU was more controversial. While some have defended the CJEU,[58] others have accused it of over-reacting by essentially requiring that the DAA itself excludes the ECtHR's jurisdiction over such cases when this is neither reflective of international practice,[59] including the EU's own treaty practice, nor strictly necessary as Member States are already prohibited from bringing such cases before the ECtHR. Moreover, the decision in respect of Article 344 TFEU represents a considerable tightening of the autonomy doctrine compared to its previous iterations, most recently in the *Mox Plant* case,[60] where the CJEU accepted a clause that allowed an international court to declare a case concerning EU law inadmissible, but which fell short of automatically resulting in inadmissibility.[61] Hence the CJEU's insistence on watertight rules in the DAA, which would reduce the scope of the ECtHR's jurisdiction, were rightly seen as an over-reaction.

When it comes to practicalities, however, these issues would matter little as they can be resolved relatively easily by redrafting the DAA.[62] The same cannot be said of the mutual trust and CFSP issues, which were also the focus of much academic criticism. In doctrinal terms, many commentators remarked upon the CJEU's elevation of the principle of mutual trust to the status of 'fundamental importance in EU law'.[63] It was rightly pointed out that mutual trust is a legal fiction rather than grounded in reality, so that its being considered a supreme interest was problematic.[64] More scathingly, perhaps,

[56] K Ziegler, 'The Second Attempt at EU Accession to the ECHR: Opinion 2/13' in G Butler and RA Wessel (eds), *EU External Relations Law – the Cases in Context* (Hart Publishing, 2022) 755, 766.
[57] Lambrecht (n 39).
[58] Notably Halberstam (n 40) 118–19.
[59] Pirker and Reitemeyer (n 39) 179.
[60] *Commission v Ireland (Mox Plant)* EU:C:2006:345.
[61] Johansen (n 39) 174–75.
[62] For suggestions, see Lock (n 43).
[63] *Opinion 2/13* (n 1) para 191.
[64] Spaventa (n 6) 52.

the CJEU was accused of seeking to preserve the possibility of EU law providing 'less protection' than what would normally be required by the ECHR.[65] Interestingly, the mutual trust issue had not been considered by the negotiators at all and, as the case law of the ECtHR in this area shows, it is an issue that arises independently of accession.[66] Negotiators of a revised DAA will thus find it difficult to draft a clause accommodating the CJEU's concerns while at the same time securing the possibility of external scrutiny by the ECtHR that the EU and its Member States have lived up to the minimum standards required by the ECHR.[67]

Most problematic, perhaps, was the CJEU's demand that accession could not happen if the ECtHR was given jurisdiction to rule on CFSP matters over which the CJEU currently does not have jurisdiction. This objection has variously been described as 'pointless' given that the ECtHR in *Matthews* had already asserted jurisdiction over matters outwith the CJEU's jurisdiction;[68] as the court being 'selfish';[69] as ignoring the wishes of the Member States given that the reference to the 'specific characteristics' of EU law appears to ignore the fact that the Member States as masters of the Treaties expressly decided not to give the CJEU jurisdiction over some CFSP matters;[70] and as the 'creation of locks'[71] where there supposedly were none before, all of which imply that the CJEU was playing judicial politics rather than applying the law.

That the Opinion would go down badly in Strasbourg was therefore not surprising and a reaction followed swiftly. The then President of the ECtHR, Dean Spielmann, remarked in a speech that 'if there were to be no external scrutiny, the victims would first and foremost be the citizens of the Union'.[72]

Commentators have also warned of the wider ramifications of the Opinion. The far-reaching concept of autonomy espoused by the CJEU in *Opinion 2/13* could make it very difficult in practice for the EU to conclude international agreements and isolate the EU from international law.[73] Moreover, it raises questions of the EU's legitimacy both internally and externally if the EU is seen not to be willing or able to commit itself to external accountability mechanisms such as the ECHR.[74]

V. Follow-Up Developments – The Revised DAA

After *Opinion 2/13*, accession negotiations were on hold for many years and did not recommence until the autumn of 2020. They resulted in a revised DAA finalised in

[65] de Witte and Imamović (n 39) 701.

[66] Notably see the cases *MSS v Belgium and Greece* [2011] ECHR; and *Tarakhel v Switzerland* [2014] ECHR.

[67] On these concerns in more detail, see T Lock, The Future of EU Human Rights Law: Is Accession to the ECHR Still Desirable? (2020) 7 *Journal of International and Comparative Law* 427.

[68] Spaventa (n 6) 54.

[69] Odermatt (n 39) 791.

[70] de Witte and Imamović (n 39) 703?

[71] Wessel and Łazowski (n 39).

[72] D Spielmann, Solemn hearing for the opening of the judicial year of the European Court of Human Rights, 30 January 2015, available at www.echr.coe.int/Documents/Speech_20150130_Solemn_Hearing_2015_ENG.pdf.

[73] Ziegler (n 52) 767.

[74] ibid 771.

March 2023.[75] The approach taken by the negotiators was to work with the existing DAA and 'fix' the issues identified in *Opinion 2/13*. Some could be rectified relatively straightforwardly: concerning the co-respondent, the revised DAA leaves the decision to become a co-respondent entirely with the EU, whose 'reasoned assessment' in this regard will be 'determinative and authoritative'.[76] In addition, there will be no exceptions to the joint responsibility of the EU and its Member State(s) in such a case;[77] and the revised DAA clarifies that reservations retain their effects in respect of co-respondents.[78] Following a similar pattern, the revised DAA leaves the decision on whether or not the ECtHR must facilitate a prior involvement of the CJEU to the EU.[79] A similar solution was found for inter-party cases between EU Member States: the EU will have to make an assessment as to whether such cases concern the interpretation and application of EU law. If they do, then the procedure provided for by Article 33 ECHR is not available to them. The same will be true for all inter-party applications between the EU and one or more of its Member States.[80] The negotiators also achieved the (technically unnecessary) coordination between Article 53 CFR and Article 53 ECHR by inserting a clarifying clause into the revised DAA, which states that Article 53 ECHR shall not be construed as precluding EU Member States from applying a legally binding common level of protection of human rights, provided that it does not fall short of the level required by the ECHR.[81]

As far as the remaining issues identified by the CJEU in *Opinion 2/13* are concerned, the solutions found in the revised DAA are less certain to satisfy the CJEU's demands. On Protocol No 16, the drafters might at first glance appear to have found an elegant solution. A new Article 5 of the DAA stipulates that a court or tribunal requesting an advisory opinion in accordance with the Protocol would simply not be considered a highest court or tribunal if the question falls within the field of application of EU law. Given that only highest courts can request an advisory opinion this would seem to resolve the problem identified by the CJEU in *Opinion 2/13*. However, in contrast to the solution found with regard to inter-party cases, where the EU is entrusted with providing an answer to this question, Article 5 revised DAA is silent on who decides whether a question falls within the scope of EU law. Similarly, as far as mutual trust is concerned, the revised DAA simply states that EU accession 'shall not affect the application of the principle of mutual trust within the European Union'.[82] This, however, raises the question of what 'mutual trust' is and, much more importantly, who gets to provide an authoritative answer.

If the CJEU continues its very strict stance on the autonomy of the EU legal order which became evident in *Opinion 2/13*, these two solutions might not make the cut. At the same time, the CJEU's case law on autonomy has developed since *Opinion 2/13* was

[75] Draft revised Agreement on the Accession of the European Union to the Convention for the Protection of Human Rights and Fundamental Freedoms 46+1(2023)36.
[76] Revised DAA, Explanatory Report, para 61.
[77] Art 3(8) revised DAA.
[78] Art 2(3) revised DAA.
[79] Revised DAA, Explanatory Report, para 76.
[80] Art 4(3) and (4) revised DAA.
[81] Art 1(9) revised DAA.
[82] Article 6 revised DAA.

handed down, sending somewhat mixed messages as to how strictly the CJEU wishes to interpret that criterion. In *Achmea*,[83] the Court reaffirmed its findings in *Opinion 2/13* and tightened them in so far as the role of national courts and the preliminary reference procedure are concerned. The Court notably considered Article 344 TFEU to not only confer exclusive jurisdiction on the CJEU over disputes between Member States concerning EU law, but extended it to cover all disputes over EU law that would ordinarily fall within the jurisdiction of national courts.[84] Furthermore, the Court added a novel nuance to the autonomy principle by linking it to the preservation of the rule of law at EU level.[85]

In doing so the CJEU buttressed its strict approach to autonomy notably concerning the principle of mutual trust. Unsurprisingly, this development did not encounter much sympathy amongst academic commentators, who in this regard described *Achmea* as 'Opinion 2/13 on steroids'.[86] Roughly one year later, the Court pronounced once more on the meaning and scope of the autonomy principle in *Opinion 1/17*.[87] That Opinion featured two clarifications, which may appear obvious but had not been expressly spelled out: first, the fact that according to long-established CJEU case law any agreement concluded by the EU becomes an 'integral part of EU law'[88] does not prevent the EU from conferring jurisdiction to an international court or tribunal concerning the interpretation of that very agreement.[89] Second, such an international court or tribunal may consider EU law as fact.[90] Some commentators concluded that the Court had been 'no longer selfish'[91] or that 'it did not take the same cautious prenuptial agreement approach it took in Opinion 2/13'.[92] While subsequent case law would appear to support the thesis that *Opinion 1/17* represented continuation rather than rupture,[93] it should be acknowledged, however, that in *Opinion 1/17* the CJEU did not seek extra insurance policies against a CETA tribunal interpreting EU law, but was quite content with a clause excluding EU law from the applicable law before it.

The biggest question marks revolve around the treatment of the CFSP, however. Perhaps surprisingly the drafters decided not to include any provision on it in the revised DAA and instead left the matter to the EU to resolve. Given that EU treaty

[83] Case C-284/16 *Achmea* EU:C:2018:158.

[84] See also S Hindelang, 'Conceptualisation and application of the principle of autonomy of EU law – the CJEU's judgment in *Achmea* put in perspective' (2019) 44 *European Law Review* 383, 387–89.

[85] Note in particular the repeated references to Case C-64/16 *Associação Sindical dos Juízes Portugueses* EU:C:2018:117.

[86] X Groussot and M-L Öberg, 'The Web of Autonomy of the EU Legal Order: *Achmea*' in G Butler and R Wessel (eds), *EU External Relations Law* (Hart Publishing, 2022) 927, 933.

[87] *Opinion 1/17 (CETA)* EU:C:2019:341.

[88] Since Case 181/73 *Haegeman v Belgium* (n 48).

[89] *CETA* (n 86) para 117.

[90] ibid paras 130–31.

[91] C Rapoport, 'Balancing on a tightrope: Opinion 1/17 and the ECJ's narrow and tortuous path for compatibility of the EU's investment court system (ICS)' (2020) 57 *Common Market Law Review* 1725.

[92] C Eckes, 'The autonomy of the EU legal order' (2020) 4 *Europe and the World*, doi:10.14324/111.444.ewlj.2019.19.

[93] Argued inter alia by K Bradley, 'Investor-State Dispute Tribunals Established under EU International Agreements: Opinion 1/17' in Butler and Wessel (eds) (n 85) 959, 964 ff; see notably Case C-741/19 *Komstroy* EU:C:2021:655.

change granting the CJEU full jurisdiction over the entire CFSP is not forthcoming, the EU-internal solution will have to take a different form.

One possible resolution might come from the CJEU's own case law concerning the limits of its jurisdiction over the CFSP. In Rosneft the CJEU had already confirmed its power to annul CFSP sanctions decisions in the context of preliminary rulings despite the more restrictive wording of Article 275(2) TFEU.[94] In *Neves 77 Solutions* the CJEU recently confirmed that it also has jurisdiction to interpret a CFSP decision where the Council has failed to implement that decision on the basis of Article 215 TFEU.[95]

The question whether the CJEU has jurisdiction to review the fundamental rights compliance of all CFSP-related matters was raised in *KS and KD*.[96] These were two appeals against General Court orders denying jurisdiction over damages actions based on Article 340(2) TFEU concerning alleged human rights violations (mostly failures to investigate) by the EU's EULEX KOSOVO mission, which had been conducted under the CFSP. In her Opinion, Advocate General Ćapeta argued that these were fundamental rights cases, jurisdiction over which 'cannot be excluded simply because that breach occurred in the context of the CFSP'.[97] The CJEU, however, took a different approach and rejected this line of argument. Notably, it held that the express exclusion of jurisdiction over the CFSP contained in Article 275 TFEU could not be circumvented by reference to other Treaty provisions, such as Article 47 CFR and more generally that the 'claim that the acts or omissions which are the subject of an action brought by an individual infringe that individual's fundamental rights is not in itself sufficient to declare that it has jurisdiction'.[98] That said, the Court reiterated that even within the CFSP the EU is bound by the basic principles of the EU legal order, which includes respect for the rule of law and fundamental rights. While therefore rejecting the broader argument that the restriction of its jurisdiction should be ignored where fundamental rights are at play, the Court was adamant to confirm its case law on restrictive measures. It furthermore restricted the exclusion of its own jurisdiction to decisions 'that are directly related to … political or strategic choices' made in the context of the CFSP. Despite narrowing down the exclusion, the CJEU stopped short of cutting the Gordian knot as suggested by AG Ćapeta. This means that there are still areas of fundamental rights-relevant CFSP action conceivable that are outside the CJEU's jurisdiction, so that the CFSP question remains to be resolved either by the Court itself in future cases or some other way.

VI. Concluding Remarks

The real test of whether the CJEU has tightened or somewhat relaxed the autonomy requirements will likely be a third CJEU Opinion on EU accession to the ECHR. Given

[94] Case C-72/15 *Rosneft* EU:C:2016:381.
[95] Case C-351/22 *Neves 77 Solutions* EU:C:2024:723.
[96] Joined Cases C-29/22 P and C-44/22 P *KS and KD* EU:C:2024:725.
[97] Joined Cases C-29/22 P and C-44/22 P *KS and KD* EU:C:2023:901, Opinion of AG Ćapeta, para 93.
[98] Joined Cases C-29/22 P and C-44/22 P *KS and KD* (n 98) para 73.

that accession negotiations have been concluded, such a request is only a matter of time. The outcome of any new accession Opinion is difficult to predict. The negotiators have tried – mostly successfully – to address the CJEU's concerns in the revised accession agreement. If the CJEU shows some flexibility, it may well be satisfied that the current version of the DAA is compatible with the EU Treaties. It would then remain a matter of ratification (viz politics) whether and when EU accession will materialise. In any event, *Opinion 2/13* will remain a landmark case in EU law.

INDEX

www.ingramcontent.com/pod-product-compliance
Ingram Content Group UK Ltd.
Pitfield, Milton Keynes, MK11 3LW, UK
UKHW020231290926
15470UKWH00002B/479

9 781509 954124